Linguistic Diversity and Language Theories

Studies in Language Companion Series (SLCS)

The SLCS series has been established as a companion series to *Studies in Language*, International Journal, sponsored by the Foundation "Foundations of Language".

Series Editors

Werner Abraham
University of Vienna

Michael Noonan
University of Wisconsin, Milwaukee

Editorial Board

Joan Bybee
University of New Mexico

Ulrike Claudi
University of Cologne

Bernard Comrie
Max Planck Institute
For Evolutionary Anthropology, Leipzig

William Croft
University of Manchester

Östen Dahl
University of Stockholm

Gerrit Dimmendaal
University of Leiden

Ekkehard König
Free University of Berlin

Christian Lehmann
University of Erfurt

Robert Longacre
University of Texas, Arlington

Brian MacWhinney
Carnegie-Mellon University

Marianne Mithun
University of California, Santa Barbara

Edith Moravcsik
University of Wisconsin, Milwaukee

Masayoshi Shibatani
Rice University and Kobe University

Russell Tomlin
University of Oregon

Volume 72

Linguistic Diversity and Language Theories
Edited by Zygmunt Frajzyngier, Adam Hodges and David S. Rood

Linguistic Diversity and Language Theories

Edited by

Zygmunt Frajzyngier

Adam Hodges

David S. Rood

University of Colorado

John Benjamins Publishing Company

Amsterdam / Philadelphia

∞™ The paper used in this publication meets the minimum requirements
of American National Standard for Information Sciences – Permanence
of Paper for Printed Library Materials, ANSI z39.48-1984.

Library of Congress Cataloging-in-Publication Data

Linguistic Diversity and Language Theories / edited by Zygmunt Frajzyngier,
Adam Hodges and David S. Rood.
p. cm. (Studies in Language Companion Series, ISSN 0165–7763 ; v.
72)
Includes bibliographical references and indexes.
1. Linguistics. I. Frajzyngier, Zygmunt. II. Hodges, Adam. III. Rood,
David S. IV. Series.

P125.L493 2004
410--dc22   2004059888
ISBN 90 272 3082 X (Eur.) / 1 58811 577 1 (US) (Hb; alk. paper)

John Benjamins Publishing Co. · P.O. Box 36224 · 1020 ME Amsterdam · The Netherlands
John Benjamins North America · P.O. Box 27519 · Philadelphia PA 19118-0519 · USA

Contents

Introduction

Zygmunt Frajzyngier and David S. Rood

The chapters included in the present volume constitute a selection from the papers presented at the International Symposium on Linguistic Diversity and Language Theories held in Boulder, Colorado in May 2003. The purpose of the Symposium was to identify hitherto unstated or understated fundamental issues in linguistic theories, taking into the account the rich variation of forms and functions observed in the languages of the world. We wished to examine the goals of both theories of language structure and theories of language evolution. An expected outcome of the symposium, although not explicitly stated, was an answer to the question of whether taking into consideration a wide rage of languages will result in changes in the categories, processes, and principles postulated by linguistic theories with respect to language structure and with respect to language change.

Some of the questions put before the participants with respect to the theories of language structure were:

1. What should be the proper object for theories of language structure?
2. What should a theory of language structure explain?
3. Should there be common formal elements in the theories of language structure?
4. Should there be common functional elements?
5. What elements should a theory of language structure contain?
6. What should be the relationship between theories of language structure and the theories of cognition?

Some of the questions with respect to theories of language change were:

1. What are motivations for language change and grammaticalization?
2. What are the roles and properties of functions in language change?
3. What are the roles and properties of forms in language change?
4. Does human conscious choice play a part in language change?
5. Is there a role for adaptability in language change? What would such a role be?

Some of the participants addressed some of these questions directly, some have addressed the questions obliquely, and still others addressed different questions that they thought to be relevant to the aims of the Symposium. There was a consensus, however, that linguistic theories should take into consideration the wide variety of forms and functions found in languages of the world and therefore, theory building in linguistics must involve typological research. Questions concerning theory do involve questions concerning methodology.

Three chapters address the problems of methodology in typological research. Given that functions across languages seldom completely overlap, and that forms are always different, a typologist faces the dilemma of what should be the proper object of comparison. After providing a sketch of theoretical issues involved in linguistic typology, Lazard proposes postulating 'intuitive and explicit notions' with respect to certain functions as tools in linguistic typology. Then the actual connections found in various languages can be compared with respect to those tools. Lazard illustrates the proposed methodology with respect to transitivity, object, subject, and voice. Lazard postulates the notion of invariants, which are neither forms nor functions, but rather abstract relations between form and function. Lazard concludes his chapter by a provocative discussion of the relationship between cognitive studies in linguistics, postulating essentially that each should develop its own theory and argumentation and should not be influenced by external factors.

The fundamental issues of methodology in typology are also raised in Corbett's chapter. In order to resolve the question of how to compare categories across languages Corbett proposes postulating canonical properties of categories. A canonical definition of a given function can then be used as benchmark in the description of forms and functions in linguistic typology. The canonical properties are to serve as tools, and do not necessarily represent the most frequent set of properties. Corbett illustrates the application of the canonical approach in syntax and morphology, with data assembled and analyzed with the help of the Surrey morphological data base. With respect to syntax, the canonical method is applied to the analysis of agreement, and with respect to morphology, the canonical method is applied to the determination of syncretism and suppletion. The outcome of this approach is a set of criteria for determining a possible word. The aims of Corbett's approach are similar to Lazard's, and in a way supplement Lazard's approach by providing a method of determining how much a given form differs from the canonical characteristics of a given category.

A fundamental issue in all linguistic research is to determine the function and meaning of a linguistic form. Pierre-Yves Raccah's study starts with an explicit description of one of the traditional approaches to determine the meaning of a linguistic form, that of observing the effects the use of the forms has upon the hearer. In his own approach to semantics, the meaning of a sentence includes the pragmatic purposes for which the sentence is used. He proposes the same method for the description of the meaning of words.

Four of the chapters specifically discuss the way particular kinds of language change address topics in the theory of language change, issues that are not restricted to single languages or language families. Claude Hagège establishes that speakers often make purposeful, considered choices in language use, thus directing, consciously, some phenomena of language change; not all change is accidental or driven by language internal pressures. Describing several individual case studies, he demonstrates that intentional attempts by writers, politicians, and even linguists to change linguistic forms may actually have a lasting effect on the language. His chapter demonstrates that we need to accept the notion that speakers make conscious choices of linguistic forms and thus contribute intentionally to the evolution of language.

Robert Nicolai demonstrates that the traditional method of establishing genetic relationships among languages runs into serious problems when dealing with languages like Songhai, a language spoken in West Africa. He claims that some of the characteristics of Songhai resemble Nilo-Saharan languages, other characteristics resemble Afroasiatic languages, and still others resemble Niger-Congo languages. He proposes a new model of emergence of language as a product of interaction of many languages within the same geographical and cultural environment. In such an interaction, the newly emerging language acquires features from all languages that interact in the given area. In the process, he shows that calculating the assignment of a language to a family must include attempts to reconstruct the social situations in which the language in question is used.

Regina Pustet looks at language change and grammaticalization through the lens of Zipf's famous statistical observation that word frequency correlates with word size — short words are used more often — and argues that this observation can and should be extended to the evolution of grammatical morphemes.

Stéphane Robert observes that languages often show multiple meanings for particular grammatical or function morphemes, and proposes that these meanings can be sorted out by speakers if they can be associated with contextual cues, such as the level (word, phrase, sentence, discourse) at which they occur. At the same time, their basic meanings are also reflected at each level. She finds this reminiscent of fractal patterns, where an invariance (basic meaning) recurs at different scales (linguistic levels), albeit with some scale-conditioned variation.

Several studies in the volume address the problem of fundamental properties of languages, more specifically the issue of fundamental categories, processes and principles as found in a wide range of languages.

Juliette Blevins discusses phenomena of syncope and antigemination in several languages. The fundamental question here is why in languages that do have syncope and antigemination, the two processes do not occur in certain cases. The explanation for the blocking of the two processes is that were these processes allowed to operate, there would be a collapse of grammatical paradigm and important functions coded by language forms would be lost. The discussion in Blevins provides evidence for the functional transparency principle as postulated in Frajzyngier's chapter, because syncope and antigemination are blocked when they would result in the elimination of functional distinctions coded by the paradigmatic forms.

Whether the 'sentence' should be considered a basic unit in syntactic theory and language structure is the question addressed by Marianne Mithun. She proposes that the category 'sentence', as commonly understood, while a useful category in some languages, does not necessarily constitute a universal basic category in language. A detailed analysis of Hualapai demonstrates that certain markers of syntactic dependency have developed into markers of pragmatic dependency. Natural discourse in Hualapai is composed of pragmatically independent and dependent sentences. The existence of pragmatically dependent and pragmatically independent clauses, observed and described in languages from various families (Frajzyngier 2001; Frajzyngier with Shay 2002) transcend the distinction between syntactically main and syntactically dependent clauses.

Michael Cysouw raises the issue of the need of a very large sample in order to determine what is frequent and what is rare in languages of the world. A detailed catalog of categories and syncretisms in pronoun and pronominal agreement systems reveals that "rare" is a relative term; he calculates that some 16 per cent of languages have "rare" systems. Cysow asks, "who are we linguists to rate such 'rare' systems", which function perfectly well for their speakers, "as strange"?

Scott DeLancey takes up the issue of the definition of lexical categories, and more specifically two types of definitions, distributional and functional. His focus is adpositions, which are considered universal lexical categories in many theories. He proposes that adpositions cannot be considered universal under a distributional or functional approach, as demonstrated by the existence of languages without adpositions. Nevertheless, adpositions may be universally available as a product of grammaticalization of various constructions, such as verbs, and genitive constructions.

Zygmunt Frajzyngier addresses the issue of principles guiding language structures. In particular he postulates a principle of functional transparency, whereby the role of every element in an utterance must be transparent to the hearer. Transparency is formulated in terms of functional domains coded in the language. The application of the principle of functional transparency is illustrated using the coding of grammatical and semantic relations between verbs and noun phrases. The study demonstrates adaptability of the language, in that once the principle of functional transparency is affected, the grammatical systems undergo compensatory changes.

Each of the chapters which conclude this collection addresses a specific problem in a language or in languages, and proposes a solution which involves a new model, or some other expansion or refinement of linguistic theory.

Liang Tao recounts the history and the state of the art in the study of classifiers in Chinese, noting that in modern spoken Chinese, a new pattern is developing in which some nouns can be counted without a classifier. She proposes to account for this phenomenon by careful study of current spoken data.

Anders Soegaard examines the properties of two constituent, N–N compounds across languages, and proposes a model that, in contrast with current compounding theories, deals with all the types he finds. He is particularly interested in handling both endocentric and exocentric compounds, and proposes to expand the traditional generative lexical model into a construction hierarchy with distinct but interrelated levels of constructions. Among the parameters his new model includes is one which takes account of conceptual relations such as literal vs. metaphorical relatedness, and a diminished role for the non-universal concept of "head'" especially in exocentric constructions.

Frank Lichtenberk, in his study of Oceanic languages, demonstrates that languages can grammaticalize the means to code possession individuation, a category different from alienable and inalienable possession. He proposes a cognitive explanation for the development of various possessive constructions in Oceanic and other languages, postulating that formal distance of linguistic forms corresponds to cognitive distance.

Marina Gorlach applies the principles of sign-oriented theory to study the reasons for English speakers' choice between separated and contiguous transitive phrasal verbs (*she broke the glass up* vs. *she broke up the glass*). Using literary texts as her data and translation into Russian as an investigative tool, she concludes that the separated forms regularly encode resultative constructions, in contrast with the incompletive meaning of contiguous verb-particle constructions.

Edward Vajda demonstrates that the morphological typological category "polysynthetic" is too broad; he proposes to replace it with "holistic grammar", a categorization based on an intersection of formal (lexical, morphological, syntactic) and functional (referential, discourse, phrasal) properties. He applies this to the argument number agreement system in Ket to show how its categories enable the typologically unusual Ket system to be compared comfortably with other languages.

Evidential systems in most languages have usually been included in discussions of modality, since they often entail a speaker's degree of commitment to the truth of a statement. Ferdinand de Haan argues that this is wrong, and that evidentials are in fact deictic, marking the relationship between the speaker and an event. His primary evidence comes from the observation that evidentials seem to develop from deictics diachronically.

From the refinement of general methodology, to new insights into language from studies of synchronic and diachronic universals, to specific studies of specific phenomena, this collection demonstrates the crucial role that language data play in the evolution of useful, accurate linguistic theories. Issues addressed include what to compare and how to determine meaning when doing typology; how to refine our understanding of diachronic processes by including consideration of intentional, social, statistical, and level-determined phenomena; reconsideration of categories such as sentence, evidential or adposition and structures such as compounds or polysynthesis; the tension between formal simplicity and functional clarity both in phonology and in general; the inclusion of unusual systems in theoretical debates; and fresh approaches to Chinese classifiers, possession in Oceanic languages, and English aspect. We think the Symposium has met its goal of confronting theories of linguistics with the diversity of languages.

References

Frajzyngier, Zygmunt. 2001. *A Grammar of Lele*. Stanford Monographs in African Linguistics. Stanford: CSLI.

Frajzyngier, Zygmunt with Erin Shay. 2002. *A Grammar of Hdi*. Berlin/New York: Mouton de Gruyter.

CHAPTER 1

What are we typologists doing?

Gilbert Lazard

"An exhaustive linguistic typology is the greatest and most important task for linguistics [...] Only through typology does linguistics rise to quite general viewpoints and become a science"(Hjelmslev). In spite of its impressive development in the last forty years, typology seems to be in need of theoretical clarification. In this connection, it is claimed that the Saussurean conception of language may contribute to a better understanding of the foundations of typological research. As for methodology, the major problem is the lack of a secure independent standard for comparing languages. A way out of that difficulty is suggested: it is exemplified by briefly reviewing recent studies on such notions as subject, object, transitivity, voice. In the last sections, a few thoughts are given to the question of the nature of cross-linguistic invariants and to that of the relationships between typological linguistics and cognitive sciences.

1. What are we looking for?

"The basic question of linguistic theory can be stated very simply: in what ways do natural languages differ and in what ways are they all alike?" (Perlmutter 1980: 195). To answer this basic question is more specifically the aim of linguistic typology. This aim is to discover features common to all languages, i.e., "empirical universals" or "invariants" of language, and, correlatively, to categorize linguistic phenomena into types.

The quest for invariants is a scientific task. Natural scientists do nothing else: all their endeavour is to perceive invariant relationships, which are considered and called natural laws, across the infinite diversity of empirical phenomena. Similarly, linguistic typologists try to discover invariant relationships within the practically infinite variety of languages. In this sense, typology may be regarded as the potentially most scientific part of linguistics.

This idea was expressed already a long time ago by great linguists. In his book *Language*, whose original Danish text was published in 1963, but which apparently was written in the nineteen forties, Louis Hjelmslev wrote:

> An exhaustive linguistic typology is, in fact, the biggest and most important task facing linguistics. [...] Its ultimate aim must be to show which linguistic structures are possible, in general, and why it is just those structures, and not others, that are possible. And here it will come closer than any other kind of linguistics to what might

be called the problem of the essence of language. [...] Only through typology does linguistics rise to quite general points of view and become a science.   (Hjelmslev 1970: 96)

Emile Benveniste did not so solemnly proclaim that ambition for linguistic typology, but he had similar views. He qualifies linguistics as a discipline trying to formulate itself as a science. He characterized its development in the first half of the 20th century as "the beginning of a linguistics conceived of as a *science,* on account of its cohesiveness, its autonomy, and the aims which are assigned to it" (1971: 5; written in 1954; italics in original). In the future he saw that science as "one of relations and deductions recapturing unity of plan in the infinite diversity of linguistic phenomena" (*ibid.* 15). In his eyes it was based on the Saussurean conception of language, "that a language is form, not substance, and that the units of language can only be defined by their relationships" (*ibid.* 80). "Each one of the units of a system is thus defined by the *relations* which it maintains with the other units and by the *oppositions* into which it enters; as Saussure says, it is a relating and opposing entity" (*ibid.* 19; italics in original).

Benveniste applied those principles in several typological studies, published in 1950 and the following years. He was conscious of doing pioneering work. For instance, at the beginning of an article entitled "The relative clause, a problem of general syntax" (1957–1958), he wrote, "The purpose of this article is to test a method of comparison dealing with a certain type of clause found in languages of different families" (1971: 181). He then surveys the construction of relative clauses in Ewe, Tunica, Navaho, Chipewyan, Sumerian, Classical Arabic, Classical Greek, Old Iranian, Hittite, Latin. From the comparison and the similarities he has observed in those diverse languages he draws conclusions on the nature of the relative clause. He also states this methodological conclusion: "What can be compared in linguistic systems that differ completely from one another are the functions, as well as the relations among these functions, indicated by formal marks" (*ibid.* 192).

For the last forty years or so, linguistic typology has enjoyed a rapid development on an international scale. Its aim has not changed, but its development has not exactly followed the path suggested by Hjelmslev and Benveniste. It was prompted by the conference of Dobbs Ferry in the USA in 1961 and particularly by the program conceived by Joseph Greenberg and his article with a proposal of forty five universals, mainly concerning the order of constituents. A great number of studies have followed bearing either on the same kind of questions or on other fields and a considerable amount of data, hypotheses and provisional conclusions have been gathered. While the initial work of Greenberg was founded on a few dozen languages only, more recent investigations made use of samples of hundreds of languages, and in this way reached more accurate conclusions.

A measure of the work achieved in typology may be provided by the Universals Archive initiated by Plank and Filimonova (2000), which now includes more than two thousand potential "universals". Of course that result, impressive as it is, does not mean that two thousand invariant relationships, i.e., scientific laws of language, have been discovered and proved real. The aim is to register any proposal about a possible linguistic relationship invariant across languages and to keep it at the disposal of all linguists for further study. The form of the register is apt to include any particular of each item, including the counter-examples, and there are many of them. The Archive is a tool for typologists.

It bears witness both to the fruitfulness of the typological research which has been and is currently being done and also to its methodological characteristics. Indeed most of that activity is influenced by the typical Greenbergian style. Greenberg had a wonderful ability to deal with an enormous mass of data and to perceive particular relationships within that mass. Everybody knows his theories on genetic relationships of languages: some are widely accepted as plausible generalisations; others are considered with caution. His practice in typology is more or less of the same kind. When dealing with constituent order, he chose to base his investigation on the traditional notions of subject, object, genitive, etc. He deliberately gave up the idea of looking for the roots of those notions, because "to have concentrated on this task, important in itself, would have, because of its arduousness, prevented [him] from going forward" into the quest for invariant relationships. For that matter, "there was never any real doubt in the languages treated about such matters. There is every reason to believe that such judgments have a high degree of validity" (Greenberg 1966: 74).

This is true to a certain extent. Traditional notions are not pure fancy. They result from the observations and reflections of ancient, and more recent, grammarians about their own and other languages, and they therefore reflect important phenomena in those languages. However, they mostly cannot be given clear explicit definitions, at least at the cross-linguistic level. Moreover, having been elaborated on the basis of Indo-European languages, they may be to some degree adequate for those languages, but we cannot be sure that they are adequate also for "exotic" languages. Hence using them in typological research inevitably involves a certain measure of vagueness and uncertainty and often leaves room for an undesirable part of speculation.

Most of the typological research which has been made in the last forty years or so follows the Greenbergian path. It has produced an impressive amount of knowledge about languages and language in general. However, for the reasons given above, the knowledge gathered in such a way cannot but be marred to some extent by the vagueness involved in its premises. It seems that the need for clarifying the theoretical basis of what we are doing is more or less widely felt. In the recent years, in different countries, conferences have been organized on questions relating to the foundations of linguistics, in particular with respect to cross-linguistic research.[1] Those discussions bear witness to a certain dissatisfaction with the present state of our discipline and a hankering after a better defined aim and a more secure foundation. In this article I would like to make a modest contribution to the effort of theoretical clarification.

2. Theoretical principles

In order to get a clear understanding of what we are doing, or should do, I believe that it is useful to return to the principles which were at the basis of the conceptions of such linguists as Hjelmslev and Benveniste, to wit the principles posited by Ferdinand de Saussure (1916; 2002). I am conscious that this idea is at variance with the presently preferred orientation of linguistic studies. What is in fashion is "cognitive linguistics". Linguists are mostly looking for connections between linguistic phenomena and results or conjectures produced in the field of cognitive psychology. That trend is not new, for, in its principle, it is as old as linguistics itself. It has been today restored to favour by the progress of cognitive sciences, and also as a useful reaction against generative linguistics. However, that does not mean that the Saussurean principles are out of date. On the contrary, they are apt to help linguists to get a clearer view of what they are doing in contradistinction to what psychologists and other cognitive scientists are doing (on this point see below, § 6).

I have elsewhere stated the theoretical ideas upon which I think typological research is, or should be, founded (Lazard 1999a; 2002; in press a). I need here only to recall a few points. Typologists deal with languages as systems: they try to discover what those systems have in common and in what ways they are different. The Saussurean conception of a language as a unitary synchronic system is obviously an abstraction, for concretely a language is not exactly the same in the heads of all its speakers, and it is permanently changing. But, as shown and forcefully and repeatedly expressed by the eminent epistemologist G.-G. Granger, the "reduction" of phenomenal realities to abstract objects is necessary for a scientific approach in any field of research. In his eyes, the Saussurean reduction of language "is as radical as the Galilean-Newtonian reduction of the physical fact to spaces, times and masses" (Granger 1983: 59). As such it may be considered as a basis for a more scientific approach of language phenomena.

A language is a system of signs. A sign consists of the inseparable association of a *signifié* and a *signifiant*. A *signifié* is a fragment of the representation of the world. A *signifiant* is a sequence of elementary phonological units. A *signifiant* or a *signifié* exists as such only by virtue of its link with a particular *signifié* or *signifiant*. The sign is arbitrary. This principle, which Saussure himself placed at the top of the theory, means that the association of its two facets is not determined by their "substances", i.e., on the one hand, the phonatory or acoustical features of the phonemes of the *signifiant* and, on the other hand, the semantic or conceptual content of the *signifié*.

Not only is the association of *signifiant* and *signifié* arbitrary, but the extent of each portion of phonic substance which is the matter of a phoneme, and the extent of each region of the semantic space which is the content of a sign are arbitrary, i.e., language-specific. Each language has its own phonological system and its own grammatical and lexical system (or system of systems). Of course, since all men have the same phonatory organs, the phonic substance is the same for all; but it is sliced up differently in different languages. On the other hand, at the level of *signifiés*, the semantic substance also is the same for all, or at least it should be considered such, because in itself it is amorphous, in the sense that it does not yield secure extra-linguistic categorizations. It appears sliced up into *signifiés* differently in different languages. A language unit is thus defined only by what makes it different from other units, or in other words, by its boundaries. This is what Saussure expressed by saying that "in a language, there are only differences", or "a language is a form, not a substance". It is nothing other than an arbitrary twofold configuration imposed on the phonic and the semantic substances. Boundaries are what makes the identity of a language: the Saussurean conception of language is "a topological structuralism" (Piotrowski 1997: 13).

A consequence of these premises which is specially important for typology is that not only units, but also categories are all language-specific and there are no cross-linguistic categories.

The idea of language-specificity of categories is more or less widely accepted by linguists. However, many at the same time act as if there were cross-linguistic categories. The reason is that there are obvious resemblances between languages. For example, many languages have a verb category which it is tempting to call a perfect. Its characteristic feature is to involve a reference both to the past and to the present. Such categories in different languages thus seem to have a similar nuclear meaning, although they may also in each language convey particular shades of meaning which are not found in other languages. It may be convenient to apply the same label "perfect" to all of them, but it is necessary not to forget that they *are* different. The linguist ought to register both their similarity and their difference.

It may be hypothesized that, in the ideal multidimensional semantic space, there are particular regions which are specially apt to be grammaticalized, i.e., which are in fact grammaticalized in more languages than other regions: let us call them "focal notions" (Lazard 1992). The notion of a past event which has current consequences (a persisting result or some kind of more abstract relevance) seems to be such a focal notion. This means that in a number of languages it is selected to be part of the verb system. More precisely, those languages have a verb form whose uses include that notion and also other notions different from one language to the next. In other words, to keep to our spatial metaphor, each language has in its own way grammaticalized a variable area around the notion in question. Such phenomena have to registered and described, but they should not be mistaken for cross-linguistic categories.[2]

To make clear what I mean I think it is useful, as an example of this kind of problems, to examine the definition of the middle voice given in Kemmer's book (1993),[3] The middle voice is a grammatical notion inherited from the analysis of Classical Greek by ancient grammarians. In Classical Greek it is clearly identified by unmistakable morphological features, with variegated meanings. That notion, having subsequently been used in the description of many other languages, has become rather problematic. Kemmer examined what is called the middle voice in a sample of about thirty languages belonging to different types and different genetic families. She concludes: "The middle was identified as a cross-linguistically valid semantic category available for potential grammatical instanciation" (p.243). Its content is described in the following terms: "The middle is a semantic area comprising events in which (a) the Initiator is also an Endpoint, or affected entity and (b) the event is characterized by a low degree of elaboration" (*ibid.*). What does this mean?

Kemmer writes that "that category was defined in relation to other clause-level categories such as reflexive, reciprocal, passive, and one- and two-participant events" (*ibid.*). Thus it is of the same kind as those other categories, reflexive, reciprocal, etc., and it is different from them. It is (rightly) not claimed to be a *cross-linguistic* category, which would mean that, in different languages, certain specific forms are exclusively associated with a specific semantic content, the same for all languages concerned: we know that this is impossible. Is it attested as a *linguistic* category in certain languages? This would mean that, in those languages, a specific form (a *signifiant*) is exclusively associated with the semantic content whose description has been recalled above (its *signifié*). It is difficult to answer the question, for it seems that, in most (all?) languages of the sample, the "middle marker", in addition to the meaning of middle voice as defined by Kemmer, has also other meanings, such as reflexive, reciprocal, and passive, which she considered different categories. In other words, the *signifiés* of the categories identifiable in those languages are wider than what she calls the middle.

Anyway, Kemmer does not seem to be concerned with that question. She claims to have identified a *semantic* category available for grammaticalization. This might mean that the semantic content defined as middle is what I call a focal notion. However, it may be said to be available for grammaticalization only if there actually exist languages with a *linguistic* category of middle, which, as we have just seen, is not certain.

Kemmer says that "the semantic middle is a coherent relatively diffuse category that comprises a set of loosely linked semantic subdomains centering roughly around the direct reflexive" (p.238). It thus appears that, rather than the middle, the direct reflexive is indeed qualified for being regarded as a focal notion. What Kemmer did was (usefully) to explore and describe a region of the semantic space intermediate between the direct reflexive, the two-participant event and the one-participant event, a region which happens to be included in the *signifiés* of variable wider grammatical categories in different languages. I am afraid it is misleading to call it a category.

Concerning the notion of a *semantic* category, I would like to repeat here what I wrote a few years ago when commenting on an article in which DeLancey had analyzed the "mirative" evidential meaning as "a semantic category related to but distinguishable from evidentiality":

We must leave to philosophers the task of clarifying the status of semantic, i.e., conceptual categories considered independently of their linguistic embodiment. As for linguists, they have to do with grammatical (and lexical) categories, which appear to them as defined by the association of a *signifiant* and a *signifié*.   (Lazard 1999b: 105; cf. DeLancey 1997)

3. The problem with typology

The typological perspective implies that the diversity of languages is not infinite, that it is possible to discover invariant relationships across that diversity. Indeed, as the faculty of language is common to the whole humanity, and as all human beings are similarly shaped and live in the same world, it is reasonable to think that these common conditions to some extent determine certain common features of language in general which it must be possible in principle to discover through the analysis of languages. More precisely, it may be hypothesized that there exist three kinds of language universals: a) those resulting from the fact that language is conditioned by the capacities of the human body and, in particular, the human brain; b) those issuing from the experience of the world, which, at least at the elementary level, must be roughly the same for all humans; c) those determined by the general conditions ("laws") of communication (see Lazard 1981).

The idea that there exist language universals, i.e., invariant relationships within language structures, is not at variance with the principle of the arbitrariness of the sign. It is easily conceivable that the huge variety of language forms and structures is nevertheless limited by general constraints.[4] In other words, invariants are conceived of as frameworks within which the diversity develops. This is why, in what is called linguistic typology, the quest for invariants and properly typological research, i.e., the categorisation of phenomena into different types, are not separate tasks. They are carried out simultaneously. Types can be established only against the background of common, i.e., invariant properties; subtypes are identified against the background of the type; and so on.

The methodology followed in typological research consists in comparing languages with each other in order to perceive what they have in common and in what ways they are different. It is at this point that linguistic typology meets with its major problem. Any comparison requires a *tertium comparationis*, an independent standard of comparison. What can we use as a standard for comparison? I have dealt with this problem in the studies mentioned at the beginning of Section 2. I shall be content here with a summary.

The difficulty is that we cannot use linguistic categories, since they are language-specific. Neither can we resort to the semantic substance, which is supposed to be roughly the same for all languages, because it is in itself "amorphous", as Saussure said, or it appears to be such as long as psychologists and philosophers have not established for sure that there exist cognitive categories independent of the linguistic ones, a condition which does not seem likely to be fulfilled in the near future.

Thus neither linguistic categories nor extra-linguistic ones are available. Then what? I think the way out of the difficulty is to resort to intuition. This thesis may appear surprising, for this is precisely what is done in current research and we deem it unsatisfactory. The question is: in what ways and within what limits is it legitimate to make intuition the basis for scientific research?

It is useful to remember that many philosophers and scholars, from Descartes and Auguste Comte to Planck and Quine, have emphasized the continuity between common knowledge and scientific knowledge. In their opinion those two kinds of knowledge are not distinguished by a difference of nature, but by a difference of fineness: scientific knowledge is more *precise*. It is therefore no wonder that the results of the current typological work, though often comprising a part of speculation, are far from being devoid of objective validity. The question is then to make the results of typological research less mixed with speculation, and closer to scientific results. They only need to be made more precise and founded on a sounder ground.

It should also be remembered that to make intuition the starting-point of a research is not epistemologically unorthodox; for all sciences are ultimately based on an intuitive foundation in the shape of axioms. It is therefore legitimate to begin a research by choosing an intuitive framework, on the condition that the part of intuition shall be explicitly and clearly delimited.

The procedure which is advocated is to make what I call "arbitrary conceptual frameworks" (ACFs) the points of departure for typological research. It entails intuitive, but explicit and clearly formulated notions in the initial stage and it excludes intuition from the subsequent operations. In this way the part of intuition is strictly delimited and mixing speculation with observation and reasoning is avoided. The approach thus lends itself to positive criticism.

In the following I very briefly recall the characteristics of ACFs:

1. They consist of *clear explicit* definitions and/or propositions, relating either to linguistic phenomena or to the world at large.
2. They are *arbitrary*, meaning that they do not result from systematic observation or a strict line of reasoning, but are freely chosen by the linguist. However, it is desirable that their choice should be oriented by a wide experience of different languages.
3. They preferably concern only *limited* domains of grammatical systems or lexical fields.
4. They are *tools* for research, not hypotheses susceptible of being verified or falsified by being checked against empirical data.
5. They are *provisional*: if they do not lead to interesting discoveries, they have to be dismissed and replaced by other ACFs.

We hypothesize that by following this path it is possible to discover invariants and to establish typologies. This hypothesis is backed up by the fact that it has been actually, if implicitly, followed to some extent by various good linguists (I mentioned some of them in Lazard 1999a and 2002). I believe it is the right way for bringing linguistics closer to the status of a science. The following section will give examples of the procedure.

4. Examples

4.1. Transitivity

Transitivity is one of the major notions inherited from ancient grammarians. Like other major traditional notions, such as subject, object, etc., it is obscure. It is usually defined as the property of a sentence conveying the idea that something passes (Lat. *transit*) from a participant to another, a definition notoriously inadequate in many cases. However, as it is commonly used in connection not only with Indo-European languages, but also with other kinds of languages, it must be thought that it somehow reflects important linguistic phenomena. There are good *descriptions* of what is usually called transitivity (Tsunoda 1994; Kittilä 2002), but they do not provide a real cross-linguistically valid *definition*.

In Lazard (2002) I presented an analysis of transitivity carried out according to the methodology described above. I chose as the ACF the notion of a "prototypical action" (PrA), defined as a real discrete volitional action performed by a human agent and actually affecting a well individuated patient. It is postulated that any language has means for expressing PrAs. The construction used for that in each language (it can be shown that there is only one), whatever its shape, is called the major biactant construction (MBC).

It is easy to see that, in practically all languages, the construction usually called transitive *is* the MBC. However, in many languages the MBC is not limited to that use, but it often conveys other meanings, non-prototypical actions or even non-actions. The extension of the use of the MBC to other kinds of events than the PrA varies considerably from languages in which it is indeed limited to the PrA to such languages as English in which it is very large. On this basis it is possible to build a typology of languages.[5]

On the other hand, by comparing the MBC with other biactant constructions in a set of languages, it can be seen: (a) that those other constructions all express events different from the PrA., and (b) that, in each language, they have common morphosyntactic properties with the (major) uniactant construction, so they may be considered as intermediate between the MBC and the uniactant construction. A correlation thus emerges between semantic deviation from the PrA and morphosyntactic intermediate position. This situation may be expressed in terms of *scalar transitivity*. The relationships observed by Hopper and Thompson (1980) are in this way inserted in a clear and systematic picture and the notion of scalar transitivity is provided with a firm ground.

4.2. The differential treatment of the object

Differential object marking is a well known phenomenon. Differential object agreement is closely akin to differential object marking, for it roughly correlates with the same factors. They are here considered together under the heading of differential object treatment. Differential object treatment is found in a great number of languages of different types and different parts of the world. The main semantic correlates of object marking and object agreement are definiteness and animacy of the object. That correlation seems to be a real invariant.

However the correlation is rather complex (see Lazard 2001b). Definiteness and animacy are scalar properties and they are not relevant to the same degree in all languages, and often there is some measure of free variation within the same language, so that in most languages it is difficult to formulate a clear rule. Moreover other semantic or pragmatic factors may also be involved in the treatment of the object: in particular a thematic (topical) object tends to be marked and/or to trigger agreement. It is also important to note that the marked and the unmarked objects and the object with or without agreement have not the same syntactic properties. The unmarked object and the object with no agreement is generally tightly linked to the verb and the group object + verb tends to function as a syntactic unit, while the marked object or the object with agreement has more freedom within the clause. In addition, in various languages the differential treatment of the object also correlates with aspectual variations and/or the meaning of the verbal lexeme.

On the whole there does not seem to be any doubt about the existence of a cross-linguistic invariant relationship in the differential treatment of the object. However, due to the complexity of the phenomena, the invariant cannot be formulated in perfectly accurate terms. In order to get a clearer view of the relationships, it is first of all necessary to clarify the very notion of an object.

What is an object? Like transitivity, it is an obscure traditional notion which dimly reflects important phenomena. Our task is to identify those phenomena. A possible way towards this aim is to resort to the same ACF as in the case of transitivity, to wit the notions of the PrA and the MBC.[6] The MBC comprises two actants, one of which represents the agent of the PrA and the other the patient. We may define the object as the actant of the MBC representing the patient in the prototypical use of the construction. However, the term of object is often used more widely and loosely. There are many kinds of more or less problematic "objects", a sort of constellation of actants characterised by various particular properties, but all more or less similar to the actant mapping the patient in the MBC. They may be analysed as being at varying (grammatical) "distances" from. the verb. I proposed to call the grammatical space they occupy the *object zone* (Lazard 1998a: 80–96; 2003b). The actant representing the patient in the MBC must be distinguished from those various other objects. As the MBC, by definition, expresses prototypical actions, the actant representing the patient in this construction may be identified as the "prototypical object".

If we consider differential object treatment in the light of this ACF and of this definition, it is clear that, in the languages where the phenomenon exists, the MBC is the construction with marked object and/or object agreement, since a) the definition of PrA includes the notion of a well individuated patient and b) object marking and object agreement involve a more definite and/or more animate object, i.e., a better individuated one. Thus the marked object and the object of a clause with object agreement are identified with the prototypical object. What is regarded as an unmarked object or the object in clauses with no object agreement takes place in the object zone among the non-prototypical "objects". It often tends to be a mere qualifier of the verb rather than a term of the clause.

This observation converges with what was said in the precedent subsection about transitivity. Indeed differential treatment of objects is one of the components of transitivity. Within the framework of the scalar conception of transitivity, clauses with marked object and/or object agreement are to be analysed as more transitive than clauses with unmarked object and/or no object agreement, in any language where the object may be treated differentially,

I shall not here proceed further towards refining the invariant of the differential treatment of the object, because this would exceed the limits of this article. I hope that what has been said is enough to show the usefulness of the procedure.

4.3 The question of the subject

Is it possible to give a valid definition of the subject in a cross-linguistic perspective? The question is more complex than that regarding the object. For this reason I think it is better approached from (at least two) different points of view (see Lazard 1998a: 97–118; 1998b: 19–21, 110–113; 2003a; in press b).

4.3.1

The first one is to resort once more to our ACF, the PrA and the MBC. We may decide that the actant in the MBC which represents the agent (when the MBC conveys the meaning of an action) is to be identified as the subject in any language. This is what implicitly most linguists actually do. That current practice implies two propositions: (a) the construction whose two actants represent an agent and a patient is a model for other two-actant sentences whose meaning is not an action, (b) the actant which may represent an agent is called the subject.[7] There is nothing wrong with those propositions. What is wrong is to keep them implicit, which makes the notion of the subject obscure.

Thus it is not illegitimate to define the subject, from a cross-linguistic perspective, on the basis of the MBC and to say that it is, in this construction, the actant able to represent an agent (which does not mean that it is an actant always representing an agent). This definition is unambiguous, since the MBC, whatever its shape, can be identified in any language. However it is undesirable, for, as will be seen below, it may happen to be at variance with the distribution of "subject properties".

It is nevertheless useful to retain the MBC and its two actants as fixed landmarks in the comparison of languages. For that task the actants need a name. I proposed a long time ago to designate them by symbols: X is the actant able to represent an agent, Y is the other one (the prototypical object[8]).

It is useful to add a third symbol Z for the single actant in the (major) uniactant construction. In the current practice, this actant is universally considered as a subject along with actant X, although these two "subjects" do not always share the same "subject properties" (see below, § 4.3.3).

4.3.2

It is well known that, in many languages, the actant called the subject is characterised by a number of specific morphosyntactic properties.[9] Let us recall a few of the most frequent ones, among others:

- coding properties: obligatoriness; "zero" case (nominative/absolute or no pre- or postposition); control of verb agreement;
- referential properties: control of reflexives and reciprocals; omissibility in coordination or subordination; accessibility to relative construction; also initial position (to be mentioned here rather than among the coding properties, because, in case of partition, it goes with the control of reflexives, etc., see below);
- transformational properties: "raising"; absence with the verb in the infinitive.

I proposed to call the set of subject properties in a given language the "subject configuration" of that language. The subject configuration varies considerably from one language to the next, in different ways:

1. It may include a large number of properties, as is the case in Western European languages. In other languages it is much more restricted, comprising only a few constituents. Lezgian, for example, seems to exhibit only one subject property (Haspelmath 1993: 294–297). Some languages of East Asia perhaps have none.
2. Its composition is widely variable, as shown by Keenan (1976: 312): "We have not been able to isolate any combination [...] of properties which is both necessary and sufficient for an NP in any sentence in any L[anguage] to be the subject of the sentence. Certainly no one of the properties is both necessary and sufficient." In other words, the subject configuration in a given language may comprise any subset of the set of properties considered as subject properties. It is theoretically possible that the subject configurations of two different languages might have no common member.
3. In one and the same language it may be divided into two subsets characterising two different actants. That situation was observed by Schachter (1976) in Philippine languages: some subject properties belong to the so-called "topic", others to

the "actor". Differently, in some ergative languages, coding properties (obligatoriness, zero case, control of verb agreement) belong to the "object", while referential properties (initial position, control of reflexive, etc.) belong to the actant mapping the agent. A similar partition is found in many languages in "experience sentences", in which the actant mapping the experiencer possess referential properties, while the actant mapping the stimulus has coding properties. That partition seems to be particularly frequent: it may be described by distinguishing a "subject of predication", possessing the coding properties, and a "subject of reference", having referential properties; our traditional subject of Indo-European languages is a conflation of those two kinds of subject.

4.3.3

In 4.3.1. we completed our primitive ACF (the PrA and the MBC) by defining the actants X, Y and Z, which are unambiguously identifiable in any language. Now, we may build a second ACF on the basis of the relationships traditionally considered as subject properties, by choosing a list of those properties, let us say, for instance, the few properties mentioned above as coding properties and referential properties. By means of these two ACFs we can sketch a tentative typology of languages with regard to the question of the subject.

We must of course keep apart the languages devoid of subject properties, if such languages really exist. In those languages the notion of a subject is irrelevant. For others (the vast majority), if we tentatively retain the distinction between subject of predication (S_p) and subject of reference (S_r), we perceive four types of languages, as a result of the combination of two oppositions:

- between languages in which X and Z have the same properties, as English, and languages in which they have different properties, as many ergative languages, in which Y has the same properties as Z;
- between languages in which experience sentences have the same construction (the MBC) as action sentences and languages in which they have different constructions, i.e., in which the actant mapping the experiencer (EXP) has referential subject properties.

We get the following types:

    I. X and Z have both coding and referential properties, action and experience sentences have the same construction, as in English; this may be symbolized by a formula:

        1. $S_p = S_r \rightarrow X / Z$,

    II. Y and Z have coding properties, X and Z have referential properties, action and experience sentences have the same construction, as in Basque:

        1. $S_p \rightarrow Y / Z$

        2. $S_r \rightarrow X / Z$,

III. X and Z have both coding and referential properties, action and experience
sentences have different constructions, as in Russian:
1. $S_p \rightarrow X / Z$
2. $S_r \rightarrow X / Z / EXP$,

IV. Y and Z have coding properties, X and Z have referential properties, action and
experience sentences have different constructions, as in Chechen:
1. $S_p \rightarrow Y / Z$
2. $S_r \rightarrow X / Z / EXP$.

4.4 Voice

This example is taken from Croft (2001: 283–319). He claims to follow these principles:

> I will argue that typologists will be unsuccessful in identifying universal cross-lin-
> guistic construction types. Constructions are language-specific, and there is an
> extraordinary range of structural diversity of constructions encoding similar func-
> tions across languages. But I will also argue that this fact does not preclude the pos-
> sibility of discovering and formulating language universals.   (p. 283–4)

I entirely agree with this position. Actually, on these points and on others as well,
Croft appears to come close to the Saussurean conceptions, although he does not
say so (in his book, he mentions Saussure's name only once in connection with the
question of arbitrariness in language, p.364) and perhaps he is not fully aware of
that convergence.

Croft studies the constructions which are currently given the labels of passive
voice and inverse voice in a series of different languages. His aim is to compare and
to characterize them in relation to one another, and to locate them in relation to the
"conceptual space" formed by the three persons involved in any discourse, namely
the speaker, the hearer and the thing spoken of, considered in the roles of agent and
patient.

The first step is to identify the "basic voice" in each language, i.e., the unmarked
construction. The simplest criterion is frequency: the basic voice is the most frequent one. It is relatively easy to recognize: the author says we may follow the judgment of grammarians. All right. The basic voice, by definition, is the "active". Definitions of the "subject" and of the "object" follow. The (active) subject is defined
as "the A participant", the (active) object, is defined as "the P argument"[10]. An actant which is neither subject nor object is an "oblique". As for the passive and inverse
voices, they are described in each language, not "in functional terms", but "in structural terms", by comparison with the active. For instance, in the English passive, A is
coded as an oblique, P is coded as a subject, V is morphologically distinct from V in
the active. Similarly, the Cree inverse is described by the following properties: A is
coded like an object, P is coded like a subject, V is morphologically distinct from V
in the direct (the basic voice).

This set of definitions is the framework taken as the point of departure of the study. It is clearly formulated. It calls however for two remarks. The first one concerns the terms A and P. The author says (p.284) that "A and P are clusters of participant roles, as defined in §4.2.1." In that previous chapter, we read that they are used as "a common denominator of comparison", and we find this formula: "A = "subject" of transitive verb (from a Eurocentric perspective), B = "object" of transitive verb." It is of course right to look for a common denominator for comparing languages (cf. above, § 3). But "subject" and "object" of European languages are not a precise standard[11]: they represent "clusters of roles", which vary across languages. It would have been more secure to explicit the idea (implicit in many current typological works) that the prototypical use of the transitive construction of European languages is to express an action, and to define A and P as the actants (or arguments) mapping the agent and the patient respectively in action sentences. Which amounted to constructing a theory of transitivity, as we did (cf. above, § 4.1).

The second remark is the following. Morphosyntactic variations involving the actants and the verb may be correlated with semantic variations: such variations are not mentioned in Croft's study. This probably means that the research does not concern all kinds of voice variations; it concerns only those which do not involve a modification of the relationships between the action and the participants, but only a change in the relationships between the semantic roles and the syntactic functions. This condition should have been explicitly stated among the premises.

With these reservations, the framework is well defined: it conforms to the requirements of an ACF. With this tool at his disposal Croft examines the relationships between the passive and inverse voices and the conceptual space constituted by the three persons in the roles of agent and patient. In certain languages there is no correlation between voice and person: this is the case, for example, in Philippine languages. But most languages exhibit a correlation. There is a large variety of situations depending on the language in question. Not only are the morphosyntactic forms variable, but the distribution of voices in the framework of person relationships varies more or less from one language to another. However an invariant relationship may be perceived in the overall picture.

The author resorts to a semantic map to make that result clearly visible. The person markers are arranged in a square table, vertically as agents (*I, you* sg., etc.) and horizontally as patients (*me, you*, etc.): this table is what Croft calls "the conceptual space". The voices used with the persons as agents and patients are located in the table. It then appears that, in all languages, the use of active voice is located towards the upper right corner of the table, i.e., in the region where the agent is first or second person and the patient is third person. Conversely, the use of the passive or the inverse voice is found towards the opposite corner, i.e., the region where the third person is agent and the first or second person is patient. This invariant, which is the conclusion of the research, is stated in the following terms (p.315):

> If there is a contrast between a basic and a non-basic voice (as defined [above]), then the semantic map of the basic voice will include the upper right corner of the

conceptual space in Figure [above], and the semantic map of the nonbasic voice will include the lower left corner of the conceptual space.

This conclusion is not unexpected. It is part of a general hierarchy of animacy (or humanness) which is currently referred to. However, Croft's study deserves attention because of its methodology. It is carried on in a clearly delimited field. It is founded on precise definitions, with the above reservations. The author thoroughly investigates the morphosyntactic data, brings them together with a well defined conceptual space, and arrives at the discovery of an accurately formulated invariant, which consists of a constant relationship emerging from the diverse shapes of the correlation between structure and function or, in another terminology, between *signifiant* and *signifié*. What was partly intuitive knowledge has become a firm and precise conclusion attained by a strict procedure.

5. On the nature of invariants

In this section I would like to comment briefly on the nature of invariants (or empirical universals) in the light of the basic Saussurean conceptions. Invariants are neither forms nor meanings; they are relationships appearing in the correlation between forms and meanings. In virtue of the arbitrariness of signs, not only forms (*signifiants*) are different across languages, but meanings or, better, *signifiés* also are all different because their limits are language-specific (see above, Section 2). If therefore languages have something in common, it can be found among neither *signifiants* nor *signifiés*. It must be located at a more abstract level: it cannot be anything other than a relationship or a set of relationships. Moreover I suspect that the most interesting ones, and perhaps even the only real universals, are relationships involving more than forms (*signifiants*) or regions of the semantic space (*signifiés*) only: they are relationships which themselves take place in the correlation between *signifiants* and *signifiés* at a higher level of abstraction.

The cases mentioned in the preceding section provide examples of such invariants. The most simple of them is the last one. Croft surveys the use of voice in about thirty languages of different types and different families. Active, passive and inverse are different arrangements of *signifiants* correlating with the same *signifié*. Their forms are varying. Croft has a section entitled "The structural variety of Actives and Passives", and another entitled "Blurring the Active-Nonactive Distinction", which emphasizes the variety. On the other hand, the uses of both basic and derived voices, when mapped against the conceptual space of persons as agents and patients, occupy variable areas, as showed by the many figures representing the situations in individual languages. From that twofold variety an invariant emerges, which is a correlation between person relationships (*signifiés*) and voices, i.e., the forms chosen for representing the action of an agent on a patient (*signifiants*).

In the case of differential object marking (I here leave out differential object agreement for simplification), the variety is manifold. First, there are different types of marking: case, preposition, postposition, other particle. Second, the semantic correlates, definiteness, animacy, etc., are variable across languages, and they often interplay with one another. Third, they are scalar qualities, and they are not relevant to the same degree in different languages. In other words, the boundary between the semantic factors which trigger object marking and those which do not may be located at different points of the scale. For example, if definiteness is relevant, in certain languages only pronouns, which are always definite, are marked, in others pronouns and proper names, which are also definite by nature, again in others all definite NPs, etc. However, object marking is always found in the higher part of the hierarchy. This invariant is a relationship between a bundle of qualities (*signifié*) and some kind of morphosyntactic marking (*signifiant*).

The case of transitivity is still more complex. The major biactant construction (MBC) and the (major) uniactant construction are the fixed poles of the continuum, but their forms, especially that of the former, may vary considerably: the MBC may be accusative or ergative, involve actant marking or not, verb agreement or not. "Intermediate" constructions also are variable. Moreover, across languages, they may differently correlate with diverse sorts of "deviations" from the prototypical action. Deviations from the PrA may even in certain languages be expressed by the MBC, while in other languages they trigger an intermediate construction. However from all that variety there emerges an invariant relationship, which is that intermediate constructions (*signifiants*) always correlate with deviations from the PrA (*signifiés*).

It would not be too difficult to cite other such relationships which are likely to be found invariant. I would like to mention two of them. The first one concerns the reflexive. Some languages have two reflexive constructions. For instance, Russian has the pronoun *sebja* and the clitic *–sja*, which is suffixed to the verb. Similarly there are in Latin the pronoun *se* and the passive-deponent conjugation, as *lavor* "I am washed, I wash (myself)", in Turkish the pronoun *kendi* and the suffix *–In*, etc. (see Kemmer 1993: 27). The two forms are not synonymous. The "heavy" form is used when, in an action which normally involves an agent and a patient who are two different persons, it happens that the same person is both the agent and the patient: this is what Kemmer calls "the direct reflexive". The "light" form appears in sentences expressing an action which normally somehow "returns" towards its agent; it often conveys "middle" meanings. For example, Kemmer constrasts in Russian *on utomil sebja* "He exhausted himself" with *on utomil-sja* "He grew weary". The verb with *sebja* is prototypically reflexive: it indicates coreferentiality of subject and object. With *–sja* it denotes a spontaneous event, according to Kemmer, or point of view of the subject, according to Frajzyngier (2000).

The same difference is found in other languages having a heavy and a light construction. It is found also in French between *se* + Verb and *se* + Verb + emphatic pronoun. For example, *il se soigne lui-même* "He tends himself", implies that he is ill and does not call upon a doctor's help, while *il se soigne* means more generally "He takes care of himself". In view of those few languages, it appears, as noted by Kemmer (p.121), that the construction expressing the direct reflexive is everywhere heavier than the other construction. I do not know whether systematic investigations on this point in a sufficient number of languages has been done. But it might be an invariant. If it is, here is a very simple correlation between form and function, or *signifiant* and *signifié*. The semantic opposition between the direct reflexive and "middle" meanings correlates with the difference between heavier and lighter constructions.

Another potential invariant of the same kind may be found in the relationship between so-called inalienable (or intimate, inherent, close, etc.) and alienable (or non-intimate, established, etc.) possession. In many languages all over the world, the inalienable possession is expressed by a synthetic construction; for instance, the name of the possessor directly follows that of the possessum, or the possessor is represented by a pronominal suffix or prefix, as *my-head* or *head-my*, while alienable possession requires a more complex construction, for instance one including a classifier, as *my thing basket*, meaning "my basket".

In fact, the constructions used are variable across languages. On the other hand, the two categories of nouns are far from having the same content in different languages: in other words, the boundary between possession regarded as inalienable and that which is regarded as alienable is located differently in the semantic space. However, there seems to be a constant relationship. Haiman (1983: 795, quoted by Lichtenberk, this volume) puts it in the following terms: "In no language will the phonological expression of inalienable possession be bulkier than that of alienable possession." And Nichols (1992: 117, also quoted by Lichtenberk) wrote: "In terms of its grammatical form, inalienable possession always involves a tighter structural bond or closer connection between possessed and possessor". Here again we find a clear invariant correlation between form and meaning, *signifiant* and *signifié*

These last two invariants are obvious examples of iconicity. In the constructional difference between "direct reflexive" and "middle", the heavier construction correlates with "a greater degree of distinguishability of participants", or a "higher elaboration", as Kemmer says. The invariant observed in the expression of inalienable and alienable possession is similarly iconic: the heavier construction correlates with greater distance between possessor and possessum. Both cases excellently show in what way invariants are limitations of the arbitrary in language.

6. Linguistic typology and cognitive sciences

If there are universals of language, it is reasonable to assume they are somehow grounded in cognitive abilities of the human brain and the way in which it perceives the world. It is therefore legitimate to look for connections between properties of language and cognitive activity. In this final section I would like to give a few thoughts to the question of the relationships between typological linguistics and cognitive sciences. My claim is that the typologist is concerned with those relationships only at the initial stage of his research and at the end or, better, after the end, when he has discovered language invariants, but not in his work of description and comparison of languages.

Cognitive linguistic theories explicitly aim at explaining language structures by what is known or surmised about the functioning of the human brain. To what extent do cognitive sciences contribute to these theories? Neurosciences, it seems, do not give much. In spite of their progress, there still is too wide a gap between their achievements and the problems the linguist has to tackle. Experimental psychology may in principle provide some data and suggestions.

However it seems to me that cognitive theories as used by linguists mainly rest on intuition: they are more often than not interesting conjectures about the functioning of the human mind in apprehending the world, building representations of it and elaborating their linguistic expression. Langacker (1984: 6) himself wrote:

> Some portions of the present work can be regarded as an exercise in speculative psychology. I speak unabashedly about cognitive events, and sometimes go into considerable detail about their architecture and their relationships. All of this must be accepted in the proper spirit. Since I claim no privileged access to the operation of the human mind, there is obviously a substantial (some might say intolerable) element of speculation in any such proposals concerning the specifics of cognitive activity.

Typology being conceived of as stated in the preceding sections and the connections between linguistics and cognitive sciences being such as it seems, where and how can the typological and the cognitive approach meet?

They may meet first at the very beginning of typological work, when the linguist has to build a conceptual framework (ACF) as a tool for research. Then the cognitive approach may offer interesting contributions. Since the frameworks are arbitrary, i.e., based on intuition, and since cognitive theories are mainly intuitive hypotheses, he may resort to cognitive theories among other sources of inspiration. For example, in the study of predicative structures, he may find useful ideas in the many theories on the semantics of predication, including aspectual properties and participation properties (agentivity, etc). In particular, the notion of prototypical action (PrA) could be refined in this way.

The subsequent stage is comparison of languages, which itself implies previous description of individual languages. In description, cognitive considerations can and must contribute nothing. A language has to be described in its own specific categories and structures. This task has its own methodology: it should not be disturbed by introducing external considerations.

The same goes for the main part of the research, namely the comparison of languages in order to discover invariants and to establish typologies. After the conceptual framework (ACF) has been chosen, intuition is excluded, and so are also extralinguistic phenomena. The linguist has to do exclusively with linguistic phenomena in individual languages and he endeavours to identify more abstract cross-linguistic phenomena. At this stage he does not have to look for the cognitive roots of what he observes or discovers. His task is to get as clear and accurate a view of cross-linguistic relationships rather than to search after some connection between more or less distinct universals of language and conjectural forms of mental activity. To identify linguistic invariants is one thing, to connect them with cognitive faculties is another, which ought to be undertaken only after the former task has been achieved.

When the typologist has succeeded in discovering invariant relationships, he has completed his specific task. However, he may feel the need for cognitive "explanations". Such a need was already felt a long time ago, for example, by Regamey (1954), when he commented on the actancy split (commonly and somewhat inaccurately called split ergativity) in Indo-Iranian. More recently, DeLancey (1981) presented a more refined interpretation of that phenomenon in terms of "view point" and "attention flow", which also belongs to the cognitive approach. Those considerations are interesting, but they are of a quite different nature from the operation of establishing linguistic invariants.

One may even ask whether it is incumbent upon the linguist to look for connections between his invariants and aspects of cognitive activity? I feel inclined to think not. His part is to explore languages and to present cognitive scientists with invariants firmly grounded in the comparative analysis of a variety of languages and attained by a strict methodology, i.e., with objective discoveries. They are important contributions to the knowledge of cognitive processes. It belongs to specialists of cognitive processes to exploit them and to integrate them into their theories.

Would it be a scandal to say that, in the present state of things, the potential contribution of linguistics to cognitive sciences is perhaps more important than the reverse? If, for instance, the transitivity invariant were confirmed by future research, it would shed light on the conceptualisation of processes in the world. Again, research on reflexives, middles and passives could, as it seems, more or less easily succeed in establishing some kind of invariant connection, which might highlight the representation of some part of the relationships between man and the world. The constructional differences between "prototypical reflexive" and "middle" and similarly between inalienable and alienable possession are interesting in this connection. They draw attention to conceptual distinctions which might pass unnoticed if they were not made conspicuous by morphosyntactic phenomena. It is linguistic research, because it is, or can be, more precise, which highlights cognitive processes rather than the latter which explain linguistic facts.

Notes

1. Examples: "Di cosa parliamo quando parliamo di linguistica?" (Rome, July 2002), "Linguistic diversity and language theories" (Boulder, Colorado, May 2003), "Mais que font les linguistes?" (Paris, November 2003). Discussions by e-mail may also be mentioned in this connection.

2. The notion of focal zone is close to that of "gram-type" proposed by Bybee and Dahl (1989). The difference is that it is purely semantic, while gram-types seem to be (cross-) linguistic notions.

3. I noticed in that book a series of misshapen French and Latin words: Fr. *le livre se vende bien* (p.20, instead of *le livre se vend bien*), *l'eau se bouille* (p.21, instead of *l'eau bout*), *le glace* (p.21, instead of *la glace*), *reflecher* (p.135, instead of *réfléchir*), *se bouillir* (p.144, instead of *bouillir*), *s'appuyer* (p.154, instead of *s'appuyer*), *tout les heures* (p.212, 218, instead of *toutes les heures*), Lat. *tremblo-r* (p.145, non-existent). I hope words of other languages have been better checked.

4. We do not have here to consider other kinds of limitations of the arbitrary, such as derived words, which are partly "motivated" (Saussure), and ideophones..

5. Our analysis agrees with a common feeling: many linguists speak of agents and patients even when the clause in question does not express an action, cf. § 4.3.1.

6. I am here considering those notions as an ACF, i.e., an arbitrary choice. However, I believe that I have demonstrated that the notion of the prototypical action and the major biactant construction actually occupy a specific place in the grammar of any language (see Lazard 2002: 153, 166). If that demonstration is accepted as valid, they are non longer an arbitrary framework chosen for convenience as a tool for research, but the objective result of an investigation, and as such they may legitimately be used as a firm point of departure for further research.

7. Terminology: a "participant" is a person or thing involved in an event; an "actant" is an NP representing a participant. "Participant" refers to the semantic level, "actant" to the morphosyntactic one.

8. It may be designated as "actant Y" or as "the prototypical object" as is more convenient to the current type of study.

9. For theoretical reasons, semantic properties are here left out as irrelevant for the definition of the subject.

10. It would be more correct not to confuse the semantic and the morphosyntactic level and to say that the subject is the A actant (or, in Croft's terminology, the A argument, but not the A participant) and the object the P actant (or argument), and also that in the passive the participant coded A in the active is coded as an oblique and the participant coded P in the active is coded as a subject, etc., cf. above n.8.

11. I criticized similar notions used by Dixon in Lazard (1997: 248–251).

References

Benveniste, Emile. 1971. *Problems in General Linguistics*, Mary Elizabeth Meek (trans). Coral Gables, FL: University of Miami Press.

Bybee, Joan L. and Dahl, Östen. 1989. «The creation of tense and aspect systems in the languages of the world". *Studies in language* 13: 51–103.

Croft, William. 2001. *Radical Construction Grammar: Syntactic Theory in Typological Perspective*. Oxford: OUP.

DeLancey, Scott. 1981. "An interpretation of split ergativity and related patterns". *Language* 57: 626–657.

DeLancey, Scott. 1997. "Mirativity: The grammatical marking of unexpected information". *Linguistic Typology* 1: 33–52.

Frajzyngier, Zygmunt, 2000. "Domains of point of view and coreferentiality". In *Reflexives: Forms and Functions*, Z. Frajzyngier and T. S. Curl (eds), 125–152. Amsterdam / Philadelphia: Benjamins.

Granger, Gilles-Gaston. 1983. *Formal Thought and the Sciences of Man*. Hingham, MA: D. Reidel.

Greenberg, Joseph. H. 1966. "Some universals of grammar with particular reference to the order of meaningful elements". In *Universals of Language*, J. H. Greenberg (ed), Second Edition, 73–113. Cambridge, MA: MIT Press.

Haiman, John. 1983. "Iconic and economic motivation". *Language* 59: 781–819.

Haspelmath, Martin. 1993. *A Grammar of Lezgian*. Berlin and New York: Mouton de Gruyter.

Hjelmslev, Louis. 1970. *Language*, Francis J. Whitfield (trans). Madison: University of Wisconsin Press.

Hopper, P. J. and Thompson, S. A. 1980. "Transitivity in grammar and discourse". *Language* 56: 251–299.

Keenan, Edward L. 1976. "Towards a universal definition of "subject"". In *Subject and Topic*, Li, Charles N. (ed.), 303–333. New York, San Francisco, London: Academic Press.

Kemmer, Suzanne. 1993. *The Middle Voice*. Amsterdam, Philadelphia: John Benjamins.

Kittilä, S. 2002. *Transitivity: Towards a Comprehensive Typology*. Turku: University of Turku.

Langacker, Ronald W. 1984. *Foundations of Cognitive Grammar, Vol. 1: Theoretical Prerequisites*. Stanford, CA: Stanford University Press.

Lazard, Gilbert. 1981. "La quête des universaux sémantiques en linguistique". *Actes sémiotiques – Bulletin* 19: 26–37. [Reprint in Lazard 2001a: 47–56].

Lazard, Gilbert. 1992. "Y a-t-il des catégories interlangagières?» In *Texte, Sätze, Wörter und Moneme. Festschrift für Klaus Heger*, S. Anschütz (ed), 427–434. Heidelberg: Heidelberger Orientverlag. [Reprint in Lazard 2001a: 58–64].

Lazard, Gilbert. 1997: "Ergativity, by R. M. W. Dixon" (review article). *Linguistic Typology* 1: 243–268. [Reprint in Lazard 2001a: 273–298].

Lazard, Gilbert. 1998a. *Actancy*. Berlin, New York: Mouton de Gruyter.

Lazard, Gilbert. 1998b. "Définition des actants dans les langues européennes". In *Actance et valence dans les langues de l'Europe*, J. Feuillet (ed), 11–146. Berlin, New York: Mouton de Gruyter.

Lazard, Gilbert. 1999a. "La linguistique est-elle une science?" *Bulletin de la Société de linguistique de Paris* 94(1): 67–112. [Reprint in Lazard 2001a: 3–46].

Lazard, Gilbert. 1999b: "Mirativity, evidentiality, mediativity, or other?" *Linguistic Typology* 3: 91–109. [Reprint in Lazard 2001a: 425–443].

Lazard, Gilbert. 2001a. Etudes de linguistique générale. Typologie grammaticale. Leuven, Paris: Peeters.

Lazard, Gilbert. 2001b. "Le marquage différentiel de l'objet". In *Language Typology and Language Universals, An International Handbook*, M. Haspelmath *et al.* (eds), Vol.2, 873–885. Berlin, New York: de Gruyter.

Lazard, Gilbert. 2002. "Transitivity revisited as an example of a more strict approach in typological research". *Folia Linguistica* 36: 141–190.

Lazard, Gilbert. 2003a. "Le sujet en perspective interlinguistique". In *Le sujet*, J.-M. Merle (ed), 15–28. Gap, Paris: Ophrys.

Lazard, Gilbert. 2003b. "What is an object in cross-linguistic perspective?" In *Romance Objects, Transitivity in Romance Languages*, Giuliana Fiorentino (ed)., 1–16. Berlin, New York: Mouton de Gruyter.

Lazard, Gilbert. In press a. "On the status of linguistics with particular regard to typology". *The Linguistic Review*.

Lazard, Gilbert. In press b. "Nouvelles remarques au sujet du sujet". *Cahiers de linguistique de l'INALCO* 5.

Lichtenberk, F. This volume.

Nichols, Johanna. 1992. *Linguistic Diversity in Space and Time*. Chicago and London: CUP.

Perlmutter, David M. 1980. "Relational grammar". In *Current Approaches to Syntax*, E. A. Moravcsik and J. R. Wirth (eds), 195–229. New York: Academic Press.

Piotrowski, D. 1997. *Dynamiques et structures en langue*. Paris: CNRS Editions.

Plank, Frans, and Filimonova, Elena. 2000. "The universals archive: a brief introduction for prospective users". *Sprachtypologie und Universalienforschung* 53: 109–123.

Regamey, C. 1954. "A propos de la "construction ergative" en indo-aryen". In *Sprachgeschichte und Wortbedeutung, Festschrift Debrunner*, 363–381. Bern: Francke.

Saussure, Ferdinand de. 1966 [1916]. *Cours de linguistique générale*, publié par C. Bally et A. Sechehaye. — *Course in General Linguistics*, Wade Baskin (trans). New York: McGraw-Hill.

Saussure, Ferdinand de. 2002. *Ecrits de linguistique générale*, texte établi et édité par S. Bouquet et R. Engler. Paris: Gallimard.

Schachter, Paul. 1976. "The subject in Philippine languages: Topic, actor, actor-topic, or none of the above?" In *Subject and Topic*, C. N. Li (ed), 491–518. New York, San Francisco, London: Academic Press.

Tsunoda, T. 1994. "Transitivity." In *The Encyclopedia of Language and Linguistics*, R. E. Asher (ed), 9: 4670–4677. Oxford, New York, Seoul, Tokyo: Pergamon Press.

Chapter 2

The canonical approach in typology*

Greville G. Corbett

University of Surrey

The canonical approach is designed to avoid two dangers in typology: the premature use of statistics and the failure to compare like with like. It involves taking definitions to their logical end point, in order to build theoretical spaces of possibilities. The canonical instances are not necessarily the most frequent, and may indeed be rare, but they fix a point from which occurring phenomena can be calibrated. This approach is demonstrated first in syntax, by looking at agreement. It is then applied to morphology, starting from the notion of a canonical paradigm, and showing how four major morphological phenomena can be seen as mismatches between the canonical expectation and the variety of real inflectional systems. Syncretism and suppletion are investigated as examples. The latter demonstrates how typology can be applied to an extreme case (lexical items whose constituent parts have no shared phonology), which can be extended by interactions with other morphological phenomena. The relevance of this approach is shown in its application to the construction of typological databases.

1. Introduction

We are invited to consider 'the proper object for theories of language structure'. Following Chomsky's suggestion, we should aim to define the notion 'possible human language'. As a part of that we need to develop the notion 'possible word'. We were also asked to examine 'the rich variation of forms and functions observed in the languages of the world'. This is the realm of typology, and I shall suggest that for typologists to make a full contribution we may need to refine our methods, as we move into more difficult areas of the typology of possible words.

As one way forward I suggest a 'canonical' approach. This approach sidesteps two potential dangers in typology, namely 'premature statistics' and 'not comparing like with like'. The first danger is that something which is frequently found may be treated as uninteresting, whereas there are linguistic phenomena which are common yet which, I believe, should surprise us. The second danger is that we fail to take sufficient care over our terminology and so do not see that phenomena labeled identically are in fact distinct (conversely we miss identities because of different traditions of labeling).

In a canonical approach, we take definitions to their logical end point and build theoretical spaces of possibilities. Only then do we ask how this space is populated. There are of course precedents for this approach; for instance Greenberg (1959) can be read in this light. It follows that canonical instances (the best examples, those most closely matching the canon) may well not be the most frequent. They may indeed be extremely rare, or even non-existent. However, they fix a point from which occurring phenomena can be calibrated, and it is then significant and interesting to investigate frequency distributions.

I shall illustrate this canonical approach, and present some practical outcomes. The point is to create theoretical spaces, to populate them while the languages are still there to be investigated, and to study both what is frequent and what is rare. The paper brings together material from different projects, to illustrate the canonical approach in various areas.

2. Syntax

As an instance of syntactic typology we consider the complex phenomenon of agreement. Here we are interested in canonical agreement, agreement in gender between adjective and noun in the noun phrase. Recall that by canonical, we mean 'best', 'clearest', 'indisputable' (according to the 'canon'). We shall also see weakenings of the criteria, giving instances which are less canonical, and others which are on the fringe of agreement. Just some of the criteria are given here for illustration: full justification is given in Corbett (2003c).

2.1. Definitions

"The term agreement commonly refers to some systematic covariance between a semantic or formal property of one element and a formal property of another" (Steele 1978: 610).

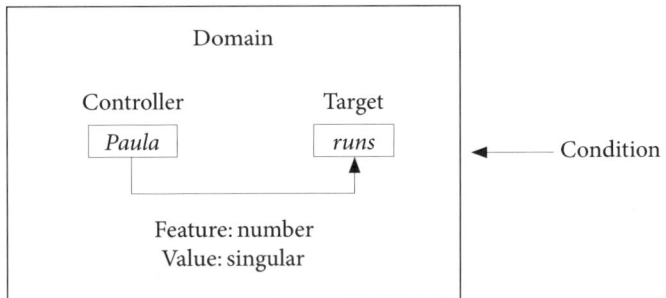

Figure 1. Framework of terms

We call the element which determines the agreement (say the subject noun phrase) the **controller**. The element whose form is determined by agreement is the **target**. The syntactic environment in which agreement occurs is the **domain** of agreement. And when we indicate in what respect there is agreement, we are referring to agreement **features**. Thus number is an agreement feature, it has the values: singular, dual, plural and so on. This is diagrammed in Figure 1.

If agreement is determined by factors which do not themselves mark agreement, then these are agreement **conditions**. Note that the controller-target relation is logically asymmetrical, but this does not imply asymmetry in the syntactic model. In fact, most modern approaches use some form of unification.

2.2. Canonical examples

As an instance of canonical agreement, consider agreement in gender in the Italian noun phrase:

Italian (Pierluigi Cuzzolin, personal communication)
(1) il   nuov-o   quadr-o
     DEF.SG.M new-SG.M picture(M)-SG[1]
     'the new picture'

(2) i   nuov-i   quadr-i
     DEF.PL.M new-PL.M picture(M)-Pl
     'the new pictures'

(3) la   nuov-a   tel-a
     DEF.SG.F new-SG.F painting(F)-SG
     'the new painting'

(4) le   nuov-e   tel-e
     DEF.PL.F new-PL.F painting(F)-PL
     'the new paintings'

Put briefly, the canonical features of these examples are as follows (they are listed in Appendix 1):

- *controller:* is present, has overt features, and is consistent in the agreements it takes, part of speech is not relevant (this is a vacuous criterion here)
- *target:* has bound expression of agreement, obligatory marking, doubling the marking of the noun, marking is regular, alliterative, productive; the target has a single controller and its part of speech is not relevant
- *domain:* agreement is asymmetrical (the gender of the adjective depends on that of the noun), local, and the domain is one of multiple domains
- *features:* lexical (in one instance), matching values, not offering any choice in values
- *conditions:* no conditions

The different canonical aspects of agreement converge so that agreement in gender of the modifier with the noun in the noun phrase emerges as the canonical instance. Phenomena which extend the instances 'outwards' are grouped under the five components of our account of agreement. For illustration we will consider just the criteria which relate to controllers.

2.3. Controller criteria

Several criteria relate to the controller. An important one is that canonical controllers are present.

Criterion 1: Controller present > controller absent
('>' is to be read as 'is more canonical than')

Compare these two similar examples:

> Russian
> (5) ty   čitaeš'
>   you read.2sg
>   'you are reading'

> Serbian/Croatian/Bosnian
> (6) čitaš
>   read.2sg
>   'you are reading'

In such sentences in Russian the controller is typically present, while in Serbian/Croatian/Bosnian typically it is not. Serbian/Croatian/Bosnian is a pro-drop language. We treat as canonical what is sometimes called 'grammatical agreement' rather than 'anaphoric agreement' (Bresnan and Mchombo 1989, Siewierska 1999, Bresnan 2001). An effect of adopting Criterion 1 is that the canonical type is restricted to relatively few languages, since pro-drop is common.

While discussions of 'dropping' concentrate on pronouns, we are making a more general point here: it is more canonical for any controller to be present rather than absent. For agreement of the adjective with the noun within the noun phrase, it is more canonical for the noun to be present; similarly in possessor-possessed agreement it is more canonical for the 'possessed' to be present.[2]

Criterion 2: Ccontroller has overt features > controller has covert features

Compare these Russian examples:

> Russian
> (7) ona spa-l-a
>   she sleep-pst-sg.f
>   'she was sleeping'

(8) ja spa-l   /spa-l-a
I sleep-PST[SG.M]/sleep-PST-SG.F
'I was sleeping' (man/woman speaking)

In (7) the controller is overtly feminine: the pronoun *ona* 'she' contrasts with *on* 'he'. In (8) the controller *ja* 'I' does not distinguish gender. We treat examples like (7) as canonical in this respect, rather than those like (8). Another way of stating this criterion is that a canonical controller marks at least as many distinctions as the target. It does so in two respects: in terms of the number of features, and in terms of their values.

On the basis of these criteria (and others not discussed here), a more general principle may be suggested (compare Moravcsik 1988: 90):

Principle-I: Canonical agreement is redundant rather than informative

In the Russian example (7), the feminine feature is available from the controller (criterion 2). In (8) it is not. Agreement in the canonical example is redundant. Similarly, English examples like *the horse is/the horses are* are more canonical than *the sheep is/are*. The situation where there is no controller present, and hence the only information about the controller is that supplied by the target (as in pro-drop constructions) is non-canonical (though, as we noted, it is commonly found); this is the point of Criterion 1.

Let us continue with other criteria relating to controllers.

Criterion 3: Consistent controller > hybrid controller

A consistent controller is one which controls a consistent agreement pattern. This is more canonical than one which controls different feature values. The notion 'consistent agreement pattern' is intuitively easy, but not quite so easy to define (for the details see Corbett 1991: 176–181). As a basic characterization, a consistent agreement pattern is the set of agreements controlled by a typical regular controller. In Table 1, it is represented by a row.

A hybrid controller, on the other hand, takes agreements from more than one such pattern. It controls different feature values on different targets. An example can be found in the Talitsk dialect of Russian (Bogdanov 1968). In this dialect, a

Table 1. Agreement patterns in Russian

Attributive adjective	Predicate	Relative Pronoun	Personal pronoun	Values
-yj	-Ø	-yj	on-Ø	singular masculine
-aja	-a	-aja	on-a	singular feminine
-oe	-o	-oe	on-o	singular neuter
-ye	-i	-ye	on-i	plural

plural verb can be used with a singular noun phrase, to indicate reference to a person or persons besides the one indicated directly. That is to say, we have an 'associative' construction, but it is indicated not by a marker on the nominal, but by plural agreement:

(9)   Talitsk dialect of Russian (Bogdanov 1968)
       moj   brat   tam tóža žýl'-i[3]
       my[SG] brother[SG] there also lived-PL
       'my brother and his family also lived there'

The plural agreement is found in the verbal predicate, but not in the noun phrase, and so we have different agreements according to the target. Of course, consistent controllers take either singular or plural agreements, irrespective of the target: that is, they have consistent agreement patterns. The inconsistent pattern does not represent a row in Table 1.

The possible patterns of agreement with hybrid controllers are tightly constrained by the Agreement Hierarchy (Corbett 1979, 1991: 225–260, 2000: 188–192; Cornish 1986: 203–211; Barlow 1991, 1992: 136–137; Kirby 1999: 92–96). The Agreement Hierarchy distinguishes four types of agreement target (see Fig. 2).

Attributive — predicate — relative pronoun — personal pronoun

Figure 2. The Agreement Hierarchy

The Agreement Hierarchy allows us to constrain possible agreement patterns as follows:

For any controller that permits alternative agreement forms, as we move rightwards along the Agreement Hierarchy, the likelihood of agreement with greater semantic justification will increase monotonically (that is, with no intervening decrease).

The considerable range of data covered by the constraints of the Agreement Hierarchy can be found in the references above.

Criterion 4: Controller's part of speech irrelevant > relevant (given the domain)

The idea is that given a domain, for instance, subject-predicate agreement, in the canonical case we do not need further information on the part of speech. Thus, in Russian we do not need to have different rules for a subject noun phrase headed by a noun as compared to one headed by a pronoun. Sometimes, however, the difference is substantial. A good example is Bayso, where the rules are rather different for pronouns as compared with nouns. For this complex situation see Hayward (1979), Corbett and Hayward (1987), Corbett (2000: 181–183). These two criteria fall under a second general principle:

Principle II: Canonical agreement is syntactically simple

Agreement varies from examples which can be captured by a relatively simple rule, to those which are exceptionally complex. The two criteria, Criterion 3 and Criterion 4, both point to agreement phenomena which can be captured by simple and general rules.

2.4. Principles of canonical agreement

Several further criteria can be grouped under a third principle:

> *Principle III: The closer the expression of agreement is to canonical (i.e. affixal) inflectional morphology, the more canonical it is as agreement.*

We return to canonical inflectional morphology in §3 below. Note that the principles, and the criteria which they summarize, never conflict. They therefore define a multi-dimensional space. The convergence of all the criteria is a point at which truly canonical agreement is described.

The canonical approach allows us to clarify some of the conceptual problems and misunderstandings that characterize the problem of agreement (see Evans 2003, Mithun 2003, Polinsky 2003, for further discussion). Having seen the gradient nature of many of the properties (as well as the ways in which they overlap), the question of 'drawing the line' between agreement and other phenomena appears secondary. It is more important to understand agreement and its related phenomena than to draw a precise line at which we might claim agreement 'stops' and some other phenomenon begins.

2.5. Relevance for a typological database

For practical purposes, however, such as the construction of a typological database, we do need to draw a line between what is included and what is not. Here the results of our approach can be of use: we can be clear where and why such a line is drawn, and users of the database can aware how the data relate to their own conceptions and analyses of the area. If they wish to define the area of investigation more tightly, the means of querying the database allow this to be done.

The Surrey Database of Agreement (Tiberius, Brown, Corbett and Barron 2002) includes detailed information on a small, carefully chosen set of genetically diverse languages: Basque, Chichewa, Georgian, Hungarian, Kayardild, Mayali, Ojibwa, Palauan, Qafar, Russian, Tamil, Tsakhur, Turkana, Yimas and Yup'ik. The database was designed and implemented in ACCESS by Dunstan Brown and Roger Gentry, and is described in Tiberius, Brown and Corbett (2002).

The design incorporates the five elements of our account in §2.1 above, which means that the researcher can query the database according to controllers, targets, domains, features (categories) and conditions. In each of these the researcher may choose to restrict the search further (and we anticipate that those who restrict their search because of a different view of agreement will often choose the more canonical instances and omit others).

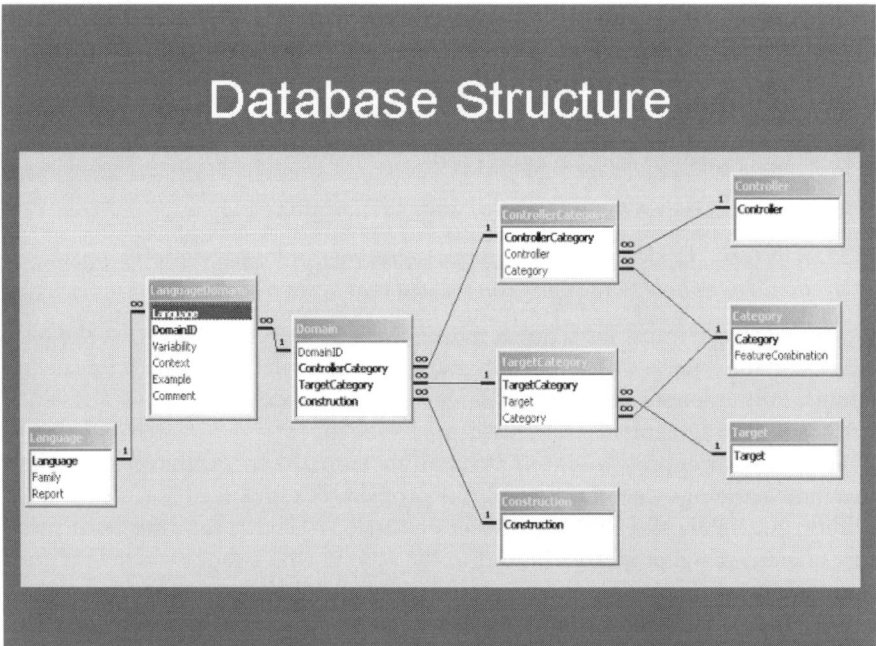

Figure 3. Structure of the Surrey Database of Agreement

The database has a relatively small number of languages. It is nevertheless quite large, because for each agreement phenomenon in each language we give a wealth of information wherever possible (thus besides straightforward subject-verb agreement, we include quantified subjects, subjects consisting of conjoined noun phrases and so on, giving the features involved, and any conditions or options). It is intended to 'open doors': to enable researchers to test hypotheses and to find data relevant to their research questions, and the sources to go further. There are links to examples in each instance; this means that the researcher can check back to the original data and so can be sure what the entries in the database mean.

For each language included there is also a prose report, written by the researcher who entered the data for the language, giving sources, and enabling the user to see how decisions were made. Since some of the analytical decisions are difficult (we are dealing with areas where there is considerable uncertainty in the field), these reports are valuable in allowing the user to see the approach of the researcher, and to treat the data accordingly. In some instances experts on the particular languages contributed a good deal and their generous help significantly strengthened the database. For more discussion of the underlying philosophy see Corbett (2003a); the database is freely available at http://www.smg.surrey.ac.uk/.

In our discussion of canonicity we have stressed that what is canonical need not be frequent. The Italian examples cited earlier (1)–(4) are familiar, but not particularly common in the world's languages. While they are familiar, it is important that we should not loose sight of their surprising nature. They show information 'in the wrong place', that is information about the noun expressed on the adjective. The information is 'displaced' (Moravcsik 1988: 90). In assigning them to a type, we should not cease to be surprised by such examples.

When discussing canonical agreement we asserted without discussion that one of the principles is that canonical agreement is expressed by canonical inflectional morphology. We take up this topic in the next section

3. Morphology

We start from the notion of a canonical paradigm, that is, an idealized morphosyntactic paradigm, for distinct word classes in individual languages. Setting this up is not always straightforward. We first have to establish the morphosyntactic features and their values (on the basis of some distinct inflectional behaviour). Then we establish which are valid for each word class. Finally we project all the logically possible feature value combinations to produce the underlying morphosyntactic paradigm. We thus 'multiply out' the logical possibilities to produce an idealized morphosyntactic paradigm. A theoretical example for nouns is given in Figure 4.

	Singular	Dual	Plural
Nominative			
Accusative			
Genitive			
Dative			
Instrumental			
Locative			

Figure 4. An abstract (morphosyntactic) paradigm

3.1. Four dimensions for a morphological typology

Suppose that the features relevant to inflection in a given language are established and we have a set of paradigms, like the one in Figure 4. We might then expect that for any given lexeme, every cell of its paradigm will be filled by the inflectional system (completeness), each form will be different (distinctiveness), the stem will be predictable, and the inflections will be predictable. A straightforward view of the function of inflectional morphology could lead to that expectation, and it provides a useful definition of canonical morphology. It can also be seen as the situation for which an Item and Arrangement model would be adequate. (See Stump 2001: 1–30 for discussion of the necessary characteristics of a realistic theory of inflectional morphology.)

The mismatches between these canonical expectations and the variety of real inflectional systems lead to our typology (see Fig. 5).

Canonical expectation	Phenomenon
Completeness of paradigm	Defectiveness
Distinctiveness of cells	Syncretism
Regularity of stems	Suppletion
Regularity of inflection	'Deponency'

Figure 5. Canonical expectations and corresponding morphological phenomena

These four phenomena are investigated in Corbett (1999). For illustration here we shall discuss just two of them, the most widespread — syncretism (§2.2), and perhaps the most challenging for a typologist — suppletion (§2.3).

3.2. Syncretism

The assumption of completeness is that each cell in a paradigm should be filled by a different form (which is what a functional view might predict). Thus in our abstract paradigm there 'should' be 18 different forms. What then if only 17 are found? The identity of form may be due to syncretism. Various fairly similar definitions of syncretism have been offered:

> Identity in form between two grammatically different inflections.   Trask (1997: 215)

> The relation between words which have different *morphosyntactic features but are identical in form.... Used especially when the identity is regular across all paradigms. [* see also 'case syncretism']   Matthews (1997: 367)

> Russian adjectives display **syncretism**, that is, a single inflected form may correspond to more than one morphosyntactic description.   Spencer (1991:45)

> In instances of syncretism, two or more cells within a lexeme's paradigm are occupied by the same form.   Stump (2001: 212)

Let us look more closely at why the cells should be claimed to be different when the forms are the same. There may be two different reasons:

1. other items of the same class have different forms. This is 'internal' syncretism, indisputably relevant to the grammar of the particular language.
2. values of a feature have a separate realization in one environment, and the projection of these values to the morphosyntactic paradigm produces the additional cell(s). This is 'external' syncretism, essential to the typologist, but not necessarily to be reflected in the grammar of the particular language.

	SG	PL			SG	PL
MASC	*byl*	*byl-i*		MASC	*byl*	
FEM	*byl-a*	*byl-i*		FEM	*byl-a*	*byl-i*
NEUT	*byl-o*	*byl-i*		NEUT	*byl-o*	

Figure 6. 'External' syncretism (Russian *byl* 'was')

The difference can be made clear by asking which is the shape of the paradigm of Russian past tense verbs (see Fig. 6). We see that Russian verbs in the past tense distinguish two numbers and three genders. This gives an abstract paradigm with six forms, as on the left. This shows that there is syncretism for gender in the context of plural number. However, no verb has more than four forms in the past tense, and our morphological description of Russian may operate with these (implying the paradigm on the right), see Brown (1995).

On the basis of this canonical approach, including external syncretism, we have created a typological database of syncretism (Baerman, Brown and Corbett 2002a,

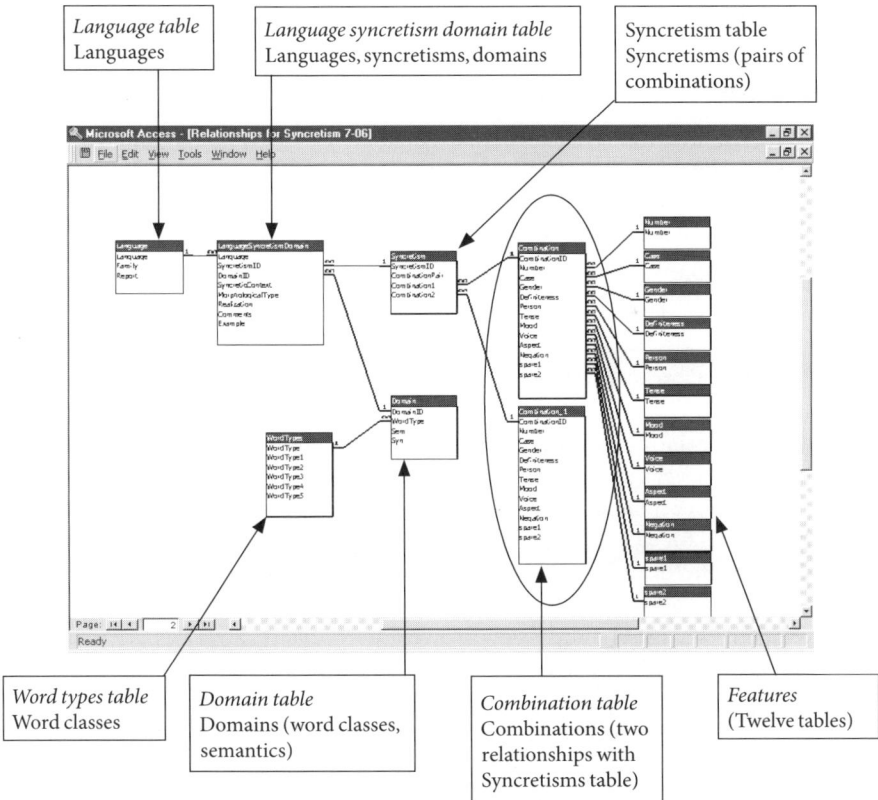

Figure 7. Structure of the Surrey Syncretisms Database

available at: http://www.smg.surrey.ac.uk/). The design is given in Figure 7, and is described in Brown (2001).

The database records all instances of inflectional homophony in thirty genetically diverse languages, comprising 1,256 separate entries. It is based on the notion of abstract morphosyntactic paradigms (discussed above) and every type of cell identity, as compared with that canonical expection, is recorded in the database. Note that the shape of the theoretical paradigm could vary according to other assumptions (and links to language reports in the database make clear what the assumptions were) but even then the notion of all cells being canonically different still holds (Matthew Baerman, personal communication).

For recent discussion of syncretism see Evans, Brown and Corbett (2001), Stump (2001: 212–241), Baerman, Brown and Corbett (2002b), which highlights the unusual syncretisms found in Indo-European, and Corbett, Baerman and Brown (2002), and for an extended account see Baerman, Brown and Corbett (forthc.).

3.3. Suppletion

Given a further assumption that canonically a lexeme will have a single stem or a series of predictably related stems (§3.1), then we must address the issue of suppletion. Suppletion has been defined as follows:

> The use of two or more entirely different **stems** in forming the inflections of a single lexical item, as in English *good/better, go/went, person/people*.   (Trask 1997: 212)
>
> Morphological process or alternation in which one form wholly replaces another. Thus in *went* either the whole form, or a stem *wen-*, is in a suppletive relationship to *go*.
>
> In **partial suppletion** only a part of the form is replaced. E.g. in *thought* (or *though-t*), the *th-* of *think* is unchanged and only *–ink* is affected   (Matthews 1997: 364)

We may think of suppletion from two slightly different points of view. One view treats it at the end case of a cline of inflectional irregularity, an instance of particularly severe irregularity (naturally with partial suppletion as less irregular than full suppletion). Another view is that suppletion represents an extreme, rather different from more minor irregularities. We shall take both points of view, since each provides illustration for a canonical approach.

If we start from the idea that suppletion is part of a cline of irregularity this might lead us to flesh out the scale, arranging items from fully regular to suppletive. This was attempted by Corbett, Hippisley, Brown and Marriott (2001) where such an irregularity scale was used to investigate in detail the distribution of the regular and irregular expression of number in Russian texts. We examined the nouns in the one million word Uppsala corpus of Russian (see Lönngren 1993 for details) and recorded all the lexemes occurring at least five times. Our dataset contains around 5440 lexemes, accounting for some 243 000 word forms from the entire corpus. Each noun in our dataset was assessed according to the irregularity scale proposed.

Having made explicit what would count as regular, less regular and fully irregular (suppletive) we had to ask what is meant by frequency. Frequency can be viewed in two ways. We might compare lexemes one with another or we could compare regular and irregular forms within lexemes. For the first approach, we could count up how many times each lexeme occurs in the plural. We call this the *absolute frequency* of a lexeme's plural. We can then compare the absolute frequency of plural of different lexemes, regular and irregular, to see if there is a relationship between irregular plurals and their absolute frequency. Alternatively we could analyse the plural by comparing it, within the lexeme, with the other available forms. For a given lexeme, we can count how often it occurs in the plural as compared with the number of times in the singular. This is the *relative frequency* of the plural. We can then compare the relative frequency of the plural in lexemes where it is irregular with that in lexemes where it is regular.

We found relations between frequency and irregularity and a certain degree of correspondence with the Irregularity Scale. Seven out of eight groups of nouns confirm the hypothesis of a relation between irregularity and absolute plural anomaly. A clear result is that the three nouns of modern Russian which show suppletion stand out dramatically. We found some evidence that the frequency of occurrence of the irregular forms, and not just frequency of occurrence of the lexeme as a whole, does relate to irregularity of the forms in question (see the cited paper). As far as (full) suppletion is concerned, though the median plural proportion is high, the result is not statistically significant. The difficulty is that there are so few nouns with suppletive stems. For the full statistical details see Corbett, Hippisley, Brown and Marriott (2001)

We now consider suppletion as an extreme, and since this is a particular challenge for typologists we devote a separate section to it.

4. Typology of the extreme

There is also good reason for treating suppletion as an extreme phenomenon. It requires us to allow for lexical items whose constituent parts have no shared phonology. If we attempt a typology of suppletion, concentrating on 'full' suppletion, this will indeed be an unusual sort of typology, a typology of extremes. The object will be lexemes, not languages. For a canonical approach here, a good starting point is Mel'čuk's definition:

> For the signs X and Y to be suppletive their semantic correlation should be maximally regular, while their formal correlation is maximally irregular.   (Mel'čuk 1994: 358)

Starting from this general definition, we can establish dimensions along which the phenomenon may vary. We can in many cases point to the 'canonical' or best instances, those which are maximally transparent in semantic terms and maximally opaque in formal terms (cf. Mel'čuk 1994: 342, forthcoming). We write 'a > b', for 'a is a more canonical example than b'. This means that we can recognise, for example, that some restrict suppletion to inflectional morphology, while others including Mel'čuk allow for suppletion in derivational morphology. Semantic correlations are typically more regular in inflectional than in derivational morphology, hence the clearer (and for some linguists the only) instances of suppletion will be found in inflectional morphology.

Corbett (2003b) proposed 15 criteria for canonical suppletion. We shall consider just some of them here, to illustrate the good perspectives that a canonical approach offers (§4.1). We shall then investigate two of the interactions of suppletion with other morphological phenomena (§4.2).

4.1. Some criteria for a typology of suppletion

For illustration we consider some of the criteria for canonical suppletion, those which deal with the elements which can be suppletive, their phonology and, most difficult, their distribution.[4]

4.1.1. *Element involved*

Criterion 1: Fused exponence > stem

This criterion is discussed in various terms. The basic notion is that if the suppletive form combines stem and inflection, this is 'more suppletive' than if the form is the stem to which appropriate inflections are added. Thus *worse* is a more canonical instance of suppletion than *better*, being more opaque, since *better* may be analysed as a suppletive stem *bett-* with the comparative marker *–er*. Nübling (1998: 78–79) talks of Segmentierbarkeit 'segmentability' versus Nichtsegmentierbarkeit, and makes the point that items with a segmentable affix are 'etwas weniger suppletiv' 'somewhat less suppletive' than those without.

4.1.2. *Phonology of this element*
This section depends on the part of the definition stating that in suppletion the 'formal correlation is maximally irregular'.

Criterion 2:   full > partial

This is also known as strong versus weak suppletion (e.g. Nübling 1998:78)

(10)   Russian: *idti* 'go' ~ *šel* 'went' (full suppletion)

(11)   English *bring ~ brought* (partial suppletion)

For suppletion there should be no formal correlation. If we take that at its simplest, we could say that (10) shows suppletion and (11) does not. However, we can take the requirement to be that there is no rule, no regularity linking the two forms. Nevertheless, the partial phonological similarity of the English forms means that they are 'less suppletive' than the Russian forms. This brings us back to the issue of viewing suppletion both as the end point of a cline and as a special extreme phenomenon.

4.1.3. *Distribution of suppletive forms*

This is one of the key issues in the typology of suppletion. Given that a lexeme has two or more suppletive forms, the question is how they can be distributed. This criterion represents the conclusion of what will be some careful discussion:

Criterion 3: Morphological > morphosyntactic

Here we follow the terms used in Stump's (2003) account of heteroclisis. Alternative terms are 'morphomic' (Aronoff 1994: 22–29) or 'morphologically systematic' versus 'featural'. The point is that the distribution of stems within a paradigm may conform to a morphological pattern or to a morphosyntactic feature specification. Stump (2002: 149–153) shows how the Network Morphology use of two default inheritance hierarchies allows us to capture this distinction. The link to the general definition is that morphosyntactic determination represents less pure semantic regularity than morphological determination (where there is no possible compromising of semantic regularity).

To see what it involved, consider the Russian lexeme in Table 2. A Slavist might well suggest that the stems are distributed according to the morphosyntactic feature of number. A Romance specialist might ask whether this example could not be described in purely morphological terms. This requires us to look at the stem patterns of Russian nouns. There are various patterns, but most give a singular-plural split (for details see Corbett 2000: 139–142).

Table 2. The Russian noun rebenok 'child'

	Singular	Plural
Nominative	rebenok	deti
Accusative	rebenka	detej
Genitive	rebenka	detej
Dative	rebenku	detjam
Instrumental	rebenkom	det'mi
Locative	rebenke	detjax

As implied above, there is a tradition in Romance linguistics of treating the distribution of suppletive forms as determined by morphological patterns or templates (Matthews 1981, Vincent 1988: 297–298, Maiden 1992: 306–307 and Aski 1995). This is based on examples set out in Table 3.

There are many French verbs which show various stem modifications, following this pattern of cells (verbs like *acheter* 'buy', to name just one). Of course, such a pattern can be described in featural terms, but the point of the Romance linguists'

Table 3. Present tense of French *aller* 'go'

	Singular	Plural
1st person	*vais*	*allons*
2nd person	*vas*	*allez*
3rd person	*va*	*vont*

claim is that the morphological pattern is established as a part of the morphological system (Maiden 2002). See Hippisley, Chumakina, Corbett and Brown (forthcoming) for further examples from outside Romance.

Before accepting morphological determination of suppletion, we should consider Carstairs-McCarthy's statement (1994: 4410) that the distribution of suppletive elements will be (morpho)syntactic or phonological. He cites examples like Italian *va(d)- ~ and-* 'go', stating that the suppletion is determined by the stress: *va(d)-* is found where the stem is stressed (Carstairs 1988: 71). An account based on stress would be possible for the French example, as long as we stay with the present tense; for the rest of the distribution, this seems less plausible.

Given that the different potential determining factors frequently overlap, we should ask which examples are available which require us to acknowledge particular types of determining factor. The Russian example (Table 2) could be treated as morphological or morphosyntactic. The French example (Table 3) could treated as morphological or possibly phonological. We need to establish which of these are required. Consider this Polish example:

Table 4. Present tense of Polish *być* 'be'

	Singular	Plural
First	*jestem*	*jesteśmy*
Second	*jesteś*	*jesteście*
Third	*jest*	*są*

Here we find a suppletive relation between the third plural and all the remaining cells (Rothstein 1993: 717; Itkin 2002). There is no phonological criterion to account for this distribution. There is, however, a morphological pattern, as shown by other verbs, where there is an irregular stem alternation, as with *wiedzieć* 'know' (Table 5).

Several verbs share this pattern (there is another pattern in which first singular and third plural are opposed to the other forms). These Polish data show that the distribution can follow a morphological pattern, rather than a phonological pattern. Like the French data, they support a morphological rather than a morphosyntactic account.

Table 5. Present tense of Polish *wiedzieć* 'know'

	Singular	Plural
First	*wiem*	*wiemy*
Second	*wiesz*	*wiecie*
Third	*wie*	*wiedzą*

We must ask which types are required. The instances of possible phonological determination can also be treated as morphological patterns. However, the Polish example is morphological in nature and is not analysable in phonological terms. Hence we need to recognize morphological patterns as a possible determiner for the distribution of suppletive stems, and it is not clear whether we need also to recognize phonological determination. The key evidence would be a paradigm where the forms could be determined by some phonological generalization and not by morphological or morphosyntactic regularities. I have not been able to find such an example, and conclude tentatively that we do not require phonological determination of suppletion.[5]

Since we need to allow for morphological determination of patterns of suppletion, we should ask whether we need morphosyntactic determination. The examples given so far do not require this. However, the Norwegian data to be discussed in §4.2.2 do suggest that morphosyntactic determination must be recognized as a possible type.

4.1.4. *Relevance for a database of suppletion*

The canonical approach has again proved useful in setting up a database of suppletion. Like the other typological databases, this one, developed by Dunstan Brown, Marina Chumakina, Greville Corbett and Andrew Hippisley has been made freely available over the web (at http://www.smg.surrey.ac.uk/. It draws on a sample of over 30 genetically diverse languages. We have adopted a strict version of Mel'čuk's definition; this means that many of the instances are relatively close to canonical ones and that claims made on the basis of the data included will be founded on clear-cut examples.

4.2. Interactions with other morphological phenomena

When we have a clear notion each of the morphological phenomena from a canonical perspective, there is another major task, namely to investigate the possible interactions between these phenomena. Here, as illustration, it makes sense to investigate the interaction between suppletion and the other phenomenon we took as a case study, namely syncretism. We then look at suppletion interacting with the 'opposite' of syncretism.

4.2.1. *Syncretism*

When discussing interactions, we mean that the same cells in the paradigm are potentially affected by the two phenomena (and not just that a lexeme independently shows an instance of both phenomena). Interactions between syncretism and suppletion are rare, but there is one remarkable instance, found in the South Slavonic language Slovene, discussed by Plank (1994), Corbett and Fraser (1997), and Evans, Brown and Corbett (2001: 215). In Slovene there are syncretisms affecting all nouns, which results in the identity of the genitive dual and genitive plural, and of the locative dual and locative plural. The unique noun *človek* 'man, person' has a suppletive stem for the plural, as distinct from singular and dual. Syncretism requires the stems to be identical while suppletion requires that they be distinct. The 'outcome' is given in Table 6.

Table 6. Slovene *človek* 'man, person' (Priestly 1993: 401)

	Singular	Dual	Plural
Nom	*človek*	*človeka*	*ljudje*
Acc	*človeka*	*človeka*	*ljudi*
Gen	*človeka*	*ljudi*	*ljudi*
Dat	*človeku*	*človekoma*	*ljudem*
Inst	*človekom*	*človekoma*	*ljudmi*
Loc	*človeku*	*ljudeh*	*ljudeh*

One interpretation is that syncretism dominates suppletion. The data have also been proposed as evidence in favour of rules of referral, since the dual forms refer to the plural in an asymmetric way.

4.2.2. *Overdifferentiation*

We take overdifferentiation as the second example of a phenomenon interacting with suppletion, because it is in one sense the opposite of syncretism. Overdifferentiated lexemes are those which have an additional form in their paradigm, like English *be* (Bloomfield 1933: 223–224). A typical case of overdifferentiation is that of an element which distinguishes three gender values in a language where normally only two are distinguished. For instance, in Kolami, there are two genders, male human and other, for almost all agreement targets. However, the numerals 'two', 'three' and 'four' — and no other agreement targets — have additional forms for female human; these three numerals are said to be overdifferentiated (Emeneau 1955: 56, Corbett 1991: 168–169).

Suppletion can interact with overdifferentiation. Hans-Olav Enger has provided the following interesting data on his East Norwegian dialect (and a comparable situation is found in some other dialects).[6] The adjective 'small' has suppletive stems as follows:

Norwegian (East Norwegian dialect, Hans-Olav Enger p.c.)

(12) en   lit-en   gutt
      ART.M.SG.INDF little-M.SG.INDF boy(M)-[SG.INDF]
      'a little boy'

(13) den   vesle   gutt-en
      ART.M/F.SG.DEF little.SG.DEF boy(M)-SG.DEF
      'the little boy'

(14) ei   lit-a   jent-e
      ART.F.SG.INDF little-F.SG.INDF girl(F)-SG.INDF
      'a little girl'

(15) den   vesle   jent-a
      ART.M/F.SG.DEF little.SG.DEF girl(F)-SG.DEF
      'the little girl'

(16) et   lit-e   barn
      ART.N.SG.INDF little-N.SG.INDF child(N)[SG.INDF]
      'a little child'

(17) det   vesle   barn-et
      ART.N.SG.DEF little.SG.DEF child(N)-SG.DEF
      'the little child'

The form *vesle* is only found in the singular definite. In the plural, irrespective of definiteness and irrespective of gender, another suppletive form namely *små* is used. While there are three genders, as the articles show, a normal adjective in the singular distinguishes masculine and feminine on the one hand, from neuter on the other. For example, *tjukk* 'thick, fat' (masculine and feminine singular indefinite) versus *tjukt* (neuter singular indefinite), Thus *lit-* is overdifferentiated, distinguishing masculine (*lit-en*), feminine (*lit-a*) and neuter (*lit-e*) indefinite singular (Enger and Kristoffersen 2000: 104).

It has a further surprise. A typical adjective does not distinguish definite plural from definite singular, for instance *tjukk-e* serves for both. In the lexeme we are interested in, *vesle* is the definite singular, but in the plural *små* is used. The lexeme is thus further overdifferentiated, distinguishing singular from plural within the definite part of the paradigm. In the positive, it has five forms where the typical adjective has three. Thus suppletion interacts with overdifferentiation, in that the suppletive form may introduce values not normally distinguished.

We now have the data to take further the discussion in §4.1.3 concerning the distribution of suppletive stems within a paradigm. We saw there that there is evidence for distribution according to a morphological pattern. Now the East Norwegian data provide evidence for morphosyntactic determination. The stems *lit-*, *vesle* and *små* are distributed according to the features of number and definiteness. The distribution does not follow a morphological pattern — adjectives do not normally make all these distinctions. Thus we have evidence for a lexeme which requires morpho-syntactic distribution of its suppletive stems.

We have sketched a part of a typology of suppletion. Our aim here was not to lay out a full typology, since that is still work in progress, but rather to show how the canonical approach in typology applies well even to 'extreme' phenomena such as suppletion.

5. Conclusion

We have looked at an approach to defining 'possible human language' and have given most attention to possible words. We have proposed a 'canonical' approach in typology, and have illustrated it with examples from syntax and morphology. We have seen how we can build theoretical spaces and then look for distributions within them. This approach works well even with extreme phenomena, as illustrated by our partial typology of suppletion. The examples which arise from the interaction of suppletion with other morphological phenomena will require us to extend our notion of what is a possible word.

Appendix: Criteria for Canonical Agreement

Canonical agreement is outlined in §2 above and full details can be found in Corbett (2003c). The criteria are listed under the five components of our account of agreement, namely controllers, targets, domains, features and conditions. Comrie (2003) provides an important addition (Criterion 12).

1. Controllers
C-1:   controller present > controller absent
C-2:   controller has overt features > controller has covert features
C-3:   consistent controller > hybrid controller
C-4:   controller's part of speech irrelevant > relevant (given the domain)
2. Targets
C-5:   bound > free
Criterion 5 can be expanded out as:
C-5´: inflectional marking (affix) > clitic > free word
C-6:   obligatory > optional
C-7:   regular > suppletive
C-8:   alliterative > opaque
C-9:   productive > sporadic
C-10: doubling > independent
C-11: target agrees with a single controller > agrees with more than one controller
C-12: target has no choice of controller > target has choice of controller (is 'trigger happy', Comrie 2003))
C-13: target's part of speech irrelevant > relevant (given the domain)

3. Domains
C-14: asymmetric > symmetric
C-15: local > non-local
C-16: domain is one of set > single domain

4. Features
C-17: feature is lexical > non-lexical
C-18: features have matching values > non-matching values
C-19: no choice of feature value > choice of value

5. Conditions
C-20: no conditions > conditions

These criteria fall under three general principles, which are given in §2.3 and §2.4.

Notes

* The support of the ESRC under grant R00027135 is gratefully acknowledged. I wish to thank the following for helpful discussion of some of the issues: Matthew Baerman, Dunstan Brown, Marina Chumakina, Andrew Hippisley and Carole Tiberius. Versions of the paper were given at the University of Kentucky 9 May 2003, and at the conference "Linguistic Diversity and Language Theories", Boulder, Colorado, 14–17 May 2003. I am indebted to both audiences for helpful discussion.

1. Glossing follows the Leipzig glossing rules (http://www.eva.mpg.de/lingua/index.html)

2. I am grateful to Andrew Spencer for this observation.

3. Bogdanov's transcription has been transliterated here.

4. For discussion of the rise of suppletion and for the complication of alternating suppletion, see Chumakina, Hippisley and Corbett (forthc.).

5. Andrew Carstairs-McCarthy points out (personal communication) that if, as here, affixes are not considered suppletive, then this makes it easier to maintain the claim that phonological determination of suppletive elements is not required.

6. In the dialect the forms given are obligatory. Other Norwegians I have asked find them acceptable, but consider the use of *vesle* optional.

References

Aronoff, Mark. 1994. *Morphology by itself: Stems and inflectional classes* (Linguistic Inquiry Monographs 22). Cambridge MA: MIT Press.
Aski, Janice. 1995. "Verbal suppletion: an analysis of Italian, French and Spanish *to go*." *Linguistics* 33: 403–432.
Baerman, Matthew; Brown, Dunstan and Corbett, Greville G. 2002a. *The Surrey Syncretisms Database*. Available at: http://www.smg.surrey.ac.uk/.

Baerman, Matthew; Brown, Dunstan and Corbett, Greville G. 2002b. "Case syncretism in and out of Indo-European." In *CLS 37: The Main Session, Papers from the 37th Meeting of the Chicago Linguistic Society, Vol. 1,* Mary Andronis, Christopher Ball, Heidi Elston and Sylvain Neuvel (eds), 15–28. Chicago: Chicago Linguistic Society.

Baerman, Matthew; Brown, Dunstan and Corbett, Greville G. forthcoming. *Syncretism.* Cambridge: Cambridge University Press.

Barlow, Michael 1991. "The Agreement Hierarchy and grammatical theory." In *Proceedings of the Seventeenth Annual Meeting of the Berkeley Linguistics Society, February 15–18, 1991: General Session and Parasession on the Grammar of Event Structure,* Laurel A. Sutton, Christopher Johnson and Ruth Shields (eds), 30–40. Berkeley: Berkeley Linguistics Society, University of California.

Barlow, Michael 1992. *A Situated Theory of Agreement.* New York: Garland.

Bloomfield, Leonard 1933. *Language.* New York: Holt, Rinehart and Winston.

Bogdanov, V. N. 1968. "Osobyj slučaj dialektnogo soglasovanija skazuemogo s podležaščim po smyslu i kategorija predstavitel´nosti." *Naučnye doklady vysšej školy: filologičeskie nauki* no. 4. 68–75.

Bresnan, Joan. 2001. *Lexical-functional syntax.* Oxford: Blackwell.

Bresnan, Joan and Mchombo, Sam. 1989. "Topic, pronoun, and agreement in Chicheŵa." *Language* 63.741–782.

Brown, Dunstan. 1995. rusverbs.dtr [a fragment of the verbal system of Russian]. Available at: ftp://ftp.cogs.sussex.ac.uk/pub/nlp/DATR/dtrfiles/rusverbs.dtr.

Brown, Dunstan. 2001. "Constructing a typological database for inflectional morphology: the SMG database for syncretism." In *Proceedings of the IRCS Workshop on Linguistic Databases,* Steven Bird, Peter Buneman and Mark Liberman (eds). Philadelphia: Institute for Research in Cognitive Science, University of Pennsylvania. 56–64. [Available at: http://www.ldc.upenn.edu/annotation/database/proceedings.html.]

Brown, Dunstan; Chumakina, Marina; Corbett, Greville G. and Hippisley, Andrew. 2004. *The Surrey Suppletion Database.* Available at: http://www.smg.surrey.ac.uk.

Carstairs, Andrew. 1988. "Some implications of phonologically conditioned suppletion." In *Yearbook of Morphology 1988,* Geert Booij and Jaap van Marle (eds), 67–94. Dordrecht: Kluwer.

Carstairs-McCarthy, Andrew. 1994. "Suppletion." In *Encyclopedia of Language and Linguistics: 8,* R. E. Asher (ed), 4410–4411. Oxford: Pergamon.

Chumakina, Marina; Hippisley, Andrew and Corbett, Greville G. Forthcoming. "Istoričeskie izmenenija v russkoj leksike: slučaj čeredujuščegosja suppletivizma". To appear in *Russian Linguistics.*

Comrie, Bernard. 2003. "When agreement gets trigger-happy." In *Agreement: A Typological Perspective* (special number of *Transactions of the Philological Society* 101), Dunstan Brown, Greville G. Corbett and Carole Tiberius (eds), 313–337. Oxford: Blackwell.

Corbett, Greville G. 1979. "The Agreement Hierarchy." *Journal of Linguistics* 15: 203-224.

Corbett, Greville G. 1991. *Gender.* Cambridge: Cambridge University Press.

Corbett, Greville G. 1999. "Defectiveness, syncretism, suppletion, 'deponency': four dimensions for a typology of inflectional systems". Guest lecture at The Second Mediterranean Meeting on Morphology, September 1999, Malta.

Corbett, Greville G. 2000. *Number.* Cambridge: Cambridge University Press.

Corbett, Greville G. 2003a. "Agreement: The range of the phenomenon and the principles of the Surrey Database of Agreement." In *Agreement: A Typological Perspective* (special number of *Transactions of the Philological Society* 101), Dunstan Brown, Greville G. Corbett and Carole Tiberius (eds), 155–202. Oxford: Blackwell.

Corbett, Greville G. 2003b. "A typology of suppletion and the notion 'Possible Word'. Paper read at the "Workshop on "Paradigm Irregularities", University of Manchester, 10–11 April 2003.

Corbett, Greville G. 2003c. "Agreement: Canonical instances and the extent of the phenomenon." In *Topics in Morphology: Selected papers from the Third Mediterranean Morphology Meeting (Barcelona, September 20–22, 2001)*, Geert Booij, Janet DeCesaris, Angela Ralli and Sergio Scalise (eds), 109–128. Barcelona Universitat Pompeu Fabra. Available at: http://www.surrey.ac.uk/LIS/SMG/projects/agreement/.

Corbett, Greville G.; Baerman, Matthew and Brown, Dunstan. 2002. "Domains of syncretism: a demonstration of the autonomy of morphology." In *CLS 37: The Panels. Papers from the 37th Meeting of the Chicago Linguistic Society*, Vol. 2, Mary Andronis, Christopher Ball, Heidi Elston and Sylvain Neuvel (eds), 385–398. Chicago: Chicago Linguistic Society.

Corbett, Greville G. and Fraser, Norman. 1997. "Vyčislitel'naja lingvistika i tipologija." *Vestnik MGU: Serija 9: Filologija* no. 2.122–140.

Corbett, Greville G. and Hayward, Richard J. 1987. "Gender and number in Bayso." *Lingua* 73.1–28.

Corbett, Greville G.; Hippisley, Andrew; Brown, Dunstan and Marriott, Paul. 2001. "Frequency, regularity and the paradigm: a perspective from Russian on a complex relation." In *Frequency and the Emergence of Linguistic Structure*, Joan Bybee and Paul Hopper (eds), 201–226. Amsterdam: John Benjamins.

Cornish, Francis 1986. *Anaphoric relations in English and French: A Discourse Perspective*. London: Croom Helm.

Emeneau, M. B. 1955. *Kolami: A Dravidian Language* (University of California Publications in Linguistics vol. 12). Berkeley and Los Angeles: University of California Press.

Enger, Hans-Olav and Kristoffersen, Kristian E. 2000. *Innføring i norsk grammatikk: Morfologi og syntaks*. Oslo: Landlaget for Norskundervisning / Cappelen Akademisk Forlag.

Evans, Nicholas. 2003. "Typologies of agreement: some problems from Kayardild." In *Agreement: A Typological Perspective* (special number of *Transactions of the Philological Society* 101), Dunstan Brown, Greville G. Corbett and Carole Tiberius (eds), 203–234. Oxford: Blackwell.

Evans, Nicholas; Brown, Dunstan and Corbett, Greville G. 2001. "Dalabon pronominal prefixes and the typology of syncretism: a Network Morphology analysis." In *Yearbook of Morphology 2000*, Geert Booij and Jaap van Marle (eds), 187–231. Dordrecht: Kluwer.

Greenberg, Joseph H. 1959. "A quantitative approach to the morphological typology of language." *International Journal of American Linguistics* 26.178–194.

Hayward, Richard J. 1979. "Bayso revisited: some preliminary linguistic observations – II." *Bulletin of the School of Oriental and African Studies, University of London* 42: 101–132.

Hippisley, Andrew; Chumakina, Marina, Corbett, Greville G. and Brown, Dunstan. 2004. "Constraints on suppletion." *Studies in Language* 28: 387–418.

Itkin, I. B. 2002. "K tipologii suppletivnyx paradigm". Paper read at the Third Winter Typological School, Moscow District, 29 January - 6 February 2002.

Kirby, Simon 1999. *Function, Selection and Innateness: the Emergence of Language Universals*. Oxford: Oxford University Press.

Lönngren, Lennart 1993. *Častotnyj slovar´ sovremennogo russkogo jazyka*. (=Acta Universitatis Upsaliensis, Studia Slavica Upsaliensis 33). Uppsala.

Maiden, Martin. 1992. "Irregularity as a determinant of linguistic change." *Journal of Linguistics* 28: 285–312.

Maiden, Martin. 2002. "Sound change, morphemic structure and the rise of suppletion in the Romance verb". Paper presented at the *Surrey Linguistic Circle*, University of Surrey.

Matthews, Peter. 1981. "Present stem alternations in Italian." In *Logos semantikos: Studia linguistica in honorem Eugenio Coseriu*, Christian Rohrer (ed), 1921–1981, vol. IV, 57–65. Berlin: de Gruyter.

Matthews, P. H. 1997. *The Concise Oxford Dictionary of Linguistics*. Oxford: Oxford University Press.

Mel'čuk, Igor. 1994. "Suppletion: toward a logical analysis of the concept." *Studies in Language* 18(2): 339–410.

Mel'čuk, Igor. forthcoming. Chapter 8 of *Aspects of the Theory of Morphology*. Berlin: Mouton-de Gruyter. [Revised version of Mel'čuk 1994.]

Mithun, Marianne. 2003. "Pronouns and agreement: The information status of pronominal affixes." In *Agreement: A Typological Perspective* (special number of *Transactions of the Philological Society* 101), Dunstan Brown, Greville G. Corbett and Carole Tiberius (eds), 235–278. Oxford: Blackwell.

Moravcsik, Edith A. 1988. "Agreement and markedness." In *Agreement in Natural Language: Approaches, Theories, Descriptions*, Michael Barlow and Charles A. Ferguson (eds), 89–106. Stanford: Center for the Study of Language and Information.

Nübling, Damaris. 1998. "Zur Funktionalität von Suppletion." *Germanistische Linguistik* 141–142: 77–101.

Polinsky, Maria. 2003. "Non-canonical agreement is canonical." In *Agreement: A Typological Perspective* (special number of *Transactions of the Philological Society* 101), Dunstan Brown, Greville G. Corbett and Carole Tiberius (eds), 279–312. Oxford: Blackwell.

Plank, Frans 1994. "Homonymy vs. suppletion: A riddle (and how it happens to be solved in …)" *Agreement gender number genitive &* (EUROTYP Working Papers VII/23) 81-86. Konstanz: University of Konstanz.

Priestly, T. M. S. 1993. "Slovene." In *The Slavonic Languages*, Bernard Comrie and Greville G. Corbett (eds), 388–451. London: Routledge.

Rothstein, Robert A. 1993. "Polish." In *The Slavonic Languages*, Bernard Comrie and Greville G. Corbett (eds), 686–758. London: Routledge.

Siewierska, Anna 1999. "From anaphoric pronoun to grammatical agreement marker: why objects don't make it." In *Agreement* (Special issue of *Folia Linguistica* XXXIII/2), Greville G. Corbett (ed), 225–251.

Spencer, Andrew 1991. *Morphological Theory: An Introduction to Word Structure in Generative Grammar*. Oxford: Blackwells.

Steele, Susan. 1978. "Word order variation: a typological study." In *Universals of Human Language: IV: Syntax*, Joseph H. Greenberg, Charles A. Ferguson and Edith A. Moravcsik (eds), 585–623. Stanford: Stanford University Press.

Stump, Gregory T. 2001. *Inflectional Morphology: A Theory of Paradigm Structure*. Cambridge: Cambridge University Press.

Stump, Gregory T. 2002. "Morphological and syntactic paradigms: Arguments for a theory of paradigm linkage." In *Yearbook of Morphology 2001*, Geert Booij and Jaap van Marle (eds), 147-180. Dordrecht: Kluwer.

Stump, Gregory T. 2003. "A theory of heteroclite inflectional paradigms." Ms. University of Kentucky.

Tiberius, Carole; Brown, Dunstan and Corbett, Greville G. 2002. "A typological database of agreement." In *LREC2002: Third International Conference on Language Resources and Evaluation: Proceedings: VI*, Manuel González Rodríguez and Carmen Paz Suárez

Araujo (eds), 1843–1846. Paris: European Language Resources Association.

Tiberius, Carole; Brown, Dunstan; Corbett, Greville G. and Barron, Julia. 2002. *The Surrey Database of Agreement*. Available at: http://www.smg.surrey.ac.uk/.

Trask, R. L. 1997. *A Student's Dictionary of Language and Linguistics*. London: Arnold.

Vincent, Nigel. 1988. "Italian." In *The Romance Languages*, Martin Harris and Nigel Vincent (eds), 279-313. London: Croom Helm/Routledge.

CHAPTER 3

What is an empirical theory of linguistic meaning a theory of?

Pierre-Yves Raccah
CNRS – CeReS

This chapter examines in depth under what conditions linguistic meaning can be the object of an empirical science. Possible answers, from the point of view of semantics, are given to questions about the proper object of theories of language structure, about what a theory of language structure explains, and about the elements a theory of language structure contains.

It is shown that the only empirical observations related to semantics are utterances and human behaviours; the semantic description of a human language is thus the description of the set of constraints that words and structures of that language impose on the construction of the senses of the utterances. Some of these constraints are imposed by articulators (connectives and operators); others by 'ordinary' words; both kinds of constraints concern the *points of view* which are necessary in order to build the senses of the utterances.

Introduction

In this chapter, I examine under what conditions linguistic meaning can be the object of an empirical science. In particular, I give possible answers, from the point of view of semantics, to the following questions:

- What should be the proper object for theories of language structure?
- What should a theory of language structure explain?
- What elements should a theory of language structure contain?

Within this inquiry, various possible reductionisms will briefly be taken into consideration, as possible directions to investigate in order to answer those questions; among those, I will study in more details the *cognitive reductionism*, and thus give a partial answer to the following question:

- What should be the relationship between theories of language structure and the theories of cognition?

It is a commonsensical belief that science is supposed to uncover the 'laws of nature'. According to that belief, scientific theories state the laws which nature allegedly obey. After briefly picturing the situation of the notion of *scientific law* with respect to the other kinds of rules, I will show that the above mentioned 'commonsensical' belief is misleading: we will discuss the conception of science that stems from it. In that discussion, we will show that scientific theories do not provide *explanations* of the phenomena, in the usual sense of the word, but rather constrained *descriptions*, of the kind I will specify. From that point of view, science could look like a formal language, a sort of representation system, with which one can also generate complex representations out of simpler ones. But scientific theories do much more, they play a crucial psychological and social role: because of the kind of constraints that science impose to possible descriptions, once a scientific theory is accepted by a community, it constitutes an inter-subjective tool to perceive phenomena: accepted hypotheses become the facts of newer theories.

Applying these views to the science of natural languages, we will examine in what sense speakers and hearers can be said to apply semantic rules. We will see that these semantic rules have to be seen as re-constructions, by the observers, of processes of sense construction, in which the meanings of sentences are the tools which operate on the hearer's knowledge for her/him to build an interpretation of the utterance of the sentence, in the situation in which it was uttered. In that sense, though semantics is obviously related to cognitive science, its objects of study are not cognitive objects.

1. Different notions of rule

This section provides a short review of the different notions of rules. This review is not exhaustive and does not aim to be so: it only pretends to put into perspective what will be said about scientific laws, preventing, thus, excessive generalisations and providing guidelines for possible extensions.

For each type of rule which we examined in the following contrastive outline, we provided some characteristics of

- the usual names given for rules of that kind,
- its domains of application,
- the kind of entities which is supposed to follow –or not– the rule,
- possible transgressions and transgressors,
- possible clearly inappropriate names for a rule of that kind; kinds of rules which are in opposition or incompatible with rules of that kind.

So, for instance, a particular law, belonging to the first line of the table, has, as its domain, human behaviour, concerns citizens or juridical entities, leaves place to cheaters (civil laws) or criminals (penal law), and cannot be taken to be a strategy, a dogma or a regularity, as soon as it is understood as a law. Table 1 sums up the main results of this short analysis.[1]

Table 1. Different notions of rules

Types (names)	Domains	Entities	Transgressors	Incompatibility
Norms, laws, contracts, procedures, orders	Legislation; more generally, human behaviour with respect to other humans and/or institutions. [General, imposed]	Citizens, judges, governments, legislators; member of an organisation.	Criminals, cheaters	Strategy; Dogma; Regularity
Rules of a game, dance, strategies	Ludic activities; more generally, human behaviour with respect to other humans. [Particular, chosen]	Players, dancers, actors.	Bad (poor) players, cheaters, marginals (?),	Law; Dogma; Regularity; Principle
Rules of a religion, dogmas, commandments	Human beliefs or behaviour with respect to non-human entities (such as divinities). [Imposed]	Members of a religious or mystical community.	Heretics	Strategy; Regularity
Moral rules and principles	Human behaviour (in general)	Any human being	Immoral, dirty, revolting	Strategy; Regularity; Dogma
Formal relations	Mathematics, Logic.	Concepts	Incoherent, inconsistent	Strategy; Dogma; Regularity
Rules of nature, scientific laws, principles	Material: physics, chemistry, etc. Immaterial: sociology, psychology, linguistics, etc.	Anything…	[No exclusion]…	Strategy; Dogma

2. Laws of nature vs principles of rationality

We often say that nature obeys laws; that natural phenomena can be explained by rules; or that some particular theory explains some particular set of phenomena. As long as these statements remain general and metaphorical, they are acceptable and harmless. However, if someone believed that nature really *obeys* some set of laws (in the sense that it would be *obedient*), (s)he would certainly be considered as mystical or, at least irrational.[2]

As a matter of fact, one must consider irrational not only the belief that nature is *obedient*, but also the belief that theories give *explanations* to natural phenomena, in the usual meaning of the word explanation. For both attitudes presuppose a very special metaphysical standpoint according to which nature is subject to *behaviours* which, in the first case, would be dictated by laws[3] and, in the second case, would be such that one could find *reasons* (or even *causes*) for those behaviours. Can we seriously pretend that the law of universal attraction is a cause (or a reason) of the movement of the Earth around the Sun, *in the same way* as Othello's jealousy was one of the causes, of the reasons, of Desdemona's death?

The only way, thus, to avoid personifying nature (with all the irrationality it would imply), is to consider that 'natural laws' cease to be natural as soon as they are laws and cease to be laws as soon as they are natural . . .[4]

2.1. On natural laws and explanations

One might want to hold that, since we can observe regularities in nature, there must be something 'out there' which is responsible for the regularities we observe. This belief – which is also mine, I must confess. . . – is not really rational:[5] the only conclusions we can draw from observable regularities is that there may be something, *either* 'out there' *or* within the observers' systems of observation, which is responsible for the regularities observed. In other words, the so called 'natural laws' should be interpreted as possible constants of the human cognitive systems, or as relating the human cognitive system to the world we observe, but not as properties of that world alone. However, once we know that whatever we think we are saying about the world is, in fact, a statement about the cognitive relationship we have with the world, we might want to simplify our statements, using the metaphor of natural laws. But we should not be blinded by that metaphor: what linguistic expressions such as 'natural law' refer to only belongs to the representations suggested by the use of language; the fact that we can *speak* of natural laws does not guarantee their existence.

It follows from these reflections that, even if we want to describe the regularities of our observations in terms of natural laws, we are not entitled to hold that these regularities exist *because of* some law: this would suppose the personification of nature which we have to reject. For, what law would force nature to obey some natural law? And, if we wanted to formulate such a law, what would force nature to obey that other law? Yet another law?

We thus have to abandon the idea that science *explains* nature. What does remain is the fact that science *describes* nature, in such a way that the descriptions it provides are often felt like explanations (hence, the use of the term *natural law*). If we consider a particular scientific theory as a set of rules which generate a description of some aspects of a class of phenomena, we get hold of a more reasonable conception of *natural laws*. That position can be called a *de dicto* conception: what we call 'natural law' is a rule which explains the description we make of some phenomenon within the framework of some theory, in the sense that the rule allows to formally generate the description. The study of physical theories very well illustrates the necessity of such an epistemological precaution.

When a fact *A* is presented as a cause of a fact *B*, it constitutes a *de re* explanation of the fact *B*. When a fact *A* is presented as a cause of the fact that one may think or say "*B happens (has happened or will happen)*", it constitutes a *de dicto* explanation for *B*. Suppose John arrives at 15:30 at a meeting where he was expected at 15:00; when asked "Why are you late", he might answer "I am late because I had a car accident on my way". He is then presenting the fact [*car accident*] as a *de re* cause of the fact [*delay*], giving thus a *de re* explanation for the fact [*delay*]. Had he answered "I am late because I arrived 30 minutes after the agreed time", independently of the social effects of such an answer, he would have presented the fact [*arriving 30 minutes after the agreed time*] as a cause for thinking or saying that he is late, that is, as a *de dicto* explanation for the fact [*delay*]. Obviously, in that example, what was expected was a *de re* answer: the *de dicto* one is deceiving in this situation. However, in other situations, the contrary happens. Suppose you hear Paul say "John is nasty" and you ask him "Why?". If Paul gives you a *de re* explanation, such as "His parents treated him badly when he was a child", you would feel deceived by that answer and would insist "Come on, I am asking why you *say* (or what makes you think) that John is nasty". In that case, the expected explanation is a *de dicto* explanation.[6] This is precisely the kind of expectations we have about scientific descriptions.

If, for instance, we considered the law for the uniformly accelerated movement, as it is expressed in

$$e = 1/2gt^2 + v_0t + e_0$$

as a *de re* explanation of the trajectory of an object with initial velocity v_0 at time $t = 0$, starting at point e_0 of the space, we would then consider the trajectory as caused by the fact expressed by the equation, which, as we have seen above, would be a mystical conception of Nature. In addition, we would also have to explain why this relation holds for this type of movements, and, after a short series of 'whys', we would end up considering the law of universal attraction:

$$F = k \cdot \frac{M.M'}{d^2}$$

as *de re* explanation of the trajectory, which would make it necessary to find an explanation for it . . . and so on.

2.2. *De re* vs. *de dicto* descriptions

Fortunately, this is not the way physicists proceed: the aim of these equations is not to provide an explanation to the 'mysteries' of nature, but to explain how the theory describes and predicts the phenomena it is supposed to account for. Scientific theories also provide more abstract laws, which account for less abstract ones, like the universal attraction law accounts for the different movement laws. These more abstract laws, as we have seen, have no intrinsic explanatory value for the phenomena: they only explain how we can describe some phenomenon E in some particular way $T(E)$, given that we describe some other phenomena, $E_1, E_2, \ldots E_n$, using descriptions $T(E_1), T(E_2), \ldots T(E_n)$.

The 'explanatory effect' produced by a scientific theory is thus external to the theory itself. In an attempt to reconstruct how this effect can occur, it can be said that it is due to the following two factors:

- our tendency to believe that nature follows rules;
- our tendency to assimilate a phenomenon with its description.

The combination of these factors seems to be operated by the following abductive reasoning:

> Since nature obeys rules and since rule S generates a satisfactory description of the natural phenomenon E, it must be this rule S that nature obeys in order to produce phenomenon E. [note the *de dicto* → *de re* shift from the first to the second occurrence of S.]

2.3. Compositionality and explicativity revisited

In order to provide systematic *de dicto* explanations, a scientific theory θ must provide means to

(a) structure a set of phenomena of the field in simple and more complex phenomena[7] (we will say that the phenomenal structure of θ rests on *external hypotheses*);

(b) assign descriptions to the phenomena of that set (let us call that a '*theory of measure*' for θ);

(c) generate descriptions out of other descriptions, with the means of theory-specific operators (called *internal hypotheses*);

(d) compare descriptions one to another (in particular, compare a description assigned to a phenomenon to a description generated).

We can thus say that a theory θ *correctly predicts* a complex phenomenon E whenever the description it *generates* is identical to the description its theory of measure *assigns* to E.

Thus, given a set of external hypotheses for an empirical theory θ, which entitle us to consider a phenomenon E as a structural complex involving the phenomena

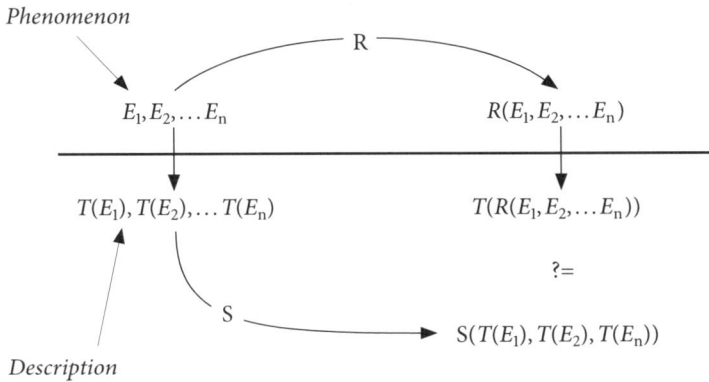

Figure 1. Structure of scientific theories: first approximation

$E_1, E_2, \ldots E_n$ (that is, $E = R(E_1, E_2, \ldots E_n)$ for some structural relation R) given a theory of measure for θ, which allows us to describe the relevant aspects of $E_1, E_2, \ldots E_n$ and E, as $T(E_1), T(E_2), \ldots T(E_n)$ and T(E), and given a theoretical operation S, the experimental contrôle of θ, consists in comparing $T(E)$, that is $T(R(E_1, E_2, \ldots E_n))$, with the description θ generates, that is, $S(T(E_1), T(E_2), \ldots T(E_n))$. Figure 1 illustrates how this functions.[8]

If Newton's law were not a *de dicto* law, we would expect any two bodies to *really* attract each other at a distance *because of* their mass; that is, we would expect the mass of the bodies to *cause* an action at a distance. This would contradict Lavoisier's second *principle* of scientific rationality ("There is no action at a distance"). This would not *in itself*, constitute an evidence against the *de re* interpretation of Newton's law (there could have been a change of paradigm from Newton's views to Lavoisier's): however, the fact that scientists do not feel Lavoisier's second principle as conflicting with Newton's law *does* constitute an evidence that Newton's law is not interpreted by scientists as a *de re* statement.

Applying that to the study of language meaning allows to understand that the question of compositionality, that was part of the constant discussion among linguists in the seventies, is ill formed: the question is not whether the meaning of a compounded expression is a function of the meaning of its parts (ontological question. . .) but whether one can describe the meaning of a compounded expression using the descriptions of the meanings of its parts.

3. On what there is. . .

In the description proposed above, phenomena $E_1, E_2, \ldots E_n$ and E are referred to without questions on how they are perceived, as if they were, so to speak, directly accessible to observation. This reconstruction is based on a metaphor according to which the world, with its structures, *appears* to our cognitive system independently of the way it functions. That is, in spite of the precautions taken for rules or laws, the position defended seems to endorse the simple objectivist point of view for entities or events. This is only an appearance, due to the necessity of the presentation. Let us now focus on the constitution of the facts in an empirical theory.

3.1. Having done with the 'scientific progress' vulgate

First, I would like to insist on the fact that the simple objectivist position cannot be grounds for a scientific activity because it relies on a non-rational belief, which I express in B:[9]

> B Our means of observation, that is, our cognitive and perceptive apparatus, occasionally augmented with some technical devices, give us a 'picture' of the world, which can be partial but still reproduces its essential features.

The two main reasons why B is not a rational belief are:

(a) We cannot know what the 'essential features' of the world are, principally because we could not be in the position to exhibit 'essential features' of the world which our cognitive system does not handle: the picture our cognitive apparatus can give us of the world is only a picture of what we can *grasp* about it... The statement of the belief B is thus circular for it really says that our means of observation, ..., give us a 'picture' of the world, which can be partial but still reproduces what our means of observation make us think that they are the essential features of the world.

(b) The 'picture' our cognitive apparatus gives us of the world cannot be directly compared to the world itself in order to exhibit their resemblance: in order to be in the position to do so, we would have to be in the position to access the world without using our cognitive apparatus so that we could have a point of comparison... There are ways to *indirectly* make that comparison (for instance, an analysis of human or non-human action on the world): but, as we will see, they need human interpretation and, thus, are not theory independent.

Thus, the role of the observer in the construction of the observable facts cannot be considered as a mere 'deformation' of a reality which would be external to her/him, but rather, as a construction of an accessible reality. The externalisation of that accessible reality constructed by the observer can only be posterior to its construction. This externalisation is the result of a social and linguistic process, which will be addressed in section 4.

3.1. Compositionality re-revisited

In the same way as we found necessary to account for the explanatory effect of scientific descriptions, we feel compelled to account for the way our observation of the world structures it into phenomena. The idea is a recursive loop of the scheme suggested above: an accepted theory forces us to perceive the world in terms of the entities and relations it predicts. In other words, consider a theory Θ^1, which describes what it considers as phenomena $E_1^1, E_2^1, \ldots E_n^1$, and E^1 as $T(E_1^1), T(Ev_2^1), \ldots T(E_n^1)$ and $S^1(T(E_1^1), T(E_2^1), \ldots T(E_n^1))$. Suppose, now, that θ_1 has been accepted by the scientific community; a member of this scientific community, while working on a theory θ^2, will identify some of θ^2's phenomena, $E_1^2, E_2^2, \ldots E_n^2$, with some of θ^1's descriptions $T(E_1^2), T(E_2^1), \ldots T(E_n^1)$; θ^2's structural relation R^2 with θ^1's theoretical operation S, and so on. So that *Figure 1* has to be modified accordingly, giving Figure 2.

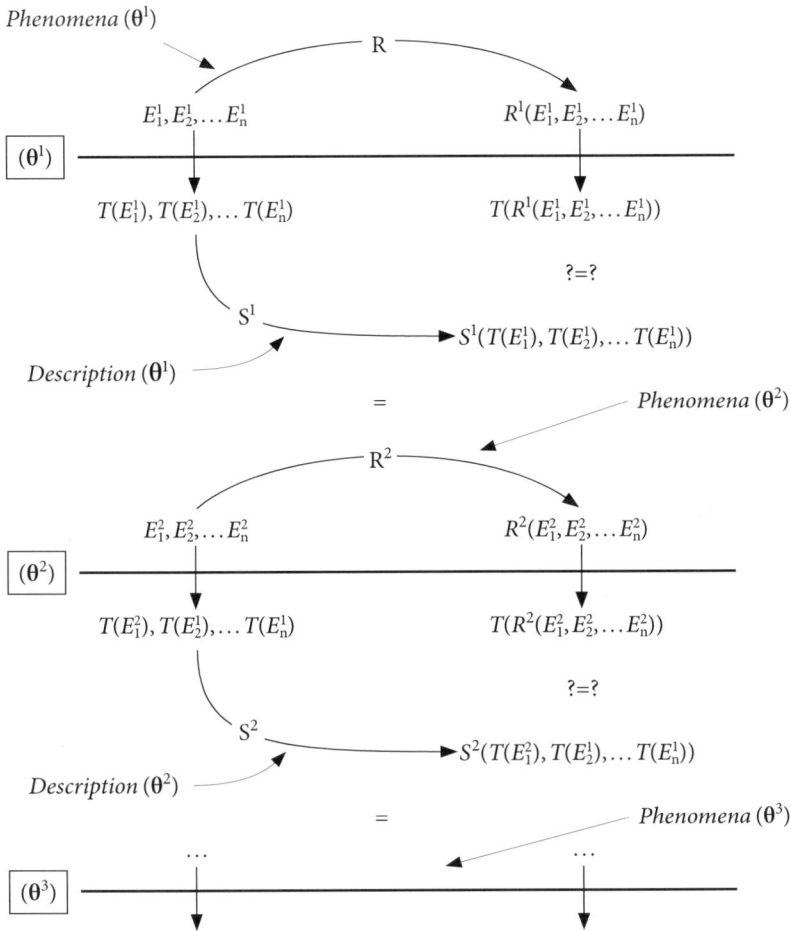

Figure 2. Structure of scientific theories: second approximation

We can thus say that the phenomena of a new theory are the theoretical constructs of accepted theories. This is easily understood when we consider that, behind any measuring device, lies a theory, like, for instance, the ammeter can be seen as a reification of the theory of electro-magnetic induction.

From a metaphysical point of view, one would, of course, need to know where all that starts from, what the first step of this loop is. But, fortunately, science does not include metaphysics: we are not concerned with this question...

We will now see the interest, from a cognitive point of view, of taking into account both the *de dicto* aspect of scientific theories and the rôle of the observer in the construction of scientific facts.

3.2. Towards a cognitive approach to scientific knowledge

According to the conceptual reconstruction developed above, scientific theories are *essentially compositional*, in the sense that what a theory describes as a complex phenomenon is necessarily described, within this theory, in terms of the parts of that phenomenon and a theoretical operation assigned to the structural rule which combines the parts of the phenomenon. Given that the correspondence between phenomena and descriptions is a matter of inter-subjective convention, it makes sense to wonder whether it is *true* or *false* that phenomenon E is assigned description $T(E)$. These characteristics partially determine the form scientific statements normally take, in order to be evaluated by the scientific community: each noun phrase must refer to one and only one scientific concept (hence, the importance of *terminology* in science); each statement to a truth value, each intransitive verb phrase to a function from scientific concepts (referred to by the subject of the verb phrase) to truth values, and so on. In the context of a communication between scientists, the responsibility for each utterance is supposed to lie with all the scientific community, not only with the speaker. If I utter

$$e = 1/2gt^2 + v_0t + e_0$$

I am not expressing my opinion (or, at least, I am not presenting myself as doing so): I am claiming that what that utterance expresses is held true by the scientific community.

This situation certainly explains why cognition has very often been reduced to a conceptual system and natural language to a logical calculus: cognition was assimilated to scientific knowledge and natural languages to scientific or technical languages, whose lexical items are not *words* but *terms*. I will now briefly show why human knowledge cannot be assimilated to a truth-conditional information system; then, I will show why the meaning of natural language expressions cannot be reduced to truth-conditional information.

The enormous amount of work that has been done in artificial intelligence often rests (though, fortunately, not always...) on the assumption that, given the conceptual and computational tools which are now available to reproduce deductive reasoning, it would be sufficient to *collect* the best experts' knowledge in some field and have it elaborated by some sophisticated *inference engine*, in order to get a perfect expert system, that is, a system which would function like (or even better than) a human expert in that field. But this assumption is unacceptable for at least two reasons:

(a) it presupposes that deductive reasoning is appropriate for any kind of expertise (and even, for that matter, at least for one...), and that the same type of reasoning is universally adequate;
(b) it considers collecting knowledge as something easy and, even, straightforward whenever you have a good expert at hand.

The first reason does not concern us very much here. Moreover, it has been recognised as a serious problem by artificial intelligence people, and has been treated, technically speaking, with many interesting exotic logical systems, such as *fuzzy logic*, *non monotonic logic*, etc.. Though the results are often interesting from a computational point of view, they are incredibly poor from a cognitive point of view.

The second reason is, actually, the heart of the question we want to address. It *seems* obvious that, since experts possess knowledge of some domain, not only can they use that knowledge properly but, that the more they know, the more they can say about what they know. But this turned out to be another non-rational belief and, in that case, it is simply false... When requested to explain why (s)he went from A to C, an expert may build a complex reasoning, with many steps, which rationally explains his/her inference. But it is usually not the process (s)he went into: the rational reasoning may take a few minutes while the expert inferred C from A in less than a second... Actually, this is precisely what experts are paid for: doing at a glance what others take time to do. But there is no reason why an expert should be, *as an expert*, expert of his/her own expertise. For that reason, experts are not the most indicated persons to consult in order to understand their own cognitive processes.

To take an example, suppose you go to your doctor with a headache and (s)he prescribes you aspirin; if you ask her/him why, (s)he, generally, can tell you that:

(i) headaches are generally due to a poor blood circulation in the cerebral membranes;
(ii) the active principle of aspirin is the ion acetylsalicilate;
(iii) the ion acetylsalicilate activates blood circulation because
   (a) it fluidifies blood,
   (b) it dilates blood vessels;

thus

(iv) the ion acetylsalicilate may fight one cause of headaches

and thus,

(v) aspirin may be indicated to fight headaches

But though this might be the explanation the doctor learnt when (s)he was a student, it is certainly not the reasoning (s)he *actually* made when prescribing aspirin. (S)he, most probably, associated a certain degree of dysfunctioning with a certain class of medicines, and activated this association forgetful of the reasons why that association was memorised. (S)he then remembers these reasons only when explicitly *thinking* about her/his knowledge, but not while *using* it.

This way of managing knowledge may be frightening: the practitioner's expertise (*as a practitioner*) is no longer guaranteed by science. However, this is precisely what makes the difference between a real expert and a beginner... The beginner applies rules (s)he has learnt and of which (s)he is conscious during their application while the expert does not apply rules consciously : there might be a way to describe her/his behaviour using rules, but they are not of the same kind as the ones the beginner applies.

4. Under what conditions the semantics of human languages could be an empirical science?

Let us admit that *semantics* is the study of what, in human languages (and, more specifically in their structures), contributes to the construction of the meaning of utterances. Taking into account the facts mentioned above, about scientificity and empiricity, it makes sense to wonder under what conditions the semantics of natural language can be an empirical science. Indeed, one can easily see that it becomes a very difficult question since, in order to be an empirical discipline, semantics has to be grounded on objective observation, while its object of study, sentence meaning, is, obviously, not directly observable. However, the following considerations could help us not despair... The situation is not very different from that of admittedly empirical sciences such as physics. It can easily be seen that gravity, for instance, is not directly observable; even forces, which appear to be closer to sensorial experience, can be observed only by means of their alleged effects. So that if we could find a way to trap, so to speak, meaning within experimental devices in such a way that it could be indirectly observed through some of its directly observable effects, semantics would not be in a situation worse than that of physics... This is what will be shown, in this section, to be possible. We will also examine some of the consequences of this approach regarding the conception one should have on language and its relationship to human communication, human cognition and ethics. In particular, it will be shown that, though semantics and cognition are tightly related, semantics is not a cognitive science and thus, the term "cognitive semantics" is void and misleading. Finally, it will be shown why, as an apparently paradoxical consequence of the empiricity and scientificity requirements, the minimal semantic units should be connected to subjective points of view, rather than to objective conditions of truth.

4.1. What are the observable phenomena of natural language semantics?

When discussing the notion of natural law, we pointed out that an essential scientificity requirement, valid for any kind of science, is that it should provide descriptions of a class of phenomena, in such a way that the descriptions of some of those phenomena provided *de dicto* explanations for the descriptions of other ones. We also pointed out that the empiricity requirements could not lead to believe that science describes the phenomena 'the way they are', since one cannot seriously believe that there is a possibility, for any human being, to *know* the way things are. Though scientific observers cannot prevail themselves of *knowing* how the world *is*, they have access to the world through their interpretation of the states of their sensorial apparatus. We also saw that that interpretation often relies on previously admitted scientific – or non scientific – theories.

If we want to apply these requirements to semantic theories, we have to find observable semantic facts, which can be accessed to through our senses. It seems that we are faced with a big difficulty, which might force us to admit that there cannot be such a thing as an empirical semantic theory: semantic facts are not accessible to our sensorial apparatus. Even if we want to distinguish, as Marcelo Dascal suggests (Dascal 1983) between *utterance meaning* and *sentence meaning*, none of them is directly accessible to our senses. We are thus in a situation in which the very object about which we want to construct an empirical science prevents its study from being an empirical study…

However, if we admit that physics is a good example of empirical sciences, we should realise that we are not in such a dramatic situation. For what the physicist can observe through her/his senses, say, the actual movements of the pendulum she/he just built, is not what her/his theory is about (in that case, the virtual movements of *any* – existing or non existing – pendulum) the object of physical theories is not more directly accessible to the observers' sensorial apparatus than the object of semantic theories. Physicists use different tricks in order to overcome that difficulty, one of which is the use of *indirect observation*: some directly observable[10] objects or events are considered to be traces of non directly observable ones, which, in some cases, are seen as one of their causes, and, in other cases, as one of their effects.

If we are willing to keep considering physics as an empirical science, we are bound to consider that that *indirect observation* strategy is not misleading; we only have to see how it could be applied to the study of meaning. In order to illustrate how this could be done, we will examine an example and will abstract from it.

Suppose an extra-terrestrial intelligence, ETI, wanted to study the semantics of English and, for that purpose, decided to observe speech situations. Suppose ETI hides in a room where several – supposedly English speaking – human beings are gathered, a classroom, for instance. Suppose now that ETI perceives that John pronounces "It is cold in here". If ETI's observations are all of that kind, there is no chance that it can formulate grounded hypotheses about the meaning of the sequence it heard. For what can be perceived of John's utterance is only a series of vibrations, which, in themselves, do not give cues of any kind as to what it can mean (except for those who understand English and interpret the utterance using their private know-how). If ETI wants to do its job correctly, it will have to use, in addition, observations of another kind. Intentional states are ruled out since they are not directly accessible to the observers' sensorial apparatus. It follows that we will have to reject any statement of the kind: "the speaker meant so and so", or "normally when someone says XYZ, he or she wants to convey this or that idea" or even "I, observer, interpret XYZ in such and such a way and therefore, that is the meaning of XYZ". ETI will have to observe the audience's behaviour and see whether, in that behaviour, it can find a plausible *effect* of John's utterance: it will have to use indirect observation. The fact that it may be the case that no observable reaction followed John's utterance does not constitute an objection to the indirect observation method: it would simply mean that ETI would have to plan other experiments. After all, even in physics, many experiments do not inform the theorists until they find the experimental constraints that work.

Before we go further, it is useful to emphasise that we have just seen that the different 'popular learned conceptions'[11] of semantics are wrong. Indeed, the observable phenomena of semantics (i) cannot be directly meanings, since these are not accessible to our sensorial apparatus; (ii) they are not just utterances, since that would not be enough to describe meaning phenomena; (iii) they are not pairs consisting of utterances and 'intended meanings', since such intentional things are not accessible to empirical observation. In our extra-terrestrial example, we suggested that they are pairs consisting of utterances and behaviours.

In the rest of this chapter, we will take that suggestion as seriously as possible: in this section, we will see how to constrain the relationship between utterances and behaviours, and examine some of the consequences of this choice.[12] In the following sections, we will present a theoretical framework based on the conception of meaning that follows from that discussion.

4.2. Three pre-theoretical hypotheses which characterise contemporary occidental rationality.

4.1.1. *The causal attribution hypothesis*
Suppose that, in our example, ETI notices that, after John's utterance, the following three actions take place: (i) Peter scratches his head, (ii) Paul closes the window and (iii) Mary writes something on a piece of paper. We all know (actually, we think we know, but we only believe . . .) that the correct answer to the question "what action was caused by John's utterance?" is "Paul's". However, ETI has no grounds to *know* it and, in addition, it may be the case that Paul closed the window not because of John's utterance (which he may even not have heard), but because *he* was cold, or because there was too much noise outside to hear what John was saying. . . Obviously, the most plausible hypothesis, in normal situations, is the one according to which

Paul's action was caused by John's utterance; but the fact that it is plausible does not make it cease to be a hypothesis...

Thus, before ETI can continue its study, it must admit the following general hypothesis

H_0 Utterances may cause behaviours

Moreover, in each experimental situation s, ETI must make specific hypotheses h_S which particularise H_0 in the situation s, and relate particular actions with the utterance under study.

It is important to remind that H_0 and the different h_S are not facts about the world but hypotheses: they do not characterise the way things are but rather the way things are conceived of in our rationality.

1.1.2. *The non materiality hypothesis*

Let us suppose that ETI shares with us the aspects of our contemporary occidental rationality expressed by H_0. This would not prevent it from believing that the way John's utterance caused Paul's action is that the vibrations emitted by John during his utterance physically caused Paul to get up and close the window. Though it hurts our contemporary occidental rationality, this idea is not absurd: the fact that we simply cannot take it seriously does not *make* it false. Moreover, utterances do have observable physical effects: a loud voice can hurt the hearers' ears, specific frequencies can break crystal, etc. What our rationality cannot accept is the idea that the linguistic effects of the utterances could be reduced to material causality. In order to rule out this idea, we need another hypothesis, which is also characteristic of our rationality rather than of the state of the world:

H_1 The linguistic effects of an utterance are not due to material causes

As a consequence of H_1, if we cannot believe that the observable actions caused by an utterance are due to its materiality, we are bound to admit that they are due to its form. In our rationality, the causal attribution requested by H_0 is constrained to be a formal causality.

1.1.3. *The non immediateness hypothesis*

If we use the term *sentence* to refer to a category of form of utterances, we start to be in the position to fill the gap between what we can observe (utterances and behaviours) and what we want semantics to talk about (sentences and meanings). However, there is yet another option that our rationality compels us to rule out: ETI could accept H_1 and believe that though the causality that links John's utterance to Paul's action is not material, it directly determined Paul's action. That is, one could believe that John's utterance directly caused Paul to close the window, without leaving him room for a choice. This sort of belief corresponds to what we can call a 'magic thinking'; indeed, in the tale about Ali Baba, for instance, there would be no magic if the "sesame" formula were recognised by a captor which would send an "open" instruction to a mechanism conceived in such a way that it could open the cave. The magical effect is due to the directedness of the effect of the formula. It is interesting to note that this feature of our rationality, which compels us to reject direct causality of forms, is rather recent and not completely 'installed' in our cognitive systems: there are many traces in human behaviour and in human languages of the 'magic thinking'. From some uses of expressions like "Please" or "Excuse me" to greetings such as "Happy new year!", an impressing series of linguistic expressions and social behaviours suggests that, though a part of our mind has abandoned the 'magic thinking', another part still lives with it. Think, for instance, about the effects of insults on normal contemporary human beings...

However, for scientific purposes, we definitely abandoned the 'magic thinking' and, again, since it is a characteristic of our rationality and not a matter of knowledge about the world, no observation can prove that it has to be abandoned: we need another hypothesis, which could be stated as follows:

H_2 The directly observable effects of utterances are not directly caused by them

The acceptance of that "anti-magic" hypothesis has at least two types of consequences on the conception one can have of human being.

The first type of consequences pertains to ethics: if utterances do not directly cause observable effects on human actions, no human being can justify a reprehensible action arguing that they have been told or even ordered to accomplish them. If a war criminal tries to do so, he or she will give the justified impression that he or she is not behaving like a human being, but rather like a kind of animal or robot. As human beings, we are supposed to be responsible for our actions; which does not mean that we are free, since a reprehensible decision could be the only way of serving vital interests. Though this type of consequences of H2 are serious and important, they do not directly belong to the subject matter of this chapter and we will have to end the discussion here. However, we think they were worth mentioning...

The second type of consequences of H2 concern the relationship between semantics and cognitive science. Indeed, H2, combined with H0 and H1, can be seen as a way of setting the foundations of a science of human cognition and of picturing its relationship with related disciplines. If we admit, in agreement with H_0, H_1 and H_2, that an utterance indirectly and non materially causes an action, we are bound to accept the existence of a non physical causal chain linking the utterance to the action, part of that chain being inaccessible to our sensorial apparatus. The object of semantics is the first link of the chain; the first internal state can be seen as the *utterance meaning*. The action is determined by a causal lattice in which the utterance meaning is a part, and which includes many other elements and links; none of these elements or links are directly observable, though indirect observation can suggest more or less plausible hypotheses about them. Different theoretical frameworks in cognitive science construe that causal lattice in different ways; they also use the variations of different observable parameters in order to form these hypotheses. In our example, the only two directly observable parameters were utterances and actions, for the part of the lattice that we are interested in is the chain that links utterances to actions. However, other kinds of cognitive science experiments could be interested in studying the variations of other directly observable parameters, such as electrical excitation, visual input, outside temperature, etc. for the beginning of the chain and movement characteristics, body temperature, attention, etc. for the end of the chain.[14]

The fact that cognitive science and semantics may share experimental devices is not sufficient to suggest that there can be a "cognitive semantics": the object of semantics (the link between utterances and utterance meanings) does not belong to the causal lattice which constitutes the object of cognitive science.

The following diagram (adapted from Raccah 2002) sums up the discussion and shows the consequences that can be drawn from it concerning the relationship between the object of semantics and that of cognitive science.

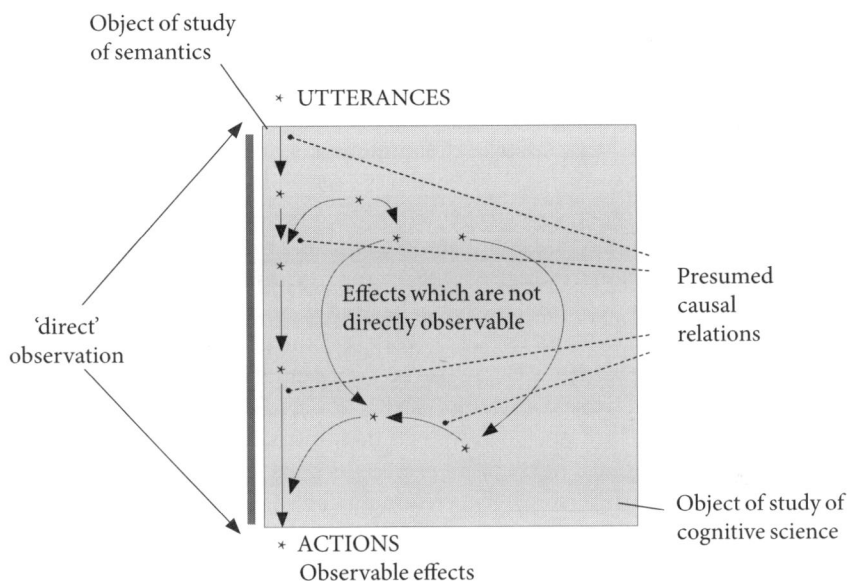

Figure 3. Non-observable causal chain between utterances and actions

4.3. Why constraints on argumentation ought to be accounted for in a scientific empirical theory of sentence meaning

We can now turn back to the question addressed by this section: Under what conditions the semantics of human languages could be an empirical science? We have seen that, in order to describe its object of study, sentence meaning, it is necessary to observe accessible traces of utterance meanings, and abstract from these observations: the sentence-meaning descriptions have to account for what is invariant in the utterance-meanings across the different situations. More precisely, if all the utterances of a sentence S share some property P whose accessible traces can be observed in the reactions of the audience in the different utterance situations, the semantic description of S must include a property P', which is responsible for the property P in all the situations. Without that constraint, there is no guarantee that the semantic description of S is (i) based on empirical observation and (ii) valid for S itself and not only for some utterances of S.

Keeping that in mind, semantics cannot limit itself do describing the informational aspects of meaning: several non-informational properties of utterances do not depend on situations and if they were not described within a semantic theory, they would be simply forgotten. . . One of these properties concerns argumentation. It is not difficult to observe that, though not all utterances are argumentations, any sentence, whatsoever, can be uttered in a situation in which that utterance *is* an argumentation. Thus, for instance, though it is true that if someone utters "It is 8 o'clock" as an answer to the question "What time is it", he/she is normally not making an argumentation; however, the very same sentence, "It is 8 o'clock" can be uttered in a situation in which the speaker is trying to have the addressee hurry up. . . Obviously, sentences cannot determine the argumentative orientations of their possible utterances (be it only because some of those utterances do not have argumentative orientation while other ones do. . .). Nevertheless, they must impose constraints on *argumentativity* since, otherwise, any sentence could be use for any argumentative purpose: and this is not the case. For instance, "It is only 8 o'clock" cannot serve the argumentative orientation *it is late*.

The fact that absolutely all sentences can be used in an argumentative utterance requires that an empirical semantic framework for human languages be able to account for the constraints sentences impose on argumentation. In the following sections, we will show that these constraints cannot be derived from truth-conditions or other 'informational' frameworks; we will then introduce the Theory of Argumentation within Language (AWL) and present its aims and functioning. We will finally go back to the relationship between semantics and cognition and discuss the interest of that approach for cognitive research.

5. Why constraints on argumentation cannot be derived from truth-conditions

Since the first studies on language, argumentation has been considered, with very few exceptions, as a phenomenon which had to be accounted for only after the meaning of the sentences under consideration had been "extracted". Indeed, until 1972, it was taken for granted that if someone used sentence A as an argument or an evidence for a conclusion C, it was in virtue of the informational content conveyed by A. According to that "commonsensical" belief, the description of the argumentative power of A had, conceptually, to be grounded solely on a description of its informational content and a characterization of the situation of utterance. After the observations of O. Ducrot and his first systematization, that naive belief turned out to be no longer acceptable (except for one who were ready to accept a particularly broad concept of informational content): see, for instance, Ducrot (1973), Anscombre and Ducrot (1983), Raccah (1984, 1987, 1990).

The theoretical framework grounded in that reconsideration of the relationship between argumentation and information (let's call it "Argumentation Within Language"; in short AWL) allows to describe, within semantics, the constraints on the argumentative orientation of utterances. AWL central hypothesis is that the warrants that allow a speaker to present an utterance as an argument for some conclusion are all instances of gradual rules presented -by the speaker- as general, in that they also apply to other cases than the one under discussion, and shared, in that the audience is assumed to accept them as such. These gradual rules, through which warrants are classified are called *topoi* (singular: *topos*).

A first class of applications of this framework is an improved description of argumentative articulators (operators and connectives), description given in terms of constraints on argumentative features.

A second class of applications of this framework stems from the following reflection: the argumentative features which are attached to the sentences whose articulators are described have to be the result of a calculus — or, at least, to be described in a more or less compositional way. The program of this class of applications is thus to build the description of the semantic argumentative features of a sentence out of the semantic description of the words of that sentence (see Bruxelles, Carcagno and Fournier 1989, Fournier and Raccah 1990, Raccah 1990 and Bruxelles and Raccah 1990). In connection with this second class of applications, I will illustrate and defend the following three claims: (i) lexical items impose biases on their denotation, (ii) these biases capture an important part of the beliefs and knowledge of the linguistic community who share these lexical items, and (iii) human expertise strongly relies on this kind of knowledge. This program is also known as ViewPoints Semantics (VPS).

In the rest of the chapter, I show why the program above had to be developed (methodological as well as empirical reasons), how it is carried on, and what it brings to semantics. I will particularly insist on (a) what there is in argumentation that cannot be satisfactorily dealt with using the classical informational concepts; (b) specific properties of argumentative inference rules in the AWL framework; (c) how and what of argumentation can be encoded within the VPS in the description of lexical items.

5.1. The relationship between information and argumentation

I will now show that it is not by virtue of the information it conveys, that an utterance is an argument for some conclusion, rejecting thus the 'classical' position on meaning, according to which meaning would be essentially accounted for in terms of information, i.e. in terms of conditions of reference.

Suppose argumentation were derived from information, that is, suppose that the argumentative content of utterances could be described in terms of the information they convey, with the possible help of argumentative rules which applied to that information. In this case, it could not happen that two sentences which conveyed the same information be uttered in the same situation with opposite argumentative orientation, since the argumentative rules, which depend on the situation, are the same (for the situations are the same) and the informational content on which they would apply would be the same, by hypothesis. This prediction, which is a direct consequence of the 'classical' position does not resist empirical tests, and this gives strong reasons to reject the 'classical' position. Consider sentences

(S4) He worked a little today.
(S5) He worked little today.

and possible continuations

(C4) He is a good boy.
(C5) He is a naughty boy.

which we will consider as possible candidates for argumentative orientations of utterances of (S4) and (S5). In a situation where it is believed that the more a boy works, the better he is, the expected continuation of utterances of (S4) is (C4) and the expected continuation of utterances of (S5) is (C5); in an abnormal (?) situation in which it were believed that the less a boy works, the better he is, the expected continuation of utterances of (S4) is (C5), and the expected continuation of utterances of (S5) is (C4). Utterances of (S4) and (S5) are thus oriented towards opposite conclusions, no matter the topos which is believed to hold between work and 'perfection'. However, the strictly informational aspects of the sense of utterances of (S4) and (S5) do not differ: the amount of work, for instance, described by utterances of (S4) and by utterances of (S5) is the same, as is attested by the fact that both (S6) and (S7) can be uttered without inconsistancy:

(S6) He worked a little, but he worked little.
(S7) He worked little, but he worked a little.

for if the amounts of work described by (S4) and (S5) were different, they could not be both uttered about the same state of affairs. It could be argued that the conception of informational content which is invoked here is too restrictive and that (S4) and (S5) do not really convey the same information. And, since they do not convey the same information, the objection proceeds, the fact that they convey opposite argumentative orientations is no longer an objection to the 'classical' position. However, there is a sense of information (call it restrictive) in which (S4) and (S5) convey the same information: the one in which we can say that utterances of (S4) or (S5) describe a small amount of work. If we want to 'extend' this (restricted) sense, in such a way that we can say that utterances of (S4) and (S5) do not carry the same information, we have to characterize the difference we want to introduce (keeping in mind that they cannot be too different, since (S6) and (S7) are not inconsistent). Obviously, the only possibility is to characterize these differences in terms of the argumentative behaviors of these utterances. That is, we have to introduce argumentation in the 'extended' concept of information. With such a conception of information, it is clear that the reasons I invoke to reject the classical conception of argumentation are not acceptable: if argumentation is already in information there is no place for another argumentative component. The structure of the two positions, so far, looks like Figure 4.

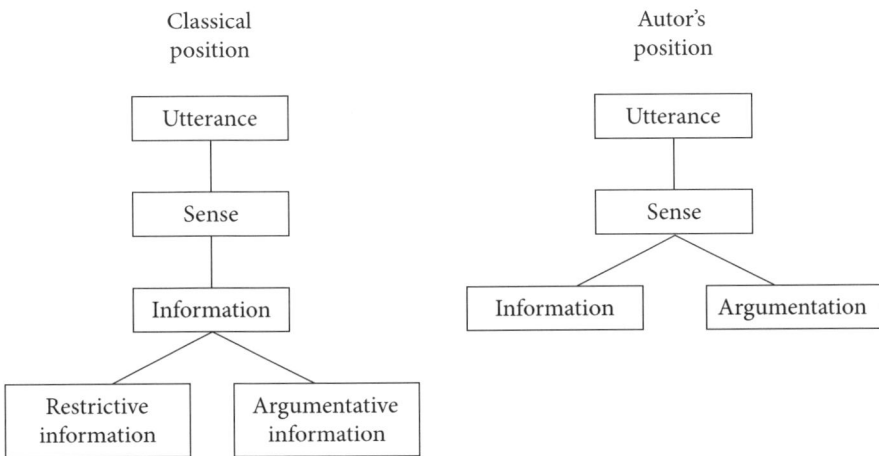

Figure 4.

In order to account for the phenomenon presented in the discussion of (S4)–(S7), the classical position has to distinguish two components of information, to maintain that argumentation depends on information: 'strict (or restrictive) information' and 'argumentative information'. Now, does 'argumentative information' depend on 'strict information'? If not, the difference between the two positions is purely terminological: what I said about argumentation and information has to be accepted about 'argumentative information' and 'strict information', the supplementary layer proposed by the revised classical position being innocuous (though useless…). If yes, then, to account for precisely the same examples, the stubborn classical position will have to make a distinction within 'strict information': 'restrictive strict information' will have to be distinguished from 'argumentative strict information'! And so on.

The discussion above suggests a shift in the conception of sentence meaning, which can be illustrated by a shift between Figures 5 and 6.

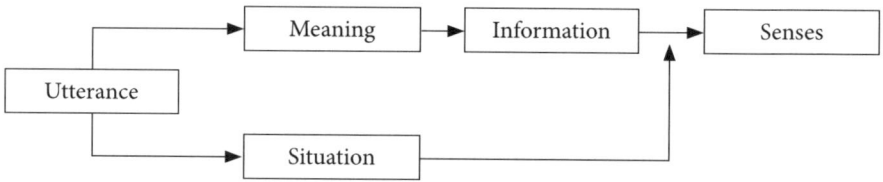

Figure 5. *Classical position*

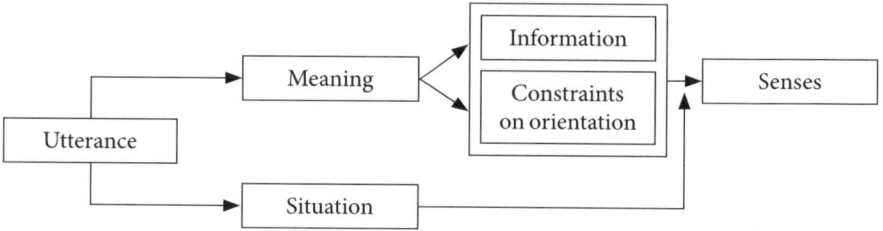

Figure 5. Author's position

5.2. Argumentative constraints in connectives and operators

In the sequel, following the terminology developed in Raccah (2002), and adapting it for English, we will use the term *connective* to refer to binary syntactic operations on sentence phrases (as opposed to sub-structures of utterances), and the term *operator* to refer to unary syntactic operations on sentence phrases.

Consider an utterance of:

(S1) It is cold, it may even be raining.

in a situation type in which the speaker was asked if she/he felt like going for a walk. Independently of the theoretical framework in which one wishes to work, the description one will have to come up with will have to account for the fact that utterances of (S1) in such situations are, indeed, answers to the question (usually negative answers). The difference between utterances of (S1) and a yes/no answer is that the former give reasons for the preferred answer. As we will see in the sequel, these reasons are based on implicit inferences, which link bad weather to refusal to go for a walk. These reasons, clearly, do not consist in essential links between weathers and walks, for a speaker who likes cold weather and rain could not use (S1) as a negative answer to such a proposal. Indeed, with such preferences, utterances of (S1) would be positive answers. . . We thus have to admit that utterances of (S1) -in classical weather preferences situations- present themselves as giving reasons to refuse to go for a walk (in addition, they perform the act of refusal: but this is another aspect of its sense). Another aspect of the sense of the utterances of (S1) is of interest here: the fact that the two parts of the sentence (*it is cold*, and *it may be raining*), linked by *even* are presented as having a different argumentative strengths. Utterances of (S1) clearly present rain as being worse than cold for going for a walk; utterances of:

(S'1) It is raining, it may even be cold.

do exactly the contrary. Rain and cold are thus presented, by utterances of (S1), as attached to some argumentative scale, relative to the particular conclusion aimed at, and depending on the particular preferences which are supposed to be admitted by both the speaker and the hearer. Note that that scale is, by no means, inherent to what rain or cold really are: that scale is *essentially* non-objective and reflects points of view.

Examples such as (S1) can easily be generalized and, once one has started, it becomes hard to find examples of utterances which do not seem to be presented as arguments for some conclusions…

5.3. Topoi and argumentative inferences

When analyzing utterances of sentence (S1), I said that they present themselves as giving reasons for yes-or-no answers, reasons based on implicit inferences. Since, as we have seen, utterances present these reasons as attached to argumentative scales, the rules which we need in order to manage these inferences have to be scalar rules. If I think that cold weather is bad to go for a walk and that rainy weather is worse, the rule which lets me infer 'no-walk' from *cold* cannot be an implication-like rule because, if it were so, it could not apply to *rain* to give 'no-walk' with more strength. What we need are rules which allow us to link degrees of bad weather to strength of refusal of the walk. Following Ducrot (Anscombre and Ducrot 1983, Raccah 1984, 1987 and Ducrot 1988) I call such rules *topoi*. A topos is an inference rule which links two gradual properties, which I call *topical fields*. Given two topical fields P and Q, a topos has one of the following four forms:

// The more X is P, the more Y is Q //
// The more X is P, the less Y is Q //
// The less X is P, the more Y is Q //
// The less X is P, the less Y is Q //

(where X and Y are members of the fields P and Q, respectively). Though, as we have just seen, there are reasons to use gradual rules such as those for the pragmatic description of argumentation, there were no a priori reasons to decide that the only rules that we will use for such descriptions are topoi. This choice corresponds to a strong hypothesis according to which these tools are sufficient for our aim. In the case of utterances of sentence (S1), in the situation described, the topos could be:

// The worse the weather, the less we want to go out //

Cold and *rainy* are degrees of BAD WEATHER and the topos applies to each of them, leading to negative degrees of 'WANTING TO GO OUT'. Moreover, the use of *even* constrains to place *rainy* higher than *cold* in the scale of BAD WEATHER, leading to a lower degree of 'WANTING TO GO OUT' for *rainy* than for *cold*. In the case of (S'1), we have the same topos, but *cold* and *rainy* are switched in the topical field. Finally, in the case of (S1), with a reverse preference (the case of people who like to walk in the rain …), the topos is obviously different:

// The worse the weather, the more we want to go out //.

Note that a statement such as "X is P to a degree d" is a meta-linguistic statement used to describe an aspect of the sense of possible utterances, and not an utterance of some sentence of the language under study. So that though topoi are inference rules, they are not rules of any natural language. Consequently, they do not link any utterances or sentences of any natural language. The fact that natural language phrases may express non-gradual properties cannot be seen as a counter-example to the hypothesis that topoi are enough for the description of argumentation: topoi do not apply to natural language phrases, but to properties attached to them, and these meta-linguistic properties may be gradual, even though the properties to which they are attached are not. For instance, a sentence like:

(S2) She is a lawyer.

can be uttered as an argument for *her* being bright, dull, wealthy, etc. in spite of its non-gradual aspect. Moreover, (S2) can be embedded in sentences which are uttered in gradual contexts and even play a gradual rôle in them, as in

(S2.1) She is a lawyer, and she is even famous,

where the property of being a lawyer and that of being famous are considered as different degrees in some topical field such as 'HAVING AN INTERESTING SOCIAL POSITION'. In the situations where

(S2.2) She is a lawyer and she is even famous: you should marry her

could be uttered (here, the sentence explicitly contains the argumentative orientation of its utterances), the second topical field (the conclusion field) concerns the interest in marrying her. The topos normally used in utterances of (S2.2) can be formulated as:

// the more interesting the social position, the more interesting the marriage //

but of course, nothing can prevent an English speaker from believing (i) that being a lawyer and being famous are degrees of dullness and (ii) that the duller the person, the more interesting the marriage. In such a twisted case, utterances of (S2.2) still present her being a lawyer and being famous as being arguments to marry *her*, but for different reasons … Thus, gradual rules of inference applied to topical fields associated with the different parts of the sentence uttered account insightfully not only for the argumentation of utterances of sentences whose parts express gradual properties, but also for the argumentation of sentences which have parts which express non-gradual properties.

5.4. A template for the description of connectives and operators

In Raccah (1987), I have shown that, in order to be able to express the facts presented above, in connection with examples (S1)–(S7), the representation system for the semantic description must include the following conceptual tools:

- distinction between asserted and presupposed indications for argumentation (not discussed here);
- possibility of expressing constraints on the form of the possible topoi (cf. the discussion above);
- possibility of expressing constraints on the selection of topoi (cf. the discussion on *but*, below);
- possibility of expressing the constraint that some properties are placed at higher, lower or similar degrees on a topical field (like in the case of *even* or *almost* -not discussed here).

For reasons exposed in Raccah (1987), we also have to distinguish between the argumentation which is *used* in an utterance and the argumentations which are only *validated* through it.[15] As a result, to adequately describe a sentence S containing a connective such as *but*, we need, in addition to the classical informational decription, to express constraints about the following argumentational aspects of the possible utterances of S:

- argumentational presupposition (let's name RR(S) the set of those constraints);
- argumentational validation (let's name it val(S));
- argumentation used (let's name it U(S)).

I will now illustrate how such a description template allows an accurate description of sentences containig *but*.

Let S be a sentence of the form A *but* B, where A and B are any sentence (possibly containing other occurrences of *but*). We want to express (i) that any utterance of S presents A and B as being opposed argumentatively (no matter the orientation of A or B); (ii) that S acknowledges that both A and B can be held and that A is indeed an argument in favor of some conclusion against which B is an argument; and (iii) that the argumentation proposed by S follows B, rather than A. Using the topoi, we get a description like the following:

$$RR(S) = RR(A) \text{ \& } RR(B) \text{ \& }$$
$$cons(top(B)) = - cons(top(A)) \text{ \& }$$
$$val(A) = \{top(A)\} \text{ \& }$$
$$val(B) = \{top(B)\}$$
$$val(S) = val(A) \text{ U } val(B)$$
$$U(S) = U(B).$$

where top(X) is the topos attached to X in the situation of utterance; cons(T) is the consequent of topos T; {a, b, c, ...} is the set containing the elements a, b, c, ...; and X U Y is the union of sets X and Y.[16]

6.2. Words and topical fields

Simple sentences (that is, sentences which do not contain such operators or connectives) do not seem, at first, to give any semantic indication on argumentation
except for the fact that any sentence whatsoever can always presented as an argument for some conclusion. However, it is now clear that the topical fields which are
associated with phrases of the language are determined by the language itself, and
not only by some beliefs or ideology. For instance, the idea that to steal one's wallet
is a degree of, say, dishonesty is an element of the meaning of *steal*, and not only a
belief or an ideology: what belongs to the realm of beliefs is the topos according to
which the more dishonest, the worse (think, for instance of the corresponding topoi
which hold in the mafia, among politicians, etc.). But to the same phrase of the language, one can associate several topical fields (for instance, in the case of *steal one's
wallet*, one can associate, besides dishonesty, other fields such as nastiness, mental
trouble, irresponsibility, etc.). The lexicon should thus describe each word in such
a way that a list of topical fields can be associated to each of those phrases. This
conception gives the grounds for a theoretical distinction between *words* and *terms*,
distinction that appeared to be useful in traductology.[17]

I will now show how this can be done within the VPS framework.

5.5. Topoi associated with topical fields

As suggested above, the VPS main idea is that sentences do not merely convey information, but also give conventional indications on how this information is seen
by the speaker. The role of topical fields is to represent these conventional indications. Thus, a topical field can be seen as a point of view on some information, that
is, as a valuation of a conceptual field. We can thus represent topical fields as ordered
pairs <CONCEPTUAL FIELD, *valuation principle*>, where the *valuation principle* can
be either a judgment (in that case, we have an *elementary* topical field), or another
topical field (in that case, we have a *compounded* topical field; see Raccah (1990) for
more about topical fields). Given a compounded topical field <CF,TF>, there exists a
unique topos // <CF,TF>,TF //, which represents the implicit gradual inference rule
attached to that topical field. Let us say that that topos is *canonically associated* to
that topical field.

5.6. Lexical topoi

In order to account for the argumentation suggested by the words, we add a list of
topical fields to the lexical description of certain words. These *lexical topical fields*
are uniquely characterized by the topoi canonically associated to them; we call them
lexical topoi. I will now illustrate this point with an example. Consider the adjective
rich, and suppose we have an informational description for it, such as the one given
by the conceptual field of POSSESSION. Such a description cannot account, by itself,

for the particular semantic effect of utterances of a sentence like

(S10) This baby is rich

which is acceptable, although it is strange to say that a baby is rich. When analyzing this impression, one realizes that the use of the adjective *rich* to express that some-one possesses suggests that the possessor is in such a situation that he/she can do something with his/her possessions. Thus, in normal cases, a speaker would not use the word *rich* to express possession unless he/she sees that possession as source of power. Utterances of (S10) are odd because they force to see the baby referred to as granted power because of its wealth.[18] VPS accounts for these facts by adding to the lexical description of *rich* a lexical topical field <POSSESSION, *power*>, which is characterized by the topos

//<POSSESSION, *power*>, *power* //,

which can be re-formulated as

// the more one possesses, the more powerful //.

5.7. Doxal and non-doxal utterances

A lexical topos may be directly used in an utterance, or it can be the first element of a chain leading to another topos, which will be used in that utterance. In the first case, we say that the utterance is *doxal*; in the second case, it is non-doxal. Doxal utterances do not add anything to the meaning of the words: they are but banalities (without being too pessimistic, that applies to most of our everyday exchanges...). Here are examples of sentences suggesting doxal utterances:

(S12) He has been working a lot; he must be tired
(S13) He is rich, he can invite you

Non-doxal utterances add knowledge or beliefs to the plain meaning of the words, as illustrated by the following examples:

(S14) He has been working a lot; his colleagues will hate him
(S15) He has been working a lot; he will have a promotion
(S16) He is rich, he will invite you
(S17) He is rich, he must have friends

where the added beliefs are straightforward.[19]

6. Conclusions

Our study of the conditions under which natural language meaning could be the object of an empirical science lead us to understand that, in spite of the close relationship between semantics of human languages and cognitive science, their objects and their empirical fields are different.

In the attempt to answer the question "What should a theory of language structure explain", we ended up with the idea that such a theory has to explain the way language structure compels the hearers to build the meaning they build, for the utterance of each sentence, in the particular situation in which it has been uttered. More precisely, we saw that the semantic description of a human language is the description of the set of constraints that words and structures of that language impose on the construction of the meaning of the utterances. This description is utterance independent since it concerns the constraints that language imposes on the interpretation of the utterances, and not the result of the interpretation. It is also empirically grounded, since it is based on the observation of the utterances and of the traces of their interpretations.

We saw that some of those constraints are imposed by articulators (i. e. connectives and operators): they can be very different in different languages; we also saw that some words impose positive (resp. negative) judgments wherever they are used, and whoever uses them: this is the case of euphorical adjectives such as 'honest', 'interesting', ..., or the corresponding dysphorical ones.

Combining the constraints of the articulators with the euphorical/dysphorical properties allows to 'compute' the ideological force of other words in utterances such as "John is a republican but he is honest". Other words, thus, impose more sophisticated judgments which are to be described as micro-programs provided by the language which they belong to. Here the diversity across languages is even stronger than what it is with respect to articulators.

Turning back to the initial question, our answer is: yes, meaning in natural languages can be the object of an empirical science, if it is considered as the constraints, invariant across utterances, under which the interpretation is built by the hearers, keeping in mind that interpretations are only indirectly observable and that, of course, constraints on them require even more theoretical work in order to be indirectly observed. In sketching and justifying the theoretical apparatus required in order to make these entities indirectly observable, we gave detailed answers to the fundamental issues, listed in the introduction, regarding the proper object and the kind of explanation attached to such theories.

Notes

1. As a recreational exercise, the reader can try to place, in this table, the famous *Murphy Law*, according to which "anything that happens happens in order to worsen the situation, unless it had been predicted by the present law"...

2. This attitude is relatively recent: think of the not so old belief according to which *nature abhors a vacuum* ...

3. Like the laws imposed on humans by some god?

4. In van Fraasen (1985), Bas van Fraasen holds a similar position, using evidences from a historical analysis of philosophical ideas.

5. See below, section 3.1.

6. The distinction between *de dicto* and *de re* causality is treated in different ways in different languages. There are not many linguistic studies about these different treatments. One of these studies, which deals with the grammatical differences between *de re* and *de dicto* clauses can be found in Frajzyngier (1991).

7. We will shortly see that presupposing the pre-theoretical phenomenal structure of the world is not theoretically neutral. But, for the time being, since that remark pushes in the direction of my argument, we can safely put that question aside...

8. Note, however, that it is still misleading, since it does not account for the fact that $E_1, E_2,$ ...E_n and E are not given (see the note above; see also next paragraph).

9. And this, of course, does not mean that it is false: it only means that no scientific method or conception can be based on it. I happen to share that belief, but this does not entail, of course, that it is a rational belief...

10. Though we have shown that nothing can be *directly observable* by a human being (since anything requires the interpretation of the state of our sensorial apparatus), we will use that expression to refer to objects or events whose access is granted by the interpretation of the effect they directly produce on our sensorial apparatus. This terminological sloppiness is introduced for the sake of legibility...

11. That is, the conception an educated person could have about semantics without having learnt and reflected about it previously... This is, it must be admitted, the conception held by many people who speak or write about language!

12. For more details, see Raccah (2002).

13. Some Buddhist sects seek the "language of nature" in which the words emit the exact vibrations which correspond to the objects they refer to.

14. We obviously didn't choose realistic nor very interesting parameters... but our purpose is only illustrative.

15. As it is shown in the paper cited, this allows for a compositional description of connectives and operators, and also allows to account for important non-informational differences between connectives (such as the French *mais* and *justement*).

16. Some of the features represented in that description have not been discussed in this chapter: this is only an illustration. For more details, see Raccah (1987).

17. See Raccah (2000) for details on that subject.

18. There is independent diachronic evidence for that explanation: the word *rich* comes from the Francique word °*riki*, which meant 'powerful' (cf. *Reich* 'power'). Though etymology does not explain contemporary meaning, one cannot help feeling that a synchronic description, motivated by the present state of a language system, is strengthened when it meets what is known about the evolution of that system.

19. Notice, however, the difference between (S13) and (S16).

References

Anscombre Jean-Claude and Oswald Ducrot. 1983. *L'argumentation dans la Langue*. Bruxelles: Mardaga.

Bruxelles Sylvie, Denis Carcagno, Corinne Fournier. 1989. 'Vers une construction automatique des topoi à partir du lexique'. *Communication, Cognition and Artificial Intelligence* 6(4): 309–328.

Bruxelles Sylvie and Pierre-Yves Raccah. 1990. 'Argumentation et sémantique: le parti-pris du lexique'. In *Énonciation et Parti-pris*, Walter De Mulder, Franc Schuerewegen and Liliane Tasmowski (eds), 59–73. Antwerpen: Rodopi.

Dascal, Marcelo. 1983. *Pragmatics and the philosophy of mind 1: Thought in Language*. Amsterdam and Philadelphia: John Benjamins.

Ducrot Oswald. 1973. *La preuve et le dire*. Paris: Mame.

Ducrot, Oswald. 1988. 'Topoi et formes topiques'. *Bulletin d'études de linguistique française* 22: 1–14. Tokyo.

Fournier, Corinne and Pierre-Yves Raccah. 1990. 'Argumentation and artificial intelligence: from linguistic models to knowledge management'. In *Computers in Literary and Linguistic Research*, Yaacov Choueka (ed.), 176–196. Genève: Champion-Slatkine.

van Fraasen, Bas. 1985. "Que son las leyes de la naturaleza?" *Dianoia* 31: 211–262 (appeared in 1986).

Frajzyngier, Zygmunt. 1991. "The de dicto domain in language". In *Approaches to Grammaticalization*, Vol. 1: *Focus on theoretical and methodological issues*, Elizabeth Closs Traugott and Bernd Heine (eds.), 219–251 (Typological Studies in Language 19:1). Amsterdam: John Benjamins.

Raccah, Pierre-Yves (1984). "Argumentation in Representation Semantics". *COLING 84*, 525–529. Stanford.

Raccah, Pierre-Yves. 1987. "Modeling Argumentation and Modeling *with* Argumentation", Technical report URA 962-CNRS, Paris; published in *Argumentation*, 4: 447–483, Brussels 1990.

Raccah, Pierre-Yves. 1990. "Signification, sens et connaissance: une approche topique". *Cahiers de Linguistique Française*, 11: 179–198.

Raccah, Pierre-Yves. 2000. "Lexical and dynamic topoi in semantic description: A theoretical and practical differentiation between words and terms". In *Language, Text and Knowledge*, Lita Lundquist et al. (eds), 11–29. Berlin and New York: Mouton.

Raccah Pierre-Yves. 2002. "Lexique et idéologie : les points de vue qui s'expriment avant qu'on ait parlé". In *Les facettes du dire: Hommage à Oswald Ducrot*, Marion Carel (ed.), 241–268. Paris: Kimé.

CHAPTER 4

Language processes, theory and description of language change, and building on the past

Lessons from Songhay

Robert Nicolaï

Institut universitaire de France and Université de Nice

Il faut résister à un positivisme de premier examen. Si l'on manque à cette prudence, on risque de prendre une dégénérescence pour une essence   (Bachelard 1934: 159)

[Prima facie positivism must be avoided. Carelessness here could lead us to take a degenerative form for an essential one.]

This chapter is a continuation of earlier work on the controversial genetic classification of Songhay as Nilo-Saharan (Nicolaï 2003), where I show that the results thus far (cf. Bender 1995, Ehret 2001) are unsatisfactory. This is attributable to the authors' models and methods, the assumptions these rest upon, the nature of the data, and *a priori* factors in research.

I discuss theoretical hypotheses regarding the ways in which languages change, the methods and procedures used by scholars, and the ways in which empirical data are used. This leads me to ask the following questions at the outset:

1. Are we entitled to make explicit use of virtual or real multilingual/multidialectal factors as normal theoretical parameters in building models of language change and proposing long-distance relationships? (This would imply changes to the classical tree representations and facilitate the incorporation of areal and contact phenomena.)
2. Would it be helpful to postulate an anthropologically defined setting for the interaction of structural linguistic forms, basic cognitive processes, and punctual input from historical contingencies, resulting in rearrangements of norms of use and formal structures? (This question is vital to the study of areal phenomena and situations lying beyond the theoretical constraints of the standard genetic model.)

These questions are in line with others raised during the Symposium with regard to the relations between theories of language structure and theories of cognition, the degree of conscious motivation for processes of language change and grammaticalization, and adabtability in language change and functionalization. In answering them, I make a number of suggestions based on my overall views on the practice of comparative linguistics, the construction of theoretical frameworks, and my recent empirical results in Nilo-Saharan and Afroasiatic.z

Lessons from Songhay

It is always instructive to see methods of proven efficiency encounter serious difficulties in a particular instance. This awakens us to the possibility of widening our viewpoint, rearranging our theoretical and methodological apparatus to deal with the rebellious data, and defining previously unrecognized problems. A striking example of this in the field of problematic genetic classification has recently been provided by the Songhay group in Africa, composed of languages, most of which are trade languages with no written tradition, spoken mainly in the region of the Niger bend and displaying little internal differentiation beyond a division into northern and southern subgroups. Let us examine this case more closely.

I will divide my discussion into three parts. The first is empirical, the second looks to the future, and the third draws conclusions. To provide a concrete illustration, I will begin by summarizing the latest ideas on the genetic classification of Songhay which will show both the inadequacy of tree diagrams for representing language change and the fundamental importance of language contact in the origin and development of this particular language (for further details, see Nicolaï 2003). I will also account for the participation of Songhay in what seems to be an area of convergence with the Mande languages.

In view of these results, I will suggest changes to our analytical framework which will give a central role to language contact phenomena and sociolinguistic hypotheses while in no way diminishing the importance of the more traditional approach. I will try to show that the resulting change in factor ranking will be crucial to the understanding of processes of language change.

Finally, I will make a few remarks on the possible impact of modelization in the field of language change.

Apparent genetic relationship

The inclusion of Songhay in the Nilo-Saharan family, first suggested by Greenberg (1964), was subsequently impugned (Lacroix 1969, Nicolaï 1990), and then ostensibly confirmed by studies of Nilo-Saharan as a whole (Bender 1995, Ehret 2001), though these two authors disagree regarding its position on the family tree. The latest study[1] (Nicolaï 2003) provides a detailed critique of the works which attach Songhay to Nilo-Saharan, and attempts to show that the models (tree model of language diversification) and methods (reconstructions, phonetic correspondences; isoglosses) they use, their basic theoretical assumptions (linear development), the nature of the data (no written tradition), and *a priori* factors in research[2] all contribute to a mistaken conclusion in this sense. Consequently, it is no longer possible to maintain that Songhay belongs to Nilo-Saharan, if 'belonging' is taken in its usual genetic sense and 'Nilo-Saharan' is meant to be a family (or a family-like phylum) of genetically related languages capable of being represented by a tree diagram.

My own analysis, founded on the entirety of the available Songhay dialectological data, has led me to seek hypotheses which might explain the absence of clear morphological correspondences with other Nilo-Saharan languages and the high proportion of likely Afroasiatic lexical items[3] which are neither obvious recent loans from Arabic (e.g. *àlbésèl* **bṣl** 'onion', *àlkámà* **qmḥ** 'wheat', etc. or the religious vocabulary of Islam) nor the result of other bounded contacts (e.g. *àddà* 'machete' from Hausa, *tukamaaren* 'cheese' from Tuareg, etc.) but part of basic vocabulary; and not isolated units but sets covering complex lexical domains down to their fine structure (see Table 1). Songhay is thereby *reoriented* towards Afroasiatic, which is not to say that it stands in any genetic relationship with this family.

Stratification of structural isomorphism and isoglosses

At the same time, the typological structure of Songhay shows marked morphosyntactic affinity to that of the Northern Mande languages. The examples in Table 2 and 3 show how extensive the isomorphism is. But once overall isomorphism is recognized, its linguistic and geographical stratification must then be examined in full detail. Such examination has led us to observe that the structural processes operating in the subsystems of the language have been differently conditioned by the historical factors in play:

- phonological change seems more sensitive to the effects of contact than morphosyntactic change,
- morphosyntactic change seems more sensitive to functional phenomena of simplification deriving from use as a trade language.

At the same time, the contexts of language use (which may change over time) give rise to processes which can modify prior configurations. Thus, we find continual Songhay-Mande contact bringing about an intensification of apparent convergence on some points through the creation of a *Sprachbund*. This is evident from a detailed study of the geographical and linguistic stratification of the shared features (e.g. the geographically bounded merger of /s/ and /z/ in western Songhay in direct contact with Mande languages). Elsewhere, however, we find that convergence has been obscured by subsequent change resulting from the use of the languages in contexts requiring simplification (e.g. the loss of SOV word order in western and northern Songhay). For all these reasons, the phenomena of *linguistic stratification* themselves require particular attention; otherwise, should they be ignored, the resulting input will necessarily lead to mistaken interpretations (see Nicolaï, in press b, on these points).

Table 1. Lexical designations of body parts.

head *bòŋ* [Kbl:[a] *abbay* 'head; cranium']

goiter *bókò*, *soft spot below the lower jaw* *bokolo* [Kbl: *ffeqlej* 'be flabby, fat, soft']

palate *dáanà* (*dayna*) [Kbl: *aney/iney*; Amh: *sənag, tənag*, vh*lanqa* palate]

gums *díinì* [Hgr: *tăyne* 'gums'; Tmz: *taniwt* 'gums']

hair/feather *hámní; himbiri* [Ar: *ḥabl* 'string'; *aîbal* 'thick, tightly-woven rope'; Hgr: *éhafiilen* 'long body hair'; *téhafilt* 'short body hair'; Wlm: *abəndal* 'hairy man']

nerve, tendon *linji* Ar: *Sirq* 'root'; Tmz: *lɛer* 'nerve, tendon, vein, artery']

fontanelle *lòŋgò* [Hgr: *élengeou* 'large nape of neck (derisive)'; Wlm: *thalləka sinciput* // fontanelle]

mouth *mê* [Hgr: *émi* 'mouth', Tmz, Wlm: *imi* 'mouth, entry, orifice'], *eye mòy, mò* [*mghb: m-mm-w* 'iris of eye', Hgr: *emmah* 'pupil of eye'; Kbl, Tmz: *mummu* 'pupil, iris of eye']

face *mòydúmà* [Hgr: *ôudem* 'face'; Kbl, Tmz: *udem* 'face']

cheekbone/smile *múmúsú* [Tmz: *smummey* 'smile, pout'; Wlm: *fəmməfməf* 'smile']

sweat *súŋgéy* [Hgr: *enǧi* 'trickle'; Kbl: *ssengi* 'cause to flow'; Gz: *ʔngy, sngy, sng, sgd(d), gy* 'melt, flow, sweat']

sneeze *tísôw* [Hgr: *tôusou* 'cough regularly'; Kbl: *tusut* 'whooping cough'; *entez* 'sneeze'; Gz: *Saṭasa* 'sneeze']

have diarrhea *sóorú* [Ar: *isha⁻l* diarrhea; *Saṣara* press; Kbl: *esrem* cause diarrhea; Tmz: *nmarsi* diarrhea; Tms: *zarrat* diarrhea; Gz: *Saṣara* press out, press, squeeze, wring out]

'tear(s)' *múndì* [Ar: *damaʕa* 'tear(s)'; Hgr: *ămit* 'tear(s)'; Kbl: *imeṭṭi* 'tear(s)'; Tmz: *ameṭṭ* 'tear(s)']

urinate *tòosì* [Hgr: *ăsẹ́as* 'bladder'; Tms: *tasəyast* 'bladder']

'spit' *túfà* [Ar: *taffa* (*tff*) 'spit'; Hgr: *soutef* 'spit'; Kbl: *ṭṭeftef* 'foam with wrath'; Gz: *taf'a* 'spit, spit out']

defecate *wá* [Gz: *Səbā* 'dung']

drool *yólló* [Hgr: *ălidda* 'drool' (n); Kbl: *aledda* 'drool' (n); arch: *rayyal* 'drool, foam, salivate']

vulva *bùtè* [Ar: *bud*, 'vulva']

chin *danka* [Ar: *ḍaqan* 'chin'; *ḍaqn* 'beard, whiskers']

breast *fòfè* [Ar: *Subb* 'breast, gusset'; Hgr: *éfef* 'breast, teat'; Kbl: *iff* 'teat']

arm/hand *kàbè* [Ar: *kîb* 'ankle, heel'; *kaff*, *kaffah* 'palm of hand']

lung *kùfú* [Hgr: *ekef* (be) inflated; Kbl: *ikuftan* foam]

liver *tásà* [Hgr: *tẹ́sa* 'belly' (of person or animal); Kbl, Tmz: *tasa* 'liver']

Note: these are only a few examples. Nicolaï (2003: 296–306 and 384–497) contains an extensive list of useful items. Even that list, however, is neither exhaustive nor definitive.
[a] Abbreviations: Kbl: Kabyl; Amh: Amharic; Hgr: Tahaggart; Tmz: Tamazight; Ar: Arabic; Wlm: Tawellemmet; Gz: Gueze; Tms: Tamajaq.

In conclusion, we may assume that, barring future evidence to the contrary, Songhay arose in a complex way from a *lingua franca*, an ancient sort of trade language, whose precise nature (Berber, earlier or later form of Semitic, Ethiosemitic, or other) remains to be established. This language, which was not necessarily homogeneous

Table 2. Examples of Mande-Songhay structural isomorphisms

Derivation		*Word formation: derivation and compounding:*
abstract quality: *ya*	*tàráy*	
mòko ~ mòkoyá 'humanism'	*bòró ~ bòrtàráy* 'humanism'	Overall, both groups use comparable derivational processes and have highly productive compounding according to identical formal patterns; reduplication is also very productive.
Compounding		
jòli 'blood', *síla* 'road'	*kúrí* 'blood', *fŏndò* 'road'	
jòlisíla 'vein'	*kúrífóndò* 'vein'	
Reduplication		
hùlá 'two', *sìdi* 'tie'	*ìhínká* 'two', *háw* 'tie'	
hùlahulasídi 'tie two by two'	*háw ìhínkahínká* 'tie two by two'	
Genitive construction[a]		*Noun modification:*
Mdk *dèndikoo jifoo*	*bànkàaraa zíibàa*	Noun-modification structures are often parallel, including the use of two reversed orders: {Modifying Noun + Modified Noun}, {Modified Noun + Modifying Adjective}.
the garment ~ the pocket	the garment ~ the pocket	
'the pocket of the garment'	'the pocket of the garment'	
Adjectival modifier		
móngón kéren nù 'the green mangos'		
mángu bóogóo 'the green mango' ~ *mángu bóogu* 'a green mango'		
Transitive proposition		*Predicative propositions:*
sékù dí mìsí sàn	*dáwdà nà háwó dáy*	There are clear similarities in the structure of predicative propositions {S Aux O V Cpl} and numerous affinities in the TAM system and the negative conjugation.
'Seku bought the cow'	'Dawda bought the cow'	
séku mán mìsí sàn	'Seku did not buy the cow'	
dáwdà màn háwó dáy	'Dawda did not buy the cow'	

Grammaticalization of lexical items: In both Mande and Songhay, the heads of adjunct phrases are noun suffixes. Some of these derive from still extant lexical items (this phenomenon is of course far more widespread).

Semantic structure: Subject to further information, these affinities in the structure of semantic fields and categorization would seem to be shared with languages across all of West Africa, rather than being characteristic of the Songhay-Mande alone.

Note: these examples are taken from Mandinga and Zarma, important representatives of West Mande and Songhay, respectively.
[a] Juxtaposition expresses inalienable possession in Mandinga. This is the structure chosen here. It corresponds exactly to Songhay; the presence of the connective in inalienable possession does not affect the parallel in constituent order. The four examples marked "Mdk" are from Mandinka, cf. Creissels (2001). The choice of Mandinka rather than Malinke does not mean that the structures illustrated do not exist in Malinke; rather that the data available to me for the latter do not contain a suitable example.

Table 3. Phonological systems: primacy of disyllabic lexemes. The table lists a few indicative similarities, to which may be added structural features such as the absence of /p/ and the absence of /r/ in initial position.

West Mande	Songhay
Seven-vowel systems (five in western Mandinga and Soninke, six in Kita Maninka)	Five- or seven-vowel systems
Relatively large medial consonant inventories, particularly in the north	Full consonant inventory in medial position
Length contrast in non-final position in many languages (in all positions in Mandinka)	Length contrast in all positions
Two tones; transition to accent systems in Mandinka, Kagoro, and some Jallonke dialects; three-tone systems reducing to two-tone systems in Kpelle	Two level tones + rising and falling contours analyzable as a succession of level tones; transition to accent systems (northern Songhay); loss of prosodic contrasts en eastern and western Songhay

Note: this table summarizes Vydrine's (2000) conclusions, which stress the difference between West Mande and Mani-Bandama.

and probably of a simplified nature, took on stable form when it was appropriated by populations which originally spoke neither Semitic nor Berber languages. Two hypotheses in this respect are possible *a priori*, neither of which can be excluded at this stage:

- a no longer existent *lingua franca* strongly impacted on and widely relexified another regional language, giving rise to Songhay, or
- that *lingua franca* "was" (in a sense yet to be defined) what has now become Songhay; in such case, Songhay was simply the result of the nativization[4] of this language.

Inferences

The language formation hypothesis illustrated by the Songhay data is concordant with the generally recognized criteria for the development of stabilized pidgin languages, and furthermore accounts for the impossibility (or perhaps merely the difficulty) of establishing strict phonetic correspondences despite the kinship in basic vocabulary.

At the same time, Songhay's continued status as a trade language, the anthropological diversity of its speakers, and the correspondence of the current situation to what we know of the medieval African world are all historical features which fit well with this hypothesis. It thereby becomes easier to understand the following three things:

1. The diversity of the Afroasiatic sources to which the Songhay lexicon can be related.

We would expect that a putative *lingua franca* with an Afroasiatic base spreading over white and black Africa would have taken over the lexical material required for its use from a number of languages, from Cushitic to Egyptian and Arabic to Berber. What we know of the Mediterranean *lingua franca* suggests variation of lexical sources (Venitian, Genovan, Provençal, etc.) over time showing that change in a comparable situation can be fairly fast.

2. The extent of lexical diffusion of the Afroasiatic vocabulary shared by Songhay with neighboring African languages.

If there really was such a *lingua franca* as I am suggesting, it is to be expected that many of its lexical items would have been incorporated into the neighboring Northwestern Mande languages, Wolof, the Saharan languages, and many others including the "truly" (?) Nilo-Saharan ones. A process of this kind would explain the amount of shared "ancient" lexical items revealed by a study of lexical diffusion over the entire West African region. It would also account for the similarities with Mande or Chadic that have been noticed (cf. Creissels 1981, Mukarovsky 1989, Nicolaï 1977, 1984, Zima 1988).

3. The morphologization of the pidginized language into the prevalent typological framework of the Mande area vs. the relexification of Mande.[5]

This is the phenomenon reflected in Songhay-Mande isomorphism, the extent of which is apparent from illustrations given above. Indeed, Songhay morphosyntax is relatively simple (economical in Houis's 1971 terminology), typologically similar to Mande, and classifiable as type B2 (as defined by Heine 1975) with respect to syntactic ordering.

Genealogical hypotheses and apparent areal convergence

Clearly, once Songhay is assumed to be a Nilo-Saharan language, it follows that Mande and Songhay belong to two distinct genealogical units. Thereupon, any isomorphism *can also be logically interpreted* as the result of convergence between two groups of languages in close contact. But if the Nilo-Saharan affiliation of Songhay is incorrect, then the present form of the Songhay language is conceivably (or better, in all likekihood) *not an outcome* of a process of linguistic convergence; though long-term contact may reinforce the apparent convergence and end up superimposing a *Sprachbund* situation on the original one. It is *impossible*, on the basis of either of the two hypothetical modes of the creation of Songhay suggested above, to interpret this overall isomorphism with Mande as simply a phenomenon of language convergence in the sense of the archetypal phenomena observed, for example, in the Balkans. This impossibility, as implied by my modified conclusions, is methodologically instructive insofar as it illustrates the degree of interdependence among rival explanations and the effect any ill-founded empirical hypotheses will have on the construction and defence of an overall explanatory system; see Nicolai (in press b) for further discussion of the implications of Songhay-Mande isomorphism.

In sum, we are led to the conclusion that convergence is only apparent in the Songhay-Mande case. Rather than highly unlikely 'generalized convergence', we may assume that a 'new variety' of language displaying the major typological features of one preexistent group of languages and containing much of the lexical stock of another must have appeared in a specific sociological contact situation (or sequence of situations). It can be shown that only later did some 'classical' convergence phenomena, particularly of a phonological nature, affect the resulting languages on a limited scale.

The lesson to be learned is that not all observed isomorphisms can be attributed to what is generally known as a *Sprachbund* or area of convergence. Indeed,

- the identification and interpretation of what might seem *a priori* to be an area of convergence is intrinsically linked to the cultural and anthropological setting in which the languages involved arise. Comparable systemic features and a common geographical location are thus insufficient evidence on which to base a conclusion regarding the kind of process whose outcome is the current situation, particularly when the historical facts are poorly documented;
- isomorphisms which cannot be explained by genetic relationship may just as well result from processes of language creation as from processes of modification of preexistent languages.

An inventory of the kinds of contact situation which give rise to isomorphisms should therefore be established. This involves taking into consideration not just the analytical operations conducted by speakers, but *also* those of the descriptive linguist himself. While it may be absurd or simply wishful thinking to try to establish a one-to-one relationship between types of language development and types of contact situation or anthropological setting, such an attempt provides the groundwork for shaping hypotheses and in any case is essential to the descriptive process.

The consideration of these facts leads to two more conclusions of a more general nature:

- Whenever a model is improperly imposed on recalcitrant data, there is a danger that *conceptual arm-twisting* will give rise to fallacious representations (see Nicolaï 2003). Forcing Songhay into the Nilo-Saharan framework provides a good example of this.
- Whenever the *shape* of a phenomenon (e.g., an area of convergence as defined by the set of isomorphisms found there) is established by linking concurrent factors and underlying processes without regard for any theoretical framework or

prior analysis, there is a danger of a *semantic cover-up*, as when Songhay-Mande isomorphism is characterized as a convergence phenomenon (see Nicolaï, in press b).

In the light of this case study, I should like to consider the frameworks which can be helpful in apprehending phenomena of language change. Their use as points of reference and the way they are linked to wider typological questions should, I believe, be seen in the light of two other issues, *the role of multiple codes*[6] and *the anthropological context of their use*, though I am hardly able to provide definitive judgments on either of these points. My questions are:

- Should real or virtual multilingualism/multidialectalism not be one of the normal parameters of theoretical models of language change and long-distance relationship? If so, the shape of traditional tree diagrams is liable to change, and it becomes easier to integrate the effects of language contact and areal phenomena.
- Should an "area" not be defined on the basis of anthropological criteria within which language structures, elementary cognitive processes, and matters of historical contingency all come into play in the recomposition of norms and codes? This would be vital to the study of areas of convergence and situations which do not fit well within the standard genetic model.

Any attempt to answer these questions should lead to a clearer view of the entire problem of language change in situations where the appearance of languages is inherently linked to contact phenomena and an anthropological dimension. I shall thus try to establish a connection between two deceptively complex intuitive notions which can be subsumed under the terms 'contact' and 'genetic origin'. In trying to do this, I shall keep in view what seems to me to be the essential nature of language itself: its social dimension and the inherent heterogeneity in the way humans exercise the cognitive capacity to restructure and rationalize what they construct as a language.

The invariables of language change

Linguistic situations of the Songhay type have shown how great the need is for analytical models of language change which give suitable priority to considerations regarding language contact and social behavioral contexts in processes of linguistic communication. Such considerations have, of course, never been totally ignored; yet they have often been treated as epiphenomenal on the basis of ordinary models of individual language structure within a given theoretical framework. Consequently, contact phenomena have been described as (unnecessarily) complicating a simple situation, rather than as part of a basically complex initial state of affairs, the very frame of study. Must we accept that linguistic processes can be correctly apprehended only on the basis of the theoretical *a priori* hypothesis that the right way to start is by postulating a homogeneous structural system? Or would we not be wiser to avoid such reductionism and try to set out from an initial postulate of complexity?

This choice of initial postulate is fundamental insofar as it must affect the framework for the explanation of the observed phenomena, as we shall see below from the interconnection of the four themes which I shall develop within the framework of an avowedly multilingual approach. It must nevertheless be said explicitly that this approach is *tentative* and does not aspire to be strictly theoretical. *A priori* strictness is precisely one of the defects I wish to reject, along with the absence of any theoretical framework whatsoever.

The multilingual approach

1. *Multilingualism and/or multidialectalism[7] are both fundamental to, and commonplace in language in general*: this is the canonical situation for the description of linguistic communication and the analysis of the processes it involves. The need to deal with more than one linguistic and/or other code is evident even in such extreme situations as monolingual groups which reject everything extraneous and condemn all departures from the norm (e.g., the Bororo Fulani, adolescent groups, etc.). This ineluctable diversity of codes is one of the necessary conditions[8] of symbolic behavior in general and language behavior (the interaction of language use and language structure) in particular. This is why it must be brought to the fore in all analytical discussions.

The apparently simpler option of taking monolingualism as the *normal* state of affairs is the result of a rationalization which cannot account for the commonest situations of communication and hence fails to provide the means for describing them properly. Indeed, the analytical process is thereby blinded insofar as the dynamics of multilingualism cannot be (re)constructed by the mere induction of complexity from a set of juxtaposed monolingual situations. This, of course, has nothing to do with any holistic philosophical assumption; in this connection, we might recall Bachelard's notion of "generalization by negation": "Generalization by negation must appropriate the negated term. All the last century's advances in scientific thought can be set down to such dialectical generalizations which appropriate what they negate, as non-Euclidean geometry appropriates Euclidean" (Bachelard 1940: 137). The inversion of the canonical situation as suggested here allows the monolingual situation to be appropriated as simply a particular case of the multilingual one.

Hence, the first component of any explanatory approach must obviously be this requirement that more than one code be available to speakers. Whether such codes are actually different languages is less important than the recognition of their availability and possibilities of development. The consequence, though trivial, should be made explicit: this fact that codes can be altered within a specific anthropological setting which guarantees their meaningfulness provides the basis for the processes of emergence and material transformation of languages.

2. *The communities within which language processes take place are likewise not homogeneous.* They must therefore be considered to be areas of contact by definition (this again is not simply a *factual observation* but also a *theoretical postulate*), whose features predetermine the processes of communication. It is perhaps preferable to speak of *social fabrics* (with emphasis on texture or structure) rather than *communities* (with emphasis on partition and borders), since the participants have a concrete apprehension (whether conscious or not) of the nature and rules of the communicational structure within which they interact and the reasons why they are engaged in it (what good it is to them). On the other hand, they do not generally find it helpful to have a *precise* idea of the limits of their community or a symbolic representation of it. Hence, the first practical object of study is not linguistic structure, which is a *construct*, but exchange and the contact of languages and speech varieties within social fabrics through the interplay of the available ranges of codes.

A *language community* can be variably defined according to the boundaries or set of boundaries recognized by the participants in a given act of exchange or how they categorize it. *Language community* is thus a derived notion. Consequently, a general *condition of heterogeneity* must be regarded as an elementary principle of language behavior. The norm for the linguist should thus be that any linguistic exchange in a given functional setting must be stably defined as a potentially multilingual or multidialectal situation.

There are two corollaries to this: first, contact situations are inherent in the constitution of any language community whatsoever. This means that, even in an ideal case where there is null internal (lectal and/or social) differentiation, some such differentiation would ultimately emerge and become established *de facto*. Secondly, linguistic exchanges necessarily transcend the limits of any ostensibly homogeneous community (cf. in particular Nicolaï 2001). An offshoot of this is that the boundaries of any language, dialect, or other lect, so often viewed as essential, are a social construct which can be manipulated and reshaped according to the strategic needs of the moment.[9]

Let us nevertheless not forget that, for obvious reasons, this does not entail that any empirical process in a multidialectal context will have the same outcome and be directly comparable to one in a multilingual context (we need only recall here the case of koines). It simply implies that the two contexts will be subject to the same *heterogeneity condition* which governs any exchange.

3. *The 'finely layered range' of codes (rather than the 'languages') potentially available to the individual and/or the community constitutes a continuum for linguistic rearrangement.* This continuum is not a *finite space*: it can always be structurally replicated merely through the use made of it. I relate fine layering to all speech activity

in the course of which norms and expressive traditions are created, new ways of speaking come into existence, and customary uses of language (often reified by linguists as *registers* or *genres*) are utilized. Such activity, definable rather in terms of communicational situations than with reference to any specific language, may give rise equally well to stable and lasting speech forms as to ephemeral phenomena. For example, today, in France, the highly symbolic speech forms which have arisen among the young, particularly in the housing estates of the poorer suburbs of large cities, can thus be apprehended as an illustration of fine layering. Any differential speech activity whatsoever could, however, be interpreted in this way, provided it carries with it the production of a new norm or expressive tradition.

As a process, fine layering operates by putting out and picking up those phonetic, prosodic, morphological, lexical, syntactic, discursive and conversational features, selected from an available repertoire, which have as one of their functions the ability to serve as contextual cues in discourse (cf. J. Gumperz 1982). The use and reuse of such features is closely monitored by *legitimate* participants in the given type of speech activity and treated as indicators, in conjunction with other symbolic and behavioral markers, of the continual formation and dissolution of transient human groupings. The reuse of any linguistic feature more for its contextual significance than for its referential value is *technically* one of the procedures involved in fine layering. I shall speak in this case of the *anaphorization* of past uses. This is ordinary behavior and no language can fail to show evidence of it. Let us look at two correlative aspects of fine layering: layering as *activity* and layering as *outcome*.

As *activity*, fine layering can be seen as the *generating force* for paradigm building,[10] given that creation, retention, or rejection of this or that expression brings about change, whether simplification or complication, in the entities contained in the non-finite space of the repertory[11] within which the outcome is being built up. Correlatively, it should be obvious that such alteration / retention / suppression of linguistic features by virtue of this eminently sociolinguistic process has the effect of constraining the linguistic results which can be attributed to the "structural mechanics" alone of a given language; for this is the true locus of transformation and reorganization of linguistic structures through the processes manifested in the contingent and continuously interpreted historical unfolding of verbal activity.

As *outcome*, fine layering can be apprehended in the *concrete stratification* of the repertory available to the speaker: it involves on the one hand the specific forms and units which speakers *choose* (consciously or unconsciously) because they value them highly, and use strategically in communication, and on the other hand, the use of specific discursive or conversational sequences, which are no less identifiable for being procedures rather than components. Differently stated, this aspect involves both the functionally essential components of a *linguistic structure* (e.g., the alteration, retention, or suppression of morphosyntactic constructions) and the functionalized *positive signs* (e.g., the choice of lexical items or phonetic or prosodic features) used in a signalling system lending itself either to further development or to rejection. It is further determined by that cognitive operation which organizes lin-

guistic processes according to its own inherent structural principles and whose apprehension is the ultimate object of typological description.

In sum, we may say that there is a *fine internal layering* of the repertory which is
essential both to the language faculty itself (as activity: it provides the generating
force) and to that of the functionalization of individual languages (as outcome: new
layers can always be added), and that this factor cannot be ignored in the description of language change. I therefore use the expression *fine layering* to refer to the
capability of any language repertory to behave as a *source* for the reworking and, on
occasion, even the splitting off of lects and verbal practices created by the refunc-
tionalization of features, linguistic forms, and materially available discursive and at-
titudinal fragments (Nicolaï 2001).

In even more synthetic terms, let us say that the notion of fine layering rests on
the following hypotheses:

- within the range of layers delimited by each *de facto* exchange, whatever their
  number (drawing from the lattice of languages, lects, habits, forms, standards,
  interpretations, etc.), a restructuring of the given set is always possible without
  the intervention of external factors, and
- a new layer can always be added or an existing one eliminated by the simple self-
  referential process of fixing upon a linguistic feature of some previous discourse,
  whether this be anaphorization, cross-discursiveness, or something else again.

It thus becomes possible to grasp the overlay, the interweaving, and the multiplicity of the variants and practices in the repertory without the *a priori* assumption of
their structural homogeneity.

Fine layering is thus both the outcome and the substance of a *continuous stratification* giving no guarantee of any inherent regularity which would allow us to anticipate the development of the layers or the shape they will ultimately take on.

Finally, to the extent that we concern ourselves with speakers' *repertories* rather
than with the *languages* they know, we can see that all the speech norms, both conscious and "infraconscious" (whether subject to negotiation or not), the lects, and
the manners of speaking which mutually define, contrast with, and condition one
another are being constantly impacted upon by a variety of factors including continual splitting and regrouping, which may bring into play the individual's consciousness of his own identity; and this is precisely the process by which language
undergoes change and acquires stability.

4. *The anthropological setting: All of the above suggests that the processes of language
change with all their relevant parameters occur within a conventional, contingent, historical setting.* Hence, if acquired and transmitted *linguistic forms* (these of course
include norms, regular variations, particular lexical and phonetic features, syntactic constructions, and so forth, all of which are potentially vectors of identity and
sociocultural classification) other than structural organizations in the structuralist
sense and the elementary cognitive schemata which underlie various contemporary

theoretical approaches are to play a role in the explanation of language change, we must apprehend these forms as *anthropological constructs* arising from a particular *anthropological setting*, which can be defined as the *substrate* for their appearance.

The intervening space

Lastly, the theoretical and methodological clarity of language description will be enhanced (even in the absence of any empirical necessity) by the definition of the framework within which these anthropological constructs and the processes they involve are to be situated. I call this framework the *intervening space*.

The intervening space is thus a *theoretical construct* deriving from the requirement that any description be articulated according to the full set of factors which allow us to apprehend the dynamics of language change as set forth above. This space is the locus of neither the 'subject' of the psychologist, nor the 'speaker' of the linguist, nor the 'group', the 'network', or the 'community' of the sociolinguist, but rather of another 'agent' which I shall call the *homo loquens* and which I shall define as an *active entity* whose form of activity remains to be described. For our purposes, we need simply assume that this *homo loquens* is none other than the agent, theoretically constructed, cognitively and historically specified, but not linguistically determined, required by the anthropological constructs which take form, then structure and define one another over and again according to the necessities of the moment within a communicational space where the fine layering of the always non-finite repertory has been identified in its full linguistic specificity.

Specific processes of the kind observable in Songhay, no less than the phenomena of areal convergence, analyzable in terms of metatypical processes (cf. Ross 1997), which depend on other determining factors, provide good examples of change which can be set down to processes directly determined at the level of the collective representations generated in the intervening space. But the reference to this coordinating framework is even more useful when one stands on the limits of language apprehension in situations of need and structural crisis of the kind envisaged by Manessy (1995) in his study of creole languages, which led him to develop the notion of *semantax*. All of these cases involve processes which cannot be accounted for by mere structural and cognitive contrasts, lie beyond the domain of the language as unit of reference, and assume a higher degree of complexity.

My answer to my two original questions is thus strongly affirmative. The multilingual/multidialectal dimension must indeed be made an explicit component of models of linguistic processes, and a relevant anthropological setting extending beyond the individual language must be defined if the processes the latter undergoes are to be properly accounted for. We may conclude with another relevant remark by Bachelard (1934: 142), who observed that "the Cartesian method is reductive rather than inductive, and reductive in a way that distorts analysis and hinders the extensive development of objective thought. [...] The Cartesian method, so successful in explaining the world, is incapable of complicating experience, as all objective research should".

Tools

At this point, a distinction must be made between the attempt at theorization and the task of creating descriptive tools. I shall refer here to a few tools which various scholars have used in recent years to account for some of the processes involved in language contact. My list will not, of course, be exhaustive; I shall limit myself to mentioning some of the notions and/or images which can be used for internal or external models.

I use the expression '*internal models*' to refer to those which are intended to represent *shapes* (see above) in terms of processes such as *pidginization, creolization, koinization*, and so forth. These are notions which bear the imprint of the historical context in which they appeared, but which have evolved through efforts to conceptualize them in a context-free manner. These efforts have made it possible to shift them from reference to empirical observations towards reference to a notional process.[12]

Terminological inflation is an obvious problem in this field: pidgin, creole, vernacular language, trade language, continuum, prepidgin, postcreole, semipidgin, semicreole, creolization, pidginization, recreolization, decreolization, etc. These are all terms which are often hard to correlate with at least identifiable if not stable contents, to relate to their historical substrate, and to take over into a theoretically stabilized explanatory structure. We might thus find ourselves speaking of Western Songhay as partially pidginized, or of Dendi (the Songhay dialect spoken in the Niger–Benin–Nigeria border region) as a revernacularized trade language.

As an example, let us take the notion of 'vernacularization' used by Manessy (1995: 96), who defines it as

> "the effect produced on a variety of languages by two complementary processes: the simplification of grammatical structures and the compensatory development of other means of expression. In a way, simplification is given at the outset [...] It results [...] from the relaxation of a sociocultural tradition so as to free a language from normative constraints. The common factor in all these situations is that the use of a simplified variant is interpreted not simply as a way to achieve common understanding but as an expression of solidarity which transcends ethnic differences within a given framework such as town, region [...] or nation state [...] This solidarity is manifested through the communality of discourse conventions".

Clearly, the essential point from the linguistic standpoint is the existence of phenomena of simplification in the form of perceptible changes each time a given community uses one of the languages in its range and restricts its use, whether deliberately or not, to some part of the functions which it might otherwise have. Psychosocially speaking, the development of a situation of *complicity* is the factor which stabilizes a given linguistic form by creating specific conventions of discourse.

Vernacularization is thus linked both with pidginization (insofar as both are marked by the same type of simplification) and with creolization (insofar as the latter implies the normative stabilization of a simplified variety of language). This is the process which gives rise to a representation of the speech practices of a community which do not as yet show the increased complexity characteristic of creolization, though they are its precondition. Vernacularization is thus the first stage in the process of creolization, as Manessy stresses when he says (1995: 129), "We propose to use the term 'vernacularization' to designate the set of linguistic processes which are set in motion within a given language variety as it is appropriated". The process of appropriation, which is psychosocial in nature, is thus the essential factor in this development. The field of application of the notion has been defined; it now remains to organize the theoretical field within which it must apply and prove its validity.

The question may be stated as follows: once these notions have been extracted from their historical context and defined, to what extent do they capture the elementary linguistic processes involved and/or to what extent are they the representation of still vaguely defined operative phenomena which remain to be analyzed within an as yet undeveloped theoretical framework[13]? This question cannot necessarily be answered here; it is even unclear whether it has an answer. At the same time, there is no reason to think that the absence of an answer constitutes a handicap for understanding the observed phenomena.

In any case, the processes (such as those which bring vernacularized forms into being) are neither described nor explained simply because they have been given a name. At best, the term 'vernacularization' delimits a category of empirical phenomena which are classified together on the basis of supposedly shared features such as simplification; not because they are less historically marked do they become more precise. Processes are thus notions which require an explanation and not tools for providing one.

Of more recent origin, *external models* make use of mathematical representations or schemata of regular processes. In developing metaphorical extensions of models applied in other domains to apprehend complex phenomena which are beyond the reach of a deterministic approach, they abandon explanatory aspirations and try only to account for processes which can be characterized geometrically or topologically. This is modest on the one hand, in that ineradicable pretentions of explaining linguistic facts are set aside, and ambitious on the other, in that a new pretention of shifting the domain of relevance comes to the fore. Recourses to catastrophe theory (Thom 1974), fractal theory (Mandelbrot 1975), dissipative structure theory (Prigogine and Stengers 1979), and chaos theory (Ruelle 1991) fit into this category.

Among those who have taken an interest in the heuristic capabilities of this kind of model for the study of language processes and language change is Lass (1997). His perceptive study explores the explanatory potentialities at the intersection of biological models and metaphorical conceptualizations drawn from chaos theory (cf. *point attractors*, *sinks*, *limit cycles*; *cyclical attractors*; *arrows and cycles*; *flow*;

chreods; *drift*, etc.). He postulates contingent topologies (*epigenic landscapes*, etc.), which are not far removed from the substrate spaces of catastrophe theory, correlated with the identification of causal mechanisms and evolutionary configurations (cf. *stasis, punctuation*) which relate explicitly to the biological evolutionary models of Gould and Eldredge (1977).

The question which arises, whenever a model is to be exported, is exactly what is being modelled and what relationship exists between the properties of the model and those of the objects to which it applies. Do the former mask or illuminate the latter? Do they have an effect on perspective? What is added by the newly transferred model to the already available perceptions? Could one perhaps identify a specific anthropological setting such as the one characteristic of the emergence of the Songhay languages in terms of processes occurring in a definable "epigenic landscape" which differs structurally from some other type of anthropological setting, such as the one characteristic of the Oceanic et Melanesian area, which has given rise to the notion of metatypy (Ross 1997)? More importantly, is anything to be gained from such a modification in terms of general linguistic theory and an understanding of the phenomena of language change?

Moreover, there can be more than one level of models corresponding to incommensurate scales in the apprehension of the phenomena. For example, the tree model of language change operates on a level which is totally unrelated to those on which morphological representations of the *Cusp of Whitney* found in catastrophe theory (cf. Thom 1974: 157) or the *strange attractors* of chaos theory (cf. Ruelle 1980: 131) might conceivably apply. The fractal approach, which apparently has applications in demography (cf. Le Bras 2000), might provide a broad-scale approximation to phenomena of linguistic diffusion.[14] In these cases, are the metaphors involved (for these are indeed still metaphors at this stage[15]) of heuristic interest or, on the contrary, do they create opacity?

Bricks and metaphors: What are bricks for? For building houses, obviously. Well, both internal and external models referred to above provide nothing more than "conceptual bricks". There are other equally well organized, factually oriented approaches which have made contributions to the same edifice (cf. Thomason and Kaufmann 1988 and their analysis of interference, Manessy 1995 and his development of semantax, and Lass 1997 and his thoughts on the processes of change). Each of these conceptual bricks bears its factory imprint (i.e., metaphorically speaking, is referenced). This is both enriching and problematic. In the end, however, the important thing is what can be built from the bricks and the architectural idea which brings the whole together,[16] since that idea must be anchored in empirical reality and lead beyond self-reference.

The aim is thus not simply to find / invent a local or overall model which captures certain apparent phenomenal regularities. It is also to evaluate the extent to which this translation can account for properties whose relevance has previously been recognized / posited / envisaged on a theoretical level, given a few *a priori* principles and an at least momentary correspondence to a particular class of empirical phenomena. The import of these apparent regularities and the way in which the model helps to make them meaningful must also be evaluated. In short, the thing apprehended must be conceptually grasped in its initial coherence (which is thereby put to the test) and in the characterization of its relevant functions; and the model must be found capable of magnifying precisely the desired defining functions and relations by making them explicit and translating them. We thereby return to the subject of metaphor.

When reflecting on the process of conceptual elaboration, Lass (1997:42) remarks that "[a]mong the important constructivist devices available to the historian is the creation of metaphors; metaphorical images can define and create new natural or conceptual kinds, which then become legitimate objects of exploration, and enrich the discipline's universe". Again, "we may notice (a) that [our own metalanguage] is much more metaphorical than we think, and (b) how important these metaphors are as devices for framing our thinking, and how much of our theory they actually generate", and this is in a way evident. To this, Bachelard's reply (1947:38) might have been, "*A science which a*ccepts imagery is the most vulnerable to metaphors. This is why the scientific method must constantly struggle against imagery, analogy, and metaphor". Or again (1947:81), "The danger of immediate metaphors for the development of scientific thought is that they are not always transitory images; they instigate autonomous thought and tend to expand and reach fullness in the domain of imagery". The debate remains open.

Perspectives

The issues and the framework for the issues: The discussion hitherto should suggest a framework whose objective would be to retain the explanatory power of existing theories while placing them in context (see the remarks on negative generalization above). An aim of this kind helps to place the problems of language processes and description of change in a new focus. It is in this respect that my concerns merge with others expressed at this symposium trying "to identify hitherto unstated or understated fundamental issues in linguistic theories taking into account the rich variation of forms and functions observed in the languages of the world". Some of these "*unstated or understated issues*" are illustrated by the preceding debate, since there is no assumption of the multicode reference framework I have been suggesting in the stance that makes comprehensible utterances such as "What should be the proper object for theories of language structure?" or "What should a theory of language structure explain?". This is also so of questions such as "What are the motivations for language change and grammaticalization?" or "Does human conscious choice play a part in language change?". Taking a position from the outset that recognizes multicodism as a defining feature of communication will entail changes in the analyses. Allowing for processes within what I have called the intervening space will reorient analyses in directions which it is far too early to spell out.[17] At the same time, the focus on the need for models suggests that we should be far more demanding before we agree to use them.

Grammaticalization can thus be set down to a process governed by the dual effects of wear and cognitively oriented reorganization of language structures (dominant and recessive structural types, shift from concrete to abstract, etc.[18]). But are these two processes what they seem or do they, like the notions mentioned above, rather stem simply from giving a name to an outward appearance or an *a priori*? Are they not modified by the postulate of multiple codes?

Is the suggested link between dominance and improved cognitive adequacy anything other than a hypothesis based on the consideration of a known contingent process of formal structuring? Is the expansion of a given form / structure necessarily linked to its effectiveness within a cognitive and neo-Darwinian conceptual background or are there other perhaps less intuitive alternatives? How can this expansion be justified without circularity? Is this anything other than the kind of shaping which one of the external models which account for the creation of order in accumulations might provide? Or could other models originating from interactional sociology not be used via, say, the interplay of agents involved in a system of interdependence with the development of an emerging phenomenon? Even without lengthier analysis, several possible approaches appear clearly, each relying on a given level of explanation and system of relevance.

Again, is it true that the concrete precedes the abstract and what might this mean? How could we imagine, even at the "beginning", a language without the inherent correlative abstraction which a symbolic system implies by and for its very existence? Perhaps in this case, another process should be conceived which, on a given occasion, might look at first sight like a passage from the concrete to the abstract of the kind which is axiomatic in many works on natural semantics. Finally, it might also be better here to apprehend this fundamental duality as a complex phenomenon rather than trying *a priori* to assign a *direction* from one facet to the other of a process of symbolization and find proof / traces of this in language change.

Finally, what we find here is that no one model will suffice to account for the phenomena under consideration. While it is clear that each subdomain is apprehended through a system of relevance and that each model gives preference to its own representation, the set of subdomains is in constant interaction, and this in turn validates other models and brings out new relevancies. There is thus nothing surprising in the fact that questions originate in different *temporalities* and refer back to different dimensions so as to support heterogeneous modelizations.

In the same way (initially, there is no alternative), their apparent simplicity disguises a formidable semantic plurality: to speak of "human conscious choice" is to bring in the potential effect of all manner of legislative activities; yet there is action without explicit legislation and without reference to institutionalized normative representations (cf. the development of discursive and/or linguistic norms in many communities). But here again, on what scale is the effect of choice being recorded (from the level of the temporary interactive group to that of a splitting of the community; from the interpretation of a process as a function of contemporary use to the recording of change over several thousand years, etc.)?

Finally, if it is accepted that neither the individual nor the speakers have any direct effect on their language, what inferences can be drawn regarding the construction of a collective entity referring back to a potentially active *homo loquens*, which is as much of a construct as the *'speaker'*: an entity with no consciousness though necessarily possessed of memory and normative references defined at a level independent of the one on which the structural processes of languages are built; an entity which can be defined to the dimensions of an anthropological space whose limits are not necessarily those of a given language since it comes under the effects of linguistic, cognitive, and cultural dimensions all at once?

I am fully conscious of going beyond the limits of what can be expressed within the framework of a symposium. It is likely that such issues could only be dealt with in a fully fledged program of new research.

Towards a conclusion

In this chapter, I have discussed the nature of language contact and diverse aspects of language change in the light of a particularly difficult case. I have also set forth a number of theoretical considerations which will help to grasp the importance of certain aspects of language change which I feel have too often been neglected. Finally, I have briefly suggested ways in which notions of model making might be used to describe the results of these processes. No one of these three themes is directly dependent on any other, none can be induced in any way from another. It is nevertheless obvious that they require correlative consideration and development. The implications of a number of simple ideas require closer examination. Fuller appreciation of the complexity of the structures we deal with must be sought, and descriptive models[19] need to be developed which identify agents which are intrinsically active in their field of reference (intervening space, linguistic space, etc.) and provide more than unanalyzed representations from this standpoint (such as those which are characterized as processes deriving directly from the consideration of historical phenomena: "tendencies" such as convergence).[20]

In the *intervening space*, for example, to what extent would models in terms of systems of interdependence with their emerging forms not be better adapted to interpreting linguistic transformations so as to provide feedback for refocussing certain strictly formal processes? The appearance of normative representations and their structuring could probably be interpreted, according to the context in which they are realized, as emerging effects of a complex system in which functional role and interdependence work together. And this is equally true of the description of processes apprehended over their historical development. But this is perhaps oversimplifying. Finally, in order to stress the fact that my discussions are creating a *local norm*, I shall conclude with a counterpoint in the initial key.

Science on Cartesian principles quite logically complicated the simple, but contemporary scientific thought tries to read real complexity beneath the simple appearances of adjusted phenomena. It tries to find pluralism beneath identity, imagine occasions when identity might be broken down beyond immediate experience, itself too readily compacted into a broad view. These occasions do not come of their own, they are not found on the surface of being, in fashions, in the picturesque aspects of shimmering, orderless nature. They must be picked out of the heart of substance from within the contexture of its attributes.   (Bachelard 1934:143)

Notes

1. Bibliographical recapitulation: (1) Songhay is an isolated unit (Westermann 1927), typologically close to Mande (Delafosse); (2) Songhay is a member of Nilo-Saharan (Greenberg 1964); (3) hypothesis impugned by Lacroix (1969); (4) Songhay is a Tuareg-Mande creole (Nicolaï 1990); (5) return to Nilo-Saharan (Bender 1995, Ehret 2001); (6) Songhay derived from a Afroasiatic *lingua franca* (Nicolaï 2003).

2. I distinguish 'assumptions' relating to the model (thus, the tree model of language diversification *assumes* a linear development) from 'a priori factors in research' relating to the sociological and at times *emblematic* features of scholarly activity (thus, choosing Bachelard rather than Feyerabend or Lakatos as one's epistemological reference necessarily categorizes the proponent).

3. Not previously identified owing precisely to *a priori* factors in earlier studies. There is no space here to present the data and analyses which support this affirmation. Nicolaï (2003) provides a detailed discussion. See Nicolaï (in press a) for a summary version. A few examples are nevertheless appended.

4. Let us speak of 'nativization' of a language as we might speak of 'ethnicization' of a culture. Ethnic groups, like languages, are not necessarily formed by genetic descent; they may quite well come into being without *deriving from* some other one, and then only later provide themselves with a history.

5. cf. Creissels (1981), Lacroix (1969), Nicolaï (1977, 1984, 1990) for remarks on Songhay grammatical morphemes akin to Mande. For a broader view, see Nicolaï (in press b).

6. I use the term "code" here in the widest sense to refer to any formal feature shared under an explicit or implicit convention, which allows a meaningful distinction to be made in a communicational exchange.

7. Note that multidialectalism should not be treated as a first stage to multilingualism, even though there are models which consider it to be historically prior. Rather, multilingualism and multidialectalism appear concomitantly.

8. Rhyming slang, pig Latin, and other language games can be interpreted as proof of this necessity. The social functions of these practices as identity-building and exclusivist are founded on the functional dynamics of multiplicity.

9. See Canut (1998:163–164) and Juillard (2001) for an approach to heterogeneity and the construction of boundaries.

10. By this expression I designate the operation, usually enriching the repertory, which consists of assimilating alternative, discursively developed forms and manners of speaking for subsequent use. These constitute a paradigm insofar as, despite having identical reference, they have different meaning (cf. Frege 1892). Note however that this operation does not invariably involve enrichment; in a suitable anthropological setting, the result can be the impoverishment of the range of paradigmatic choices.

11. In another area of paradigm building, we might also see a fine layering effect in the stratification of the utterances which are potentially entailed by the paraphrasablity of utterances produced in any verbal exchange; indeed, there is rarely only one way of saying what one wants to say, with regard either to intended reference or to implicit correlates and any symbolic intentions.

12. This discussion forcefully recalls Bachelard's comments on the strength of imagery. Discussing the importance of the image of the sponge in the 18th century to explain a number of phenomena of physical extension, he cites Réaumur and remarks (1947:75), "His entire thought derives from this image, and is incapable of progressing beyond this primary intuition. When he tries to erase the image, its function persists [...] He might ultimately agree to give up the sponge, but he wants to hang on to sponginess. This is proof of an exclusively linguistic development entailing the conviction that, by associating an abstract word with a concrete one, an intellectual advance has been achieved. A coherent doctrine of abstraction would require a greater degree of detachment from primary images". Bachelard is speaking here of historical configurations, but the fact remains that vigilance is required whenever we come across notions whose definition is overloaded by their reference or their connotation. There are many of these.

13. Obviously, there is another level where these same context-free notions are examined and analyzed so as to permit their definition by more abstract operators such as the processes of simplification or complexification, increasing complexity which also require definition.

14. The reader can profitably consult the approach developed by Stéphane Robert in this same volume to apply this model internally to linguistic construction in order to account for apparent scaling in transcategorial phenomena.

15. It should not be forgotten that all these theories have mathematics as their domain, and that the relationship between the formal properties of a model and the objects to which it applies must be established or at least explicitly set out in order for the exportation to go beyond the level of the approximate metaphor, however enlightening this may be in itself.

16. Thus Lass (1997:293) finds his tools helpful but stresses that "what counts is the image of an evolving system as a kind of 'flow' in some n-dimensional space, and the existence of regions in that space towards which the flow tends to converge".

17. We are no longer faced with a simple process of change which can be analyzed almost deterministically with perhaps some allowance for contextual effects (the ordinary framework for the a posteriori explanation of a clearly identified and localized change) but are not yet (far from it) in a situation governed by chance and preconstrained by a specific substrate. The most accurate prediction in the treatment of complex phenomena of any kind (in meteorology, economics, etc.) remains that of the margin of error.

18. All of these are notional tools from the conceptual arsenal whose history could doubtless be followed back via a cross-disciplinary analysis of scientific discourse. Their common

use and status as elementary concepts do not make them accurate descriptions nor *a fortiori* valid explanations.

19. These must be neither opacifying (hiding what they are intended to illuminate) nor residual (oversimplifying what they are supposed to account for). In either of these cases, the problem is avoided, and the sum of the knowledge acquired is either nul or negative.

20. Like many others, I once found notions of processes such as pidginization, creolization, etc. stimulating and perhaps heuristic. I do not now renounce them but, after further reflection, I hope to have assigned them to their proper place. This is proof of their usefulness and opens the way to moving beyond them.

References

Bachelard, Gaston. 1934 [1999]. *Le nouvel esprit scientifique*. Paris: PUF.

Bachelard, Gaston. 1940 [2002]. *La philosophie du non*. Paris: PUF.

Bachelard, Gaston. 1947. *La formation de l'esprit scientifique*. Paris: Vrin.

Bender, Lionel M., 1995. *The Nilo-Saharan languages, a comparative essay*. München: LINCOM Europa.

Canut, Cécile. 1998. "Perception des espaces plurilingues ou polylectaux et activité épilinguistique". *Language and location in space and time*, ed. by Petr Zima and Vladimir Tax, 155–170, München: LINCOM Europa.

Creissels, Denis. 1981. "De la possibilité de rapprochements entre le songhay et les langues Niger-Congo (en particulier mandé)". *Nilo-Saharan*, ed. by Thilo C. Schadeberg and M. Lionel Bender, 185–199. Cinnaminson: Foris Publications.

Creissels, Denis. 2001. "Catégorisation et grammaticalisation: la relation génitivale en mandingue". *Leçons d'Afrique, Filiations, ruptures et reconstitution de langues*, ed. by Robert Nicolaï, 433–454. Louvain-Paris: Peeters.

Dixon, R. M. W. 1997. *The rise and fall of languages*. Cambridge: Cambridge University Press.

Ehret, Christopher. 2001. *A historical-comparative reconstruction of Nilo-Saharan*. Köln: Köppe.

Frege, Gottlob. [1892] 1971. *Ecrits logiques et philosophiques*. Paris: Le Seuil.

Gould, Stephen Jay and Eldredge, Niles. 1977. "Punctuated equilibria: the tempo and mode of evolution reconsidered". *Paleobiology* 3. 115–151.

Greenberg, Joseph H. 1963. *The languages of Africa*. Bloomington: Indiana University Press.

Heine, Bernd. 1975. Language typology and convergence areas in Africa. *Linguistics* 144. 27–47.

Houis, Maurice. 1971. *Anthropologie linguistique de l'Afrique noire*. Paris: PUF.

Juillard, Caroline. 2001. "Une ou deux langues ? Des positions et des faits". *La Linguistique* 37 (2). 3–31.

Lacroix, Pierre-Francis. 1971. "L'ensemble songhay-jerma: problèmes et thèmes de travail". *Actes du 8e Congrès SLAO, 1969*, Annales de l'Université d'Abidjan, Linguistique, Série H, Abidjan. 87–99.

Lass, Roger. 1997. *Historical linguistics and language change*. Cambridge: Cambridge University Press.

Le Bras, Hervé. 2000. *Essai de géométrie sociale*. Paris: Odile Jacob.

Mandelbrot, Benoît. [1975] 1995. *Les objets fractals*. Paris: Flammarion.

Manessy, Gabriel. 1995. *Créoles, pidgins, variétés véhiculaires, Procès et genèse*. Paris: Editions du CNRS.

Mukarovsky, Hans. 1989. "Songhai – eine tschadische Sprache?". *Frankfurter Afrikanistische Blätter* 1. 16–29.

Nicolaï, Robert. 1977. Sur l'appartenance du songhay. *Annales de l'Université de Nice* 28. 129–35.

Nicolaï, Robert. 1984. *Préliminaire à une étude sur l'origine du songhay*. Berlin: Dietrich Reimer.

Nicolaï, Robert. 1990. *Parentés linguistiques (à propos du songhay)*. Paris: Editions du CNRS.

Nicolaï, Robert. 2000. *La traversée de l'empirique. Essai d'épistémologie sur la reconstruction des représentations de l'évolution des langues*. Paris: Ophrys.

Nicolaï, Robert. 2001. "La "construction de l'unitaire" et le "sentiment de l'unité" dans la saisie du contact des langues". *Langues en contact et incidences subjectives*, 359–386. Montpellier: *Traverses* 2.

Nicolaï, Robert. 2003. *La force des choses ou l'épreuve 'nilo-saharienne'. Questions sur les reconstructions archéologiques et l'évolution des langues*. Köln: Köppe.

Nicolaï, Robert. in press a. "Aux marges de l'espace chamito-sémitique: songhay et diffusion aréale. *Les langues chamito-sémitiques (afro-asiatiques)*", ed. by Amina Mettouchi and Antoine Lonnet. Paris: Ophrys.

Nicolaï, Robert. in press b. "Mande-Songhay: Facts, questions, frames". *Africa as a linguistic area / Areal typology and African languages*, ed. by Bernd Heine and Derek Nurse. Cambridge Univ. Press.

Prigogine, Ilya and Isabelle Stengers. 1979. *La nouvelle Alliance. Métamorphose de la science*. Paris: Gallimard.

Ross, Malcom S. 1997. "Social networks and kinds of speech-community event". *Archeology and Language* 1, ed. by Roger Blench and Matthews Spriggs, 207–261. London/New-York: Routledge.

Ross, Malcom S. 2001. "Contact-Induced Change in Oceanic Languages in North-West Melanesia". *Areal and Genetic Inheritance. Problems in Comparative Linguistics*, ed. by Alexandra Y. Aikhenvald and Robert M.W. Dixon, 134–166. Oxford: Oxford University Press.

Ruelle, David. 1980. "Strange attractors". *The Mathematical Intelligencer* 2. 126–137.

Ruelle, David. 1991. *Hasard et chaos*. Paris: Odile Jacob.

Thom, René. 1974. *Modèles mathématiques de la morphogenèse*. Paris: Christian Bourgois.

Thomason, Sarah. 1996. *Contact languages, a wider perspective*. Amsterdam - Philadelphie: John Benjamins.

Thomason, Sarah G. and Terrence Kaufman. 1988. *Language contact, creolization, and genetic linguistics*. Berkeley: California University Press.

Vydrine, Valentin. in press. "Areal and genetic features in West Mande and Mani-Bandama (East Mande) phonology: In what sense did Mande languages evolute?". *JAWL International Symposium "Area Typology of West Africa"* ed. by Bernard Comrie and Ekkehart Wolff.

Westermann, Diedrich. 1927. *Die Westlichen Sudansprachen und ihre Beziehungen zum Bantu*. MSOS Beiheft (Jagrg. 30). Berlin: De Gruyter.

Zima, Petr. 1988. "Songhay, Hausa and Chadic (Preliminary notes on lexical affinities)". *Progressive Traditions in African and Oriental Studies: Asia, Africa, Latin America* 21. 185–192.

Chapter 5

On the part played by human conscious choice in language structure and language evolution

Claude Hagège

Collège de France

Most linguists consider that the categories used and classified by human languages as tools of expression of the universe are not the result of a conscious building activity. The present paper tries to show that, in contradistinction to this position, speakers-hearers, here conceptualized as LEs (Language Engineers), are aware of a part of their own activity with respect to language construction. This awareness can be observed in the lexicon, as may be expected, but also in phonology, and even in morphosyntax. Thus, although speakers-hearers do not analyze every device as professional linguists do, they evince a certain amount of metalinguistic activity. This applies both synchronically and diachronically.

1. Introduction

It is usually taken for granted among linguists of various schools that language structure and language evolution are unconscious processes. "Unconscious" is not used here in its Freudian sense, but in its common meaning: unconscious processes are those that human beings perform without being aware of this fact. Boas's is an explicit claim: "The linguistic classifications never rise into consciousness [...] The great advantage that linguistics offers [...] is the fact that on the whole, the categories which are formed always remain unconscious, and that for this reason the processes which lead to their formation can be followed without the misleading and disturbing factors of secondary explanations." (1911: 70–71).

In fact, the validity of Boas's claim depends on the language component to which it is applied. In many respects, human beings may be conceived of as language engineers (LEs). In this paper, after briefly recalling the work of certain famous LEs (section 2), I will try to show voluntary human activity in the fields of morphosyntax (section 3), phonology (section 4) and the lexicon (section 5).

2. "First grammarians" and famous language engineers

So far, we know of no language whose creation *ex nihilo* can safely be ascribed to the initiative of a particular individual. However, the history of human languages is replete with cases in which, at a certain moment in the evolution, someone, alone or with a group of associates, played a leading role in the standardization or reform of one of its parts. I will only recall some facts here (for more details, cf. Hagège 1983).

The norm for Icelandic was established in the 12th century by an anonymous "first grammarian". In the 16th century, the translations of the Bible by Luther, Sylvester, and Agricola, established a large part of the religious, learned and abstract lexicons of German, Hungarian and Finnish respectively. In the 18th century, Lomonosov laid the foundations of modern literary Russian, as opposed to the old norm, strongly influenced by Church Slavonic. In the beginning and at the end of the 19th century, many nationalist fighters were also scholars, dictionary-makers and/or philologists, among them Arana-Goiri, Korais, Štúr, Aasen, and Karadžić, who proposed unified or modernized forms, respectively, of Basque, Greek, Slovakian, neo-Norwegian and Serbo-Croatian (Šulek, departing from Karadžić, later set up a specific norm for Croatian). Finally, in the 20th century, at least six cases may be mentioned: Ben Yehuda established the lexical base of modern Hebrew by gathering the main written records from all the periods of the history of Hebrew and drawing from them as much material as possible; Mustafa Kemâl (Atatürk) rid Turkish of many learned Arabic loanwords and heavy Arabicized wordings; Kasravi tried to do the same for Persian; Aavik coined many words and proposed various simplifications for Estonian; and Prince Wan and Alisjahbana worked out a modernized lexicon of Thai and Indonesian, respectively.

None of these actions would deserve more than passing mention if they had not been generally successful. Of course not all proposals made by these reformers met with general acceptance, but many did, and to the extent that those of them which had to do with the written form of a given language were followed by most writers, including popular ones, they also had an indirect influence on spoken usage. Thus conscious human choice, through the action of various reformers, has played a part, if not the main part, in the evolution of many languages. Having recalled this aspect of the subject, it is now time to examine what part is played, in language structure and evolution, by average speakers, since they also make conscious linguistic choices that result in changes in their language.

3. Conscious human choice in morphosyntax

I will first examine cases of morphological analysis of complex words by lay speakers (3.1). I will then show how users' consciousness may lead to an explicit knowledge of grammar and thus influence its evolution (3.2). Finally, I will present various cases of publicly claimed, and successful, actions on morphosyntax (3.3).

3.1. Morphological analysis of complex words by lay speakers

Ordinary speech in various languages often exhibits complex words whose constituting parts are split off from one another, even though it would seem that they are
not separable. This is shown in examples (1) and (2) for case and plural markers respectively:

(1) Tokharian A (Schmidt 1969: 107)
     kukl-as   yuk-as   öṅkälm-ās-yo
     cart-OBL.PL horse-OBL.PL elephant-OBL.PL-INSTR
     'with carts, horses and elephants'

(2) Turkish
     bayan ve   bay-lar
     lady   and gentleman-PL
     'ladies and gentlemen'

In (1), *kukl* and *yuk* are both oblique plurals, as is *öṅkälm*, but only the latter receives
an instrumental case marker, although all three nouns are in the instrumental; in 2,
it is the plural marker *-lar* which is split off from *bayan* although this noun is plural
just like *bay*, which bears the marker in question.

Derivational affixes may also be split off, whether adverbial (example (3)) or adjectival (example (4)):

(3) Spanish
     clara y precisamente
     'clearly and precisely'

(4) German
     tradier–   aber nur schwerlich entlehnbar
     transmit– but only uneasily   borrowable

In (3), the adverbial suffix *-mente* applies both to *clara-* and to *precisa-* but is separated from the former; in (4), the adjective-forming suffix *-bar*, although it has no
autonomous existence, is severed from the first verbal stem, and treated as common
to two stems.

In these cases, selected from among many, we can see that lay speakers are often
quite aware of the structures allegedly hidden in their language. They even make
some conscious choices which influence the structure and evolution of their language, as we will now see.

3.2. Poetic activity as reflecting an explicit knowledge of grammar, and its role in language evolution

Jakobson wrote (1968: 600) that parallelism (*parallelismus membrorum*), a characteristic poetical device, gives us "a direct insight into the speakers' own conception

of the grammatical equivalences". Parallelism is pervasively found in the archaic Canaanite tradition reflected in the style of the Bible, as well as in Russian folksongs such as the *byliny* (heroic epics), in the oral poetry of Finno-Ugric, Turkic, Mongolian and Tungusic peoples, and in the learned classical tradition of ancient China.

The latter is an especially interesting example, because parallelism played an important role in the very history of grammatical thought in China. Classical Chinese poetry has a striking characteristic: in the first verse of a distich a word may occupy the same position as another word in the following verse only if these two words are semantically parallel. Accordingly, Chinese poets needed to set up word pairs containing parallel members. In order to make the choice easier, they divided the whole lexicon of Chinese into two lists (cf. Hagège 1975: 23–24), both of which contained all the parallel words among which two words could be selected. One list contained so-called full words, i.e. names of tangible objects, as well as most verbs referring to actions. The other list contained what were considered to be empty words, i.e. nouns and verbs referring to thoughts, feelings, some actions, as well as adverbs, prepositions and conjunctions, to use modern terminology. Later on, this distinction became the very basis of traditional Chinese grammar. Thus, an early form of linguistic thought was prompted by the needs of poetical activity. Even tough it is quite likely that many nouns and verbs ascribed to the list of empty words in old Chinese grammar would not be so classified by modern linguists, the interesting thing is that in these remote times well-read Chinese speakers (admittedly a small part of the population) were aware of grammatical mechanisms, and reflected this awareness in the way they established the norms for poetic creation.

Now the most striking phenomenon is that a number of tools that have been created in the course of the history of Chinese by a process of grammaticalization, mostly prepositions, are historically derived from verbs belonging to the "empty words" list, like *bǎ* 'take', *gěi* 'give', *yòŋ* 'use', *gēn* 'follow', etc. In other words, although it cannot be ascertained that poets have directly influenced the evolution of the language, it remains likely that their constant use of such verbs as parts of verses in which they were parallel with words which appeared in the other verse of the distich and which were long-established prepositions, such as *yú* "to", *yīn* "because of", *zì* "from", *yǐ* "by means of", contributed to the grammaticalization of these verbs.

3.3. Publicly claimed action on morphosyntax

3.3.1. *Voluntary intervention by political authorities*

Cases of such voluntary intervention are not widespread. At least one, however, is beyond any doubt and, to some extent, spectacular: modern Hebrew. Between 1952 and 1964, the state of Israel, whose birth had taken place only a few years earlier, was the site of a long linguistic controversy. Strange as it may appear, this controversy, which took the form of a national debate, centered around the use of the preposition *ʔet* before definite objects (Hagège 1993: 34–35)! In Biblical and, to a lesser extent, in Mishnaic Hebrew (the language of rabbinic literature devoted to the Bible), definite objects are normally marked by ʔet, this stage of the language being comparable, in this respect, to other languages with a definite (often definite + human) object marker, like Spanish (*a*), Persian (*-râ*), Turkish (*-i/ -u/-u*), Mongolian (*-yg*), Aymara (*-ru*), etc. D. Ben Gurion, the first Prime Minister and one of the founders of the state, claimed that the cases where ʔet can be useful, namely those where it serves to clarify who is the agent and who is the patient, are very rare: the context is usually sufficient for that purpose. Ben Gurion added that Rabbi Aqiba (second century) objected to the use of ʔet, and that Maimonides, the famous philosopher of the 12th century, almost never used it. Moreover, according to Ben Gurion, the number of occurrences of ʔet regularly decreased from the earlier to the later books of the Bible. Finally, the Prime Minister claimed that using too many ʔet made the style clumsy, wasted paper, printing ink, money and time in a young state which could not afford all that. Therefore, he concluded, ʔet should be discarded. Many letters were written by Ben Gurion to various periodicals, and many people wrote for or against ʔet in famous newspapers, such as *Ha-Tsofeh* ('The Observer'), *ʕal Ha-Mišmar* ('On Guard'), *Davar* ('The Word').

Among the many opponents to Ben Gurion's position was the writer and grammarian Yuri Avineri, who debunked Ben Gurion's arguments one after the other. According to Avineri, the context is usually insufficient for distinguishing the subject from the object; moreover, it is simply not true that writers of the Mishnaic period avoided ʔet, and it can only be said that if Maimonides' texts exhibit slightly fewer uses of *etʔ* than the Bible, it is just because, writing in Hebrew in Arabic-speaking countries or regions, where he also wrote in Arabic (Moslem Andalusia, Morocco, Palestine and Egypt), he was strongly influenced by classical Arabic, which marks the patient not with a preposition, but with a case ending; as for the Prime Minister's counting, Avineri said, it was wrong: statistics tend to show the pervasive presence of ʔet throughout the Bible. The conservative view eventually prevailed, and Ben Gurion was forced to withdraw his project. The most striking fact is that none of the many journalists, writers, and ordinary people who participated in this public controversy had any training in linguistics. This did not prevent them from acting as language users quite conscious of such a technical, and allegedly mechanical, point as the marking of a syntactic relationship between a transitive verbal predicate and a definite patient.

Thus we see that in certain cases, rare though these cases may be, language users are LEs: by voluntary intervention, they literally make the syntax of their language, deciding for example, like here, that a morphological tool belonging to classical stages has an important syntactic role to play, and should therefore not be dismissed from the modern stage they are consciously reconstructing!

3.3.2. *Official decisions made in the field of nominal morphology*
Gender is a domain open to official action in various languages. Limiting myself to European examples, I will mention two cases. One is Dutch. A group of language experts, the Van Haeringen Committee, was asked, in the beginning of the 1950s,

to study the possibility of giving up the feminine in Dutch. In 1955 the governments of the Netherlands and Belgium gave political status to the conclusions of this Committee, and the feminine was officially abandoned. Of course, this does not mean that those relatively few speakers who traditionally used the feminine all of a sudden rejected it. Nor does it mean, on the other hand, that the Committee imposed its view on a population that was not prepared to accept it. In fact, since the end of the 16th century the use of the feminine had long been declining, especially in the northernmost part of the Dutch-speaking area, but also elsewhere. Only due to the pressure of purists who wished to remain faithful to the Latin model did the feminine survive, to a large extent artificially. Thus we may see that conscious actions on morphology are not necessarily effected by unreliable language reformers prompted by their dreams. Rather, their success is often conditioned by an already existing and widespread trend, whose final purpose is to modify the state of things.

In a comparable way, a human decision effected a change in nominal gender in neo-Norwegian, this time in the opposite direction. The feminine had disappeared in Danish and Swedish, as well as in the danicized norm of Norwegian, which, starting from the beginning of Danish rule (early decades of the 16th century), had been official in Norway for almost four centuries. But the feminine was restored in *nynorsk* (neo-Norwegian), a language created, in the wake of nationalist claims among 19th century intellectuals, by Ivar Aasen (cf. section 2, and Hagège 1983: 47–48). The latter drew on South-West dialects, in which the feminine had remained in use. Thus, a man whose action was certainly not quite isolated but who was the main contributor was able to build, on the basis of pre-existing dialects, a new norm, applied to such an apparently unconscious grammatical phenomenon as gender. This shows that a human community, or even a group of individuals, can make, on the basis of living material, a linguistic means of communication that is accepted by a part of the population of a country: Nynorsk is one of the two official languages in Norway today, and was spoken in 1976 by 16,5% of children attending primary school (Gundersen 1983: 157).

3.3.3. *Successful actions on verbal inflection and on the counting system*
Many examples could be mentioned here. I will select two. The18th century language promoters of Hungarian introduced in the literary style, and even in spoken usage, the verbal inflection with an -*ik* suffix, which was beginning to get confused with another type of verbal inflection. Secondly, a decree made in 1951 by the Norwegian government decided that the numeral system for tens and units, which is traditionally, as in Swedish, of the sequential type <unit + 'and' + ten>, should become, as in English or French, <ten + unit>, e.g. *tjue-to* 'twenty-two' or *trettifem* 'thirty-five', instead of *to-og-tjue* and *fem-og-tredve*. It is not certain, in this case, however, that the new system obtained a real consensus (cf. Tauli 1968: 153).

3.3.4. *Actions on verbal and nominal inflections.*
Only one example will be given here. As early as the middle of the 16th century, per-

son and case endings had disappeared in most dialects of spoken Finnish, as a result of the weakening of unstressed short vowels in final position. Thus, *tule-mme* 'we come', *metsä-ssi* 'in the forest', *isä-si* 'your father' had become, respectively, *tule-m*, *metsä-s* and *isä-s*. While the products of this weakening are those which are found in closely related Estonian, where Aavik (cf. section 2) proposed many other such reductions aiming at more 'simplicity', Finnish reformers imposed the return to the non-apocopated forms.

3.3.5. *Modifying word order*
A single example will again be given. In 1920, the Czech government recommended following, with respect to clitic position, the rule given in Gebauer's *Grammar*, which had been republished several times since its first publication in 1890. According to this rule, when a stressed word appears at the sentence outset, the reflexive clitic must occupy the second position just after it ("Wackernagel law"), thereby reflecting the spoken usage, which is opposed to the literary style. This has become the norm in contemporary Czech.

4. Language users' signature in phonology

It is easy to notice that most human communities resort to certain pronunciation strategies in order to be recognized as possessing a distinctive identity (4.1): this is observed for the two sexually defined parts of mankind (4.1.1), as well as for various nationwide groups (4.1.2). Furthermore, in various countries, political authorities have often taken steps to change certain pronunciations officially, as will be shown here with two examples (4.2).

4.1. Affirming one's identity through one's pronunciation

4.1.1. *Women vs men*
The specific pronunciation features that distinguish women from men have often been mentioned. I will limit myself here to a few of them. Women, in many languages, have a tendency to diphthongize vowels much more than men. In words with an affective meaning or connotation, women also tend to pronounce initial sibilants, when followed by a vowel, as hushing sounds.

Another typically feminine sound feature is the clearer pronunciation of vowels. Japanese vowels, in particular, are much less harsh in women's speech that in that of men, as if a virility code required that men should pronounce their vowels more gutturally. The use of vowels as sexual identity markers is even responsible for an interesting phenomenon which might lead to an important change in the pronunciation of French in France. Among the words ending, phonetically, in [-vowel+consonant], some, like *fil* 'thread', which come from late Latin words whose masculine or neuter ending disappeared at an early stage, are written without a final '-e', while others, like *jambe* 'leg' or *chasse* 'hunting', are written with a final '-e'. This reflects the fact that until the end of the 15th century, the vowel corresponding to '-e', whose origin is the final *-a* of the late Latin etyma, was pronounced as a syllabic schwa, just as it is today in Southern regional French, under the influence of Provençal. However, in Northern contemporary French, the pronunciation of all these words ends in a consonant, whatever their history. It is therefore striking to observe that since the middle of the 1970s, many women, especially young ones, have begun introducing a schwa at the end of such words. Thus, the three words mentioned above are pronounced, respectively, [žábə], [šásə], [fílə]; the same applies to abbreviated words, like [pʁɔ́fə] instead of [pʁɔf], from [pʁɔfɛsœ́ʁ] 'professor'. This phenomenon is developing at an increasing speed, and it involves not only words whose final consonant was either historically, or never, followed by a schwa, but even words ending in vowels, including [wi] 'yes', often pronounced [wíə].

It appears that we have to do here not with a purely mechanical phenomenon but with a voluntary search for identification. This is corroborated by comparable facts that are found in some phonetic features of American English as spoken by women, especially as far as vowels are concerned. According to Labov (1972: 303–4), "there are of course physical differences between the vocal tracts of men and women to be taken into account, and the shorter length of women's vocal tracts does predict higher formant positions." However, he adds that "spectrographic studies show that in many dialects the difference is much more than an upward shift: women use a wider range of formant positions, overlapping men's formants in all directions, with much greater distances between vowel locations. The sexual differentiation of speakers is therefore not a product of physical factors alone, or of different amounts of referential information supplied by speakers, but rather an *expressive posture which is socially more appropriate for one sex or the other* [italics provided, CH]. On Martha's Vineyard, men are more "close-mouthed" than women, and use more contracted areas of phonological space; conversely, women in New York City and Philadelphia use wider ranges of phonological space than men, with more extreme lip-spreading, lip-rounding, for vowels, more blade-affrication and palatalization of consonants."

Given these facts, Labov's conclusion does not come as a surprise: "The sexual differentiation of speech", he writes (1972: 303), "often plays a major role in the mechanism of linguistic evolution." Admittedly, this sexual differentiation is not always the result of a totally conscious choice. However, a simple experiment shows that it is by no means unconscious: when asked to pronounce the three words above without a final [ə], the French women whose speech I have studied answer that this final [ə] belongs to their way of pronouncing them.

4.1.2. *Phonetic signatures of various nations*
I will only present four geographic and cultural areas. Further details can be found in Hagège and Haudricourt 1978: 139–140. In Gascony, communities living in the most peripheral zones of an area distinguish themselves from their neighbors living

across the border by certain phonetic peculiarities. Thus, the Gascon variety spoken by inhabitants of the Val d'Aran, located close to the Catalan area, has voiceless stops after nasals and sonorants, yielding, for example, *crampa* 'room' or *lenca* 'language', instead of ordinary Gascon *cramba, lenga*. Another example is the *əi* diphthong of Scottish colonists who settled in Ulster at the end of the 17th century and imitated the prestigious English of other presbyterian colonists who had settled in Ulster after 1603 and had, like the speakers who had remained in England, started to transform middle-English *ī* into *əi*. Later, this diphthong became *aɪ* in final open syllables, while in standard British and American English, this evolution was extended to all contexts, as is well-known. However, in certain rural dialects spoken by descendents of these Scottish colonists, the former diphthong, preserved in some words as an identifying feature, did not disappear; hence various pairs like [bəi] 'bay' / [baɪ] 'by' or 'buy', [stəi] 'stay' / [staɪ] 'sty'.

A third example is provided by the Israeli Hebrew area. A characteristic case of identity claim has to do with the placement of stress: due to the fact that the pioneers who founded the state of Israel had stressing habits that came from their mother tongue, Yiddish, where bisyllabic words are usually stressed on the first syllable as opposed to the Hebrew stress pattern, several word-pairs were created, in which only stress is distinctive; *tikvá* for example, means 'hope', whereas *tíkva*, which is stressed according to the Yiddish model, refers to a specifically Israeli object: the national hymn.

The fourth illustration is provided by preglottalized consonants in Vietnamese. These consonants had been ruled out of the language spoken by Vietnamese mandarins, influenced by the prestigious language of the Chinese, who had conquered and occupied the country (there are no glottalized consonants in Chinese). However, when the Chinese left in the middle of the 12th century, the glottalized consonants reappeared in Vietnamese, despite the contemptuous feelings of urban societies towards the mountain dwellers who had conserved these sounds, as a conscious sign of national identity.

4.2. Voluntary modifications of certain pronunciations

Among the examples given here, one shows the effects of voluntary intervention by political authorities on the natural course of phonetic evolution, while the other concerns the process by which a part of a country's society imposes its phonetic norm on the other part.

4.2.1. *Imposing "correct speech" over "slack-jawed speech": Icelandic vowels.*
Guðfinnsson, an author of investigations into Icelandic vowels, showed (1947, 1964) that in the early 1940s 38.55% of all his informants in the capital Reykjavik merged the front vowels /ɪ/ and /e/ as well as the back vowels /y/ and /ø/. According to these studies, the merging, which had originated among fishermen in the 19th century and "spread rapidly in the west, east and north of the country" (Håkon Jahr 1989:

106), was almost becoming the norm in the middle of the 20th century. This change was in line with a long historical development of the Icelandic vowel system, of which it represented the last step. One of its effects was the homophony of words like *viður* 'wood' / *veður* 'weather', or *flugur* 'flies' (plural) / *flögur* 'slabs, flakes'.

However, as Håkon Jahr recalls (*ibid.*), "Guðfinnsson himself published a normative guide in pronunciation where several pages were dedicated to the fight against" this vowel merging, called *flámæli*, i.e. "slack-jawed speech", as opposed to *réttmæli*, i.e. "correct speech". An intensive campaign of eradication was launched against *flámæli* by the language planners of Iceland, a country with 230.000 inhabitants, in which it is relatively easy to reach a great part of the population. The reason for this campaign was simply that the natural outcome of this vowel change was considered to be unacceptable. The campaign was an impressive success. Around forty years after Guðfinnsson's first study, Þráinsson and Árnason (1984) did a new survey investigation in Reykjavik. When compared with Guðfinnsson's, this survey shows a rather dramatic change: in the early 1980s 2.6% of those studied in Iceland's capital were found to have *flámæli*, and among the younger generation, this feature was totally absent. A question arises: was this very surprising reversal of an historical development of the Icelandic vowel system due to the low social status of *flámæli*, or was it the reaction initiated by school teachers and normative grammarians? Håkon Jahr (1989: 107) mentions the case of a dental *l*-allophone, which, although it was on its way to being replaced by an alveolar or retroflex allophone in Oslo Norwegian after the vowels /a/ and /ɔ/, nonetheless remained lateral: Oslo speakers halted this change because such a pronunciation sounds exceedingly rural to them. By contrast with the Norwegian situation, there is no evaluation of sounds according to the urban/rural parameter in Iceland. The determining factor was another extralinguistic element: language planning, which itself is based on a certain type of social evaluation.

4.2.2. *Norm appropriation in Israeli Hebrew*
When the state of Israel was founded (1948), it was officially decided that the pronunciation norm of Hebrew would correspond to that of the Sephardic communities, especially those that came from the Near East and the Maghreb. The way these communities pronounce Hebrew is closer to Semitic habits, as exemplified by Arabic, which possesses the pharyngeal consonants /q/, /ʕ/, and /ħ/, as well as the laryngeal /ɦ/. All these consonants must have been pronounced as such in ancient Hebrew. But nowadays, Ashkenazic Jews, whose background is European, and who spoke Yiddish, from which these sounds are absent, do not pronounce them: /q/ is merged with /k/, /ʕ/ with /ʔ/, and /ħ/ with /χ/. This pronunciation, being that of the settlers who founded the state of Israel, has become the norm. Thus the majority of the population have consciously shifted to a phonetic behavior which enjoys some prestige, even though it does not conform to the phonology of a Semitic language, and is not officially recognized.

5. The conscious shaping of the lexicon

The lexical component of languages is not as sharply structured as the morphosyntactic and phonological components. It is therefore even more open to voluntary actions. Two types of such actions will be chosen here as evidence: marking-reversal (5.1) and neological activity (5.2).

5.1. Marking-reversal

Marking-reversal (Witkowski and Brown 1983) is only one among many cases of the voluntary action of speakers on the lexicon of their language. It could be claimed that the change by which the name of a familiar entity is, at a given time, applied to another, imported, entity does not result from an explicit and collective decision. But we can just as well consider that users act as conscious LEs, when they add linguistic material in order to distinguish a previously unknown object from an object belonging to their culture. This is observed, for example, in Fijian. A bow was called *dakai*, and a wooden axe *matau* in this language. But when guns and metal axes were introduced, they were called, respectively, *dakai ni vâ lagi* and *matau ni vâ lagi*, i.e. 'bow/axe from overseas'. In the long run, as bows and wooden axes were becoming less and less usual, *dakai* and *matau* became the names of guns and metal axes respectively. As a result, to refer to the bow, for instance, the speakers ended up saying *dakai ni viti*, literally 'gun from Fiji'. It also happens that the specification, instead of being added, becomes the name of the former entity. Thus, in many South-American languages, newly introduced animals whose cultural importance was becoming predominant were eventually designated by a word which, formerly, denoted a familiar animal; and the latter received a new name referring to a particular feature. In contemporary Huastec, for instance, *bičim*, which meant 'deer' in pre-colonial times, today means 'horse', whereas 'deer' is *icĩamal*, literally 'horned'. We may conclude that LEs shape the lexicon according to social and cultural evolution: the lexicon is restructured when a foreign object is introduced and when it progressively overtakes, by its cultural importance, a familiar object, to which a certain name was given prior to acculturation; this name ceases being applied to that object, and becomes the name of the new object.

5.2. Neological activity

Word-coining, in literate societies but also in oral societies, is a worldwide enterprise, aimed at giving names to new objects, new techniques, new relationships, etc. This activity results in the making of what is called technolects in Hagège 1983: sets of technical terms, each set being proper to a certain field of human life and work. Characteristic examples may be taken from languages which have long been the targets of reform movements led by (groups of) individuals or states (cf. section 2). For instance, from the last quarter of the 18th to the middle of the 19th century, Hungarian reformers successfully coined many words, like *rovar* 'insect', from *rovátkolt* 'grooved' + *barom* 'animal, cattle', both truncated, or *iroda* 'office', from *ír* 'to write' + -*da*, a suffix which, having been hypothesized from word-endings, was not accepted without lengthy discussions, in which writers, professors, and even non-specialists participated. In modern Hebrew, the reformers proposed to the public of readers, through newspapers, new words that they had coined in various ways. For example Biblical Hebrew, in sharp contrast with Israeli Hebrew, but like Arabic and other Semitic languages, favors derivation much more than compounding, which is much rarer. But Israeli reformers, following the English and French models, introduced many compounds, despite Ben Yehuda's views which, on this matter, were much more conservative. Examples of such compounds are *kadur-sal* (ball-basket) 'basket-ball', *kxol-ʕeynayim* (blue-eyes) 'blue-eyed', *šmar-taf* (sit-baby) 'baby sitter', *ben-xayil* (possessor (lit. 'son')-success) 'smart fellow', *ʕiver-tsvaʕim* (blind-colors) 'color-blind', i.e., respectively, tatpuruṣa, bahuvrīhi, synthetic, possessive and viewpoint compounds. In all of these compounds, we observe that the speakers, acting as LEs who choose certain processes but not others, did not follow the English word-order, even though they took English as one of their models to cope with the dearth of compound formation which was characteristic of Biblical Hebrew. Not only did Israeli speakers invent these new patterns in nominal morphology; they also acted on derivation, a technique which, as recalled above, was much more widespread in Biblical Hebrew: they gave up irregular or morphophonemically complex processes, while at the same time reviving some others, which were moribund in Mishnaic Hebrew, like the agent noun-ending -*an*, relational adjectives in -*i*, or, in verbal morphology, the *puʕal* and *šafʕel* derived forms, as well as the scheme called *piʕel* in the Hebrew grammatical tradition, because it exhibits a succession of two vowels /i/ and /e/, which may be combined with the consonants of a borrowed word: on this model, Israelis have collectively coined and spread such verbs as *tilfen* 'to telephone', *diklem* 'to declaim', *pitrel* 'to patrol', *pister* 'to pasteurize', etc. Thus, foreign roots were hebraicized in a way that reduced their foreign look: by forcing them into Hebrew morphology.

6. Conclusion

It will not come as a surprise that vocabulary is the linguistic component which is most open to human actions on language structure. It is more surprising, however, that the morphosyntax and the phonology of human languages are far from being unconscious structures. Thus, there is a metalinguistic activity carried out by ordinary users, either synchronically when they appear to be aware of certain ways in which languages function, or diachronically when they perceive an ongoing change and act upon it, and often both synchronically and diachronically. It is true that they belong to a very specific type of engineers, since there is a great deal of variation in the degree of awareness they have of the very process by which they build their languages; and of course, one cannot say that lay speakers' work or vocation is to unearth the hidden or underlying mechanisms on which professional linguists work. But their awareness as a whole cannot be denied. This is what the facts examined in the present paper have tried to show.

References

Boas, F., 1911, "Introduction", in *Handbook of American Indian Languages*, 5–83, Washington, D.C.: Government Printing Office.

Fodor, I. and C. Hagège, eds., 1983–1994, *Language Reform: History and Future*, 6 volumes, Hamburg: Buske Verlag.

Gudfinnsson, B., 1947, *Breytingar á framburði og stafsetningu*, Reykjavík: Ísafoldarprentsmiðja H.F.

Gudfinnsson, B., 1964, *Mállyzkur II um íslenzkan framburð*, (Studia Islandica 23) Reykjavík.

Gundersen, D., 1983, "On the development of modern Norwegian", in Fodor and Hagège, eds., vol. II, 157–173.

Hagège, C., 1975, *Le problème linguistique des prépositions et la solution chinoise (avec un essai de typologie à travers plusieurs groupes de langues)*, Paris : Société de Linguistique de Paris / Louvain : Peeters.

Hagège, C., 1983, "Voies et destins de l'action humaine sur les langues", in Fodor and Hagège, eds., vol. I, 11–68.

Hagège, C., 1993, *The Language Builder, An Essay on the Human Signature in Linguistic Morphogenesis*, Amsterdam/Philadelphia: John Benjamins.

Hagège, C. and A.-G. Haudricourt, 1978, *La phonologie panchronique*, Paris : Presses Universitaires de France.

Håkon Jahr, E., 1989, "Language planning and language change", in L. E. Breivik and E. Håkon Jahr, eds., *Language change, Contributions to the study of its causes*, Berlin/New York: Mouton de Gruyter, 99–113.

Jakobson, R., 1968, *Selected writings*, vol. V, The Hague/Paris: Mouton.

Labov, W., 1972, *Sociolinguistic patterns*, Philadelphia: University of Pennsylvania Press.

Schmidt, K. H., 1969, "Agglutination und Postposition im Tocharischen", *Münchner Studien zur Sprachwissenschaft* 25, 105–112.

Tauli, V., 1968, Introduction to a theory of language planning, (*Acta Universitatis Upsaliensis* 6) Uppsala: Almqvist and Wiksells.

Þráinsson, H. and K. Árnason, 1984, "Um reykvísku", in *Íslenskt mál og almen málfræði* 6, 113–134.

Witkowski, S. R. and C. H. Brown, 1983, "Marking-reversals and cultural importance", *Language*, 59, 3, 569–582.

Chapter 6

The challenge of polygrammaticalization for linguistic theory:

Fractal grammar and transcategorial functioning

Stéphane Robert

Centre National de la Recherche Scientifique – LLACAN

Transcategorial morphemes share the common ability to be used synchronically across different syntactic categories (synchronic grammaticalization). This paper first shows that transcategoriality is a general property of linguistic systems, variously exploited by languages, then addresses the theoretical questions raised by these morphemes. A new model accounting for this transcategorial functioning, named "fractal grammar", is proposed and illustrated by various examples. The analysis for this particular functioning relates the polysemy of these morphemes to their syntactic flexibility in a dynamic way: the variation of the syntactic scope of the morpheme ("fractal functioning") is triggered by its environment and produces its polysemy (variation of the semantic scope). Fractal grammar is thus defined by two basic mechanisms: the construal of a common image-schema ("scale invariance"), accounting for the unity of the morpheme, and the activation of "scale (or level) properties", accounting for the semantic and syntactic variations. A typological sketch of transcategoriality is then sketched, in relation to the strategies used by linguistic systems for the distribution of grammatical information. Three types of transcategorial strategies are distinguished: "oriented", "generic", and "functional" transcategoriality. The status of linguistic categories is then discussed in the light of the analysis of these particular morphemes.

1. Introduction

1.1. From grammaticalization to transcategoriality

During the past twenty years, the revival of the study of grammaticalization has raised a number of important issues on the pathways and constraints of language change. Notably, the most common approach to grammaticalization was mainly based on Indo-European languages and adopted a historical perspective, focusing on the processes whereby items become more grammatical through time. These two characteristics are probably connected since, for structural reasons (*i.e.* because they are inflectional languages), in Indo-European languages grammaticalization is mainly (though not absolutely) an oriented and diachronic process requiring a morphological erosion of the grammaticalized item.

However, as mentioned by several authors (Traugott and Hopper 1993: 17, Heine *et alii* 1991, Heine and Kilian-Hatz 1994), African languages provide some challenging cases for the standard linguistic theories, because they show striking cases of what one may call "synchronic grammaticalization": the same linguistic unit is used synchronically in different syntactic categories. For instance, *bé* in Ewe, functions both as a verb 'to say' and as a complementizer (Lord: 1976); *ginnaaw* in Wolof can be used synchronically as a noun ('the back'), as a preposition ('behind' or 'except') or as a subordinating conjunction with the meaning of (causal) 'since' (Robert: 1997). As shown by Heine and Kilian-Hatz (1994), there can be extraordinary semantic and morphosyntactic variation of some items, such as the morpheme *tɛ* in Baka, which may behave like a preposition, an auxiliary, or a coordinating or subordinating conjunction, and which is at the same time associated with a number of different semantic domains and grammatical functions, such as case marking, subordination, diathesis, predication, derivation, tense-aspect, and modality (see section 1.2.).

These cases of synchronic grammaticalization or "polygrammaticalization" (Craig 1991) are far from being restricted to African languages and actually are widespread cross linguistically: Ewe *bé*, for instance, has correspondents in many languages from different families (Güldemann and Von Roncador 2002). These morphemes reveal a property of linguistic systems which is variously exploited by languages: a variable proportion of morphemes in a language is used synchronically in different syntactic categories. Since these morphemes function synchronically in various syntactic categories (be they both lexical and grammatical or only grammatical), I would rather speak of "transcategorial morphemes" and transcategorial functioning, in order to distinguish the diachronic process of category change, classically designated by the term "grammaticalization", and the syntactic and semantic flexibility shown in synchrony by these transcategorial morphemes. In the case where the transcategorial functioning is common and recurring in a language, the category change cannot be considered a marginal phenomenon or a transitory phase or stage of grammaticalization; it is rather a typologically important feature of the linguistic system. Actually, synchronic and diachronic grammaticalization are not separate phenomena. In this view, grammaticalization is the diachronic aspect of the more general phenomenon of transcategoriality that we have to account for.[1]

1.2. The challenge

In some cases, the semantic and morphosyntactic variation of the item is not restricted to the shift from a lexical to a grammatical use but can cross many grammatical categories, as illustrated by the morpheme *tɛ* in Baka. As sown in Figure 1, extracted and adapted from Heine and Kilian-Hatz (1994)[2], the various uses of this morpheme are organized in a complex network of semantic and syntactic values: *tɛ* may behave like a particle, a preposition, an auxiliary, or a co-ordinating or subordinating conjunction,[3] involving various semantic domains such as space, time, aspect, cause, purpose, manner, instrument, case marking and more.

The analysis of transcategorial functioning, of which *tɛ* is an especially clear case, raises some important theoretical questions. First of all, how can we account for the semantic and syntactic variation while maintaining the unity of the morpheme? The existing models[4] dealing with polysemy are either only semantic or conceptual, such as those based on semantic networks and family resemblance (Lakoff 1987, Langacker 1987, Taylor 1989); or they essentially describe the evolution of syntactic patterns, as does the model of "grammaticalization chains" (Craig 1991, Heine *et alii* 1991, Heine 1992). They do not explicitly relate semantic and syntactic variation. Correlatively, what is the status of the linguistic categories when the linguistic units show such syntactic flexibility? Are these "transcategorial" morphemes instances of fuzzy categories? All languages present cases of transcategorial functioning but the extent and modalities of transcategorial functioning are different across languages. In English, for instance, participles (such as *considering*) can be used as prepositions, inflected verb forms as subordinating conjunctions (*suppose, imagine…*), or temporal adverbs as discourse particles (*now, still*), but there is nothing comparable to the Baka *tɛ*. Some languages make extensive use of this capacity of the linguistic systems, while in others, the transcategorial functioning seems to be more limited and to follow different patterns. However, as pointed out by Anward (2000), part-of-speech recycling might be a much more common situation than usually thought. So finally, can we draw a typological sketch of transcategoriality and explain its various modalities in relation to different linguistic systems?

In this chapter,[5] besides pointing to transcategoriality as a common and important feature of linguistic systems, I want to make a few proposals concerning the way we can account for this striking but well regulated variation of the linguistic units. First, I propose a dynamic model for the analysis of transcategorial function-

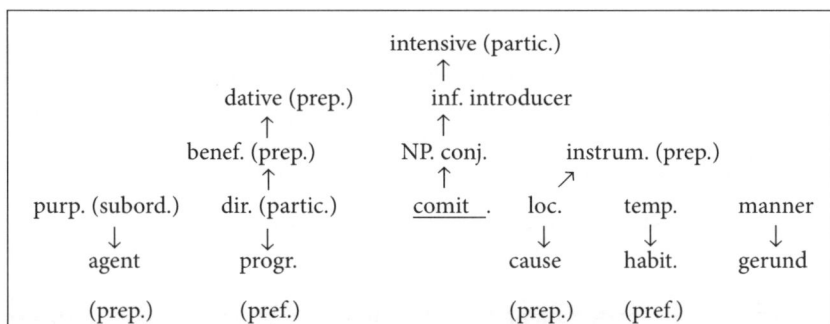

Figure 1. The uses of *tɛ* (Baka), from Heine and Kilian-Hatz 1994

ing; then, I present a typological sketch of transcategoriality, and finally, I conclude with a few thoughts on the status of linguistic categories.

2. A dynamic model: fractal grammar

2.1. Why are transcategorial morphemes fractal?

Transcategorial morphemes share the common ability to be used synchronically in different syntactic categories. The proposed analysis for this particular functioning relates the polysemy of these morphemes to their syntactic flexibility in a dynamic way: first, the context (more precisely the co-text) specifies the syntactic category in which the item is used; then the variation of the syntactic scope of the morpheme produces its polysemy by triggering variation in its semantic scope and the activation of contextual properties. I name this model of analysis "fractal grammar" (Robert 1997, 2003a). This is not a mathematical model. I have taken from fractals (Mandelbrot 1975) two properties that were enlightening to me for the analysis of the functioning of transcategorial morphemes:

1. Objects are said to be fractal (Sapoval, 1997: 73, 136; Gleick, 1991: 128) when they have the property of scale invariance and self-similarity: *a similar structure* appears at different scales and objects are invariant when undergoing a *dilatation in the scope* of the observation. A coast, a tree branch or a snow flake for instance are fractal objects, because the structure they show when observed at different scales is similar: a broken line in the case of a coast or a ramified structure for a tree branch.
2. The common structure appearing at different scales is similar but not strictly identical: each scale also has specific scale properties so that there is no strict identity between the structures appearing at different levels. Rather, we have an *analogical* structure.

In the case of transcategorial morphemes, the analysis I propose in order to account for the syntactic and semantic flexibility of the linguistic units, relies on two basic mechanisms that are comparable to these two properties of the fractal objects. By definition, a transcategorial morpheme is used on different syntactic levels with a different syntactic scope (for instance, as a noun, as a preposition, as a subordinating conjunction). The linguistic "scale" corresponds here to the "syntactic level" at which the unit functions. The transcategorial functioning can be explained by the two following mechanisms:

1. Through the different syntactic uses of the term, a similar semantic structure (a "schematic form") is abstracted and preserved, which constitutes the unity of the morpheme.
2. In each use, the category change activates different properties specific to the syntactic category in which the term functions; therefore in the different uses (*e.g.*

as a noun, as a preposition or as a subordinating conjunction…), the semantics of the morpheme undergoes a dilatation of its syntactic scope (see below for details) along with particular specifications that produce the variations among the different uses. I call the semantic and syntactic properties specific to each syntactic category, "level (or scale) properties". Thanks to these properties, the semantic structure common to the different syntactic uses is *similar* (or analogical) but not strictly identical.

When a linguistic unit, besides being used as a preposition, is also used as a subordinating conjunction (e.g. *ginnaaw* presented in 2.2.), the constituent modified by the unit is one of greater complexity and belongs to a higher level of the structural hierarchy (here, a clause *vs* a noun phrase). Therefore, considering that a similar semantic structure is applied in these different uses of the transcategorial morpheme, one can say that, from one use to another, the semantics of the morpheme undergoes "a dilatation (or expansion, increasing) of its syntactic scope": the scope element (or domain of application) of the transcategorial morpheme corresponds to a larger and more complex unit of the syntactic hierarchy (cf. scale properties 2, in 2.4.: "domain of application and scope of the term").

I have to add an important factor in the dynamics of this model: in the case of transcategorial morphemes, since the morphosyntactic category of the term is not specified *a priori* (the unit can function in different categories, such as preposition or subordinating conjunction…), the *context* is the triggering factor for the activation of the syntactic properties (level properties) of the category in which the morpheme functions in each of its uses, because its syntactic role and status is defined by its place and environment inside the utterance. All linguistic morphemes are context-sensitive in the way that their semantic value depends partly on their semantic environment (*tender* does not have the same meaning in *a tender steak* and in *a tender man*) but transcategorial morphemes have a particular property: they are also syntactically context-sensitive. This means that their morphosyntactic status depends on their position inside the utterance and on their syntactic environment: for instance, when English *now* is used after a verb, it functions as a temporal adverb, while before a clause it functions as a discourse particle; in the same way, when the Wolof *ginnaaw* is used after a verb ad before a noun phrase, is functions as a preposition, while before a clause it functions as a subordinating conjunction.

I am now going to present this model in greater detail by illustrating it with various examples. But one can already see what is meant by the notion of 'fractal' functioning. The transcategorial morphemes are said to be fractal because of their ability to be used synchronically in different syntactic categories with increasing (or decreasing) syntactic scope; here the semantic structure (or schematic form) common to the various uses plays the role of the "scale invariance" and the semantic and syntactic properties specific to each syntactic category producing the variation play the role of the "scale properties" of fractals. The different scales here are not scales of observation (as for fractals objects) but scales of functioning, *i.e.* they correspond to the syntactic levels defined by the syntactic categories in which the transcategorial morphemes are used. The scale properties of linguistic units are general properties of the syntactic categories; they are activated in the particular uses of the transcategorial morpheme and interact with its common semantic structure in order to produce its sense in the particular use.

2.2. Scale invariance: the common "schematic form"

Let us first take a simple example. In Tupuri (Adamawa, Cameroon), the verb 'to enter' is also used as an ingressive auxiliary, *kàl* (Ruelland 2003). This is a very common case of grammaticalization of a movement verb into an aspectual auxiliary.

The common semantic properties of these two uses, and therefore the semantic unity of the term, can be accounted for by considering that through the different syntactic uses of the term, a similar semantic structure is abstracted and preserved but mapped onto two different domains. This common semantic structure corresponds here to the notion (or the schema) of 'entrance'; in the use as a movement verb, the domain in which it applies is a place (entrance into a physical space), while in the use as an aspectual auxiliary, it is a process (entrance into a process). Note that this common semantic structure is not a concept but an abstract semantic schema, what Culioli ([1978 and 1987] 1990: 115–135) calls a "schematic form", Lakoff (1987) "an image schema", or Michaelis (1996), a "semantic super-structure". The use of this schematic form as an aspectual morpheme is made possible by the fact that aspect is conceptualized as a topological domain whose properties are comparable to those of space. Probably because of a fundamental analogy between space and time existing in our cognitive processes[6], the schematic form common to a movement verb and an ingressive auxiliary seems to be quite obvious. However, the different domains onto which the common schematic form is mapped can be more abstract than space and time.

In Nêlêmwa (Oceanic, New-Caledonia), for instance, the morpheme *r/toven*[7] functions as a verb 'to finish' (*cf.* 1), as an aspectual modifier with a terminative value (2), and as a nominal quantifier with a totalizing value, 'all' (3).

(1) *co toven o khiiboxa pwaxi-m   tavia!*
     2SG finish LOC beat   child-POSS.2SG dog
     'Stop beating your dog!'

(2) *i   u   keva wany xe wagiik . . . xa keva roven wany hleny*
     3SG ACC build boat TOP a . . .   also build finish boat this.DEICT
     'He has built a boat... and this boat is finished'

(3) *hla vhaa agu   roven*
     3PL talk people all
     'Everybody is talking (about it)'

Following Bril (2003) from whom these data are taken, we can state that through these different uses, this morpheme indicates a single semantic operation which constitutes the common schematic form of the term, namely a totalizing quantification of a domain that can be (1) the temporal extension of an event, (2) the aspectual phase of a process, and also (3) the set of elements constituting a (nominal) class.

With a third example, I would like to show that the increase in the syntactic scope of transcategorial morpheme (and the "dilatation" of its semantic scope) can reach the highest linguistic level, namely the discourse level. I have chosen the case of *ginnaaw* in Wolof (Atlantic, Senegal) because this morpheme, interestingly, functions in three different syntactic categories and, thanks to a detailed study of its uses in context, I have been able to propose a unitary analysis of the common schematic form underlying its various uses (Robert 1997). But I want to point out that fractal functioning at the discourse level is very common, although most of the time the analysis of the schematic form is not easy to provide because it is very abstract. In fact, most discourse particles are fractal morphemes: they apply at different syntactic levels with various syntactic scope, the discursive (or argumentative) use being only the widest one (see Hansen 1998). Thus, as pointed out by M. Mithun (article in this volume), many languages show an extension of grammatical constructions from the domain of sentence-internal syntax into discourse. For instance, the Navajo =(*g*)*o* construction evolved from a derivational adverbializer, used for forming vocabulary, into a marker of subordinate clauses, and finally has been extended to function at the discourse-level, connecting sentences and marking their informational status (backgrounded, descriptive, subsidiary, explanatory, or evaluative information). In the same way, the Hualapai -*k*/-*m* constructions originated in inflectional oblique case endings, then evolved into markers of syntactic dependency among clauses within a sentence, and, finally, with a wider scope, they signal textual cohesion and mark statements that together comprise a larger discourse unit. These cases are typical instances of fractal functioning whereby the scope of the morpheme is increased and reachs the highest level of the discourse macro-units.

Turning now to Wolof, *ginnaaw* occurs synchronically in three different grammatical categories. As a noun, it names a body part, the 'back'; as a preposition it means 'behind', in some restricted uses 'after',[8] but also 'except'. *Ginnaaw* also has a more striking use as the subordinating conjunction 'since' in its causal meaning, much like French *puisque* with its argumentative properties. Examples (4) to (7) exemplify the different uses.

Table 1 *ginnaaw*'s uses and senses

Noun (4)	back (body part)
Preposition (5, 6)	behind; after; except
Subordinating conjunction (7)	since (causal not temporal)

(4) *Jigéén-u   Senegaal dañu-y   boot   seen*
woman-CONN. Senegal VBFOCUS3PL-IMPERF carry their
doom   ci   ginnaaw
children PREP. ginnaaw
'Senegalese women carry their children on their backs'

(5) *Mi . . . ngi   deck ci   ginnaaw jàkka   ji*
3SG . . . PRESENTATIVE live PREP. ginnaaw mosque the
'He lives behind the mosque'

(6) *Ginnaaw yaay   bi,   ñépp ñëw   nañu*
ginnaaw mother the, all   come PERF3PL
'Except for the mother, they all came'

(7) *Ginnaaw faral   nga   ko, maa . . . ngi   . . . dem*
ginnaaw to.side.with PERFECT.2SG him, 1SG . . . PRESENT . . . go
'Since you have taken his side, I am leaving'

Detailed analysis of *ginnaaw*'s uses (Robert 1997) allows me to state that *ginnaaw* defines an asymmetrical space with a front / back orientation proceeding from a landmark (or locator) and refers to the space behind it (excluding the landmark). This schematic form is illustrated in Figure 2, where the shaded part designates the space referred to (*i.e.* the figure or profiled substructure, Langacker 1991) by *ginnaaw*.

With this common schematic form, we can account for the observed polysemy, according to the nature of the element functioning as the landmark inside the utterance. So the landmark is the variable producing the polysemy: its syntactic nature defines the category in which *ginnaaw* functions, and, therefore, its semantic and syntactic scope, and the domain onto which it is mapped. When *ginnaaw* is in nominal function no other term in the utterance plays the role of the landmark; the morpheme has extra-linguistic scope and a referential value: the landmark is the primary landmark, namely the human body, hence the meaning 'the back'. When *ginnaaw* governs a noun and is used as a preposition, the landmark is the noun governed by *ginnaaw* (here 'the mosque') and *ginnaaw* refers to the space behind this landmark ('he lives behind the mosque'). If *ginnaaw* is moved to the front of the clause, the scope of the *ginnaaw* phrase is the entire proposition (not just the

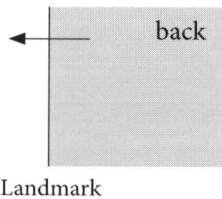

Figure 2. *ginnaaw's schematic form*

verb): *ginnaaw* refers to (thus validates) the 'space' behind the landmark, excluding the landmark; the proposition 'they all came' is true only behind the landmark 'the mother'. Hence the sense 'except for the mother, they all came'.

When the landmark is a clause, *ginnaaw* functions as a subordinating conjunction: it expresses a locational relationship between two clauses but not a temporal sequencing (*behind = after P, there is Q). How does *ginnaaw* come to mean 'since' in its causal sense? The answer relies on understanding what a 'landmark' is in discourse. In this third use, the syntactic scope of *ginnaaw* is a clausal complement, not a noun. We are dealing with a complex sentence at the discourse level. According to *ginnaaw*'s semantics, the clause P ('you have taken his side') is the landmark behind which the clause Q ('I am leaving') is located and *ginnaaw* refers to the space behind this landmark. Thus, the main clause ('I am leaving') is the scope of assertion, the focus, and the *ginnaaw*-clause is presented as the starting point of the utterance, that is a topic. This point is confirmed by the syntactic constraints on the order of the clauses: in contrast with another causal morpheme (*ndax* 'because'), *ginnaaw*-clauses always appear first (*I am leaving, since-*ginnaaw* you have taken his side); furthermore the *ginnaaw* clause can't be used in an answer to a question ('why are you leaving?')[9], which confirms its topical status. So taking this topical status into account, we can gloss the *ginnaaw*-complex sentence as following:

> 'Behind (*i.e.* given) the fact that you have taken his side (P),
> there is the fact that I'm leaving (Q)'.

Ginnaaw validates the main clause as a following consequence of the topic in discourse. That is what I have called "argumentative causality" (Robert 1997). So the space validated by *ginnaaw* here is the assertive space, i.e. the discourse organization: the proposition is stated as the resulting consequence of a first proposition. Hence the meaning 'since you have taken his side, I'm leaving' and the argumentative effects of the *ginnaaw* assertion: I (the speaker) am not responsible for the situation and its consequences, I'm only describing what results from an already validated statement (*cf.* the epistemic status of the topic as an already known and established fact). Noticeably, this use of a spatial morpheme for expressing argumentative causality and clause chaining shows that discourse is conceptualized here as a space with topological properties, analogical to the properties of physical space. In metaphor theory (Lakoff 1987), we could say that the metaphor at work here is the metaphor of the discourse as a landscape which the speaker is moving in, with independently established landmarks (topics, statements), point of view, back-front orientations and progression.

So, through these different uses of *ginnaaw*, we can see the construal of a common schematic form (or image-schema), as sketched in Figure 2, which is abstracted from one use to another and mapped onto different domains (the referential domain of lexicon when used as a noun, the domain of noun phrase when used as a preposition, and the domain of the clause when used as a subordinating conjunction), with a corresponding increase in its syntactic and semantic scope (lexicon, prepositional noun phrase, subordinating clause). Therefore this schematic form can be said to be the "scale invariance property" of the morpheme and to constitute the unity of the transcategorial morpheme.

2.3. Schematic form: beyond semantic generalization, a matrix form

The semantic change happening in grammaticalization has often been analyzed in terms of desemantization (Meillet 1912), semantic bleaching (Givón 1975) or erosion (Lehmann 1982), that is as a semantic reduction or loss. In the shift from a lexical to a grammatical use, there is a loss of "semantic flesh". But more needs to be said, because grammatical morphemes do have meaning, too. Concerning the semantics of grammaticalized terms, several authors (Hagège 1993: 212, Hopper and Traugott 1993: 96, Bybee *et alii* 1994: 9) have noted that, most of the time, the lexical units entering into grammaticalization have a general meaning (they are hyperonyms or super-ordinate terms corresponding to basic level terms): 'go' (rather than 'run'), 'give' (rather than 'offer'), 'have' (rather 'own'). Following Langacker's analysis (1987, 1991), we can account for this fact by considering that hyperonyms are more schematic than hyponyms, which are more specific: since the semantics of grammar is more schematic than that of the lexicon, it is natural that the most schematic elements of the lexicon are those which tend to evolve into grammatical morphemes. But the same authors have also noted that this general rule is not absolute and suffers from a number of exceptions: less general (or more specific) terms can also grammaticalize, as in the case of anteriors arising from 'finish', 'throw away', and 'pass by'; of futures arising from 'want' or 'desire'; and obligation markers from 'be proper or fitting' and 'owe' (Bybee *et alii*: *ibid.*). The proposed explanation of these exceptions to the rule of 'general meaning' is that, in order to enter into a grammaticalization process, the morpheme first has to undergo 'semantic generalization' (*ibid.* and Bybee 2003). So the semantic changes which lead to grammaticalization are characterized by these linguists as changes that increase the generality of the meaning of terms.

I want to point out that the fractal model can bring more precise answers to these questions concerning the semantics of transcategorial morphemes and the nature of semantic change in the process of grammaticalization. First, although the semantic change from a lexical to a grammatical meaning does involve a kind of semantic generalization, the notion of generalization is nevertheless not sufficient to account for the precise semantics of the gram. One has to describe what is retained from the lexical meaning in the grammatical use, not only in order to account for the semantic change and the commonalities between the different uses of the term, but also in order to describe the specific semantics of the gram: not all futures, for instance, have the same meaning (e.g., there are futures expressing probability *vs.* certainty); in other words, they do not necessarily rely on the same schematic form or construal (Langacker 1991). The analysis of grammaticalization in terms of a topologically structured schematic form, abstracted and preserved from one domain to another as is proposed here (see also Sweetser 1988, Talmy 2000), gives a more precise account of the grammatical meaning: from the lexical meaning only a schema is retained, and what is preserved in the grammatical use is not simply a 'feature' (like the feature 'future') but a semantic structure, 'a form'. This preserved schematic form gives its shape to the meaning of the gram. So the semantics of the gram is shaped by the schematic form abstracted from the lexical use.

Let us take an example. Tupuri has two terms that can be used as prepositions with the meaning 'in, inside': one (*nēn*) comes from the noun 'eye', the other one (*bíl*), from the noun 'belly' (Ruelland 1998): the same spatial value seems to have been abstracted from two different lexical units. However, the constraints on their grammatical uses reveal that the two are not synonymous: two different conceptions of 'interior' are involved. In our terms, we would say that the spatial uses of (*nēn*) and (*bíl*) rely on two different schematic forms (or topological configurations), abstracted from their different lexical meanings: in the case of 'eye', the interior is a compact domain, while in the case of the 'belly' it is a hollow interior. Therefore, 'belly' cannot be used to say 'inside the forest', because a forest is a compact domain, not a hollow; conversely, 'belly' will be used to say 'in a hole', where 'eye' is not possible because a hole is not a compact domain.

Thus, the schematic form is not a simple semantic feature, it is a semantic form that serves as a *matrix* for the construal of new meanings, when mapped onto new domains: it is a form used for generating new meanings in a dynamic process. This concept can explain how grammatical semantics can emerge from lexical meaning and also account for apparent but deceptive grammatical synonymy. As a corollary, it can explain why potentially all kinds of terms (general or specific) can grammaticalize and also why hyperonyms do so more often. A schematic form can be abstracted from any lexical term presenting such a form in its (poorer or richer) semantics, because it consists of the *selection of a substructure* inside the lexical meaning; such a form can be present in the semantic structure of very different terms. For instance the discrepancy between a temporal starting point and a prospective targeted point, as expressed by future in many cases, can be abstracted from movement verbs (French *aller*), but also from verbs of will (English *will*), of transformation (German *werden*), or of permission (Maltese *halli* 'let'), because they all have such a schema (or substructure) in their various meanings. But hyperonyms grammaticalize more easily because they are more schematic and less stuff of the lexical component has to be eliminated in the process of schematization. In this way, the fractal model explains how grammaticalization (or more generally semantic change) is motivated (and not random) but not strictly deterministic: certain terms are more likely to grammaticalized because their semantic structure is closer to the schematic semantics of grammatical categories, but one cannot strictly predict from which term the schematic form of the grammatical morpheme will be abstracted.

The second aspect on which the fractal model can shed new light is precisely that of semantic loss and gain between lexical and grammatical uses. Everyone agrees that during the grammaticalization process, the morpheme loses some semantic components of its lexical meaning. How can we describe what is lost and by which linguistic mechanism it happens? Furthermore, as noted by several authors (Sweetser 1988, Hagège 1993, Bybee *et alii* 1994), in its grammatical uses, the gram is also enriched by the semantics of the new domain it is applied to and therefore gains new semantic specifications. The fractal model accounts for this "resemantization" of grammatical uses, and more generally for the difference between the various uses of a transcategorial morphemes, with the mechanism of "scale properties" (or level properties). In fact, the schematic form does not represent the semantics of the term in its different uses but the *common schema* underlying the various senses and grounding the unity of the morpheme, *i.e.* the matrix of the change. In language use, the schematic form never appears as such, it is always instantiated in a particular use and therefore enriched by its specific properties. Even in the case of the most grammatical uses, the semantics of the transcategorial morpheme is not reducible to the schematic form. There is also another mechanism at work in the meaning construal of each sense of the transcategorial morpheme. That is what I am going to present now.

2.4. Scale properties and the construction of variation

Despite a common semantic structure, a transcategorial morpheme shows different syntactic and semantic properties in its various uses. The mechanism explaining the semantic and syntactic variation from use to use is the activation of different "scale properties" in each use, according to the following process: (a) the position of the term inside the utterance speficies its categorial status (as a noun, as a preposition, or as a verb suffix, e.g.); (b) its functioning in a specific category triggers the activation of the properties of this category, that is, properties specific to the syntactic level and category in which the morpheme functions in its various uses ("scale properties"). Indeed, the specificity of transcategorial morphemes is that they show a syntactic flexibility by which they are recategorized in discourse or, depending on the language type, simply categorized in discourse (cf. section 2.5.3.): according to their particular use in discourse, they will acquire the different properties of the morphosyntactic category (or part-of-speech) in which they function.

I am going now to present and illustrate the different scale properties that I have observed. The list is certainly not exhaustive since the scale properties involve all the properties of linguistic categories. But what is presented here is an explanatory mechanism. It is worth noticing that the nature of scale properties is language specific (they can vary according to the categories, structures and rules of the given language) but that their existence is postulated as universal.

1. *Triggering factor.* The position of the term in the utterance, and the nature and order of the surrounding terms specify the syntactic category in which the term functions in its particular use, according to the patterns of sequential arrangement of the language. For instance, according to the syntactic pattern of Wolof, the position of *ginnaaw* before a noun activates its functioning in the category of prep-

ositions; before a clause, in the category of subordinating conjunctions. It is worth noticing that this dynamic model supposes that, in language comprehension, the syntactic status of the transcategorial morpheme can be retroactively specified after a (short) phase where it is ambiguous, with possible garden-path effects: for instance, in Wolof, a sentence can begin with a noun, so when *ginnaaw* appears first, it can be understood either as a noun, or as a preposition ('except'), or as a subordinating conjunction. However, most of the time (i.e except in generic uses), the Wolof noun is followed by a noun modifier (article or demonstrative), so when the noun modifier appears after *ginnaaw*, the morpheme is clearly understood as to be functioning as a noun in a noun phrase (e.g. "the back is the most fragile body part"). When followed directly by a noun (or a noun phrase), *ginnaaw* can be interpreted either as a preposition ('except') governing this noun, or as a subordinating conjunction followed by the subject of the clause, but this ambiguity will be solved with the next component: if it is a verb, then *ginnaaw* is in its subordinating use and the noun is the subject of this verb, if it is another noun or a pronoun, *ginnaaw* is a preposition. When followed by a verb, *ginnaaw* is necessarily interpreted as a subordinating conjunction (cf. example 7).

In the same way, according to the syntactic pattern of Nêlêmwa, the postposition of *roven* to another verb activates its functioning in the category of verb modifiers, its postposition to a noun, in the one of nominal modifiers.

The functioning in a specific category activates the following scale (or level) properties:

2. *Domain of application and scope of the term.* At the nominal level, the term has *referential* scope, a denotational value; the schematic form is instantiated in a specific domain (*e.g.* the body, in the case of *ginnaaw*), which is not deducible from the linguistic context but encoded in the language. The schematic form is then enriched by two scale properties of the lexicon; the specific referential domain it applies to, and also what I have called the "depth dimension" of the lexicon (Robert 1999), that is the semantic frames, the various scenarii, the physico-cultural properties, and the connotations associated with the term.

These properties are not present in the grammatical uses. In contrast to the lexical uses, in its grammatical functioning, the morpheme has *relational* and intradiscursive scope: the domain onto which the schematic form is mapped is the one defined by the modified term (*e.g.* 'the mosque' in the example of the prepositional use of *ginnaaw*, the complexe sentence in its subordinating use).

For instance, in its nominal use, *ginnaaw*'s meaning is enriched by the physico-cultural properties and connotations associated with the body-part 'the back', in the depth-dimension of the lexicon: that is a part of himself that the person cannot see, where things can happen to him without being foreseen; that is also where Senegalese women carry their children but not their burdens (which are carried on the head).

So, what is lost going from a lexical to a grammatical use is the referential properties and the depth-dimension of lexicon. What is preserved is the schematic form.

What is gained is, first, the properties of the domain defined by the modified term, and second, the following linguistic properties.

3. *Paradigmatic properties.* In each use, the term belongs to a different paradigm with specific oppositions that contribute to specify its sense. One can suppose that the different paradigms to which the item belongs in its particular uses contribute to specify its sense because the unit then occupies a certain place in a variable semantic space defined by the set of items constituting this paradigm. For instance, as a noun, *ginnaaw* belongs to the paradigm of body-part terms as it is conceptualized and categorized in Wolof; in its prepositional use it belongs to another paradigm, the one of prepositions, which is made of a restricted number of body-part terms but also of other terms. So the representational space occupied by *ginnaaw* is different in the two cases. In its subordinating use, *ginnaaw* contrasts with another causal subordinating conjunction (*ndax*), by its topical (*vs* focused) status; this paradigmatic opposition certainly contributes to specify *ginnaaw*'s meaning in its subordinating use.

4. *Syntactic properties of the structural level.* At each level of the syntactic hierarchy a number of specific syntactic properties are attached. The different structural levels generate structures and structural expectations into which the transcategorial morpheme automatically enters. Therefore, when used in a given category, the transcategorial morpheme is subject to the constraints of this category, acquires its functions and receives its specifications. I cannot list exhaustively these well-known properties and rules because they are those of the whole syntax. My point is only to show that they function as rules applying regularly and differently in each use of the term, thus contributing to specify its syntactic behavior and semantic structure. For instance, a nominal phrase requires modifiers, has an argumental function in the clause, can be complemented and so on. Depending on the rules of the particular language, a verb phrase may require aspecto-temporal specifications, have a certain valence, create a nuclear relation with the subject when used as a predicate, etc. At the clause level, the structure of the predicative relation is activated, and has to be saturated.

More generally, the various constructions in which the morpheme can be used and the meaning of these constructions also contribute to specify the semantics of the morpheme in its particular use; construction grammar (Fillmore *et alii* 1988, Goldberg 1995, Croft 2001) is also a component of scale properties in this fractal model.

Finally, I want to emphasize that the discourse level also has scale properties: it implies a set of specific components that will be activated and have to be filled in: a point of view (including aspectual perspective), a modal value (assertion, interrogation, epistemic status...), a discursive landmark (the topic), and a focus ; in a complex clause, the nature of the relationship between the clauses must also be specified (temporal or causal sequencing, or argumentative orientation), as was the case in the subordinating use of *ginnaaw*, which can explain how the common schematic form can acquire the meaning of causal 'since' when these discourse level properties are applied to it: the schematic form of *ginnaaw* then structures the relation between the two clauses as an orientation at discourse level, *i.e.* as an argumentative orientation of the discourse grounded in the spatial shaping of clause linking.

5. *Semantics of the category, semantics of the function, semantics of the position.* Not all linguists agree on the specific semantics of syntactic categories and syntactic functions, but most of them agree that there is a semantics of morphosyntactic categories (noun, adjective, verb…) and a semantics of grammatical functions (subject, object, predicate, modifiers, etc.) that can be attached at least to the prototypical members of these categories or functions. These properties also work as scale properties because they bring to the schematic form of the transcategorial morpheme the additional semantic features of the category in which it functions and those of the syntactic function it has in the particular utterance. For instance, A. Wierzbicka (1986) ascribes to the category of the noun the specific semantic feature of 'classification' and to the adjective, that of 'description'. Concerning the semantics of grammatical functions, Langacker (1991) defines the semantic role of the subject as the profiling of a primary figure for the predicative phrase; Croft (1994) characterizes subject and object as 'delimiters' of the verbal causal segment, its initiator and endpoint respectively. In any case, there is a specific semantics attached to the grammatical function independently of the lexical semantics of the term. Once again, these properties are language specific, in the sense that a category might or might not be relevant or have a different status in one language compared to another: for instance, the grammatical function of subject is not relevant in the same way in ergative languages, subject prominent languages or in topic prominent languages. Less controversial and better known is the semantics of the position. In French, for instance, the pre-posing of an (otherwise postposed) adjective changes its meaning from a descriptive to an evaluative one: *un homme grand* ('a tall man'), *un grand homme* ('a great man'). In Nêlêmwa, according to the general rules of the language that apply to numerals too, the meaning of *roven*, when used as a nominal quantifier, depends on its position: before the nominal phrase, *roven* indicates a fraction of discrete units (*roven*+NP = 'all the…'), while postposed to the noun, it refers to a globality: NP+*roven* = 'the whole…' (Bril 2003).

6. *Restrictions or loss of combinatory restrictions specific to the category* also function as scale properties. For instance, when used as an auxiliary, a verb loses the restrictions on the selection of the subject (or complement) it had in its lexical uses: the subject of 'go' as a movement verb has to be capable of physical or fictive motion (as in *the road goes to the beach*), while it does not when the verb is used as an temporal auxiliary.

7. *The scope of anaphora and co-reference* are also defined by the category in which the unit functions. As exemplified by Haspelmath and König (1995), when converbs grammaticalize in prepositions, they lose the constraint of subject co-reference, as in *considering his age, he has made excellent progress in his studies.*

This list is certainly not exhaustive; for instance, intonation should be added as another scale property that shapes the meaning and function of the item in a particular use. However it outlines a powerful mechanism explaining how the variation of the meaning of transcategorial morphemes is regularly constructed and specified in discourse, thanks to the general properties of syntactic categories and parts of speech.

2.5. Limits and refinement of the model

The fractal model does not intend to account for all cases of polysemy, but only for those correlated with a change of category, *i.e.* for transcategorial functioning. However, even when restricted to this specific case, this model still presents some limitations and should be refined.

2.5.1. *Persistence (or remanence) of scale properties*

As we said, different scale properties are supposed to be activated in the various uses of the transcategorial morpheme. This implies that the scale properties of one syntactic level are inhibited when those of another one are activated. However, when one use emerges from a previous one (diachronic grammaticalization), some properties of the former use may remain in the new one: specific features of a syntactic category can persist even though the item is used in another syntactic category. Several authors have noted that some semantic features of a previous lexical use can persist when a morpheme is grammaticalized; this phenomenon is called "persistence" by Hopper (1991) and "retention" by Bybee *et alii* (1994). The persistent features of a previous (or another) use of a transcategorial morpheme in another one are not only semantic; they can also be syntactic. What I call the persistence (or remanence) of scale properties" is the fact that semantic or syntactic features of the previous syntactic category the morpheme was functioning in before can be retained in its new use. Such cases of persistence are well attested and can explain some heterogeneities in linguistic systems. While using other terms for describing this phenomenon, Hagège (1990: 138), for instance, gives a clear illustration of it. In French, some participles have grammaticalized into prepositions, such as *durant* ('during') or *excepté* ('except') in *durant des années* ('during (several) years') and *excepté les fillettes* ('except the little girls'). The origin of these adpositions in participles is visible in some residual uses of them as postpositions, with a non canonical word order (French otherwise uses the system of pre-positions) as in: *que tout le monde sorte, les fillettes excepté* ('everyone leave, except the little girls'); as a relator *excepté* does not agree with the noun (*les fillettes*); however in this use, the nominal phrase presents an unusual word order (the relator is postposed to the complement). This heteregoneity in a system of adpositions comes from the retention, in their use as relators, of the specific word order of the categories from which the adpositions have arisen (here the participles). The same is true and even more systematic in Chinese, which has both prepositions and postpositions (*ibid.*: 139). Chinese prepositions come from verbs and have maintained, in their use as relators, the word order of verb phrases (verb+object > relator+complement) as exemplified in (8), while postpositions are derived from from nouns and have retained the word order of noun phrases (complement+head noun > complement+ relator), as in (9):

(8) *song gei   xuescheng*
     send give/to student
     'to send to a student'

(9) *zhuozi shang*
     table   summit/on
     'on the table'

Heterogeneities in syntactic systems, as in the case of French or Chinese adpositions, appear to be produced by regular rules, if we just admit that syntactic categories are not fixed and static entities, but patterns of functioning which constantly operate in discourse, reshaping the linguistic units and their categorical status, as stated also in the framework of emergent grammar (Hopper 1987) and radical construction grammar (Croft 2001).

2.5.2. *On grammaticalization chains and extensions*
As presented here, the fractal model relates each particular use of the transcategorial morpheme to a common matrix (the schematic form); it does not integrate the particular "chains" connecting the various uses together. Now, as exemplified by Craig (1991) or Heine and Kilian-Hatz (1994), in some cases, the different uses of the term do not seem to be directly related to a common matrix, but rather to one another in a network of polydirectional grammaticalization chains. In the analysis of *tɛ* presented by Heine and Kilian-Hatz (see Figure 1), the different uses of *tɛ* are related to a central value, the one of comitative, but, for most of them, through the mediation of one or several other uses: for instance, the use as an introducer of purpose subordinating clause is only *indirectly* related to this central value, through the mediation of the use as a directional particle. This does not mean that the different uses are not also connected to a common schematic form, but the fractal model should include the dimension of grammaticalization chains (Heine 1992). Furthermore, it is well known that grammaticalization may also be produced by various extensions such as metonymy or by grammaticalization of pragmatic inferences, or semiotic metonymy (Frajzyngier 1996). In such cases, the matrix of change is clearly not a schematic form. Therefore, if the process of metonymic extension does coexist with the one of schematization for a particular morpheme, a more comprehensive model of language change should add another dimension. This model could then be represented as in Figure 3.

2.5.3. *Typology of transcategoriality*
Before coming to a conclusion, I want to mention briefly how the theoretical questions raised by transcategorial morphemes could be refined by a typological study on transcategoriality. In a preliminary study (Robert 2003b), which I will summarize in

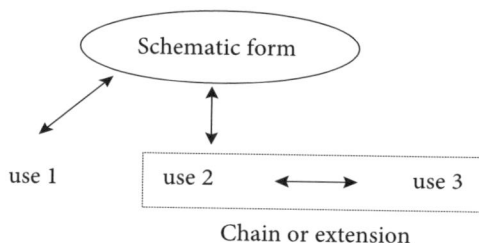

Figure 3. Refined model

a nutshell, I have investigated the various modalities of transcategorial functioning in fifteen languages from different families. This analysis was based on a collective work (cf. Robert ed. 2003), a questionnaire that I have submitted to my colleagues of the LLACAN,[10] and also occasional personal incursions into other languages (Basque and Japanese). The languages on which this first sketch relies were mainly African languages (Niger-Congo and Nilo-Saharian), but also included Afroasiatic, Oceanic, Japanese and Basque. In these languages I have examined:

- the relative proportion of transcategorial morphemes in the language compared to the morphemes whose categories are fixed
- the nature of the class change (noun to preposition, verb to particles...)
- the scope of change in each case
- the marking (*vs.* non marking) of class change
- the synchronic *vs.* diachronic character of transcategoriality
- the morpho-syntactic characteristics of the languages

The results showed different kinds of transcategorial functioning. Depending on the language, transcategoriality is:

- massive *vs.* more restricted
- more synchronic *vs.* more diachronic
- oriented (and marked) *vs.* non oriented (direct)

Interestingly these different modalities of transcategorial functioning correspond to different morpho-syntactic types of languages. So there are structural tendencies to transcategoriality that can be related to the economy of the linguistic systems, crucially to the different strategies for the distribution of grammatical information. I have identified three types of transcategorial strategies which I call oriented transcategoriality, generic transcategoriality, and functional transcategoriality.

(1) In languages with heavy morphology (*e.g.* inflectional languages, such as the Hausa, Maltese and Modern South Arabic languages in the study), the category change is limited (mostly to the verb) and directed from a source category to a target one, mostly through a diachronic process: for instance, full verbs are the main source of auxiliaries, of some adverbs, subordinating conjunctions or discourse

particles; the grammaticalization of nouns is rarer and essentially concerns body part terms giving rise to spatial prepositions. Noticeably polyfunctionals (*i.e.* grammatical morphemes used in different categories without lexical use) are very rare; if they do exist, they always arise from other grammatical categories, such as deictics or indefinite pronouns.

This type is called "oriented" transcategoriality and corresponds to the classical cases of grammaticalization. It can be related to a synthetic and grammatical strategy for the distribution of syntactic information. Because of inflectional morphology, the language units are here altogether semantic (notional) units, category indicators and relational nodes or centers. Since the syntactic categories are marked on the units, the units tend to be more fixed in a given category, so they have a restricted combinatory latitude (they combine with a more restricted number and type of constituents) and transcategorial functioning in synchrony: the category changes require time, morphological erosion and lead to freezing (the unit is fixed into the new category). The counterpart of this categorial rigidity is the synthetic character of the distribution of information.

(2) In languages with light morphology (*e.g.* isolating languages, Banda-Linda, Gbaya, Sängö, Tupuri, Dagara, Ikwere and Nêlêmwa, in the study), the language units appear as generic notions which are either not categorized at all or (are) only weakly pre-categorized and can be instantiated in various categories; their syntactic status is specified by the discourse (these are known as "type-token" languages); most of the time, one use can hardly be derived from another. Transcategoriality is then massive, polydirectional (weakly oriented from a source category to a target), unmarked most of the time, synchronic and transparent. Body part nouns, for instance are used as spatial prepositions but also as morphemes expressing "self", reciprocal (Sängö), or temporal or causal conjunctions (Tupuri). Unlike the previous type, in these languages, connectors and subordinating morphemes come from other categories (nouns, verbs, adverbs, . . .). We can also notice that, most of the time, these languages have one (or two) "archi-relators" (archi-fractals), with highly variable syntactic scope (introducing complement nouns, dependent predicates, relative clauses, circumstantial subordinating clauses, or marking topic or focus).

This type is called "generic" transcategoriality: it arises from an initial categorial under-specification and can be related to an analytical and lexical strategy for the expression of grammatical relations. There is no morphological marking of syntactic categories and syntactic relations in these languages; so the morphemes appear as generic units that are underspecified in some aspect (their referential domain in the lexicon, their syntactic categories in utterance) and have therefore a large combinative latitude (derivation is limited while compounding is highly productive). In the economy of these systems, more compositionality is the counterpart of the flexibility of the units and their high combinatory latitude.

(3) Finally, a third type of transcategorial operation is exemplified by some agglutinating languages like Basque or Japanese. The Basque language combines two distinct processes for the distribution of information in the sentence: (a) the case

markers which indicate the semantic roles of the components, and (b) the agreement markers on the predicate, which specify their syntactic roles. This dissociation between semantic and syntactic roles allows the case markers to function with different components, on different syntactic levels. For instance, when the scope of the morpheme k indicating the semantic role of source or origin, is on a noun, it indicates the source of a process (the agent) or its spatial or temporal origin, but when it has scope over a clause, this morpheme indicates that the clause with k is the origin of the following clause and turns it into a conditional clause (Bottineau 2003).

In this case, transcategoriality does not proceed from category crossing (as for oriented transcategoriality), or from category specification in discourse (as for generic transcategoriality) but from the functional distribution of semantic *vs.* syntactic roles. I call it "functional transcategoriality". It corresponds to a selective strategy for grammatical information (semantic roles and syntactic roles are expressed by distinct units). Due to this functional distribution, the morphemes expressing semantic roles can apply to various syntactic structures whose status is specified by argument markers.

Through these different cases, we have caught sight of the important part played in the propensity of a language for transcategoriality by the distribution of the grammatical information and the dissociation of conceptual components from relational components. The more autonomous the grammatical markers are (analytical strategy), the easier the category changes for linguistic components are. The various predispositions of a language to transcategoriality can be related to the nature of the linguistic system and are therefore at least partly predictable.

Conclusion

As a conclusion, I would like to return to the question of the status of linguistic categories raised by transcategorial morphemes. When linguistic units function synchronically in different categories, does the unity of categories and speech parts vanish in their various uses? Do we have fuzzy categories or continuous categories, as in the prototype model? If the categorial status of a linguistic item is constructed in discourse, does it mean that the linguistic categories are emergent (Hopper 1987, Bybee and Hopper 2001)? This depends on the level of analysis we are considering: the pattern of the language system, *or* the way the categories work in discourse. What fractal functioning reveals is *categorial flexibility* on the part of certain units. However, even if the membership (of these units) in a category is constructed in discourse and triggered by the position of the morpheme and its environment in discourse, it is nevertheless the case that the category pre-exists *in the linguistic system* as a model of functioning. Furthermore, as pointed out by Croft (2001: 78), even in the languages that are claimed to lack part-of-speech distinctions, a distributional analysis shows that the parts of speech do exist but are covert. In other words, (1) in every language, even the massively transcategorial languages, *models and types of categories* do exist, with discrete boundaries, but all languages allow, to various degrees and with various constraints, certain units to change their categories and therefore to adopt the functional features of the new category. Such are the dynamics of linguistic systems. (2) Fractal grammar shows that there is continuity in semantics through the schematic form, but the (level or) scale properties introduce discontinuity into the semantic continuum. (3) During their historical development, languages may "crystallize" certain uses; the membership of a unit in a category is then frozen. That is the endpoint of the classic case of grammaticalization. (4) Languages also show a variable propensity for categorical flexibility *vs.* rigidity, which defines different types of transcategorial functioning.

Notes

1. Echoing L. Michaelis's discussion on the subject (1996: 180), I make no presuppositions about the fact that the various synchronic uses of a transcategorial morpheme necessarily reflect or can be equated with the path of historical development which yielded the latter.

2. Table 25 in the cited article presents a semantic network, where the grammatical categories are not specified; when possible, I have inferred the grammatical categories from the related examples in order to add them in this partial figure. Possible mistakes are mine.

3. The different uses of *tɛ* are only grammatical and don't include a lexical functioning, I call that subtype of transcategorial morpheme, a polyfunctional.

4. For an overview of the different models, see Heine *et alii* (1991: 108 sqq).

5. This paper is largely based on two recent articles of the author (Robert 2003a and 2003b), published in French in S. Robert (éd.), 2003, *Perspectives synchroniques sur la grammaticalisation: Polysémie, transcatégorialité et échelles syntaxiques*, Collection *Afrique et Langage* n°5, Editions Peeters, Louvain.

6. Aspect can be defined as the "situation-internal time" (Comrie 1976: 5).

7. *Toven* is the strong form for the verb, *roven* the weak form for the verb modifier and nominal quantifier (Bril 2003). According to Nêlêmwa's morphology, the two forms are clearly two variants of the same stem. Concerning the question of transcategoriality, we can consider that this split into two distinct forms corresponds to what Anward (2000: 32) has called "marked recycling" of parts-of-speech *vs* "simple recycling"; for reasons of space, I cannot present this aspect of transcategorial functioning, i.e. morphologically marked *vs* unmarked category change (see Robert 2003b), but even if the case of the verbal use is left out of the discussion because it is morphologically not strictly identical to the two other uses, the two other cases can nevertheless be explained by fractal grammar.

8. The temporal sense of *ginnaaw* is possible in its prepositional use but seems to be restricted to the cases where it governs a noun involving time, such as in *ginnaaw ëllëg* (ginnaaw tomorrow) '(the day) after tomorrow', or *ginnaaw añ* (ginnaaw lunch) 'after lunch'. In that case, the temporal domain is shaped as a space. This temporal value is impossible when *ginnaaw* is used as a subordinating conjunction. The subordinating conjunction 'after' is expressed with another morpheme (*bi/ba*): *Bi mu lekkee la dem* (when AOR3SG eat+ANTERIOR. FocusComp3sg go) 'After he had eaten, he left'.

9. Or only when the sentence is marked by a special cohesive anaphoric intonation which confirms its topical status.

10. Isabelle Bril for Nêlêmwa, Bernard Caron for Hausa, France Cloarec-Heiss for Banda-linda, Alain Delplanque for Dagara, Marcel Diki-Kidiri for Sango, Sylvester Osu Ikwere, Paulette Roulon-Doko for Gbaya, Suzanne Ruelland for Tupuri, Marie-Claude Simeone-Senelle for Modern South-Arabic, Martine Vanhove for Maltese. Special thanks go also to Didier Bottineau for his contribution on Basque. Possible mistakes are mine.

References

Anward, Jan. 2000. "A dynamic model of part-of-speech diffentiation." In *Approaches to the Typology of Word Classes*, Petra M. Vogel and Bernard Comrie (eds), 3–45. Berlin: Mouton de Gruyter.

Bottineau, Didier. 2003. "Syntaxe génétique et typologie cognitive : la genèse des énoncés basques, anglais et japonais." Paper presented at the 10ème Colloque International de Psychomécanique du Langage, Oloron-Sainte-Marie.

Bril, Isabelle. 2003. "Quantification, aspect et modalité : phénomènes de portée et d'échelle, quelques exemples en nêlêmwa." In *Perspectives synchroniques sur la grammaticalisation: Polysémie, transcatégorialité et échelles syntaxiques*, Stéphane Robert (ed), 53–68. Louvain: Editions Peeters.

Bybee, Joan, Perkins, Revere and Pagliuca, William. 1994. *The Evolution of Grammar. Tense, Aspect and Modality in the Languages of the World*. Chicago and London: The University of Chicago Press.

Bybee, Joan and Hopper, Paul (eds). 2001. *Frequency and the Emergence of Linguistic Structure. Typological Studies in Language 45*. Amsterdam/Philadelphia: John Benjamins.

Craig, Colette. 1991. "Ways to go in Rama: a case study in polygrammaticalisation." In *Approaches to grammaticalization*, Elisabeth Closs Traugott and Bernd Heine (eds), 455–492. Amsterdam/Philadelphia: John Benjamins.

Croft, William. 1994. "The semantics of subjecthood." In *Subjecthood and Subjectivity. The status of the subject in linguistic theory*, Marina Yaguello (ed), 29–76. Paris/Gap/London: Ophrys/Institut français du Royaume-Uni.

Croft, William. 2001. *Radical construction grammar: syntactic theory in typological perspective*. Oxford: Oxford University Press.

Culioli, Antoine. 1990. *Pour une linguistique de l'énonciation, Vol. 1, Opérations et représentations*. L'Homme dans la langue. Paris/Gap: Ophrys.

Fillmore, Charles F. 1988. "The mechanisms of 'construction grammar.'" Paper presented at the Annual Meeting of the Berkeley Linguistics Society.

Frajzyngier, Zygmunt. 1996. *Grammaticalization of the Complex Sentence. A case study in Chadic: Complementary Series to the Study in Language 32*. Amsterdam/Philadelphia: John Benjamins.

Givón, Talmy. 1975. "Serial verbs and syntactic change: Niger-Congo." In *Word order and word order change*, Charles N. Li (ed), 17–112. Austin: University of Texas Press.

Gleick, James. 1991. *La théorie du chaos*. Paris: Flammarion.

Goldberg, Adele E. 1995. *Constructions. A Construction Grammar Approach to Argument Structure: Cognitive Theory of Language and Culture*. Chicago/London: The University of Chicago Press.

Güldemann, T. and von Roncador, M. (eds) 2002. *Reported Speech: A Meeting Ground for Different Linguistic Domains*. Amsterdam/Philadelphia: John Benjamins.

Hagège, Claude. 1990. *The Dialogic Species. A Linguistic Contribution to the Social Sciences*. New York: Columbia University Press.

Hagège, Claude. 1993. *The Language Builder*. Current Issues in Linguistic Theory 94. Amsterdam/Philadelphia: John Benjamins.

Hansen, Maj-Britt Mosegaard. 1998. The function of discourse particles. A study with special reference to spoken standard French. Amsterdam/Philadelphia: John Benjamins.

Haspelmath, Martin and König, Ekkehard (eds). 1995. *Converbs in cross-linguistic perspective: structure and meaning of adverbial verb forms, adverbial participles, gerunds*. Empirical Approaches to Language Typology 13. Berlin: Mouton de Gruyter.

Heine, Bernd. 1992. "Grammaticalization chains." *Studies in language*, 16(2): 335–368.

Heine, Bernd; Claudi, Ulrike and Hünnemeyer, Friederike. 1991. *Grammaticalization: A conceptual framework*. Chicago: University of Chicago Press.

Heine, Bernd and Kilian-Hatz, Christa. 1994. "Polysemy in African languages: An example from Baka." In *Sprachen und Sprachzeugnisse in Afrik. Eine Sammlung philologischer Beiträge Wilhelm J.G. Möhlig zum 60 Geburtstag zugeeignet*, Thomas Geider and Raimund Kastenholz (eds). Köln: Rudiger Köppe Verlag.

Heine, Bernd and Kuteva, Tania. 2002. *World Lexicon of Grammaticalization*. Cambrigde: Cambridge University Press.

Hopper, Paul. 1987. "Emergent Grammar." *Berkeley Linguistics Society*, 13: 139–157.

Hopper, Paul. 1991. "On some principles of grammaticization." *Approaches to grammaticalization*, Elisabeth Closs Traugott and Bernd Heine (eds), 17–35. Amsterdam/Philadelphia: John Benjamins.

Lakoff, George. 1987. *Women, fire and dangerous things: What categories reveal about the mind*. Chicago: University of Chicago Press.

Lakoff, George. 1993. "The contemporary theory of metaphor." In *Metaphor and Thought*, A. Ortony (ed), 202–51. Cambridge: Cambridge University Press.

Langacker, Ronald W. 1987. *Foundations of cognitive grammar, vol.1*. Standford, California: Standford University Press.

Langacker, Ronald W. 1991. "Cognitive Grammar." In *Linguistic Theory and Grammatical Description*, Flip G. Droste and John E. Joseph (eds), 275–306. Amsterdam/Philadelphia: John Benjamins.

Lehmann, Christian. 1995. *Thoughts on Grammaticalization*. Muenchen: Lincom Europa.

Lord, Carol. 1976. "Evidence for syntactic reanalysis: from verb to complementizer in Kwa." Paper presented at Chicago Linguistic Society. Parasession on Diachronic Syntax, Chicago.

Mandelbrot, Benoît. 1975. *Les Objets fractals, forme, hasard et dimension*. Paris: Flammarion.

Meillet, Antoine. 1912 [1948]. "L'évolution des formes grammaticales". *Scientia*, XII.

Michaelis, Laura A. 1996. "Cross-world Continuity, and the Polysemy of Adverbial *Still*." In *Space, Worlds and Grammar*, Gilles Fauconnier and Eve Sweetser (eds), 179–226. Chicago and London: The University of Chicago Press.

Mithun, Marianne. In this volume. "On the notion of the sentence as the basic unit of syntactic structure."

Robert, Stéphane. 1997. "From body to argumentation: grammaticalization as a fractal property of language (the case of Wolof *ginnaaw*)." *Proceedings of the 23th Annual Meeting of the Berkeley Linguistics Society (Special Session on Syntax and Semantics in African Languages)*: 116–127.

Robert, Stéphane. 1999. "Cognitive invariants and linguistic variability: from units to utterance." In *Language Diversity and Cognitive Representations*, Catherine Fuchs and Stéphane Robert (eds), 21–35. Amsterdam/Philadelphia: John Benjamins.

Robert, Stéphane (ed). 2003. *Perspectives synchroniques sur la grammaticalisation: Polysémie, transcatégorialité et échelles syntaxiques: Afrique et Langage 5.* Louvain: Editions Peeters.

Robert, Stéphane. 2003a. "Polygrammaticalisation, grammaire fractale et propriétés d'échelle." In *Perspectives synchroniques sur la grammaticalisation: Polysémie, transcatégorialité et échelles syntaxiques*, Stéphane Robert (ed), 85–120. Louvain: Editions Peeters.

Robert, Stéphane. 2003b. "Vers une typologie de la transcatégorialité." In *Perspectives synchroniques sur la grammaticalisation: Polysémie, transcatégorialité et échelles syntaxiques*, Stéphane Robert (ed), 255–370. Louvain: Editions Peeters.

Ruelland, Suzanne. 1998. "Je pense et je parle comme je suis: le corps, le monde et la parole en tupuri." *Faits de langues*, 11–12: 335–358.

Ruelland, Suzanne. 2003. "Verbes, auxiliaires et déplacements dans l'espace en tupuri." In *Perspectives synchroniques sur la grammaticalisation: Polysémie, transcatégorialité et échelles syntaxiques*, Stéphane Robert (ed), 127–148. Louvain: Editions Peeters.

Sapoval, Bernard. 1997. *Universalité et fractales*. Paris: Flammarion.

Sweetser, Eve. 1988. "Grammaticalization and semantic bleaching." *Proceedings of the 14th Annual Meeting of the Berkeley Linguistics Society*, 389–409.

Talmy, Leonard. 2000. *Toward a Cognitive Semantics*. Cambridge MA: MIT Press.

Taylor, John R. 1989. *Linguistic categorization: Prototypes in linguistic theory*. Oxford: Oxford University Press.

Traugott, Elisabeth Closs and Hopper, Paul. 1993. *Grammaticalization*. Cambridge: Cambridge University Press.

Wierzbicka, Anna. 1986. "What's a noun? (or: how do nouns differ in meaning from adjectives ?)." *Studies in Language*, 10: 353–389.

Wischer, Ilse and Diewald, Gabriele (eds) 2002. *New Reflections on Grammaticalization*. Typological Studies in Language 49. Amsterdam/Philadelphia: John Benjamins.

CHAPTER 7

On discourse frequency, grammar, and grammaticalization

Regina Pustet

University of Munich/University of Colorado

The point of departure for the present investigation is G. K. Zipf's postulate of an interdependence between the length of words and their frequency in discourse: the shorter a word is, the more frequently it will occur in discourse. In this paper, it is argued that this statistical correlation holds not only at the word level, but at the morpheme level as well. The study further uncovers obvious analogies between Zipf's model and recent findings in research on language change and grammaticalization. One of the central claims of both approaches concerns the relationship between the structural complexity of linguistic items and their frequency in discourse. In Zipf's model, this correlation is phrased almost exclusively in synchronic terms; in discourse-sensitive scenarios of language change, the correlation materializes itself in the fact that the shortening of linguistic items over time is typically accompanied by an increase in their discourse frequency.

1. Zipf's model of language vs. grammaticalization theory

George Kingsley Zipf (1902–1950) can be considered one of the most influential linguists of his time. Although human language was the original focus of his comprehensive statistical research, his work finally came to embrace numerous other scientific domains as well. In linguistics, Zipf is remembered mainly for discovering the presumably universal statistical correlation that holds between the discourse frequency of linguistic items and their structural complexity or length ("the more frequent, the shorter") which is known as Zipf's Law. In the attempt to develop a general theory of human ecology, Zipf found that the systematic correlation between frequency and structural complexity describes a fundamental statistical regularity that does not only apply to language, but also to many areas of research in a vast spectrum of disciplines such as physics, biology, economics, art, the social sciences, and library science. As a matter of fact, Zipf's analyses capture properties of the physical world which are so profound that the famous Zipf curves can be put on a par with the Gaussian distribution (cf. Mandelbrot 1977: 423). Particularly within the natural and social sciences, which have, by now, provided a wealth of evidence for the validity of Zipf's Law, Zipf curves have long been accepted as a basic constant in statistical analysis. Paradoxically, Zipf's work has, so far, not attracted a comparable amount of attention in theoretical linguistics. Quoted only sporadically and never in great detail, in general language theory, Zipf's monumental and eminently useful framework has, so far, not been explored as thoroughly as it deserves.

In the meantime, however, research in functional-typological language theory spanning several decades by now has produced insights that should kindle renewed interest in Zipf's work. On closer inspection, Zipfian theories show a high compatibility, if not to say a striking overlap, with many core tenets of functionalism which concern both synchronic and diachronic aspects of language structure.

The aim of this paper is twofold. It will, first and foremost, propose and then verify a hypothesis which is long overdue in linguistic theorizing: that Zipf's findings are valid not only for lexical systems, but for grammatical systems as well. Zipf's methods are such that Zipf-style analyses, in the majority of cases, merely allow statements about the behavior of discourse units which happen to form coherent words in a given language. This method, in essence, filters out lexical items as units of investigation, and neglects grammatical items. In what follows, Zipf's method will be modified in such a way that specifically, and exclusively, grammatical items are targeted. In order to determine whether Zipf's statistical correlations hold within the grammatical systems of individual languages, this new method will then be tested out on discourse data from four different languages: Armenian (Indo-European language family), Lakota (Siouan language family), Taiwanese (Sino-Tibetan language family), and Thai (Austro-Tai language family).

Upon substantiating the assumption that grammatical systems do indeed comply with Zipfian principles, this study will, secondly, deal with the obvious analogies between Zipf's model and grammaticalization theory. It will be argued that these two frameworks are too strongly intertwined to ignore the connection. A synthesis of Zipf's model and grammaticalization theory should turn out to be extremely fruitful and inspiring because Zipf's approach sheds some more light on certain aspects of grammaticalization which have invited a lot of guesswork in the more recent literature—most notably, the unidirectionality principle of grammaticalization (e.g. Campbell 2001, Croft 2000, Haspelmath 1999, Janda 2001, Newmeyer 2001, Norde 2001).

1.1. Zipf's model of language, in a nutshell

Zipf's model of language evolves around three basic variables: the discourse frequency, the structural complexity, and the semantic complexity of linguistic elements (Zipf 1965a, 1965b). The specific formula referred to by the term "Zipf's Law" defines the statistical correlation between discourse frequency and structural complexity. According to Zipf (1965a: 25), the structural complexity of linguistic items "tends, on the whole, to stand in an inverse (not necessarily proportionate) relationship to the number of occurrences". The contrast of the English article *the* [ðə],

maximal

↑

discourse
frequency

↓

minimal

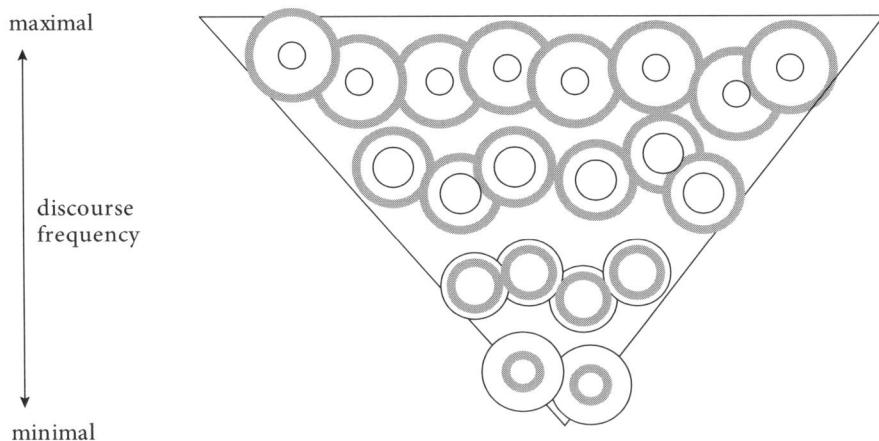

Figure 1. Schematic representation of discourse according to Zipf's model

which is structurally simple and extremely frequent in discourse, and the English
pronoun *themselves* [ðəmselvz], which is structurally more complex and far less
frequent in discourse, illustrates this principle.

What is less widely known is that Zipf also established statistical correlations between discourse frequency and the parameter of semantic complexity. Zipf's data
on English show that the number of meanings of linguistic elements increases as
their discourse frequency increases (Zipf 1965b:28). The empirical method Zipf
used to verify this correlation was counting dictionary translations for lexical items.
This aspect of Zipf's work is confirmed by more recent investigations such as Breiter
(1994) for Chinese and Levickij et al. (1996) for Modern German, which also employ dictionary counts. Since, further, discourse frequency correlates with structural complexity, Zipf argues that all three of the variables listed above are interdependent. These correlations constitute the basic skeleton of Zipf's framework; they
are schematically represented in figure 1 (for more details, cf. Pustet (2004). Black
circles symbolize the variable of structural complexity, while gray circles symbolize
the variable of semantic complexity. The size of the circles stands for relative structural or semantic complexity. The number of circles of a specific type represents
their relative frequency in discourse. The number of circles of each type contained
in this diagram is, of course, in no way representative of the respective quantitative
proportions in real discourse samples.

It must be kept in mind that the above schematic representation, which is of necessity abstract, glosses over the fact that the Zipfian correlations are never perfect:
presumably, in any language, there are extremely short linguistic items which are
not very frequent in discourse, such as the English noun *tea* [tiː], or structurally
complex elements which are relatively frequent, such as the English preposition *towards* [təwɔːdz].

1.2. Grammaticalization theory, in a nutshell

Incidentally—or maybe for a very good reason --, the purely synchronic Zipfian correlations which hold between the variables of discourse frequency, structural complexity, and semantic complexity are echoed by the general rules which determine diachronic change at the level of morphemic units:

(1) As the semantic complexity of a linguistic item increases and its structural complexity decreases, its frequency increases.

The postulate of the co-occurrence of these processes can be regarded as one of the major tenets of grammaticalization theory. The generalizing formula (1) is actually a conflation of the joint results of two very influential paradigms in contemporary non-generative approaches to language change. Within the framework which will henceforth be referred to as "Classical Grammaticalization Theory" (CGT), whose scope is defined by works such as Heine et al. (1991), Heine and Kuteva (2002), Hopper and Traugott (1993), Lehmann (1982), Traugott and Heine (1991), the variable of discourse frequency does not play a very decisive role. The relative insignificance of discourse frequency within CGT may be due to its specific goals and the nature of the empirical research required to achieve these goals. CGT investigates grammaticalization processes over long time spans which often extend over hundreds of years or even longer periods of time. Typically, CGT is concerned with the development of grammatical items from lexical items, such as the development of benefactive case markers from verbs which express the concept 'to give', or with the development of "more" grammatical items from "less" grammatical items, such as the development of subject or object markers from oblique case markers. Research in CGT tends to focus on non-Indo-European languages. For such languages, documentation covering longer time periods is often sparse, and existing grammatical descriptions are not always supplemented with suitable text samples, which can be used for determining the discourse frequency of individual linguistic items. Given this, research into "long distance grammaticalization" does not usually provide the empirical data which would be necessary for integrating the frequency factor into the overall picture.

In contrast, discourse frequency is a very crucial factor in approaches to language change for which designations such as "Emergent Grammar" and "Usage-Based Models" have been proposed. Influential publications in this tradition include Barlow and Kemmer (2000), Bybee (1985), Bybee (2001), Bybee and Hopper (2001), Hopper (1987), Langacker (1987). Like CGT, emergent Grammar and Usage-Based Models (henceforth, EG&UBM) deal with the mechanisms of structural and semantic change, but in contrast to CGT, EG&UBM typically investigate change taking place within short time spans. At the "microscopic" level, EG&UBM confirm the findings that CGT proposes for the "macroscopic" level. By and large, language change proceeds from the semantically more specific to the more abstract, and from the structurally more complex to the structurally simpler. It has to be conceded as this point, however, that this generalizing formula does not come without exceptions, and that it is not fully supported by all scholars working in the area of grammaticalization (for details, cf. section 3). To name just two examples for the purpose of illustration, changes observed by CGT concern the development of the progressive aspect marker *- hą* in Lakota, i.e. of a semantically abstract element, from the semantically more specific verb *hą* 'to stand'; or the development of the Modern Greek future marker *θa* from a complex construction comprising the verb *thel-* 'to want' and the complementizer *hina* (Joseph 2001: 178ff.). In the latter case, semantic change is accompanied by extreme structural reduction. Changes observed by EG&UBM tend to be more subtle, both at the semantic and at the formal level. For instance, it can be shown that the English complementizer *that* originates in the demonstrative pronoun *that*. Berkenfield (2001: 291) argues that during this development, the element *that* has extended its semantic scope: the function of complementizer is semantically more abstract than the function of demonstrative pronoun. During the process of grammaticalization of *that*, reductive change has taken place at the structural level as well. On the average, the demonstrative pronoun *that* exhibits longer vowel duration (133 ms) than the complementizer *that* (84 ms) (Berkenfield 2001: 291).

EG&UBM systematically add the variable of discourse frequency to the overall scenario of language change, and provide a wealth of empirical evidence for the diachronic correlation of increase in discourse frequency with decrease in structural complexity and increase in semantic complexity. It should be noted, however, that this correlation is an idealization. In practice, none of these changes is necessarily concomitant with simultaneous or near-simultaneous changes within the other two dimensions. For instance, cases in which semantic change is not accompanied by structural change are richly documented. The idealized model of language change, in which changes in frequency, structural complexity, and semantic complexity coincide, can be rendered schematically as follows:

Figure 2 is to be taken as a simplification for yet another reason. The diagram implies that individual linguistic elements develop into a single innovative element only. As a matter of fact, however, a linguistic element often develops into various new elements.

For the sake of clarity, it must be pointed out that the usage of the term semantic complexity in this paper differs from the usage encountered in some of the more prominent publications on grammaticalization. For instance, Heine et al. (1991: 15f.) argue that "the more grammaticalization processes a given linguistic unit undergoes, … **the more it loses its semantic complexity**, functional significance, and/ or expressive value" (boldfacing added); similarly, cf. Givón (1975: 98). Thus, according to these authors, during the process of grammaticalization, the semantic complexity of linguistic elements decreases rather than increases. This is, at least at first glance, in stark contrast to the claim made in the present paper: according to what is said above, in grammaticalization, linguistic items **gain** in semantic complexity. As a matter of fact, however, these seemingly contradictory usages of the

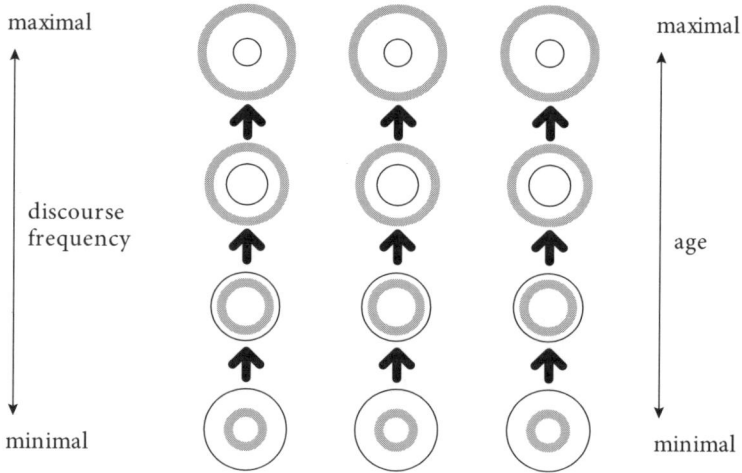

Figure 2. Schematic representation of diachronic change in linguistic structure

term semantic complexity actually describe the same concept in different ways. In dealing with the semantic complexity of linguistic elements, the above authors refer to **intensional** content, i.e. to the number of semantic features needed to define the meaning of the latter. The more abstract the meaning, the fewer semantic features are contained in the overall semantic profile of a linguistic item. A low number of defining features corresponds to low semantic complexity. Thus, the semantic profile of 'dog', which is composed of features such as 'mammal, quadruped, carnivorous, furry, barks' is less complex than that of 'chow chow', which includes all these features plus several other characteristics such as 'has flabby skin, a tail that curls over its back, and a purplish tongue'. However, alternatively, the **extensional,** rather than the intensional, content of linguistic items can be taken as the basis for the definition of semantic complexity. The extensional content of a concept is defined in terms of the number or range of its meanings. In this reading of the concept of semantic complexity, low semantic complexity is tantamount to a low number of different meanings and/or contextual interpretations. In this case, 'dog' will be considered semantically more complex than 'chow chow'. The concept 'dog' can be used in a greater number of contexts than 'chow chow'; the meaning of 'chow chow' is included in the meaning of 'dog'. A fundamental axiom of logic, however, states that high intensional content of concepts correlates with low extensional content, and vice versa. Consequently, in grammaticalization, semantic concepts lose in intensional complexity, but they gain in extensional complexity. The present study operates exclusively with the extensional definition of semantic complexity.

1.3. Synthesis

A glance at figures 1 and 2 reveals that the latter, in essence, have a lot in common. One crucial difference between Zipf's model and grammaticalization theory, which also emerges from the graphic representations, is that grammaticalization theory is concerned with the properties that **individual** linguistic items exhibit with respect to the variables of discourse frequency, structural complexity, and semantic complexity, while Zipf's model (ideally) captures the properties of **all** linguistic items that make up a given language system with respect to these three variables. Secondly, grammaticalization theory per se focuses on changes in the properties of linguistic elements over time. This dynamic component is lacking in the basic version of the Zipf model depicted in figure 1. But since Zipf's approach to language is holistic, it can be concluded that the comprehensive Zipf model also provides the backdrop for the course of events in language change. On the assumption that the linguistic items contained in a linguistic system comply with the Zipfian blueprint for the architecture of languages at all times, changing the value of one variable for any linguistic item in a given language is likely to entail changes in the values for the other variables. More specifically, if the frequency of a linguistic item increases in diachronic change, chances are that at the same time, its semantic complexity increases and its structural complexity decreases. If structural complexity decreases, this process is, more likely than not, coupled with frequency increase and expansion of semantic complexity. If semantic complexity increases, structural complexity can be expected to decrease, while frequency increases. On these grounds, the behavior of linguistic items in language change becomes predictable, at least to a certain degree, and the respective predictions are completely in line with the empirical observations made in research on grammaticalization.

Given this, it does not come as a big surprise that Zipf's own studies implicitly reveal a statistical correlation between the frequency and the age of linguistic items as well. On the basis of empirical data on consecutive lexical borrowings from Scandinavian, Romance, and other languages into Middle English and modern English, as compared to those lexical items that were present in the earliest stratum, i.e. Old English, Zipf claims that the discourse frequency of lexical items is, on the whole, "inversely related to their age" (Zipf 1965b: 120). Thus, in any given language, "the longer and less frequent words tend to be the younger ones" (Zipf 1965b: 120). Needless to say, these findings strongly support the hypothesis advanced above—grammaticalization theory can be embedded into Zipf's comprehensive model of language.

As plausible as this may sound so far, there is a little catch to the argument: there are no investigations to date that confirm the hypothesis that grammar—at the synchronic level—abides by Zipfian rules. Zipf's preferred method of determining frequency values was better suited for capturing lexical rather than grammatical items, as section 2.1 will show, and Zipf's successors have, so far, done little to remedy this. However, at least for the lexicon, Zipf's own research provides data on reductive change at the structural level which conform to the claims made by grammaticalization theory. For instance, in the variety of American English spoken at Zipf's time, shortening of *gasoline* to *gas*, *moving picture* to *movie*, *omnibus* to *bus*, and *telephone* to *phone* could be observed.

But since grammaticalization theory is, first and foremost, about grammar, a synthesis of grammaticalization theory and Zipf's model presupposes explicit proof of the hypothesis that grammar complies with Zipfian principles. The following section will provide positive empirical evidence for this hypothesis on the basis of discourse data from four languages. This issue is in need of clarification not only with regard to future studies in grammaticalization. If Zipf's model is valid for grammar as well, this fact about human language is fundamental enough to deserve in-depth treatment for its own sake.

2. The interaction of discourse frequency, structural complexity, and semantic complexity in grammar

The conclusions drawn in this paper are derived from discourse data from the following, genetically unrelated, languages: Armenian (Indo-European), Lakota (Siouan), Taiwanese (Sino-Tibetan), and Thai (Austro-Tai). A major difficulty in collecting discourse data suitable for this project lies in the fact that ready-made frequency data which fulfill the methodological requirements addressed in section 2.1 are not available because discourse analyses of the kind introduced in sections 2.1 and 2.2 have not been carried out so far. In contrast, there exist a multitude of quantitative data obtained on the basis of classical Zipf-style discourse analyses because Zipf's theories have been tested time and again on various languages. But, as will be made clear in section 2.1, such data cannot be used for the present study.

Unfortunately, even raw data suitable for the analyses described in section 2.1 are difficult to come by. Although there are comprehensive text corpora for most of the major languages of the world, these analyses require a high degree of familiarity with the grammar of the languages under investigation on the part of the analyst. The existence of thorough interlinear glosses and detailed grammatical descriptions could be considered an alternative to extraordinary language competence, but language documentations that meet these standards are extremely hard to find.

These considerations suggest that the best line of attack in compiling discourse data for this study is collaboration with native speakers who provide their own discourse samples. This renders the process of data compilation a very time-consuming task, and consequently, the discourse samples must remain relatively small. But as it will turn out in section 2.2, even small samples yield relevant data in this case.

2.1. Method

In what follows, a decisive methodological step away from Zipf's original quantitative discourse analyses will be taken. Zipf's method is, in and of itself, unimpeachable, but it is not compatible with the specific goals of this study, which aims at verifying whether Zipfian principles are operative in grammar or not. The major drawback of Zipf's method from this perspective is its insensitivity to the internal morphological structure of words, on the one hand, and to the semantic individuality of linguistic items, on the other. In most cases, Zipf merely counted words, irrespective of their morphological composition; differences in the meaning of phonetically identical linguistic items are equally irrelevant in Zipf-style analyses. Today, this method is still in use (e.g. Balasubrahmanyan and Naranan 1996).

An example from Latin—the opening line of Virgil's Aeneid—will be discussed in detail to illustrate Zipf's analytical method.

(2) *arm-a*   *vir-um-que*   *can-o*
     arms-ACC.PL man-ACC.SG-and sing of-1SG.PRS.IND
     'I sing of arms and the man.'

All three words contained in this simple clause are potentially ambiguous. *arma* can, for one, be analyzed as the nominative or accusative plural form of the neuter plural noun *arma* 'arms'; but *arma* is also the imperative singular of the verb *armare* 'to arm, furnish with weapons, stir up, provoke, rouse'. *virumque* can be broken down into the components *vir* 'man', *-um* 'accusative singular', and the coordinator *-que* 'and'. But *virum* is also the accusative singular form of *virus* 'slime, poison, power, force, vigor'. *cano* can be analyzed as the first person singular present indicative of the verb *canere* 'to sing of'; alternatively, *cano* can be analyzed as the dative or ablative singular masculine/neuter form of the adjective *canus* 'gray, white, hoary'. In a classical Zipfian discourse analysis, all occurrences of the form *cano* are added up in the count as instances of the occurrence of a single linguistic unit, regardless of whether *cano* means 'I sing of' or 'gray.DAT/ABL.SG' in individual cases. Since, further, morphologically complex word forms are left unsegmented in classical Zipfian analyses, words are always counted as a whole. Thus, in the case of *cano*, instead of the morphological units *can-* and *-o*, only the complex word form *cano* enters a classical Zipf-style analysis as a countable unit.

Grammatical items, however, exhibit a strong tendency to figure as affixes, rather than as free elements. Consequently, this method of counting captures only part of the grammatical inventory of a given language. The percentage of grammatical items that end up in a classical Zipf-style analysis depends on the morphological type of the language in question. The more synthetic a language is, the fewer grammatical items will be captured; the more isolating a language is, the more grammatical items will be included in the analysis.

It has to be annotated at this point that at least for some Native American languages (Lakota, Nootka, and Plains Cree, cf. Zipf 1965b: 78ff.), Zipf conducted morphology-sensitive analyses as well. However, the methodological and empirical details of these analyses remain obscure, so that these materials cannot be used for the purposes of the present study.

Grammaticalization theory is concerned with the behavior and properties of **individual** linguistic items, i.e. elements that constitute a unit both at the semantic and the morphological level. In the attempt to determine whether grammar and grammaticalization follow Zipfian principles, Zipf's method of counting must, therefore, be modified in such a way that elements which form independent units at the semantic and at the morphological level are targeted systematically. The method employed in the analysis of the discourse samples discussed in section 2.2, for one, operates with full morphological segmentation of words, and secondly, acknowledges homonymy relations between phonetically identical units.

To revert to the Latin example given above for purposes of illustration, within the modified Zipf analysis, the form *cano* yields several countable units: the roots *can-* 'to sing of' and *can-* 'gray, white, hoary'; and the suffixes *-o* 'first person singular present indicative', *-o* 'dative singular masculine', *-o* 'dative singular neuter', *-o* 'ablative singular masculine', and *-o* 'ablative singular neuter'. For each of these units, the number of occurrences in a given stretch of discourse is determined separately.

Since this study focuses on grammatical rather than lexical items, only grammatical items were included in the discourse counts whose results are presented in section 2.2. It is, admittedly, not always easy to decide whether a given linguistic item is part of grammar or part of the lexicon; the grammar vs. lexicon distinction is anything but clear-cut. However, in the long history of grammar writing, undeniably, an implicit consensus on what linguistic items should be included in a grammar has developed. There is an invariant set of categories which, if present in the categorical inventory of a given language, show up in the grammatical description of any language, regardless of its genetic affiliation. The checklist of grammatical items this study operates with is based on this consensus. This list of items, at least for the four languages investigated in this study, comprises the following functional domains and categories: semantic roles (both inflectional case markers and adpositions count as markers of semantic roles), pragmatic roles (topic, focus etc.), number, gender/noun classification, (in)definiteness, demonstratives, person (independent personal pronouns count as person markers), tense, aspect, modality, valence change (e.g. passive, antipassive, causative), auxiliaries, predicators (including copulas), gradation, intensification, diminution, emphasis, linkers/subordinators (levels: sentence, clause, constituent).

After counting the discourse occurrences of individual linguistic items in the discourse samples, the structural complexity of the latter is determined. This does not pose any particular problems insofar as structural complexity is simply measured in phonemes (Zipf sometimes counted syllables rather than phonemes).

2.2. Data

In order to obtain schematic representations of the frequency distribution of linguistic items relative to the variable of structural complexity, the raw frequency data from the four languages investigated, i.e. Armenian (Indo-European language family), Lakota (Siouan language family), Taiwanese (Sino-Tibetan language family), and Thai (Austro-Tai language family) are processed as follows.

For each language, the average discourse frequency of all those elements which share a specific value of structural complexity is calculated. For this purpose, their individual frequency values are added up, and the total (F) is divided by the number of group members (M). F/M indicates the average discourse frequency for the grammeme group in question, which is defined in terms of structural complexity. This procedure yields the figures set out in Tables 1–4. In the graphical representation of the figures given in Tables 1–4, the average frequency values F/M are plotted against the complexity values of the linguistic items occurring in the language-specific samples (see Figs. 3–6). On comparing Figures 3–6, it turns out that by and large, all four graphs exhibit a gradual slope from left to right, which is tantamount

Table 1. Discourse frequency and phonemic complexity of grammemes in Armenian (sample size: about 1,700 words)

	Grammeme group as defined by number of phonemes							
	1	2	3	4	5	6	7	8
Total of frequencies F	493	581	361	115	15	26	2	1
Total of group members M	16	35	24	19	6	6	1	1
F/M	30.8	16.6	15.0	6.1	2.5	4.3	2.0	1.0

Table 2. Discourse frequency and phonemic complexity of grammemes in Lakota (sample size: about 1,200 words, corpus taken from Pustet forthcoming)

	Grammeme group as defined by number of phonemes									
	1	2	3	4	5	6	7	8	9	10
Total of frequencies F	3	520	84	212	59	48	13	3	10	4
Total of group members M	3	44	10	34	17	13	8	3	3	3
F/M	1.0	11.8	8.4	6.2	3.5	3.7	1.6	1.0	3.3	1.3

Table 3. Discourse frequency and phonemic complexity of grammemes in Taiwanese (sample size: about 1,100 words

	Grammeme group as defined by number of phonemes						
	1	2	3	4	5	6	7
Total of frequencies F	53	281	80	9	1	3	1
Total of group members M	5	37	16	7	1	2	1
F/M	10.6	7.6	5.0	1.3	1.0	1.5	1.0

Table 4. Discourse frequency and phonemic complexity of grammemes in Thai (sample size: about 2,000 words)

	Grammeme group as defined by number of phonemes					
	2	3	4	5	6	7
Total of frequencies F	43	488	167	6	6	4
Total of group members M	4	45	17	2	3	2
F/M	10.8	10.8	9.8	3.0	2.0	2.0

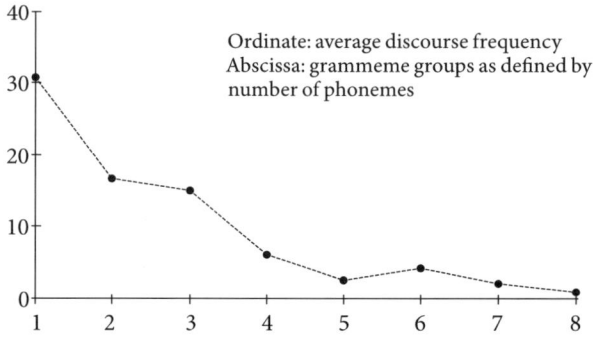

Figure 3. Discourse frequency and phonemic complexity of grammemes in Armenian

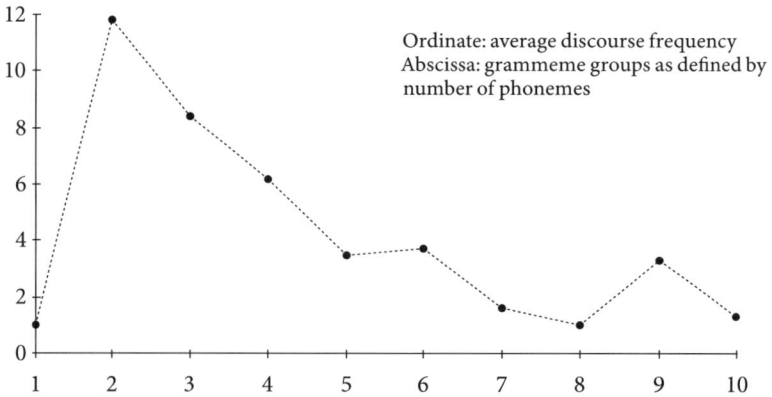

Figure 4. Discourse frequency and phonemic complexity of grammemes in Lakota (corpus taken from Pustet forthcoming)

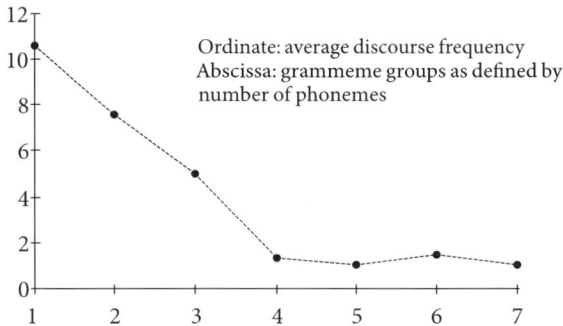

Figure 5. Discourse frequency and phonemic complexity of grammemes in Taiwanese

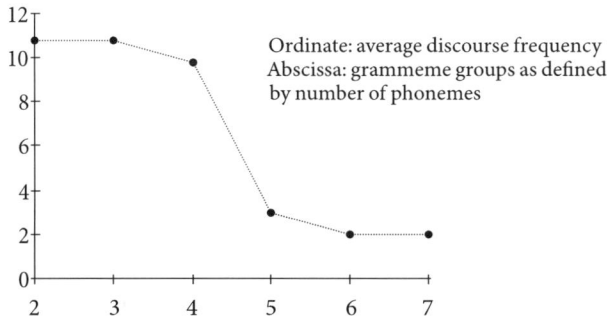

Figure 6. Discourse frequency and phonemic complexity of grammemes in Thai

to stating that in general, in all four languages, the values for structural complexity increase as the values for discourse frequency decrease. The hypothesis that Zipf's Law holds for the internal structure of grammatical systems is thus borne out.

Zipf's Law concerns the variables of structural complexity and discourse frequency only. But, as stated in section 1.1, Zipf also postulated a correlation of the latter variables with the variable of semantic complexity. It is in this area that Zipf's framework could be substantially elaborated on, if the nature of the subject under consideration, i.e. semantics, were more accessible to "hard" empirical research and, in particular, offered possibilities of quantificational description. Discourse frequency is quantifiable by counting discourse occurrences, and structural complexity is quantifiable by counting phonemes. But how should the meaning of linguistic items be quantified? Zipf's solution to this problem was counting dictionary translations (cf. section 1.1), but such a methodology can, of course, only be regarded as a first pioneering approximation to the issue. Tackling this problem is a task for future research, but certain observations regarding the structure of grammatical subsystems, such as case marking, suggest that ultimately, the question of whether semantic complexity correlates with frequency the way Zipf's theories predict will be answered in the affirmative. The statement that core cases, i.e. those cases which code valence-bound arguments (subject, object, ergative, absolutive) have a higher semantic scope than oblique cases, such as locative, directional, comitative, instrumental etc., should not be disputable. The mere fact that core arguments are valence-bound inevitably catapults core case markers to the top of the frequency hierarchy of case markers. Markers of oblique case roles are less frequent in discourse. But, as every practicing typologist would probably confirm, there is a cross-linguistic tendency for core case markers to be structurally less complex than oblique case markers, to the point at which the shortest possible expression format, i.e. zero expression, is employed. Thus, in the grammatical subdomain of case marking, higher semantic complexity, higher frequency, and lower structural complexity coincide. There is no reason to assume that these correlations do not hold in grammatical systems as a whole.

2.3. Interim conclusions

On the basis of the empirical data presented above, it seems safe to link grammaticalization theory with Zipf's model because grammatical systems do in fact exhibit at least one of the correlations which have been found to be constitutive for both grammaticalization theory and Zipf's model: within grammar, by and large, the length of linguistic items decreases as their discourse frequency increases (Zipf's Law). Moreover, it is more than likely that within grammatical systems, the variable of semantic complexity also abides by Zipfian principles.

It is important to note that Zipf's Law applies to grammatical systems **as a whole**, both in synchrony and diachrony. As for diachrony, particularly the research conducted within EG&UBM has already shown, in many ways, that **individual** grammatical (and lexical) items comply with Zipf's Law: frequency increase tends to entail shortening. But only a holistic approach of the kind laid out in Zipf's framework brings out the algorithmic nature of the interaction of discourse frequency and structural complexity. As diagrams 3 to 6 show, within a grammatical system, all individual elements seem to partake in an overall organizational pattern that, by and large, requires a specific value of structural complexity to converge with a specific frequency value in a given discourse sample in a given language. Thus, in the Armenian sample, the frequency of grammemes which have a structural complexity of three phonemes condenses around the value 15.0 (cf. table 1); in the Lakota sample, the frequency of grammemes which have a structural complexity of four phonemes condenses around the value 6.2 (cf. table 2); in the Taiwanese sample, the frequency of grammemes which have a structural complexity of seven phonemes condenses around the value 1.0 (cf. table 3); and so on. This powerful blueprint, which dictates the architecture of language-specific discourse structure, prescribes an approximate frequency value for every complexity value, whereby on the whole, the frequency value rises continually as the complexity value drops. Because Zipf's own method does not specifically target grammatical items, this area of research into language structure has, so far, been entirely uncharted territory.

An important side effect of these findings is a better understanding of the basic mechanisms underlying grammaticalization. The concomitance of frequency increase, structural reduction, and semantic expansion, which has been observed in countless case studies within grammaticalization theory, appears less mysterious if it can be identified as a reflex of the universal pattern of the organization of language systems which is proposed in Zipf's theories.

One aspect of grammaticalization, however, has puzzled theorists more than anything else: the fact that all processes which take place in grammaticalization are, for the most part, unidirectional. As the next section will show, embedding grammaticalization theory into Zipf's model should also be extremely helpful in the attempt to account for the much-debated unidirectionality of grammaticalization.

3. The unidirectionality of grammaticalization

The unidirectionality principle of grammaticalization is one of the hallmarks of grammaticalization theory. It states that all processes involved in grammaticalization are, on the whole, irreversible:

> As conceptual manipulation leads from lexical or less grammatical meanings to more grammatical ones, this process is unidirectional, and so are all developments in the process of grammaticalization. Although cases in the opposite direction have been reported, they may be viewed as exceptions to the unidirectionality principle.   (Heine et al. 1991: 212)

Unidirectionality phenomena have been known for centuries. Givón (1975) can be credited with initiating the theoretical discussion of unidirectionality in the more recent literature. For an extensive list of references which support the unidirectionality tenet, cf. Janda (2001: 298).

Grammaticalization theory describes a vast array of processes of language change. The claim that all developments in grammaticalization are, by and large, unidirectional, refers to all these processes, including, for instance, the alleged irreversibility of the developmental path from free element to clitic to affix, or from lexical to grammatical element. One important objection that has always been raised against grammaticalization theory is that there are numerous exceptions to the unidirectionality principle (for an extensive list of references on this, cf. Janda 2001: 292). Interestingly, many of these counterexamples are encountered in the latter two subdomains of grammaticalization, i.e. in the development from free element to clitic, and from lexical to grammatical element. Thus, to cite two almost overused examples one more time, the English noun *ism* originates in the suffix *-ism*; the English prepositions *up* and *down*, which can be considered grammatical or at least semi-grammatical elements, can nowadays be used as verbs, as in *he upped and left* and *he downed two tequilas*. For various additional examples of this kind, cf. Norde (2001: 235). Frajzyngier (1996, 1997b) acknowledges the overall unidirectionality of change from lexical to grammatical items, but explicitly challenges the unidirectionality tenet for cases in which a grammatical item develops from another grammatical item on the basis of the observation that in the domain of grammar, bidirectional change is relatively frequent. For instance, in Chadic languages, historical developments from temporal clause marker ('when') to conditional protasis marker ('if'), as well as from conditional protasis marker to temporal clause marker, have taken place (Frajzyngier 1997b).

The present study focuses exclusively on those three aspects of grammaticalization theory which also constitute the most basic components of Zipf's model. These parameters are structural complexity, semantic complexity, and discourse frequency. Other facets of grammaticalization theory will not be dealt with here, although many of these have, in fact, also been anticipated in Zipf's work (Zipf 1965a, 1965b).

Of the three basic Zipfian parameters, semantic complexity is clearly the most frequently discussed when it comes to producing arguments against the unidirectionality of grammaticalization, but most of this discussion actually evolves around developments from grammatical to lexical elements. However, it is questionable if such cases of grammaticalization reversal are really to be taken as examples of a reduction of semantic complexity. Why, for instance, should the English verbs *to up* and *to down* be regarded as semantically less complex than the prepositions *up* and *down* they are derived from? The problem which surfaces here is that semantics still defies investigation in scientifically accurate ways, and this, of course, includes the task of measuring semantic complexity. Semantic change is often so gradual, minor, and elusive that intuitions regarding changes in semantic complexity are difficult to verify. For instance, the Lakota verb *ohómni* 'to go around' has all the trappings of a full-fledged transitive verb. But *ohómni* 'to go around' has also developed into the postposition *ohómni* 'around', which has the morphosyntactic features which are characteristic for Lakota postpositions (Pustet 2000: 163f.). In certain morphosyntactic positions, however, neither verbal nor postpositional morphosyntax is present, and in many such contexts, a translation as both verb and postposition is adequate. Especially in such cases, it is hard to tell which interpretation of *ohómni* 'to go around/around' is the correct one, and, what is more, if the distinction matters at all, at least to the Lakota speaker. Fortunately, there do exist linguistic items which unequivocally illustrate the reversibility of semantic change, i.e. a development from a more abstract to a more specific meaning. For instance, the English noun *hound* used to mean 'dog in general'. Today, *hound* has assumed the more specific meaning of 'long-eared hunting dog which follows its prey by scent' (Campbell 2001: 135). An analogous example from the domain of grammar is diachronic change which transforms complementizers into sequential markers, as attested in Chadic languages:

> The development of complementizers into sequential markers … is evidence that grammaticalization may proceed from the more abstract to more concrete, con-

tradicting the unidirectionality hypothesis which assumes only change from more concrete to more abstract.   (Frajzyngier 1996: 467)

Sequential markers code relationships between events in the ontologically relatively tangible dimension of time, while complementizers code relationships between syntactic elements and can therefore be considered conceptually more abstract (Z. Frajzyngier, p.c.). Likewise, grammaticalization of nominal and verbal plural markers from the semantically more abstract category of demonstratives can be postulated in Chadic languages (Frajzyngier 1997a).

The possibility of reversing the increase of the discourse frequency of linguistic items in diachronic development, further, is not considered very strongly in CGT, in which the frequency parameter never figured that prominently. However, in practice, frequency decrease is a very common phenomenon—its pseudonym is obsolescence.

Although the unidirectionality principle has been, and is being, challenged at all levels (e.g. Campbell 2001, Newmeyer 2001), the extant literature hardly ever provides examples which document the reversibility of the structural reduction of linguistic elements. This is noteworthy because the development of structurally simpler from more complex forms plays such a crucial role in grammaticalization theory. In section 3.2, potential examples for the lengthening of linguistic items in diachronic change are given. For now, suffice it to say that the development of the Estonian question marker *es* from the affixal question marker *-s* (Campbell 2001: 128) attests the increase of the structural complexity of a grammatical element in the course of time.

The threat posed by counterexamples to the unidirectionality principle to the status of grammaticalization theory as a basic component of the theory of language in general has often been overestimated. Arguing that the mere existence of counterexamples to unidirectionality suffices to reject grammaticalization theory clearly overstates the case. As long as there is a statistical imbalance between changes that comply with grammaticalization theory and those that do not, to the effect that the former predominate significantly, grammaticalization will have to be acknowledged as a remarkable fact about language that is well worth theorizing about in its own right. Unfortunately, empirical data that determine the relative percentage of the two types of changes are not available, which is not surprising, given the complexity of the research required to compile the relevant data for only one language for only a short period of time. Newmeyer (1998: 275) estimates the ratio of grammaticalization processes proper and counterdirectional processes of language change at roughly 10:1. If this figure is correct, the quantitative imbalance between the two types of processes is statistically highly significant.

3.1. Explaining the (quasi-)unidirectionality of structural change

Although the need to explain the (quasi-)unidirectionality of grammaticalization is increasingly being recognized, few people have ever taken up this task, and none of the extant studies (e.g. Croft 2000: 158ff., Givón 1975, Haspelmath 1999) has made extensive use of the Zipfian framework. Phenomenologically speaking, the unidirectionality principle of grammaticalization is implied in Zipf's model (cf. figures 1 and 2): given that the older expression units are, on the whole, more frequent, shorter, and semantically more abstract than the newer ones (cf. section 1.2), linguistic elements can, on the whole, only be "upgraded" from less frequent to more frequent, from structurally "heavier" to structurally "lighter", and from semantically less complex to semantically more complex in diachronic change. The opposite developments would contradict the systematic link of high frequency, low structural complexity, and high semantic complexity with relative age which is part of the architecture of Zipf's model. This observation, however, does not yet clarify the **motivations** of the unidirectionality of grammaticalization. In what follows, it will be argued that Zipf's model also has the potential of providing a new and plausible explanation for the unidirectionality principle, at least as far as the (quasi-)irreversibility of structural reduction is concerned.

It should not be too far-fetched to assume that Zipf's parameters discourse frequency, structural complexity, and semantic complexity are, one way or another, interdependent. As will become evident in what follows, the nature of the relationship between frequency and structural complexity is well understood. However, opinions on the role of semantics relative to that of frequency and structural complexity diverge. In this theoretical context, particularly the relationship between semantics and frequency has been addressed in the extant literature. Frequency might determine semantic complexity, or semantic complexity might determine frequency. Especially in Bybee's work, evidence supporting both positions can be found. The two parameters might indeed stand in a relation of mutual dependency. For instance, Bybee and Hopper (2001: 13) and Bybee and Thompson (1997: 380) claim that frequency determines semantic complexity, while Bybee (2001: 165) argues that semantics determines frequency. Given the present state of the art, it is too early to settle the question about the potential causal connections between semantics and frequency, and between semantics and structural complexity. For this reason, the issue of the (quasi-)unidirectionality of semantic change will not be pursued any further in this study.

In contrast, there seems to be complete agreement on the nature of the relation of discourse frequency and structural complexity. Apparently, Zipf's assumption that frequency increase causes structural reduction, while the reverse does not apply, has never been called into question (for a confirmation of Zipf's view, cf. Bybee (2000: 72), Bybee (2001: 9).

> ... on the whole the comparative length or shortness of a word cannot be the cause of its relative frequency of occurrence because the speaker selects his words not according to their lengths, but solely according to the meanings of the words and the ideas he wishes to convey.   (Zipf 1965a: 29)

> Until it can be shown that lengthenings occur from frequency or shortenings from rarity, we may reasonably presume ... that, where frequency and abbrevia-

tory substitution are connected, the frequency is the cause of the abbreviatory substitution.   (Zipf 1965a: 36)

According to Zipf (1965a, 1965b), the causal connection between the variables of frequency and structural complexity is established by the **principle of least effort**, or **economy**, which Zipf regarded as the basic motivation of all statistical correlations he discovered, both in linguistics and beyond linguistics. Speech can be made more economical in terms of articulatory effort if higher-frequency items are kept short. A confirmation of this view can be found, for instance, in Newmeyer (1998: 253ff.).

Accepting the Zipfian argument that structural reduction is, via economy pressure, conditioned by frequency increase solves the problem of explaining the unidirectionality of structural change. If the discourse frequency of linguistic items dictates their structural complexity, and if the frequency of linguistic items, via obsolescence, may decrease in diachronic development, the result of frequency decrease should be an increase in structural complexity. But cases of increase in the structural complexity of linguistic items seem to be extremely rare. The reason for this asymmetry is immediately obvious if the economy principle is held responsible for the structural reduction of linguistic items in the event of frequency increase. Economy pressure applies in one direction only: it is plausible that economy causes shortening when frequency increases, but there is no compelling reason why linguistic items should be lengthened when their discourse frequency drops.

Under specific circumstances, lengthening processes may occur nevertheless. This, however, is not to be interpreted as a violation of the Zipf-based systemic connections sketched out above, but rather, as the logical consequence of yet another economy principle which is also addressed in Zipf's work.

3.2. Reductive vs. expansive economy and the lengthening of lexical items in Chinese languages

The empirical facts that exemplify processes of lengthening of linguistic items in diachronic change presented in this section are widely known. But these data have, so far, not been used as evidence against the unidirectionality of structural change.

In Chinese languages, lexical items tend to be semantically polyfunctional, the consequence being a high degree of ambiguity in language production. Within linguistic systems, ambiguity can be tolerated to a certain extent only, lest communication becomes ineffective. The solution to this problem, in Chinese languages, is large-scale compounding. Homonymy is effectively reduced by combining linguistic items with other elements which specify the meaning of the former:

> ... the threat of too many homophonous syllables has forced the language to increase the proportion of polysyllabic words, principally by means of ... compounding.   (Li and Thompson 1981: 14)

The feeling that there is a need to counteract the pervasive ambiguity of Chinese lexemes by means of compounding is also shared by native speakers of Chinese languages, and it is echoed in Haiman's (1985: 24f.) comment on the Chinese situation:

> The tendency to minimize the inventory of forms, while militating against synonymy, will tolerate homonymy, but not beyond the point where confusion may result. Beyond this point, another kind of 'linguistic therapy' may come into play, whereby homonyms are eliminated by a variety of ad hoc means, typically including borrowing and compounding.

Compounds which consist of elements which are synonyms or at least near-synonyms are not uncommon. This constellation is exemplified by the Mandarin lexeme $t\!s^h\!i$-$t\!\varc^h\!\acute{y}\varepsilon n$ 'to save (money, food etc.), to store, storage'. The components of this lexeme are $t\!s^h\!i$ 'to save, to store' and $t\!\varc^h\!\acute{y}\varepsilon n$ 'to save, to put in a storage room, to put money in the bank for saving'. The usage of these three lexemes is illustrated in examples (3) to (5).

(3) wǒ jào $t\!s^h\!i$-$t\!\varc^h\!\acute{y}\varepsilon n$ ʂáɹ u
     1SG want save   food stuff
     'I want to save food.'

(4) wǒ jào $t\!s^h\!i$ ʂáɹ u
     1SG want save food stuff
     'I want to save food.'

(5) wǒ jào $t\!\varc^h\!\acute{y}\varepsilon n$ ʂáɹ u
     1SG want save   food stuff
     'I want to save food.'

For $t\!s^h\!i$ 'to save, to store', the following additional translations are listed in a Mandarin dictionary (the order and grouping of the translations in the dictionary has been adopted unchanged):

(6) Additional meanings of $t\!s^h\!i$ 'to save, to store':
     1. besides, to eliminate, except, to exclude, divided by
     2. kitchen, cupboard
     3. to uproot, to hoe, hoe
     4. to alternate, deputy
     5. closet, cabinet
     6. to slaughter, butcher
     7. to hesitate
     8. little kid, chick
     9. name of a river in China
     10. rake for sowing and harvesting rice
     11. normal rake, name of city in Hunan province, disagreeing
     12. to cut grass, to feed, hay
     13. toad

16. to can
17. calf
18. to cut down smaller plants
19. bamboo used for weaving mats, name for a disease
20. tent-like mosquito screen

$ts^h\acute{\imath}$ thus has a total of 21 meanings, but such multifunctionality is by no means rare in Mandarin. As a matter of fact, lexemes with 50-odd different meanings are not exceptional in this language. By altering the tonal structure of $ts^h\acute{\imath}$, about 20 additional meanings can be obtained.

In contrast, the verb $t\varsigma^h\acute{y}\varepsilon n$ 'to save, to put in a storage room, to put money in the bank for saving', which merely has three additional meanings, is only mildly polyfunctional by Mandarin standards:

(7) Additional meanings of $t\varsigma^h\acute{y}\varepsilon n$ 'to save, to put in a storage room, to put money in the bank for saving':
  1. to survive, to live, to keep, to exist
  2. to squat, to crouch
  3. savings book

Do such instances of lengthening of words via compounding, which can be rated as counterexamples to the principle of the unidirectionality of structural change, have to be viewed as evidence against the validity of Zipf's model as well? No, because deeper immersion intoh Zipf's work suggests that this specific type of counterexample results from an additional economy principle which also has a great impact on linguistic structure.

The first economy principle, which is operative in the reduction of structural complexity during frequency increase, can be labeled the **reductive economy principle**. Earlier in this section, this principle has been discussed in relation to the structural complexity of individual linguistic items. But according to Zipf (1965b: 20), the reductive economy principle is also relevant for the size of the inventory of linguistic items a linguistic system as a whole is composed of:

> From the viewpoint of the speaker (the *speaker's economy*) who has the job of selecting not only the meanings to be conveyed but also the words that will convey them, there would doubtless exist an important latent economy in a vocabulary that consisted exclusively of one single word—a single word that would mean whatever the speaker wanted it to mean. Thus if there were m different meanings to be verbalized, this word would have m different meanings. For by having a single-word vocabulary the speaker would be spared the effort that is necessary to acquire and maintain a large vocabulary and to select particular words with particular meanings from this vocabulary.

It should be noted that **both** speaker and hearer profit from small categorical inventories in terms of reduced acquisition and storage efforts because both speaker and hearer have to acquire and store linguistic items. This minor issue aside, it is plausible that the economy-driven minimization of linguistic substance does not only manifest itself in the frequency-dependent number of **phonemes** per **expression unit**, but also in a tendency of keeping the number of (both lexical and grammatical) **categories** that make up complex **linguistic systems** as small as possible. Zipf continues:

> But from the viewpoint of the auditor (the *auditor's economy*), a single-word vocabulary would represent the acme of verbal labor, since he would be faced by the impossible task of determining the particular meaning to which the single word in a given situation might refer. Indeed from the viewpoint of the auditor, who has the job of deciphering the speaker's meanings, the important internal economy of speech would be found rather in a vocabulary of such size that it possessed a distinctly different word for each different meaning to be verbalized. Thus if there were *m* different meanings, there would be *m* different words, with one meaning per word. This one-to-one correspondence between different words and different meanings, which represents the *auditor's economy*, would save effort for the auditor in his attempt to determine the particular meaning to which a given spoken word referred. (Zipf 1965b: 21)

The Chinese "compounding hype" can be attributed to the general principle which is described in this quote. Since, via homonymy reduction, this principle acts to increase, rather than to reduce, the number of categories in a linguistic system, it will be referred to as the **expansive economy principle**. This principle arises from the cognitive effort invested in the act of decoding linguistic utterances and assigning meanings to them. If the number of categories within a given system is too small, the semantic load associated with individual categories is too heavy. As a consequence, ambiguity becomes rampant, and the coding system becomes ineffective and thus uneconomical.

Reductive and expansive tendencies have to be well balanced for a linguistic system to be maximally effective:

> Thus if there are an *m* number of different distinctive meanings to be verbalized, there will be (1) a *speaker's economy* in possessing a vocabulary of one word which will refer to all the *m* distinctive meanings; and there will also be (2) an opposing *auditor's economy* in possessing a vocabulary of *m* different words with *one* distinctive meaning for each word. Obviously the two opposing economies are in extreme conflict. (Zipf 1965b: 21)

In Chinese languages, inconvenient homonymy relations are eliminated by achieving greater distinctiveness of forms by means of compounding. The Mandarin lexeme $t\dot{s}^h\acute{i}$-$t\dot{c}^h\acute{y}\varepsilon n$ 'to save (money, food etc.), to store, storage' merely illustrates the first stage in the "lengthening" of words, during which both lexical components are still used as independent lexemes, as examples (4) and (5) demonstrate. Later, the lexical components involved might, one by one, become unproductive as full lexemes. Finally, their only remaining function might be that of a morphological component of the bipartite form in question. If both components lose their original status as full lexemes, and only the compound survives, a new, and structurally more complex, linguistic item has been created. Such developments are attested in all varieties of Chinese.

Thus, several pieces of the multi-faceted puzzle presented by grammaticalization theory ultimately fall in place if grammaticalization theory is integrated into Zipf's framework. The latter offers a motivation for the unidirectionality of structural change, and it also accounts for processes of Chinese-style lengthening of words which could be taken as prima facie evidence against the unidirectionality principle. In the Chinese case, the phenomenon of lengthening via compounding must be interpreted as the flip side of the economy coin, more specifically, as the response of the expansive economy principle to homonymy pressure.

4. Towards frequency-based approaches to language typology and language change

In sum, the preceding section has shown that Zipf's frequency-based framework can be used to account for various aspects of grammaticalization. Even more importantly, the language data presented above demonstrate that grammar abides by Zipfian principles. This study, in addition to the work which is currently done in the context of usage-based models of language, intends to stimulate a popularization of both cross-linguistic and diachronic approaches to language in which the parameter of discourse frequency receives the attention that it obviously deserves.

Pustet (2003), in which the usage of copulas with lexical items is investigated at the cross-linguistic level, illustrates just one of the various research opportunities that emerge from the Zipfian framework. This study discloses a global rule of copula distribution which can be directly derived from the parameter of discourse frequency and thus, from Zipfian principles. If only one of the three parts of speech noun, verb, and adjective is compatible with a copula in a given language, the copula combines with nouns, rather than with verbs and adjectives. Languages which employ copulas in combination with two parts of speech will employ them with nouns and adjectives but not with verbs. In some languages verbal predicates contain copulas, but in all these languages, nouns and adjectives are also combined with copulas in predicate position. This scale of copula compatibility, in which nouns rank over adjectives, while adjectives rank over verbs, is mirrored by an analogous scale of frequency of appearance in predicate position. In the context of a Zipfian argumentation the parallelism of the two scales can be motivated. In the ten languages investigated in Pustet (2003), nouns are least frequent in predicate position, adjectives are more frequent in predicate position, and verbs are most frequent in predicate position. Since copulas per se add on to the structural complexity of predicate phrases, Zipf's economy principle demands that the most frequent predicate types, i.e. verbal predicates, should be kept as short as possible. Next in line in terms of structural complexity are adjectival predicates, according to their rank in the scale of frequency of occurrence in discourse. On these grounds, as elements that increase the structural complexity of predicate phrases, copulas are least likely to occur with verbs, more likely to occur with adjectives, and most likely to occur with nouns.

Reverting to grammaticalization at this point, it remains to be clarified in what way the fairly theoretical findings of the present paper could be productively incorporated into more down-to-earth work in the area of grammaticalization. One of the claims made in this investigation concerns the potentially decisive role of discourse frequency in language change. If the research agenda for future studies of grammaticalization over longer time spans, as conducted within the framework of CGT, included systematic compilation of frequency data, the Zipf-based hypothesis which maintains that grammaticalization in the form of reductive change and/or development towards greater semantic complexity within long time periods is generally accompanied by frequency increase, would become testable. Further, the Zipfian model might add new perspectives to research into grammaticalization if the principle of the correlation of the parameter of discourse frequency with the parameters of semantic and structural complexity is exploited in detail. For instance, on the basis of the fact that specific values of structural complexity of linguistic items correlate strongly with specific frequency values, the occurrence of reductive change, i.e. shortening, of linguistic items in the process of language change should become more or less predictable. That is, as soon as a given element reaches a certain threshold value on the frequency parameter, reductive change can be expected to take place.

Despite its relatively ambitious goals, it seems realistic to conclude that the present study only touches upon the tip of an iceberg of dormant dimensions in linguistic research. Frequency-based approaches should, in due time, spawn a multitude of innovative and inspiring projects in the cross-linguistic and diachronic study of language.

Acknowlegdements

I am indebted to the following native speakers of Armenian, Lakota, Mandarin, and Thai for acting as language consultants for this study: Karen Kanokwan Benjasiriwan, Christina Yu-Wen Chen, †Mary Light, Armik Mirzayan, Florine Red Ear Horse, Shogher Shahverdyan, †Neva Standing Bear, and Garnik Tonoyan. I would also like to thank Zygmunt Frajzyngier for numerous thought-provoking comments on the original version of this paper.

References

Balasubrahmanyan, V. K. and S. Naranan. 1996. "Quantitative linguistics and complex system studies". *Journal of Quantitative Linguistics* 3: 177–228.

Barlow, M. and S. Kemmer (eds.). 2000. *Usage-based models of language*. Stanford: CSLI.

Berkenfield, C. 2001. "The role of frequency in the realization of English *that*". In J. L. Bybee and P. Hopper (eds.), 281–307.

Breiter, M. A. 1994. "Length of Chinese words in relation to their other systemic features". *Journal of Quantitative Linguistics* 1: 224–231.

Bybee, J. L. 1985. *Morphology: a study of the relation between meaning and form*. Amsterdam: Benjamins.

Bybee, J. L. 2000. "The phonology of the lexicon: evidence from lexical diffusion." In Barlow, M. and S. Kemmer (eds) (eds.), 65–85.

Bybee, J. L. 2001. *Phonology and language use*. Cambridge: Cambridge University Press.

Bybee, J. L. and P. Hopper (eds.) 2001. *Frequency and the emergence of linguistic structure*. Amsterdam: Benjamins.

Bybee, J. L. and P. Hopper 2001. "Introduction to frequency and the emergence of linguistic structure". In Bybee, J. L. and P. Hopper (eds.), 1–24.

Bybee, J. L. and S. Thompson. 1997. "Three frequency effects in syntax". *BLS* 23: 65–85.

Campbell, L. 2001. "What's wrong with grammaticalization?" *Language Sciences* 23: 113–161.

Croft, W. 2000. *Explaining language change. An evolutionary approach*. Harlow, UK: Longman.

Frajzyngier, Z. 1996. *Grammaticalization of the complex sentence: a case study in Chadic*. Amsterdam: Benjamins.

Frajzyngier, Z. 1997a. "Grammaticalization of number: from demonstratives to nominal and verbal plural." *Linguistic Typology* 1: 193–242.

Frajzyngier, Z. 1997b. "Bidirectionality of grammaticalization." In: Herbert, R. K. (ed.), *African Linguistics at the crossroads. Papers from Kwaluseni*, 17–38. Cologne: Köppe.

Givón, T. 1975. "Serial verbs and syntactic change: Niger-Congo". In *Word order and word order change*, C. N. Li (ed.), 47–112. Austin: University of Texas Press.

Haiman, J. 1985. *Natural syntax. Iconicity and erosion*. Cambridge: Cambridge University Press.

Haspelmath, M. 1999. "Why is grammaticalization irreversible?" *Linguistics* 37: 1043–1068.

Heine, B., U. Claudi and F. Hünnemeyer 1991. *Grammaticalization. A conceptual framework*. Chicago: University of Chicago Press.

Heine, B. and T. Kuteva. 2002. *World lexicon of grammaticalization*. Cambridge: Cambridge University Press.

Hopper, P. J. 1987. "Emergent grammar". *BLS* 13: 139–157.

Hopper, P. J. and E. C. Traugott. 1993. *Grammaticalization*. Cambridge: Cambridge University Press.

Janda, R. D. 2001. "Beyond "pathways" and "unidirectionality": on the discontinuity of language transmission and the counterability of grammaticalization". *Language Sciences* 23: 265–340.

Joseph, B. D. 2001. "Is there such a thing as "grammaticalization"?" *Language Sciences* 23: 163–186.

Langacker, R. 1987. *Foundations of cognitive grammar. Vol. 1: Theoretical prerequisites*. Stanford: Stanford University Press.

Lehmann, C. 1982. "Thoughts on grammaticalization. A programmatic sketch." Köln: Institut für Sprachwissenschaft [*akup* 48].

Levickij, V. V., J. J. Kiiko and S. V. Spolnicka. 1996. "Quantitative analysis of verb polysemy in Modern German". *Journal of Quantitative Linguistics* 3: 132–135.

Li, C. and S. Thompson. 1981. *Mandarin Chinese. A functional reference grammar.* Berkeley: University of California Press.

Mandelbrot, B. 1977. *The fractal geometry of nature.* New York: Freeman.

Newmeyer, F. J. 1998. *Language form and language function.* Cambridge, MA: MIT.

Newmeyer, F. J. 2001. "Deconstructing grammaticalization". *Language Sciences* 23: 187- 229.

Norde, M. 2001. "Deflexion as a counterdirectional factor in grammatical change." *Language Sciences* 23: 231–264.

Pustet, R. 2000. "Lakota postpositions". *International Journal of American Linguistics* 66: 157– 180.

Pustet, R. 2003. *Copulas. Universals in the categorization of the lexicon.* Oxford: Oxford University Press.

Pustet, R. Forthcoming. *Lakota texts.* Lincoln: University of Nebraska Press.

Pustet, R. 2004. "Zipf and his heirs." *Language Sciences* 26: 1–25.

Traugott, E. C. and B. Heine (eds.) 1991. *Approaches to grammaticalization.* 2 Vols. Amsterdam: Benjamins.

Zipf, G. K. 1965a [1935]. *The psycho-biology of language.* Cambridge, MA: MIT.

Zipf, G. K. 1965b [1949]. *Human behavior and the principle of least effort.* New York: Hafner.

Chapter 8

On the assumption of the sentence as the basic unit of syntactic structure

Marianne Mithun

University of California, Santa Barbara

The goal of most syntactic theories has been the specification of the structure of the sentence. The sentence is a useful point of departure, but various kinds of evidence suggest that it may not be the basic, universal, impermeable, privileged cognitive unit often assumed, systematically delineated by coinciding prosodic, semantic, and grammatical boundaries. Here evidence is presented from the development of certain markers in Hualapai, which have been extended from the domain of the sentence, where they specify syntactic dependency, into discourse, where they signal pragmatic dependency. This development suggests that linguistic structure does not necessarily stop at the sentence.

∿

Most syntactic theories have taken the sentence as the fundamental unit of grammatical structure. It is of course recognized that clause boundaries *within* sentences may not always be sharp, as when lexical verbs are in the process of evolving into auxiliaries, but it is generally taken for granted that the outer boundaries of sentences are easily delineated. As an idealization, the sentence is certainly a useful starting point for syntactic analysis. It may, however, define realistic boundaries for grammatical structure. Here we will examine evidence of the permeability of these boundaries from Hualapai, also known as Walapai, a language of the Yuman family spoken in Arizona.

In languages of the Yuman family, dependent clauses are identified by suffixes termed 'switch-reference' markers, following an important 1967 article on such patterns by William Jacobsen. Munro described the phenomenon as follows.

> The suffixes -*k* and -*m* are subordinators ("switch-reference" markers) whose function is to show whether the subject of the marked verb is the same as (-*k*) or different from (-*m*) that of a following or, generally, syntactically "higher" verb. (Munro 1976a: 100–101)

Examples of these markers can be seen in the Hualapai sentences in (1). (Slightly different orthographic conventions are used in the various sources on the language, some designed for the community, others for academic purposes. In examples cited here, the conventions of the primary sources are retained.)

(1)   Hualapai switch reference: Watahomigie et al. (2001: 413)

    a. *Marych*   *he'h*   *nyitu:yk̲*
        Mary-ch   he'-h   nyi-tu:y-k̲
        Mary-SUBJECT dress-that SUBORDINATE-take.off-SAME
        'After Mary took off her dress,
        đathgwi:lkwiny.
        đathgi:l-k-wi-ny
        wash-SAME-do-PAST
        she washed it.'

    b. *Malindach vak*   *nyiva:m̲*
        Malinda-ch va-k   nyi-wa:-m̲
        M-SUBJECT this.place-at SUBORD-come.here-DIFFERENT
        'When Malinda came here,
        Cindych   *đu Banyà:nyuwá ya:mkyuny.*
        Cindy-ch   đu Banya:nyuwa ya:m-k-yu-ny
        Cindy-SUBJECT just Phoenix   go-SAME-be-PAST
        Cindy had just gone to Phoenix.'

Such 'switch-reference' constructions have received extensive discussion in articles and grammars (Langdon 1970, 1978, Couro and Langdon 1975, Kendall 1975, 1976, Chung 1976, Munro 1976a, 1976b, 1981, Winter 1976, Yamamoto 1976, Slater 1977, Langdon and Munro 1979, Redden 1980, Gordon 1983a, 1983b, 1986, Haiman and Munro, eds. 1983, Hardy 1979, 1982, 1983, Hardy and Gordon 1980, Hinton 1984, Miller 1992, Watahomigie et al. 2001, and others.) Winter 1976 and Langdon 1978 have shown that the pattern and the markers themselves, *-k for 'same subject' and *-m for 'different subject' can be reconstructed for Proto-Yuman. Researchers have noted that the marked clauses need not be subordinate, but just dependent. The -k and -m markers may link semantically coordinate clauses, as in (2).

(2)   Hualapai coordinate clauses: Watahomigie et al. (2001: 61, 415)

    a. *Rhiánnonch* *he'h*   *tuyk̲*   *đathgwi:lkwiny.*
        Rhiannon-ch he'-h   tuy-k̲   đathgwi:l-k-wi-ny
        R-SUBJECT   dress-that take.off-SAME wash-SAME-do-PAST
        'Rhiannon took off the dress and washed it.'

    b. *Johnach*   *Mary baeqm̲*   *mi:kiny.*
        John-ch   Mary beq-m̲   mi:k-i-ny
        J-SUBJECT Mary hit.with.fist-DIFFERENT cry-SAME-say-PAST
        'John hit Mary and she cried.'

The markers are pervasive throughout the Yuman languages. Many simple sentence structures in English have complex sentence counterparts in these languages.

(3) Hualapai complex constructions: Watahomigie et al. (2001: 414)
  a. 'Wi:hch   'i:l<u>k</u>   vayúmkyu.
      'wi:-h-ch   'i:l-<u>k</u>   va-yum-k-yu
      canyon-that-SUBJ be.steep-<u>SAME</u> INTNS-be.intensely-<u>SAME</u>-be
      'The canyon is very steep.'
      (lit. 'The canyon is steep and it is very much so.')
  b. Nyach   vo:<u>k</u>   jigmi:ml   ya:myuny.
      nya-ch   vo:-<u>k</u>   jigmi:m-l   ya:m-yu-ny
      I-SUBJECT 1.walk-<u>SAME</u> canyon-into 1.go-be-PAST
      'I walked down into the canyon.'
      (lit. 'I walked and into the canyon I went.')

The -k and -m suffixes are even more pervasive than might be expected due in part
to the extensive use of auxiliary constructions. The alert reader may have noticed
that most of the final verbs in the examples above are complex, containing both a
lexical verb root such as 'wash' or 'go' and a more general suffix such as 'be' or 'do'. The
four Hualapai auxiliaries are -yu 'be', -wi 'do', -i 'say', and -yi 'feel'. The first tends to
be used in intransitive clauses, the second in active, transitive clauses, the third in
clauses involving noise, and the fourth in clauses indicating emotion. Langdon 1978
reconstructs the auxiliary constructions to Proto-Yuman. Their diachronic source
is easily traced to complex sentences in which the modern auxiliaries were matrix
verbs, and the modern lexical verbs were subordinate to them. The embedded lexical verbs carried same-subject markers, since their subjects were coreferential with
those of the matrix clause. This suffix remains embedded within the auxiliary constructions in the modern languages.

(4) Hualapai auxiliary constructions: Watahomigie 2001: 413, 414
  a. Đathgwi:l<u>k</u>winy.
      đathgi:l-<u>k</u>-wi-ny
      wash-<u>SAME</u>-AUX.do-PAST
      'She washed it.'
  b. Cindych   du Banyà:nyuwá ya:m<u>k</u>yuny.
      Cindy-ch   du Banya:nyuwa ya:m-<u>k</u>-yu-ny
      C-SUBJECT just Phoenix   go-<u>SAME</u>-AUX.be-PAST
      'Cindy had just gone to Phoenix.'
  c.. Vayúm<u>k</u>yu.
      va-yum-<u>k</u>-yu
      INTENSIFIER-be.intensely-<u>SAME</u>-AUX.be
      'It is very much so.'

There has been extensive discussion of the factors governing choices between the
two switch-reference markers. Langdon and Munro conclude that clauses linked
by the same-subject marker do not in fact always show the same subject. Neither do
they show coreference of agents or of topics.

The evidence presented in this paper should demonstrate that languages with the switch-reference device present their speakers with situations where the choice of one or the other cannot be based on purely grammatical grounds. We have shown that the choices speakers make in these circumstances are not unmotivated and in some instances agree across languages, but that no single category, grammatical or semantic, can be invoked as the unique determinant of the choice of same or different markers, although the examples discussed have been shown to each have their own rational motivation. It appears, then, that when the obvious criteria fail, other ones are chosen in ways that are compatible with one or several of the components (syntactic or semantic) of the formal function involved.   (Langdon and Munro 1979: 340)

The issue of interest to us here is actually not the choice between *-k* and *-m*, but when such a marker is used at all. The conditions of use vary across the languages. The Hualapai tale in (5) below was tape-recorded by Werner Winter in 1956, then later transcribed and translated. (Winter's linguistic transcription is retained, with spaces separating auxiliaries from their associated verbs. Winter provides morpheme-by-morpheme glossing as well, omitted here for reasons of space.) The tale opens with a series of four sentences, each translated as an independent sentence in English followed by a period, but ending in the same-subject marker *-k*. (Some of the lines are themselves complex sentences, with internal switch-reference markers as well.)

(5) Hualapai tale: Winter 1998: 149-151, T. McGee, speaker (1956)
   1. *Pa' pqi' hwak-:y-k ha-k ñ-wa:y-θ-k̲.*
      'A man and a woman were living together.
   2. *Mat-ka-v-yu-k pa:y-k-yu-k̲.*
      The two of them lived somewhere.
   3. *Va-m pe:m-k̲.*
      From there they went away.
   4. *He' s-ya:v-k va-m pe:m-k̲.*
      Starting from there, the two left.
   5. *Ha:-k-t-kwi-:v-a-k va:-m-:ca'.*
      They came to Peach Springs.
   6. *Wi:-k-ña-k va:-m-:ca'.*
      They came to Blue Mountain.'

The tale continues with a direct quotation without a switch-reference marker, but then resumes with two more independent sentences, each ending in a marker.

   7. *Swa-v-te' ñu' qwa:w-m ma:'hk̓e'.*
      "'You carry a big olla on your head.
   8. *Ka-k ha-:v-c ke' yu-m '-θi-:ca' '-t-'op-hi-k 'i-m̲.*
      There will be no water for us to drink," [the man] said.
   9. *Va-m '-pe:m-k va-m '-pe:m-k̲.*
      The two of us went on and on.

10. *Ha-yo:-wo' si:'.*
    He identified a water hole.
11. *Mat-si:-k wi:-vak 'i'.*
    He called the place Awl Rock.'

This section is followed by another series of 10 lines carrying switch-reference markers before there is another unmarked sentence. Some of the marked lines might be comparable to conjoined clauses in English, such as (14) and (15), but others were translated and punctuated as English independent sentences.

12. *Ha-m va' '-pe:m-k̲.*
    'So we went on.
13. *Wil-m '-ñ-t-miñ-m̲*
    As we crossed [a thicket of] bushes,
14. *kθar-ña-sram-:v-c v-lel-:v ñ-'i-m̲;*
    my coyote shawl was torn;
15. *wil-:h-c ñ-lel-m̲.*
    the brush tore it.
16. *Wa-ñ-c-c-pe-m̲.*
    He scolded me.
17. *Va'-va'-yu-k va-m '-pe:m̲.*
    In this way we went on.
18. *Mat-si:-k wi:-k-mol-:v-o' 'o-k̲.*
    He named the places; [one] he called Lone Rock.
19. *Mat-k-skyal-a' '-k mat-qa:y-k-wa-:c 'i-k '-k̲.*
    [Another one] he called Open Place; [a third one] Where-There-Is-Plenty-of-Mud.
20. *Wi:-k-htat 'i-k wi:-ka-re-:v-a' 'i-k mat-si:-k̲.*
    He identified Cactus Mountain and Rock-Where-They-Play; he named the places.
21. *Ha'v-'im-k c-ya:m-k̲.*
    He said that and made [me] go on.
22. *Ha-v-k-lav-lav-a' ha' c-va:-ma'.*
    He made me reach Dripping Water.'

The final section consists of four marked lines, before the final independent sentence.

23. *Va-m '-pe:m-k '-pe:m-k̲.*
    'We went on from there.
24. *Ña '-sram ñ-lel:v-m̲.*
    My shawl was torn;
25. *wa-ñ-c-c-pek va'v-'i-k va'v-'i-m̲.*
    he kept scolding me.

26. *Tu 'va'va' '-yu-k̲.*
I was just [ashamed] all the time.
27. *Na-mi:r '-vok-:c-'-yu-ñ.*
At last we [turned around and] came back home.'

The switch-reference markers can be seen to chunk the text as in (6). Each sentence ending in a switch-reference marker has been grouped with the following sentence. A line is skipped after sentences with no switch-reference marker.

(6)   Text pattern: Winter (1998:149-151), from Tim McGee in 1956

A man and a woman were living together.	SAME
The two of them lived somewhere.	SAME
From there they went away.	SAME
Starting from there, the two left.	SAME
They came to Peach Springs.	
They came to Blue Mountain.	
"You carry a big olla on your head.	
There will be no water for us to drink,"	
the man said.	DIFFERENT
The two of us went on and on.	SAME
He identified a water hole.	
He called the place Awl Rock.	
So we went on.	SAME
As we crossed a thicket of bushes,	DIFFERENT
my coyote shawl was torn;	DIFFERENT
the brush tore it.	DIFFERENT
He scolded me.	DIFFERENT
In this way we went on.	DIFFERENT
He named the places; one he called Lone Rock.	SAME
Another one he called Open Place;	SAME
a third one he called Where-There-Is-Plenty-of-Mud.	SAME
He identified Cactus Mountain and Rock-Where-They-Play;	SAME
he named the places.	SAME
He said that and made me go on.	SAME
He made me reach Dripping Water.	
We went on from there.	SAME
My shawl was torn;	DIFFERENT
he kept scolding me.	DIFFERENT
I was just ashamed all the time.	SAME
At last we turned around and came back home.	

The proportion of marked dependent clauses to unmarked independent sentences in (6) is typical of the extensive set of Hualapai texts recorded by Winter. The density of such structures, along with their distribution, suggests that the -*k* and -*m* markers are no longer restricted to marking strict syntactic dependency within single sentences. They apparently link pragmatically-related, independent sentences. The earlier function of marking syntactic dependency has been extended beyond the boundary of the sentence into discourse, where the switch-reference suffixes link elements of larger events

We might question whether the diachronic development did indeed move from within the clause outward into discourse. Within Hualapai (and throughout the Yuman family), the diachronic sources of the markers can still be identified. Suffixes with the same shapes as the switch-reference markers appear elsewhere in the grammar. Earlier researchers wondered whether the various occurrences of -*k* and -*m* should be treated as separate items related by homonymy; or as single, polysemous markers; or as single markers each with one unifying, abstract meaning. Munro (1976a, 1976b), Winter (1976), and Langdon (1978) have proposed that relations among the markers in their various functions might be diachronic. In light of what we now know about processes of grammatical change, this last approach makes the most sense.

Alongside of the same-subject marker -*k* is a locative noun case suffix -*k* translated variously 'at, on, near, close to, to, toward'. It can indicate location at a place, or direction toward the speaker or another deictic center. Alongside of the different-subject marker -*m* is an ablative/instrumental/comitative noun case suffix translated 'from, away, along, over, by, with'. It can indicate motion at a distant location, or direction away from the speaker or another deictic center. The same noun case suffixes appear throughout the Yuman family.

(7) Hualapai locative case -*k*: Watahomigie et al. (2001: 40, 45, 45)

    a. *Óloch*   *'ha:h<u>k</u>*   *skwi:kyu.*
        olo-ch   'ha:-h-<u>k</u>   skwi:-k-yu.
        horse-SUBJECT water-that-<u>LOCATIVE</u> stand-SAME-be
        'A horse is standing at the water.'

    b. *Nya đálach*   *'wa:va<u>k</u>*   *va:kyuny.*
        nya đála-ch   'wa:-va-<u>k</u>   va:-k-yu-ny.
        I   father-SUBJ house-this-<u>LOCATIVE</u> come-SAME-be-PAST
        'My father came to this house.'

    c. *Nyach hé'va*   *gwèjámo<u>k</u>*   *'yo:winy.*
        nya-ch hé'-v-a   gwčjámo-<u>k</u>   '-yo:-wi-ny.
        I-SUBJ dress-this-DEF dump-<u>LOCATIVE</u> 1-get-do-PAST
        'I got this dress at the dump.'

(8) Hualapai ablative/inst -*m*: Watahomigie et al. (2001: 46, 43, 43)

    a. *Nya jíđach*   *'wa:v-<u>m</u>*   *jibámkyuny.*
        nya jiđa-ch   'wa:-v-<u>m</u>   jibam-k-yu-ny
        I   mother-SUBJ house-this-<u>ABLATIVE</u> go.out-SAME-be-PAST
        'My mother went out of this house.'

   b. *Ba:hch*   *'háđa*   *i'ívm*   *a:vkwiny.*
      ba:-ha-ch   'háđ-a   i'ív-<u>m</u>   a:v-k-wi-ny
      man-that-SUBJ dog-DEF stick-this-<u>INST</u> hit-SAME-do-PAST
      'The man hit the dog with the stick.'

   c. *Cindych Joriginem*   *hwak'k*   *gwe*   *májkwi.*
      Cindy-ch Jorigine-<u>m</u>   hwak-k   gwe   ma-j-k-wi
      C-SUBJ   J-<u>COMITATIVE</u> together-SAME thing eat-PL-SAME-do
      'Cindy is eating with Jorigine'
      = 'Cindy and Jorigina are eating together.'

The markers can locate events in time, in association with nouns or larger phrases.

(9)   Hualapai temporal adverbial *-m*: Watahomigie et al. 2001: 58-9
   a. *Nyach*   *màkanya:m*   *gwe*   *'đinyu:đ'winy.*
      nya-ch   màkanya:-<u>m</u> gwe   '-đinyu:d-'-wi-ny
      I-SUBJECT yesterday-<u>at</u> thing 1-write-1-do-PAST
      'I wrote (<u>at</u>) yesterday.'

   b. *Yapa:ch vilwi:vm*   *'vo:may'yu.*
      yapa:ch vilwi:v-<u>m</u>   '-vo:m-ay-'-yu.
      night   be.in.middle-<u>at</u> 1-go.home-IRREALIS-1-be
      'I will go home <u>at</u> midnight.'

It is easy to see how such case markers could be extended from inflectional markers on nouns to larger constituents, forming adverbials. Redden provides the example of a clause inflected as an instrument with the ablative/instrumental *–m*. He notes that the *-m* at the end of the clause 'when it eats food' cannot be serving as a different-subject marker, since that clause has the same subject as the matrix clause 'a child grows'.

(10)   Hualapai adverbial *-m*: Redden (1980: 68)
     Hmány-a-č   *kwček-má-v*   *nyi-má-m*
     child-the-SUBJECT something-eat-this SUBORDINATE-eat-<u>m</u>
     táy-ò-k-wi
     grow.big-get-SAME-do
     'A child grows when it eats food.'

Redden suggests that a more literal translation would be 'With/by eating food, a child grows'. He observes that the *-m* suffix at the end of the first clause in (11) below could be interpreted either as a cause/instrument of my getting up, or as a switch-reference marker, since the subjects of the two clauses are indeed different.

(11)   Hualapai adverbial *-m*: Redden (1980: 69)
     Hmány-a-č   *nyi-mí-m*   *mán-ik.*
     child-the-SUBJECT SUBORDINATE-cry-<u>m</u> arise-k
     'When the baby cries, I get up.'

Comparative evidence confirms the direction of development of the Hualapai dependency markers. The use of -*k* and -*m* as inflectional case endings on nouns, and as markers of syntactic dependency on clauses, can be reconstructed for Proto-Yuman. Individual languages show further developments in various directions, but the extension of the markers into discourse is not a general phenomenon in the family.

3. From syntactic dependency to pragmatic relatedness

The use of originally syntactically dependent clause structures as independent sentences is considerably more widespread than is often recognized. It has been described in languages of the Eskimo-Aleut family by Kalmár (1982), Jacobson (1995), Miyaoka (1997), Mithun (2002a, 2003) and others; in Japanese by Iwasaki (1993, 2000) and others; in languages of the Carib family of South America by Gildea (1997, 1998); in Barbareño Chumash by Mithun (2002b); in Navajo by Mithun (2002a); in a number of African languages by Frajzyngier (2001, 2004), Frajzyngier with Shay 2002,), and in other languages as well. An extensive survey of such phenomena in languages from a variety of families and areas is in Evans (to appear). It appears that the development of erstwhile syntactically-dependent structures into independent sentences can come about in several different ways.

Gildea (1997, 1998) has proposed that some independent sentences in the modern Carib languages are descended from earlier nominalized clauses. He hypothesizes that some of these originated as nominalized complements of copular sentences of the form *It is/will be the city's destruction by the enemy*. The pronominal subject *it* was lost, and the original copula and nominalizer were reanalyzed together as a tense marker. Other independent sentences are hypothesized to have originated as the objects of complements of postpositions in copular sentences: *He is on the destruction of the city*. The postposition and nominalizer were reanalyzed together as a tense marker.

The development of auxiliary constructions in Yuman languages shows certain parallels with the Carib developments, though no nominalization was involved. As noted earlier, many sentences contain the same-subject suffix -*k* inside of the matrix verb. This is presumably due to the diachronic origins of auxiliary constructions in complex sentences, whose matrix verbs eroded into the modern auxiliary enclitics 'be', 'do', 'say', 'feel', etc. The lexical verbs in such constructions, such as 'run' in (12) below, originated in clauses subordinate to those matrix verbs. Since the subjects of the subordinate clauses were always coreferential with those of the matrix clause, the subordinate clauses ended in the same-subject marker –*k*, which remains inside the modern verb forms.

(12)   Hualapai auxiliary construction: Watahomigie et al. (2001: 163)
    Amúch   *viyámkyu.*
    amu'-ch   viyam-k-yu.
    mountain.sheep-SUBJECT run-SAME-AUX.be
    'A mountain sheep is running.'

Since third person subjects are not overtly represented within the verbal morphology, none appears within the modern auxiliary construction, either in association with the auxiliary or the lexical verb. (Third person subject prefixes are often included by grammarians in the glosses of verbs because of their meaningful absence, which contrasts with the first and second person subject prefixes: 3.run-SAME-AUX. be '[he/she/it] ran'.) The process described for Carib does not appear to underlie the extension of the Yuman switch-reference construction to independent sentences, however.

In his broad-based study of the use of dependent structures as independent sentences, Evans (to appear) explicitly excludes cases like those discussed by Gildea (as well as the Yuman auxiliary constructions) from what he terms 'insubordination'.

> My definition also requires that the resultant construction draw its material from only the old subordinate clause. This is to distinguish it from cases of clause union which end up including elements of an erstwhile subordinate clause (e.g. participial forms, or a causativized verb root) in addition to elements of the erstwhile main clause (e.g. an auxiliary, or a causativizing element) ... Also excluded are cases where former main verbs are reduced to particles or suffixes to an erstwhile subordinate verb which has become the new main verb.' (ms: 15)

Evans traces the development of all insubordinate constructions to the ellipsis of a matrix clause. Differences in function among the various types of insubordinate constructions are attributed to the different matrix clauses that have been omitted.

The missing matrix analysis is certainly a reasonable hypothesis about the source of the constructions discussed by Evans, but it cannot account for the Hualapai developments. In Hualapai, the dependent markers indicate pragmatic relations of sentences to the discourse as a whole, rather than to a particular missing matrix clause. Long series of sentences may be marked as background information to the overall storyline in narrative, or as closely-related sequences of events within larger episodes.

Evans does note that the functions of some modern 'insubordination' constructions may not always be directly derived from the ellipsis of a matrix clause. Sometime after their original development through matrix clause ellipsis, he proposes, insubordination constructions may take on new meanings associated with the circumstances of their use. Yuman switch-reference suffixes on independent sentences do appear to have taken on certain meanings from their contexts of use in the various languages, but it is not clear that their antecedents should be traced to structures from which specific matrix clauses were omitted. For Hualapai, Redden notes that a final different-subject marker -*m* 'can indicate that some sort of consequences or results are expected, required, or necessary' (1980: 70). He provides the examples in (13) below.

(13) Hualapai expected consequences: Redden 1980: 70

    a. *Ólo-č*   *wí-l*   *yá-č-m-a-<u>m</u>.*
        horse-SUBJECT rock.canyon-into go-PL-TENSE-<u>DIFFERENT</u>
        'The horses went down into the canyon.'

    b. *Kúl-a-č*   *wí yá-l*   *yúr-<u>m</u>.*
        rabbit-the-SUBJECT rock this-into enter-<u>DIFFERENT</u>
        'The rabbit went in under there.'

    c. *Nyi-kwáy*   *vi-táy*
        SUBORDINATE-clothes intense-heavy
        'Their winter clothes
        nyi-wí-č-o-č   *páy-a qáč-<u>m</u>.*
        SUBORDINATE-have-PL-that-SUBJ all-the be.small-<u>DIFFERENT</u>
        are all too small.'

Redden describes their meaning as follows.

> In the above sentences, the speaker expects the hearer to draw certain conclusions from the conditions stated. The final *-m* is much like a final *and* in English spoken with a level, sustained intonation. In the first sentence, the implication is that it will be a lot of trouble to find the horses that have wandered down into the canyon. In the second sentence, the hearer is expected to do something about getting the rabbit out of the hole. In the third, it is implied that the children will have to have new winter clothes since the old ones are too small.   (Redden 1980: 70)

Unlike the constructions described by Evans, these constructions with sentence-final different-subject marker *-m* do not appear to have originated with the deletion of any particular matrix clause. They do appear to have taken on certain connotations through association with circumstances typically surrounding their use, the fact that the different-subject marker *-m* originally signaled the dependent status of its clause, creating the expectation that another clause would follow.

In any case, the Hualapai independent *-k/-m* construction does not appear to have arisen through the mechanisms outlined by Gildea and Evans. There is no trace of copular material resembling that in the Carib constructions described by Gildea, nor of specific, identifiable, deleted matrix clauses along the lines described by Evans.

A third kind of mechanism by which dependent structures can evolve is proposed by Iwasaki (1993, 2000) in his discussion of the development of certain Japanese independent sentence types from dependent clauses. In Japanese of the Heian period (circa ninth through twelfth centuries), relative clause (attributive) constructions came to be used as independent sentences with specific functions: marking background information in prose, and exclamation or suppressed assertion in poetry. In Middle Japanese the formal distinction between the finite and attributive forms disappeared as a result of phonological change. But the functional contrast was subsequently renewed with different grammatical material when nominalized clauses came to be used as independent sentences. Iwasaki notes that the modern nominalized sentences are characterized as having an explanatory flavor, 'expressing the background for some facts' (1993: 25). The originally dependent syntactic structures came to be used as independent sentences precisely to convey the 'dependent, background nature of a sentence in relation to foreground conclusive sentences in textual structure' (2000: 237-238). Iwasaki proposes that the illocutionless nature of the earlier subordinate forms gave rise to the discourse dependency of the later forms, often interpreted as explanation. The mechanism proposed by Iwasaki, that is the direct extension of syntactically dependent clause constructions to uses beyond the boundaries of the sentence, is more in line with the scenarios apparently behind the Hualapai developments seen here.

4. Conclusion

The goal of most syntactic theories has been the specification of the structure of the sentence: simple, compound, or complex. The sentence is certainly a useful point of departure for understanding much about the syntactic structure of many languages. At the same time, it may not be the universal, impermeable, cognitive unit often assumed, systematically delineated by coinciding prosodic, semantic, and grammatical boundaries.

In Hualapai, which has developed explicit markers of syntactic dependency, these markers have been extended beyond the domain of the complex sentence into discourse. The same general process of extension can be seen in both languages, from marking syntactic relations among clauses to pragmatic relations among syntactically independent sentences. In discourse, the Hualapai dependency markers are exploited to signal cohesion, marking statements that together comprise a larger discourse unit.

Our view of the sentence as a distinctive, static, even innate category may be overly simplistic, perhaps colored by the norms of European literacy. Most of us are all too familiar with the run-on sentences typical of early student papers; in many cases, the structure of the sentence is something that must be taught. If our syntactic analyses are based uniquely on written renditions of single sentences constructed or elicited in isolation through translation, we may miss some of the subtleties of the syntactic structures we are trying to understand, as well as the forces that create them.

Abbreviations

AUX	Auxiliary	INTNS	Intensifier	POSS	Possessor
DEF	Definite	OBJ	Object	SUBJ	Subject
INST	Instrumental	PL	Plural	SUBORD	Subordinate

References

Chung, Sandra. 1976. "Compound tense markers in Tolkapaya." In *Proceedings of the First Yuman Languages Workshop* [University Museum Studies 7], James Redden (ed.), 119-128. Southern Illinois University at Carbondale.

Couro, Ted and Langdon, Margaret. 1975. *Let's Talk 'Iipay Aa: An Introduction to the Mesa Grande Diegueño Language.* Banning and Ramona, Calif.: Malki Museum Press and Ballena.

Evans, Nicholas to appear. "Insubordination and its uses." In *Finiteness,* Frans Plank and Irina Nikolaeva (eds), Berlin: Mouton de Gruyter.

Forsyth, John. 1970. *A Grammar of Aspect: Usage and Meaning in the Russian Verb.* Cambridge: Cambridge University.

Frajzyngier, Zygmunt. 2004. *A Grammar of Lele.* Stanford Monographs in African Linguistics. Stanford: Center for the Study of Language and Information.

Frajzyngier, Zygmunt. 2001. In press. "Tense and aspect as coding means." In *Journal of West African Languages: West African Language Typology: Papers from the International Symposium on Areal Typology of West African Languages,* Bernard Comrie and Ekkehard Wolff (eds).

Frajzyngier, Zygmunt and Shay, Erin. 2002. *A Grammar of Hdi.* Berlin: Mouton de Gruyter.

Gildea, Spike. 1997. "Introducing ergative word order via reanalysis: Word order change in the Cariban family." In *Essays on Language Function and Language Type.* Joan Bybee, John Haiman, and Sandra Thompson (eds), 145-161. Amsterdam: John Benjamins.

Gildea, Spike. 1998. *On Reconstructing Grammar: Comparative Cariban Morphosyntax.* Oxford: Oxford University.

Gordon, Lynn. 1983a. "Switch-reference, clause order, and interclausal relationships in Maricopa." In *Switch-reference and Universal Grammar,* John Haiman and Pamela Munro (eds), 83-104. Amsterdam: John Benjamins.

Gordon, Lynn. 1983b. "Some Maricopa auxiliaries." In *Proceedings of the 1982 Hokan Languages Workshop and Penutian Languages Conference* [Occasional Papers on Linguistics 11]. James Redden (ed.), 1-11. Department of Linguistics, Southern Illinois University at Carbondale.

Gordon, Lynn. 1986. *Maricopa Morphology and Syntax.* University of California Publications in Linguistics 108.

Haiman, John and Munro, Pamela (eds). 1983. *Switch-reference and Universal Grammar.* Amsterdam: John Benjamins.

Hardy, Heather. 1979. *Tolkapaya Syntax: Aspect, Modality, and Adverbial Modification in a Yavapai Dialect.* Ph.D. dissertation, University of California, Los Angeles.

Hardy, Heather. 1982. "Pragmatics and the syntax of switch reference in Tolkapaya." *Southwestern Journal of Linguistics* 5. 85-99.

Hardy, Heather. 1983. "The use of auxiliaries as a cohesive device in Tolkapaya." In *Proceedings of the 1982 Hokan Languages Workshop and Penutian Languages Conference* [Occasional Papers on Linguistics 11], James Redden (ed.), 15-22. Department of Linguistics, Southern Illinois University at Carbondale.

Hardy, Heather and Gordon, Lynn. 1980. "Types of adverbial and modal constructions in Tolkapaya." *International Journal of American Linguistics* 46. 183-196.

Hinton, Leanne. 1984. *Havasupai Songs: A Linguistic Perspective.* Tübingen: Gunter Narr.

Iwasaki, Shoichi. 1993. "Functional transfer in the history of the Japanese language". *Japanese/Korean Linguistics* 2. 20-32.

Iwasaki, Shoichi. 2000. "Suppressed assertion and the functions of the final-attributive in prose and poetry of Heian Japanese." In *Textual Parameters in Older Languages*, Susan. Herring, Pieter. van Reenen, and Lene. Schøsler (eds), 237-272. Amsterdam: John Benjamins.

Jacobsen, William Jr. 1967. "Switch-reference in Hokan-Coahuiltecan." In *Studies in Southwestern Ethnolinguistics: Meaning and History in the Languages of the American Southwest*, Dell Hymes and William Bittle (eds), 238-263. The Hague: Mouton.

Jacobson, Steven A. 1995. *A Practical Grammar of the Central Alaskan Yup'ik Eskimo Language*. Fairbanks: Alaska Native Language Center.

Kalmár, Ivan. 1982. "The function of Inuktitut verb modes in narrative texts." In *Tense-aspect: Between Semantics and Pragmatics*, Paul Hopper (ed.), 45-64. Amsterdam: John Benjamins.

Kendall, Martha. 1975. "The /-k/, /-m/ problem in Yavapai syntax." *International Journal of American Linguistics* 41. 1-9.

Kendall, Martha. 1976. *Selected Problems in Yavapai Syntax: The Verde Valley Dialect*. New York: Garland Press.

Langdon, Margaret. 1970. *A Grammar of Diegueño: The Mesa Grande Dialect*. University of California Publications in Linguistics 66.

Langdon, Margaret. 1978. "Auxiliary verb constructions in Yuman." *Journal of California Anthropology Papers in Linguistics* 1. 93-130.

Langdon, Margaret and Munro, Pamela. 1979. "Subject and (switch-) reference in Yuman." *Folia Linguistica* 13. 321-44.

Miller, Amy 1992. "-*k* and -*m* in Yuma narrative texts." In *Papers from the 1992 Hokan-Penutian Languages Conference* [Occasional Papers on Linguistics 17], James Redden (ed.), 69-81. Department of Linguistics, Southern Illinois University at Carbondale.

Mithun, Marianne. 1989. "The grammaticization of coordination." In *Clause Combining in Grammar and Discourse* [Typological Studies in Language 18], John Haiman and Sandra Thompson (eds), 331-359. Amsterdam: John Benjamins.

Mithun, Marianne. 1992. "External triggers and internal guidance in syntactic development: coordinating conjunction." In *Internal and External Factors in Syntactic Change* [Trends in Linguistics 61], Marinel Gerritsen and Dieter Stein (eds), 89-129. Berlin: Mouton De Gruyter.

Mithun, Marianne. 2002a. "From downstairs to upstairs: A quiet evolution from dependent to independent clause structures and its implications." Paper presented at the Oxford-Kobe Seminar on Language Change and Historical Linguistics. Kobe, Japan, May 2002.

Mithun, Marianne. 2002b. "Rhetorical nominalization in Barbareño Chumash." *50th Anniversary Conference* [Survey of California Languages Report 12], 55-63. University of California, Berkeley.

Mithun, Marianne. 2003. "From discourse to syntax and back." Paper presented at the Georgetown University Round Table in Languages and Linguistics (GURT), Washington D.C., March 2003.

Miyaoka, Osahito. 1997. "A chapter on the Alaskan Central Yupik subordinative mood." In *Languages of the North Pacific Rim*, O. Miaoka and M. Oshima (eds), 61-146. Kyoto, Japan: Graduate School of Letters, Kyoto University.

Munro, Pamela. 1976a. "Subject copying, auxiliarization, and predicate raising: The Mojave evidence." *International Journal of American Linguistics* 42. 99-112.

Munro, Pamela. 1976b. *Mojave syntax*. New York: Garland Press.

Munro, Pamela. 1981. "Mojave *k* and *m*: It ain't necessarily so." In *Proceedings of the 1980 Hokan Languages Workshop* [Occasional Papers on Linguistics 9], James Redden (ed), 124-129. Carbondale: Department of Linguistics, Southern Illinois University.

Redden, James. 1980. "On Walapai /-k/ and /-m/." In *Proceedings of the 1979 Hokan Languages Workshop* [Occasional Papers on Linguistics 7], James Redden (ed), 68-71. Carbondale: Department of Linguistics, Southern Illinois University.

Slater, Carol. 1977. "The semantics of switch-reference in Kwtsaan." *Proceedings of the Berkeley Linguistics Society* 3. 24-36.

Watahomigie, Lucille J., Bender, Jorigine, Watahomigie, Philbert Sr., and Yamamoto, Akira Y., with Mapatis, Elinor, Powskey, Malinda, and Steele, Josie. 2001. *Hualapai Reference Grammar* [Endangered Languages of the Pacific Rim Publications Series A2-003]. Kyoto: Nakanishi Printing Co.

Winter, Werner. 1976. "Switch-reference in Yuman languages." *Hokan Studies*, Margaret Langdon and Shirley Silver (eds), 165-174. The Hague: Mouton.

Winter, Werner. 1998. *Walapai (Hualapai) Texts*. Native American Texts Series. Berlin: Mouton de Gruyter.

Yamamoto, Akira. 1976. "Notes on the interpretation of /-m/ and /-k/ in Walapai." In *Proceedings of the First Yuman Languages Workshop* [University Museum Studies 7], James Redden (ed), 149-152. Carbondale: University Museum, Southern Illinois University.

CHAPTER 9

Adpositions as a non-universal category

Scott DeLancey

University of Oregon

A basic empirical fact about language is that morphemes can be sorted into categories according to their syntactic behavior. There are two long-standing problems in the study of lexical categories: how they are to be defined, and whether there is some set of categories which occur in all languages. Recent work on the problem of categories shows that these are essentially the same problem, since the universality or otherwise of major categories like Noun, Verb, and Adjective depends very much on how they are defined: functionally-defined categories can plausibly be argued to be universal, while reliance on purely distributional definitions makes it much more difficult to argue for the universality of categories like Adjective and Adverb. In this chapter I will argue that there is no useful sense in which the category of Adposition can be considered a linguistic universal, although it is universally available, in that it is the most natural outcome of the grammaticalization of certain types of construction (verb phrases and genitive constructions) which occur in any language.

1. Lexical categories

In traditional grammar syntactic categories like *noun* and *preposition* are given partially or completely notional definitions. Throughout most of the 20th century orthodox linguists shunned such definitions, insisting that syntactically relevant categories could only be defined on purely distributional grounds. This approach has the advantage of preventing the careless analyst from introducing into the analysis of one language categories which are assumed to exist on the basis of their occurrence in some other. On the other hand, it notoriously makes it difficult to compare the categories of different languages, and thus to come to any objective conclusions about the universality of any particular category. (This issue has been extensively discussed in recent years; see e.g. Croft 1991, 2000, 2001). In the generative tradition, definitions are usually eschewed altogether, the lexical categories being taken as given a priori by "universal grammar". This approach obviously offers us nothing of relevance to the empirical question of whether or not a given category is actually universal in some objective, replicable sense.

More recently, linguists interested in the functional motivations for linguistic structure, and especially in the development of syntactic categories through grammaticalization, have once again found value in functional definitions of syntactic categories in terms of semantics and discourse function (see Givón 2001, Croft 2000, 2001). This is not necessarily a matter of incompatible theoretical viewpoints, although it is too often taken as such. In fact structural and functional definitions are both essential parts of linguistic theory and analysis, but they have quite different roles (DeLancey ms., Croft 2000, 2001).

Structural definitions, unlike notional ones, are diagnostic--they let us identify categories in a language, and assign category membership to individual forms. Given a sentence like *Could you schlep this across for me*, one does not have to know the meaning of *schlep*, or even recognize it as an English word, in order to be able to identify it as a verb. The problem with distributional definitions is that they have no explanatory value--the facts about English which let us identify an unknown form as a verb or noun do nothing to explain why there should be such things as verbs or nouns.

This, of course, is exactly what functional definitions are for. The problem with notional definitions, and the reason for their banishment from respectable linguistic discourse during the structuralist era, is that they cannot be used to identify members of the category in question--knowing (or believing) that verbs are words which denote events or states will not help us in determining the lexical category of *schlep*, but it could help us to understand why there is such a category. To truly understand how language works, one must be able to both identify the actual categories which exist in actual languages, and to explain why those are the categories which exist, and this requires both structural and functional definitions.

Thus it is no surprise that recent universalist proposals (e.g. Givón 2001, Dixon ms.) define universal categories such as Adjective in functional rather than structural terms. In the spirit of Croft's and Givón's proposals, we may say that it is the functional categories which are universal, while languages may vary in the means which they adopt to carry out the functions. But as categories grammaticalize, these various means will tend to show convergent grammaticalization as they adapt to the universal functions.

In the later part of the chapter I will argue that Klamath, a Penutian language of Oregon, lacks an adposition category altogether. I will then devote several pages to trying to show that one form in the language which does behave much like a postposition and expresses a very typical adpositional function doesn't really have to be analyzed as one. An obvious question is, why bother? Is a singleton category enough to establish the presence in a language of a putatively universal category? I will argue that if it is, then the "universality" of that category, at least of the category of adposition, is reduced to an uninteresting triviality, and that Klamath--unlike more familiar languages which rely heavily on relator nouns and/or serial verbs to do adpositional detail work--in fact is clear evidence that the adposition category is not a universal solution to the problem of marking spatial and other case-like relations of nominals.

2. Adpositions and their ilk

Most languages manifest some prepositional or postpositional category whose members take a nominal argument and specify the semantic relation of that argument to the clause. In this section we will briefly survey some of the variations on this general pattern.

2.1. Adpositions

Adpositions constitute a peculiar syntactic category, in that they seem to straddle the boundary between lexical and grammatical categories. In some languages the adpositional category is a small, closed, highly grammaticalized set, often involving the marking of core grammatical relations as well as adverbial relations. In others it is a large, permeable set of words with very lexical meanings and functions. But even in such languages some members of the category have clearly grammatical functions, for example the use of English *to* and German *zu* in infinitival constructions, or both of these and French *à* as markers of the indirect object relation.

From a distributional point of view, adpositions are like verbs in that they take an NP argument, but unlike verbs in that they are not predicates themselves; the **pre-/postpositional phrase (PP)** formed by the adposition and its argument functions not as a VP but as an adverbial (and, in some languages, also adnominal) modifying phrase. It is impossible to provide a comprehensive and clear semantic definition of the category, as adpositions within a given language often show a range of rather distinct semantic functions. However, one functional criterion which is often mentioned in connection with adpositions is spatiotemporal meaning. While we might be able to imagine a distributionally-defined adposition category which had no connection with the encoding of spatial relations, in attested languages with adpositions, one of the major and prominent functions of PP's is to indicate spatial and temporal relations, including most essentially the location, direction, or goal of the event denoted by the verb of the clause. That is, if a language has adpositions at all, we can expect that some of them will have a spatial function. This association with spatiotemporal meaning is so characteristic of adpositions that it is regularly incorporated into dictionary and other definitions; conversely, linguistic and psycholinguistic discussions of the grammar of spatial relations sometimes seem to assume that adpositions are the universal mechanism for the expression of location and direction (e.g. Miller and Johnson-Laird 1976, cf. DeLancey 2003). Certain other case-like functions are frequently associated with adpositions; these prominently include the associative, instrumental, and benefactive relations.

There is substantial variation in the size of the adpositional class across languages which manifest such a category: Japanese or Tibetan have fewer than half-a-dozen postpositions, while English and Russian have scores--English probably over a hundred. With this difference in size we find, inevitably, a considerable difference in lexical specificity. Modern Lhasa Tibetan, for example, has exactly five postpositions: ergative/instrumental *gis*, locative/dative *la*, genitive *gi*, ablative *nas*, and associative *dang*.[1] The latter three have quite close equivalents in English: 'of', 'from', and 'with', respectively. But there are no Tibetan equivalents even for other prepositions which an English speaker might regard as quite basic, such as *in* or *on*, much less for semantically complex prepositions like *among, via, despite*, or *for*. The kinds of lexical information which distinguishes the prepositions in English is, in languages like Tibetan, encoded in a category of **relator nouns** (Starosta 1985).

2.2. Adposition-like categories

Doubts about the universality of the adposition category are often connected to recognition of one or both of two widespread constructions which carry out functions associated with adpositions in other languages, but which are often analyzed as involving specialized subcategories of verbs or nouns rather than adpositions per se. These constructions, **serial verbs** and **relator nouns**, are clearly closely-related to adpositions, and can be shown to be common sources for new adpositions, and (especially in creole languages) to be likely sources for the innovation of an adposition category in a language which lacks such.

The behavior of these types of construction casts serious doubt on the possibility of clearly defining a discrete and unambiguous adposition category in some languages (cf. Li and Thompson 1974, Hagège 1975, Starosta 1985, DeLancey 1997). While this certainly constitutes a significant problem for many established conceptions of what word classes are and how they behave, it does not necessarily automatically vitiate the hypothesis of adposition as a universal category. Indeed, the strong tendency of serial verbs and relator nouns to grammaticalize to the point where they can be reanalyzed as adpositions can be taken as evidence for the universality, if not of a structural adposition category, at least of an adpositional **function** (cf. DeLancey 2001), and thus for the "universality" of adposition in the dynamic, functionally-driven sense of Croft or Givón.

2.3. Serial verbs

In Southeast Asia and West Africa we find languages which provide abundant data which on their face seem to pose difficulties for universal claims about adpositions as a category--problems which have been known for generations now in connection with the study of Chinese. In Chinese, as in other non-Tibeto-Burman languages of mainland Southeast Asia, we find functional equivalents of prepositions which are transparently verbal in origin, the majority of which continue to function as lexical verbs while also filling a prepositional function. Thus their categorial status is not obvious, and has been a matter of considerable controversy. In an important study, Li and Thompson (1974) demonstrated that this is in fact a syntactically heterogenous set of words, in terms of the degree of verbal syntax which they manifest.

To illustrate the nature of the problem, consider the status of the coverb *yong*, which is one of the common ways of indicating the Instrument relation (all examples taken or adapted from Li and Thompson 1974):

(1) yong kuaizi   chi fan
     use   chopsticks eat food
     'eat with chopsticks'

From the perspective of a European language, it is easy to identify *yong* as a preposition, which takes a nominal argument to create an adverbial phrase. But, as indicated in the gloss, *yong* is a verb in its own right, meaning 'use'. And Chinese makes frequent use of unmarked sequences of verb phrases in what amounts to a clause-chaining construction, as in:

(2) hui   jia   chi fan
     return home eat food
     'go home and eat'

If ex. (2) is analyzed as a sequence of verb phrases, as it must be, then there is no obvious reason not to analyze (1) the same way. Given the close association between chopsticks as instruments and eating, it is hard to tease apart the instrumental and independent verbal senses in ex. (1), but with an example in which chopsticks would be a less prototypical instrument, it is easier to get all possible readings. Thus ex (3):

(3)   yong kuaizi   zhuo cangying
        use   chopsticks catch flies

can translate 'catch flies with chopsticks', but it can equally well mean 'use chopsticks and then catch flies', or, for that matter, any of the other possible interpretations of a chain of independent verb phrases: 'use chopsticks and catch flies at the same time', 'use chopsticks and catch flies (in alternation)'. Thus we have good reason to analyze ex. (1) as a sequence of clauses, more analogous to English *use chopsticks to eat* than to *eat with chopsticks*. And, indeed, *yong*, even in its preposition-like use, shows basically verbal syntax; for example, it accepts aspectual marking:

(4)   ta yong-le kuaizi   chi-fan yihou
        he use-seq chopsticks eat   after
        'After he had used the chopsticks to eat with …'

Li and Thompson demonstrate that, among the set of "coverbs", there is a wide range of syntactic behaviors. Some, like *yong*, are not really distinguishable from verbs on distributional grounds, except in occurring with considerable frequency as the first of two chained verb phrases. Others, such as *cong* 'from', while demonstrably verbal in origin, occur synchronically primarily as prepositions, and have lost most or all of their verbal syntax, and thus could be considered to be true prepositions. These facts, interpreted from a purely synchronic perspective, might be taken to suggest that Mandarin is in the process of developing a distinct preposition category. But when we examine the historical attestation of Chinese, we see that the synchronic Mandarin situation is pretty much how the language has always been throughout its attested history. At any given stage, we can identify a set of coverbs, some highly grammaticalized, some hardly at all. Over time, it seems that the tendency is for highly grammaticalized items to disappear (at least from the spoken language), being replaced by newer candidates.

Thus at any given historical stage of Chinese we find an inventory of coverbs, some of which are barely grammaticalized and still behave essentially as verbs, while others are highly grammaticalized to the point where we are forced to analyze them as belonging to a distinct category. In other words, even if the preposition category is always permeable and fluid, it is nevertheless always present in the language.

2.4. Relator nouns

The other major strategy for supplementing and refilling the adposition category is through a **relator noun** construction. This very widespread category has not been widely recognized in descriptive or theoretical work. Relator noun categories are frequently the topic of discussion, and sometimes extended controversy, as to whether they are nouns or adpositions (see e.g. Frajzyngier 1974).

For all the confusion that they seem to engender, relator nouns are not an unfamiliar phenomenon to anyone, being easily recognized in such unexotic languages as French and English. Since each of these languages has a robust and thriving adposition category, relator nouns constitute a relatively marginal category, but a number of them are quite frequent in occurrence and encode fairly basic concepts: *à côté de, on top of, in front/back of, on behalf of*, etc. Such constructions can be a source of new prepositions, e.g. English *atop < on top of, beside < by side of.*

In languages which invest less in a lexical category of adpositions, relator nouns may constitute a substantial and important category. Tibetan (Delancey 1997) is an example of a language with a very small and specialized adposition category. Modern Lhasa Tibetan has only two spatial postpositions, locative/allative *la* and ablative *nas*. The great bulk of the work done by English prepositions is performed by a large class of relator nouns:

> *rkub=kyag-gi **mdun**-la* 'in front of the chair'
> *rkub=kyag-gi **mdun**-nas* 'from in front of the chair'
>
> *rkub=kyag-gi **rgyab**-la* 'behind the chair'
> *rkub=kyag-gi **rgyab**-nas* 'from behind the chair'
>
> *rkub=kyag-gi **'khris**-la* 'beside the chair'
> *rkub=kyag-gi **'khris**-nas* 'from beside the chair'

The relator noun construction consists of an NP of which the RN is the head, and the lexical noun a dependent marked with the genitive *gi*. The RN is thus phrase-final and takes the spatial postposition. Relator noun constructions are used in non-spatial functions as well: *blo=bzang-gi **don=dag**-la*   'for Lobsang, for Lobsang's benefit'.

In Tibetan too we can watch these relator nouns slide toward the postposition category. Classical Tibetan had the same relator noun construction:

(5) dbyug=pa=can-gyis ba=glang de
     P.N.-ERG   OX   DEM
     khyim-**gyi nang-du** btang-ba
     house-GEN **inside**-LOC let.go
     'Yugpacan let the ox go **inside** the house.'

The relator noun *nang* in ex. (5) is one of the commonest. In Classical texts it occurs in a well-behaved relator noun construction, that is, it is clearly the head noun in a PP construction, with the lexical noun (*khyim* 'house') obligatorily marked as genitive.

In Modern Lhasa Tibetan, *nang*, along with several other erstwhile relator nouns, no longer governs genitive marking:

(6) zim=chung(??/*-gi) nang-la
     bedroom(??/*-GEN) in-LOC
     'in the bedroom'

This indicates a significant categorial shift: the reason why the genitive occurs in the RN construction, as in:

   rkub=kyag-gi **mdun**-la 'in front of the chair'

is because *mdun* 'front' is a head noun, and *rkub=kyag* is a dependent noun, and the genitive marks this relationship. Tibetan does not allow two nouns together as part of the same NP unless one is marked as a dependent with the genitive. If the genitive is no longer allowable with *nang*, that strongly implies that *nang* is no longer a noun. Exactly what it *is*, is far from clear (see DeLancey 1997), but it certainly appears to be on its way to becoming some sort of a postposition.

The small set of ex-relator nouns which now behave like *nang* does not constitute a semantically or syntactically definable set. As grammaticalization theory would predict, it does seem to be the most frequently used meanings which grammaticalize first; the *nang* set also includes *sgang* 'on' and *'og* 'under', while, as we have seen, *mdun* 'front', *rgyab* 'behind', and *'khris* 'beside' still behave as nouns.

2.5. Adposition as a functional universal?

Data from languages such as Chinese and Tibetan clearly demonstrate that an adposition category need not be a discrete, clearly definable category such as is envisioned in most structuralist and generativist accounts of lexical categories. But in a functional sense these data nevertheless are very consistent with the hypothesis of a universal category of adposition. The first relevant fact, of course, is that in both languages there are some forms which cannot synchronically be analyzed as verbs or nouns, and which must therefore be assigned to a distinct adpositional category. Even if we were to look instead at a language like either of these, but where there were no fully-grammaticalized adpositions, we still see a persistent tendency to grammaticalize forms in a particular direction, and there is no way to characterize that direction except in terms of some abstract, cross-linguistic concept of adposition. And even if this were not the case, and we were dealing only with fully verb-like coverbs or fully noun-like relator nouns, we still have a language in which there are forms, be they verbs or nouns, which in certain constructions act just like adpositions, i.e. they occur with a nominal argument and indicate an adverbial relation between that argument and the main clause.

What we see, in the case of both serial verb and relator noun constructions, is a **functional attractor**, which draws unwary verbs or nouns into its orbit. From an autonomous syntax perspective this isn't really helpful in establishing the idea of prepositions as a universal category. From a functional viewpoint, though, it suggests strongly that not only that there is a universal function which can be carried out by adpositions, but that some kind of adposition-like construction is the way that languages will find to carry out this function.

3. La solution Klamath

I believe that the conclusion suggested at the end of the previous section is supported by the facts of a substantial majority of the world's languages. But there are other types of language which manage things quite differently. In this section we will look at facts from one such language, Klamath, a Plateau Penutian language of southern Oregon.[2]

The elements of interest in these examples are the locative suffix -*dat*, and the **locative-directive stems**, or **LDS**'s. The LDS's and the words which gloss them are in boldface: [3]

(7) coy honk ?at c'wiididiks domna,
     then DEM now killdeer   hear
     Goos-dat *cak'aay'*-ank
     tree-LOC *sit.***up.high**-PRT
     'Then Killdeer heard, sitting **up in** a tree …' (Barker 1963: 4.1;55)

(8) *gawl*-apga-bli   lac'as-dat
     *go.***on.top**-back-again house-LOC
     '[He] climbed back up on the house.'

(9) sqel   *go***Lii**   limaas-am ciis-dat
     Marten *go.***into** limaas-GEN dwelling-LOC
     'Marten went into the Limaas' house.' (Stern Ms.)

(10) coy sa q'ay siktgi-st *dosqan*-ca   Gome-tdat
      then they NEG move-NOM *few.run*.**out**-just cave-LOC
      'When she didn't move, they ran out of the cave.' (Gatschet 1890: 122)

These examples represent location/direction concepts which we might expect to see lexicalized in any mildly ambitious adpositional system. Other LDS's represent concepts which seem less familiar from an Old World perspective. Along with {acw} 'on the head, hair', exemplified in (11), we find LDS's meaning 'in the mouth', 'on the face', and 'on the male genitals':

(11) sdiy'a sa ńos-dat s-*i?a*cwa   woniibi weew'anwis
      pitch 3pl head-LOC REFL-*pl.obj*.**on.hair** foursUBJ women
      'Then they smeared pitch on their heads, the four women.' (Gatschet 1890: 101)

The LDS {iGog} in (12) does not mean simply 'inside', but inside an enclosed space that serves as a container:

(12) ?at sa honk *slan*Goga   slowaa
      now 3PL DEM *mat.***in.container** lynx
      cakl'a-tdat *ksi*Goga sa   ?aysis-as
      basket-loc *living.obj*.**in.container** 3pl Aisis- obj
      'Now they spread out a lynx skin inside a storage basket and put Aisis into it.' (Gatschet 1890: 101)

It could not mean 'inside' as 'inside a house', or 'within a space', or 'in a hole', or 'in a corner or cupboard', each of which is represented by a distinct LDS. The very common LDS {ew} in (13) means 'in, into water; in a flat place; in, on the female genitals':

(13) coy weleeqs   na?as gi, "dankt   hoot ?ambo-tdat *gew*-i!"
      then old.woman thus say long.time DEM water-LOC **go.in.water**-IMPER
      Then the old lady said, "Go and live in the water for a long time!" (Barker 1963: 4.1;34)

We can see from all these examples that -*dat* can be found in connection with any spatial relation: static location, as in (7), goal of motion, as in (8-9 and 11-13), or source, as in (10). These distinctions, as well as the other semantic information reflected in the English translations of the examples, are found not in the locative marker, but in the LDS's in the verb.

3.1. Locative-directive stems

The locative-directive stems in Klamath form a semantically relatively homogenous set of 120-150 or so elements which specify, often in quite specific detail, a location or path: {abaayi'} 'diagonally against, up against', {anasg} 'under the feet', (aptneeGi} 'on top of a full load', {ew} 'in water, in a flat place; in, on the female genitals', {iwy'G} 'into a container, sack, receptacle', {oditgool} 'out from under', {owi} 'spreading out, scattering', {pbeeli'} 'back and forth', etc.

Any verb of motion or location obligatorily contains one of these elements. Motion/location verbs fall into different categories according to the category of the initial element with which the LDS combines (DeLancey 1999, 2003). There are basically two varieties. In one, the LDS combines with an initial stem[4] which specifies either posture or manner of locomotion (in the following examples the initial elements are in *italics* and the LDS's in **boldface**):

*c*abay'a	'*sit* **leaning against**'
*c*al'aal'a	'*sit* **by the fire**'
*c*el'Ga	'*sit* **down**'
*t*gabaay'a	'*stand* **leaning on**'
*t*gaqaay'a	'*stand* **in the woods**'
*t*godiila	'*stand* **underneath**'
*hot*tgal	'*jump* **up**'
*hol*ʔaal'a	'*jump* **into the fire**'
*how*wa	'*run* **into water**'

In the second type, the initial element functions as a noun classifier (although it is quite possible that these may have originated as verb stems):

*ʔ*abaay'a	'*long object* **leaning diagonally against**'
*ʔ*al'aal'a	'*long object* **in(to) the fire**'
*n*al'aal'a	'*flat object* **on the fire**'
*n*ewa	'*flat object* **in water, flat place**'
*c'i*l'aal'a	'*liquid in a container* **on the fire** (as, a pot on to boil)'
*c'*iqa	'*(take) liquid* **out**'

I have glossed all of these as intransitive verbs of position, but they are in fact all indifferently stative, i.e. locational, eventive, i.e. motional, or causative, i.e. transitive (see DeLancey 1999, 2003). The essential point for our present purpose is the semantic contribution of the LDS's.

The system of verb building is definitely lexical; not all theoretically possible combinations of initial element and LDS are attested, and many of the attested combinations have specialized or idiomatic meanings. The semantic contribution of the LDS category, however, is fairly constant, specifying a path or location. If a separate locative argument is included in a sentence with such a verb, it is simply marked with the locative suffix:

(14)   st'oys-dat   *how*wa
        mudhole-LOC *jump*.**into.water**
        'jump into a mudhole' (Barker 1963: 4.1;215)

(15) coy honk has-*ncak*dan**G**a,   qeemat-dat
      then DEM CAUS-*stick*.together-IND back-LOC
      'Then she stuck them together, on the back.' [i.e. she stuck two children to-
      gether back-to-back] (Barker 1963: 4.1;48)

(16) *ceq'ya*   honk doo   wqepl'aqs-dat
      sit.**in.doorway** DEM over.there summer.house-LOC
      'She sat at the door of the house.' (Barker 1963: 4.1;107)

(17) coy honk ?at hadakt *l*osa
      then DEM now there   *round.obj*.**underneath**
      kyem-mat, mee-maqlat-dat,   honk-l'am n'os.
      fish-LOC   DIST-waterfowl-LOC DEM-POSS head-OBJ
      'Then she buried it there under the fish, under the waterfowl, her head.'
      (Barker 1963: 4.1;129)

(18) coy daats   honk, hom'as hak
      then however DEM   that.way EMPH
      gosanc'a   sa, honkant sneyl'aqs-dat
      go.**down.into**.just 3pl DEM.LOC hearth-LOC
      'And then, however, they went down into the hearth ashes.' (Barker 1963:
      4.1;144)

(19) coy honk ?at honkant *kc'is***G**a,   niil-lat
      then DEM now DEM.LOC *crawl*.**through.tube** fur-LOC
      'Then she crawled into it, into the fur.' (Barker 1963: 4.1;190)

Given the semantic range and richness of the LDS category, and the fact that a LDS
will be present in almost any clause of motion or location, it is hard to see what purpose would be served by any additional specification of spatial information outside
the verb.

At least in this area of the grammar the difference between Klamath and more
familiar languages like English does not necessarily reflect any fundamental difference in the conceptualization of motion and location. The difference seems to be
essentially typological. The Klamath LDS and the English preposition category are
in many ways quite comparable, in terms of semantic function and range, numbers,
and degree of openness of the class. The essential difference between the languages
is that in English--a "configurational" language if ever there was one--these forms
form a constituent with the NP which is their semantic argument, while in the quasi-
polysynthetic[5] Klamath they incorporate in the verb.

3.2. The expression of non-spatial oblique relations

As one would expect from a generally head-marking language, which would include nearly any North American language, Klamath indicates most other typically
oblique relations, i.e. benefactive and instrumental, in the verb rather than on the

noun. The single exception to this generalization is the free form *dola*, which marks the associative relation. Since this is a free form, and has a strong tendency to occur contiguous to a nominal argument, it is the best candidate for adposition status to be found in Klamath. In this section I will quickly illustrate the obviously non-adpositional constructions, and then consider the question of the categorial status of *dola*.

3.3. The instrumental case

Instrumental, like locative, is marked with a case suffix, and also in some cases by "instrumental prefixes"[6] in the verb. In (20), the instrumental prefix *s-* 'sharp instrument' provides some information about the nature of the instrument, while *-tga* marks the instrumental noun 'knife':

(20)   ho-ha-*s***dapg**a deqiis-tga
       DIST-REFL-*sharp.inst*.**hit** knife-INST
       '[They] were stabbing one another with knives.' (Gatschet 1890: 114)

However, often *-tga* is the only indication of the instrumental relation. This form is clearly a case suffix, not a postposition; like the object suffix, it occurs on dependent as well as head elements of the NP (Barker 1964: 244-5):

(21)   coy honk ?at sn'eweeck'a mna-**tga**   dalc'i-**tga** slin
       then DEM now little.girl 3sPOSS-INST arrow-INST shoot
       'Now then that little girl shot with her arrow' (Barker 1963: 4.1;85)

3.4. The benefactive LDS

Klamath has no benefactive marker that occurs in construction with a nominal argument; the only benefactive construction is an applicative suffix on the verb. The benefactive suffix is, by morphophonemic behavior, a member of the locative-directive stem category, though it has migrated to a more peripheral position class (Barker 1964: 160, DeLancey 1991). Barker glosses the form {oy} as 'give singular object', a sense which is plausibly consistent with the general motion/location/path semantics of the LDS category. And examples illustrating this sense of {oy} can be found, indeed the only way to express the sense of 'give' with a singular Theme argument is with a bipartite stem consisting of {oy} in construction with a classifying lexical prefix (see DeLancey 1999):

(22)   *ney*   ?is   mi   qmo
       flat.obj.**give** 2sgSUB/1sgOBJ 2sgPOSS basket.hat
       "Give me your cap." (Stern ms.)

Unlike the more semantically typical members of the LDS class,[7] but like benefactive applicatives the world around, the suffix {oy} licenses an extra object argument, semantically identifiable as a beneficiary. And in the available texts the benefactive function of {oy} is considerably commoner than the 'give' use illustrated in ex. (22).

In ex. (23), the benefactive suffix adds an object argument, *sas* 'them' (nominative form *sa*), to the otherwise intransitive verb *sbok'wa* 'have/put one's leg across':

(23)   coy s?aaMaks gi-wk,   *sbok'w*-iiya   sa-s
       then relative   be-because *w.leg*.**across**-BEN 3pl-OBJ
       'Then because he was a relative, he [Old Crane] put a leg across for them.'
       (Barker 1963: 1;139)

Without the benefactive, *sbok'wa* would not occur with an object-marked noun, although it might well occur with a locative form or phrase.

And in (24) we see an already transitive verb *s?ott'a* 'make' (in its irregular form /s?odee-/), with its unmarked Theme object *lolp* 'eye', add an extra valence with the benefactive suffix:

(24)   sat'waaYi ?is   gen, lolp ?is   s?odee-baly-ii-wapk
       help.IMPER 2sgA/1sgO this eye 2sgA/1sgO make-again-**BEN-FUT**
       "Help me, make some eyes again for me!" (Barker 1963: 13;102)

The pronominal clitic form *?is* refers to a 1st person object when the subject is 2nd person. Its occurrence in the second clause shows that that clause has a 1st person object in addition to the effected object *lolp* 'eye', and thus that the form *s?odeebalyii-* has three arguments: a subject and object licensed by *s?odee-*, and another object licensed by the benefactive *-ii-*.

The LDS category as a whole probably originated in a highly marked category of serialized verbs (DeLancey 2003), but there is no Klamath-internal evidence of a verbal origin specifically for the benefactive {oy}. In fact, a cognate benefactive suffix occurs in both of Klamath's nearest relatives, Sahaptian (Rude 1987) and Molala (Berman 1996), and it is clear that we can reconstruct it as an applicative suffix for Proto-Plateau Penutian (see Berman 1996). In both of these languages, however, the suffix is obviously related to an independent verb form--thus the Proto-Plateau suffix reflected in Klamath {oy} did originate in a grammaticalized verb construction.

dola: an associative adposition?

The most plausible candidate for adposition status in Klamath is the associative *dola*, which typically (though not always, see below) takes a nominal argument and directly follows it:

(25)   *doscam*-bli   hoot sa ?at, sqel   c'asgaay-'as dola
       few.run.**along**-back DEM 3pl now Marten Weasel-OBJ with
       '...now they ran back, Marten with Weasel.' (Barker 1963: 10;127)

As in ex. (25), *dola* usually[8] takes object case in any nominal which can express it, such as *c'asgaay* 'Weasel', here a myth character and thus human. It has no obvious categorial assignment in Klamath.[9] According to X' theory, since it governs case it must be either a verb or an adposition. Both of these are well-attested among comitative markers across languages. But Klamath (as we will see later) has no adposition category, unless *dola* is it. And its form makes it highly likely that it is etymologically a verb, so we might consider the verbal analysis first. *Dola* has the form of a verb in the simple indicative tense, and its syntactic behavior is in many ways what one would expect of a Klamath verb. The order of a Klamath verb and its arguments is quite free (Barker 1964: 338-42, Underriner 2002). The same is true of *dola* and its object. It usually follows its argument, as in ex. (25), but it is also found preceding it:

(26)   q'ay honk s?aywakta ka-kni   hoot sa kat dola honk-s
       NEG DEM know   DIST-someone that 3pl REL with DEM-OBJ
       '...those who were with him did not know that.' (Barker 1963: 10;108)

In this example the relative *kat* is a subject form, and the demonstrative *honks* is an object form, as we would expect of the argument of *dola*.

However, *dola* can at best be a highly defective verb, as it only ever occurs in one form--that is, out of the efflorescent inflectional and derivational possibilities of the Klamath verb (DeLancey 1991), the hypothetical *dol-* stem uses only one, the unmarked default indicative form. And it is not even the most likely one--attested Klamath does not serialize finite verbs, and the synchronically expected form for a subordinated verb would be the non-occurring participle form *dolank*. Moreover, its syntactic behaviors also include some which are not consistent with verbal status. We do not ordinarily find sequences of finite verbs within a Klamath sentence, but *dola* frequently occurs following the verb *gena* 'go', with no overt nominal argument:

(27)   coy honk ?at hok sn'eweeck'a c'osak
       then DEM now DEM little.girl   always
       gena   dola, gena   dola, gankankca
       go.hence with go.hence with hunt.around
       'Now then that little girl always went with [him], went hunting.' (Barker 1963: 4;69)

(28)   coy sa   naanok gena   dola, kat ?aysis dola swecan-damna
       then 3PL all   go.hence with REL Aisis with go.gamble-HABITUAL
       'They would all go with [him], those who used to gamble with Aisis.' (Gatschet 1890: 100)

In many parts of the world one would immediately suspect the sequence *gena dola* as being a serial verb construction, 'go accompany'. But western North America is not one of those places. Like other languages of the area, Klamath makes abundant use of the participial subordinating construction, marked in Klamath by *-ank*:

(29)   coy honk ?at sa-?iisy-ank   c'lelGa
       PRT DEM now REFL-hide-PART put.mass.obj.down
       'Then he secretly put it aside.' (Barker 1963: 1;47)

(30) Gil?-ank   p'a-wook,   q'ay sle?a, wit'eem'am'c
      hurry-PART eat-because NEG see   Old.black.bear
      'Because she ate quickly, Old Bear did not see.' (Barker 1963: 1;48)

But, as noted above, in attested Klamath sequences of verbs in the finite -*a* form do not occur within a sentence.

Example (31) further supports the argument, as we do not find in Klamath sequences of a finite verb followed by the copula *gi*: [10]

(31) hoot hok dola gi, sqel'am'c-'as
      that DEM with be Old.Marten-OBJ
      'He was together with him, Old Marten.' (Barker 1963: 10;92)

So *dola* is not synchronically a verb, though it surely was one once. And it is not self-evidently an adposition, given that it doesn't need to be adjacent to, or even to have, an argument. On the other hand, many prepositions in English have pretty much the same distribution:

(32) He ran out the door.
(33) He ran out.
(34) He's out.

And irrespective of the grammatical function of *out* in (33-34), we have no hesitation in identifying it as a preposition in (32), as it occupies a well-defined syntactic slot in the overall extremely well-defined phrase structure of Standard English.

The problem is that in Klamath there are no other adpositions to compare it to, so we don't really know how adpositions behave (or, would behave) in Klamath. And it is certainly conceivable that, had Klamath survived, *dola* was destined to be the entering wedge for the development of a new, innovative postposition category. But we can hardly maintain that in its attested form it has already grammaticalized to that extent. And, given the general patterns of recent grammaticalization in Klamath (see above and DeLancey 1991), we would more likely expect it to incorporate in the verb than to forge a career as the pioneer of a new, decentralized construction.

4. Adposition as a non-universal category

But, all that said, there is no question that if we had any reason to want to find a postposition in Klamath, we could present *dola* and consider the challenge met. By the same loose criteria by which I freely granted coverbs and relator nouns honorary adposition status, i.e. forms which in certain constructions act just like adpositions, occurring with a nominal argument and indicating an adverbial relation between that argument and the main clause, *dola* is certainly as much a postposition as Lhasa *nang* or Mandarin *yong*, and is just as certainly much less a verb than is *yong*.

Let us return to the question asked in the first section: Is a singleton category enough to establish the presence in a language of a putatively universal category?

Like the well-known coverbs of Southeast Asia, West Africa, and creole languages, *dola* is one more small example of the grammaticalization of verbs into adpositional function. That is, it is, in origin, a grammaticalized verb; in its synchronic function it marks the associative relation, and it typically occurs in construction with a nominal argument. The attestation of this process in a language whose general inclination over at least the last millenium or two has been to grammaticalize elements into the verb complex is evidence of its ubiquity--and by saying "ubiquity" rather than "universality" I want to emphasize that we are here talking not about any innately-based structure, or even any fundamental design feature of language, but simply something that happens naturally and easily.

But, unlike the coverbs of Mandarin or the relator nouns of Tibetan, the existence of *dola* as a singleton category in Klamath does not testify to the universality of a tendency for languages to create and maintain such a category, since Klamath manifestly has no interest in doing so. That is, Adposition is not a universal functional sink, in the way that Croft, Givón, or Dixon would argue that Adjective is. If a language is going to grammaticalize the functional category of property concept terms, then it will, inevitably, create something recognizable as an Adjective class. And if, as is probably the case, all languages do grammaticalize the category to some degree, then very likely there will always be a recognizable category or subcategory that can be identified as Adjective. But, despite the great popularity of adpositional systems around the world, it is not the only possible solution.

Of course we know, from a wide range of languages, that the non-spatial adpositional functions associative, instrumental, and benefactive, can be marked within the verb rather than by an adposition or case form. Klamath shows that the other typical function of adpositions, spatial relations, can likewise be incorporated in the verb rather than constituting an adnominal category, and that such a system can quite neatly do everything that even the most ambitious adpositional system can.

Notes

1. The fact that the ergative, genitive, and locative morphemes show substantial, irregular allomorphy, each having an allomorph which forms a close phonological bond with the preceding syllable, could be adduced as an argument that these are suffixes rather than postpositions. However, in terms of their distribution they are phrasal clitics, whose occurrence is limited to the end of the NP; since Tibetan NP's are not head-final, the case markers will cliticize to whatever word happens to occur NP-finally. (See DeLancey 2002).

2.   Klamath is nearly extinct. As of this writing there are only one or two fully-fluent speakers still living, although the Tribe has instituted some language classes in the local school in an attempt to revitalize the language.

3. All Klamath forms are written in the practical orthography adopted by the Department of Culture and Heritage of the Klamath Tribes. The orthography is essentially Barker's (1964) phonemic orthography with a few self-evident typographical changes. Examples taken from

Barker's *Klamath Texts* (1963) are cited with text and sentence number, i.e. 4;69 is sentence (69) in text #4. Examples from other sources are cited with page numbers.

4. Klamath verbs of this type represent a compound of two bound stem elements, of a type which Jacobsen (1980) has called "bipartite stems" (cf. DeLancey 1996, 1999, 2003).

5. North American languages show a strong tendency to combine a great deal of grammatical material with the verb in a single phonological word, which we may take as a (thoroughly informal) definition of a polysynthetic language. Klamath is polysynthetic by this definition, though not by others.

6. As suggested by Talmy (1985), these morphemes--at least in Atsugewi and Klamath--are probably not shape classifiers of instrumental arguments, as sometimes assumed, but *action* classifiers reflecting a characteristic type of motion. In a non-mechanical technology the use of particular types of implement will be characteristically associated with particular body movements. Even so, this category of verbal element does provide information about the instrument, in the same way that LDS's do about the LOCATION.

7. Another exception being {otn} 'on, against', which often seems to simply give transitive force to a bipartite stem.

8. But not always; note that it does not occur in the second clause of (28), below.

9. Barker assigns it to his "residue" category, and labels it only as an "enclitic".

10. Barker's transcription of a comma in this sentence implies that *sqel'am'c̓as* is an afterthought, but note that it is still in object case.

References

Barker, M.A.R. 1963. *Klamath Texts*. [University of California Publications in Linguistics 30]. Berkeley and Los Angeles: University of California Press.

Barker, M.A.R. 1964. *Klamath Grammar*. [University of California Publications in Linguistics 32]. Berkeley and Los Angeles: University of California Press.

Berman, Howard. 1996. "The position of Molala in Plateau Penutian". *International Journal of American Linguistics* 62: 1-30.

Croft, William. 1991. *Syntactic Categories and Grammatical Relations*. Chicago: University of Chicago Press.

Croft, William. 2000. "Parts of speech as language universals and as language-particular categories". In *Approaches to the Typology of Word Classes*, P. Vogel and B. Comrie, (eds), 65-102. Berlin and New York: Mouton de Gruyter.

Croft, William. 2001. *Radical Construction Grammar*. Oxford: Oxford University Press.

DeLancey, Scott. 1991. "Chronological strata of suffix classes in the Klamath verb". *International Journal of American Linguistics* 57: 426-45.

DeLancey, Scott. 1996. "Penutian in the bipartite stem belt: Disentangling areal and genetic correspondences". In *Proceedings of the 22nd Meeting of the Berkeley Linguistics Society: Special Session on Historical Topics in Native American Languages*, D. Librik & R. Beeler, (eds), 37-54. Berkeley: Berkeley Linguistics Society.

DeLancey, Scott. 1997. "Grammaticalization and the gradience of categories: Relator nouns and postpositions in Tibetan and Burmese". in *Essays on Language Function and Language Type: Dedicated to T. Givón*, Joan Bybee et. al., (eds), 51-69. Amsterdam and Philadelphia: John Benjamins.

DeLancey, Scott. 1999. "Lexical prefixes and the bipartite stem construction in Klamath". *International Journal of American Linguistics* 65: 56-83.

DeLancey, Scott. 2002. "Lhasa Tibetan". In *The Sino-Tibetan Languages*, Graham Thurgood and Randy LaPolla, (eds), 270-88. London: Routledge.

DeLancey, Scott. 2003. "Location and direction in Klamath". In *Motion, Direction and Location in Languages. In Honor of Zygmunt Frajzyngier*, Uwe Seibert and Erin Shay, (eds), 59-90. Amsterdam and Philadelphia: Benjamins.

DeLancey, Scott. ms. *Functional Syntax*. draft available at http: //www.uoregon.edu/~delancey/sb/fs.html.

Dixon, R. M.W. to appear. "Adjective classes in typological perspective". In *Adjective Classes: A Cross-linguistic Typology*, R.M.W. Dixon and A. Aikhenvald, (eds). Oxford University Press.

Frajzyngier, Zygmunt. 1974. "Postpositions in Awutu". *Journal of West African Languages* IX (2): 61-70.

Gatschet, Albert. 1890. *The Klamath Indians of Southwestern Oregon*. [Contributions to North American Ethnology, vol. II]. Washington: Govt. Printing Office.

Givón, T. 2001. *Syntax: an Introduction. Volume 1*. Amsterdam and Philadelphia: Benjamins.

Hagège, Claude. 1975. *Le problème linguistique des prépositions et la solution chinoise*. Paris: Société de Linguistique de Paris.

Jacobsen, William. 1980. «Washo bipartite verb stems». In *American Indian and Indoeuropean Studies: Papers in Honor of Madison S. Beeler*, K. Klar et. al., (eds), 85-99. Berlin and New York: Mouton.

Li, Charles, and S. A. Thompson. 1974. "Coverbs in Mandarin Chinese: Verbs or Prepositions?" *Journal of Chinese Linguistics* 2 (3): 257-78.

Miller, George A., and Philip Johnson-Laird. 1976. *Language and perception*. Cambridge, MA: Harvard University Press.

Rude, Noel. 1987. "Some Klamath-Sahaptian grammatical correspondences". In *Kansas Working Papers in Linguistics* 12: 67-83.

Starosta, Stan. 1985. "Relator nouns as a source of case inflection". In *For Gordon Fairbanks*, V. Acson and R. Leed, (eds), 111-33. Honolulu: University of Hawaii Press.

Stern, Theodore. Ms. *Klamath Texts*.

Talmy, Leonard. 1972. *Semantic Structures in English and Atsugewi*. Ph.D. dissertation, University of California, Berkeley.

Talmy, Leonard. 1985. "Lexicalization patterns: Semantic structure in lexical forms". In *Language Typology and Syntactic Description*, volume III, T. Shopen (ed), 51-149. Canbridge and New York: Cambridge University Press.

Underriner, Janne. 2002. *Intonation and Syntax in Klamath*. Ph.D. dissertation, University of Oregon.

Chapter 10

Understanding antigemination*

Juliette Blevins

University of California, Berkeley

A careful review of languages with and without antigemination reveals a complex interaction of phonetic, phonological and morphological effects. In the majority of languages with synchronic antigemination effects paradigm-internal anti-homophony constraints are in evidence. In one set of cases, rule inversion is also involved. In only one language, is there evidence for the natural evolution of antigemination. Combined, these findings suggest that cases of phonetically natural antigemination are extremely rare, and that the majority of antigemination effects are not consequences of the Obligatory Contour Principle, but rather illustrate blocking of syncopating sound change precisely where this sound change would result in loss of a paradigmatic contrast.

1. Introduction

Within Evolutionary Phonology (Blevins 2004a), recurrent sound patterns are argued to be a direct consequence of recurrent types of phonetically based sound change. Common phonological alternations like final obstruent devoicing, nasal-stop place-assimilation, intervocalic consonant lenition, and unstressed vowel deletion, to name just a few, are shown to be the direct result of phonologization of well documented articulatory and perceptual phonetic effects. Synchronic markedness constraints of structuralist, generativist, and optimality approaches are abandoned, and replaced, for the most part, with historical phonetic explanations which are independently necessary.

Already, this framework has proven useful in identifying new phonetic explanations for well documented recurrent sound patterns and for distinguishing sound patterns with a natural history in phonetic substance from those with an unnatural history involving rule inversion, rule telescoping, analogy, or language contact. To take just one example, consider the phonetic typology of metathesis presented in Blevins and Garrett (1998, 2004). Given the recurrent nature of certain metathesis sound patterns, but not others, phonetic explanations grounded in perceptual ambiguity and coarticulation are proposed. Nasal-obstruent metathesis is not accounted for by these phonetic explanations. Nevertheless, nasal-obstruent metathesis is attested in at least seven East Cushitic languages. In this case, as detailed by

Garrett and Blevins (2004), a seeming exception to the phonetic typology of metathesis has an unnatural history rooted in pre-existing patterns of morphophonological alternation.[1]

Within Evolutionary Phonology, it is only by understanding the precise history of language change that sound patterns with natural and unnatural histories can be distinguished. The general Neogrammarian dichotomy of regular sound change and analogy is strengthened by giving further substance to both the phonetic sources of regular sound change, and the morphological and phonological bases of analogical change.

In this chapter, I examine another recurrent sound pattern which is potentially problematic for the Evolutionary approach. The sound pattern in question is one in which phonological syncope rules are sometimes blocked from applying if their output would create a sequence of adjacent identical consonants. This recurrent sound pattern was first characterized and analysed by McCarthy (1986), who referred to it as 'antigemination'.

One case of antigemination analysed by McCarthy (1986: 220–221) is that found in Afar, an East Cushitic language of Ethiopia. The Afar data in (1) illustrates the general antigemination pattern. Unstressed pre-tonic vowels are lost from open syllables when preceded by open syllables (1a-h) unless the consonants flanking the targeted vowel are identical, in which case there is no syncope (1i-k). Unlike other instances of apparent rule-blockage, the constraint on syncope in Afar cannot be attributed to a general constraint against geminates. Geminates in Afar occur freely both within and across morphemes: *cammi* 'uncle', *aabb-uk* 'hearing', *daffe-s-s-a* 'she seated' (from /daffey-is-s-a/ 'sit-CAUS-she-IMPF').

(1)   Afar unstressed vowel syncope: $V \rightarrow \emptyset$ / [$_{word}$CVC_CV́ (Bliese 1981: 212–216; Barillot 2002)

	Stressed	Unstressed	Gloss
a.	xamíla	xamlí	'swamp grass' (acc./nom.-gen.)
b.	cagára	cagrí	'scabies' (acc./nom.-gen.)
c.	kaxánu	kaxní	'love' (acc./nom.-gen.)
d.	digíray	digré	'let him play'/'he played'
e.	gutúca	gutcé	'push(pl.)'/'he pushed'
f.	barísay	barsé	'let him teach'/'he taught'
g.	digibté	digbé	'she/he married'
h.	wagerté	wagré	'she/he reconciled'
	No syncope		
i.	xararté	xararé	'she/he burned'
j.	dananté	danané	'she/he hurt'
k.	walaltá	walalá	'she/he spoke'

McCarthy (1986) argues that antigemination is a consequence of the Obligatory Contour Principle which prohibits adjacent identical elements in phonological representations. Formerly a constraint on lexical representations, the Obligatory Contour Principle (OCP) is extended by McCarthy to exert an active influence on the mapping between underlying and phonological surface forms. A hypothetical Afar form like **danné* (from *danané*) is blocked because it contains a sequence of adjacent identical *n*'s.

Odden (1988) presents serious theoretical and empirical criticisms of the OCP-based account of antigemination. First, he highlights weaknesses related to phonological representations and notions of adjacency. Within McCarthy's model, antigemination is predicted to apply to tautomorphemic derived C_iC_i sequences, but not to heteromorphemic sequences, since morphemes are claimed to define independent 'tiers'. Where antigemination is expected but not found morpheme-internally, McCarthy analyses the segments in question as long-distance geminates. Where antigemination is not expected but attested across morphemes, tier-conflation is claimed to apply prior to syncope. As Odden notes, the freedom to represent C_iVC_i sequences as long-distance geminates when necessary to allow syncope, combined with the freedom to order tier-conflation before syncope to derive intra-morphemic antigemination greatly weakens the predictive power of the model. An important empirical observation is that antigemination is not found in certain languages. Odden concludes that OCP is not a principle of universal grammar.[2]

Within Evolutionary Phonology, where recurrent sound patterns are, for the most part, a reflection of recurrent phonetically based sound change, syncope is easily explained, but antigemination is problematic. Syncopating sound patterns like the Afar rule in (1) are widespread cross-linguistically, and numerous sound changes of precisely this type have been proposed for distinct language families. Thurneysen (1980) describes the general sound change for Old Irish:

> Nothing... has so altered the form of Irish words as the syncope of interior vowels. This takes place in every word which... had **more than two syllables**. In the normal course of development, **the vowel of the second syllable was elided**... The rule applies both to simple words and close compounds. This drastic reduction of the second syllable is the counterpart of the strong stress on the first. (67)

Similar across-the-board syncope of unstressed vowels has occurred in the history of many Austronesian languages. In Chamorro, Proto-Malayo-Polynesian schwa, an extra-short vowel, was lost in the environment VC_CV (Blust 2000: 88). A similar syncope rule is attested in the history of the Central Alaskan Yupik (Fortescue et al. 1994, Jacobson 1984) where Proto-Eskimo schwa has been lost from the second syllable of a word-initial string of open syllables. Another example of schwa syncope in open weak (odd-numbered) syllables has occurred in the history of Munsee/Delaware, an Algonquian language (Goddard 1982). These syncopating sound changes are illustrated in (2i–iv), where proto-forms are Old Irish, Proto-Malayo-Polynesian, Proto-Eskimo and Proto-Algonquian respectively.[3]

(2)   Syncope as sound change
  i.   Old Irish   *V > ø /[C$_0$V́C_CV
      *dilese   >   dilse 'ownership'
      *nameta   >   naimtea 'enemies, acc.'
  ii.   Pre-Chamorro *ə > ø /[C$_0$V́C_CV
      *qaləjaw   >   atdaw 'sun'
      *ma-gətus   >   ma-ktos 'snap, break off'
  iii. Yupik   *ə > ø /VC_CV
      *aləqaR   >   ałqaq 'older sister' (CAY)
      *qavəyaR   >   qawyaq 'sand' (CAY)
  iv.   Pre-Munsee   *ə > ø /[(C)_]$_{Weak Syllable}$
      *wetehkwani   >   wtohwan 'branch'
      *petekwesiwa >   ptəkwsəw 'he is round'

The phonetic explanation for syncope rules like those in (2) is straightforward: short unstressed vowels range in pronunciation from hyperarticulated vowels with recognizable quality to hypoarticulated segments which lack any noticeable formant structure. These hypoarticulated tokens are easily reinterpreted by subsequent generations as consonant release, or zero.[4] Syncope rules, then, have a clear natural history, which we will continue to understand better as our knowledge of speech production and perception deepens.

The problem, however, is that when we look at the potential phonetic precursors of phonological syncope rules, like those illustrated in (2), we do not see evidence of antigemination. On the contrary, McCarthy (1986) describes *phonetic* syncope effects in Odawa, Modern Hebrew, English, Japanese and Hooper Bay Chevak where unstressed vowels *may* be omitted between adjacent identical consonants. (In these and other examples, Cº indicates a consonant with audible release.) He argues that it is precisely the phonetic character of these variations, illustrated in (3), which makes the OCP irrelevant. Since the OCP is a constraint on phonological representations, it has no effect on phonetic implementation rules.

(3)   Problem I: phonetic syncope does not show antigemination (McCarthy 1986)

Language/family	Variant surface forms
Odawa /Algonquian	tətanisi, tºtanisi, ttanisi 'he stays for a while'
Modern Hebrew /Semitic	nadədu, nadºdu, naddu 'he/they wandered'
English /Indo-European	sınənım, sınºnım, sınnım 'synonym'
Hooper Bay Chevak /Eskimo	ənəni, ənºni 'house-LOC.SG'

In the historical domain, there is also evidence that regular syncopating sound changes have occurred without respecting antigemination. For the Central Alaskan Yup'ik (CAY) and Munsee developments summarized in (2iii–iv), there are apparent cases where syncope has applied between identical consonants. Relevant data for Yup'ik is presented in (4i) and that for Munsee in (4ii). In (4i.a–c) the expected reflex of intervocalic Proto-Eskimo $^*\gamma$ is CAY γ as shown by the forms in (4i.d-f).[5] Attested [x] or [xx] then reflects earlier geminate $^*\gamma\gamma$ derived via syncope. In (4ii), proto-forms with weak C_iə.C_i sequences show Munsee reflexes with vowel loss, followed by degemination. Unami maintains some adjacent identical consonants in these contexts (Goddard 1979).[6]

(4) Problem II: syncope as regular sound change does not show evidence of antigemination

    i.

Proto-Eskimo	Central Alaskan Yupik	Gloss
a. *iγəγaγ-	ixaγ-	'lean (against)'
b. *pəγəγaR-	pəxxaR-	'stay up all night'
c. *təγəγ-	təxə-	'be hard'
	təxxi-	'get hard'
d. *aγə-	aγə-	'go (over or past)'
e. *iγə-	iγə-	'swallow'
f. *təγu-	təγu-	'take'

    ii.

Proto-Algonquian	Munsee	Gloss
a. *ne-ne:me	ne:m (< nne:m)	'I see (it)'
b. *kə-kawi:(PEA)	kawi (Unami kkawi)	'he sleeps'
c. *pe-pak-	pake:w (<ppake:w)	'it is flat'

Even within the same language families that provide evidence for antigemination, one finds syncope of vowels between identical consonants. The first mention of this sound pattern in the history of linguistics could be in Sibawayh's Al-Kitab, dating from the 8th century. In his discussion of Arabic phonology, Sibawayh discusses a specific case of *Idghām* (literally 'fusing two elements together in one complex') which involves the elision of a short vowel between two identical consonants bringing them together to be produced as a geminate (vol.3: 350, as cited in Al-Nassir 1993: 56). The example he gives is */radada/ produced as *radda* 'he turned back'. Sibawayh attributes syncope in this example to a phonological rule, *Idghām*, which "avoids sequences of identical elements to achieve some degree of ease of articulation" (ibid).[7]

Just as phonetic perceptual and coarticulatory accounts of metathesis then, do not predict nasal-stop metathesis, so phonetic perceptual and coarticulatory accounts of syncope generally fail to predict antigemination (though see section 4). With no clear phonetic basis for antigemination effects, the Evolutionary approach leads us to consider alternative unnatural histories for this recurrent sound pattern. This chapter presents such a consideration, and also explores whether some aspects of antigemination may be rooted in phonetically natural processes.

In this chapter, I report strong correlations between antigemination and other sound patterns. As I illustrate in section 2, antigemination is attested in languages with pre-existing geminate-singleton contrasts and in languages with degemination, but not elsewhere. After demonstrating these correlations, I attempt to explain precisely where and how antigemination arises. In the most common cases discussed in section 3, syncope between identical consonants appears to be blocked just in case its output would give rise to neutralization of a paradigmatic opposition. This subcase comes under the general heading of 'non-homophony', 'anti-identity', or 'paradigmatic contrast' effects. Here, antigemination is a composite of natural phonetically based syncopating sound change, and independent morphological effects. In section 4, antigemination in Central Alaskan Yup'ik is claimed to have a singularly natural history. One question which arises is why the effects seen in Yup'ik are not found in other languages. Section 5 highlights distinct empirical predictions made by this account in contrast to others and briefly explore implications of this study for modern phonological theory. A strong prediction of this model is that phonetic antigemination effects will not be phonologized unless rule inversion, rule telescoping, language contact, or paradigmatic effects are also involved.

2. Languages with and without antigemination

A summary of languages with claimed antigemination effects from McCarthy (1986) is given in (5).

(5)   Languages with antigemination effects (McCarthy 1986)
    I. Pre-existing C/C: contrast   Language family
      Afar   Cushitic/Afro-Asiatic
      Iraqi Arabic   Semitic/Afro-Asiatic
      Damascene Arabic   Semitic/Afro-Asiatic
      Tunisian Arabic   Semitic/Afro-Asiatic
      Tiberian Hebrew   Semitic/Afro-Asiatic
      Central Alaskan Yup'ik   Eskimo/Eskimo-Aleut
    II. Degemination
      Tonkawa   Isolate (Texas, USA)
      Modern Hebrew   Semitic/Afro-Asiatic

The languages in (5) are organized into two classes. In class I languages, a geminate/ non-geminate contrast exists, and, it turns out, is also reconstructable for relevant proto-languages from which these languages descend.[8] In class II languages, there is no underlying length contrast, but there is evidence for degemination. Some languages in class I also show evidence of degemination in certain contexts (e.g. Iraqi Arabic, Tunisian Arabic, Damascene Arabic).

Note that while pre-existing length contrasts and degemination are sound patterns strongly associated with antigemination, they cannot be used to predict whether or not antigemination effects will be found. Syncope in Hindi shows no antigemination effects (Odden 1988: 465), but Hindi does have an underlying geminate/non-geminate contrast. In Piro (Matteson 1965), on the other hand, where underlying geminate/non-geminate contrasts are absent, there is active degemination of obstruents, yet syncope also shows no antigemination effects (Lin 1997). Some languages without antigemination effects are listed in (6).

(6)   Languages without antigemination effects
     I. Pre-existing C/C: contrast

Hindi	Indo-European
Akkadian	Semitic
Hooper Bay Chevak	Eskimo

     II. Degemination

| Piro | Arawakan |

     III. Neither

Klamath	Lutuamian (see below)
Outlier Polynesian, Mussau,	
Trukese, Iban	Austronesian (Blust 1990)

On the other hand, if a language *does not* have a robust length contrast and *lacks degemination*, then it *will not* exhibit antigemination. A language of this type is Klamath, a Lutuamian language of south-central Oregon (Barker 1963, 1964).[9] Unlike the class I languages in (5), Klamath does not have a robust underlying length contrast. Only a small number of stems are analysed as containing geminates which contrast with singletons in the same environment, though on the basis of internal reconstruction, it is clear that these are of recent origin. And unlike the class II languages in (5), there is no evidence of general degemination in Klamath. With the exception of /... s-s .../ clusters, sequences of identical consonants which arise across morpheme boundaries surface without degeminating. Some examples are shown in (7).

(7)   Another language without antigemination: Klamath (Lutuamian, Oregon, USA)

     i. Pre-existing C/C: contrast?   Highly limited.
     ii. Degemination?   No.

        a. *telli: na* 'looks off the edge'   /tel-li: na/ [D: 100]
        b. *tilnne: ka* 'rolls into a hole'   /tiln-ne: ka/ [D: 115]
        c. *tinne: ka* 'sets (of sun)'   /tin-ne: ka/ [D: 116]
        d. *lt^{h}ewwa* 'grazes in a flat place'   /lt^{h}ew-wa/ [D: 225]

In Klamath, as illustrated in (8), short vowels in open stem-initial syllables are lost when a prefix is added. This rule of syncope does not show antigemination effects.[10] Compare *qoqa* 'puts on, wears a dress' in (8a), with the causative *hosqqa* 'puts a dress on someone' from /hVs-qoqa/ via stem vowel copy, and prefix-induced syncope. In this example, as in (8b), a surface geminate is derived via syncope. In (8c) the expected form is *snoc'c'e: y'a*, however, laryngeal neutralization takes *c'c'* to *cc'* (Blevins, 1993).

(8) Klamath syncope

	Base	Syncope	Gloss
		V→ø / Prefix + [(C)C_CV …	
a.	qoqa	hosqqa< /hVs-qoqa/	'puts on a dress/CAUS' [D: 157]
b.	lalamna	sallamna < /sV-lalamna/	'puts a round obj. on back/ REFL' [D: 205]
c.	c'oc'e:y'a	snocc'e:y'a < /snV-c'oc'e:y'a/	'melts/CAUS' [D: 95]

Though there is no general degemination process in Klamath, the language does simplify derived /…s-s…/ clusters to [s] (Barker 1964: 95), as illustrated in (9a–c).

(9) Degemination of /…s-s…/ clusters in Klamath /hVs-/ causatives

	Base	Degemination	Gloss
a.	sle'a	hesle'a < /hVs-sle'a/	'sees/ CAUS' [D: 373]
b.	s'aywakta	has'i:watka < /hVs-s'aywakta/	'knows/teaches' [D: 342]
c.	sacaqʰwa	hascaqʰwa < /hVs-sacaqʰwa/	'wash (hands)/CAUS' [D: 347]

Compare:

	Base		Gloss
d.	qʰoyqa	hosqʰi:qa < /hVs-qʰoyqa/	'recognize/introduce' [D: 323]
e.	tʰsin	histʰsan < /hVs-tʰsin/	'grow/CAUS' [D: 414]
f.	c'ayalcʰn'a	hasc'yalcn'a < /hVs-c'ayalcʰn'a/	'backs up/ CAUS' [D: 83]

Compare *sle'a* 'sees' with *hesla* 'causes someone to see' in (9a), from /hVs-sle'a/. The causative prefix /hVs-/ is *s*-final, as illustrated in (9d-f). In this case, the expected surface form is **hessla*, but /ss/ degeminates to [s]. Given the suggested correlation between degemination and antigemination in the class II languages in (5), it is instructive to examine word forms in Klamath where syncope could give rise to /s-s/ sequences. Words of this type, with stem-initial /sVsV…/, are shown in (10). Hypothetical surface forms under distributive *(C)CV-* or reflexive/reciprocal *sV-* prefixation are shown in bold.

(10) Klamath sVs-initial stems

	Base	RED + hypothetical syncope + degem'n	gloss
a.	sasalk'ya	/sa-sasalk'ya/ > /sa-ssalk'ya/ > **sasalk'ya**	'quarrels' [D: 349]
b.	sesadwi	/se-sesadwi/ > /sessadwi/ > **sesadwi**	'sells' [D: 359]
c.	sosannqa	/so-sosannqa/ > /so-ssannqa/ > **sosannqa**	'wrestles' [D: 383]

As illustrated in (10), if syncope and degemination apply, causative and reflexive-reciprocal surface forms are *identical* to the base forms from which they are morphologically derived. Antigemination is clearly not the answer to why there is no evidence for syncope in (10). As shown in (8), Klamath does not show evidence of antigemination in parallel forms where degemination is not applicable. Despite morphological attempts to produce prefixed forms in (10), the phonology conspires to produce forms which are identical to their non-derived counterparts. It is precisely this sort of striking collapse of paradigmatic contrasts which, I will argue, leads to apparent antigemination effects in the majority of the world's languages.[11]

3. Unnatural history

In the following sections, I review cases of antigemination reported in McCarthy (1986) and elsewhere. In each case, I provide evidence that the constraint against syncope between identical consonants has an unnatural history. In 3.1, languages show antigemination in limited morphological contexts which suggest paradigmatic anti-homophony constraints (cf. Yip 1998, Crosswhite 1999). In 3.2 synchronic syncope constitutes diachronic rule inversion.

3.1. Paradigm-internal anti-homophony effects

3.1.1. *Tunisian Arabic*
Tunisian Arabic as described by Wise (1983: 168–170) has a rule of vowel syncope which deletes unstressed high vowels from open syllables.[12] Tunisian Arabic also has conditioned degemination: geminate consonants which are not pre-vocalic are simplified to singletons. The syncope rule is given in (11) along with several examples of its application in (11ii). Notice that in (11ii), syncope can be seen as feeding degemination.

(11) Tunisian Arabic unstressed vowel syncope: $V \rightarrow \emptyset /[\ldots \sigma. C\_CV(C)]_{Wd}$
         $[+high]$

    i. Conditions for syncope not met ii. Syncope applies (+ degemination)

zarbijja	'rug'	zarbíiti	'my rug'	< /zarbíjjiiti/
quffa	'basket'	qúfti	'my basket'	< /qúffiti/
/fumm/	'mouth'	fumha	'her mouth'	< /fúmmiha/
zarbijjítna	'our rug'			
quffítna	'our basket'			
fummi	'my mouth'			

Though McCarthy (1986: 241) suggests that regular antigemination effects are found in Tunisian Arabic, this is not the case.[13] As noted by Wise (1983: 169–170), in nouns, adjectives, and participles, syncope applies regularly, even when adjacent identical consonant sequences would be created. The examples in (12) illustrate the absence of antigemination in participles.

(12) Tunisian Arabic syncope without antigemination: participles
       i. conditions for syncope not met   ii. syncope applies (+ degemination)
       a. mityaʃʃiʃ 'angry (m.)'   mityaʃʃa 'angry (f.)' < /mityaʃʃiʃ-a/
       b. mSammim 'determined (m.)'   mSamma 'determined (f.)'
                                                < /mSammim-a/

McCarthy's reference then, must be to forms within verbal paradigms. In fact, the only place where apparent antigemination effects are observed in Tunisian Arabic is in verbs of the form $CVC_iC_iVC_j$. When these verbs take a $-V$ suffix, as shown in (13), the syncope rule operative in (11) and (12) does not apply, despite the fact that phonological environments are parallel to the participles in (12), where syncope does apply.

(13) Tunisian Arabic syncope with antigemination: inflected verbs
       i. conditions for syncope not met   ii. no syncope + degemination
                                                 where expected
       a. mityaʃʃiʃ 'angry (m.)'   yaʃʃifu 'they angered' (**yaʃʃu)
       b. /xaffif-/ 'alleviate'   xaffifu 'they alleviated' (**xaffu)
       c. /qarr-/ 'decide'   qarraru 'they decided' (**qarru)[14]

Why are syncope and antigemination blocked in inflected verbs in Tunisian Arabic, while applying freely elsewhere? As in the hypothetical Klamath derivations shown in (10), the combination of syncope and degemination results in paradigm collapse within the verb system. Many of the $CVC_iC_iVC_i$ verbs in question are causative forms of CVC_iC_i stems. Given this, the consequence of syncope + degemination is to essentially undo the templatic morphology associated with causative formation. Wise (1983) suggests this possibility, providing relevant examples:

> It is possible that the rules [of syncope and degemination: JB] are suspended in this environment to avoid clashes with verbs with a CVCC stem; most CVC-CVC verbs are in fact derived morphologically from verbs of CCVC or CVCC type and are therefore quite closely related to them semantically. For example, we find both /qarru/ 'they admitted' and /yaʃʃu/ 'they cheated' from /qarr+u/ and /yaʃʃ+u/. (170)

In other words, what appears to block phonological rule application in (13ii) is not a phonological constraint, but a morphological one. The forms in (12ii.a) and (13ii.a) provide a minimal pair: in participles, the rules apply, but in verbs, they do not. Within the participle paradigm, verb stems of the form CCVC and CVCC have CVVCVC participles, with vowel length in the first syllable (e.g. ʃaad 'he pulled', ʃaadid 'pulling, have pulled'). As a result, there is no possibility of homophony arising via syncope between these members of the paradigm, as there is within the class of finite verbs.

The OCP-based account of antigemination in (13ii) can only be rescued by assuming that tier-conflation applies before suffixation of verbal inflection, but after suffixation of nominal inflection, or by equivalent domain restrictions on the OCP itself.[15] This strictly phonological account relies heavily on the manipulation of tier-conflation (or its non-derivational equivalent), and misses the generalization true for both Tunisian Arabic and Klamath: regular phonological alternations may be blocked or unobservable precisely where they result in obliteration of paradigmatic contrasts.

3.1.2. *Iraqi Arabic*

In Iraqi Arabic as described by Erwin (1963: 56–58), a syncope rule deletes short vowels from stem-final open syllables when vowel-initial suffixes are added. Iraqi Arabic also has conditioned degemination: as in Tunisian Arabic, geminate consonants which are not pre-vocalic undergo degemination. The syncope rule is given in (14) along with several examples of its application in (14ii).

(14)   Iraqi Arabic unstressed vowel syncope: $V \rightarrow \emptyset / [\ldots \sigma . C\_CV(C)]_{Wd}$
   i. conditions for syncope not met   ii. syncope applies (+ degemination)
   ʃaʕar 'hair'   ʃaʕrak 'your hair' < /ʃaʕar-ak/
   xaabar 'he telephoned'   xaabrat 'she telephoned'
                                        < /xaabar-at/
   ybaddil 'he changes'   ybadluun 'they change'
                                        < / ybaddil-uun/
   ykassir 'he breaks'   ykasruun 'they break' < /ykassir-uun/

Notice that, as in Tunisian Arabic, examples like *ybadluun* in (14ii) show syncope feeding degemination: /ybaddil-uun/ → /ybaddluun/ → *ybadluun*.

   As in Tunisian Arabic, syncope without antigemination is attested. In (15), certain inflected adjectives undergo syncope giving rise to adjacent identical segments. Erwin (1963: 242) makes it clear that syncope in this context is optional; nevertheless, it occurs, and leads one to question McCarthy's general claim that antigemination is a consequence of a general constraint on phonological representations.

(15)   Iraqi Arabic syncope without antigemination: inflected adjectives
   i. conditions for syncope not met   ii. syncope applies (optionally)
   mitraaSiS 'crowded together (m.)'   mitraaSiSa, mitraaSSa 'crowded
                                        together (f.)'
                                        mitraSiSiin, mitraaSSiin 'crowded
                                        together (pl)'

However, syncope is consistently blocked in inflected verbs, whether they are associated with CVCCVC (class II) or CVVCVC (class III) templates, as shown in (16).

(16)   Iraqi Arabic syncope with antigemination: inflected verbs
   i. conditions for syncope not met   ii. no syncope + degemination where
                                           expected
   a. dallal 'he pampered'   dallilaw 'they pampered' (**dallaw)
   b. jaddad 'he renewed'   jaddidaw 'they renewed' (**jaddaw)
   c. ħaajaj 'he argued'   ħaajijaw 'they argued' (**ħaajjaw)
   d. traaSSaS 'he moved close'   traaSSaSaw 'they moved close together'
                                        (**traaSSaw)

As in Tunisian Arabic, the failure of syncope to apply in (16ii) appears to be determined by a seeming anti-homophony constraint. If verbs of the form $CVC_iC_iVC_i$ or $CVVC_iVC_i$ undergo syncope and, in the first case, automatic degemination, under suffixation, they will collapse with inflected CVC_iC_i stems from which they are typically derived (Erwin 1963: 65–66). For example Class II *tammam* 'to complete' is derived from /tamm/ 'to be complete'. A hypothetical form like **tammaw* 'they completed' (< /tammam-aw/) is indistinguishable from *tammaw* 'they are complete'. As in Tunisian Arabic then, the failure of syncope to apply between identical stem consonants in Iraqi verbs may better be explained in terms of paradigm collapse under potential homophony than OCP effects.

3.1.3. *Damascene Arabic*

The facts described for Damascene (Syrian) Arabic by Cowell (1964) are even more strikingly inconsistent with an OCP account than those noted above for other Arabic dialects. In Damascene, syncope optionally applies between adjacent identical consonants if they are both short (17d-eii), but fails to apply between identical consonants if they would produce a $C_iC_iC_i$ cluster (17iii).[16] Precisely in this latter context, degemination is the norm.[17] Notice that the morphological make-up of the cluster is not a factor: In examples like (17d) the identical sequence which results from syncope is tautomorphemic, while in (17f) syncope is blocked in tautomorphemic identical sequences.

(17)   Damascene Arabic syncope: $\{e,o\} \to ø\,/\,[\ldots\sigma.\,C\_CV(C)]_{Wd}$

	i. conditions for syncope not met		ii. syncope	
a.	btəskon	'you dwell'	btəskni	'you (f. sg.) dwell'
b.	bisaaʕed	'he helps'	bisaaʕdu	'they help'
c.	GalTet	'mistake of'	GalTTi	'my mistake'[18]
d.	bihaaʒeʒ	'to argue with'	bihaaʒʒu	'they argue with'
			(or bihaaʒəʒu)	
e.	ħaaTeT	'having put'	ħaaTTe	'having put, f.'
			iii. no syncope	
f.	bisabbeb	'he causes'	bisabbəbu	'they cause'
			(**bisab(b)bu)	
g.	mSammem	'determined'	mSamməme	'determined, f.'

In Damascene, as in the examples above, the underlying cause of antigemination effects appears to be potential loss of paradigmatic oppositions. Since there is no surface contrast between $C_iC_iC_i$ and C_iC_i in the language (Cowell 1964: 23–24, 27), in cases where syncope would give rise to $C_iC_iC_i$, the contrast between $CVC_iC_iVC_i$ and CVC_iC_i templates, so basic to the inflectional system of verbs, would be lost.

3.1.4. *Tiberian Hebrew*

McCarthy (1986) claims that Tiberian Hebrew syncope is blocked when a morpheme-internal geminate would be derived (18iii), but can give rise to adjacent identical consonants across morpheme boundaries (18ii.c).

(18) Tiberian Hebrew syncope: ə → ø /…σ. C_.CV

	i. conditions for syncope not met	ii. syncope	
a.	/zaaχər/	zaaχrúu	'they recalled'
b.	/haaləχ/	haalχúu	'they walked'
c.	/hinnen/	hinnii	'behold me' (< hinnnii < hinnən-ii)
		iii. no syncope	
d.	/Saaləl/	Saaləlúu	'they darkened'
e.	/saaβəβ/	saaβəβúu	'they surrounded'

Odden (1988: 467, n. 11) emphasizes that McCarthy's entire argument for Tiberian Hebrew rests on the phonetic interpretation of the *shewa* symbol, which can be realized as ə or as nothing, and that the assumed contrast between, e.g. *zaaχrúu* (18a) and *saaβəβúu* (18e), occurs in one of the most controversial environments for interpreting the correct phonetic value of *shewa*. Relevant factors are shown in (19). With no clear basis for McCarthy's interpretation of *shewa* as schwa vs. zero in (18), we are left to wonder whether the contrast between forms like those in (18ii) and (18iii) ever existed. [19]

(19) Tiberian Hebrew *shewa* (Malone 1986, 1993; Odden 1988)
   a. phonetic value of *shewa* is ə or nothing
   b. grapheme *metheg* is thought to support interpretation of zero, but it is nonmandatory and therefore an unreliable indicator
   c. all cited examples of antigemination in Tiberian Hebrew contain *metheg*, irrespective of surrounding consonants

3.1.5. *Tonkawa*

Our knowledge of Tonkawa, an isolate of central Texas, is based on the collected works of Hoijer (1933, 1946, 1949, 1972). In Tonkawa, as described by Hoijer, vowel syncope effects stem vowels which are non-final, preceded by at least one open syllable, and in open syllables themselves. Hoijer (1933: 1) refers to stems as 'themes' and highlights the fact that vowel elision of this type is limited to themes, and never effects the form of affixes regardless of their position within the word. The syncope rule, stated in (20), is highly lexicalized then, applying only to stem vowels which themselves are both non-final in the stem and non-initial within the word.

(20) Tonkawa syncope: V → ø /V. C_.CV
                          [+stem]   [+stem]

Alternations which this rule is meant to capture are shown in (21), where abstract trisyllabic stems /picena/ and /notoxo/ fail to surface with all three vowels intact.

(21)   Syncope alternations in Tonkawa
  a. picen   'steer, castrated one'   f. notox   'hoe'
  b. picno?   'he cuts it'   g. notxo?   'he hoes it'
  c. wepceno?   'he cuts them'   h. wentoxo?   'he hoes them'
  d. picnano?   'he is cutting it'   i. notxono?   'he is hoeing it'
  e. wepcenano? 'he is cutting them'   j. wentoxono? 'he is hoeing them'

Kisseberth (1970) notes that syncope is inhibited if a sequence of adjacent identical segments would be created. In (22), stems with regular syncope are compared with those in which syncope appears to be blocked.

(22)   Antigemination effects in Tonkawa
  i. Underlying stem   ii. syncope
  a. /notoxo-/   notxo?   (< /notoxo-o?/)   'he hoes it'
  b. /picena-/   picno?   (< /picena-o?/)   'he cuts it'
  c. /yakapa-/   yakpo?   (< /yakapa-o?/)   'he hits him'
  d. /topo-/   ketpo?   (< /ke-topo-o?/)   'he cuts me'
                        iii. no syncope
  e. /hewawa-/   hewawo?   (< /hewawa-o?/   'he is dead'
  f. /ham'am'a-/   ham'am'o?   (< /ham'am'a-o?/   'he is burning'
  g. /totopo-/   ketotopo?   (< /ke-to-topo-o?/) 'he cuts me re-
                                                          peatedly'

Though Kisseberth (1970) attributes this effect to the absence of underlying geminates in Tonkawa, McCarthy (1986) argues that antigemination in Tonkawa is another case where the OCP blocks syncope.

The reanalysis of antigemination proposed here follows Hoijer's morphological analysis of Tonkawa closely. Of primary importance is the recognition that all sequences showing apparent antigemination effects are reduplicated C_iV_i sequences. A close examination of all examples of stem-internal C_iVC_i strings in Tonkawa, where V is a potential syncope target suggest that CV-reduplication is always involved. Reduplication in Tonkawa is used to productively mark repetitive aspect as well as plural subject or object, as shown by the pairs in (23) which are shown in their underlying (non-syncopated) forms.

(23)   Productive CV-reduplication in Tonkawa (pre-syncope forms)
  i. Non-repetitive   Repetitive
     /topo-/   /totopo-/   'to cut (it) off'
     /nota-/   /nonota-/   'to touch'
     /kayce-/   /kakayce-/   'to be chopped off'
     /nawele-/   /nawewele-/   'to spread out a fabric'
     /tama?axe-/   /tatama?axe-/   'to be smashed, shattered'
     /notoxoko-/   /nototoxoko-/   'to expectorate'
     /yapece-/   /yayapece-/   'to sew, make clothes'

    ii. Non-plural subject   Plural subject/object

/nataya-/	/natataya-/	'to choose, select'
/panoxo-/	/panonoxo-/	'to bathe'
/napasxa-/	/napapasxa-/	'to play ball'
/noko-/	/nonoko-/	'to pick up'
/yatisxe-/	/yatitisxe-/	'to butt'

In some cases, reduplication holds of the first stem element like /to-to-po/ in (22g), while in other cases, it is the second stem element which is reduplicated as in /ha-m'a-m'a/ (22f). In some instances, reduplicated forms are somewhat semantically opaque, but synchronic evidence for a reduplicated base is still present. This is the case for /hewawa-/ 'die, be dead, be killed' (22e), with mediopassive prefix /he-/, to which we can compare /hehewa-/ 'to stop dying; recover (from an illness)' (Hoijer 1933: 42–43), and /ham'am'a-/ 'to burn' (22f) with /ha-/ prefix (Hoijer 1933: 39–42), and /m'a-/ theme also found in /m'a-ye-/ 'set fire to' (Hoijer 1946: 301).

As noted by Hoijer (1933: 7), reduplicated C_iV_i sequences have either the form $C_iV_iC_i$ or $C_iV_iC_iV_i$. In other words, no reduplicated string ever undergoes syncope of the first vowel of the derived C_iV_i-C_iV_i string, while some reduplicated strings will lose their second vowel, if it is in the context for syncope (20) to apply. In addition to the syncope rule in (20) then, reduplicated stems must be lexically marked as to whether their second vowel can or cannot undergo the syncope rule. Examples of these two reduplicated stem types are illustrated in (24).[20] Notice that the failure of vowels to syncopate in (24ii) is entirely independent of phonotactics: when the stem is not reduplicated, syncope occurs between the same two consonants as shown in the plural object forms.

(24)   Lexical syncope in reduplicated C_1V_1-C_2V_2 strings

i. Syncope of V_2		ii. No syncope of V_2	
yataso?s	'I stab him'	komo?s	'I suck it'
yaytaso?s	'I stab him rep.'	kokomo?s	'I suck it rep.'
/ya-yatasa-o?/		cf. wokmo?s	'I suck them'
coxno?s	'I sleep'	topo?s	'I cut it'
cocxa: yewo?	'several sleep together'	totopo?s	'I cut it rep.'
/co-coxa: -yewa-o?/		cf. wetpo?s	'I cut them'

What then accounts for the failure of syncope in forms like (22e-g)? I suggest that, as in the Arabic cases reviewed earlier, syncope is blocked just when its output would give rise to paradigm collapse. In this case, as in others reviewed, a regular degemination process is active in Tonkawa. As described by Hoijer (1946: 292): "combinations of identical consonants always unite to form a single consonant."[21] Examples of degemination across morpheme boundaries are illustrated in (25).

(25)   Regular degemination in Tonkawa
"…combinations of identical consonants always unite to form a single consonant" Hoijer (1946: 292)

Underlying form	Surface form	Gloss/text
a. /tanmaslak-k^{w}a:low/	tanmaslak^{w}a:low	'jackrabbit' [T2.1]
b. /yakon-nacaka- …/	yakonacka:tewa:nes	'I'll knock you un-conscious' [T1: 4]
c. /ha:csokonay-yayka'ay/	ha:csokonayayka'ay-'a:la	'wolves-quot.' [T4: 7]

Now consider the effect of syncope + degemination in the reduplicated forms where syncope appears to be blocked. Hypothetical derivations are shown in (26).

(26)   Tonkawa C_1V_1-C_2V_2 strings, syncope, and degemination

Base	RED with hypothetical syncope + degemination			gloss
a. /hewa-/	/hewawa-/ >	hewwa- >	**hewa-	'to die'
b. /ham'a-/	/ham'am'a-/ >	ham'm'a >	**ham'a-	'to burn'
c. /CV-topo-/	/CV-totopo-/	CV-ttopo-	**CV-topo-	'to cut'

As with the Klamath data in (10), if syncope and degemination apply, repetitive and plural subject/object forms derived via reduplication will be homophonous to the bases from which they are derived. Unlike Klamath, there are few if any forms outside of those involving reduplication where both syncope and degemination are applicable.[22] However, an independent rule of stem-final vowel loss can feed degemination. As shown in (27), in compounds like those in (25), stem-final vowel loss gives rise to geminates which are subject to degemination.

(27)   Final vowel loss (+ degemination): no antigemination in

a. /yakona-nacaka- …/	yakonacka:tewa:nes	'I'll knock you uncon-scious' [T1: 4]
b. /yas'ene-nacaka- …/	yas'enwencaka	'it was cutting them to death'[T19: 11]
c. /yakexe-xakana- …/	/yakexakana-/	'to push it down hard' [D: 485.1]

As in the three Arabic dialects examined above, it is not a distinction between tauto- and heteromorphemic identical sequences which determines the distribution of antigemination effects. In productive reduplications like *totopo-*, where syncope is blocked, the CV reduplicative affix is arguably a distinct morpheme in Tonkawa. McCarthy's (1986) proposal that syncope is always blocked between tautomorphemic segments, but only sometimes blocked between heteromorphemic segments, is unsuccessful in predicting precisely where antigemination effects will occur. Antigemination in Tonkawa and the other languages examined above is not a general feature of sound patterns. It is in evidence precisely where vowel loss combined with other regular sound patterns would result in the phonological identity of two morpho-syntactically distinct members of a paradigm. In the case of Tonkawa, syncope combined with degemination would result in merger of reduplicated and non-reduplicated stems which distinguish the inflectional paradigms in (23).

While the attribution of many antigemination effects to paradigm-internal anti-homophony effects may be original in the domain of modern linguistics, Sibawayh again seems to have had a similar idea. In his discussion of forms like /iqtatalu/ 'they fought each other' from the stem /qatalu: / 'they killed', Sibawayh attributes the failure of syncope between identical consonants (yielding **iqtalu < **iqttalu) to the fact that 'the affixed /ta/ morpheme is a syntactical element *used for meaning*' (Al-Nassir 1993: 59). In other words, syncope plus degemination would eliminate all phonological evidence of /ta/, making the non-infixed base indistinguishable from the infixed /ta/ form.

3.1.5. *Modern Hebrew*
McCarthy (1986) includes Modern Hebrew as a language with antigemination effects. The facts he cites in support of this are shown in (28).[23]

(28)   Modern Hebrew e/ø alternations in suffixed stems
        i. conditions for syncope not met   ii. syncope applies
        a. kaʃar   'he tied'   kaʃru   'they tied'
        b. kuʃar   'he was connected'   kuʃra   'she was connected'
        c. hitkaʃer   'he contacted'   hitkaʃru   'they contacted'
                                             iii. no syncope
        d. nadad   'he wandered'   nadedu   'they wandered'
        e. kucac   'he was cut'   kuceca   'she was cut'
        f. titpalel   'thou (m.) will pray' titpaleli 'thou (f.) will pray'

In this case, Modern Hebrew differs quite dramatically from Arabic, and Tiberian Hebrew, where stems of the form shown in (28d–f) are always CVC_iC_i ,— mono-syllabic with a final geminate, when followed by a vowel.[24] Under McCarthy's general analysis, antigemination was violated consistently in bilateral roots of this sort in the history of Arabic and Hebrew. Recall Sibawayh's 8th Century reference to this syncope as "a phonological rule which avoids sequences of identical elements to achieve some degree of ease of articulation".

A clear alternative to McCarthy's interpretation of the Modern Hebrew pattern is that, geminates in Modern Hebrew have a peculiar unnatural history themselves. The absence of length contrasts in the majority of Eastern European languages of the mid-nineteenth century, may have directly influenced the newly arising secular language. In this case, it could be that the historical geminate/non-geminate contrast was replaced with a C_i vs. C_ieC_i contrast directly. Since the syncope rule in question is not an innovation, the remapping of singleton/geminate contrasts can be seen to work on the output of the historical syncope rule. I have schematized the analysis in (29).[25]

(29)   Modern Hebrew reflections of historical C_i vs. C_iC_i contrasts
Mappings from the output of historical syncope:

Pre-Modern Hebrew   Modern Hebrew
$[\ldots C_i \ldots]_{stem}$ $\leftrightarrow$ $[\ldots C_i \ldots]_{stem}$
$[\ldots C_iC_i \ldots]_{stem}$ $\leftrightarrow$ $[\ldots C_ieC_i \ldots]_{stem}$

An alternative is to adopt an analysis parallel in nearly all respects to that made for Tonkawa above. If stems like *nadad* (28d) are viewed as partial reduplications of *nad-* , as suggested in Glinert (1989: 460), then syncope plus degemination will result in neutralization of the paradigmatic contrast.[26] Assuming regular degemination, what blocks syncope is the neutralization of distinct morphosyntactic paradigms.

3.2. Rule inversion and paradigm effects in East Cushitic

Data from Afar, an East Cushitic language, was presented in (1). The Cushitic languages are distant cousins of the Semitic languages. In a very recent quantitative and comparative study of Somali, Afar, Rendille and Oromo, Barillot (2002) demonstrates that all of these languages show evidence of root non-homorganicity effects, and templatic non-concatenative morphology, well known from studies of their distant Semitic cousins (e.g. McCarthy 1981, 1982).

Within this context, Barillot (2002) also reviews the status of antigemination in these East Cushitic languages. One of his most significant findings in this area is that, in Somali, there is a correlation between syncope and identity of vowel quality between V_1 and V_2 in CV_1CV_2C stems. The general facts for Somali verbs are summarized as in (30):

(30)   Salient characteristics of CVCVC verbs in Somali (Barillot 2002: 279)
   a.   The majority of CVCVC stems have identical vowels in both syllables.[27]
   b.   When CVCVC stems have two distinct vowels, *there is no syncope.*

From a historical point of view, it is clear that the majority of CVCVC stem have the same vowel in both syllables because they are the result of vowel copy. The historical process is illustrated in (31), where Proto-East Cushitic is abbreviated PEC.[28] Given historical evidence for vowel copy epenthesis, the generalizations in (30) follow from historical rule inversion: vowels which are historically present do not syncopate, while those which are historically inserted may take part in V/zero alternations.

(31)   East Cushitic vowel copy: $^*CV_iCC- > CV_iCV_iC- /\_\{C,\#\}$
   a.   PEC *bull-* 'flour'; Afar *bulul* 'become pulverized'; Oromo *bull-aw-* 'become pulverized'
   b.   PEC *ħizz-* 'yam, creeper'; Somali *ħidid*; Bayso *hidid*; Oromo *hidd-a*.
   c.   PEC *kilm-* 'tick'; Afar *kilim*, Oromo *film-a*.

However, in Somali, as in Afar, Rendille and Oromo, vowels are not lost between identical consonants in CVC_iVC_i stems even when vowels are identical. Barillot (2002) demonstrates that in some cases, this is because the medial consonant in Somali is (historically) geminate.[29] For the remaining cases, he posits abstract underlying forms: stems like *barar-* 'enfler', he claims, are underlying quadrilateral $C_1VC_2C_1VC_2$ stems, with an empty onset to the second syllable (op cit. p.445). By assuming that these stems involve -CVC reduplication, Barillot at once accounts for the identity in vowels and consonants. The abstract medial empty onset is part of a consonant cluster and the structural description of the syncope rule is not met.

Barillot extends this abstract analysis to Afar, Rendille and Oromo where CVC_iVC_i stems also resist syncope, as illustrated in (32).[30]

(32)   East Cushitic antigemination effects in CVC_iVC_i verb stems (Barillot
         2002: 465)

	Afar		Rendille		Oromo	
	se marier	*parler*	*avoir mal*	*se regrouper*	*traire*	*griffer*
1s/3ms	digba	**walala**	bolxa	**urura**	elma	**tarara**
2s/3fs	digibta	walalta	boloxta	ururta	elemta	tararta
1p	digibna	walalna	boloxna	ururra	elemna	tararna
2p	digibtan	walaltan	boloxtaan	ururtaan	elemtani	tarartani
3p	digban	**walalan**	bolxaan	**ururaan**	elmani	**tararani**
CAUS/	digbise	**walalise**	bolxica	**ururica**	elmama	**tararama**
PASS	*marier*	*faire parler*	*faire mal*	*regrouper*	*être trait*	*être griffé*

In (33) I summarize the descriptive facts for CVC_iVC_i stems which hold for all four East Cushitic languages, following Barillot (2002: 468).

(33)   Salient characteristics of CVC_iVC_i verbs in Somali, Afar, Rendille and
         Oromo
         a.   The second stem vowel does not alternate with zero
         b.   The final consonant is never guttural.
         c.   Vowels in the first and second syllable are identical.

Generalizations (33b,c) follow from the historical analysis presented in (31). Stems of the form CVC_iVC_i are derived from $*CV_iC_jC_j$- stems. It follows that consonants, like gutturals, which are not geminable, will not surface in these forms, and that the vowel in the second syllable will be a copy of the first, since vowel-copy epenthesis is involved. The generalization we need to account for now is that in (33a): why is it that all East Cushitic languages show antigemination in stems of this sort? Since the vowel/zero alternation originally involved vowel-insertion, not vowel deletion, there is no natural history of this process which involves a gradual evolution from phonetic to phonological syncope.

I suggest that in this case, rule inversion is coupled with clear paradigm uniformity effects. Under rule inversion, historical vowel copy in (31) is reinterpreted as vowel loss.[31] In all four East Cushitic languages under discussion, there is synchronic degemination in word-final and preconsonantal position, as stated in (34).[32]

(34)   East Cushitic degemination
       $C_iC_i \rightarrow C_i /\_\{C, \#\}$

As a consequence, under suffixation, CVC_iC_i- stems in the modern languages undergo regular degemination before consonant-initial suffixes, and word-finally. Some of these geminate final stems are lexical (Afar *obb*- 'hear'), but others appear to be the result of regular word-formation processes (e.g. Afar geminate-final imperatives). For the second class, stem-final gemination is morphological. In this case, paradigm leveling occurs precisely where syncope would give rise to a stem-final geminate which is not morphological. As in Tonkawa, it is the morphological or morphotactic non-identity of two stem types (reduplicated and non-reduplicated in Tonkawa, final geminate vs. final C_iVC_i in East Cushitic) which is maintained under antigemination.

While this analysis involving paradigm leveling has a slightly different character from the direct anti-homophony effects seen in Arabic and Tonkawa, it is supported by facts from Arbore (Hayward 1984), where leveling has not occurred in CVC_iVC_i stems which reflect historical $*CVC_iC_i$-. In (35) relevant sub-paradigms are shown for three different stem-types: CVC_iC_i- stems, CVCVC- stems where the second vowel is non-alternating, and CVC(V)C- stems where the second vowel, in parentheses, alternates with zero in precisely the environments predicted by the historical reanalysis of (31) as vowel deletion. Note that CVC_iVC_i- stems which would violate antigemination under syncope fall into two lexical classes: those where the vowel is lost (violating antigemination), and those where the vowel is maintained, as in the related languages in (32).

(35)   Some Arbore verb subparadigms (Hayward 1984: 274–285).

	2s perfect	2s imp.	1s perfect
i. CVCVC- stems			
ʔeruc- 'vomit'	ʔeructe	ʔeruc	ʔeruce
tatab- 'want'	tatatte	tatap	tatabe
kulil- 'warm oneself'	kulilte	kulil	**kulile** ⎫
harar- 'hurry, be fast'	hararte	harar	**harare** ⎭ cf. bold forms in (32)
ii. CVC$_i$C$_i$- stems			
horr- 'chase'	horte	hor	horre
fuss- 'miss'	fuste	fus	fusse
laww- 'milk'	lawte	law	lawwe
fayy- 'be saved'	fayte	fay	fayye
iii. CVC(V)C- stems			
zer(e)n- 'pierce'	zerente	zeren	zerne
war(a)b- 'fetch water'	waratte	warap	warbe
k'in(i)n- 'sting'	k'ininte	k'inin	{**k'inne**} expected under rule inversion;
k'ad(a)d- 'shut'	k'adatte	k'adat	{**k'adde**} no antigemination

Since the Arbore system comes closest to representing the sound change with rule inversion, it supports an analysis in which the extension of non-alternating CVC_iVC_i- stems in other East Cushitic languages is due to analogical change.[33]

4. Natural history

Despite the seemingly unnatural histories just examined, there is a potential natural history for antigemination effects. Antigemination could be viewed as a transient stage of phonologization which occurs when syncopating sound changes innovate in languages with pre-existing geminate/singleton contrasts. The critical observation is that, at the stage of variation before sound change occurs, unstressed vowels in the syncope environment are reduced. If a reduced vowel can be re-interpreted as consonant release, or as a simple phonetic transition from one consonant to the next, then vowel loss is phonologized. However, in languages where underlying geminates occur, the audible release between identical consonants (or homorganic ones) in the syncope context will result in temporary resistance to their categorization by language learners as the same phonological entities as underlying (full or partial) geminates. These rearticulated identical elements will resist interpretation as geminates, because for underlying long consonants, there is no release between the two 'halves' of the geminate consonant. Other consonant clusters with medial release, on the other hand, may be reinterpreted as true clusters more readily, given the optionality of release in heterorganic clusters in many languages. At the same time, patterns of coarticulation for adjacent identical consonants will be expected to reduce or eliminate the open transition over time, so that eventually, despite the perceptual basis for resistance to syncope between geminates in such languages, if no other factors interfere, syncope should eventually occur. In all of the cases examined above, there is evidence that syncope can and will apply between identical consonants, unless paradigmatic constraints are operative. However, there is at least one known language where antigemination may perhaps be seen in its pure and natural state.

In Central Alaskan Yup'ik (CAY), with underlying geminate/non-geminate contrasts, schwa syncope applies across the board to unstressed vowels in the VC_CV context, unless the two consonants are identical (Miyaoka 1971, Reed et al. 1977, Woodbury 1982, Woodbury 1987, Woodbury personal communication, 2003). In this case, there is gemination of the post-schwa consonant, since in general schwa is not licit in unstressed open syllables. In Hooper Bay Chevak, the usual situation is for schwa to delete even when surrounded by identical consonants.[34] Following Woodbury (1982), McCarthy (1986: 245) is very explicit about the output of syncope in Hooper Bay Chevak: "The result of deleting schwa between identical consonants in no case merges with a true one-to-many geminate. Rather, the cluster of identical consonants is produced with a medial release that, in sonorant environments, is a full-fledged vowel . . . In no case does the derived cluster merge with a true geminate." Representative forms are shown in (36).

(36)   Syncope and antigemination in Central Alaskan Yup'ik

	/kəmə-ni/	/kəmə-mi/	/ənə-ni/
General CAY	kəmni	**kəməmmi**	**ənənni**
Hooper Bay Chevak	kəmni	kəm°mi	ən°ni
	'his own flesh'	'of his own flesh'	'house-LOC.SG'

McCarthy's account of the two differing dialects relies on representational differences which result from tier conflation. Morphemes are represented on separate tiers, which are conflated at some point in the derivation. If morphemes are on separate tiers, and syncope applies between identical consonants in different morphemes, the output of syncope will not violate the Obligatory Contour Principle, since adjacency is only defined tier-internally. The account is summarized in (37).

(37)   An OCP-based account of Yup'ik dialect differences in vowel syncope
       (McCarthy 1986)

	Antigemination	Rule type	Tier conflation
General CAY	yes	post-lexical	yes
Hooper Bay Chevak	no	late lexical	no

To my knowledge, no additional support for the distinction in rule type proposed by McCarthy exists, nor is there any evidence that syncope in Hooper Bay Chevak is anything but post-lexical. It is clearly not structure preserving, producing rearticulated adjacent identical consonants, and also follows other rhythmic rules which appear to be post-lexical (Woodbury 1982, 1987). McCarthy (1986: 245) himself admits that "the distinction in the domain of syncope cannot as yet be independently motivated."

I suggest that the difference between General CAY and Chevak reflect the natural evolution of syncope rules. While pre-existing length contrasts and morphological effects may inhibit the progress of syncope between identical consonants, coarticulatory effects may eventually win out, as in the phonetic alternations illustrated in (3). Central Alaskan Yup'ik stands out in the classification of languages presented in (5.I). In all other languages, templatic morphology defines whole paradigms or subparts of them. In all other languages, gemination can be the primary exponent of a morphological contrast, and this morphological contrast can, in effect, give rise to unnatural phonologization of the transient sound pattern defined by General Yup'ik.

Though the natural evolution of antigemination in Yup'ik appears to be unique cross-linguistically, this evolutionary stage (without Yupik-specific post-schwa gemination) is posited as a transient one for all phonetically natural syncopes in which a pre-existing geminate/non-geminate contrast exists. What is rare is for this transient state to be phonologized without the interference of factors external to phonetic naturalness. In all of the cases reviewed in section 3, a pre-existing morphological contrast appears to influence the grammaticization of antigemination. In Central Alaskan Yup'ik, the independent rule of post-schwa gemination (completely generalized in other dialects) may also have played a role: once unstressed $C_i \vartheta C_i$ sequences are produced as $C_i \vartheta C_i C_i$, syncope is further inhibited, since the schwa is no longer in an open syllable. Since Chevak lacks the post-schwa gemination rule, syncope is not further inhibited, and naturally extends itself to $C_i \vartheta C_i$ sequences as well.

5. Explanation in evolutionary phonology

The working hypothesis of Evolutionary Phonology is that common sound patterns typically result from common phonetically motivated sound change. Among these common sound patterns are the general syncope patterns examined above: in all but the East Cushitic case, synchronic syncope alternations mirror, to a great extent, phonetically natural syncopating sound changes. The specific question I have addressed in this study is whether the failure of syncope to apply between identical consonants in unrelated languages can also be viewed as phonologization of a phonetically natural effect. A survey of syncopating sound changes in which antigemination is not found suggests that non-phonetic processes are involved. All languages surveyed in section 3 show strong correlations between antigemination and homophony avoidance within paradigms. Nevertheless, in at least one language, Central Alaskan Yup'ik, antigemination shows no morphological conditioning and appears to have a near-natural history interrupted only by the existence of post-schwa gemination.

Does antigemination have a natural history? The answer within Evolutionary Phonology is complex: yes and no. Sequences of identical consonants which occur as variants of unstressed $C_i V C_i$ sequences will more readily resist reinterpretation as geminates in languages with pre-existing consonantal length contrasts than in languages without them. If independent self-organizing principles of morphological analysis intervene during the course of language acquisition, antigemination may emerge as a consequence. However, where pre-existing length contrasts are absent, antigemination cannot have a natural history. If it is observed, as in Tonkawa, it is predicted to fall into the class of unnatural histories. Where it is not observed, as in the history of Munsee sketched in (4), the expected natural history of syncope continues uninterrupted.

How are the same facts, correlations and tendencies to be accounted for in purely synchronic terms? In sections 1 and 2 I outlined several problems for previous synchronic accounts of antigemination. McCarthy's (1986) approach is undermined by its dependence of multi-tiered representations (including long-distance geminates) and the operation of tier-conflation which have been eliminated from standard Optimality-theoretic treatments (Gafos 1998, Keer 1999, Kager 1999). Odden's suggestion that the OCP is not a component of Universal Grammar leaves us in an even weaker position to understand the fundamental nature of the sound patterns in question.

The only well developed synchronic alternative to McCarthy (1986) I am aware of is the general account suggested by Rose (2000). Under her account, antigemination is still a phonological OCP effect, but the OCP operates only on C_iVC_i sequences, since any surface C_iC_i sequence in a given domain is claimed to be geminate and does not violate the OCP. Such geminates do, however, violate the NO-GEM constraint. The OCP and NO-GEM have distinct rankings in different languages, and McCarthy's tier-conflation is translated into domain-specific constraints. A serious empirical problem with Rose's account is her assumption that "any output sequence of two identical consonants within the same domain ... constitutes a geminate, a single consonant with long duration. This is in line with phonetic evidence, which has found no distinction between surface true and fake geminates ..." (Rose 2000: 101). However, in McCarthy's original article, he notes that in languages like Modern Hebrew and Hooper Bay Chevak, precisely this contrast occurs: derived sequences of identical consonants can be rearticulated, but underlying geminates cannot.[35]

However, the fundamental problem I see with the range of synchronic approaches is not technical or empirical, but explanatory. While it is straightforward for synchronic approaches to reframe analyses of the antigemination cases described above in terms of the interaction of phonological constraints with morphological anti-homophony constraints (Yip 1998, Crosswhite 1999), and paradigm uniformity effects (Kenstowicz 1996, Benua 1997, Steriade 2000, McCarthy 2002, etc.) such accounts fail to make the same range of predictions as the historical approach advocated here. In (38) I highlight some of these predictions, and present them as a challenge for competing synchronic analyses.

(38)   Predictions of Evolutionary Phonology for syncope and antigemination
   a.   Antigemination is strongly correlated with languages which have either lexical geminate/non-geminate contrasts or degemination.
   b.   Pure antigemination as a regular feature of an exceptionless phonological syncope alternation with origins in unstressed/weak vowel loss is rare or non-existent. (General CAY is 'impure', due to post-schwa gemination).
   c.   In languages with only open syllables, syncope between identical consonants only may reflect pre-existing gestural scores. (Blevins and Blust 2003)

The correlation in (38a) is a consequence of the unnatural histories involved in the majority of antigemination cases reported in the literature. The phonological pattern ruled out in (38b) follows from our phonetic understanding of syncopating sound changes. Though certain variable $C_1{}^VC_2, C_1{}^\circ C_2$ sequences (where '^{V}' is a short unstressed vowel) may prove more resistant to (re)analysis as C_1C_2 than others, there is strong phonetic tendency for adjacent identical consonants to merge into single segments over time. Only when non-phonetic analogical effects intervene, is there a recurrent pattern of grammaticized antigemination effects. Finally, in (38c),

I suggest a phonetic explanation for a recurrent pattern not discussed in this chapter, but clearly related: in many languages with only open syllables, syncope occurs only between identical or homorganic consonants (Blust 1990, Odden 1988). Within synchronic accounts, the OCP and No-Gem must both be low ranking, and an additional constraint must be invoked to rule out heterorganic sequences. The alternative is to note that in languages with only CV syllables, there is already an articulatory pattern that each consonantal feature complex must be released into a vowel. The only derived clusters which can be produced with this pattern intact are geminates or homorganic ones. There is no reference to the OCP, No-Gem, or any additional synchronic markedness constraints. The sound pattern is predicted by a simple interaction of vowel reduction and pre-existing patterns of C-V coarticulation.

While the primary focus of this study is antigemination, I hope to have demonstrated more generally the extent to which the central premises of Evolutionary Phonology provide a concrete model in which natural and unnatural sound patterns can be identified. General patterns of syncope are amenable to historical phonetic explanation, but the diverse and morphologically conditioned patterns of antigemination are not. In understanding the true nature of antigemination, we come closer to understanding the ways in which phonetics, phonology and morphology can interact to produce the diverse sound patterns which characterize the world's languages.

Notes

* This is a revised version of a paper first presented at the Berkeley Linguistic Society in 2003. I am grateful to that audience, and to Adrian Macelaru and Tony Woodbury for comments and corrections on earlier drafts.

1. Other cases of nasal-obstruent metathesis with unnatural histories are summarized in Blevins and Garrett (2004). For one of the first modern treatments of sound changed conditioned by morphological paradigms, see Malkiel (1968).

Abbreviations used in glosses are: caus = causative; dist = distributive; impf = imperfective; acc = accusative; refl = reflexive; rep = repetitive; quot = quotative; nom = nominative; gen = genitive; loc = locative; sg = singular; pl = plural; m = masculine; f = feminine. Language abbreviations used are: CAY = Central Alaskan Yup'ik; PE = Proto Eskimo; PEA = Proto Eastern Algonquian.

2. In Optimality-theoretic terms we might rephrase his conclusion: that the OCP (and antigemination) are violable constraints. This is the approach taken in, e.g. Rose (2000), where the OCP is paired with a constraint No-Gem, whose interactions are claimed to account for the same range of antigemination effects. See Section 5 for further discussion of this proposal.

3. These sound changes are written segmentally for the sake of exposition. They can all be stated in prosodic terms: an unstressed vowel is deleted from weak position in a foot, when

the vowel is non-final. This is clearly the correct statement for Old Irish, since in words of five or more syllables, the vowel of the fourth syllable is also lost (Thurneysen 1980: 67).

4. The failure of short unstressed vowels to delete in final position may reflect prosodic domains of coarticulation as well as an inhibiting effect of phrase-final lengthening.

5. In other vocalic contexts, e.g. *a_i, a_u*, the reflex of *γ is zero: PE *$qayuR$ CAY, *qauq* 'forehead'.

6. Interestingly, degemination is also in evidence in the history of Central Alaskan Yupik, and must have preceded syncope. Consider, for example the following correspondences: PE *$annəviy$ 'place or time of going out', CAY *anvik*; PE *$nałəkkay$ 'crotch (of trousers)' CAY *nałkiik* (dual); PE *$qatəŋŋun$ 'half-sibling' (?), CAY *qatŋun*. Since syncope in all other cases is limited to VC_CV environments, these sets show that degemination preceded historical syncope. At the time that syncope applied then, CAY may have lacked a geminate/nongeminate contrast. See sections 2 and 3 where this correlation becomes relevant.

I have scoured available sources for particular instances in which the Old Irish and Chamorro sound changes noted might give rise to adjacent identical consonants. No reflexes of proto-forms with the relevant unstressed *C_iVC_i sequence were found.

7. See Al-Nassir (1993: 58–61) for a detailed discussion of Sibawayh's treatment of *Idghām* in identical segments separated by short unstressed vowels. Within Sibawayh's typology of phonological processes, there is no general term for vowel syncope. The term *Ikhfā'* 'concealing' is used for unstressed vowel reduction (Al-Nassir 1993: 58).

8. For reconstructed geminate/singleton contrasts, see Sasse (1982) for Proto-East-Cushitic, Moscati et al. (1964) for Proto-Semitic, and Fortescue et al. (1994) for Proto-Eskimo.

9. Austronesian languages with syncope between identical consonants are discussed in Blust (1990), and others in Odden (1988). For an analysis of syncope between identical consonants only, see Blevins (2004a), and Blevins and Blust (2003).

10. Odden (1988: 465) cites (3a). Other examples he provides of vowel loss in C_iVC_i are cases where the two consonants have distinct laryngeal feature specifications either underlyingly (e.g./k^hek'-/) or in the base for prefixation (e.g. *qoq'a: k* 'little river', with reduplication and syncope, *qoqq'a: k* 'dist. little rivers').

11. That syncope did apply historically in exactly these contexts is supported by entries in Gatschet (1890), where geminate fricatives are recorded. Compare, for example the following non-distributive/distributive pairs, where 'sh' writes Barker's /s/: *shéshatui/shéshshatui* 'to trade, barter/dist.'; *shashága/shashshága* 'to take care of oneself/dist.'; *shashálkia/shshshálkia* 'to quarrel/dist.'; *shishókish/shishshókish* 'fighter; warrior/dist.' Evidently sound change of *$ss > s$ occurred sometime between Gatschet's field work at the end of the 19th century, and Barker's fieldwork in the middle of the 20th century. After this sound change, prefixation (resulting in homophony) appears to be blocked (Blevins 2004b). The attested base forms in (10) cannot be interpreted as instances of prefixed stems.

12. Syncope is obligatory for high vowels, and optional for non-high vowels.

13. McCarthy (1986: 241, note 14) notes "difficulties" in the Tunisian Arabic data.

14. Recall from note 12 that syncope is optional for non-high vowels. Wise's point is that syncope never occurs in these verbal paradigms, whether the vowel is high, or not.

15. See Rose (2000) where just such morphological domain restrictions on the OCP are proposed.

16. Cowell (1964: 80) states: "If the last two radicals are alike (as in *ħāžаž* 'to argue with') the imperfect stem vowel *e* is commonly dropped when *-i* or *-u* are suffixed: *biħāžžu* or else *ə* may come between the like radicals as in Pattern II verbs . . . . *biħāžəž*." I assume that the common application of syncope reflects the general case, with the non-syncopated pattern on analogy with Pattern II verbs. Later Cowell (1964: 203) states that "e is not dropped but is changed to *ə*, when it comes between a double and a single consonant which are alike."

17. The example provided by Cowell (1964: 15) is ʃak(k)kon /ʃakk + kon/ 'your (pl.) suspicion' which can be pronounced longer than simple geminates, but "are normally reduced to the same length as double ones." Cowell makes it clear (op cit, p. 27) that consonant length is only contrastive in Damascene in prevocalic position: in pre-consonantal position, or at the end of the phrase there is neutralization of the length contrast. One other place where syncope is blocked is in quadriradical CVCCVC bases, where the 3rd and 4th radicals are alike (op cit, p.118): *baxʃaʃ* 'to tip', *ybaxʃəʃu* 'they tip' (**ybaxʃʃu*). Since not all CCC clusters derived from potential syncope in this context are licit in the language, it is unclear whether the absence of syncope in this context it so be attributed to general CCC phonotactics in the language, specific constraints on post-consonantal geminates, or to analogy with biliterals like *sabbeb* discussed in the text.

18. Note in this example that syncope is followed by progressive assimilation of pharyngealization, which gives rise to a surface geminate [TT]. Examples like this one provide counterevidence to McCarthy's (1986: 42) suggestion that the autosegmentalization of voicing and pharyngealization features within the feature geometry gives rise to adjacent identical segments, and therefore, to antigemination effects under the OCP. The data he examines is the following, where there is no syncope between /d, T, D/ and /t/:

i. conditions for syncope not met		ii. no syncope	
a. madd-et	'she stretched'	maddəto	'she stretched it'
b. ħaTT-et	'she put'	ħaTTəto	'she put it'
c. fEDD-et	'silver of'	fəDDəto	'your (f. sg.) silver'

As with the cases noted in the text, it is the identical $C_iC_iC_i$ output sequence which appears to blocks syncope in these cases, not the OCP. In sum, a general OCP-based account cannot explain why syncope does apply in GalTTi 'my mistake' from /GalT-et-i/, but not in the forms above, since morphological structures are parallel.

19. McCarthy's analysis, in this case, depends on ordering of tier-conflation before syncope within cyclic domains. However, Odden (1988) argues that syncope is post-lexical in Tiberian Hebrew, making McCarthy's analysis untenable. Notice that in Tiberian Hebrew, as interpreted by McCarthy, the situation is the reverse of Damascene Arabic in terms of output conditions. In forms like *hinnii* (18c) from /hinnən-ii/ syncope gives rise to a trigeminate cluster which is reduced via degemination, while blocking is found in verbs like *Saaləlúu*, where a licit intervocalic geminate might otherwise surface.

20. Hoijer (1933) suggests that the synchronic C_1V_1-C_2V_2 pattern where V_2 resists syncope could be from earlier *C_1V_1-C_2V: $_2$, with a levelling of vowel length in the non-reduplicated theme.

21. McCarthy (1986: 224) gives precisely the same page reference to Hoijer (1946: 292) but a different interpretation, concluding that when geminates arise via morphological concatenation they are "only optionally simplified." Hoijer (1946: 289) makes it clear that he has "made several important changes in both the orthography and the phonological discussion."

One of these appears to be the recognition of regular degemination, as stated in the quoted passage. Confirmation of this is found in Hoijer's (1972) published texts, where all combination of identical consonants across morpheme boundaries appear as single consonants. Compare, for example, Hoijer (1933: 614.b) *ha:csokonay-yeyka'ay* 'wolves:big coyotes' with Hoijer (1972: text 4, par.7) *ha:csokonayayka'ay'a:la*.

22. One potential example is *makay* 'dun-colored' possibly from /makik-ay/ via /makkay/. Compare *makik* 'yellow, orange'.

23. McCarthy (1986: 238) also supplies the following nouns and adjectives for comparison, though no evidence is provided that these nouns must be derived from CVCVC bases with syncope: *dabran* 'talkative', *zaxlan* 'very slow', and *malxut* 'kingdom' vs. *zalelan* 'glutton', *xatetan* 'meddler' and *noxexut* 'presence'.

24. Some authors of modern grammars, in comparing triliteral CVCVC templates to bilateral CVCC, continue to refer to this process in terms of synchronic vowel loss. For example, Cowell (1964: 41) states that when the CVCVC verb pattern is "applied to a root whose last two radicals are alike, such as *d-l-l*," the stem "loses its second vowel *a*, and the two radicals cohere as a double consonant: *dall* 'to indicate' (not "*dalal*")."

25. This mapping is the historical equivalent to McCarthy's (1986: 239) synchronic rule of geminate epenthesis. This rule inserts a schwa between the two halves of an underlying geminate. Since there are no intramorphemic contrasts between geminate and non-geminates in Hebrew, this synchronic analysis is highly abstract, positing underlying geminates which never surface. It also presents an apparent violation of geminate integrity, though McCarthy argues that representation of vowels and consonants on separate tiers makes epenthesis possible.

26. McCarthy (1986: 238), based in part on Bolozky (1977) states that degemination is optional and only occurs in "fast or casual speech." For this analysis, it is only necessary that degemination was non-contrastive at some point in the history of Modern Hebrew, a fact suggested by the elimination of all geminate/singleton contrasts once present in the Biblical language.

27. Verb stems with non-identical vowels fall into three classes: those where historical identity has been altered by phonetic effects of an adjacent consonant; those where Arabic loans are replaced with the *a-i* melody; a remainder of the three verbs *sumad* 'marquer au fer rouge', *subag* 'étaler du beurre' and *umal* 'enrager' (Barillot 2002: 277). In other words, of the 329 CVCVC- Somali verb stems in the database, only three have unexplained non-identical vowels. Adrian Macelaru (personal communication, 2003) suggests that non-identical vowels in these three verbs could be the result of sporadic *a>u triggered by a following labial consonant.

28. This is not Barillot's (2002) analysis. He treats verbs of the form $C_1V_1C_2V_1C_2$ as underlyingly $C_1V_1C_2C_1V_1C_2$ from final - $C_1V_1C_2$ reduplication plus medial cluster reduction. Within the Government Phonology framework, these stems have empty C positions which block syncope. See Barillot (2002) for a thorough view of the facts from these East Cushitic languages, and for a clear exposition of his own analysis, which also eliminates reference to antigemination as a consequence of the OCP.

29. Barillot posits abstract synchronic underlying geminates in these positions, though degemination of the consonants in question is exceptionless. It is straightforward, however, to reinterpret his results in historical terms. These stems had medial geminates historically,

and hence did not meet the structural description of the syncope rule. Once degemination occurred for the consonants in question, the syncope rule became opaque.

30. Stems of the form CVCVy- also typically resist syncope in Afar (Barillot 2002: 455). Bliese (1981: 215–216) attributes this to a general phonotactic constraint against surface *Cy* clusters in the language. In section 5 I return to general remarks about the evolution of syncope rules and potential constraints on their application.

31. The term 'rule inversion' refers to cases where a historical sound change involving *A > B/Z has synchronic reflexes involving A alternating with B, where this alternation is interpreted synchronically as B →A (usually in the complement environment to Z). Though some instances of historical rule inversion can be eliminated (e.g. Frajzyngier 1976), the historical reinterpretation of deleted segments as inserted segments is common (Blevins, to appear).

32. See Barillot (2002, chapter 1) where Somali phonotactics are presented, including a reanalysis of certain surface singletons as underlying geminates.

33. Of the non-alternating stems in (35i), *ʔeruc-* and *kulil-* show distinct vowels, suggesting original *CVCVC- stems, while *tatab-* and *harar-* appear to involve historical CVC- reduplication (*tabtab > tatab-* and *harhar > harar*) also with no history of V/zero alternations.

34. For some younger speakers, the general CAY pattern is found, but Woodbury (1982: 87) suggests that the constraint on syncope "insofar as it exists there, has the status of a loan" with younger speakers possibly influenced by GCAY speakers in Bethel. More recently, Woodbury (personal communication, 2003) notes that the failure of syncope between identical consonants for Chevak speakers was "a transient phenomenon, barely worth reporting."

35. Similar facts are detailed for Imdlawn Tashlhiyt Berber by Dell and Elmedlaoui (1996).

References

Al-Nassir, A. A. 1993. *Sibawayh the Phonologist: A Critical Study of the Phonetic and Phonological Theory of Sibawayh as Presented in his Treatise Al-Kitab*. Library of Arabic Linguistics. Monograph no. 10. New York: Kegan Paul International.

Barillot, Xavier. 2002. Morphophonologie gabaritique et information consonantique latente en Somali et dans les langues est-couchitiques. Thèse de doctorat en linguistique théorique et formelle, Université Paris VII Denis Diderot, UFR do Linguistique.

Barker, M. A. R. 1963. *Klamath Dictionary*. University of California Publications in Linguistics 31. Berkeley: University of California Press.

Barker, M. A. R. 1964. *Klamath grammar*. University of California Publications in Linguistics 32. Berkeley: University of California Press.

Benua, Laura. 1997. Transderivational identity: phonological relations between words. PhD dissertation. University of Massachusetts, Amherst.

Blevins, Juliette. 1993. "Klamath laryngeal phonology". *International Journal of American Linguistics* 59: 237–279.

Blevins, Juliette. 2004a. *Evolutionary Phonology: The Emergence of Sound Patterns*. Cambridge: Cambridge University Press.

Blevins, Juliette. 2004b. Klamath sibilant degemination: Implications of a recent sound change. *International Journal of American Linguistics* 70: 279–289.

Blevins, Juliette. To appear. "Consonant epenthesis: Natural and unnatural histories". In J. Good (ed.), *Proceedings of the Workshop on Explaining Universals*. Cambridge: Cambridge University Press.

Blevins, Juliette and Robert Blust. 2003. Towards a theory of drift: patterns of Austronesian syncope. Ms., University of California, Berkeley.

Blevins, Juliette and Andrew Garrett. 1998. "The origins of consonant-vowel metathesis". *Language* 74: 508–556.

Blevins, Juliette and Andrew Garrett. 2004. "The evolution of metathesis". In Bruce Hayes, Robert Kirchner, and Donca Steriade (eds.). *Phonetically Driven Phonology*. 117–156 Cambridge: Cambridge University Press.

Bliese, Loren F. 1981. *A Generative Grammar of Afar*. Arlington, Texas: Summer Institute of Linguistics.

Blust, Robert. 1990. "Three recurrent changes in Oceanic languages". In J.H.C.S. Davidson (ed.), *Pacific island languages: Essays in honour of G. B. Milner*. 7–28. London: University of London, School of Oriental and African Studies.

Blust, Robert. 2000. "Chamorro historical phonology". *Oceanic Linguistics* 39: 83–122.

Bolozky, Shmuel. 1977. "On the status of fast speech in natural generative phonology". In J. Kegel, D. Nash, and A. Zaenen (eds.), *Proceedings of the Seventh Annual Meeting of the North-eastern Linguistic Society*. Cambridge, MA: MIT.

Cowell, Mark W. 1964. *A reference grammar of Syrian Arabic*. Washington, DC: Georgetown University Press.

Crosswhite, Katherine. 1999. "Inter-paradigmatic homophony avoidance in two dialects of Slavic". *UCLA Working Papers in Linguistics 1, Papers in Phonology 2*. 48–67.

Dell, François and Mohammed Elmedlaoui. 1996. "On consonant releases in Imdlawn Tashlhiyt Berber". *Linguistics* 34: 357–395.

Erwin, Wallace M. 1963. *A Short reference grammar of Iraqi Arabic*. Washington, DC: Georgetown University Press.

Fortescue, Michael, Steven Jacobson, and Lawrence Kaplan. 1994. *Comparative Eskimo Dictionary with Aleut Cognates*. Fairbanks: Alaska Native Language Center.

Frajzyngier, Zygmunt. 1976. "Rule inversion in Chadic: An explanation". *Studies in African Linguistics* 7.2: 195–210.

Gafos, Adamantios I. 1998. "Eliminating long-distance consonantal spreading". *Natural Language and Linguistic Theory* 16: 223–278.

Garrett, Andrew and Juliette Blevins. To appear. "Morphophonological analogy". In Sharon Inkelas and Kristin Hanson (eds.). *The nature of the word: Essays in Honor of Paul Kiparsky*. MIT Press.

Gatschet, Albert S. 1890. *The Klamath Indians of Southwestern Oregon*. Washington, DC: Government Printing Office.

Glinert, Lewis. 1989. *The grammar of Modern Hebrew*. Cambridge: Cambridge University Press.

Goddard, Ives. 1979. *Delaware Verbal Morphology: A Descriptive and Comparative Study*. New York: Garland.

Goddard, Ives. 1982. "The historical phonology of Munsee". *International Journal of American Linguistics* 48: 16–48.

Hayward, Richard. 1984. *The Arbore language: A First Investigation*. Hamburg: Helmut Buske Verlag.

Hoijer, Harry. 1933. *Tonkawa: An Indian language of Texas*. Extract from Handbook of American Indian Languages, Vol. III. New York: Columbia University Press.

Hoijer, Harry. 1946. Tonkawa - An Indian language of Texas. In C. Osgood (ed.), *Linguistic Structures of Native America*. New York: Viking Fund Publications in Anthropology 6.

Hoijer, Harry. 1949. *An analytical dictionary of the Tonkawa language*. University of California Publications in Linguistics 5(1). Berkeley: University of California Press.

Hoijer, Harry. 1972. *Tonkawa Texts*. University of California Publications in Linguistics 73. Berkeley: University of California Press.

Jacobson, Steven A. 1984. *Yup'ik Eskimo Dictionary*. Fairbanks: Alaska Native Language Center.

Kager, René. 1999. *Optimality Theory*. Cambridge: Cambridge University Press.

Keer, Edward W. 1999. Geminates, the OCP and the Nature of Con. PhD dissertation, Rutgers University, New Brunswick, NJ.

Kenstowicz, Michael. 1996. "Base identity and uniform exponence: alternatives to cyclicity". In J. Durand and S. Laks (eds.), *Current Trends in Phonology: Models and Methods*. 363–393. European Studies Research Institute and University of Salford.

Kisseberth, Charles. 1970. Vowel elision in Tonkawa and derivational constraints. In J. Sadock and A Vanek (eds.), *Studies presented to Robert B. Lees by his Students*. Papers in Linguistics, Monograph Series I. Champaign, Ill: Linguistic Research, Inc.

Lin, Yen-Hwei. 1997. "Syllabic and moraic structures in Piro". *Phonology* 14: 403–436.

Malkiel, Yakov. 1968. The inflectional paradigm as an occasional determinant of sound change. In W. P. Lehmann and Y. Malkiel (eds.), *Directions for historical linguistics*. Austin: University of Texas Press.

Malone, Joseph. 1986. The obligatory contour principle, tier conflation and bracket erasure: A new alignment from Hebrew. Ms., Barnard College.

Malone, Joseph. 1993. *Tiberian Hebrew Phonology*. Winona Lake, IN: Eisenbrauns.

Matteson, Esther. 1965. *The Piro (Arawakan) Language*. Berkeley: University of California Press.

McCarthy, John J. 1981. "A prosodic theory of nonconcatenative morphology". *Linguistic Inquiry* 12: 373–418.

McCarthy, John J. 1982. "Prosodic templates, morphemic templates, and morphemic tiers". In H. van der Hulst and N. Smith (eds.), *The Structure of Phonological Representations I*. Dordrecht: Foris.

McCarthy, John J. 1986. "OCP effects: Gemination and antigemination". *Linguistic Inquiry* 17: 207–263.

McCarthy, John J. 2002. *A Thematic Guide to Optimality Theory*. Cambridge: Cambridge University Press.

Miyaoka, Osahito. 1971. "On syllable modification and quantity in Yuk phonology". *International Journal of American Linguistics* 37: 219–226.

Moscati, Sabatino, Anton Spitaler, Edward Ullendorf and Wilhelm von Soden. 1964. *An Introduction to the Comparative Grammar of the Semitic Languages: Phonology and Morphology*. Wiesbaden: Otto Harrassowitz.

Odden, David. 1988. "Anti Antigemination and the OCP". *Linguistic Inquiry* 19: 451–475.

Reed, E. Irene, Osahito Miyaoka, Steven Jacobson, Paschal Afcan, and Michael Krauss. 1977. *Yup'ik Eskimo Grammar*. Fairbanks: Alaska Native Language Center and Yup'ik Language Workshop.

Rose, Sharon. 2000. Rethinking geminates, long-distance geminates and the OCP. *Linguistic Inquiry* 31: 85–122.

Sasse, Hans-Jürgen. 1982. *An Etymological Dictionary of Burji*. Hamburg: Helmut Buske Verlag.

Steriade, Donca. 2000. Paradigm uniformity and the phonetics-phonology boundary. In J. Pierrehumbert and M. Broe (eds.), *Laboratory Phonology V: Acquisition and the Lexicon*. 313–334. Cambridge: Cambridge University Press.

Thurneysen, Rudolf. 1980. *A Grammar of Old Irish*. Dublin: The Dublin Institute for Advanced Studies.

Wise, H. 1983. "Some functionally motivated rules in Tunisian phonology". *Journal of Linguistics* 19: 165–181.

Woodbury, Anthony C. 1982. Study of the Chevak dialect of Yup'ik Eskimo. Phd dissertation, University of California, Berkeley.

Woodbury, Anthony C. 1987. "Meaningful phonological processes: A consideration of Central Alaskan Yupik Eskimo prosody". *Language* 63: 685–740.

Yip, Moira. 1998. "Identity avoidance in phonology and morphology". In S. LaPointe, D. Brentari, and P. Farrell (eds.), *Morphology and its relations to phonology and syntax*. 216–246. Stanford, CA: CSLI Publications.

Chapter 11

What it means to be rare:
The variability of person marking

Michael Cysouw

Zentrum für allgemeine Sprachwissenschaft (ZAS), Berlin
Max Planck Institute for Evolutionary Anthropology, Leipzig

The marking of person in language is a relatively well-described aspect of linguistic structure. However, even in this case, linguistic theory can use an update on the empirically attested linguistic variation among the world's languages. In this paper, I present a summary of the results of various wide-scale typological investigations in the realm of person marking that I have conducted over the last few years. On this basis, I argue that there is a continuous cline from common to rare structures of person marking without a clear division between 'regular' cases and 'exceptions.' This situation poses a problem for any current theoretical analysis. When only the structures with the highest frequency are included, the theory looks regular; but there are many counterexamples. When the more unusual structures are also captured by the theory, this leads to many rather ad-hoc stipulations in the theory. An ideal theory of language should not distinguish between 'regular' and 'exceptional', but capture the relative frequencies of attestation.

1. Introduction

One goal a linguistic theory might aim for is to account for the linguistic diversity of the world's languages. However, that linguistic diversity is probably much greater than many a theorist might realise (cf. Noyer 1997, Dalrymple and Kaplan 2000, Harley and Ritter 2002). Only when the full extent of linguistic variability is taken into account can a theory be evaluated as to its explanatory force. The question then becomes a practical one: how much of the variation should be explained by a theory for it to be considered 'sufficient' or even 'good'?

In this paper I will present as an exemplary case the variation attested in the marking of person. The main reason to choose person marking is that data are rather easily found for very many languages, as basic person marking facts will be described in even short sketches or family surveys. For that reason, I have been able to collect many examples of structures that would normally be classified as 'rare'. But what does it mean to be rare? A structure found in, for example, one language out of a sample of 200 of the world's languages (which is really rare indeed) is — when extrapolated to the 5,000–10,000 languages presently spoken — still a structure that is attested statistically in about 25 to 50 languages. Can all these languages be simply disregarded as 'exceptions'?

This paper is organised as follows. In Section 2, some methodological issues are discussed. Then, in Section 3, the commonly attested structures are reviewed. In Sections 4 through 8 various rare phenomena are discussed. These sections present the basic data for this paper. Finally, in Section 9, a summary is presented and some possible theoretical approaches to explain the variation are discussed.

2. Methodological musings

This paper is a summary of the investigation into the variability of person marking that I have been conducting over the past few years. Various aspects have been published already, some are forthcoming and there are also some data which are still being recorded. I will not discuss the complete data on which the present paper is based, but rather limit myself to a survey of the frequencies of attestation. For each frequency, a list of the languages that show that particular phenomenon is given in the appendix.

I will focus on oppositions that are found in paradigms of person markers. Person markers occur in various guises. They can be morphologically independent pronouns or morphologically bound inflections; they can code for various syntactic and/or pragmatic functions; and they can be used obligatorily with each verb or only sparingly in highly marked contexts. I will look at all the person paradigms attested in a language, independently of form and function, because I am only interested in the internal structure of the paradigm. This means that many languages are included in the present paper because of only one aberrant paradigm. Some languages will appear more than once in different sections, because different paradigms in these languages show different 'rare' patterns. An important limitation is that I will disregard number marking when person and number are marked separately. This is the case most clearly in languages that have person prefixes and number suffixes (the reverse is extremely rare for some unknown reason, cf. Cysouw in preparation-a). In such cases, the paradigm included here will then consist only of the person prefixes, since number is undetermined in the paradigm (see Cysouw 2003: 4–15 for an extensive discussion of these and other definitional issues).

The main body of this paper will be a rather dry survey of paradigms of person marking in which some seemingly disparate categories are marked by identical linguistic means. Such a combination can be called a structural ambiguity, a syncretism, or simply homophony or homonymy. I will use the term syncretism, which is intended as a neutral, empirical cover-term for all the observed cases (cf. Luraghi 2000). Furthermore, I do not distinguish between languages in which this syncretism is a meaningful ambiguity, reflecting the conceptualisation of reality of a particular speech community, and languages in which the syncretism is only an accidental result of phonological merger. Actually, I doubt that this distinction can be made consistently throughout a large collection of languages. And even if a particular structure is the result of a seemingly random historical merger, this still leaves the question of why the resulting combination of categories does not force the speakers of such a language to disambiguate the two. There are some cases included in this paper in which the structure of the language regularly disambiguates the syncretism, but in most examples this is not the case.

The rare structures of person marking that I will discuss are often attested in closely related languages, or are a recurring structure in larger genetic units. To give an indication of the genetic diversity of the frequencies attested, I will interpret not only the number of cases attested, but also the number of genera and the number of stocks to which these languages belong. Both levels of classification are used rather freely, and no claims on genetic (sub)groupings are intended (see the appendix for the classifications used). Most importantly, I have decided to count 'Papuan' (i.e. the non-Austronesian languages from New Guinea and the surrounding islands) and non-Pama-Nyungan (i.e. the Australian languages that do not belong to the Pama-Nyungan family) as stocks, although the comparative evidence for them is non-existent or meagre.

The present collection of cases is a result of rather *ad hoc* sampling. A consistent typological sampling strategy (cf. Rijkhoff and Bakker 1998) is not suitable for an investigation of rare phenomenona. In a standard typological sample, rare structures do not appear, or appear only as exceptions (depending on the size of the sample). This touches on a central problem with strict sampling procedures in typology. A sample can show which linguistic types are common among the world's languages, but it cannot be used to analyse a type that is possible, yet uncommon. It is good practice to amend each large-scale typology with a detailed investigation of uncommon types. A fine example of this method is the paper on gender/number marking by Plank and Schellinger (1997). That paper starts with the well-known Greenbergian universals, which state (roughly summarised) that gender distinctions in the plural imply gender distinctions in the singular. However, the authors then show that on closer inspection a large set of 'counterexamples' exists. By investigating such 'exceptional' examples, a deeper understanding of the possible variability of human language can be reached.

Because I have not controlled the sample of the present collection of cases, it remains enigmatic what it means if I report, for example, twelve cases for a particular rare phenomenon — call it phenomenon X. The following calculation gives a rough estimate of the meaning of such frequencies. In total, I will report on 501 examples of more or less rare patterns of person marking as attested in 373 different languages. Naively calculated, twelve cases of phenomenon X out of a sample of 373 languages amounts to 3.2%. However, the present 373 languages are not at all representative of all the world's languages. To get an indication of the relative meaning of these 373 languages, I compared this collection to the basic sample of the *World Atlas of Linguistic Structures* (WALS, Haspelmath *et al.* forthcoming), which consists of 200 languages.[1] Of the 373 languages, only 63 are part of the WALS-200-sample (also counting near matches, i.e. close relatives). No other languages in the WALS-200-sample show any unusual patterns of person marking. This means that my 373 languages are roughly comparable to a hypothetical typological sample of about 373*(200/63) = 1184 languages. The twelve examples of phenomenon X are thus to be taken relative to an 1184-language sample, which amounts to 1.0%. Such percentages are not to be taken too seriously, though they help to provide an impression of the relative importance of the frequencies as reported here.

Before I discuss the data in detail, a short note on terminology is in order. I will use the term 'clusivity' as a cover term for various forms in which languages express concepts that are traditionally called 'inclusive' and 'exclusive' first person. On the one hand, there are languages like English that do not mark clusivity at all.[2] On the other hand, there are very many different ways in which languages can mark a difference between inclusive and exclusive (cf. Cysouw 2003: Ch. 3). All these different structures are combined when I use the term 'clusivity.'

3. The common patterns

Before turning to the rare patterns, I will first discuss the commonly attested structures of person marking. Ingram (1978: 218–219) designated four paradigmatic structures of person marking as 'more common than others'. These four structures are shown in Figure 1. First, there is a six-person paradigm with three persons in both the singular and the plural. Then there is a seven-person paradigm adding a separate inclusive to the six-person system. Further, dual forms can be added to both the six-person and the seven-person paradigm, leading to nine-person and eleven-person paradigms. These four patterns are what most linguists would expect when looking for personal pronouns (or any other kind of person marking paradigm).

Without clusivity — Without dual

I	we
you	you'all
s/he	they

With clusivity — Without dual

	I + you('all)
I	I + others
you	you'all
s/he	they

Without clusivity — With dual

I	we two	we
you	you two	you'all
s/he	they two	they

With clusivity — With dual

	I + you	I + you'all
I	I + one other	I + others
you	you two	you'all
s/he	they two	they

Figure 1. The common person paradigms

Table 1. Frequencies of person paradigms (based on the data from Forchheimer 1953 as counted by Ingram 1978)

Kind of paradigm	Frequency	Percentage
Six- or nine-person paradigm	24	33.8
Seven- or eleven-person paradigm	25	35.2
Other structures	22	31.0

Ingram's reason for designating these paradigmatic structures as 'more common than others' is shown in Table 1. The four common paradigmatic structures constitute the patterns found in about 70% of all languages. He obtained these data by counting all the examples in Forchheimer (1953), but he did not realise that the languages as presented by Forchheimer were not meant to be representative of the genetic diversity of the world's languages.[3] Nevertheless, the proportion of about 30% of 'other' structures seems to be roughly accurate. As discussed above, I found that 63 out of the 373 languages in the present collection are also among the WALS-200-sample. This means that if I had taken the WALS-sample for this investigation, I would have found that $63/200 \times 100 = 31.5\%$ of the languages in the sample have a deviant structure somewhere in their person marking.

Among the roughly 31% of deviant structures, the paradigms shown in Figurz are the most widespread. These paradigmatic structures are known as 'minimal/augmented' and 'unit-augmented'. The minimal/augmented paradigm is like the seven-person paradigm, but adds an opposition between a minimal inclusive (you.SING and I) and an augmented inclusive (you.PL and I). The minimal inclusive in such paradigms is necessarily dual in nature, but it is better not to analyse it as a dual. The reason for this claim is that virutally all languages with a minimal inclusive have no other dual forms anywhere in the structure of the language (Cysouw 2003: 85–90).

The unit-augmented paradigm is the 'dual' variant of a minimal/augmented paradigm. However, because the 'dual' of the inclusive (you-two and I) actually consists of three persons, this 'dual' is called 'unit-augmented' (following McKay 1978), meaning one unit (i.e. participant) more than the basic category.

Minimal/augmented (8 person)

I + you	I + you'all
I	we
you	you'all
s/he	they

Unit-augmented (12 person)

I+you	I + you two	I + you'all
I	I + one other	I + others
you	you two	you'all
s/he	they two	they

Figure 2. Two relatively common person paradigms

Table 2. Attested cases of minimal/augmented and unit-augmented paradigms (data from Cysouw 2003; extended in Cysouw in preparation-b)

	Stocks	Genera	Languages	Pronouns
Eight- or twelve-person paradigm	12	24	79	78

These two paradigmatic structures might seem exotic, though Siewierska and Bakker (forthcoming) found 15 cases of such paradigmatic structures in a representative sample of 393 of the world's languages (3.8%). I have extensively searched for cases and currently know of 79 languages with one of these two paradigmatic structures, almost all to be found as independent pronouns (see Table 2). Examples are commonly attested in the Philippines, among the non-Pama-Nyungan languages in Australia and in the Chadic languages in Africa and the surrounding non-Chadic languages. Outside these core areas there are incidental examples all over the world. Using the approximation proposed in section 2, the attested 79 languages make up about 6.7% of the world's language. This percentage is somewhat higher than the 3.8% as attested in Siewierska and Bakker's study. The reason for the difference between the two figures is that the distribution of minimal/augmented patterns appears to be strongly areal. The three main areas mentioned above show a rather dense distribution of these patterns. Likewise, the genetic diversity in the set of minimal/augmented paradigms is relatively low, as can be seen in Table 2. The 79 languages are found in only 24 different genera. Because of this skewed distribution, a sample-study (like Siewierska and Bakker's) will result in a somewhat lower percentages than my instance-based counts. The other phenomena to be presented in this paper will show much less areal/genetic clustering, so the approximations of the typological frequency that I present there will be more accurate.

The six most common paradigmatic structures, as presented in this section, account for the person marking in roughly three quarters of the world's languages. In the remaining quarter of the world's languages, there are at least some person paradigms that do not belong to any of these six. It is this last quarter that will be the main theme of the rest of this paper.

4. Number syncretisms

The difference between singular and plural does not have to be marked in a person paradigm. All examples attested with overlap between a singular and a non-singular category are summarised in Table 3. The first thing to note is that, in almost all cases, the overlap between singular and plural is in the same person. Only the last three rows of Table 3 show that there are a few deviant cases. Most examples of singular/plural overlap are like English *you*, which is used for second person in both the singular and the plural. However, English is atypical in that it is only the second

Table 3. Attested cases of number syncretism (data from Cysouw 2003 with a few examples added)

	Stocks	Genera	Languages	Pronouns
3rd no number			(many)	
2nd and 3rd no number	12	16	39	7
1st, 2nd and 3rd no number	25	30	60	20
1st no number	2	4	5	2
2nd no number	3	3	9	3
1st and 2nd no number	2	2	4	0
1st and 3rd no number	3	3	3	1
1 singular = 2 plural	2	2	2	0
2 singular = 1 plural	2	2	5	1
3 singular = 2 plural	2	2	2	0

person which shows this overlap. As can be seen from the first three rows in the table, it is more common for the overlap to follow the person hierarchy 1>2>3.[4] The overlap is first attested low on the hierarchy (with the third person) and only subsequently extended upwards.[5] This hierarchy has been known for some time; the first clear reference to it was made by Forchheimer (1953: 12).

Although this hierarchy is well known and widely quoted, it turned out to be rather difficult to find examples of its various stages. The number of cases (see Table 3) is even lower than the number of minimal/augmented paradigms (see Table 2). The structure that was most difficult to find is the paradigm that marks number only in the first person. The 39 cases in my collection approximate to 3.0% of the world's languages — a percentage that can only be interpreted as rare indeed.

In person paradigms that also have dual forms, one might expect the same hierarchy of overlap, this time between dual and plural. However, Plank (1989: 305) already argued that this hierarchy is not as straightforward as the one between singular and plural. As can be seen from the data in Table 4, I would argue — even more

Table 4. Attested cases of number syncretisms involving the dual (data from Cysouw 2003)

	Stocks	Genera	Languages	Pronouns
3rd no dual	4	4	5	5
2nd and 3rd no dual	4	5	5	5
1st no dual	3	3	3	3
2nd no dual	4	4	4	3
1st and 2nd no dual	4	5	6	2
1st and 3rd no dual	1	1	1	1

strongly — that there is no hierarchy at all in paradigms with dual marking. All the possible forms of overlap are more or less equally frequent. Note that there is no row listing cases with dual/plural overlap in all three persons — first, second and third — as this would mean that there is no dual being marked at all in the paradigm.[6]

Summarising, human languages show a preference to follow the person hierarchy 1 > 2 > 3 for the marking of number. In total, I have collected 99 examples of paradigms that are in line with this hierarchy, which is 8.4% of the world's languages (using the approximation as proposed in section 2). However, there is a lot of variation, a point that will appear recurrently in this paper. Simply dismissing all other variants as being unusual or exceptional is a rather crude decision. After all, we are talking about a total of 49 'exceptions' (4.1%), half as many as the number of examples that are in line with the hierarchy. A theory that deals only with the main generalisation (i.e. the person hierarchy) has limited explanatory force: it explains 99 cases, but it cannot explain another 49 cases.

5. Person syncretisms

A commonly repeated supposedly universal characteristic of human language is the distinction among the three persons (first, second and third). Although indeed all languages may have some way to distinguish among references to speaker, addressee and other, it is not true that this threefold division is obligatorily made in each person marking system of every language. There are quite a few cases in which the distinction among the persons is blurred to some extent.

For the analysis of person categories, Heath (forthcoming) discusses three different theoretical possibilities. The first possibility is called the 'speech-roles model', opposing participants (first and second person) to non-participants (third person). The second model is named the 'consciousness model', opposing the first person to the combined second and third person. Finally, Heath proposes an addressee-centric 'pragmatic model' opposing the second person to the combined first and third person. In other discussions of person marking in the literature only one of these possibilities is discussed, implying that there is something special about one of these models. For example, Noyer (1997: 112–113) discusses only examples of the third versus non-third structure and uses the existence of such cases to argue for a feature [±participant] in morphology. Another example is Sasse (1993: 670), who only notes 'rare reports of neutralisation of 2nd and 3rd person'. My findings present quite a different situation.

In Table 5, the frequencies of person syncretisms are shown as attested in the singular. Clearly, the 'consciousness model' (first versus non-first) is the most frequent when looking at the number of languages. However, at the level of stocks and genera, the difference from the next most frequent syncretism (third versus non-third, i.e. the 'speech-role model') is not that large. In fact, the recorded high frequency of the first versus non-first syncretism is due to its relative ubiquity in Indo-European and

Table 5. Attested cases of person syncretisms in the singular (data from Cysouw 2003)

Singular	Stocks	Genera	Languages	Pronouns
First versus non-first	10	15	31	1
Third versus non-third	9	10	11	1
Second versus non-second	3	4	8	0
Completely syncretic	2	3	4	0

Papuan inflection. The unusual character of all these syncretisms is emphasised by the observation that almost all cases are attested in inflectional paradigms. Only the first versus non-first and the third versus non-third are attested incidentally in independent pronouns (in Winnebago and Qawesqar, respectively).

A comparable situation is found with person syncretisms in the non-singular, as shown in Table 6 (in this table, only person syncretisms are included that do not involve clusivity — these will be discussed in the next section). Again, the opposition first versus non-first is clearly the most common, followed by third versus non-third. In contrast to the singular syncretisms, both these structures are regularly attested in independent pronouns. In these independent pronouns, it is almost never the case that singular and plural both have a person syncretism. In contrast, in the inflectional cases, the same syncretism is attested regularly in both the singular and the non-singular.

These frequencies highlight the need for a two-tiered kind of explanation of the structural possibilities of human language. On the one hand, there are clear differences in frequency between the various theoretical options. Some syncretisms are more ubiquitous than other — a fact that has to be explained in a theory of language. On the other hand, all the theoretical possibilities are attested — a range of variation the can not be neglected. Simply stating that the preferred structure for person syncretisms is first versus non-first (although true) only accounts for 73 of the 137 syncretisms as listed in the two tables (53%). A theory that only accounts for slightly more than half of the cases attested can hardly be called sufficient.

Table 6. Attested cases of person syncretisms in the non-singular (data from Cysouw 2003)

Non-singular	Stocks	Genera	Languages	Pronouns
First versus non-first	16	23	42	15
Third versus non-third	11	15	24	11
Second versus non-second	5	10	11	0
Completely syncretic	3	5	6	0

6. Syncretisms involving clusivity

The situation becomes a bit more complicated once the possibility of a distinction between inclusive and exclusive is taken into account. In traditional terminology, the inclusive and exclusive were seen as subcategories of the first person plural. The rationale behind this intuition is that when a language does not overtly mark an inclusive/exclusive opposition, then both kinds of reference are made by use of the first person plural 'we'. However, once there is an inclusive/exclusive opposition marked overtly, then there is good reason to interpret the exclusive as the first person plural and the inclusive as something different (cf. Daniel forthcoming).

The case of the Algonquian person prefixes is recurrently quoted in the literature as showing that there also exists a link between inclusive and second person (e.g. Zwicky 1977; Plank 1985; Daniel forthcoming). Their argument roughly runs as follows. In Algonquian, the same person prefix is used for the inclusive and for the second person. This combination makes sense as both inclusive and second person refer to the second person (among others). This is a second person based structure. In contrast, the European style first person plural pronoun 'we' combines inclusive and exclusive reference because both refer to first person (among others). This is a first person based structure. Languages appear to have both options.

I investigated the cross-linguistic validity of these options by collecting examples of syncretism between inclusive/exclusive and some other person, either singular or plural (Cysouw forthcoming-b). I only included languages that overtly distinguish between inclusive and exclusive. The results are summarised in Table 7. It is clear from these frequencies that the situation is not symmetric at all.

There is a clear asymmetry between the ubiquity of the exclusive/first person syncretism (34 cases, approximately 2.9% of the world's languages) and the almost complete absence of the inclusive/first person syncretism (one exceptional case only). This asymmetry can be accounted for by noting that the exclusive is the plural counterpart of the first person singular. The exclusive/first person syncretism is thus a kind of number syncretism.

Table 7. Attested cases of syncretisms between inclusive/exclusive and other persons (data from Cysouw forthcoming-b)

	Stocks	Genera	Languages	Pronouns
Exclusive = first person[a]	17	20	34	14
Inclusive = first person	1	1	1	0
Exclusive = second person	3	6	15	1
Inclusive = second person	9	9	14	2
Exclusive = third person	7	7	19	0
Inclusive = third person	4	8	15	1

[a] These cases are a subset of those cases listed in Table 3 having no number in the first person

There are four theoretically possible syncretisms between inclusive/exclusive on the one hand, and second/third person on the other. All four are roughly equally frequent. They occur with a mean of 15.8 cases, which is approximately 1.3% of the world's languages. These four kinds of syncretism are clearly less frequent than the exclusive/first person syncretism and they are almost unattested among independent pronouns.

Judging from such numbers, the Algonquian case should not be overvalued for the development of a theory of linguistic structure. Its structure shows an intriguing possibility of human language, but it is not more important than other structures, which do not make much sense semantically (e.g. inclusive combined with third person). Further, all these figures have to be compared to the 33.8% of the world's languages that do not have clusivity at all (cf. Table 1). The extremely rare 'second person based' structure like in Algonquian is clearly far less important (as far as frequency counts) than the 'first person based' structure as found in English.

7. Different kinds of clusivity

Another field of variation is the specific interpretation of the inclusive/exclusive opposition. In section 3, I argued that two variants are rather common: the normal inclusive/exclusive opposition (see Figure 1) and the minimal/augmented variant (see Figure 2). However, there are some more possibilities attested, as will be summarised in this section. These variations will be analysed as syncretisms, but this term is only intended as a descriptive tool — it might be better to see the oppositions as special semantic variation on the inclusive/exclusive theme (cf. McGregor 1996).

The first two variants are shown in Table 8. The structures that are listed there are analysed as variants of the minimal/augmented paradigm. In the minimal/augmented paradigm, there are three different forms that are to be translated into English as *we*. Theoretically, then three different syncretisms are possible. First, minimal inclusive and augmented inclusive can be combined into one form: this leads to the regular inclusive/exclusive opposition (and will not further be discussed here). The other two options, as shown in the table, are much rarer. Greenberg (1988) and McGregor (1989) discuss incidental examples, but I have searched further to see how frequent these structures really are. It appears that they are rare, though more common than one might have thought (cf. Table 8).

Table 8. Attested cases of variants of minimal/augmented (data from Cysouw 2003; extended in Cysouw forthcoming-b)

	Stocks	Genera	Languages	Pronouns
Minimal inclusive = exclusive	5	5	6	5
Augmented inclusive = exclusive	5	8	11	7

Table 9. Attested cases of syncretisms between various forms of clusivity (data from Cysouw 2003)

	Stocks	Genera	Languages	Pronouns
Dual inclusive = dual exclusive	3	6	7	5
Plural inclusive = plural exclusive	3	3	3	1
Dual inclusive = plural inclusive	3	3	3	3
Dual exclusive = plural exclusive	2	2	2	2

The first variant from Table 8 opposes the augmented inclusive (you and I and others) to the combination of minimal inclusive (you and I) and exclusive (I and others). McGregor says about this combination that it 'excludes one of the two non-speaker roles, either the addressee or another third person' (1989: 439). He calls this form 'restricted'. This structure is uncommon, yet there are a few more cases attested, showing that McGregor's case is not a singularity among the world's languages.

The other possibility opposes the minimal inclusive (you and I) to the combination of the augmented inclusive (you and I and others) and exclusive (I and others). Greenberg (1988) calls this the 'Assiniboine type'. This structure appears to be somewhat more common than the former, yet I do not think that this difference is significant. The totals for both structures are simply too low to allow for any definitive conclusion.

Other variants on the inclusive/exclusive theme are shown in Table 9. These cases can be seen as variants of the 11-person system (see Figure 1). All paradigms included here have an inclusive/exclusive opposition and some dual forms — at least a second person dual and a third person dual. However, the interaction between the dual and the inclusive/exclusive opposition varies. Four different variants have been attested, although they are all rare. There are more theoretical options which are not (yet) attested, for example the combination 'dual inclusive = plural exclusive'. In fact, the four structures attested each neatly neutralises exactly one semantic opposition — either the dual/plural opposition or the inclusive/exclusive opposition. This observation suggests that there are also interesting generalisations possible distinguishing between structures that are rare and structures that are extremely rare (or even unattested).

All the cases discussed in this section are rare. However, in total we are talking about 30 languages, which is about 2.6% of the world's languages using the approximation as developed in Section 2.[7]

8. Honorific usage of clusivity

Person markers often differ in their referential value according to the social setting in which they are used. Head (1978) gives a useful survey of the linguistic possibilities for expressing respect. One phenomenon that he found recurrently among the world's languages is to use a plural form instead of a singular, thereby implying respect. However, in his sample of 'more than hundred languages' (Head 1978: 151), he only found two cases in which an inclusive or exclusive pronoun was used to express respect (Head 1978: 178): one case in which the exclusive expresses respect (Auca) and one in which the inclusive expresses respect (Hawaiian). In Table 10, I have summarised the number of cases that I have found.[8]

The most common honorific usage of clusivity is to express polite address using an inclusive (17 cases). Interestingly, it is not immediately clear why this usage should be so (relatively) widespread. It is even hard to explain this usage at all using the politeness framework of Brown and Levinson (1987). In their framework, they distinguish between two different kinds of politeness: positive politeness and negative politeness. Positive politeness "anoints the face of the addressee by indicating that in some respects, [the speaker] wants [the addressee's] wants" (Brown and Levinson 1987:70). In other words, being positively polite roughly amounts to sharing the addressee's attitudes. Negative politeness "consists in assurances that the speaker recognizes and respects the addressee's ... wants and will not ... interfere with the addressee's freedom of action" (Brown and Levinson 1987: 70). In other words, being negatively polite roughly amounts to leaving the addressee alone as much as possible.

Not all sources give concise information on the precise contexts in which the inclusive can be used as a polite form of address. As far as the descriptions allow an interpretation, the inclusive seems to be preferred in formal situations in which it is necessary to give deference to the addressee. This usage of an inclusive is a kind of negative politeness, because it is a less direct way to refer to the addressee than a blunt second person pronoun.[9] However, this does not yet explain why the inclusive can be used to express a difference in status. Including oneself in the reference is an implicit threat to the addressee's negative face — and thereby potentially impolite (cf. the so-called 'doctor's we', as in 'how are we doing today?' asked by a doctor to his patient — a usage found to be offensive by many). Maybe there is an influence from the inherent asymmetry between speaker and addressee. The speaker, simply by the fact of being speaker, exercises control over the speech situation. The action of speaking itself is inherently threatening the negative face of the addressee. By using an inclusive form, the speaker offers to disregard this inherent supremacy,

Table 10. Attested cases of honorific usage of clusivity (data from Cysouw forthcoming-a)

	Stocks	Genera	Languages	Without Austronesian
Inclusive as polite second person	5	9	17	4
Inclusive as humble first person	1	3	5	0
Inclusive as bonding first person	3	3	3	3
Inclusive as impolite first person	2	3	4	4
Exclusive as polite first person	4	6	8	5

which means that by including himself, the speaker implicitly abases himself. Interpreted this way, using an inclusive instead of a second person form is a way to give deference — one of the many ways to be negatively polite (cf. Brown and Levinson 1987: 178–186).

Overall, the inclusive appears to be clearly more viable for honorific usage compared to the exclusive. However, the inclusive does not always have to express respect: there are even some cases in which the inclusive is used to be rude. This apparently strange usage is completely in line with expectation, because an inclusive is an implicit threat to the addressee's negative face (see above). Again, the general impression that remains is one of variation. The variation might be skewed, yet this only leaves one more phenomenon to be explained: the variation itself and the skewing of the variation.

9. Interpreting variation

Having now reviewed 501 cases of (more or less) rare structures of person marking, the first remark to be made is that I do not claim this survey be either complete or exhaustive. However, I have tried to show that the variation in the structure of person marking in the world's languages is large. Trying to account for this large variation is a challenge to any theory of linguistic structure. Of course, any generalisation or theory will leave some examples unaccounted for. However, the central question is where we would want to place the cut-off point between explained and unexplained variants of human language.

To bring home this point, I have summarised all the frequencies discussed in this paper in Figure 3. All the structures are listed in this graph, ordered by the frequency of attested cases. There are (at least) two possible ways to look at this graph. The CATEGORICAL VIEW sees a breaking point after the sixth case 'third versus non-third (non-singular)'. All phenomena above the breaking point are frequent; all below this divide are rare. In this view, all frequent phenomena can be summarised by a nice short list of generalisations. Either

– the paradigm is complete (as in Figure 1 and Figure 2); or
– there is number syncretism according to the person hierarchy 1 > 2 > 3; or
– there is a speaker-centred reduction of person marking to first versus non-first.

However, these three generalisations leave 250 cases from 194 different languages unaccounted for, which amounts to some of the person marking in approximately 16% of the world's languages. The generalisations are fine, though the power of their explanation is limited. One could go on adding sub-generalisations, but this is not a real solution. First, each such sub-generalisation is limited to just a few cases and, second, there will still remain some cases that fall out of any generalisation. A 100% account of variation by discrete generalisations can only be achieved at the cost of including 'generalisations' that account for singular cases only.

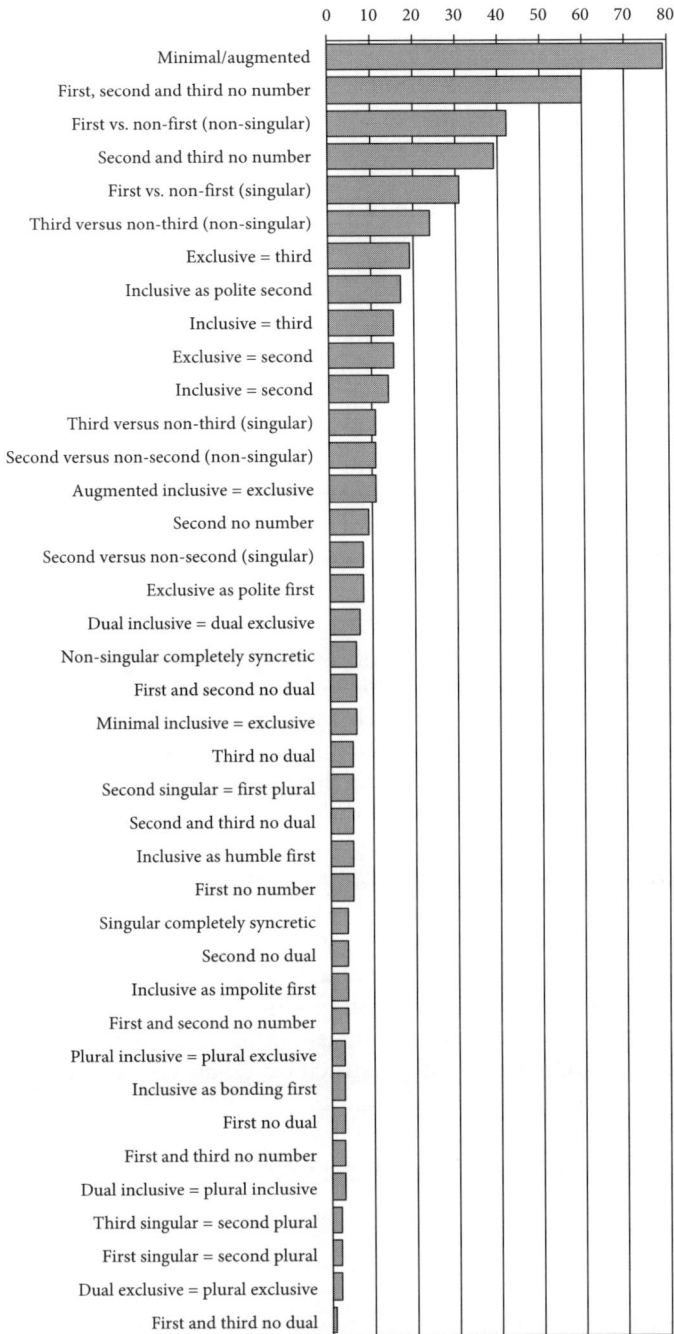

Figure 3. Various rare variants of person marking, ordered to frequency

In contrast to this categorical view, a SCALAR VIEW sees a continuum of diminishing frequencies without a clear break between common and rare cases. The main generalisation is that everything is possible, though not everything is equally likely to occur. However more pleasing such a view is in principle, it is difficult to see how this scalar view might be reworked into a real theory about the structure of human language.

One might think in the direction of optimality theory, in which preference is accounted for by a ranking of constraints. Though it is appealing, I feel that such an approach merely models the data at hand, instead of providing an explanation. The problem is that I do not see a possibility for proposing constraints that interact, without being trivial. Of course, one could propose, for example, three constraints 'first vs. non-first', 'second vs. non second' and 'third vs. non-third'. These three constraints interact, and by ordering them the empirical situation as described in this paper can be modelled. However, the basic principle of an optimalisation approach seems to disappear then, as there is no external rationale for the constraints. Simply all theoretically possible constraints have been included.

A more telling approach would be to include only the constraint 'first vs. non-first', as this is cross-linguistically the most prominent (a kind of 'external' evidence for the validity of the constraint). However, I cannot think of any other cross-linguistically salient constraint that can override this constraint and lead, for example, to a third vs. non-third system.

The situation attested here for person marking is probably also typical for other aspects of the variation among the world's languages. Some structures are clearly more common than others (an important insight that has to be explained), but rare structures also exist. Often it will even be the case, as shown here in Figure 3, that there is no clear division between what should be classified as common and what should be counted as rare. There is simply a continuum from the more common to the rarer cases. If this situation indeed generalises to other linguistic structures, then it becomes difficult to maintain an essentialistic theory of human language. Any proposed essence or absolute universal of language arbitrarily qualifies some part of the continuum as 'right' and degrades the rest as 'wrong'.

Until a good solution is found for dealing with such continua in a theory of linguistic structure, we are left with the problem of the meaning of 'exceptions'. Are they less functional kinds of linguistic structure? Or are they expected to change rapidly into a more common kind of linguistic structure? Probably not, but then we are left with rare structures that work just fine for their users/speakers. Who are we linguists to rate such a working structure as exceptional?

Appendix

The counts that were presented in the present paper are based on the data described in various other publications by the present author (Cysouw 2003, forthcoming a, b, in preparation a, b). In these publications, complete reference to and full discussion of all examples is presented. For reasons of space, I will not repeat these lengthy discussions here, but simply list the names and genetic affiliations of the languages. The language names are ordered roughly according to geographical origin, starting in Africa, through Eurasia into the Pacific, followed by the Americas from north to south. Note that I have interpreted Papuan (i.e. the non-Austronesian languages from the Pacific) and non-Pama-Nyungan (i.e. those languages from Australia that do not belong to the Pama-Nyungan family) as stocks. Although I acknowledge that the genetic affiliation of these clusters is not demonstrated (but see Blake 1988 on non-Pama-Nyungan), I have nevertheless used these classifications because they show considerable similarity in their pronoun systems (cf. the 'unity in diversity' principle from Foley 1986: 9). The language names in italics are those in which the particular structure is attested in the independent pronouns. For these languages, I have not indicated here whether the same structure is also attested in any inflectional paradigm or not (in most languages listed this is not the case).

Languages as counted in Table 2

- Minimal/augmented paradigms
Yag Dii, Koh (Adamawa, Niger-Congo); *Ebang, Moro* (Kordofanian, Niger-Congo); *Ngiemboon, Babungo, Limbum, Ghomala, Akoose* (Bantoid, Niger-Congo); *Dan, Northern Looma* (Mande, Niger-Congo); *Nuer* (Nilotic, Nilo-Saharan); *Gula Sara* (Central Sudanic, Nilo-Saharan); *Marghi, Gude, Lamang, Hdi, Lele, Fyer, Kulere, Sha, Dafo-Batura, Bokas* (Chadic, Afro-Asiatic); *Nivkh* (isolate); *Andaman* (Isolate); *Atta, Isnag, Itneg, Ilocano, Kalinga, Bontoc, Balangao, Kankanay, Ifugao, Kallahan, Agta, Ibaloi, Pangasinan, Sambal, Pampangan, Hanunoo, Tagalog, Tagbanwa, Batak, Binukid, some variants of Manobo, Maranao, Kalagan, Tboli, Blaan, Sangir, Tausag, Samal* (Philippines, Austronesian); Hatam (West Papuan, Papuan); Montain Koiali (Koiarian, Papuan); *Kemtuik* (Nimboran, Papuan); *Weri* (Goilalan, Papuan); *Santa Cruz, Nanggu, Reefs* (East Papuan, Papuan); *Maranungku, Malakmalak* (Daly, non-Pama-Nyungan); *Wardaman, Rembarrnga, Ngandi, Mangarayi, Nunggubuyu* (Gunwingguan, non-Pama-Nyungan); *Bardi, Nyulnyul, Nyikina* (Nyulnyulan, non-Pama-Nyungan); *Ndjébanna* (Burarran, non-Pama-Nyungan); *Tiwi* (Tiwian, non-Pama-Nyungan); *Uradhi* (Pama-Nyungan); *Ute, Northern Paiute, Kawaiisu, Tübatalabal* (Uto-Aztecan); *Southern Sierra Miwok* (Miwok); *Chayahuita* (Cahuapanan).

Languages as counted in Table 3

- 2nd and 3rd no number
Mbay (Central Sudanic, Nilo-Saharan); Turkana, Teso, Lotuho, Maasai (Eastern Nilotic, Nilo-Saharan); Georgian, Svan (South Caucasian); Chukchee, Koryak, Kamchadal (Chukotko-Kamchatkan); *Berik* (Tor, Papuan); *Kuman* (East New Guinea Highlands, Papuan); *Jéi* (Trans-Fly, Papuan); *Karo Batak, Acehnese* (Sundic, Austronesian); *Mekeo* (Oceanic, Austronesian); Mandan, Assiniboine, Lakhota (Siouan); Coahuilteco (isolate); Kwakiutl, Heiltsuk (Wakashan); Xerente, *Maxakali* (Gé); Chulupi (Mataco-Guiacuruan); Huallaga Quechua (Quechuan); Kariña, Tiriyó, Carijona, Kashuyana, Wai Wai, Hixkaryana, Waimiri-Atroari, Arekuna, Akawaio, Wayana, Dekwana, Bakairí, Txikão (Carib).

- 1st, 2nd and 3rd no number
Ngiti, Logbara, Mamvu (Central Sudanic, Nilo-Saharan); Svan (South Caucasian); Lak, Megeb (Nakh-Dagestanian); *Chrau* (Mon-Khmer, Austro-Asiatic); *Nimboran* (Nimboran, Papuan); *Imonda, Amanab* (Border, Papuan); *Salt-Yui, Golin* (East New Guinea Highlands, Papuan); Kiwai (Trans-Fly, Papuan); Nasioi (East Papuan, Papuan); Winnebago, Hidatsa,

Crow (Siouan); Maricopa, Mojave, Dieugueño, Yavapai, Yuma (Yuman); Nez Perce (Sahaptin); Wichita, Caddo, Pawnee (Caddoan); Menomini, Cree, Fox, Eastern Ojibwe, Southwestern Ojibwe, Passamaquoddy-Maliseet (Algonquian); *Acoma Keresan* (Keres); Kutenai (isolate); Washo (isolate); Huave (Huavean); Sierra Popoluca, Coatlán Mixe (Mixe-Zoque); *Chalcatongo Mixtec, Ocotepec Mixtec, Yosondúa Mixtec, Diuxi-Tilantongo Mixtec* (Mixtecan, Oto-Manguean); *Chocho* (Popolocan, Oto-Manguean); Pame, Chichimeco Jonaz, Ixtenco Otomí (Otopamean, Oto-Manguean); *Jaqaru* (Aymaran); *Canela-Kraho,Xerente* (Gé); *Asheninca, Nomatsiguenga, Caquinte* (Campa, Arawakan); Maká, Abipon, Mataco (Mataco-Guaicuruan); Tarma Quechua (Quechuan); Ayoreo (Zamucoan); Awa Pit, *Paez* (Barbacoan-Paezan); *Pirahã* (Mura).

- 1st no number

Marind (Marind, Papuan); Gadsup, *Usarufa* (East New Guinea Highlands, Papuan); Binandere (Binanderean, Papuan); Warrwa (Nyulnyulan, non-Pama-Nyungan).

- 2nd no number

English (Germanic, Indo-European); *South American Spanish* (Romance, European); Lamalera, Dawanese, Kisar, Sika, Roti (Timor, Austronesian); Koiari (Central and Southeastern, Papuan); *Xokleng* (Gé).

- 1st and 2nd no number

Big Nambas, Kwamera, Lenakel (Southern Oceanic, Austronesian); Warrwa (Nyulnyulan, non-Pama-Nyungan.

- 1st and 3rd no number

Classical Ainu (isolate); *Tairora* (East New Guinea Highlands); Dargi (Nakh-Dagestanian).

- 1 singular = 2 plural

French (Romance, Indo-European); Vanimo (Sko, Papuan).

- 2 singular = 1 plural

Suki (Gogodali-Suki, Papuan); Pipil, Milpa Alta Nahuatl, North Puebla Nahuatl, Huasteca Nahuatl (Aztec, Uto-Aztecan).

- 3 singular = 2 plural

German (Germanic, Indo-European); Midob (Central Sudanic, Nilo-Saharan).

Languages as counted in Table 4

- 3rd no dual

Gothic (Germanic, Indo-European); *Nganasan* (Uralic); *Limbu, Camling* (Bodic, Sino-Tibetan); *Kewa* (East New Guinea Highlands).

- 2nd and 3rd no dual

Kilivila (Western Oceanic, Austronesian); *Rapanui* (Polynesian, Austronesian); *Arapesh* (Toricelli, Papuan); *Yidiɲ* (Pama-Nyungan); *Kadiwéu* (Mataco-Guicuruan).

- 1st no dual

Classical Arabic (Semitic, Afro-Asiatic); *Ancient Greek* (Indo-European); *Aleut* (Eskimo-Aleut).

- 2nd no dual

Mansi (Uralic); *Sedang* (Mon-Khmer, Austro-Asiatic); *Yareba* (Central and Southeastern, Papuan); *Dhuwal* (Pama-Nyungan).

- 1st and 2nd no dual

Buin (Bougainville, Papuan); Kapau (Angan, Papuan); Kwamera, Lenakel (Tanna, Austronesian); *Tunica* (Isolate).

- 1st and 3rd no dual
Dizi (Omotic, Afro-Asiatic).

Languages as counted in Table 5

- First versus non-first (singular)
Kenuzi-Dongola (Eastern Sudanic, Nilo-Saharan); Dutch, Icelandic (Germanic, Indo-European); Old Church Slavonic, Bulgarian, Macedonian, Serbocroatian (South Slavonic, Indo-European); Hindi (Indo-Aryan, Indo-European); Chukchee, Koryak, Kamchadal (Chukotko-Kamchatkan); Tsakhur, Akhvakh, Zakatal', Megeb (Nakh Dagestanian); Akha (Burmese-Lolo, Sino-Tibetan); Bunan, Dumi, Monpa, Newari, Tibetan (Bodic, Sino-Tibetan); Awyu, Wambon, Kombai (Central and South New Guinea, Papuan); Moraori (Trans-Fly, Papuan); Siroi (Rai Coast, Papuan); Chitimacha (Isolate); Awa-Pit, Guambino (Barbacoan); Lengua (Mascoian); *Qawesqar* (Alcalufan).

- Third versus non-third (singular)
Krongo (Kordofanian, Niger-Congo); English (Germanic, Indo-European); Lak, Hunzib (Nakh-Dagestanian); Svan (South Caucasian); Maltese (Semitic, Afro-Asiatic); Amele (Mabuso, Papuan); Waskia (Pihom-Isumrud-Mugil, Papuan); Nez Perce (Sahaptin); *Winnebago* (Siouan); Pame (Oto-Manguean).

- Second versus non-second (singular)
Icelandic, German, Gothic (Germanic, Indo-European); Spanish, Siciliano (Romance, Indo-European); Koiari, Ömie (Central and Southeast, Papuan); Ika (Chibchan).

- Completely syncretic (singular)
Italian, French (Romance, Indo-European); Icelandic (Germanic); Kapau (Angan, Papuan).

Languages as counted in Table 6

- First versus non-first (non-singular)
Wolof (Atlantic, Niger-Congo); Kunama (Nilo-Saharan - with clusivity in first person); Icelandic (Germanic, Indo-European); Slovene, Upper Sorbian (Slavonic, Indo-European); Bunan, Rongpo (Bodic, Tibeto-Burman); Chukchee, Koryak, Kamchadal (Chukotko-Kamchatkan); Megeb (Nakh-Dagestanian); Kati, Kombai, Wambon, Awju (Central and South New Guinea, Papuan); Gadsup, *Kalam, Fore, Wiru*, Yagaria, Kewa, Kuman (East New Guinea Highlands, Papuan); *Baruya*, Kapau (Angan, Papuan); *Amele* (Mabuso, Papuan); Siroi (Rai Coast, Papuan); Magi, *Yareba* (Central and Southeastern, Papuan); Moraori, Kiwai (Trans-Fly, Papuan); *Nez Perce* (Sahaptin); *Northern Paiute* (Uto-Aztecan - with clusivity in first person) Chitimacha (isolate); Lengua (Mascoian); *Warekena* (Arawakan); *Warao* (isolate); Awa-Pit (Barbacoan); *Qawesqar* (Alcalufan); *Mauritian Creole, Seychellois Creole, Réunion Creole, North Haitian Creole* (French-based Creoles).

- Third versus non-third (non-singular)
Dogon (Niger-Congo); *Fongbe* (Kwa, Niger-Congo); Kenuzi-Dongola (Eastern Sudanic, Nilo-Saharan); Tinan, Manchad, Primi (Bodic, Tibeto-Burman); Svan (South Caucasian); Lak, Dargi (Nakh-Dagestanian); *Awa, Usarufa* (East New Guinea Highlands, Papuan); Mombum (Central and South New Guinea, Papuan); Waskia (Pihom-Isumrud-Mugil); Tetun (Timor, Austronesian); *Slave, Apache, Navaho, Kato, Hupa* (Athabascan); Nez Perce (Sahaptin); Ika (Chibchan); *Southern Haitian Creole* (French Based Creole); *Ndyuka, Sranan* (English based Creoles).

- Second versus non-second (non-singular)
Bagirmi (Central Sudanic, Nilo-saharan); Midob (Eastern Sudanic, Nilo-Saharan); Dogon

(Niger-Congo); Wolof (Atlantic, Niger-Congo); French (Romance, Indo-European); Hindi (Indo-Aryan, Indo-European); German (Germanic, Indo-European); Omié (Koiarian, Papuan); Orokaiva, Korafe (Binanderean, Papuan).

• Completely syncretic (non-singular)
Dutch, English (Germanic, Indo-European); Rongpo (Tibeto-Burman); Koiari (Central and Southeastern, Papuan); Waskia (Pihum-Isumrud-Mugil, Papuan); Una (Mek, Papuan).

Languages as counted in Table 7

• Exclusive = first person
Ngiti (Central Sudanic, Nilo-Saharan); Svan (South Caucasian); *Chrau* (Mon-Khmer, Austro-Asiatic); Kwamera, Lenakel, (Tanna, Austronesian); *Nimboran* (Nimboran, Papuan); *Imonda, Amanab* (Border, Papuan); Tiwi (Tiwian, non-Pama-Nyungan); Warrwa (Nyulnyulan, non-Pama-Nyungan); Winnebago (Siouan); Wichita, Caddo, Pawnee (Caddoan); Menomini, Cree, Fox, Eastern Ojibwe, Southwestern Ojibwe, Passamaquoddy-Maliseet (Algonquian); *Chalcatongo Mixtec, Ocotepec Mixtec, Yosondúa Mixtec, Diuxi-Tilantongo Mixtec* (Mixtecan, Oto-Manguean); *Chocho* (Popolocan, Oto-Manguean); Huave (Huavean); Sierra Popoluca (Mixe-Zoque); Maká (Mataco-Guaicuruan); Tarma Quechua (Quechuan); *Jaqaru* (Aymaran); *Canela-Kraho* (Gé); *Asheninca, Nomatsiguenga, Caquinte* (Campa, Arawakan).

• Inclusive = first person
Binandere (Goilalan, Papuan).

• Exclusive = second person
Southern Udihe (Tungusic); Lamalera, Dawanese, Kisar, Sika, Roti (Timor, Austronesian); Buma, Yabem, Sobei, Mekeo, *Nehan*, Central Buang (Western Oceanic, Austronesian); Ulithian (Micronesian, Austronesian); Burarra (Burarran, non-Pama-Nyungan); Tiwi (Tiwian, non-Pama-Nyungan).

• Inclusive = second person
Diola-Fogny (Atlantic, Niger-Congo); Kulung (Kiranti, Sino-Tibetan); Acehnese (Sundic, Austronesian); Lavukaleve (East Papuan); Tiwi (Tiwian); Menomini, Cree, Fox, Eastern Ojibwe, Southwestern Ojibwe, Passamaquoddy-Maliseet (Algonquian); Kiowa (Tanoan); *Sanuma, Itonama* (Isolates).

• Exclusive = third person
Diola-Fogny (Atlantic, Niger-Congo); Buduma (Chadic, Afro-Asiatic); Hatam (West Papuan); Binandere (Goilalan); Shuswap (Salish); Kiowa (Tanoan); Kariña, Tiriyó, Carijona, Kashuyana, Wai Wai, Hixkaryana, Waimiri-Atroari, Arekuna, Akawaio, Wayana, Dekwana, Bakairí, Txikão (Carib).

• Inclusive = third person
Kwamera, Lenakel, North Tanna, Southwest Tanna, Whitesands (Tanna, Austronesian); Atchin (Remote Oceanic, Austronesian); Nalik, Buma (Western Oceanic, Austronesian); Muna (Sulawesi, Austronesian); Hatam (West Papuan); Athpare, Camling, Dumi (Kiranti, Tibeto-Burman); Huave (Huavean); *Tupinambá* (Tupí).

Languages as counted in Table 8

• Minimal inclusive = exclusive
Yaouré (Mande, Niger-Congo); Sar (Sudanic, Nilo-Saharan), *Tumak* (Chadic, Afro-Asiatic), *Kunimaipa* (Goilalan, Trans-New Guinea); *Bunaba, Gooniyandi* (Bunaban, non-Pama-Nyungan).

- Augmented inclusive = exclusive
Kunimaipa (Goilalan, Papuan); *Hatam* (West Papuan, Papuan); Bardi, Nyulnyul (Nyulny-ulan, non-Pama-Nyungan); *Burarra* (Burarran, non-Pama-Nyungan); *Tiwi* (Tiwian, non-Pama-Nyungan); *Assiniboine, Lakhota,* Iowa (Siouan); *Pech* (Chibchan); *Guató* (Macro-Gé).

Language as counted in Table 9

- Dual inclusive = dual exclusive
Jiarong (Tibeto-Burman); *Tuaripi* (Eleman, Papuan); *Guhu-Samane, Korafe* (Binanderean, Papuan); Moi (West Papuan, Papuan); Yava (Geelvink Bay, Papuan); *Kuku-Yalanji* (Pama-Nyungan).

- Plural inclusive = plural exclusive
Samo (Central and South New Guinea, Papuan); Tanimbili (Remote Oceanic, Austronesian); Coos ('Oregon Penutian').

- Dual inclusive = plural inclusive
Savosavo (Yele-Solomons, Papuan); *Ngankikurungkurr* (Daly); *Yagua* (Isolate).

- Dual exclusive = plural exclusive
Wik-Munkan (Pama-Nyungan); *Ponapean* (Micronesian, Austronesian).

Languages as counted in Table 10

- Inclusive as a polite second person
Muna, Konjo, Bajau, Wolio, Sa'dan, Duri, Palu (Sulawesi, Austronesian); Toba Batak, North Maluku Malay, Sulawesi Malay (Sundic, Austronesian); Tetun (Timor, Austronesian); Mala-gasy (Borneo, Austronesian); Hawaiian (Polynesian, Austronesian); Ainu (Isolate); Limbu (Kiranti, Tibeto-Burman); Cuzco Quechua (Quechuan); Tamil (Dravidian).

- Inclusive as a humble first person
Sawu (Bima-Sumba, Austronesian); Toba Batak, Sulawesi Malay (both Sundic, Austrone-sian); Duri, Palu (both Sulawesi, Austronesian).

- Inclusive as a bonding first person
Galela (West Papuan); Tzeltal (Mayan); Tamil (Dravidian).

- Inclusive as an impolite first person
Santali (Munda, Austro-Asiatic); Vietnamese (Mon Khmer, Austro-Asiatic); Malayalam, Tamil (both Dravidian).

- Exclusive as a polite first person
Minangkabau, Malay (both Sundic, Austronesian); Malagasy (Borneo, Austronesian); Kharia, Ho (both Munda, Austro-Asiatic); Vietnamese (Mon Khmer, Austro-Asiatic); Tamil (Dra-vidian); Auca (unclassified).

Notes

1. In fact, the WALS-sample is not an ideal sample. This sample was compiled to cover both the genetic diversity and the areal distribution of the world's languages, meaning that gen-etic units that are spread out over a large territory are slightly overrepresented (in particular the Bantu languages and the Austronesian languages).

2. It has been claimed that the first person plural clitic =*s* in English, like in *let's do it*, is an

inclusive form (cf. Hopper and Traugott 1993: 10–14). Indeed, this clitic can only have an inclusive reading, though that is the result of the hortative context, not of the clitic itself (cf. Dobrushina and Goussev forthcoming).

3. Forchheimer investigated much many more languages than were included in his book (1953: 2). He deliberately only showed those paradigms that were different from each other in their internal *morphological* structure (e.g. whether the plural was regularly derived from the singular or not). Forchheimer did not intend to represent the diversity of *paradigmatic* structure as counted by Ingram.

4. Overlap in the first person for languages with an inclusive/exclusive opposition almost universally means an overlap between first person singular and exclusive (see section 6).

5. I did not collect an exhaustive set of examples of the overlap between third singular and third plural only (i.e. the first row in the table) as I expected this to be common from the start. I did not want to waste my time on this seemingly common phenomenon, because I wanted to focus on rare structures.

6. The paradigm that has been called minimal/augmented here (see Figure 2) has a category minimal inclusive, which is traditionally called a dual inclusive. If this category is analysed as a kind of dual (which is, for example, done by Plank 1989), then dual marking in the inclusive only is clearly more frequent than all other options from Table 4. However, I think it is better to analyse the minimal inclusive as a group that consists of speaker and addressee and consider the fact that these are two individuals to be an epiphenomenon (cf. Cysouw 2003: 85–90).

7. Siewierska and Bakker (forthcoming) even find 18 cases (combining their categories Min-Incl, AugIncl and SplInclExcl) in a sample of independent pronouns from 393 languages, which amounts to 4.6%.

8. This collection consists only of published accounts of honorific usages of clusivity. This collection might not be representative of the world's linguistic diversity because honorific usage is very often not described at all. More than half of all cases that I have been able to find come from Austronesian languages (cf. Lichtenberk forthcoming). The preference for the usage of the inclusive as polite address disappears when all Austronesian examples are removed, so an alternative explanation for this phenomenon is to interpret it as an Austronesian idiosyncrasy.

9. Cf. the explanation for this phenomenon in Limbu by van Driem: 'the apparent psychological reasoning behind the polite inclusive is that one implicates and, if such be the case, incriminates oneself in the verbal scenario' (1987: 221) and in Austronesian by Lichtenberk (forthcoming): 'by placing herself in the addressee's sphere, the speaker blurs the distinction between the addressee and herself, which may serve to mitigate potentially face-threatening acts.'

References

Blake, Barry J. 1988. "Redefining Pama-Nyungan: towards the prehistory of Australian languages." *Aboriginal Linguistics* 1: 1–90.
Brown, Penelope and Stephen C. Levinson. 1987. *Politeness: Some Universals in Language Usage* (Studies in Interactional Sociolinguistics; 4). Cambridge: Cambridge University Press.

Cysouw, Michael. 2003. *The Paradigmatic Structure of Person Marking*. (Oxford Studies in Typology and Linguistic Theory). Oxford: Oxford University Press.

Cysouw, Michael. Forthcoming-a. "Honorific uses of clusivity." In *Clusivity*, Elena Filiminova (ed). Amsterdam: Benjamins.

Cysouw, Michael. Forthcoming-b. "Syncretisms involving clusivity." In *Clusivity*, Elena Filiminova (ed). Amsterdam: Benjamins.

Cysouw, Michael (in preparation-a). "The asymmetry of person marking."

Cysouw, Michael. In preparation-b. "Dual inclusive revisited."

Daniel, Michael. Forthcoming. "Understanding inclusives." In *Clusivity*, Elena Filiminova (ed). Amsterdam: Benjamins.

Dalrymple, Mary and Ronald M. Kaplan. 2000. "Feature indeterminacy and feature resolution." *Language* 76 (4): 759–798.

Dobrushina, Nina and Goussev, Valentin. Forthcoming. "Inclusive imperative." In *Clusivity*, Elena Filiminova (ed). Amsterdam: Benjamins.

Foley, William A. 1986. *The Papuan Languages of New Guinea*. (Cambridge Language Surveys). Cambridge: Cambridge University Press.

Forchheimer, Paul. 1953. *The Category of Person in Language*. Berlin: Walter de Gruyter.

Greenberg, Joseph H. 1988. "The first person inclusive dual as an ambiguous category." *Studies in Language* 12 (1): 1–18.

Harley, Heidi and Elizabeth Ritter. 2002. "Person and number in pronouns: a feature-geometric analysis." *Language* 78 (3): 483–526.

Haspelmath, Martin, Matthew Dryer, David Gil and Bernard Comrie (eds). Forthcoming. *World Atlas of Language Structure*. Oxford: Oxford University Press.

Head, Brian F. 1978. "Respect degrees in pronominal reference." In *Universals of Human Language, Vol. 3: Word Structure*, Joseph H. Greenberg (ed), 151–212. Stanford: Stanford University Press.

Heath, Jeffrey. Forthcoming. "Person." In *Morphology: An International Handbook on Inflection and Word-Formation, Vol. 2*. (Handbücher zur Sprach- und Kommunikationswissenschaft; 17), Geert Booij, Christian Lehmann and Joachim Mugdan (eds). Berlin: Walter de Gruyter.

Hopper, Paul J. and Elizabeth Closs Traugott. 1993. *Grammaticalization*. (Cambridge Textbooks in Linguistics). Cambridge: Cambridge University Press.

Ingram, David. 1978. "Typology and universals of personal pronouns." In *Universals of Human Language, Vol. 3: Word Structure*, Joseph H. Greenberg (ed), 213–248. Stanford: Stanford University Press.

Lichtenberk, Frantisek. Forthcoming. "Inclusive-exclusive in Austronesian: An opposition of unequals." In *Clusivity*, Elena Filimonova (ed). Amsterdam: Benjamins.

Luraghi, Silvia. 2000. "Synkretismus." In *Morphology: an International Handbook on Inflection and Word-Formation, Vol. 1*, Geert Booij, Christian Lehmann and Joachim Mugdan (eds), 638–647. (Handbücher zur Sprach- und Kommunikationswissenschaft; 17). Berlin: Walter de Gruyter.

McGregor, William B. 1989. "Greenberg on the first person inclusive dual: Evidence from some Australian languages." *Studies in Language* 13 (2): 437–451.

McGregor, William B. 1996. "The pronominal system of Gooniyandi and Bunaba." In *Studies in Kimberley languages in honour of Howard Coate*, William McGregor (ed), 159–173. München: Lincom Europa.

McKay, Graham R. 1978. "Pronominal person and number categories in Rembarrnga and Djeebbana." *Oceanic Linguistics* 17: 27–37.

Noyer, Rolf. 1997. *Features, Positions, and Affixes in Autonomous Morphological structure.* (Outstanding Dissertations in Linguistics). New York: Garland.

Plank, Frans. 1985. "Die Ordnung der Personen." *Folia Linguistica* 19: 111–176.

Plank, Frans. 1989. "On Humboldt on the dual." In *Linguistic Categorization*, Roberta Corrigan, Fred Eckman and Michael Noonan (eds), 293–333. (Current Issues in Linguistic Theory; 61). Amsterdam: Benjamins.

Plank, Frans and Wolfgang Schellinger. 1997. "The uneven distribution of genders over numbers: Greenberg Nos. 37 and 45." *Linguistic Typology* 1 (1): 53–101.

Rijkhoff, Jan and Dik Bakker. 1998. "Language sampling." *Linguistic Typology* 2 (3): 263–314.

Sasse, Hans-Jürgen. 1993. "Syntactic categories and subcategories." In *Syntax: ein internationales Handbuch zeitgenössischer Forschung. Vol. 1*, Joachim Jacobs, Arnim von Stechow, Wolfgang Sternefeld and Theo Vennemann (eds), 646–685. (Handbücher zur Sprach- und Kommunikationswissenschaft; 9). Berlin: Walter de Gruyter.

Siewierska, Anna and Dik Bakker. Forthcoming. "Inclusive/exclusive in free and bound person forms." In *Clusivity*, Elena Filimonova (ed). Amsterdam: Benjamins.

Van Driem, George. 1987. *A Grammar of Limbu.* (Mouton Grammar Library; 4). Berlin: Mouton de Gruyter.

Zwicky, Arnold M. 1977. "Hierarchies of person." *Chicago Linguistic Society* 13 (1): 714–733.

Chapter 12

The principle of Functional Transparency in language structure and in language evolution

Zygmunt Frajzyngier

University of Colorado

The present study proposes that the principle of Functional Transparency plays a causal role in language structure and language evolution. The principle states that every utterance has a transparent role in a discourse and that every constituent has a transparent role within an utterance. 'Transparency' refers to the functional domains coded in the language rather than to the addressee's need to understand the role of the constituent in some real world. The study describes the components of the principle and how the principle is realized, provides cross-linguistic evidence for its existence within the domain of grammatical and semantic relations in a clause, and states the implications resulting from the principle.[1]

1. Introduction

One of the aims of linguistic theory is to explain why languages are similar and why they are different. Within the domains of phonetics and phonology the reasons for differences and similarities are fairly well understood, even though there are many open questions there. Outside these domains, similarities and differences among languages have to do with whether languages code the same functional domains or the same functions within these domains and whether languages use the same formal means to code these functions. Two languages may be similar, for example, if they both code the functional domains of aspect and tense, if they code the same aspectual and tense distinctions within these domains, and if they code these distinctions by the same formal means, e.g. verbal inflection or auxiliaries. Languages differ if they code different functional domains or different sub-domains within the same functional domains. One language might code the functional domain of aspect while another language might have no such category at all. Two languages might code the domain of aspect, but if one language codes four aspects and the other only two, then the two languages have different internal structures for this domain. Two languages with a four-aspect system might code these aspects using different formal means.

Linguistic theory is not yet able to explain why languages differ in the functional domains they code and the internal structures of these domains. The goal of the present study is to illustrate some of the reasons why languages differ in the means they use to code the same or similar functional domains, in this case, the relationship between the predicate and the noun phrase.

2. Motivations for grammaticalization: Previous proposals

The term 'evolution' is understood as a continual process of adaptation. The term 'grammaticalization', as used here, refers to the emergence of grammatical structures in general rather than to the narrower phenomenon of the emergence of grammatical morphemes from lexical items as taken by some scholars, e.g. Heine and Kuteva 2002: 2. While not every phenomenon of evolution involves grammaticalization, every instance of grammaticalization is an instance of evolution. Motivations for grammaticalization proposed thus far put into one basket the motivation and the effects of grammaticalization, to include various aspects of speaker-hearer relations, economy, simplification, communicative need, routinization, and the conventionalization of implicatures (Hopper and Traugott 1993). Simplification may very well be an effect of grammaticalization. Heine, Claudi, and Hünnemeyer propose that human creativity is also one of the main motivations for grammaticalization and that metaphor is the main force in grammaticalization (1991: 48). Human creativity, including the devising of metaphors, is a means of grammaticalization rather than its motivation.

Although communicative need may be useful for explaining similarities among languages, it is not a viable tool for explaining their differences. Other motivations that have been proposed, with the exception of human creativity should also result in languages being similar in forms and in functions coded by these forms. The present study proposes a motivation that plays an important role in the emergence of specific syntactic structures, a motivation that has been missed in the previous studies.

3. Hypothesis and implications

3.1. Hypothesis

One of the motivations for grammaticalization, i.e. for the emergence of grammatical structures, is the principle of Functional Transparency. The principle of Functional Transparency has three components. The first is that every utterance has a transparent role in a discourse. The second is that every constituent of the utterance has a transparent role within the utterance. The third component of the transparency principle is that the choice of the role of the constituent in the utterance is dictated by the functional domains coded in the language and often in a specific types of constructions, rather than by the addressee's need to understand the role of the constituent in some real world. The present paper concentrates on the latter two components. The first component is merely illustrated.

Illustration of the first component: If the role of an utterance in discourse is not transparent, the discourse is incoherent and is not acceptable. As an illustration consider the following fragments from the London–Lund Corpus (A and B are different speakers. Various markers indicate intonation, pauses, and stresses. These markers can be omitted in the interpretation of the examples here). The sequence of utterances below is quite incoherent, in that the utterances represented on various lines are not connected by anything other than the order in which they are printed:

A> be^cause I !have to adv=ise# .
A> ((a)) ^couple of people who are !d\oing [dhi: @]
A> *and ^can* you ass\ess ^can you . [k@v'ae ?]
      ^what's the w\ord# .
A> con^nect them in 'such a 'way that they :just go \on#
B> I ^can't see 'what the ob'jection of the 'heads of de!p\artments _is# .
B> how^\ever# .
B> [i] I ^did the !timetable for 'last . for "^th\is y/ear# .²

Now consider the same fragments in their actual environment in discourse: Each fragment is followed by a propositional connector such as 'well', 'so', and 'and', which code very specific relations, albeit not always relations well described in the literature:

1_1_0 <11 A> be^cause I !have to adv=ise# .
1_1_0 <12 A> ((a)) ^couple of people who are !d\oing [dhi: @]
1_1_0 <13 B> well ^what you :d\/o#
1_1_0 <14 B> ^is to - - ^this is sort of be:tween the :tw\/o of _us#

1_7_0 <1261 A> *and ^can* you ass\ess ^can you . [k@v'ae ?]
      ^what's the w\ord# .
1_7_0 <1262 A> con^nect them in 'such a 'way that they :just go \on#
1_7_0 <1263 A> **so ^nobody can de:t\ect ((it))#**

3_4_0 <593 B> I ^can't see 'what the ob'jection of the 'heads of
      de!p\artments _is# .
3_4_0 <594 B> how^\ever# .
3_4_0 <595 B> [i] I ^did the !timetable for 'last . for "^th\is y/ear# .
3_4_0 <596 B> ^=and [@:m]# .
3_4_0 <597 B> "^most 'classes be^cause of the com!{pl\exity of our} s\/ylla'bus
      you see#
3_4_0 <598 B> which [wi @?@?i] it con^tains a'bout [@:] ^y\/ou know# .

Illustration of the second component: The second component of the principle of Functional Transparency is that every constituent of the utterance has a transparent role within the utterance. If a constituent in an utterance is not marked for its role, the role of that constituent cannot be identified, and the utterance is ungrammatical. Consider the following utterances:

(1)   *Mary drove Boston her car.
      *Mary Boston her car drove.
      *Mary her car Boston drove.
      *Mary her car drove Boston.

Once the elements have their roles properly marked, a grammatical sentence obtains:

(2)   Mary drove her car to Boston.

Illustration of the third component: The listener's interpretation of an utterance is guided by the functional domains coded in the given language and in the given type of construction rather than by the need to understand the role of the constituent in some real world. The functional domains are those domains that are coded through the grammatical system of the given language (Frajzyngier and Mycielski 1998). The listener does not expect information that is not coded in the given language through lexical or grammatical means. Thus, many Chadic languages obligatorily code the category 'ventive' (movement toward the place of speech or some other deictic center) and less often the category 'centrifugal', movement away from the place of speech. If a language codes one of these categories and the situation described allows for one of these categories to apply, such a category must be coded in the utterance. These categories are not coded in English, and the speaker of English would be quite annoyed were he or she to get information in every clause indicating whether the event occurred in the place of speech or somewhere else and there was a subsequent movement toward the place of speech.

3.2.   The principle of Functional Transparency and ambiguity

The principle of Functional Transparency has implications for the issue of ambiguity in language. One of the implications is that for a functional domain that has been coded in the language, there may be no systemic ambiguity throughout the grammatical system. Thus, if a language codes the distinction of number for nouns and verbs, there will not be systemic and systematic ambiguity as to whether a given noun or verb is singular or plural. There may be occasional ambiguity in individual expressions, due to a particular choice of lexical items or phonological changes occurring across lexical items. A case in point is French sequence [lom kila vü], which may mean either 'the man whom he saw' or the 'man who saw him', ambiguity that does not exist in the written form of the language:

(3)   *l'homme qui l'a vu*
l'homme qu'il a vu (I am grateful to Michel Denais, CNRS, Nice, for drawing my attention to this ambiguity in French)

Ambiguity resulting from a choice of specific lexical items in specific tenses or aspects, etc., in no way affects the validity of the principle, because of its limited distribution in the grammatical system.

3.3. The principle of Functional Transparency and language change

The principle of Functional Transparency provides powerful motivation for the continuing evolution of syntactic structures, since the addition of any element to an utterance requires some coding means to make the function of that element transparent within some functional domains of the given language. Although this aspect of the transparency principle involves functional domains, it is quite independent of any specific functional domain. Functional domains coded in the language provide just a set of options for the coding of the new element.

The loss of a coding means in the language, whether due to either phonological changes or other processes, requires compensatory changes to preserve the function of a given constituent, lest the function be lost. Quite often, the loss of the function does occur. It is not clear whether there is ever a loss of the complete functional domain, such as the coding of number, tense, or aspect, or of the coding relationships between the predicate and noun phrases.

In the present study, the argumentation in support of the existence of the principle is provided by a cross-linguistic analysis of the relationships between noun phrases and predicates, a functional domain coded in many languages. The term 'relationship' is used here in a very general way, to include the grammatical relations 'subject' and 'object', the semantic relations 'agent' and 'patient' (Mithun 1991, Mithun and Chafe 1999), and languages in which the relations between the verb and the noun phrases include both grammatical relations and a variety of semantic relations. Such a language is Hausa, where the relations include subject, affected subject, non-affected second argument, partially affected second argument, and affected second argument (Frajzyngier and Munkaila, to appear). Not every language, however, codes the categories subject and object, or agent and patient. Mandarin seems to be the case in point. Moreover, even if a language codes a distinction between subject and object or agent and patient, it does not have to do it in all constructions. Thus Amharic, Arabic, and Hebrew do not have to formally distinguish between subject and object in relative clauses with the third-person subject and object sharing the features of gender and number (cf. Frajzyngier and Shay 2003).

The paper is organized as follows: I first discuss the properties of coding means, in particular, the lexicon, linear order, inflection, and phonological means. That is followed by a discussion of the coding of relations between verbs and arguments in structures where the predicate cannot serve as a reference point for two noun phrases.

4. The coding means

The coding means used across languages, but not necessarily in every language, include:

- The lexicon
- Linear order
- Adpositional coding, including prepositions and postpositions
- Conjunctions and 'function words'
- Inflectional coding on nouns, verbs, and other lexical categories
- Phonological means

The interaction of these means allows the hearer to compute the function of every element in the utterance within the functional domains coded in the given language.

The lexicon: In many languages, lexical items inherently code the role of an element in larger constructions. Thus the category 'verb' is inherently a predicate, the category 'noun' is inherently an argument, the category 'adjective' is inherently a modifier (Lyons 1996, Frajzyngier 1986, Hengeveld 1992, Frajzyngier and Shay 2003). The use of an element in a function other than the one that is its inherent property requires the use of other coding means, e.g. derivational morphology, linear order, adpositions, articles, or phonological means such as tone and intonation.

Linear order: the position of a given lexical item with respect to some reference point, which could be another lexical category

Adpositional coding: the use of prepositions and postpositions

Conjunctions, and other free morphemes, often called 'function words'

Inflectional coding: used on nouns, verbs, and adjectives, but may also be used on numerals, conjunctions, adpositions, complementizers, and possibly other lexical categories

Phonological means, including *sandhi* phenomena, tone and intonation, vowel harmony, and pauses

I start with linear order, possibly the simplest coding means in language (cf. Frajzyngier, Krech, and Mirzayan 2002), and one that, very likely, codes some function or other in all languages.

5. Linear order as a coding means

The fundamental requirement for coding through linear order is a reference point. Potential reference points are the beginning of an utterance, the end of an utterance, or another lexical category (not another lexical item). The beginning and the end of an utterance may serve as reference points only if these are specifically marked as such by some morphological or phonological means. Otherwise, in the process of speech, it is not possible to determine the beginning and the end of an utterance, hence neither the beginning nor the end of an utterance can serve as reference points.

In order for linear order to be available as a coding means, several conditions must be met. First, there must be only one instantiation of the given lexical category in the utterance. Thus, in a language that uses linear order and that has a distinction between nouns and verbs, it is a verb, not a noun, that serves as the reference point, since a clause contains only one verb but may contain more than one noun. Second, the lexical category that is to serve as a reference point must have one or more readily identifiable characteristics that distinguish it clearly from all other categories. These characteristics may include phonological structure, morphological structure, or external markers of categoriality. In Slavic languages, verbs code tense, aspect, person, and mood, while nouns do not. In Semitic languages, verbs have a different phonological structure from nouns. In some Chadic languages, verbs may begin only with a consonant, while nouns may begin with either a consonant or a vowel (Frajzyngier with Shay 2002). In most instances of coding by linear order, it is a lexical category that serves as the reference point for the linear order. It is very likely that if a language does not have a class of words that can serve as potential reference points, linear order alone may not be a viable coding means. Such a situation is examined later in this study.

If a lexical category serves as a reference point, the theoretical possibilities for coding grammatical relations through linear order are quite large. The following schema represents five coding positions to the left and right of the reference point, giving us a possibility of coding ten relationships between the verb and the nouns:

(4)　　—　　—　　—　　—　　—　　V　　—　　—　　—　　—　　—
　　　　−5　−4　−3　−2　−1　REF　1　　2　　3　　4　　5

In this schema, it is possible to identify the role of any element either to left or right of the verb if and only if (a) each verb has a fixed number of elements with which it **must** occur and (b) all elements are present in the utterance. These two conditions present the following disadvantages: Condition (a) will preclude the language from ever being able to acquire new verbs, because the hearer will never know with how many nouns (or noun phrases) the new verb **must** occur, and therefore the hearer will not be able to interpret the roles of nouns occurring with the new verbs. With respect to condition (b), if even one element is missing, there is no way to establish the identity of the remaining elements on that side. Therefore, despite the theoretical possibilities offered by linear order, only two positions can unambiguously serve as the coding means: the position before and the position after the reference point:

(5)　　＿＿ VERB ＿＿

If the verb happens to occur at the beginning or the end of the clause, the theoretical possibilities are still quite large:

(6) a. ___ ___ ___ ___ VERB
                 4   3   2   1

     b. VERB ___ ___ ___ ___
                     1   2   3   4

The same theoretical constraints as the ones explained for the left- and right-branching languages apply. Therefore, in a left-branching or a right-branching language, the only coding position available is before or after the verb:

(7) a. ___ VERB
              1

     b. VERB ___
                 1

The ramifications of the theoretical and practical limitation resulting from the verb-initial or verb-final position are that some other coding means must be used if more than one argument occurs in the clause and the language codes relations between the verb and the noun phrases. One possibility is to introduce another lexical item that may serve as a reference point. This lexical item brings with it at least one, and at most two, coding positions. A lexical item that is introduced for the sake of providing a new coding position eventually becomes a preposition or a postposition, depending on where it was introduced. It can then become a prefix or suffix, and may finally end up as an inflectional marker. The process of change from verbs to adpositions and eventually to affixes is attested time and again in unrelated languages all over the world (Heine, Claudi, and Hünnemeyer 1991, Heine et al. 1993, Lehmann 1995, and papers in Giacalone Ramat and Hopper 1998). Since all linguists are familiar with the linear order used for coding grammatical relations in languages that have arguments to the left and right of the verb, as in English, I first examine languages having only one coding position, i.e. languages in which the verb occurs in either clause-final or clause-initial position. Following the terminology used by Dryer (1992), languages in which the verb is in clause-final position are called left-branching languages, while languages in which the verb is in clause-initial position are called right-branching languages.

6. Left-branching languages

Left-branching languages use a variety of means to code grammatical relations, including inflectional case marking, adpositions, and coding on the verb.

6.1. Coding by nominal inflection

Amharic (Ethio-Semitic), a verb-final language, has the categories 'subject' and 'object'. The verb codes the categories 'person', 'gender', and 'number' of the subject. Amharic uses subject-object-verb order as a **coding means** if and only if the following conditions apply: (a) all of the arguments required by the minimal argument structure of the verb are present; (b) the subject immediately precedes the object (i.e. there are no elements in between the two categories); and (c) no material intervenes between the noun phrase arguments and the reference point.

If a clause contains the two unmarked noun phrases that the verb can take, the first argument is the subject and the second the object:

(8)   *wəš↓š↓a-w l əǧ↓*   *näkkäsä*
      dog-DEF   child bit:3M:SG:PRF
      'The dog bit a child.' (Leslau 1968: 68; glosses by ZF)

If a clause contains only one third-person argument and this argument is the subject, the word order is SV and the NP is unmarked:

(9)   *ləǧ↓-u*   *wäddäqä*
      child-DEF fall:3M:SG:PRF
      'The child fell.' (Leslau 1968: 68)

If the sole NP is the **object**, word order is OV and the NP is marked by the suffix *-n*:

(10)   *bärr-u-n*   *käffätä*
       door-DEF-OBJ open:3MSG:PRF
       'He opened the door.' (Leslau 1968: 68)

If the **object** occurs in clause-initial position, followed by the subject, this constitutes a disruption of the SOV coding system. Consequently, the categoriality of the noun phrase as object must be marked, and this is done through the suffix *-n*:

(11)   *ləǧ↓-u-n*   *wəš↓š↓a-w näkkäsä*
       child-DEF-OBJ dog-DEF   bite:3MSG:PRF
       'The dog bit the child.' (Leslau 1968: 68)

The same is true when another constituent in the clause, such as a prepositional phrase, intervenes between the object and the verb, resulting in the order S-O-PP V:

(12)   *abbat-ye*   *gommän-u-n*   *ba-tkəlt*   *bota zärra*
       father-1SG cabbage-DEF-OBJ PREP-garden place plant
       'My father planted the cabbage in the vegetable garden.' (Cohen 1970: 341; glosses by ZF)

One could claim, as one of the participants at the Symposium did, that such clauses do not need marking, because nobody will believe that 'a cabbage has planted my father in the garden', or some other, similarly nonsensical meaning. However, it is precisely because of such constraints on the interpretation of reality that the above examples are interesting. A language does not code the relationships in reality but rather the relations within the functional domains coded in the specific language.

An analysis based on what is possible and what is not possible in reality would give the correct interpretation of the relations in reality. Nevertheless, each element in the clause is coded for its role in the functional domain coded in the language, viz. subject and object, and not for its possible role in reality.

6.2. Coding on the verb and postpositional coding

Dahalo (East or South Cushitic, depending on whose classification one accepts [cf. Tosco 1991]) is verb final. The language is said to have the categories 'subject' and 'object'. The verb codes the person and number of the subject. When both arguments are present, the structure is Subject Object Verb. Neither the subject nor the object has inflectional markers or adpositions (data from Tosco 1991, with his glosses):

(13)   *múnta+da guho   b'urú-i[e]   líimamummi*
       farm-LOC people maize-HAB work-3P
       'They cultivate maize in the farm.' (Tosco 1991: 85)

Because the subject is coded on the verb, a single argument occurring before the verb is interpreted as the object if its person does not match the person coded on the verb:

(14)   *nat'á+t[o]*   *'ini te   lúbuto*
       woman+that-F FOC AFF beat:2s
       'You are going to beat the woman.' (Tosco 1991: 86)

Adjuncts are marked by adpositions:

(15)   *'ani+j[e] ali+nto   háasoobo*
       1SG+HAB Ali+ASSOC speak.1SG
       'I converse habitually with Ali.' (Tosco 1991: 85)

When a noun phrase is moved into clause-initial position for topicalization, its role as the object is coded by pronouns suffixed to the subject:

(16)   *gwíttsa 'úku 'ini gaano-ku lúbbi*
       child   that FOC man-that hit-3M
       'The child, the man beats him.' (Tosco 1991: 85. 'that' stands for demonstrative in Tosco's glosses)

If a noun follows the verb, as in focus constructions, its role as the object is marked by the postposition *kabé*. Thus, the role of noun phrases within the domain of relations between the predicate and the noun phrases is kept transparent:

(17)   *'áata 'életo   dawa kabé*
       you know-2SG Dawa ACC
       'Do you know Dawa?' (Tosco 1991: 88)

A pronominal object is marked twice, once as a suffix to the verb and again as an independent pronoun followed by *kabé*:

(18) 'áata 'életo+'i   'án kabé
      you know-2s-1sg 1sg acc
      'Do you know me?' (Tosco 1991: 88)

The data from Dahalo support the proposed hypothesis in that if only one argument is used, or if the Subject Object Verb linear order is disturbed, the language uses means other than linear order to code the roles of arguments.

6.3. Appositional coding

In Japanese and Korean, the verb is in clause-final position and noun phrases are marked by postpositions, sometimes called case markers:

(19) a. *John ga   kita*
          John nom come
          'John came.'
      b. *John ga   tegami o   yonda*
          John nom letter   acc read
          'John read the letter.' (Kuno 1973: 10)

The omission of postpositions is common in colloquial speech (cf. Martin 1975:50). However, if the nature of the verb and the NPs is such that the roles of the arguments could be misinterpreted, postpositions must not be omitted:

(20) *John ga   Mary o   butsu*
      John nom Mary acc beat
      'John beats Mary'

In Old Japanese (about 700 AD), an object did not have to be marked by the postposition *o* if it immediately preceded the verb:

(21) *ware wa   imo omou*
      I   top wife think
      'I think of my wife.' (Miyagawa 1989: 205)

Contemporary spoken Korean provides ample evidence for the existence of the principle of Functional Transparency. If the subject and object are both present, the object tends not to be marked by the accusative case marker *–(l)ul* (all data and analyses from Yang MS):

(22) *nay-ka   Barbara-Ø manna-se*
      1sg-nom Barbara   meet-conn
      'I meet Barbara and …'

When the subject is omitted and the object is the only argument, the marker *–(l)ul* is used because its role cannot be deduced from the structure of the clause:

(23) a. *ayei sangkak-ul mos ha-ess-ney*
          at all thought:ACC not do-PST-FP
          '(I) didn't think (about it) at all.'

A participant at the Symposium observed that 'thought' cannot be the subject of the verb 'do' and can be interpreted only as the object; and therefore, the coding of the object is not required by the principle of Functional Transparency. Note that this observation is based on some perceived relationships between two referents represented by a noun and a predicate in the real world. Neither the observation nor the interpretation is correct. The noun 'thought' in English, especially its plural form, can be a subject of a verb, as in the following examples:

(23) b. your thoughts do not help me (elicited)

10_6_1 <136 a> and I wonder what 'thoughts are 'going through her 'head#
(LLC)

In the following examples from Polish, the noun *myśl* 'thought' is the subject:

(24) *sprowadzimy*   *takie dziewczyny. Myśl   dobra*
      bring:FUT:PRF:1PL such girls.   thought:NOM good
      'We will bring over such girls. That's a good thought.' (lit. 'The thought is good.')

The following example clearly indicates that the noun corresponding to 'thought' can be construed as agentive in the subject role:

(25) *pragniemy*   *uratować nasze dzieci,   zabezpieczyć je,   zanim*
      desire:PRES:1PL save   our   children protect   3PL:ACC before
      mogłaby   im   zagrozić jakaś zbrodnicza myśl
      could:F:HYP 3PL:DAT threaten some criminal   thought:NOM
      'We want to save our children, to protect them before some criminal thought were to threaten them.' (Polish sources)

The interpretation that the coding of the object is not required by the principle of Functional Transparency is not correct, because the principle of Functional Transparency does not have in its scope the addressee's need to understand the reality, but rather the addressee's need to understand the interrelationship of elements within the functional domains coded in the language. The examples from Korean are interesting precisely because, even if one could think, based on some analysis of reality, that *sangkak* 'thought' could only be an object, this noun is nevertheless marked as object in the clause. This is the evidence that the language marks the constituents of the clause as to their role in the clause, not their role in reality, which presumably would not need to be marked.

7. Right-branching languages

Coding strategies used in right-branching languages are illustrated by data from
Hdi and Hona (Central Chadic) and Lakhota (Siouan). The two Chadic languages
have different coding means and different properties. Hdi is right branching in
all tenses and aspects, whereas Hona is right branching only in the perfective aspect. Accordingly, the coding means in the perfective and the imperfective aspect in
Hona differ. The mere existence of the different coding means in different aspects
provides the necessary evidence for the proposed principle. The Lakhota examples
illustrate the use of an additional verb to code an additional argument.

7.1. Coding by preposition and linear order

In Hdi, in clauses that do not involve marked pragmatic functions such as topicalization or focus, the first noun phrase following the verb is the subject. The second
noun phrase is marked by the preposition *tá*. Coding by the preposition is a necessary means for distinguishing between the two noun phrases:

(26)   a.   *tsghà-dá-f*   *xáxən **tá** sánì*
        put up-ALL-UP 3PL   OBJ one
        'They sent up one [bag].'

      b.   *lá-mà zíngá dà*   *tùghwázàk kà* *hlà-ná-ghá-tá-tsí*   ***tá***
        go-IN Zinga PREP hibiscus   SEQ find-DEM-D:PVG-REF-3SG OBJ
        pákáwá ghúvì kà   *ks-ú-tá-tsí*
        hyena   SEQ touch-SO-REF-3SG
        'When Zinga entered the hibiscus, he found Hyena and devoured him.'

The preposition *tá* is not used with the second argument if the verb has the referential suffix *tá* and the second argument immediately follows the verb:

(27)   a.   *mbàɗ ká*   *pákáwá ghúvì kà* *klà-á-**tá***   *vàrà*
        then   COMP hyena   SEQ take-PART-REF beans
        'Hyena took some beans.'

      b.   *dghàd-áy-tàn dghàd-áy-tàn mbàɗ ká*   *krì kà* *klà-gá-f-tá*
        chew-PO-3PL chew-PO-3PL then   COMP dog SEQ take-INN-UP-REF
        ìr-á   *zwáŋ-á*   *pákáwá ghúvì*
        eye-GEN child-GEN hyena
        'While they were chewing it, Dog picked up an eye of a child of Hyena.'
        (Frajzyngier with Shay 2002)

7.2. Coding on the verb

Hona has SVO order in the imperfective aspect and VSO in the perfective. Subject
pronouns are suffixed to the verb:

(28)   *dád-ì*
    run away:PRF-1SG
    'I ran away.'
    dá-n-nà
    run-PRF-2SG
    'You ran away.'
    pár-dá   háy
    jump-3SG down
    'He jumped down.'
    pár-dá   sə́
    jump-3SG up
    'He jumped up.'

In the perfective, if the verb is followed by all the nouns required by its argument structure, i.e. by the nominal subject and object, the verb is not marked by any affixes, since all expected arguments are present (all data from independent field notes by Frajzyngier and Laurie Jordan. For some data, tones were not recorded):

(29)   *fí   nú-nà   łúwà*
    bake wife-1SG meat
    'My wife baked meat.'

If there is only one argument following the verb, linear order alone (i.e., the absence of any additional coding means) indicates that this argument is the subject:

(30)   *ngwálà łúwà*
    finish   meat
    'The meat is finished.'

If there is only one noun phrase following the verb and the verb is marked by a subject suffix, the noun phrase after the verb is the object. If the object is definite, it is coded on the verb as well:

(31)   a.   *ky-án-ɗ   łú-dì   pát*
        eat-OBJ-3SG meat-DEF all
        'He ate all the meat.'
    b.   *s-án-ɗ   ám-dì   pát*
        drink-OBJ-3SG water-DEF all
        'He drank all the water.'

If there are two arguments following the verb, the definiteness of the second argument (the object) is coded on the verb:

(32)   a.   *łe-n   Ali hur-yen*
        slaughter-OBJ Ali neck-3SG
        'Ali slaughtered it.' (lit. 'Ali cut its neck.')

  b. *ngwálà-ŋ-dì łú-dì*
    finish-OBJ-1SG meat-DET
    'I finished the meat.'

If the canonical coding means in the perfective aspect is disturbed, e.g. if an argument is moved into clause-initial position for focusing or topicalization, some additional means must be used to identify the role of the fronted argument. The subject role of the fronted noun phrase is coded by the third-person subject pronoun (singular or plural) following the verb:

 (33) *wá-nà fan-d*
    child-1SG wash-3SG
    'My child washed.'

Cf. the non-fronted subject:

 (34) *fàn wá-nà*
    wash child-1SG
    'My child washed.'

 (35) *pàshí-nà péred wí-ndà*
    friend-1SG all leave-3PL
    'All my friends left.'

Cf. the non-fronted subject:

 (36) *wí pashí-nà*
    leave friend-1SG
    'All my friends left.'

The object suffix occurs on the verb:

 (37) *Ali łe-n-dǝ*
    Ali slaughter-OBJ-3SG
    'Ali slaughtered'

In the imperfective aspect, Hona has SVO order. Given the availability of two positions, one preceding the verb and the other following it, the grammatical roles are coded by the linear order alone, and there is no need to mark them by other means, more specifically by subject and object suffixes:

 (38) *bǝní-fà kí sɔ̀ydírá wà*
    man-INDEF eat vultures NEG
    'One does not eat vulture meat.'

The object can be coded on the verb to mark its definiteness:

 (39) *nà nú-nà à tsáb-àŋ lú-nnà-d*
    IMPRF wife-1SG FUT wash-OBJ shirt-1SG-ALL
    'My wife will wash my shirt.'

When it has VSO linear order, Hona has to use means other than the linear order to code grammatical relations if the object occurs alone in the clause or if either the subject or the object occurs in clause-initial position. With SVO linear order, there is no need to use means other than the linear order to code the role of arguments.

7.3. Coding an additional argument by adding a verb

Across languages, one of the most common means of coding an additional argument is to add another verb to the clause, thus providing at least one new coding position. This is one motivation for the emergence of serial verb constructions in many African and Asian languages. In particular, the addition of the dative argument to verbs that do not take the dative as their unmarked argument is done with the equivalents of the verb 'give'. This means can also be found in Lakhota (Siouan). Lakhota is an active-stative (split-intransitive) SOV language. The semantic roles of active or non-active arguments in the first and second person are coded by affixes to the verb. The third-person singular argument, whether active or non-active, has no overt marking on the verb:

(40)   *a-ma-ya-phe*
       hit-1SG-2SG-hit
       'You hit me.'

       a-ma-phe
       hit-1SG-hit
       'He hit me.'

       aphe
       hit
       'He hit him.'

If a first- or a second-person argument marked on the verb is dative or benefactive, this is indicated by the verbal affix *ki* (recall that the third-person object is unmarked):

(41)   *a-ma-ki-pha-pi*
       hit-1SG-DAT-hit-PL
       'They hit him for me.'

According to David Rood, p.c., in Lakhota one cannot have two overt object pronouns on the same verb. It appears, however, that the coding of the third-person dative, unlike the third-person direct object, requires the addition of another verb if the direct object of the clause is first- or second-person pronoun. Unlike in other languages with serial verb constructions, this verb must be preceded by a conjunction and it codes the active subject through the number suffix:

(42) *a-ma-pha-pi   na é-či-chu-pi*
hit-1SG-hit-PL and do-DAT-do-PL
'They hit me for him.' (lit. 'They hit me and they did it for him.') (data courtesy of David Rood, p.c.)

The introduction of an additional argument to a clause in Lakhota thus requires an introduction of a new verb.

8. Evidence from languages with SVO order

Further evidence for the existence of the principle of Functional Transparency is provided by the interaction among coding means in languages in which the SVO order is the coding means for grammatical relations in pragmatically neutral clauses. In Mina (Central Chadic), other coding means must be used when the SVO order is disturbed or is not available as a coding means. In English, only certain perturbations of the SVO order are allowed.

Even if a language codes the roles of arguments through linear order, and even if that linear order exploits the positions to the left and to the right of the verb, there must be a means of coding grammatical relations when the SVO order is disturbed. The assumption that a noun phrase carries its argument role when it is moved out of its position is proved wrong by the fact that some means must be used to code the role of such a noun phrase. If there are no special means deployed, the role of such a noun phrase can be computed from the formal coding means used in the rest of the clause. Otherwise, the noun phrase loses the role for which it was coded, and consequently, the movement out of the position that codes the role of the noun phrase is disallowed. Below are examples of each of these variants available for the erstwhile SVO languages. The disallowed movement is illustrated only partially for reasons that are described later in this study.

8.1. Compensatory means and the role computation

The situations in which the preservation of the role of the moved element is coded by a preposition or computed from the rest of the clause are illustrated on data from Mina, a Central Chadic language. Mina codes the roles 'subject' and 'object' through the position preceding and following the verb (all data from Frajzyngier, Johnston, with Edwards, in press):

(43) *ká lám bíŋ   zà*
INF build house EE
'He built a room.'

(44) *bìɮáf vàl-á-k   mbà táŋ*
God give-OBJ-1SG child DEF
'God gave me that child.'

If the object is in focus, it is moved to the position before the verb. The presence of two arguments before the verb creates an ambiguity concerning their roles. Either argument preceding the verb could be the subject or the object. This ambiguity is resolved by the use of the preposition *n* before the object:

(45)   á   n   kɔ́dɔ̀m   ngɔ̀n ɓɔ̀t   ábɔ̀   nd-á   ngɔ̀n wɔ̀tá
        3SG PREP calabash 3SG   take ASSC go-DIST 3SG village
        'Then she took her calabash and returned home.'

If the object is topicalized, it is moved into the position preceding the verb. Theoretically, we could have the same ambiguity as in the preceding sentence. However, there is one important difference. The form *í* '3PL' can only be the subject pronoun. Since this form is interpreted as the subject pronoun, the noun phrase that precedes the subject must be interpreted as the object:

(46)   wɔ̀l   màsálád í   ndí gám   kà
        woman lazy   3PL HAB chase POS
        'The lazy woman is chased away.'

The important conclusion from the data in Mina is that a noun phrase does not carry its role in a clause, and therefore its role either must be marked through a preposition or otherwise be computed from the formal means available in the rest of the clause.

8.3. The disallowed movement from the object position

The situation in which the movement is disallowed is illustrated on data from English. The fact that English has SVO linear order by itself does not explain constraints on the second argument. However, the fact that the fundamental and the only coding means for the category 'direct object' in English is the position following the verb does. The coding of the object is illustrated by the following example:

1_1_0 <6 B> ^actually !Joe 'set the :p\aper# (LLC)

In written and, more rarely, in spoken English one can encounter clauses with two noun phrases occurring before the verb without any other segmental coding means accompanying either of the noun phrases:

(47)   No, sorry. We're out of bagels. **A bran muffin** I can give you. (Birner and Ward 1998: 33).

Such sentences are attributed to the influences of Yiddish on some dialects of English (Birner and Ward 1998). Whenever I have presented this type of clause in my courses in Colorado, native speakers of English consistently and without exception rejected them as ungrammatical. In a conversation from the London Lund Corpus comprising 1,211 utterances, there is not a single instance of mere fronting of the erstwhile object without some additional means, such as existential 'there is …'-constructions, cleft sentences, relative clauses, and passive sentences:

1_1_0 <819 B> **there`s an^\other - fight** I`ve 'got on my hands at the m/oment#

Passive clauses are means of topicalizing the affected argument, which is nevertheless coded as the subject rather than the object:

1_1_0 <845 B> this ^English L\anguage p/aper#
1_1_0 <846 B> has ^been be'devilled 'long e"!n\ough#
1_1_0 <847 B> by th((o))se ^l\iterature w/allahs#

1_2_1 <39 B> [@:m] . we`re ^not [@ . @] :given [dhi] ((the)) :title of de"!p\/art-ment#
1_2_1 <40 B> because this ^means going to the . :chapter and :c\/ouncil# .

Relativization of the object is a good example of putting the noun phrase having the grammatical role of object before the subject:

1_1_0 <480 B> ((he   said   as   a))   ^matter   of   fact   **the**   :only   ones I "!c\an guarant/ee#
1_1_0 <481 B> and I can ^guaran:tee these abso!l\utely#
1_1_0 <482 B> if they`re ^used according to ((di!r\/ection))#
1_1_0 <483 B> ((are ^**those that** I`ve got !!h\ere#))

David Rood pointed out (p.c.) that one can have topicalized objects in clause-initial position in dialects of English not affected by Yiddish:

(48)   We were sorting pencils. The red ones Mary put into a box. The green ones Mike took home with him. But the blue ones nobody wanted. (David Rood, p.c.)

Such constructions are actually quite frequent in Shakespeare. An explanation of why a noun phrase can occur before the subject and still be interpreted as an object lies in the computation that the hearers perform. This computation probably has the following steps: The verb is preceded by a noun phrase; therefore, this noun phrase is the subject. The noun phrase that precedes the subject is not marked by any preposition. There is no preposition following the verb. Therefore, the noun phrase preceding the subject may only be an object.

Even though one can in some constructions and in some dialects of English put a noun phrase before a subject and expect it to be decoded as an object, there is no such possibility with post-posing, or right dislocation, e.g. putting a noun phrase after a prepositional phrase and expect it to be interpreted as an object:

(49)   I actually ^got it for y/ou#))
       *I actually got for you it

1_2_2 <1082 A> it`s ^got ((the)) con:tinuous :history for him :h\/ere#
       * it`s got for him the continuous history here

The position after the verb codes the category 'object' even if a verb is followed by a particle:

(50)   I looked for a job for him
       *I looked for him for a job

The reason why a noun cannot occur after the prepositional phrase is that in this position it is no longer coded as an object, its role in the clause remaining unmarked. The same constraint is responsible for not allowing two or more noun phrases to occur after the verb, instead of one occurring before the verb and one after the verb, without some additional marking:

2_7_0 <1294 a>someone gave me a very nice smile in Dillon's
       *gave me someone a very nice smile in Dillon's
       *gave me a very nice smile someone in Dillon's

When the two noun phrases occur after the verb in English, the principle of Functional Transparency has been violated, because one cannot determine which noun phrase is the subject and which is the object. The evidence that the principle of Functional Transparency has been violated is additionally provided by the following discussion.

9.   SVO order as compensatory means

In a language with rich nominal inflection, the distinction between arguments is coded through case marking on nouns, and word order codes functions other than grammatical relations, as illustrated in the following examples from Polish:

(51)   *banda*   *spali-ł-a*   *stodoł-ę*
       gang:NOM burn:PRF-PAST-SG:F barn-ACC
       'A gang burned down the barn.'

       banda   *stodoł-ę*   *spaliła*
       gang:NOM barn:-ACC burn:PRF-PAST-SG:F
       'A gang burned down the barn.'

       spaliła   *banda*   *stodoł-ę*
       burn:PRF-PAST-SG:F gang:NOM barn-ACC
       'A gang burned down the barn.'

       stodoł-ę   *spaliła*   *banda*
       barn-ACC burn:PRF-PAST-SG:F gang:NOM
       'A gang burned down the barn.'

When the distinction between nominative and accusative case marking is neutralized, case marking cannot be used to distinguish between the subject and the object, and instead, SVO word order must be deployed. Such neutralization occurs with masculine non-human nouns and with neutral nouns:

(52) a. *Autobus   minął   samochód*
          bus:NOM/ACC pass:PRF:3M:SG car:NOM/ACC
          'A bus passed a car.'

      b. *Samochód   minął   autobus*
          car:NOM/ACC pass:PRF:3M:SG bus:NOM/ACC
          'A car passed a bus.'

Putting two nouns before or after the verb results in ungrammatical clauses:

(53) **Autobus   samochód   minął*
       bus:NOM/ACC car:NOM/ACC pass:PRF:3M:SG
       for 'A bus passed a car.'
       *minął   autobus   samochód
       pass:PRF:3M:SG bus:NOM/ACC car:NOM/ACC
       for 'A bus passed a car.'

The same is true of clauses whose arguments belong to the neutral class:

(54) *cielę   przestraszyło   szczenię*
      calf:NOM/ACC frighten:PRF:SG:NEUT puppy:NOM/ACC
      'The calf frightened the puppy.'

(55) *szczenię   przestraszyło   cielę*
      puppy:NOM/ACC frighten:PRF:SG:NEUT calf:NOM/ACC
      'The puppy frightened the calf.'

(56) **cielę   szczenię   przestraszyło*
      calf:NOM/ACC puppy:NOM/ACC frighten:PRF:SG:NEUT
      for 'The calf frightened the puppy.'

In Polish, SVO order codes grammatical relations if and only if nominal inflection, the primary means of coding grammatical relations, is neutralized. In all other instances, the word order codes other functions.

10. Evidence from language change

Language change provides compelling evidence for the principle of Functional Transparency and at the same time poses new questions for further investigation. If a coding means is lost, two things may happen: (a) the coding of the function is lost; (b) new means must be used to code the functions previously coded by the lost coding means. Languages attest to both alternatives. The loss of a function is illustrated by the loss of the category 'dual' in many Indo-European languages.

Support for the principle of Functional Transparency comes from languages where a decay of one coding means is compensated by grammaticalization of another means to carry all or some of the functions carried by the decayed coding means. Three well-known cases of language change illustrate compensatory changes. Old English had an extensive system of subject-person and number coding on the verb and of inflectional coding on the noun. Because of phonological changes, both of these coding means have been largely reduced. Linear order has been grammaticalized to carry the distinction between subject and object. Unlike most other Slavic languages, Bulgarian does not have inflectional coding for case. Similarly to English, Bulgarian has grammaticalized linear order to code the distinction between subject and object (Sławski 1962). A similar process took place in Palestinian Arabic, where the loss of case marking motivated the grammaticalization of the SVO linear order as the coding means for grammatical relations.

Another good example of compensatory change is the development of articles in French and other Romance languages. Latin had inflectional coding on nouns, which indicated not only case but, more important, also gender. These two categories performed different functions in the language. Case was used for many functions involving relationships between the predicate and noun phrases and relationships among noun phrases. Gender was a fundamental means for the reference system. With the weakening of word-final vowels and consonants, both the case system and the gender coding of nouns were affected. The decay of gender coding posed a serious problem for the reference system because the gender of nouns was no longer marked. Hence, the development in all Romance languages of the system of articles, which, in addition to whatever function they may have in the coding of definiteness or indefiniteness, also indicate the gender of the noun and thus allow for the coding of reference across discourse.

11. Conclusions and open questions

Linear order, adpositions, verbal inflection, nominal inflection, and phonological changes are coding means for specific functions. The existence of every coding means may be explained in terms of the function it performs and its interaction with other formal means.

When one coding means is not available, the language must use another means if the same function is to be expressed. Otherwise, the function is lost. With respect to the functional domain, this study allows us to explain why languages have prepositions and postpositions, the conditions and the constraints on linear order as coding means, and the conditions and consequences of changes in the canonical word order. The proper understanding of the functions of various coding means makes it unnecessary to postulate traces as a means to decode grammatical or semantic relations within a clause, as proposed in generative grammars that represented the function of arguments through their position in the clause.

An open question is whether one can establish a hierarchy of functional domains such that some functional domains will be preserved throughout the history of language and other functional domains may be lost once their coding means are lost. An example of such a functional domain is the category 'dual' in Indo-European languages. I would predict that if the functional domain were one that must be coded in every clause, it probably would not be lost. The functional domains with a narrow scope may well be lost. However, an empirical study with respect to the nature of the domains has yet to be made.

As a motivation for language evolution, the principle of Functional Transparency is neither as arbitrary nor as hard to define as the principles of economy, simplification, and creativity, which have been proposed elsewhere as motivations for evolution in syntax. The principle of Functional Transparency is motivated by the function it serves. The explanatory power of the principle lies in the fact that the existence of every formal device used in language, which is to say every coding means, may be explained in terms of the function it performs and its interaction with other formal means coding related functions.

Abbreviations

ACC	Accusative	INDEF	Indefinite
AFF	Affirmative	LOC	Locative
ALL	Allative	M	Masculine
ASSOC	Associative	NEUT	Neutral
COMP	Complementizer	NOM	Nominative
CONN	Connector	OBJ	Object
DEF	Definite	PART	Partitive
DEM	Demonstrative	PAST	Past time reference
DET	Determiner	PL	Plural
EE	End of event marker	PO	Potential object
F	Future	POS	Point of view of subject
FOC	Focus marker	PRF	Perfective
FUT	Future	PVG	Point of view of goal
GEN	Genitive	REF	Referential
GO	Goal	SEQ	Sequential marker
HAB	Habitual	SG	Singular
IMPRF	Imperfective	SO	Source orientation
INF	Infinitive	TOP	Topic
INN	Extension coding location within an enclosed space	UP	Extension coding upward movement or goal

Notes

1. Some data used in this paper were gathered with the support of the NSF Grant 'Grammars of Gidar, Mina, Lele and East Dangla'. The work on this study started while I was a guest of the Max Planck Institute for Evolutionary Anthropology in Leipzig. The work continued while I was Associated Researcher of the Centre National de la Recherche Scientifique at the University of Nice. I would like to thank participants at my talks at the Universities of Zurich, Frankfurt, Bayreuth, Rice University (Houston), and at the Max Planck Institute for Evolutionary Anthropology in Leipzig for comments on various aspects of this paper. Some of the ideas presented in the present study are more fully developed in Frajzyngier and Shay (2003). I also would like to thank Erin Shay and David Rood for comments on an earlier version of this paper. Marian Safran, through her expert editing, made sure that this paper is less obscure that it otherwise might have been.

2. The data from the London–Lund Corpus are presented in the original transcription as provided on the ICAME disks. For the description of the corpus and of the coding system used there see http://khnt.hit.uib.no/icame/manuals/LONDLUND/INDEX.HTM and Svartvik 1990. The phonetic features of the utterances in the examples quoted have no bearing on the issues discussed and can be ignored.

References

Birner, Betty J., and Gregory Ward. 1998. *Information status and noncanonical word order in English*. Studies in Language Companion Series 40. Amsterdam/Philadelphia: John Benjamins.

Cohen, Marcel. 1970. *Traité de langue amharique (Abyssinie)*. Paris: Institut d'ethnologie.

Dryer, Matthew S. 1992. "The Greenbergian Word Order Correlations." *Language* 68: 81-138.

Frajzyngier, Zygmunt. 1986. "Propositional characterization of categories." In Scott DeLancey and Russell Tomlin (eds.), *Papers from the First Pacific Linguistic Conference*, 108-119.

Frajzyngier, Zygmunt. 1994. Review of Tosco 1991. *Sprachtypologie und Universalienforschung*. 234-236.

Frajzyngier, Zygmunt. 1996. *Grammaticalization of the Complex Sentence: A case study in Chadic*. Amsterdam/Philadelphia: John Benjamins.

Frajzyngier, Zygmunt, and Jan Mycielski 1998. "On some fundamental problems of mathematical linguistics." In Carlos Martin-Vide (ed.), *Mathematical and computational analysis of natural language*. Amsterdam/Philadelphia: John Benjamins, 295-310.

Frajzyngier, Zygmunt, Holy Krech, and Armik Mirzayan. 2002. "Motivation for copula in equational clauses." *Linguistic Typology* 6.2, 155–198.

Frajzyngier, Zygmunt, with Erin Shay. 2002. *A Grammar of Hdi*. Berlin: Mouton de Gruyter.

Frajzyngier, Zygmunt, and Erin Shay. 2003. *Explaining language structure through systems interaction*. Amsterdam/Philadelphia: John Benjamins.

Frajzyngier, Zygmunt, Eric Johnston, with Adrian Edwards. (in press). *A Grammar of Mina*. Berlin/New York: Mouton de Gruyter.

Frajzyngier, Zygmunt, and Mohammed Munkaila. (To appear). *Grammatical and semantic relations in Hausa: Point of view, goal, and affected object*. Cologne: Koeppe.

Giacalone Ramat, Anna, and Paul J. Hopper (eds.). 1998. *The limits of grammaticalization*. Amsterdam/Philadelphia: John Benjamins.

Heine, Bernd, Ulrike Claudi, and Friederike Hünnemeyer. 1991. *Grammaticalization*. Chicago: University of Chicago Press.

Heine, Bernd, Tom Güldemann, Christa Kilian-Hatz, Donald A. Lessau, Heinz Roberg, Mathias Schladt, and Thomas Stolz. 1993. *Conceptual shift. A lexicon of grammatical-*

ization processes in African languages. Afrikanistische Arbeitspapiere 34/35.

Heine, Bernd, and Tania Kuteva. 2002. *World lexicon of grammaticalization.* Cambridge: Cambridge University Press.

Hengeveld, Kees. 1992. "Parts of Speech." In Michael Fortescue, Peter Harder, and Lars Kristoffersen (eds.), *Layered structure and reference in a functional perspective.* Amsterdam/Philadelphia: Benjamins, 29-55.

Hopper, Paul J., and Elizabeth Closs Traugott. 1993. *Grammaticalization.* Cambridge: Cambridge University Press.

Kuno, Susumo. 1973. *The structure of the Japanese language.* Cambridge, Mass.: MIT Press.

Lehmann, Christian. 1995. *Thoughts on grammaticalization.* Munich: Lincom Europa.

Leslau, Wolf. 1968. *Amharic Textbook.* Wiesbaden: Otto Harrassowitz.

Lyons, John. 1996. *Linguistic semantics: An introduction.* Cambridge: Cambridge University Press.

Martin, Samuel Elmo. 1975 (1988). *A reference grammar of Japanese.* Yale University Press: New Haven.

Mithun, Marianne. 1991. "Active/Agentive case marking and its motivations." *Language* 67: 510-546.

Mithun, Marianne, and Wallace Chafe. 1999. "What are S, A, and O?" *Studies in Language* 23.3: 579-606.

Miyagawa, Shigeru. 1989. "Structure and case marking in Japanese." *Syntax and Semantics* 22. San Diego: Academic Press.

Sławski, Franciszek. 1962. *Gramatyka języka bułgarskiego.* Warsaw: Państwowe Wydawnictwa Naukowe.

Svartvik, Jan (ed). 1990. *The London Corpus of Spoken English: Description and Research.* Lund Studies in English 82. Lund University Press.

Tosco, Mauro. 1991. *A Grammatical Sketch of Dahalo.* Cushitic Language Studies 8. Hamburg: Buske.

Van Valin, Robert D. 1997. *Syntax. Structure, meaning and function.* Cambridge: Cambridge University Press.

Yang, Hyun Jung. Ms. Object coding through linear order in Korean. University of Colorado.

CHAPTER 13

The importance of discourse analysis for linguistic theory

A Mandarin Chinese illustration[1]

Liang Tao

Ohio University

Four different theoretical proposals from typological, formal synchronic, diachronic and discourse-functional approaches are examined concerning the Mandarin Chinese numeral classifier system. The study promotes usage-based discourse analysis in the study of language and cognition, with the belief that linguistic theories should cover the dynamic nature of language, which is constantly changing over everyday usage. Discourse analysis should be considered a fundamental means for developing a linguistic theory. Grammaticalization can be the product of everyday language usage without speakers' conscious choices.

1. Introduction

Linguistics is the study of language. But there are several approaches to language data collection and data analysis. This paper presents a case study of the Mandarin Chinese classifier system from four different approaches to promote the importance of usage-based discourse analysis in the study of language and cognition.

Discourse analysis in this paper refers to the linguistic study of language (Tannen 1989) that draws from the properties of human communication (e.g. Fox, Jurafsky and Michaelis 1999) to generalize instances of usage that reflect what the language users actually do in their interactional communication. This study proposes that discourse analysis offers the most comprehensive solution to the question of the possible relationship between form and function in natural language (e.g. Fox 1995). It is a quantitative approach using the analysis of both written and naturally occurring conversational data to take into account the range of human interactional needs that influence the choice of given patterns. Therefore, this approach offers insight into the interpretation of different grammatical patterns in a sentence based on its discourse context. It also explains language development through usage (e.g. Barlow and Kemmer 2000).

This study agrees with the view that language is a dynamic phenomenon, changing constantly during everyday language usage, and argues that if it fails to acknowledge this point, a linguistic theory may provide at best a partial explanation of language. Examination of four different approaches on the form and function of the Chinese numeral classifier system serves as an illustration supporting this proposal.

The theoretical discussions of the numeral classifier system in Mandarin Chinese that this study examines come from diachronic (Wang 1958, 1985), typological (Bisang 1998, 1999; Greenberg 1990a, b), formal synchronic (Cheng and Sybesma 1999) and discourse-functional analyses (Tao 2002). Using data collected from both written and recorded natural conversation discourse, this study demonstrates that the classifier system in modern Mandarin Chinese does not reflect a complete departure from its early form, syntactic position or semantic function. Further, the study shows that usage variations in naturally occurring conversational discourse have led to language change. Lack of data from actual discourse usage has led to inaccurate observations of the Mandarin numeral classifier system from some previous studies. It has also led to their negligence of grammaticalization through current language change.

In modern Chinese, the classifier is considered obligatory in a noun phrase containing a number and/or a demonstrative (e.g. Aikhenvald 2000[2]; Chao 1968; Li and Thompson 1981; Ding et al. 1979; Lü 1982, 1990; Wang 1958, 1985; Zhu 2000; etc.), in the patterns *Demonstrative/Numeral+Classifier+Noun* (Dem/Num+Cl+N), or *Demonstrative/Classifier+Noun* (Dem/Cl+N) when the nominal referent is singular and so the numeral *one* is implied (e.g. Lü 1990; Wang 1958). In a specific discourse context where the nominal presents known information, the pattern may appear as *Num+Cl*, in which the nominal referent is represented by its designated classifier. This study focuses on the numeral classifier NP without the demonstrative, but always with an overt noun.

Specifically, this study analyzes the numeral NPs in three interrelated areas: (1) Form: the presence and absence of the numeral or classifier, and their relative positions in the numeral classifier NP; (2) Syntactic Position: these NPs before or after the verb in a sentence; (3) Semantic Function: the referential status, i.e., definiteness and specificity of these NPs in discourse. The study shows that, due to their lack of discourse analysis, previous studies have provided only partial explanation to the numeral NPs in all three areas. Further, those studies have overlooked current change in Mandarin numeral NPs. Specifically, concerning the Form, there are inaccurate beliefs in claiming the obligatory presence of the classifier in a numeral NP (e.g. Bisang 1998; Cheng and Sybesma 1999; Sackmann 2000), and in identifying the diachronic origin of certain NPs (e.g. Wang 1958). Cheng and Sybesma (1999) are among the first to study the syntactic position and semantic interpretation of the numeral classifier NPs. But the discourse data from this study contradict their theoretical claims.

Previous linguistic analyses of the Chinese classifier system are mainly based on the presumption that the classifier is obligatory when a nominal is associated with a numeral or a demonstrative. The main function of the Chinese classifier is to individualize and to classify count nouns (e.g. Bisang 1998, 1999; Greenberg 1990a). However, in actual practice, this obligatory rule is never followed fully in modern Mandarin Chinese, and the classifier does not always appear in an NP that contains either a numeral or a demonstrative. These *exceptional* NPs can be observed in both formal written texts as well as informal spoken discourse, in the patterns *numeral+N (Num+N)* and *Demonstrative+N*. The latter pattern has been noted in previous studies and is quite readily accepted (e.g. Chao 1968; Ding et al. 1979). The present study focuses on the exceptional pattern *yi55+N: one+N* without a classifier in between. The study suggests that this exceptional NP pattern actually comes from two sources: diachronic language development and current language change. One interesting result of current language change is the numeral NP *one+N* that appears exactly the same in form as an old Chinese NP, which is still in use in formal written discourse. Traditionally, in written discourse, the pattern *one+N* is identified as some relics of classical Chinese (e.g. Chao 1968: 585; Lü 1982). This study shows that the new syntactic pattern *one+N* can be differentiated from the old pattern by two conditions: a. the formality of the language in written discourse, and b. the tonal difference in spoken discourse. The exceptional NPs in the form *one+N* are not merely stylistic variations of numeral classifier NPs in Mandarin Chinese; they actually reflect language change through everyday usage, leading to grammaticalization. Therefore, this study proposes that the classifier is not always obligatory in Mandarin Chinese, as previous studies claim. Although the classifier NP still constitutes the mainstream grammatical pattern in Mandarin Chinese, it is only one of the ways (though maybe a preferred way at present) to present nominal referents in Mandarin Chinese.

To illustrate the history and current language change in Mandarin numeral NPs, Section 2 presents data from both classical Chinese and spoken and written discourse of modern Mandarin Chinese. Section 2.1 briefly introduces previous findings on the form, syntactic position and function of the numeral classifier NPs in modern Mandarin Chinese. Section 2.2 presents a brief introduction of the Mandarin Chinese tone system as background information. Section 2.3 presents data to illustrate the history of major Chinese numeral classifier NPs. Introduction and analysis of diachronic data provide the reader with background information on the development of the Mandarin classifier system. Section 2.4 analyzes data from written and conversational discourse of modern Chinese while examining the three interrelated areas: Form, Syntactic position and Function of numeral classifier NPs. Section 3 discusses previous theoretical approaches in dealing with the Chinese classifier system. The study points out limitations and even fallacies of some of the previous proposals due to their negligence of discourse analysis.

Section 4 concludes the study by proposing that the impact of human cognitive processes (Anderson 1993) on language production leads to language variation and grammatical change, which is a continuous process over language usage. Only through detailed analyses of actual language in discourse can a linguistic theory provide adequate explanations to the Chinese classifier system.

2. Mandarin Chinese classifiers, past and present

This section presents data from both diachronic and modern Chinese discourse, including written and naturally occurring conversational discourse of modern Mandarin Chinese. Data analysis serves as an illustration of the importance of discourse analysis to support the argument that the actual usage of the numeral classifier NPs in modern Mandarin Chinese contradicts some claims from previous studies that have not based on discourse analysis. Further, taking into consideration both the past and present changes in Mandarin Chinese offers comprehensive data supporting the proposal to view the numeral classifier system as a dynamic, ever changing phenomenon through language usage.

It is important to differentiate two written styles in historical Chinese documents: *wen35yan35 wen35: classical Chinese,* and *bai35hua51 wen35: vernacular prose.* Classical Chinese was used in formal written discourse all the way up to about 1919 (the May 4th campaign, which abandoned classical Chinese). The vernacular prose was used for at least seven hundred years (also until 1919). This style adopts some spoken Chinese, but still with heavy influence from classical Chinese. Diachronic data include both styles.

Examples presented here are single sentences, but analyses of the nominal referents are based on the discourse context from which the sentences are extracted; therefore, the interpretation of the choice of these NP patterns is not based solely on their syntactic roles within the sentence, but is based on the discourse context that warrants the choice of the interpretation. This approach provides objective information to the study of the form and function of the numeral classifier NPs in Mandarin Chinese.

2.1. Mandarin chinese numeral classifiers: form, syntactic position and semantic function

Mandarin Chinese classifiers often cover two semantic categories: the classifier and the measure word, often grouped together under the term *liang51 ci35*: measure word or classifier (e.g. Chao 1968: 584; Ding et al. 1979: 168) because both categories occur in the same syntactic slot in an NP. Concerning their functions, the classifier may individualize and classify a count noun (e.g. Bisang 1998, 1999). The measure word sets off boundaries to mass nouns (e.g. Chao 1968[3]; Ding et al. 1979). When a nominal referent is not paired with a numeral or a demonstrative, there is no difference syntactically between a count and a mass noun, both may express a mere concept of the object/mass they represent (Bisang 1998, 1999; Greenberg 1990a). In this study, the term classifier covers both categories (i.e. the classifier and the measure word).

The analysis of this study centers on three areas: the numeral classifier NP form, their syntactic position and semantic function. It is shown that in all three areas the discourse data contradict some claims from previous studies.

Concerning the form of the numeral classifier NPs, this study proposes that in contemporary Chinese, the numeral classifier NPs appear in four patterns:

(1) (A) Noun + Numeral + Classifier (N+Num+Cl);
     (B) Numeral + Classifier + Noun (Num+Cl+N);
     (C) Classifier + Noun (Cl+N); and
     (D) Numeral + Noun (Num+N).

Pattern (A) has a narrow function in discourse (e.g. Chao 1968; Lü 1982, 1990; Wang 1958, etc.), with roots from diachronic Chinese. Patterns (B) and (C) are the most well-examined in Chinese. Of the two, (B) is the most widely used; therefore it is considered the representative of the Mandarin numeral classifier NP. Most of the studies on the Chinese numeral classifier NPs center on this form (e.g. Aikhenvald 2000; Bisang 1998, 1999; Chao 1968; Erbaugh 1986; Greenberg 1990a, b; Li and Thompson 1981; Sackmann 2000, etc.).

Pattern (C), *Cl+N*, expresses a singular nominal referent. But there are different explanations to the origin of this pattern. One view (Cheng and Sybesma 1999) claims that (C) differs from (B) in its underlying representations. The other view maintains that this pattern is the elliptical form of (B) with the numeral *yi55: one* omitted (e.g. Ding et al. 1979; Lü 1990; and Wang 1985).

Lü (1990: 174) points out that the omission of *yi55: one* in pattern (C) is made possible under two conditions: the numeral *yi55* is unstressed, and it is placed after a verb while in the same intonation unit with the verb. Lü maintains that one of the pragmatic functions of the word combination *yi55 (one) + Classifier* in Chinese resembles that of the indefinite article in English, a function in which the numeral *yi55: one* is unstressed in spoken discourse. Since the verb expresses important information in an utterance and thus receives stress, the unstressed numeral after the verb is often lost in this intonation unit. For the same reason, a stressed numeral *yi55: one* is retained even after the verb. Based on this analysis, Lü maintains that, concerning the syntactic position, *Cl+N* is always placed after the verb in modern Chinese discourse.

Contrary to Lü, Cheng and Sybesma (1999) propose that it is the different underlying representations that have predetermined the different syntactic positions of patterns (B) *Num+Cl+N* and (C) *Cl+N*, the former may occur either before or after the verb, whereas the latter only after the verb.

Concerning the semantic function of patterns (B) and (C), only Cheng and Sybesma's study (1999) has examined this issue with the claim that the two differ in that (B) may take an *indefinite specific* or *nonspecific* interpretation, whereas (C) can only take an *indefinite nonspecific* interpretation. They further claim that since the pre-verb position does not allow an indefinite nonspecific interpretation, *Cl+N* can only occur after the verb. Data presentation in Section 2.4 reflects inaccuracy of some of their theoretical claims, while specific examinations of Cheng and Sybesma's proposals are presented in Section 3.

Pattern (D), *Num+N*, differs from the other three patterns in that it does not contain a classifier when the nominal referent is associated with a noun. This pattern was used in classical Chinese, and it is still considered to be a copying of classical Chinese (e.g. Chao 1968: 585; Lü 1982) in modern Chinese discourse. As a result, it has not been fully acknowledged as current usage in modern Chinese grammar. Therefore this pattern is the focus of this current study.

The next two sub-sections present analysis of the Mandarin Chinese numeral NPs on their form, syntactic position and semantic functions, while comparing claims on these three areas from previous studies.

The most widely used classifier in Mandarin Chinese is *ge51*, a general classifier that is associated with the most varieties of nominal referents. The original essence of *ge51* refers to an individual (piece of bamboo or arrow) or thing (Wieger 1965: 611; Lindqvist: 1991: 231; Wang 1958: 238; also see discussions in Erbaugh 1986). Over time *ge51* has extended its function to become the general classifier in Mandarin, mainly for humans (e.g. Lü 1990). In actual language use, this general classifier is often paired with nominal referents whose default classifiers are not *ge51* (e.g. Erbaugh 1986; Lü 1990). Naturally *ge51* is used more frequently than are other classifiers (Lü 1990), which makes *ge51* highly prone for change (e.g. Bybee 2000; Bybee and Hopper 2001). The language change discussed in this study focuses on this classifier.

2.2. Mandarin Chinese tones and the classifier system

Chinese is a tone language. Presentation of data from Mandarin Chinese is incomplete without indication of the tones. Further, the discourse functional study of current language change reported here involves one specific tonal change in Beijing Mandarin Chinese. Therefore, this section begins with a brief introduction of the Mandarin Chinese tones.

There are four basic tones in Mandarin; every stressed syllable bears one of these tones to differentiate lexical meaning. The smallest unit of the Mandarin lexicon is formed with one syllable, in the pattern (C)V (+nasals (n/ng)), plus a tone. Using numbers 1–5 to represent the pitch value of the tones, with 5 representing the highest and 1 the lowest pitch (Li and Thompson 1981: 8; see also Chao 1968), the following is an illustration of the tones.

(2)   First tone: 55   High-level
      Second tone: 35   High-rising
      Third tone: 214   Dipping/falling-rising
      Fourth tone: 51   High-falling

The pitch register of the syllable remains at level 5 in the high level tone 55. In the high-rising tone 35, the pitch register of the syllable starts in the middle level and rises high to level 5. In the dipping or falling-rising tone 214, the pitch register begins at a low level 2, goes even lower to 1, then rises to level 4. With the high falling tone 51, the pitch register starts high at level 5 and falls sharply down to 1. In addition, there is a neutral tone in Mandarin, which is no tone on an unstressed syllable, often seen on a grammatical particle.

The four basic tones illustrated above are in their citation forms. In natural connected speech, a set of tone sandhi changes is strictly followed. (e.g. Li and Thompson 1981: 8–9; Chao 1968: 36). Further, there are two words in Mandarin whose tones are conditioned by the tone immediately following them. One of the words, *yi55: one*, is related to the discussion of language change in this study; therefore, a brief sketch of this tone sandhi rule is presented below. The numeral *yi55* has three tone variations (Examples in (3) are hypothetical).

(3) a.   *yi55*: one, as the numeral one in counting, especially the last two digits
      of a numeral
      e.g. *yi51 bai214 yi55shi35yi55 ge51 ren35*: one.hundred
      eleven.classifier.people: 'one hundred and eleven people'
   b.   *yi35*: one, before a syllable with a high-falling tone (51)
      e.g. *yi35 ge51ren35*: one.classifier.person: 'one/a person'
   c.   *yi51*: one, before a syllable with any other three tones
      e.g. *yi51 che55 xi55gua*: 'one car(load) of watermelon'
      yi51 chuan35 ren35: 'a boat(load) of people'
      yi51 ben214 shu55: 'a (copy of a) book'

Tone sandhi rules are very strictly followed in natural speech because a wrong tone could disrupt the intonation flow and/or the intended meaning; thus when an improper tone is uttered, a repair often occurs: speakers pause and repeat the syllable to produce the correct tone (Tao, Fox and Gomez de Garcia 1999).

In this study, written discourse data are presented with syllables containing their default tones unless a syllable is unstressed (i.e. the neutral tone). Tone sandhi changes are assumed to be present. However, sometimes *yi55* is presented with its default tone when it is unclear how its tone would be pronounced (2.4). For diachronic data, words are coded with their pronunciation in modern Mandarin Chinese, not their possible pronunciations historically.

2.3. Historical development of the Chinese classifier

Chinese classifiers originally were associated with single objects of a cultural value (Wang 1958). Systematic classification developed in the language from around 220 AD (Bisang 1998, 1999; Wang 1958). Historically, there are mainly five word order patterns of Chinese NPs associated with the numeral and classifiers. According to Wang (1958), the earliest NP pattern with classifiers is in the word order: *N+Num+Cl* (4), where the classifier is associated with a specific object to indicate quantities. Later in around 700–400 BC, three more patterns were also in use, though not as widely, *N+Num* (which is no longer in use in modern Chinese discourse), *Num+N* (5) and *Num+Cl+N* (6). The wide use of the pattern *Num+Cl+N* could have started around the 2nd to 5th centuries AD (Six Dynasties, Wang 1958: 243). But after the mid antiquity (3rd–9th centuries AD), *Cl+N* (7) became widely used and the numeral *one* was omitted.

(4)   N+Num+Cl

    a.   (Du Guangting: Qiuran Ke Zhuan: The Legend of Qiuran Ke. 850–933 AD)

       Bi51   si51shi35 ren35, luo35lie51   yan35 qian35.

       servant:girl forty   Cl   spread:line-up extend front[4]

       '(There were) forty maids lined up in a row extending in front (of them).'

    b.   (Dong Yong: The Legend of Dong Yong. 317–420 AD)

       dan51 ling51 jun55 fu51 wei51 wo214 zhi55

       only let   2SG   wife for   1SG   weave

       jian55   bai214   pi214.

       Fine.silk hundred Cl

       'Just let your wife weave me a hundred reams of fine silk.'

(5)   Num+N

    a.   (Analects of Confucius (Lunyu), 5th century BC)

       San55 ren35 xing35, bi51 you214 wo214 shi55   yan55.

       three people walk   must exist   1SG   teacher Int.

       'Whenever there are three people, there should be someone among them who can teach me.'

    b.   (Du Guangting: Qiuran Ke Zhuan: The Legend of Qiuran Ke, 850–933 AD)

       yi35 ji51 you21 shu55se51, zhi35 hong35fu35,

       one maid has   rare.beauty hold red:whisk

       '(There was) a maid with rare beauty holding a red whisk.'

    c.   (Sima Qian: Shiji: Sima Xiangru Zhuan: The Legend of Sima Xiangru, 163–85 BC)

       Mai214 yi51 jiu214she51 gu55 jiu214,

       buy   one liquor.hut sell liquor

       (He) bought a liquor house to sell alcohol.

(6)   *Num+Cl+N*

    a.   (Du Fu: 721–770 AD)

       Liang214 ge51 huang35li51 ming35 cui51   liu214

       two Cl   oriole   sing   emerald:green willow

       'Two orioles are singing in the lush green willow.'

    b.   (Su Shi: Sanduo Hua Shixu: Preface of three flowers, 1036–1101 AD)

       Fang35zhou55 you214 yi51   ren35 chang35 dai51 san55

       Fangzhou exit extraordinary person often wear three

       duo214 hua55.

       Cl   flower

       'There was a supernatural person in Fangzhou who often wore three flowers.'

(7)   *Cl+N*
  a.   (Mencius Philosophy, 372–289 BC)
       Bei55 shui214 che55 xin55.
       cup   water   cart   firewood
       'One cup of water tries to put off the fire from a cartload of firewood
       (utterly inadequate help).'
  b.   (Zhuangzi: Neipian, 369–286 BC)
       Fu51 bei55 shui214 yu35 ao51tang35   zhi55shang51.
       Pour cup   water   at   concave.place Mod.top
       'Pour a cup of water into a concave site.'
  c.   (Truism from Classical Chinese)
       Yi35 cun51 guang55 yin55 yi35 cun51 jin55, cun51 jin55 nan35
       one inch   time   one inch   gold   inch   gold   difficult
       mai214 cun51 guang55 yin55.
       buy   inch   time
       'An inch of time is as precious as an inch/ounce of gold, yet an inch/
       ounce of gold cannot buy an inch/ounce of time (Time is more pre-
       cious than gold).'
  d.   (Feng Menglong: Jiang Xingge Chonghui Zhenzhu Shan: Jiang
       Xingge's Reunification with the Pearl Chemise, 1574–1646, AD)
       . . . *jian51 ta55 dai51 ge hai35zi dao51lai35,*
          see   3SG   bring Cl child   arrive:come
       '(They) saw that he brought a child with him.'

One can see from examples (4)–(7) that the four numeral NP patterns may occur
either before or after the predicate verb diachronically. All examples except (7d) are
from classical Chinese. Example (7d) is from the vernacular prose. Example (4a)
presents an indefinite yet specific NP before the verb; (4b) presents an indefinite
nonspecific NP after the verb. The pre-verb NP in (5a) presents the concept 'when-
ever there are three people,' with an indefinite and non-specific interpretation. The
pre-verb NP in (5b), however, refers to a specific maid, the protagonist of the story;
therefore the classifier individualizes this referent as an indefinite yet specific referent. In (5c) the post-verbal NP introduces a new, indefinite yet specific bar just being bought.

Example (6a) *Num+Cl+N* comes from the first line of a famous poem. The pre-
verbal NP individualizes two orioles that are highly specific to the poet's (or the
reader's) eye. The post-verbal NP in (6b) refers to an indefinite non-specific referent (three flowers).

The pattern *Cl+N* in (7a) has become a proverb now. It does not contain a verb,
yet the concept presented entails a pre- and post verb referent, both indefinite nonspecific. In example (7b), the post verb NP has an indefinite nonspecific interpretation. Example (7c) is an idiom with no specific date as to when it was first used, yet
it clearly originated from classical Chinese. The second phrase of (7c), with the pat-

Table 1. Syntactic and functional distributions of numeral NP patterns in Classical Chinese

	Preverb				Postverb			
	Def.	Ind.spec.	Ind.nonsp.	Gen.	Def.	Ind.spec.	Ind.nonsp.	Gen.
N+Num+Cl	–	+	–	+	–	–	+	+
Num+Cl+N	–	+	–	–	–	–	+	–
Cl+N	–	–	+	+	–	+	+	+
Num+N	–	+	+	–	–	+	–	–

Note: Def: Definite; Ind.spec: Indefinite specific; Ind.nonsp: Indefinite nonspecific; Gen: Generic

tern *Cl+N*, is often used alone without the first one. The two patterns *Num+Cl+N* and *Cl+N* in (7c) present the same generic interpretation in this example. The NP in (7d) introduces an indefinite specific referent in the post verbal position, in the vernacular prose of written Chinese.

Table 1. summarizes the form, syntactic position and semantic function of the numeral classifier NPs from the data. Information from this table only illustrates possible semantic functions of NPs in classical Chinese.

In summary, historically, the four numeral NP patterns can occur before or after the verb. None of the NPs found from the data express a definite referent. The information can be compared with that found from data in modern Mandarin discourse to illustrate language change.

2.4. Classifiers in Modern Chinese Grammar

This section presents analysis of data illustrating the form, syntactic position and discourse function of the numeral NPs in modern Chinese. The analysis may demonstrate the inaccuracy of some of the claims from previous studies. The contradictory issues are presented in the data analysis, but detailed discussions of these theoretical issues are presented in Section 3.

There are four basic numeral classifier NP patterns used in contemporary Mandarin Chinese discourse: the main pattern *Num+Cl+N*, plus its three variances *(Num)+(Cl)+N* (e.g. *N+Num+Cl*, *Cl+N*, and *Num+N*). The data presented here come from both written and naturally occurring conversational discourse. Examination of data from both spoken and written discourse allows the study to cover different discourse genres in which all possible classifier NP patterns may occur in modern Chinese.

The conversational data are collected by the author over a decade (1987–2003). Most of the data come from audio and video recorded conversations of native Beijing Mandarin speakers. A few come from the author's written records of casual conversations. The written discourse data are taken mainly from two sets of books, both recent best-sellers in China. The two differ in the formality of the language. One is a series of fictions depicting the early history of the Manchu Dynasty (Eryuehe 1996,

1997, 1999, V. 2–4), where the language can be relatively formal. The other book is produced after the success of a highly popular TV series (Guo 2001) about a medicine family in Beijing. The genre of this book resembles that of a script, with background description and direct speeches. The language in this book in general is a direct reflection of spoken Beijing Mandarin, following its TV series. It is important to note that this script-like book takes a different genre from most other books. The numeral classifier NPs may serve as a means to lead the readers into a *mental observation* of the actions and scenes of the TV play while reading the book.

The NP pattern *N+Num+Cl* has a relatively restricted function: to indicate quantity in counting (e.g. Lü 1982; Ding et al. 1979). Example (8) is a direct quotation of a pawnshop employee telling the accountant to keep a record of an item, in an informal spoken language style. The NP presents a specific referent.

(8) *Xie214—...puo51   miar51   lan51 ao214 yi35 jian*
       write   broken.shell worn-out padded.coat one Cl
       'Write down—...one worn-out padded coat with torn shell!' (Guo 2001:
       386)

The numeral classifier NP pattern *Num+Cl+N* is most widely used in modern Chinese. The pattern may occur both before and after the main verb, and it is used in both formal written discourse and conversational discourse. There are few disputes concerning the form or function of this pattern; so data analysis presented here is brief.

(9) a. *yi35 ge ren35   yi51wan35 shui214.* (Beijing 97[5])
           one Cl person one Cl   water
           'Each person (of the group) (gets) one bowl of water...'
      b. *Lu51biar55shang ge55 le yi35 da51kuai51 tie214*
           road.side on place.PERF one big Cl   iron
           'There was a huge piece of iron placed on the roadside.' (Beijing 87: 27)
      c. *Ba214 y 35ge da51jiao214zhi35tou nei51 zhi55jia gar51*
           BA one Cl big.foot.toe   that nail.cover
           gei214 xian55 le. (Beijing 87: 27)
           to.one's.loss lift Asp
           A: (He) got one (of his) big tone nails chipped up.

(10) *Liang214 ge ren35   dou55 shi51 jing55 ming35 ren35.*
       two   Cl person both   be   astute person
       'The two of them are both extremely astute.' (Eryuehe 1996: 483)

In example (9a) the two NPs present the meaning: *for every person x, x gets water (in the amount of one bowl)*, in which the first NP refers to a group of people emphatically. In example (9b), the post verb NP *a huge piece of iron* introduces an indefinite yet specific object, evidenced by the perfective particle *-le*. The NP in (9c) occurs in the BA construction, which marks a highly affected specific direct object. However, the NP in (10) presents a *definite* interpretation: the two people who just entered the

room (and immediately sensed something wrong . . .). This interpretation contradicts the claim that the numeral NP in Mandarin cannot take a definite interpretation (Cheng and Sybesma 1999).

The next group of examples covers the NP pattern *Cl+N*, presenting a singular
nominal referent with the numeral *yi55: one* implied (Ding et al. 1979; Lü 1990: 166;
Wang 1958). The examples presented here may cover the most usage range of *Cl+N*,
which involve mainly the most frequently used classifier *ge51*. This approach is in
agreement with at least one previous analysis (Lü 1990), which uses *ge+N* as a representative of the pattern *Cl+N* because of the broad functions *ge+N* covers.

In modern Mandarin Chinese, *Cl+N* is found to occur in two syntactic positions:
an indefinite NP in the post-verb position (11a–c) and (12), and a highly specific
NP in two syntactic constructions, (13a, b) and (14a–c).

(11)   a.   *Sheng35li214 lai35 le ge pu214cha35.* (Beijing 87: 6)
            province.in come.PERF Cl general-examination
            'The province gave a general (medical) examination.'
       b.   *You214 jian51 shi51   yao51 gen55 ni214 shuo55shuo.*
            have   Cl   matter need with 2SG   speak.speak
            '(I) have something to discuss with you.' (Athens 2003)
       c.   *Dai51 ben214 za35zhi51 lu51shang kan51.*
            bring Cl magazine   road.top read
            '(I'll) bring a magazine to read during the trip.' (Athens 2003)

(12)   *Ni214men na! Bu51zhi55dao51 dang55 ge nü214ren35*
       2PL INT   NEG know   be Cl woman
       you214 duo55nan35! (Guo 2001: 706)
       have how difficult
       'You people! (You) just don't understand how hard it is to be a woman!'

(13)   a.   *Hao214 jing55zhi51 ge xiao214yuar51!*
            good/what:a exquisite Cl little courtyard
            'What an exquisite little courtyard!' (Guo 2001: 136)
       b.   *Hao214 ge Qian35long35ye35 yu35yong214 ke214jia214.*
            good Cl Q   residual.strength worth praise
            'What an Emperor Qianlong! His strength was truly commendable.'
            (Er 1997, 4: 269)
       c.   *Guang55 ge zhu214xi35 ye214 zuo51 bu51 cheng35 shi51.*
            only. Cl   chair still   do.NEG.complete matter
            A chairman alone cannot get things done. (Ding et al. 1976: 177)

(14)   a.   *Ba214 ge hu51bu51 da51tang35, neng51 de*
            BA Cl Finance-Dept. big.Hall make up-to
            chou51qi51 si51 yi51. (Er 1999, 4: 91)
            stinking-smell four-side emit
            '(They) made the Grand Hall of the Finance Department into (a
            place) with out-bursting stinking odor.'

b. *Leng51   ba21 ge Yang35 Jiu21 hong35*
    obstinately BA   Cl Y
    xiang214 bu51 qi214lai35 le. (Guo 2001: 434)
    think   NEG up:come ASP
    '(He) just could not get Yang Jiuhong recalled from his memory (cannot remember who Y. is).'

c. *Ta55 ba214 ge dao55 xi214 le.* (Athens 2003)
    3SG BA Cl knife wash Asp
    'She got the cleaver washed (It was my job!)'

Concerning the semantic functions, the NPs in examples (11a-b) both introduce indefinite yet specific referents, contrary to Cheng and Sybesma's claim that *Cl+N* can only take a nonspecific interpretation. In (11a), the NP refers to a medical campaign (to check the infection of blood flukes among urban people who used to work in infected rural areas), a specific piece of new information. The classifier *ge51* individualizes the medical examination as one specific event. In (11b), the NP presents a specific matter that the speaker has in mind to discuss with the hearer. In (11c) the NP has an indefinite nonspecific interpretation because the speaker has not decided which magazine to bring. But it could be potentially specific if the speaker had a specific copy in mind. In (12), the general classifier *ge51* identifies a specific class of people, i.e., women; therefore, the NP presents a generic interpretation. Notice that this interpretation also contradicts the theoretical proposal from Cheng and Sybesma (1999: 511), who claim that *Cl+N* cannot take a generic interpretation.

Examples (13a) and (13b) involve the general classifier *ge51* in a highly productive construction as an exclamation to comment on a definite and specific referent (13a) or to serve as a topic to a comment (13b). Example (13c) contains *Cl+N* in the pre-verb position. The referent is indefinite, but it could be specific, or nonspecific (i.e., any chairman in the leadership position). It is important to note that the classifier still follows a syllable, although in a pre-verb position. Examples (14a–c) are cited from three different sources, formal (14a) and informal (14b) written texts, and a naturally occurring conversation (14c). All three contain the BA construction where the NPs are pre-verbal following the direct object maker BA, which marks a specific direct object that is highly affected by the predicate verb. These examples indicate that *BA-ge+N* may appear in both formal written as well as informal spoken discourse of Mandarin Chinese (also noted in Lü 1990). Examples (11a, b) and (13–14) indicate that the pattern *Cl+N* may present specific nominal referents in two syntactic positions in modern Mandarin Chinese.

The classifier-free numeral NP pattern *Num+N* used to be a rather productive pattern that may occur in both pre- and post-verb positions (e.g. (5a–c)). This pattern is still productive in written Chinese discourse, especially with the use of the numeral *yi55: one*, contrary to the general belief that a Chinese classifier is obligatory in a numeral NP (e.g. Bisang 1998; Chao 1968; Cheng and Sybesma 1999; Ding et al. 1979; Li and Thompson 1981). Recently, the pattern has increasingly appeared in informal spoken Beijing Mandarin. This study argues that the pattern *one+N* actually evolves from two different routes. This issue is explained in detail in Section 3.5. For now it is important for readers to note the tonal differences on the numeral *yi55: one* – in formal expressions, the numeral *yi55* changes its tone to follow the tone sandhi rules (3), whereas in the newly developed pattern the numeral *yi35* has a fixed high-rising tone that does not follow the tone sandhi changes.

The classifier-free form of *Num+N* poses a grave challenge to most of the previous studies on the numeral classifier system of modern Mandarin Chinese. But this pattern has not been fully examined in previous studies; therefore, it deserves more detailed examination.

The first set of examples all contain numerals higher than *one*. The numeral *two* in Mandarin has two different forms, the standard numeral in counting: *er51* (15a), and *lia214* (15b, c). The latter is the result of a phonologically reduced chunk *liang214ge51: two+Cl* (Ding et al. 1979). Notice that the falling-rising tone in *lia214* follows a general tone sandhi change: it turns into a high-rising tone when preceding another falling-rising tone (15c), and it turns into a low tone when preceding any of the other three tones (15b).

(15) a. *Er51 ren35 xia51 de   mei35gan21 shang51 qian35 . . .*
          two.people scare to.degree NEG.dare   go:up   front
          'The two of them were so scared that they didn't dare to move forward.'
          (Guo 2001: 374)
      b. *Lia21 xia51 qi35 de bu35 gan51 le.*
          two   play chess REL NEG do   ASP
          'The two (who were) playing chess would not take it now.' (Guo 2001: 561)
      c. *Yi35ge tuir21 ta55 dao51 tour35 fen55 lia35 jiao214 a!*
          one:Cl leg it arrive end split two feet Int.
          'At the end of one single leg it splits into two feet!'   (Beijing 97)

(16) *Wu214 ren35 zhan51zai51 men35 qian35.*
      five   people stand at   door front
      'The five of them stand in front of the door.' (Guo 2001: 537)

The pre-verb numeral NPs in examples (15a) and (16) both present a definite referent (not any people but the two/five named in the immediately preceding context). This function is similar to that of the NP pattern *Num+Cl+N* in (10). Similarly, the pre-verb NP in (15b) also introduces a definite referent – two specific chess players that have been introduced in the preceding context. The post-verb NP in (15c) presents an indefinite nonspecific referent: some general information of the leg-feet combination. Such usages of the numeral NP in examples (15a–c) seem to bring the reader to the actual scenes in the TV show while narrating the story. It could be due to the genre of this script type of book that such usages are adopted. Therefore, given the right genre, the numeral NP pattern *Num+N* in modern Mandarin Chinese can take the pre-verbal syntactic position with a definite and specific interpretation. This type of usage resembles those found in classical Chinese (e.g. 5a, c) but they should not be taken as direct copies of classical Chinese. Such pre-verb NPs are called for by a specific discourse genre of modern Mandarin Chinese. They are not embedded in fixed idiomatic expressions passed down from classical Chinese, nor are they in a context that calls for a formal language from classical Chinese usage; therefore examples (15a, b) and (16) illustrate productive usage of the pattern *Num+N* that should be included as part of modern Mandarin Chinese grammar.

Next are examples all containing the pattern *yi55+N: one+N*. This pattern has two different origins. In spoken language the two origins can be easily differentiated by a tonal variation: the numeral *yi55* follows tone sandhi changes as specified in (3) if the pattern has its origin from classical Chinese. The recent language change leaves the numeral *yi35* with a high-rising tone irrespective of its immediately following tone. However, when an expression is presented with an informal, spoken language style in written discourse, it is difficult to judge whether the tone of the numeral *yi55* follows the sandhi changes in data presentation. In this case the default tone *yi55* is used (e.g. 19c, d)[6].

Concerning the syntactic position, the pattern *yi55+N* may occur either before the verb (17a–c) or after the verb (18), (19a–d).

(17) a. *Yi51 yu214   ti35xing214 le   Fang55lan35.*
          one language remind   Perf. Fanglan
          'The single remark alerted Fanglan.' (Eryuehe 1999, 3: 437)

      b. *Yi55 huo214ji tui55 men35 jin51 lai35, . . .*
          one employee push door   enter come
          'An employee pushed-opened the door and came in.' (Guo 2001: 156)

      c. *Yi55 ren35   you214 yi55 ren35 de   ming51.*
          one person has   one person POSS fate
          'Everybody has his/her own fate.' (Guo 2001: 666)

(18) a. *Bai21xing51   you51 duo55 yi35 hu51min35   qing55guan55.*
          Hundred.surname also   gain one protect.people clear.official
          'Common people will gain one more honest and upright official who
          protects them.' (Eryuehe 1999, 2: 393)

      b. *Yan51shan55 wu214shu51 shan51 shi51*
          Y   martial.art fan   be
          yi51 ji35ti214 wu214dao214 xiang51mu51
          one collective dance   item
          'The Yanshan Martial Art Fan is a collective dance item.' (*Yanshan
          Wushu Shan*, report from *Changcheng Zaixian*: Great Wall Online: he-
          bei.com.cn. Saturday, 10 Jan. 2004).

(19) a. *Wo21m'n yi35 tong35xu35, zhei51c'i51:: ta55m'n jia55 zhu51:*
          1PL.   one classmate   this:time   3PL   home live
          nar21,
          there (Beijing 87: 19)
          'A classmate of ours, this time, his family lives at there . . .'
      b. *Wo35 gao21le   yi35 ma35zui51 qiang55.*
          1SG   design.Perf one anesthesia gun
          'I designed an anesthesia gun.' (Beijing 87: 26)
      c. *jinr55 gen55 yi55 gan214 da51 che55 de   da214jia51.*
          today with one drive-big-cart   REL-marker fight
          'Today (I) had a fight with a horse-cart driver.' (Guo 2001: 623)
      d. *Jiu214hong35 yi55 ren35 zuo51zai51 chuang35yan35 shang51 fa55*
          J.   one person sit at   bed   side   top
          dai55.
          stare.blankly
          'Jiuhong sat on the bedside alone, staring blankly.' (Guo 2001: 682)

All NPs in the pattern *yi55+N: one+N* in examples (17a–c) are in the pre-verbal sentence-initial position. But the three differ in their diachronic origin and their semantic functions. The expression in (17a) is from the formal written discourse that resembles classical Chinese. The tone of the numeral *yi55* follows the Mandarin tone sandhi rule (3c). The referent of the NP here is definite and specific, referring to the comment immediately preceding this sentence.

Example (17b) comes from the book/TV script. The NP introduces a specific referent (though indefinite) that enters into the room. Such a pre-verbal usage of the pattern *yi55+N* has been rather common in this book, and all instances function to introduce someone specific entering into the scene. Therefore, this usage may occur at least in a specific genre: as descriptions of scenes in a script that brings the reader into a viewer's realm. The expression *huo214ji* is an informal term for employees of a small shop, so this sentence is in an informal style. The first NP in (17c) seems to be a general term covering all human beings in an emphatic manner: for every person x, x has a fate designated only to x. The second NP in (17c) is specific in reference to the first NP.

The NPs in example (18a, b) both occur post-verbally with an indefinite yet specific interpretation. Example (18a) resembles usage from classical Chinese, evidenced by the formality of the language. Example (18b), however, is commonly seen in news reports in modern Chinese.

In examples (19a - d), the NPs *yi35+N* also occur after the verb. These NPs reflect the result of a recent language change in spoken Beijing Mandarin that eliminated the general classifier *ge51* (Tao 2002, further explained in Section 3.4). Concerning the functions of these NPs, the one in (19a) is presented as a topic of the utterance, whose nominal referent is new yet highly referential, introduced by means of the pronoun *wo214men*, an elliptical expression of *wo214men you214*: we have.

Table 2. Syntactic and functional distributions of numeral NP patterns in Modern Chinese

	Preverb					Postverb			
	Def.	Ind.spec.	Ind.nonsp.	Gen.	BA	Def.	Ind.spec.	Ind.nonsp.	Gen.
Num+Cl+N	+	+	+	−	+	−	+	+	−
Cl+N	−	?	?	−	+	−	+	+	+
Num+N	+	+	+	−	−	−	+	+	−

Note: Def: Definite; Ind.Spec: Indefinite Specific; Ind.Nonsp: Indefinite Nonspecific; BA: Pre-verb direct object marker, the BA construction; Gen: Generic

The NPs in (19b, c) are both indefinite yet specific. The NP in (19d) enumerates the singleness of the grammatical subject as an apposition, an emphatic function of the numeral NP. Examples (19c) and (19d) are extracted from the script-like book. These two examples are grouped here because, a. the language style of these examples reflects spoken usage of these NPs; and b. this observation has actually been supported in a pronunciation test, in which *native* Beijing Mandarin speakers chose to pronounce *yi35* with a high-rising tone in the two examples, irrespective of the tone sandhi rules (see (3)). However, *non*-Beijing Mandarin speakers did not seem to know how to treat this tone, so they used the default tone yi55 to pronounce the numeral.

In summary, there are four numeral NP forms: (A) *N+Num+Cl*, (B) *Num+Cl+N*, (C) *Cl+N*, and (D) *Num+N* in modern Chinese. Table 2 presents the syntactic position and semantic function of these NPs. Excluded from the Table are NPs that occur without a verb, including: the pattern *N+Num+Cl* (8), which mainly enumerates quantity, patterns *Cl+N* and *Num+N* with the semantic functions of exclamation (13a), discourse topic (13b, 19a) or emphasis (19d).

Table 2 indicates that the pattern *Cl+N* occurs mainly at the post-verb position in modern Mandarin Chinese with either a specific (11a, b, 14a–c), nonspecific (11c) or generic (12) interpretation. It can occur pre-verbally in the BA construction (14a–c), and sometimes as the grammatical subject (13c). Patterns *Num+Cl+N* and *Num+N* both may take a definite interpretation in the preverbal position (10, 15a, b, 16). The fact is not surprising given the general discourse pressure of information flow (e.g. Chafe 1994; Du Bois 1987; Fox 1987). In the post verb position, the semantic function of all three NP forms can be indefinite nonspecific (9a, 11c, 15c, 18b, 19b, c) or indefinite specific (9b, 11a, b, 17c, 18a). So far only the pattern *Cl+N* has been found to take a generic interpretation (12). Only *Num+N* has not been found in the *BA* construction.

2.4. Interim summary

This section has analyzed data from both diachronic and modern Chinese discourse on the form, syntactic position and semantic function of the numeral classifier NPs in Mandarin Chinese. The data show that there are mainly four numeral classifier NP forms in modern Chinese, and all four can be seen in classical Chinese. Comparison of Tables 1 and 2 reflect a slight change of the syntactic position and semantic function of these NPs. Specifically, the semantic function of *N+Num+Cl* has narrowed to an independent expression enumerating quantity. The classical usage of *Cl+N* (7a, c) in the pre-verb position no longer exists in modern Chinese; however, a new pattern in the same form emerged in vernacular Chinese (7d), which occurs mainly in the post verb position.

The pattern *Num+N* is reasonably productive in different discourse genres of modern Mandarin Chinese. One may argue that *Num+N* is a direct copy of classical Chinese, which should not be included into the grammar of modern Mandarin Chinese. But this study proposes to include the pattern in modern Mandarin grammar because *Num+N* can be used productively in written texts of a specific genre (e.g. 18b). This view, nevertheless, may pose some challenge to the general belief that a classifier is obligatory in an NP containing a numeral.

Finally, the data from diachronic and modern Chinese discourse show contradictions to some previous studies. The issue is discussed in Section 3.

3. Previous studies of the Chinese classifier NPs

This section mainly examines four previous studies on Mandarin numeral classifier NP to promote the importance of discourse analysis in linguistic study. Section 3.1 examines a diachronic study of the classifier NPs (Wang 1958). Section 3.2 discusses typological studies of the classifier system (Bisang 1998, 1999; Greenberg 1990a). Section 3.3 examines the synchronic study (Cheng and Sybesma 1999). These three approaches share one common view: the classifier is obligatory in Mandarin Chinese when a nominal referent is associated with a numeral. The discourse functional analysis of current language change in the classifier NP is presented in 3.4 (Tao 2002; Wiedenhof 1995).

3.1. Diachronic study of the classifier NP

This section discusses an inaccurate observation on the development of the numeral classifier NP pattern *Yi35ge51+N*, caused by lack of detailed discourse analysis (Wang 1958). Citing Honglou Meng (Cao 1982[1700]), Wang maintains that before 1919 (the May 4th literary campaign to ban classical Chinese as the written form), *yi55ge51+N* was used when there was a need to enumerate the singleness of the referent or to emphasize the quantity (e.g. *ni214 yi35ge51 ren35*: only you, ibid: 465); otherwise the numeral *yi55*: *one* was omitted, leaving *ge51+N* as the main NP form. The phenomenon was true at least in the vernacular prose of the early 1700s (Wang 1958: 465). Since 1919, *yi55ge51+N* was used more frequently with a function of an indefinite article, and this increased usage was the result of heavy influence of the indefinite article from Indo-European languages (ibid: 465).

Wang's observation on the developmental history of the pattern *yi55ge51+N* seems inaccurate. Using a quantitative approach, this present study conducted a rough analysis of the occurrence frequency of *yi35ge51+N* and *ge51+N* from three chapters of *Honglou Meng* (Cao 1982[1700]), one of the most famous Chinese fictions written in the early 1700s. The book brings spoken language into the text, especially in direct quotations. It is found that, contrary to Wang's claim, *yi35ge51+N* and *ge51+N* occur about equally frequently. The difference of the two lies in pragmatic preferences. Specifically, in the narrative discourse *yi35ge51+N* constitutes about 85% of all the instances of the two patterns, indicating that *yi35ge51+N* was used in a relatively formal style. The emphatic usage of this pattern and the *ge51+N* pattern each occurred only 7% of the time. In quotations of direct speech, however, *ge51+N* occurred 61% of the time, exclusively in the post-verb position, so it is highly likely that *ge51+N* was used more informally in the spoken language of that time. The emphatic form of *yi35ge51+N* and other normal usage of this pattern occurred 18% and 20% of the time respectively.

Considering the fact that the book uses spoken language in its quotations, it could be the case that during the 1700s, *yi35ge51+N* was used predominantly in a relatively formal vernacular prose. The emphatic semantic function of this pattern only occurred in a small usage percentage; therefore, this function of *yi35ge51+N* cannot be its main function of that time, contrary to Wang's claim. In other words, it is inaccurate to state that the wide usage of *yi35ge51+N* was due to influence of European languages in the early 20th century.

Concerning the origins of the pattern *Cl+N*, Lü (1990) has offered a more compelling explanation. Lü (1990: 174) proposes that *Cl+N* is a phonologically reduced form of the pattern *Num+Cl+N*. The reduction takes place when the numeral *yi55* is unstressed after a verb while in the same intonation unit with the verb. If Lü's prediction is accurate, then the pattern *yi35ge51+N* has to be present before *ge51+N* appears. This process seems possible because the wide use of the pattern *Num+Cl+N* started in the 2nd–5th centuries AD (Six Dynasties, Wang 1958: 243). The phonologically reduced pattern *Cl+N* became widely used later, after the mid antiquity (3rd–9th centuries AD, Wang 1958: 243). In fact, instances of both patterns have been found from historical documents, and indeed *Num+ge51+N* (7a, from 700 AD) may have been used much earlier than was *ge51+N* (7d, from 1500 AD). Therefore, lack of discourse analysis has led Wang to an inaccurate conclusion on the development of the pattern *yi35ge51+N*.

The data from this study offer two additional amendments to Lü's proposal. Lü (1990) argues that modern Chinese *Cl+N* did not descend from classical Chinese because *Cl+N* in classical Chinese could occur pre-verbally (e.g. (7a, c)); whereas modern Chinese *Cl+N* can only occur after the verb because it is the verb that has triggered the phonological reduction and deletion of the numeral *yi55: one*. However, Lü has not made it clear that such a language change also happened historically. Example (7d) contains the general classifier *ge51*, commonly seen in the vernacular prose style of the 1500s; thus *Cl+N* comes from a diachronic language change as well. Further, examples (13a–c) indicate that *Cl+N* may not be restricted to the post-verb position when they follow other modifications, indicating that the phonological reduction may be triggered by *either* modifications *or* the predicate verb preceding *yi55*. Nonetheless, the origin of *Cl+N* exemplifies the impact of spoken language on language change.

Wang's proposal on the historical development of the patterns *yi35ge51+N* may mislead the readers to the belief that the general usage of the pattern *yi35ge51+N* only flourished in the early 20th century due to the influence of the indefinite article from western languages. Therefore, lack of quantitative discourse analysis has led to inaccuracy in Wang's analysis.

3.2. Synchronic study of the Classifier

The syntactic position and semantic function of the numeral NPs, especially those of the pattern *Cl+N* (examples (11)–(14)), have posed a challenge to a formal synchronic study of the numeral classifier NP in Chinese (Cheng and Sybesma 1999). Cheng and Sybesma have examined three NP forms in Mandarin and Cantonese, a *bare noun* (i.e. a noun presented alone without any association of a numeral or demonstrative), and two classifier NP patterns *Num+Cl+N* and *Cl+N*. Presented here are their theoretical claims on the classifier NP patterns *Num+Cl+N* and *Cl+N* in Mandarin Chinese, which do not include measure words that involve quantifiers (e.g. a *cup* of).

Cheng and Sybesma propose that the two numeral classifier NPs differ in their interpretations because they have stemmed from different structural representations (21—Example 39, ibid: 529). In Mandarin Chinese, the two patterns *Num+Cl+N* and *Cl+N* both have (21) as their underlying representation, except that the pattern *Cl+N* does not contain an overt Numeral. Number plays a decisive role in this argument. In (21), the structural representation NumeralP entails an indefinite interpretation. The *Numeral* may be overt or non-overt in the NP. Overt numerals present quantifications, which are indefinite in nature, but it may allow specific or nonspecific interpretations. Therefore, noun phrases with overt numerals (i.e. *Num+Cl+N*) yield an indefinite interpretation, which may be specific or nonspecific (ibid: 528–9). On the other hand, a non-overt numeral (i.e. *Cl+N*) only allows for a nonspecific interpretation (ibid: 530).

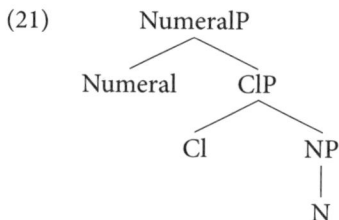

(21)   NumeralP
        ╱╲
   Numeral   ClP
            ╱╲
          Cl   NP
                |
                N

To explain the different interpretations of the two NPs, Cheng and Sybesma suggest that for the indefinite interpretation, the *Cl+N* pattern has stemmed from NumeralP (21). When the numeral is non-overt, the *Cl+N* pattern can only take a nonspecific interpretation. The pattern *Cl+N* contains an overt classifier that 'cannot appear without a Numeral' (ibid: 529), although the numeral may be overt or non-overt (ibid: 529–30). Since the *Numeral* only allows a non-specific interpretation, it is natural that *Cl+N* can only take a non-specific interpretation. However, Cheng and Sybesma admit that the reason behind this argument is still unclear (ibid: 529).

The generic interpretation needs a definite, kind-referring noun phrase, which neither of the two patterns *Cl+N* and *Num+Cl+N* provides, due to their (overt) involvement with the Numeral. Therefore neither can take the generic interpretation (only the bare noun may do so).

In terms of syntactic positions, Cheng and Sybesma propose that the two Chinese NPs have different distributions constrained by their limited range of different interpretations. They propose (ibid: 512–28) that *Num+Cl+N* can occur both pre- and post verbally, however, it can only take an indefinite interpretation due to the presence of the overt numeral. The pattern *Cl+N* can only occur post-verbally to take an indefinite nonspecific interpretation. Support for the indefinite nonspecific interpretation of *Cl+N*, according to Cheng and Sybesma, is that *Cl+N* cannot go after the direct object marker BA, which marks a highly affected specific NP preceding the predicate verb.

Cheng and Sybesma's argument is based on an arbitrary premise that the pre-verb syntactic position allows only a specific interpretation; whereas the post-verb position can take a nonspecific interpretation. But no explanation is given as to why such restrictions exist syntactically. On the other hand, from the discourse functional approach, it is found that the syntactic position and semantic function of a nominal are correlated due to the discourse pressure of information flow. Roughly speaking, the nominal argument functioning as the grammatical subject before the verb often carries given information. New information is often introduced as the grammatical object following the predicate verb (e.g. Chafe 1980, 1994; DuBois 1987; Fox and Thompson 1990, etc.). When new information is first introduced, it is often indefinite, inaccessible to the hearer; therefore, it has to be grounded with reference to the ongoing discourse.[7] This practice has been supported in the discourse of typologically diversified languages and has been found to correlate with human cognitive processes. From this point of view, it is not the underlying representation of the nominal NPs, but the discourse pressure out of the interactive needs of communication, that determines the syntactic position and semantic interpretation of the NPs. For the same reason, Lü's explanation (1990) of the origin of *Cl+N* seems to make more sense, i.e., it is phonologically reduced from *Num+Cl+N*, and the reduction took place at the post verb position historically through spoken discourse.

In essence, Cheng and Sybesma argue that the function of the classifier in Chinese is to classify and individualize nominal referents. The classifier is the *locus* of grammatical number in Chinese. And *Number* plays a crucial role in the syntactic distribution and NP interpretation of the two different NP forms. Their theoretical proposals presume that the form, syntactic position and semantic function of the two NP patterns are pre-determined by a theory-internal, formal, underlying structural representation.

The functional definition of the classifier from Cheng and Sybesma does not seem to differ much from previous functional and/or typological studies (e.g. Bisang 1998, 1999; Chao 1968; Greenberg 1990a; Li and Thompson 1981) on the transnumeral nature of Chinese. Their syntactic analysis of the two numeral classifier NP patterns has provided some valuable insight into different functional distributions of the classifier NPs in Mandarin Chinese. However, Cheng and Sybesma's study has neglected one important aspect – the dynamic nature of language that can only be fully appreciated through discourse analysis. Language is for the purpose of communication. Through everyday usage, language is subject to the effect of diachronic change, and it is also experiencing constant change through everyday usage on its surface form (e.g. Joseph 2003). A synchronic syntactic analysis of the Chinese classifier system without consideration of its past history or its current change can only result in partial coverage of the system. Indeed, the theoretical proposal of Cheng and Sybesma has neglected two major aspects: the classifier-free numeral NP *Num+N* (examples (17b), (19a–d)) and the generic (12) and specific interpretations carried in the NP *Cl+N* (e.g. (11a, b), (13a, b), and (14a–c)).

The productive usage of the numeral NP pattern *Num+N* contradicts Cheng and Sybesma's theoretical claim that the classifier is the locus of grammatical number. In this pattern, the numeral (although not the *Numeral* projector in their theory) has to be overt, yet the classifier may not be (e.g. (15)–(19)). Cheng and Sybesma propose that an overt numeral allows only for an indefinite interpretation. But this claim cannot explain the pre-verbal occurrence of the patterns *Num+Cl+N* and *Num+N* with a definite interpretation (e.g. (10), (15a, b), (16)). More contradictions to Cheng and Sybesma' theoretical claims are the pattern *ge51+N* with a *generic* interpretation (12), and the *specific* interpretation of *Cl+N* after the verb (11a, b, 12) and in the *BA* construction (14a–c). This classifier NP *Cl+N* cannot take (21) as its structural representation because (21) specifies that without the overt numeral the NP can only be *non-specific*.

The counter-examples to Cheng and Sybesma's theoretical proposal serve as an illustration that, without looking at language in its actual usage in discourse, theories that stem from a purely synchronic syntactic approach may face constant challenges from actual discourse data, which changes over everyday usage. This type of theory will face continuous needs for revision if it tries to offer a valid explanation of language.

3.3. Typological Studies of the Chinese Classifiers

It is generally believed that Chinese classifiers are obligatory in an NP that is associated with a numeral and/or a demonstrative. Many linguists have suggested that the obligatory use of the classifier is caused by the fact that the language does not have compulsory marking of number in nouns, (i.e. transnumerality (Bisang 1998: 39, 1999; Greenberg 1990a, b)). Greenberg (1990a: 184) proposes that in a numeral classifier language, which lacks compulsory marking of plurality in nouns, the classifier is an individualizer which performs the same function as a singulative derivational affix in languages with the collective/singulative distinction. Bisang (1998, 1999) proposes that the Chinese noun expresses a mere concept of its referent, which is indeterminate. The noun has to be further individualized by the classifier before it can be enumerated or specified for the status of the referent it denotes. Therefore, to sum up, to these studies the classifier is compulsory in Chinese due to transnumerality. Bisang further argues that the Chinese classifier system is developed to provide a way to individualize and to classify the referent (Bisang 1998: 39, 1999), and the classifier mainly serves the purpose of classification and identification.

There are two issues that contradict the claims from these previous studies. In actual language use, the Chinese noun does not always present a mere concept. The syntactic construction can make the referent of a single noun concrete. For instance, when people are waiting for a bus at a bus stop, one may produce the utterance *che55 lai35 le: vehicle come: Asp*, meaning that the bus is arriving. In this case the vehicle becomes a definite referent that the speaker refers to. In the next example, the single noun presents a definite referent, evidenced from its immediately preceding discourse context and the direct object marker BA.

(20)   *Ta55 ba214 jiao214 gei214   ke55 le.*
       3sg   BA   foot   to.one's.loss hurt ASP
       'He got (his) foot hurt.' (Beijing 1987)

In the context where this utterance is produced, the speakers were talking about one specific person, and the single noun *jiao214: foot* refers to that person's foot with the ownership implied. This example indicates that a single noun in Chinese does not necessarily present a mere concept of a referent. Its interpretation depends on the syntactic construction and its discourse context.

The second issue that contradicts these previous claims is the productive usage of the classifier-free pattern *Num+N* (e.g. examples (15)–(19)) in modern Mandarin Chinese. If we accept this pattern as part of modern Mandarin grammar, then usage of this pattern in discourse indicates that the classifier may not always be obligatory in modern Mandarin Chinese. Consequently, a transnumeral language may not entail a correlation with the obligatory usage of the classifier as Bisang proposes (1998 1999).

Greenberg has also noticed this phenomenon. He points out that transnumerality in a language does not imply the presence of numeral classifiers. The correlation of the two is just implicational but not a logical equivalence. Specifically, he points out that there are indeed transnumeral languages that have measure words but not classifiers. Nevertheless, he considers the phenomenon a general problem in relation to the main thesis of his study, a puzzle in need of resolution (1990a: 189). As is discussed later in Section 3.4, the current language change may provide an answer to Greenberg's puzzle.

3.4. Discourse functional study and the phono-syntactic conspiracy

The discourse functional study of the Mandarin Chinese classifier system reports a current language change out of a process named the *phono-syntactic conspiracy* (Tao 2002). This current study proposes the view that, although the classifier may be a preferred system in a transnumeral language, the classifier should be considered only *one way* for individualizing a nominal referent in the transnumeral language. This proposal is based on a current language change in spoken Beijing Mandarin Chinese, which results in the elimination of the general classifier while retaining the numeral, resulting in a numeral NP pattern *yi55+N: one+N* (e.g. 19a – d). The occurrence of this pattern challenges the theoretical claim from most of the previous studies, which states that the Chinese classifier is obligatory when a noun is associated with a numeral.

This *phono-syntactic conspiracy* describes a language change from the pattern *yi55+ge51+N: one+Cl+N*. It starts on the phonological reduction of the syllable *ge51*, but ends in a syntactic change in spoken Beijing Mandarin *yi35+N*, resulting in the deletion of the highly frequently used Mandarin classifier *ge51* while retaining the numeral *yi35: one*. The results of the conspiracy are: a, a *frozen tone*, a tone that does not follow Mandarin tone sandhi rules (e.g. (3)); b, a syntactic *classifier-free* practice, and c, a *syntactic tone*. Mandarin tones have been lexical because they differentiate lexical meaning. The addition of the syntactic tone marks the beginning of a new tonal function in the language. There are four steps in the conspiracy, illustrated in (22) (Tao 2002: 279)[8].

(22)   Phono-syntactic Conspiracy
1. Tone-sandhi rule application: *yi55 → yi35ge51 + Noun*
2. Vowel reduction: *ge* adopts a neutral tone. The vowel is reduced to a schwa /ə/: *yi35ge51 -> yi35gə + Noun*
3. Intervocalic consonant deletion: *yi35gə -> yi35ə + Noun.*
4. Vowel sequence simplification: *yi35ə -> yi35 + Noun.*

Step 1 of the conspiracy describes how the high level tone in *yi55* turns into a high-rising tone *yi35* when preceding the high-falling tone in *ge51*, a practice following the Mandarin tone sandhi rule as specified in (3b). Because *yi35ge51* often comes out together, they have become a phonological unit with one stress on the numeral *yi35*, so *ge51* is often unstressed, losing its contrastive, relative pitch. In spoken Beijing Mandarin, the unstressed vowel in the classifier *ge51* is further reduced into a schwa /ə/, as illustrated in Step 2. Step 3 involves a re-analysis of the syllable structure in which the two syllables *yi35ge* become one chunk. Then an intervocalic consonant is fused phonologically. In this case, /g/ is reduced phonologically -- it turns into a glide, and sometimes the glide is completely dropped. Step 4 is the final product of the conspiracy: completely eliminating the classifier *ge51* while leaving the word *yi35* with a high-rising tone. Conditioned by the high-falling tone in *ge51*, which has been completely dropped by now, the high-rising tone in *yi35* is frozen in that it no longer follows Mandarin tone sandhi rules (cf. (3c)): it neither triggers nor undergoes tone sandhi. Thus this frozen tone is emancipated (Haiman 1994) from the tone sandhi rules. The emancipated frozen tone now serves a new syntactic function – an indicator of a classifier-free or bare NP in spoken Beijing Mandarin. Note that the segmental changes only develop (Steps 3 and 4) when a nominal expression follows the combination *yi35ge*.

The 4-step phono-syntactic conspiracy illustrates synchronic variations of the syllable structures in Mandarin noun phrases involving *yi35ge51+Noun: one+Cl+N*. Currently, all 4 steps of the conspiracy coexist in spoken Beijing Mandarin. The final product of the conspiracy is illustrated in examples (19a–d).

It has been well documented that frequency and chunking play a decisive role in language change (e.g. Bybee 2000; Bybee and Hopper 2001; Bybee and Scheibman 1999; Haiman 1994; Hopper 1998; Zipf 1968 [1935]). In naturally occurring conversations, the more often two elements are produced together, the more likely they are produced as a phonological chunk. Thus it is more likely they will be fused or bonded phonologically. This process describes exactly how the phono-syntactic conspiracy takes place in spoken Beijing Mandarin.

The numeral *yi55: one* and the classifier *ge51* are high frequency words (#8 and #12 among the 4000 high frequency words in daily conversations, Beijing Language Institute 1986). A frequency count out of data of 5 hours of naturally occurring conversations indicates that the combination of *yi35ge51+N: one+Cl+N* far exceeds the occurrence of *yi55* in combination with all other lexical items. In the conversational data of five hours, 78% of the instances of *yi55*-combinations come from this single pattern *yi55+ge51+N*. Concerning the difference between *yi35ge51+N* and *ge51+N*, there is no definitive answer to this question, yet it is found that the former is used much more frequently than the latter: in a conversation of 90 minutes, there are 43 instances of *yi35ge51+N*, 85% of which are after the verb, but only two cases of *ge51+N*.

The result of the phono-syntactic conspiracy leads to a classifer-free NP *yi35+N: Num+N* with a frozen high-rising tone. One may question whether the frozen tone is still conditioned by the general classifier *ge51* as a non-overt underlying classifier. Tao (2002) suggests that although this explanation is possible, there are instances of *yi35+N* where the designated classifier of the N is not *ge51* (19b, where the designated classifier for gun in Mandarin is *ba214: handle* or *zhi55: branch*). The fact indicates that *yi35+N* may have been emancipated from its original environment to become grammaticalized in this new form. So far the pattern *yi35+N* is only found in the post-verb position in spoken discourse, although in informal written discourse it may appear in the pre-verb position (17b).

This discourse functional study of current language change offers additional explanation to the increased usage of the classifier-free numeral NP *yi35+N* in spoken

Beijing Mandarin. This NP has also been adopted in written texts (e.g. Guo 2001) in an informal style of Mandarin Chinese. However, in the written texts where the language style is formal, a similar pattern *yi55+N* is also often seen (e.g. (17a), (18)). But, in this case the formality of the written language can differentiate the origins of the two NPs. In a pilot study in which native Beijing Mandarin speakers were asked to read a set of sentences containing the pattern *yi55+N* (e.g. example (19c)), it is found (Tao, in press) that native Beijing Mandarin speakers chose to pronounce the numeral by following tone sandhi rules (as specified in (3)) if the written language was formal. They chose the frozen tone *yi35* to pronounce the numeral if the written language was in the informal style. The results of this pilot study indicate that at least the newly developed NP *yi35+N* has an impact on the mental representation of native Beijing Mandarin speakers. To them the two identical NP patterns in print actually differ in their genre of usage.

Tao (2000 2002) further notes that with a group of special measure words, the frozen tone on the numeral *yi35* has become an indicator of the grammatical function of the *N* (23), which marks the beginning of a syntactic tone in Mandarin Chinese (recall that Mandarin tones have been lexical). For the same written form as illustrated in the following examples, tonal variations on the numeral *yi55* trigger two different interpretations:

(23) a. 一本 *yi35ber214*: a notebook; *yi51ber214*: one copy (of a book/note-book)
  b. 一枪 *yi35qiang55*: a gun; *yi51qiang55*: one gunshot
  c. 一车 *yi35che55*: a vehicle; *yi51che55*: a carload (of ...)

The findings of this discourse functional study may explain the increasing usage of the classifier-free numeral NP in Beijing Mandarin. It illustrates how frequency of usage leads to language change.

3.5. Interim summary

The newly developed classifier-free numeral NP *yi35+N* and the productive use of its mirror-image *yi55+N* in Mandarin Chinese discourse provide counter examples to the theoretical assumptions from the three previous studies whose analyses either propose (Wang 1958) the obligatory presence of the classifier, or are based on the premise of the claim that a classifier is obligatory in an NP associated with a numeral (Greenberg 1990a; Bisang 1998, 1999; Cheng and Sybesma 1999). Discourse usage of the classifier-free numeral NP also challenges the theoretical proposal of Cheng and Sybesma (1999), which presumes that the overt classifier is always associated with a number (the number being overt or covert). In the classifier-free numeral NP, the classifier is not overt, yet the number is.

One may argue that the general classifier *ge51* may have presented a unique case different from the other classifiers in Mandarin Chinese. In any case, this classifier has been found to pair with nouns that have different designated classifiers (e.g. Erbaugh 1986; Lü 1990, etc.). If that is true, then any exceptional function of *ge51* is just exceptional but not representative of the Mandarin numeral classifier system. Contrary to that view, Lü (1990: 166) takes *ge51* as a representative of the Chinese classifiers just because of the wide usage of this general classifier. This present study agrees with Lü (1990) and proposes that there is another stage of language development caused by semantic leveling and human motor skills in language production. The spreading of the general classifier demonstrates that the semantic function of the Mandarin classifier may have been gradually bleached out, leaving only a grammatical function to fill in the slot of the classifier in a numeral NP. Secondly, if we accept the standpoint that linguistic change and grammaticalization often start in high frequency words through daily usage, then it is highly probable that the high usage frequency of *ge51* has triggered its change. Therefore the usage of *ge51* does not pose any exceptional cases in discourse. Instead the word may just be the one that is more likely to start the variation and change than are other less frequently used classifiers in Mandarin Chinese. Consequently, the discourse function of *ge51* may actually reflect a developmental path of language change concerning the numeral classifier system in Mandarin Chinese.

4. General discussion

Admittedly, all four types of theoretical analyses of the Mandarin Chinese classifier system have provided valuable insights into the study of the classifier in general, and the Chinese classifier system in particular.

Specifically, Wang's contributions to the theoretical study of Chinese language have been generally acknowledged and considered invaluable. However, due to lack of actual discourse analysis, his observations of Mandarin Chinese appears to be limited, resulting in the negligence of the actual function of the two NP patterns *yi35+ge51+N* and *ge51+N* in the development of Mandarin Chinese.

Greenberg's typological study (e.g. 1990a, b) of the classifier systems has provided an insight explanation of the correlation of transnumeral languages and classifiers. The cognitive explanation has been further extended (e.g. Bisang 1998, 1999; Broschart 2000; Sackmann 2000). Nevertheless, these studies have not examined actual language uses in discourse; therefore their theoretical proposals have neglected the pragmatic function of syntax. For instance, even though English has an indefinite article, the language still does not avoid the ambiguity between pure concept and concrete referent by using them (cf. as a pure concept: I wish I had *a cat*, or as a concrete, specific new referent: There's *a cat* outside your door (Menn, personal communication)). Similarly, in the preverbal position, or after the direct object marker BA, a single noun in Chinese also presents a concrete and specific referent. Therefore, the pragmatics of the whole referential context must be taken into account in explaining the choice of the NP, and the practice has to be carried out by discourse analysis.

Cheng and Sybesma's (1999) synchronic analysis of the Chinese NPs has provided an insight view and detailed explanations of the differences between single nouns and classifier NPs in Mandarin Chinese. The study has provided some explanations of the correlations of syntactic positions and semantic functions of these NPs. However, without consideration of actual language use in naturally occurring discourse, the formal theoretical claims in this study cannot offer a valid, full explanation of the Mandarin classifier NPs.

The discourse functional study (Tao 2002) proposes to modify claims from most of the previous studies. The proposal is to view the Mandarin Chinese classifier system as one way to deal with transnumerality in Chinese. The reason for proposing this modification comes from the belief that grammatical patterns reflect human observations of the physical world around them. Cognitively, an object can be conceived at any given moment as a mere concept of a type, or as an individual item. Languages may develop different coding systems to cope with these physical human observations. However, although the human cognitive representation may be constant, the linguistic coding system does not have to (nor will it) remain the same. The newly emerged pattern $yi35+N$ provides support for this argument. This classifier-free NP poses a violation of the general belief that the Chinese classifier is compulsory for this transnumeral language when an NP is associated with a numeral.

The process of phono-syntactic conspiracy exemplifies a usage-based language change through fusion, which is directly related to the impact of usage frequency to language change. According to Anderson (1993), there are two types of long-term memory in human cognition: declarative and procedural knowledge. The former is conscious knowledge that can be reported; the latter can be observed as an efficient production of a task through compiled practice, reflected by automaticity in performance. Phono-syntactic conspiracy demonstrates language change through phonological fusion in language production, conditioned by a frequently used word combination $yi35ge51+N$. This process may be related to human motor skills in language production, not caused by semantic motivations as most of the previous studies center around (e.g. Bisang 1998; Craig 1986; Erbaugh 1986; Greenberg 1990a; Hopper 1986). Therefore, this study again reflects the fact that language change is the change of its surface form, not the change of some abstract theoretical representations (Joseph 2003).

Figures 1a and 1b illustrate the major difference between the three previous studies and the discourse functional study on the form and function of the numeral classifier system in Mandarin Chinese. Figure 1a illustrates the view that classical Chinese and modern Mandarin grammar are two separate entities; further, language variation is just variation in form within modern Mandarin grammar. The three previous approaches in the study of Mandarin Chinese numeral classifier NPs (Cheng and Sybesma's study (1999) in particular) seem to have adopted this view because they have all excluded certain usages such as the $Num+N$ pattern from modern Mandarin grammar. Some linguists consider $Num+N$ to be $wen35yan35wen35$: classical Chinese (e.g. Chao 1968: 585), a valid consideration if the pattern is within

Classical Chinese NP   Modern Mandarin Classifier NP NP Variations

Classical Chinese NP   Modern Mandarin Classifier NP NP Variations

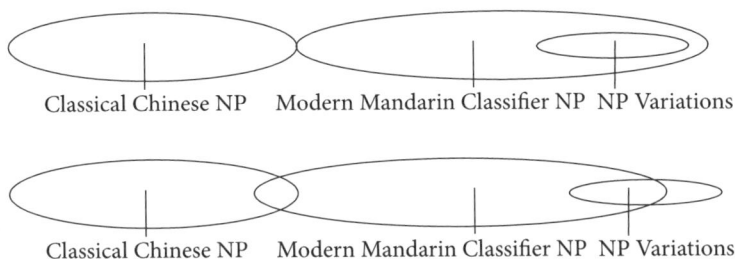

Figure 1. Top: classical Chinese and modern Mandarin grammar are two separate entities; bottom: classical Chinese and modern Mandarin grammar are not two separate entities

a fixed expression (e.g. *Yi51mao35 bu51 ba35*: one-hair-Neg-pull: extremely stingy). However, if a pattern can be used productively in different syntactic constructions, such as the *ge51+N* pattern in the BA construction (e.g. examples 14a–c), or the *Num+N* pattern (e.g. examples 15–19), then these usages should be considered part of the modern Chinese grammar, although they may appear in different discourse genre. This point is illustrated in Figure 1b.

Figure 1b illustrates the viewpoint based on findings from current discourse functional studies on the form, syntactic position and semantic function of Mandarin Chinese numeral classifier NPs. In this view, classical Chinese and modern Mandarin grammar are not two separate entities. They overlap during language development. Therefore, although the pattern *Num+N* in formal written discourse has originated from classical Chinese, current productive use of this pattern should warrant its inclusion into modern Chinese grammar. Further, language variations, such as the numeral classifier NP *yi35ge51+N* in different variation stages as specified in the phono-syntactic conspiracy, are not mere variants of the same form. The variation may become grammaticalized, leading into future language change. So language variation should not be contained as mere variations within modern Mandarin grammar. It may have a potential for future grammatical change.

This study does acknowledge, however, that *Num+Cl+N* is the mainstream numeral classifier NP pattern in modern Chinese grammar. It should be taught as such in pedagogical grammar of Mandarin Chinese. It is true that the classifier may not be dropped freely in every instance of a numeral classifier NP at the present time. On the other hand, linguistic analyses should not only observe the mainstream usage by neglecting the past and present development of a language because language is changing through everyday usage.

In summary, the numeral classifier system in modern Mandarin Chinese should be observed as a dynamic, ever-changing phenomenon. At any given moment in time, language usage in discourse may contain an expression with its root from the past, as well as instances of usages that may be deviant from the modern grammar. Failure to account for these exceptional cases may be neglecting actual language itself. Therefore, this present study proposes that a linguistics theory should take discourse analysis seriously by observing what is actually used in the language. Discourse analysis should be taken as the fundamental means for the study of language.

Notes

1. The author would like to thank Barbara Fox and Lise Menn for their encouragement of this study, and to thank the editors of this volume for their encouragement and constructive comments and suggestions for the chapter. Any error in this chapter remains the sole responsibility of the author.

2. Aikhenvald's study (2000) is based on data from other researchers. The data sometimes are flawed. For instance, the citation on the pairing of the plural marker *–men* and the numeral (2000: 208) was wrongly attributed to the numeral higher than one, not the fact that the indefinite measure word/quantifier *yi51xie55: a few* can only be paired with the numeral *yi55: one*, not with other numerals (e.g. *san55xie55: *three few).

3. These classifiers and measure words are not two discrete categories. Many differ in their syntactic function as classifiers or measure words. For detailed discussion of these differences, see e.g. Chao (1968); Ding et al. (1979 [1961]); Lü (1990) Wang (1958).

4. Abbreviations of grammatical markings include the following: Asp: Aspectual marker, BA: the direct object marker; Int: Interjection; Neg: negative marker; Perf: perfective particle; Poss: Possessive marker; Rel: relative clause marker.

5. Each citation of the data from naturally occurring conversations is accompanied by a place name (e.g. Beijing, Athens, Changsha, etc.) to indicate where the data were recorded. The year following the place names (e.g. 97, 2003, etc.) indicates the time when the recording was conducted or when the quotation was noted, and the page number from the transcripts.

6. This author has noticed that in a mini TV series, *yi55* in the same NP is pronounced differently depending on the formality of the utterance. It follows the tone sandhi change in a formal utterance; *yi35* takes a high-rising tone when the same NP is used in an informal utterance (e.g. *yi51/yi35 shan55ye214 lang35zhong55:* one/a herb medicine man, from: *Shenyi Xi Laile*: Magic Medicine Man Xi Laile).

7. In the following example: 'There's *a woman* in my class who's a nurse.' The new information *woman* is first introduced after the verb, and grounded by means of the speaker (*my* class) and the relative clause (who's a nurse); thus making the new information relevant to the ongoing conversation (Fox and Thompson 1990: 301).

8. The classifer-free NP has also been noted in Du (1993), who only points out the phenomenon, and in Wiedenhof (1995), who proposes a phonological explanation. But neither has studied usage frequency leading to this change. Tao's study is independent of the previous two.

References

Aikhenvald, A. 2000. *A Typology of Noun Categorization Devices*. Oxford: Oxford University Press.
Anderson, J. R. 1993. *Rules of the Mind*. Hillsdale, NJ: Erlbaum.

Barlow, M. and Kemmer, S. (eds.). 2000. *Usage-Based Models of Language*. Stanford: CSLI Publications.

Beijing Language Institute. 1986. *Xiandai Hanyu Pinlü Cidian* (Word frequency dictionary of contemporary Chinese language). Beijing, China: Beijing Language Institute Press.

Bisang, W. 1998. "Grammaticalization and language contact, constructions and positions". In *The Limits of Grammaticalization*. A. Ramat and P. Hopper (eds.), 13–58. Amsterdam: John Benjamins.

Bisang, W. 1999. "Classifiers in East and Southeast Asian languages: Counting and beyond". In *Numeral Types and Changes Worldwide*. J.Gvozdanovic (ed.), 113–185. Berlin: Mouton de Gruyter.

Broschart, J. 2000. "Isolation of units and unification of isolates: The gestalt-functions of classifiers." In *Systems of Nominal Classifications*. G. Senft (ed.), 239–269. Cambridge: Cambridge University Press.

Bybee, J. 2000. "The phonology of the lexicon: Evidence from lexical diffusion." In *Usage-Based Models of Language*. M. Barlow and S. Kemmer (eds.), 65–85. Stanford: CSLI Publications.

Bybee, J. and Hopper, P. (eds.). 2001. *Frequency and the Emergence of Linguistic Structures*. Amsterdam: John Benjamins.

Bybee, J. and Scheibman, J. 1999. "The effect of usage on degrees of constituency: The reduction of don't in English." *Linguistics*. 37 (4): 575–596.

Cao, X. 1982[early 1700]. *Honglou Meng* (Dream of the Red Mansion/ The Story of the Stone). Beijing, Renmin Wenxue Chuban She: Peoples' Literature Press.

Chao, Y.R. 1968. *A Grammar of Spoken Chinese*. Berkeley: University of California Press.

Chafe, W. (ed.). 1980. *The Pear stories: Cognitive, cultural, and linguistic aspects of narrative production*. Norwood, N.J.: Ablex Pub. Corp.

Chafe, W. 1994. *Discourse, Consciousness, and Time: The flow and displacement of conscious experience in speaking and writing*. Chicago: University of Chicago Press.

Cheng, L. L-S. and Sybesma, R. 1999. "Bare and not-so-bare nouns and the structure of NP." *Linguistic Inquiry*. 30 (4): 509–542.

Craig, C. (ed.). 1986. *Noun Classes and Categorization*. Amsterdam: Benjamins

Ding, S.; Lü, S.; Li, R.; Sun, D.; Guan, X.; Fu, Q.; Huang, S.; and Chen, Z. 1979 [1961]. *Xiandai Hanyu Yufa Jianghua* (An Outline of Modern Chinese Grammar), 6th edition. Beijing: Shangwu Yinshu Guan (Commercial Press).

Du Bois, J. 1987. "The Discourse Basis of Ergativity." *Language*, 63(4): 805-855.

Du, Y. 1993. "Beijing hua zhong de Yi+ming (the construction of Yi+Noun in Beijing Mandarin)." *Zhongguo Yuwen* (Chinese Language). 2: 142.

Erbaugh, M. S., 1986. "The development of Chinese noun classifiers historically and in young children." In *Noun Classes and Categorization*, C. Craig, (ed.), 399–436. Amsterdam: Benjamins.

Eryuehe. 1999. *Kangxi Dadi* (The Great Emperor Kangxi). Kaifeng, China: Henan Wenyi Chuban She (Henan Literature Press).

Eryuehe. 1997. *Qianlong Huangdi* IV (The Emperor Qianlong). Beijing, China: Xinshijie Chuban She (New World Press).

Eryuehe. 1996. *Qianlong Huangdi* I (The Emperor Qianlong). Kaifeng, China: Henan Wenyi Chuban She (Henan Literature Press).

Fox, B. 1987. *Discourse Structure and Anaphora*. Cambridge: Cambridge University Press.

Fox, B. 1995. "Introduction." In *Studies in Anaphora*. B. Fox (ed.), vii–xi. Amsterdam: John Benjamins.

Fox, B, A., Jurafsky, D. and Michaelis, L. A. 1999. "Preface." In *Cognition and Function in Language*. B. Fox, D. Jurafsky and L. Michaelis (eds.), vii-viii. Stanford: CSLI Publications.

Fox, B. and Thompson, S. 1990. "A discourse explanation of the grammar of relative clauses in English conversation." *Language*. 66 (2): 297–316.

Guo, B. 2001. *Da Zhai Men* (Great High Residence). Beijing, China: Zuojia Chubanshe (Writer's Press).

Greenberg, J. 1990a. "Numeral classifiers and substantive number: Problems in the genesis of a linguistic type." In *On Language: Selected writings of Joseph H. Greenberg*, K. Denning and S. Kemmer (eds.), 166–193. Stanford: Stanford University Press.

Greenberg, J. 1990b. "Dynamic aspects of word order in the numeral classifier." In *On Language: Selected writings of Joseph H. Greenberg*, K. Denning and S. Kemmer (eds.), 227–240. Stanford: Stanford University Press.

Haiman, J. 1994. "Ritualization and the development of language." In *Perspectives on Grammaticalization*. W. Pagliuca (ed.), 3–28. Amsterdam: John Benjamins.

Hopper, P. J. 1998. "The paradigm at the end of the universe." In *The Limits of Grammaticalization*, A. G. Ramat and P. Hopper (eds.), 147–158. Amsterdam: John Benjamins.

Hopper, P. J. 1986. "Some discourse functions of classifiers in Malay." In *Noun Classes and Categorization*, C. Craig, (ed.), 309–326. Amsterdam: Benjamins.

Joseph, B. 2003. "Language Change: Change in language or something else." Talk given at the Colloquium of the Department of Linguistics, Ohio University. January 28, 2003.

Li, C. and Thompson, S. 1981. *Mandarin Chinese: A functional reference grammar*. Berkeley: University of California Press.

Lindqvist, C. 1991. *China: Empire of Living Symbols*. New York: Addison-Wesley Publishing Company, Inc.

Lü, S. 1990. *Hanyu Yufa Lunwen Ji* (Essays on Chinese Grammar), Vol. 2. Beijing, China: Shangwu Yinshu Guan (Commercial Press).

Lü, S. 1982. *Zhongguo Wenfa Yaolue* (A Brief Sketch of Chinese Grammar). Beijing, China: Shangwu Yinshu Guan (Commercial Press).

Sackmann, R. 2000. "Numeratives in Mandarin Chinese." In *Approaches to the Typology of Word Classes*, P. Vogel and B. Comrie (eds.), 421–477. Berlin: Mouton de Gruyter.

Tannen, D. 1989. *Talking Voices: Repetition, dialogue, and imagery in conversational discourse*. Cambridge: Cambridge University Press.

Tao, L. 2000. "Prosody and word recognition in Beijing Mandarin: A case study." In: *Proceedings of SWAP*, A. Cutler, and J. M. McQueen (eds.), 175–178. Nijmegen, the Netherlands: Max Plank Institute for Psycholinguistics.

Tao, L. 2002. "Phono-syntactic Conspiracy and Beyond: Grammaticalization in Spoken Beijing Mandarin." In *New Reflections of Grammaticalization*, I. Wischer, and G. Dieward (eds.), 283–299. Amsterdam: Benjamins.

Tao, L. In press. "Classifier loss and frozen tone in spoken Beijing Mandarin: The *yi+ge* phono-syntactic conspiracy". *Linguistics*.

Tao, L., Fox, B., and Gomez de Garcia, J. 1999. "Tone–choice repair in conversational Mandarin Chinese". In *Cognition and Function in Language*, B. Fox, D. Jurafsky and L. Michaelis (eds.), 268–281. Stanford: CSLI Publications.

Wang, L. 1958. *Hayu Shigao* (Outline of the History of the Chinese Language), Vol. 2. Beijing: Science Press.

Wang, L. 1985. *Zhongguo Xiandai Yufa* (Modern Chinese Grammar). Beijing, China: Shangwu Yinshu Guan (Commercial Press).

Wiedenhof, J. 1995. *Meaning and Syntax in Spoken Mandarin*. Leiden, The Netherlands: Research School CNWS.

Wieger, L. S. J. (1965 [1927]). *Chinese Character, their Origin, Etymology, History, Classification and Signification: A Thorough Study from Chinese Documents*. 2nd ed., English and revision according to the 4th French ed. New York: Paragon Book Reprint Corp.

Zhu, D. 2000 [1982]. *Yufa Jiangyi* (Lectures on Grammar). Beijing: Shangwu Yinshu Guan (Commercial Press).

Zipf, G. K. 1968 [1935]. *The Psycho-Biology of Language*. Cambridge: MIT Press.

CHAPTER 14

Compounding theories and linguistic diversity

Anders Søgaard

University of Copenhagen

This chapter presents a typologically grounded theory of composition in compound semantics. Relevant background information on the history of compounding theories is first provided. One branch of theories, slot-filler theories, is especially promising, but unfortunately most existing slot-filler theories are highly anglocentric. In this chapter, a richer characterization of lexical constituents and a construction hierarchy provide the basis for a typologically better slot-filler theory. Constituents are characterized by feature structures, and the approach presented here is compatible with most unification-based theories of natural language. In sum, the chapter provides both an overview of compounding theories and a constructive theory of compound semantics. Finally, the role of discourse in compound interpretation is briefly addressed.

෴

What should a theory of compound semantics explain? Practical aims include to identify kinds of compounds that exist in some languages but not in others, as well as getting at meaning differences relevant for translation. If the ambiguity of *ice knife* is relevant for translation, then we need to get at the proper distinction. In fact, the ambiguity is relevant in Italian, where *ice knife* translates into either *coltello di ghiaccio* or *coltello da ghiaccio*. The translation equivalents mean, respectively, 'knife made out of ice' and 'knife for cutting ice'. For simplicity and clarity of exposition, I consider two-constituent N–N compounds only.

1. Existing compounding theories

Simple compositional accounts of compounding rely on the enumeration of possible semantic relationships between constituents. Unfortunately, the set of compounding relationships is not easily exhausted. Even proscribed relationships, such as 'A is between two B's', are experimentally attested. It was such findings, as well as speculating about seemingly irreducible compounds, which led Downing (1977) to claim that the set of compounding relationships is infinite. For this and other reasons, compounding is sometimes taken to be a case of linguistic non-compositionality (see Coulson 2000). On this view, a two-constituent compound, AB, is interpreted via an unspecified "connected-with" relationship. Here, simple compositional accounts are called reductionist theories, whereas the non-compositional accounts are called pragmatic theories. Two other kinds of theories, transformational theories and slot-filler theories, interpret AB via constituent-dependent compounding relationships.

Compounding theories thus come in four different flavors. *Reductionist theories* have proposed a limited number of primitive relationships between the constituents in a compound: 'A is in B', 'B is in A', 'A is the goal of B', 'A is the source of B', etc. However, such an account is by definition both arbitrary (Bauer 1978; van Santen 1979) and incomplete because of the infinite set of compounding relationships. For illustration, try to place a compound such as *car thief* in the four-way typology given in the parenthesis above; such a typology was proposed by Hatcher (1960). Is a car thief a 'car in a thief', a 'thief in a car', a 'thief as the goal of a car' or a 'thief as the source of a car'?

Transformational theories typically claim that compounds are derived from relative clauses, e.g. *ignition key* from *key which causes ignition* (Rhyne 1976). Such theories seem to be falsified by L1 acquisition studies that show compounds are acquired earlier than relative clauses (Fanselow 1981). Further, a 'man, who carries garbage' is not necessarily a 'garbage man'. Rather, it seems there is an inherent meaning difference between compounding constructions and relative clauses. Unrecoverable deleted material is also theoretically inadequate in the transformational framework. In addition, such unrecoverable semantics would lead to massive and unmotivated ambiguity.

Many contemporary theories are so-called *slot-filler theories*, in which constituents are conceptualized as bundles of features, and the modifying constituent simply "adds" a feature to the other constituent. I claim that current slot-filler theories face serious challenges. A first challenge is that even in endocentric compounds, modifying constituents very often add more than one feature. A second one — and this seems a more serious challenge to contemporary theories — is that exocentric compounding is productive in many languages. Though often less productive than endocentric compounding, it needs to be accounted for. Finally, some languages exhibit less conservative conceptual type distribution than slot-filler theories typically account for. For the notion of conceptual type distribution, see below.

Finally, *pragmatic compounding theories* claim that there is only one relationship between the constituents of a compound, but that its meaning be derived from pragmatic knowledge about the world. Thus, pragmatic theories are essentially non-compositional. Furthermore, pragmatic theories claim that compounds comprise maximal information in minimal linguistic structure. However, many languages show a great deal of "redundant" compounding. Also, there need not be a direct relationship between the two constituents at all. Consider the Danish compounds *spaghettiwestern* ['Italian western'] and *kartoffelwestern* [potato-western; 'Danish western']. Here, no link exists between the food and the film; rather, the food and the country are linked, and then, so are the country and the film. Finally, pragmatic theories are uninteresting in many respects, since they make no distinction between different kinds of compounds, and unless they are equipped with a world knowledge component, e.g. a probabilistic reasoning module, they cannot help us in translation or in determining ontological relationships between compounds and their constituents.

Since only slot-filler theories and pragmatic theories are left on the market today, I will not discuss reductionist or transformational theories in greater detail. To represent the former theories, I have chosen some promising proposals, from which our treatment of compounding phenomena will benefit. The slot-filler theory dealt with in this chapter was formulated within the generative lexicon framework. The pragmatic theories that we are concerned with are that of Bauer (1978, 1979) and the one formulated by cognitive semanticists within the conceptual blending framework.

2. Pragmatic compounding theories

According to pragmatic theories of compounding, the internal compounding relationship in AB should be glossed 'is connected with' or 'there is a connection between' (Bauer 1979). The connection is such that the hearer can predict the meaning of AB on the basis of semantic and pragmatic knowledge. The reference to pragmatic information is crucial, since it leads researchers to question, if compound interpretation can be formalized at all. For illustration, Coulson and Fauconnier (1999), explicitly adhering to the conceptual blending framework, state that "because the overt language of a nominal compound such as 'stone lion' provides minimal clues to how the integration of input frames is to proceed, the language user is forced to rely on contextual information and background knowledge." In this sense, pragmatic theories are unrestricted polymorphic languages.

In the first part of the chapter, I claimed that pragmatic theories often make wrong predictions with regard to the existence of redundant compounds and indirect compounding relationships. The above quote points to yet another problem. Namely, lack of generalization. Is it really the case that *stone lion* provides minimal clues to its own interpretation for a speaker, who presumably is aware of the existence of compounds such as *plastic gun* and *snow man*? In our view, it would be quite natural to assume the existence of a "privative" compounding construction (or some type shifting operation extending the denotation of the head noun). Lack of generalization also makes pragmatic theories incapable of adequately accounting for systematic ambiguities in compound interpretation.

As Liberman and Sproat (1992) point out, it is impossible to disprove the "connected-with" hypothesis by itself in positive terms; but systematic ambiguities suggest that it is wrong. One may argue that systematic ambiguities stem from common properties of background knowledge. But some seem to depend solely on the existence of multiple compounding constructions. Consider for example the apparent ungrammaticality of **butcher knife* in English. The equivalent in Danish, *slagterknif,* is grammatical. On the other hand, while **knivslagter* is ungrammatical in Danish, *knife butcher* seems fine in English. It is hard to come up with ontological reasons for such differences. If multiple compounding constructions are posited, it is easy to block systematic gaps, e.g. that human denoting modifiers are absent in productive endocentric compounding in English.

That compounds are often many-ways ambiguous is immediately clear. According to Hatcher (1951), the endocentric compound, ανδρο-γυνος [man-woman] is found with several comic writers of ancient Greece as "a designation of effeminate or perverted men"; however, in Plato's writings, ανδρο-γυνος gets a copulative interpretation, used to describe "the perfect soul in which the two 'halves', man and woman, were once united." Consider other copulative compounds, such as *vodka juice* and, a Mandarin Chinese compound, *fumu* [father-mother; 'parents']. Could not these be given endocentric interpretations also? Something along the lines of 'juice flavored with vodka' and 'a mother who acts like a father'? In Danish, *farmor* [father-mother] denotes ones father's mother. This ambiguity also goes for most narrative compounds, such as the Vietnamese compound *com-nuóc* [rice-water; 'cooking']. A narrative compound refers to an event, of which the constituents denote salient parts.

What are the important insights of recent pragmatic theories? Pragmatic theories by definition stress the importance of context in compound interpretation. In our model, the role of context is formalized by the interplay of a number of features in the so-called "k-structure" and discourse structure. Also, as argued below, pragmatic frameworks such as conceptual blending provide means for testing formal analyses of compounds and getting at their meaning in its full complexity (though for most practical purposes, we may only be interested in partial meanings). For reasons not to be discussed here, the cognitive semiotics framework is adopted for this purose in Section 6 on the expense of more traditional blending theories (see Søgaard 2002 for a full discussion).

3. The generative lexicon approach to compounding

The standard generative lexicon approach to compounding is basically a slot-filler approach. In the generative lexicon, composition in compounds is conceived of as "specification of one of the semantic components within the qualia of the head noun" (Johnston and Busa 1999). This slot-filler mechanism relies on a strong version of the head-modifier asymmetry.

> In the case of *lemon juice*, the AGENTIVE role of the head noun *juice* specifies a creation event which, for convenience, we express as the relation **made_from**. Such a relation holds between **juice** and a natural kind-entity such as **fruit** or **vegetable**. Thus, in the compound *lemon juice* the modifying noun *lemon* is to further subtype this component of the meaning of *juice*. This is possible because **lemon** is a subtype of fruit.   (Johnston and Busa 1999: 175)

Johnston and Busa posit a single compounding construction to capture that a pre-modifier in English can specify the semantic type of one of the arguments in the qualia of the pointer.

It is of course beyond the scope of this chapter to present the generative lexicon framework in its full complexity, or even to present it crash course style, but some properties are crucial to our model. In the generative lexicon, semantic expressions result from a fixed set of generative devices including type coercion and co-composition. These mechanisms take four levels of structure as their input, one of them being qualia structure (Pustejovsky 1991). Traditionally, qualia structure is given by the Aristotelian four-way distinction: formal, constitutive, agentive, and telic. The formal quale (Q_f) is just the location of that specific type in an inheritance hierarchy. The constitutive quale (Q_c) contains any part-whole relationship that is relevant to establishing its set of referents. The agentive quale (Q_a) is a predicate, telling us how things denoted by that semantic type come about (the origin of the things referred Xto). Finally, the telic quale (Q_t) denotes the purpose of the things referred to. Constitutive qualia refer to partonomies (and functions), the remaining qualia refer to taxonomy-like hierarchies. However, not every quale need be relevant to every lexical entry.

Qualia structure is an intuitively appealing way to link lexical information with commonsense metaphysics. These two components are probably distinct modules, but the lexical component may utilize standard conceptualization patterns. Recalling Frege's famous analogy, the qualia structure is a telescope for observing a referent; only, it comprises four distinct modes of representation, i.e. optical images.

4. What the generative lexicon explains

Since the generative lexicon is a semi-polymorphic language, it is designed to account for a range of polysemy phenomena. The relevance of this property is somewhat indirect to us, but as Copestake and Briscoe (1995) argue, different compounds, AB and AC, often utilize different senses of a constituent, A. Compounding might be seen as "stressing the lexicon", if for some new compound a new sense must be added to the lexical entry for A or B. Fortunately, since qualia structure incorporates multiple modes of representation, few new senses should be added. Consider two compounds, *gun wound* and *hand wound*. The schematic meaning of *gun wound* can be paraphrased 'A causes B', whereas the meaning of *hand wound* is something like 'B on A'. No new sense should be added, since in the first case, A fills the first argument slot of the agentive quale in B, whereas in *hand wound*, A is an argument of a constitutive quale in B. Consider also *ice knife* again. The 'knife made of ice' reading comes from constitutive qualia, while the 'knife for cutting ice' reading is licensed by the telic role.

Compounds in which both constituents refer metonymically to the referent can be subdivided into copulative compounds and narrative compounds, depending on whether the referent is an individual or an event. Copulative compounds are also called "dvandvas" (the Sanskrit word for 'twins'), and their distribution, cross-linguistically, appears to have strong areal biases (Bauer 2001). Copulative compounds can again be further subdivided. One division is between generalizing and non-generalizing compounds. Hatcher (1951) divides non-generalizing compounds into three semantic kinds. One kind denotes 'two objects seen as one', another denotes a half-half composition or 'one object seen as two', whereas the third kind denotes a blend of two things. To highlight one of the advantages of the generative lexicon, some further distinctions among generalizing compounds are made, and a proper treatment of copulative compounds is presented. For this demonstration, we reject Johnston and Busa's claim that languages such as English only have one compounding construction. In part six, the formal underpinnings of our approach are explicated.

Our analysis of generalizing copulative compounds is closely knit to the generative lexicon representation of different kinds of lexical inheritance networks. In fact, it is based on it: Generalizing compounds denote collective categories via constitutive (partonomies), telic (functional categories), and agentive relationships. Also, some classes, such as heterogeneous classes, are based on multiple qualia role inheritance (for discussion, see Wierzbicka 1985). In our model, these relationships are included in the value set of the TAX | QUALIA attribute.

To denote collective categories, the two constituents must share a qualia role and thus be salient members of the same lexical inheritance network. Examples include (1) and (2). The first example is from Vietnamese, the latter from Mandarin Chinese.

(1)   *bàn-ghê*
       table chair
       'furniture'

(2)   *shubào*
       books periodicals
       'reading matter'

(1) denote a functional category of members sharing the purpose of 'furniture'; likewise, (6) denote a set of nodes in a hierarchy, tied together by the telic role read(x,*y*).

It is argued below that such compounding constructions constitute a subtype of a conceptual type, $[P(m_1)-P(m_1)]$. This CONC value reads: "The first constituent of the compound, A, is a metonymic pointer, and the second constituent, B, is a metonymic pointer." Considering two-constituent compounds only, the denotation of generalizing copulative compounds is $\{[[A]], \ldots [[B]], \ldots\}$, whereas the denotation of non-generalizing copulative compounds is $\{[[A]], [[B]]\}$.

Generalizing compounds thus denote collective categories via different qualia roles. Contrarily, non-generalizing compounds denote finite partonomies. Typically, such partonomies have only two or three daugther nodes, since in order to qualify as a non-generalizing compound, every node must be represented by a constituent.

5. What the generative lexicon fails to explain

Recall Johnston and Busa's analysis of _____ *juice* compounds. In the British National Corpus, 928 out of 1897 occurrences of *juice* are compound pointers with noun modifiers. The most common modifiers were fruits and vegetables such as *lemon* (256 occurrences), *orange* (217), *apple* (37), and *tomato* (26). All modifiers share the same taxonomic level, except *fruit* (176). This illustrates a point to be made later on; namely, that some compounding constructions specify for taxonomic levels. Johnston and Busa account for most cases, but it is important also to stress that they exclude compounds such as *pan juice, cooking juice,* and *stomach juice.* All such compounds must then be labeled opaque and idiosyncratic, and they are to be explained only by semantic drift. This is of course unattractive, since such patterns may be or become productive.

Johnston and Busa face problems of making sense of exocentricity and multiple feature exchange. A problem of a more formal nature concerns feature percolation. The feature percolation problem is tied up with certain trends in lexicalist morphology.

Most slot-filler theories do not distinguish between formal and conceptual percolation. (By "formal percolation", I wish to point out what others have called "morphosyntactic locus" or "category determinant"; see Zwicky 1993.) This distinction is crucial to compounding theory, as well as to morphology in general. Many Romance languages exhibit grammatically exocentric compounding. Mandarin Chinese and Vietnamese provide even clearer evidence for the existence of grammatically exocentric compounding. In fact, in 30% of all compounds in Mandarin Chinese, none of the constituents belong to the same grammatical category as does the compound itself (Huang 1998). In our model, conceptual pointer information is represented as CONC values. Our simple solution for constituent structure representation here will be to posit some "empty" daughter as phrasal head. The constituents are both taken to be adjuncts.

Simple slot-filler theories cannot account for languages with free pointer-modifier distribution. In one third of all languages, the ordering of the constituents is inconsistent with respect to conceptual percolation (Bauer 2001). For relatively consistent languages, the distribution is typically correlated with possessor noun and pointer order. For example, most European languages have right constituent pointers for both genitive and compounding constructions. But through loans, even very conservative languages like English and Tagalog may be slightly inconsistent for specific lexical fields. In English, this is the case when it comes to lexical fields like FOOD and LAW.

Vietnamese exemplifies a genuinely inconsistent language. As for Romance languages, the symmetric distribution is explained by orthogonal historical influences (Nguyên 1997).

(3)   *bút-lông*
      pen hair
      'brush'

(4)   *tô-quô´c*
      father land
      'ancestor country'

6. Extending the generative lexicon model: The construction hierarchy of compounding

To improve the generative lexicon model and to make it account for conceptual exocentricity, I propose a construction hierarchy comprising distinct, but interrelated levels of more or less schematic constructions. The inherent meaning difference between compounding constructions and relative clauses results from root type information; compounds are nouns (names), whereas relative clauses are clauses. Every level is associated with a specific formal or semantic feature.

Some of the features employed by our model are conventional, including phonology, argument structure (ASTR), event structure (ESTR) and qualia structure (Q). Novel features include CONC, TAX and BACKGROUND.

The structure that describes compounding constructions is called basic k-structure. K-structure represents the minimal conceptual semantics of linguistic expressions. Our design is a straight-forward extension of LFG architecture (see Kaplan and Bresnan 1995, for a formal introduction), but our approach is also compatible with HPSG (Pollard and Sag 1987; 1994). Just as φ is a mapping from c-structure into f-structure, κ is a mapping from c-structure into k-structure. K-structure easily translates into logical form.

Regarding the CONC attribute: Our conceptual typology is based on a distinction between literal (l), metonymical (m_1), and metaphorical (m_2) relatedness. There is no clear-cut distinction between literal and metonymical relatedness, whereas the distinction between metonymical and metaphorical relatedness is sharp. (This is very clear in compounding, since most metonymic modifiers exhibit condensation, rather than displaced reference; see Lock 1997.) However, a compound may of course have two or more interpretations, in some of which the modifier's conceptual status changes.

A two-constituent compound consists of at least one pointer and at most one modifier. The traditional notion of head is misguiding, since it does not allow for gradience between literal and metonymical relatedness, and since it does not distinguish between grammatical and conceptual percolation. In this typology, a compound inherits its profile or conceptual structure (or parts of it) from the pointer. Whereas a head entails literal relatedness, literal relatedness entails a pointer - not the other way around. In other words, only pointers are literally related to the object. Also, if two constituents are related to the object in similar ways, they are both assigned pointer status.

Logically, there are 36 conceptual types, i.e. non-extended constructions. Our constraints leave us only 11 possible types: (a) A two-constituent compound cannot have two modifiers; (b) two pointers are related to the object in similar ways; (c) if two constituents are related to the object in the same way, they are both assigned pointer status; and (d) modifiers are not literal.

In the graphs below, we represent conceptual types by feature structures with the attributes, STATUS and REF. STATUS specifies the conceptual status, i.e. whether the constituent is pointer or modifier. REF specifies its mode of referring. Here, we abbreviate such feature structures. So, CONC|STATUS(A) = P $\land$ CONC|REF(A) = L $\land$ CONC|STATUS(B) = P $\land$ CONC|REF(B) = L corresponds to [P(l)-P(l)].

1. [P(l)-P(l)]: This compound type has three subtypes: (a) What traditionally has been called appositional compounds, such as *maiden girl* and *μητρο-παρθενος* [mother-virgin; 'Mary']; (b) redundant compounds, in which the left constituent contains redundant information, such as *bahay-kubo* [house-hut; 'hut'] and *hanging-amihan* [wind-breeze; 'breeze'] in Tagalog; and (c) redundant compounds, in which the right constituent contains redundant information, such as *palm tree*. Note that contrary to Ryder (1994), I claim that redundant information is not possible only in the default pointer position (in English, this is the right position; in Tagalog, it is the left). A clear counterexample to Ryder's hypothesis is found in Tagalog, namely *bayad-utang* [payment-dept; 'payment']. Cross-linguistically, this type is often used to mark gender and diminution; for example, by compounding with 'child' (Bauer 2001:699). The distinction between appositional compounds and redundant compounds is set-theoretical: If the union of the denotations of the two constituents is a proper subset of one of the constituents, the compound is redundant.

2. [P(m$_1$)-P(m$_1$)]: Subtype a) corresponds to copulative compounds, such as *space time*. Subtype b) is called narrative compounds and include compounds such as *basag-ulo* [fracture-head; 'fight'] in Tagalog and *com-nuóc* [rice-water; 'cooking'] in Vietnamese. The constituents of a narrative compound do not point at the constituents of an object; rather they point at salient constituents of an event or narrative. If narrative compounding is productive, the interpretation of such compounds probably make reference to event structure and coherency constraints. For further subdivisions, see part four. Formally, the difference between type one and type two is that type two constituents refer to parts of the referents, whereas type one constituents refer to the whole (or more) of the referents.

3. [P(l)-M(m$_1$)]: Endocentric compounds with left constituent pointers, such as *punong-mangga* [tree-mango; 'mango tree']. Cross-linguistically, compounds with one literal pointer are often specific-level terms, as noted by Croft (1991:183).

He also notes that the pointer-modifier asymmetry "reflects a daughter-parent structure of the taxonomy."

4. $[M(m_1)$-$P(l)]$: Endocentric compounds with right constituent pointers, such as *lawn tennis* and *maraschino cherries*. This is by far the most celebrated type in compounding theory. Theorists such as Spencer (1991) have mistakenly argued this to be the only productive type, cross-linguistically. Such arguments illustrates the somewhat anglocentric character of traditional compounding theory.

5. $[P(l)$-$M(m_2)]$: Endocentric compounds with metaphorical right constituent modifiers, such as *sundalong-kanin* [soldier-cooked rice; 'cowardly soldier'] in Tagalog. Note that the REF value of the modifier has no impact on subsumption; all endocentric compounds are subtypes of their pointer constituent.

6. $[M(m_2)$-$P(l)]$: Endocentric compounds with metaphorical left constituent modifiers, such as *méʔkʼinobal* [mother-haze; 'rainbow'] in Tzotzil. Type six is the reverse of type five, just like type four was the reverse of type three.

7. $[P(m_1)$-$M(m_2)]$: Because of the existence of $[M(m_2)$-$P(m_1)]$, I also assume the existence of this type. However, no example occurred in my data. If such an assumption is valid is left for future research to evaluate. An alternative suggestion is that both these types are the result of sense extension (metonomy).

8. $[M(m_2)$-$P(m_1)]$: Exocentric compounds with metaphorical left constituent modifiers, such as *duck bill* and *shovel head*. Such compounds are not subtypes of their conceptual pointers; that is, a 'shovel head' is not a kind of head, but a subspecies of sharks.

9. $[P(m_2)$-$M(m_1)]$: Exocentric compounds with metaphorical left constituent pointers, such as *panawag-pansin* [panawag (calling-instrument)-attention; 'one, who gets or wants attention'] in Tagalog. Similarly, a 'panawag-pansin' is not a calling instrument, but a person.

10. $[M(m_1)$-$P(m_2)]$: Exocentric compounds with metaphorical right constituent pointers, such as *dust-bowl*. The difference between *shovel head* and *dust bowl* is that, while a shovel head is a shark, whose head looks like a shovel, a dust bowl is a valley-like configuration in which dust or sand storms are trapped. In other words, in *shovel head* the modifier is metaphorical, while the pointer is metaphorical in *dust bowl*.

One type that didn't occur is $[P(m_2)$-$P(m_2)]$. One explanation is that this is due to the need for anchoring a metaphor in its target domain. (It seems impossible to blend two BACKGROUND values and produce a third.)

Many languages have four to six different conceptual types for N-N compounds. For example, English has at least the types one, two, four, six, eight and ten. On the other hand, Tagalog has the types one, two, three, five, and nine. Other types may be added. In fact, a single loan word might constitute a more specific construction that licenses the use of a conceptual type (through extraction of conceptual type information), e.g. a speaker of English might coin compounds that are analogical to *Code Napoleon*, which seems to be a type three compound. That compounds are by default symmetric until they are linked to conceptual type constructions, allows us to account for non-conservative pointer-modifier distribution. For processing, it is important that conceptual types can be largely derived from TAX and Q_f information (see part seven).

Compounding constructions also specify for taxonomic level. According to the Sprogteknologisk Orddatabase corpus of Danish written language, the frequency of generic-level modifiers in compounds derived from the analogy base or schema, ____-*gård* [yard], such as *andegård* [duck-yard] and *hundegård* [dog-yard], is twice or three times as high as that of life form-level modifiers as in *dyregård* [animal-yard]. Other compounding constructions such as ____-*bod* [stall] only select for upper-level modifiers. Taxonomic specification largely results from Gricean pragmatics. However, pragmatics can't handle all cases, e.g. the restrictions on slot-filling in ____-*bod*. The TAX attribute takes feature structures as its values. Such feature structures have four appropriate attributes: INDEX, TYPE, LEVEL and QUALIA. INDEX specifies the (local) inheritance hierarchy, TYPE specifies whether it is a taxonomy or a partonomy, LEVEL specifies the taxonomic level, and QUALIA specifies which quale structures the given inheritance hierarchy. For example, constitutive qualia always structure a partonomy.

The BACKGROUND values specify the kind of discourse situation in which the compound typically is used. Or, in what semantic domain (what kind of narratives), you are likely to find it. Note the difference between formal qualia and BACKGROUND. *Sea-legs* shares its formal quale with *conference legs*, but BACKGROUND values percolate from the k-structures of the modifiers, *sea* and *conference*.

Lexical item specific constructions have partially specified phonology (PHON) values. (5) highlights the need for lexical item specific constructions. Though *sea-legs* is probably fully lexicalized, nonce compounds too provide irregular analogy bases for novel compounds, as well as for the reinterpretation of blocked compounds.

(5) As we parted I said I would stay on for a little while to get my conference legs. She looked puzzled, as well she might, by this ponderous trope. 'As in sea-legs,' I explained. (David Lodge, *Thinks....*)

Cognitive semiotics (Brandt and Brandt 2002) provides a framework for dealing with novel sense extensions in their full complexity. In (5), the "parting situation" constitutes a semiotic base space, which is presented in the first input space of the meaning construction network. A represented scenario (the second input space), i.e., the 'sea-legs' scenario, is mapped onto the presented scenario, and a preliminary matching of components is licensed by establishing a blended space. This output is constrained by relevance information from base space, and then returned to base space to evoke the appropriate inferences. Such an account is useful to us, since it highlights important mechanisms in the interpretation of the novel compound, namely, (a) that the compound is interpreted via a direct analogy relationship to 'sea-legs', and (b) not overruled by relevance constraints, the licensed inferences are coherent with those inferences attributed to the representation space. In terms of our model, it follows that we should expect 'conference legs' to look much like 'sea-legs', formally, and that vital links to the schematic situation are preserved (licensing inferences that the subject wishes to stay at the conference place to get used to the whole "conference situation"). This can be done by introducing complex force dynamic schemes or by enriched lexical entries containing eventive information. In our model, Q provides the relevant information via telic and agentive qualia in a constrained fashion.

The lexical representation of a compounding construction is now straight-forward. The graph in Figure 1 represents the lexical item specific construction *sea-legs*. It is clear that *conference legs* is not fully analogous to *sea-legs*; in fact, the differences,

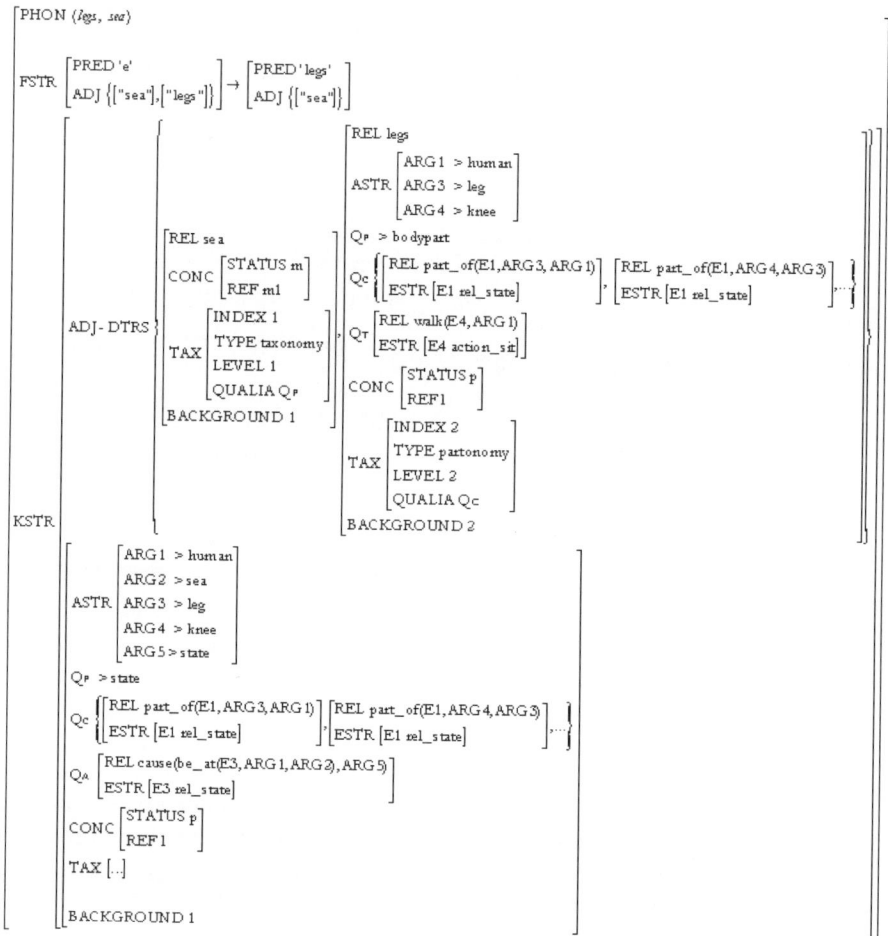

$$
\begin{bmatrix}
\text{PHON } \langle \textit{legs, sea} \rangle \\[4pt]
\text{FSTR} \begin{bmatrix} \text{PRED 'e'} \\ \text{ADJ } \{["sea"],["legs"]\} \end{bmatrix} \rightarrow \begin{bmatrix} \text{PRED 'legs'} \\ \text{ADJ } \{["sea"]\} \end{bmatrix} \\[20pt]
\text{KSTR} \begin{bmatrix}
\text{ADJ-DTRS} \left\{ \begin{bmatrix} \text{REL sea} \\ \text{CONC} \begin{bmatrix} \text{STATUS m} \\ \text{REF m1} \end{bmatrix} \\ \text{TAX} \begin{bmatrix} \text{INDEX 1} \\ \text{TYPE taxonomy} \\ \text{LEVEL 1} \\ \text{QUALIA } Q_P \end{bmatrix} \\ \text{BACKGROUND 1} \end{bmatrix} , \begin{bmatrix} \text{REL legs} \\ \text{ASTR} \begin{bmatrix} \text{ARG1} > \text{human} \\ \text{ARG3} > \text{leg} \\ \text{ARG4} > \text{knee} \end{bmatrix} \\ Q_P > \text{bodypart} \\ Q_C \left\{ \begin{bmatrix} \text{REL part\_of(E1,ARG3,ARG1)} \\ \text{ESTR [E1 rel\_state]} \end{bmatrix}, \begin{bmatrix} \text{REL part\_of(E1,ARG4,ARG3)} \\ \text{ESTR [E1 rel\_state]} \end{bmatrix}, \ldots \right\} \\ Q_T \begin{bmatrix} \text{REL walk(E4,ARG1)} \\ \text{ESTR [E4 action\_sit]} \end{bmatrix} \\ \text{CONC} \begin{bmatrix} \text{STATUS p} \\ \text{REF1} \end{bmatrix} \\ \text{TAX} \begin{bmatrix} \text{INDEX 2} \\ \text{TYPE partonomy} \\ \text{LEVEL 2} \\ \text{QUALIA } Q_C \end{bmatrix} \\ \text{BACKGROUND 2} \end{bmatrix} \right\} \\[40pt]
\text{ASTR} \begin{bmatrix} \text{ARG1} > \text{human} \\ \text{ARG2} > \text{sea} \\ \text{ARG3} > \text{leg} \\ \text{ARG4} > \text{knee} \\ \text{ARG5} > \text{state} \end{bmatrix} \\ Q_P > \text{state} \\ Q_C \left\{ \begin{bmatrix} \text{REL part\_of(E1,ARG3,ARG1)} \\ \text{ESTR [E1 rel\_state]} \end{bmatrix}, \begin{bmatrix} \text{REL part\_of(E1,ARG4,ARG3)} \\ \text{ESTR [E1 rel\_state]} \end{bmatrix}, \ldots \right\} \\ Q_A \begin{bmatrix} \text{REL cause(be\_at(E3,ARG1,ARG2),ARG5)} \\ \text{ESTR [E3 rel\_state]} \end{bmatrix} \\ \text{CONC} \begin{bmatrix} \text{STATUS p} \\ \text{REF1} \end{bmatrix} \\ \text{TAX } [..] \\ \text{BACKGROUND 1} \end{bmatrix}
\end{bmatrix}
$$

Figure 1.

i.e. the TAX and Q_f values of the modifier constituents, are what makes *conference legs* slightly humorous — and ponderous.

Note that composition is not just "specification of one of the semantic components within the qualia of the head noun." The construction provides the agentive role on its own. (We do not want to say that it is part of the semantics of 'legs' that, though probably true, they are caused by our "being-on-the-ground".) Also, this is a case of multiple feature exchange, since the modifier contributes with a BACK-GROUND value too.

Consider again the Mandarin Chinese compound *fumu* [father-mother; 'parents']. Its representation is given in Figure 2.

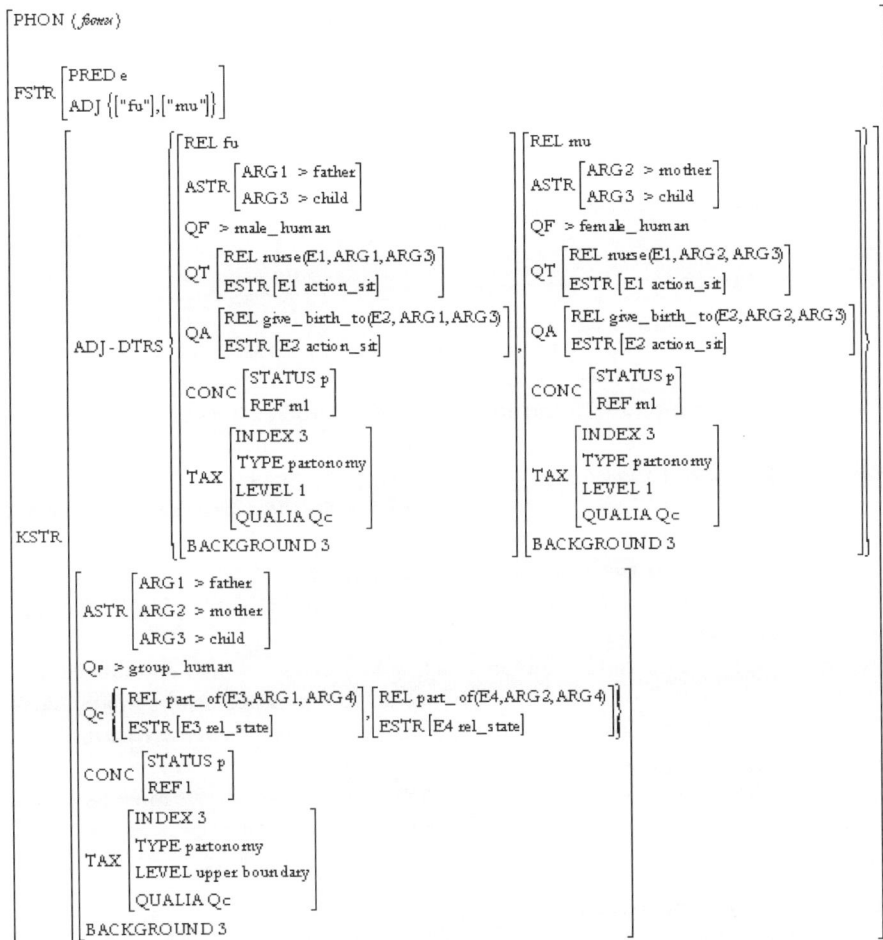

Figure 2.

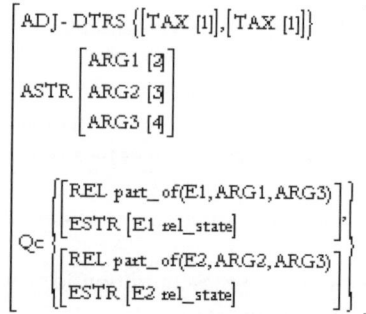

$$\begin{bmatrix} \text{ADJ-DTRS } \{[\text{TAX } [1]],[\text{TAX } [1]]\} \\ \text{ASTR } \begin{bmatrix} \text{ARG1 } [2] \\ \text{ARG2 } [3] \\ \text{ARG3 } [4] \end{bmatrix} \\ \text{Qc } \left\{ \begin{bmatrix} \text{REL part\_of(E1, ARG1, ARG3)} \\ \text{ESTR } [\text{E1 rel\_state}] \end{bmatrix}, \begin{bmatrix} \text{REL part\_of(E2, ARG2, ARG3)} \\ \text{ESTR } [\text{E2 rel\_state}] \end{bmatrix} \right\} \end{bmatrix}$$

Figure 3.

The underlying schematic construction used to coin such compounds in Mandarin Chinese is presented by Figure 3. The feature structures for the ADJ-DTRS attribute can be read as constraints on the constituents.

So far so good. Even if we assume that our representational framework describes the relevant features of every possible compound in any natural language, it is still somewhat unclear how compounds are interpreted by speakers. How do constructions apply, and how are compounds disambiguated?

7. Interpretation

At the level of c-structure, two nouns constitute a noun phrase headed by an empty string, i.e. an underspecified structure. At the level of f-structure, the compound is analysed as a PRED modified by an adjunct. The PRED value refers to the functional head of the compound; any of the conceptual pointers in the k-structure might be the functional head. Thus, the f-structure refers to the k-structure. Once the f-structure decides on its PRED value, we can also disambiguate the c-structure, so as not to violate economy principles on syntactic analysis.

(This analysis differs from the traditional LFG analysis of compounds, in which compounds are treated as endocentric constructions directly mapping onto endocentric f-structures (see Butt et al. 1999). The f-structure of the modifier constituent is represented in the overall f-structure as a member of a set, which is a value of the COMPOUND attribute. In most cases, our analysis by inference results in an analysis compatible with this, but as demonstrated above, for an exhaustive treatment of compounds, additional flexibility is crucial.)

For the k-structure to "inform" the f-structure, the CONC values must be determined. As noted above, such values can be derived from TAX and Q_f values, listed in the inheritance hierarchy in the lexicon. Derivation rules include:

(6)   If the domain values of the two constituents cannot be unified, then one of the constituents must be metaphorical, i.e., $Q_f(A) \leftrightarrow Q_f(B) = \perp \leftrightarrow$ CONC | REF(A) = M2 ∨ CONC | REF(B) = M2.

(7)   If the two constituents share taxonomy values, the compound is either
       of type 1 or 2, i.e., TAX(A) = TAX(B) → (CONC | STATUS(A∧B) = P∧
       CONC | REF(A∧B)=L) ∨ (CONC | STATUS(A∧B) = P ∧ CONC | REF(A∧B)=M1).

On top of such universal principles for compound interpretation, language specific
default principles probably exist. Some languages (like English) might lexicalize for
default constructions. Psycholinguistic experiments prove some conceptual types
to be easier to process (see, for example, Libben 1998). One explanation is that dif-
ferent modes of referring (CONC | REF values) involve more complex cognition than
others. Or it might be that some conceptual types are tested by speakers as default
interpretations.

Though conceptual types are constrained by postulates such as these, compounds are still ambiguous. Some ambiguities are part of natural language, and we
are obliged to let them be. We should not disambiguate, what is inherently ambiguous. But compounds may be disambiguated in discourse. Any theory of compounding should thus allow relevant interaction with discourse structure or, conforming
to standard LFG architecture, d-structure by a δ-projection.

Consider the two standard interpretations of *cotton bag*, discussed in Copestake
and Lascarides (1997): a 'bag made of cotton' and a 'bag to contain cotton'. The two
interpretations depend on two different constructions of the same conceptual type.
In the first construction, the modifzzier is an argument of a constitutive quale; in the
second, it is an argument of the telic quale. Such ambiguities can be treated within a
standard generative lexicon model by a disjunctive k-structure, see Figure 4.

The only difference here is what quale is modified. But as argued in part two, there
are ambiguities that cannot be resolved by the standard generative lexicon model.

Let us return to the Greek compound ανδρο-γυνος [man-woman] and its two
interpretations: 'a designation of effeminate or perverted men' and 'the perfect soul
in which man and woman were once united'. These interpretations are of two different conceptual types, namely [P(l)-M(m$_2$)] and [P(m$_1$)-P(m$_1$)]. Since the metaphorical interpretation involves visual metaphor, the constitutive quale contour(*x*,
contour1) percolates in the k-structure. In Figure 5, irrelevant features are omitted.

In discourse, one sense may be prompted. Consider the two discourse pieces:

(8)   Mary sorted her clothes into various large bags. She put her skirt in the
       cotton bag.

(9)   Mary sorted her clothes into various bags made from plastic. She put her
       skirt in the cotton bag.

Sentence (8) is ambiguous, though the constitutive interpretation is more likely.
This statistical fact can be represented by language-specific probability features in
the schematic constructions. But (9) is inconsistent with a constitutive reading of
the compound. Logically, the only possible interpretation is the telic interpretation.
For the Greek compound, similar inconsistencies arise, e.g. when a pronoun is used
to refer to its denotation.

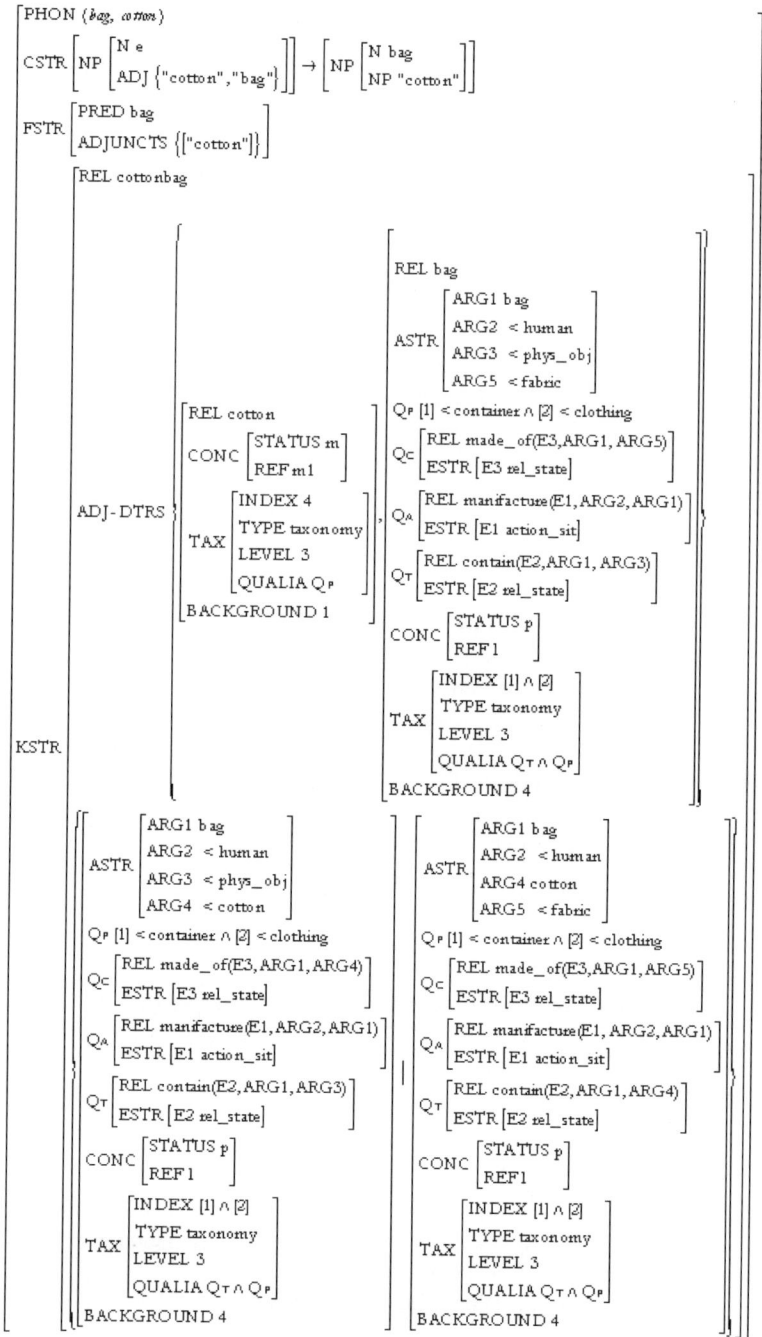

PHON ⟨*bag, cotton*⟩

CSTR [NP [N e / ADJ {"cotton","bag"}]] → [NP [N bag / NP "cotton"]]

FSTR [PRED bag / ADJUNCTS {["cotton"]}]

KSTR [REL cottonbag

ADJ-DTRS {

[REL cotton
CONC [STATUS m / REF m1]
TAX [INDEX 4 / TYPE taxonomy / LEVEL 3 / QUALIA Q_P]
BACKGROUND 1]

,

[REL bag
ASTR [ARG1 bag / ARG2 < human / ARG3 < phys_obj / ARG5 < fabric]
Q_P [1] < container ∧ [2] < clothing
Q_C [REL made_of(E3,ARG1,ARG5) / ESTR [E3 rel_state]]
Q_A [REL manifacture(E1,ARG2,ARG1) / ESTR [E1 action_sit]]
Q_T [REL contain(E2,ARG1,ARG3) / ESTR [E2 rel_state]]
CONC [STATUS p / REF 1]
TAX [INDEX [1] ∧ [2] / TYPE taxonomy / LEVEL 3 / QUALIA Q_T ∧ Q_P]
BACKGROUND 4]

}

{

[ASTR [ARG1 bag / ARG2 < human / ARG3 < phys_obj / ARG4 < cotton]
Q_P [1] < container ∧ [2] < clothing
Q_C [REL made_of(E3,ARG1,ARG4) / ESTR [E3 rel_state]]
Q_A [REL manifacture(E1,ARG2,ARG1) / ESTR [E1 action_sit]]
Q_T [REL contain(E2,ARG1,ARG3) / ESTR [E2 rel_state]]
CONC [STATUS p / REF 1]
TAX [INDEX [1] ∧ [2] / TYPE taxonomy / LEVEL 3 / QUALIA Q_T ∧ Q_P]
BACKGROUND 4]

|

[ASTR [ARG1 bag / ARG2 < human / ARG4 cotton / ARG5 < fabric]
Q_P [1] < container ∧ [2] < clothing
Q_C [REL made_of(E3,ARG1,ARG5) / ESTR [E3 rel_state]]
Q_A [REL manifacture(E1,ARG2,ARG1) / ESTR [E1 action_sit]]
Q_T [REL contain(E2,ARG1,ARG4) / ESTR [E2 rel_state]]
CONC [STATUS p / REF 1]
TAX [INDEX [1] ∧ [2] / TYPE taxonomy / LEVEL 3 / QUALIA Q_T ∧ Q_P]
BACKGROUND 4]

}

]

Figure 4.

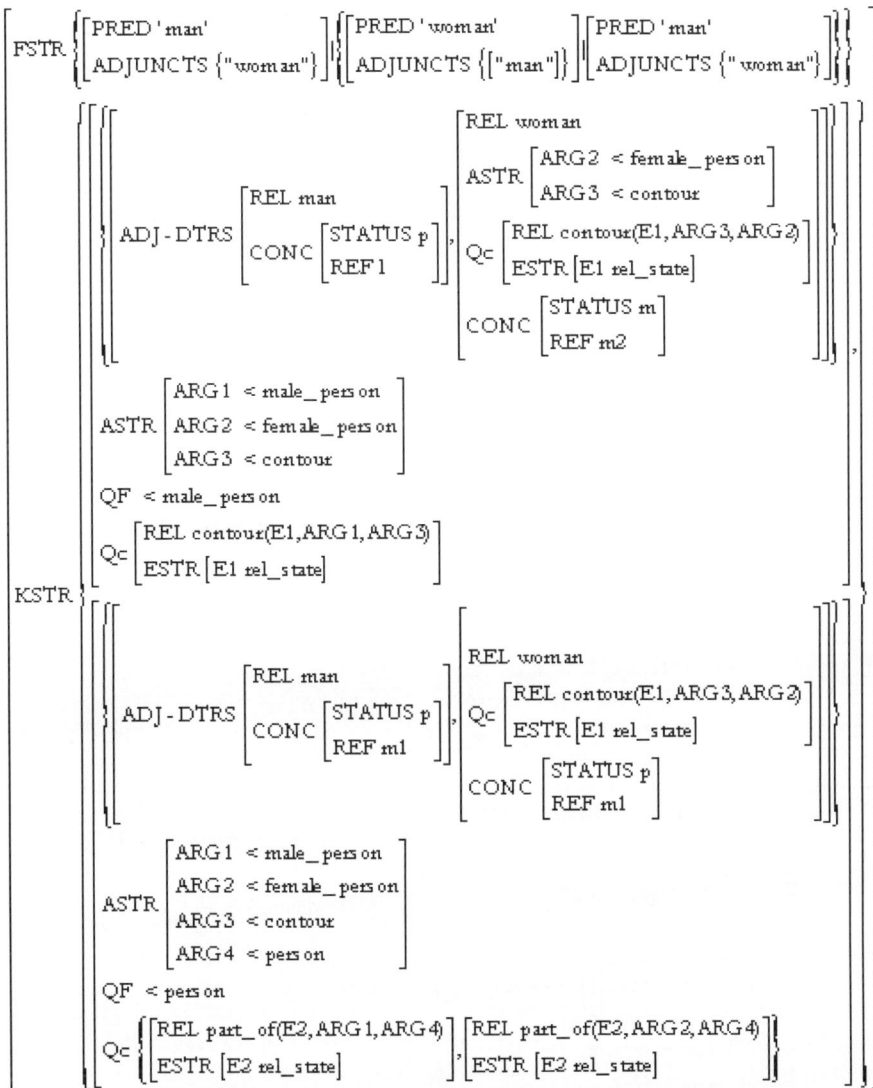

$$
\left[\text{FSTR} \left\{ \begin{bmatrix} \text{PRED 'man'} \\ \text{ADJUNCTS } \{\text{"woman"}\} \end{bmatrix} \left| \left\{ \begin{bmatrix} \text{PRED 'woman'} \\ \text{ADJUNCTS } \{[\text{"man"}]\} \end{bmatrix} \right| \begin{bmatrix} \text{PRED 'man'} \\ \text{ADJUNCTS } \{\text{"woman"}\} \end{bmatrix} \right\} \right\} \right.
$$

$$
\text{KSTR} \left\{ \left[\begin{array}{l} \left[\text{ADJ-DTRS} \left\{ \begin{bmatrix} \text{REL man} \\ \text{CONC} \begin{bmatrix} \text{STATUS p} \\ \text{REF 1} \end{bmatrix} \end{bmatrix}, \begin{bmatrix} \text{REL woman} \\ \text{ASTR} \begin{bmatrix} \text{ARG2 < female\_person} \\ \text{ARG3 < contour} \end{bmatrix} \\ \text{Qc} \begin{bmatrix} \text{REL contour(E1,ARG3,ARG2)} \\ \text{ESTR} [\text{E1 rel\_state}] \end{bmatrix} \\ \text{CONC} \begin{bmatrix} \text{STATUS m} \\ \text{REF m2} \end{bmatrix} \end{bmatrix} \right\} \right] \\ \text{ASTR} \begin{bmatrix} \text{ARG1 < male\_person} \\ \text{ARG2 < female\_person} \\ \text{ARG3 < contour} \end{bmatrix} \\ \text{QF < male\_person} \\ \text{Qc} \begin{bmatrix} \text{REL contour(E1,ARG1,ARG3)} \\ \text{ESTR} [\text{E1 rel\_state}] \end{bmatrix} \end{array} \right., \right.
$$

$$
\left[\begin{array}{l} \left[\text{ADJ-DTRS} \left\{ \begin{bmatrix} \text{REL man} \\ \text{CONC} \begin{bmatrix} \text{STATUS p} \\ \text{REF m1} \end{bmatrix} \end{bmatrix}, \begin{bmatrix} \text{REL woman} \\ \text{Qc} \begin{bmatrix} \text{REL contour(E1,ARG3,ARG2)} \\ \text{ESTR} [\text{E1 rel\_state}] \end{bmatrix} \\ \text{CONC} \begin{bmatrix} \text{STATUS p} \\ \text{REF m1} \end{bmatrix} \end{bmatrix} \right\} \right] \\ \text{ASTR} \begin{bmatrix} \text{ARG1 < male\_person} \\ \text{ARG2 < female\_person} \\ \text{ARG3 < contour} \\ \text{ARG4 < person} \end{bmatrix} \\ \text{QF < person} \\ \text{Qc} \left\{ \begin{bmatrix} \text{REL part\_of(E2,ARG1,ARG4)} \\ \text{ESTR} [\text{E2 rel\_state}] \end{bmatrix}, \begin{bmatrix} \text{REL part\_of(E2,ARG2,ARG4)} \\ \text{ESTR} [\text{E2 rel\_state}] \end{bmatrix} \right\} \end{array} \right\}
$$

Figure 5.

8. Conclusion

In this chapter, a theory of compositionality in compounds was provided. Contrary to traditional compounding theories, which with few exceptions all seem to be based on English or Indo-European data, this theory is typologically grounded. In addition, an attempt was made to formalize some of the empirical insights. In sum, it was found that since both endocentric and exocentric compounding are productive, the semantics of compounding is not explained by listing every single compound. Nor is it explained by enumerating semantic relationships or by deriving compounds from relative clauses; or simply by passing the job on to trash can pragmatics. Rather, the meaning of a compound should be compositionally derived from the input constituents, a more or less schematic construction, and discourse information. In dealing with compounding (and to explain semi-systematic ambiguities), it thus seems crucial to allow for multiple compounding constructions. Since different compounding constructions possibly apply in the interpretation of a compound, the semantic output is a result of relatively complex inferences. Evidence for such complexity is given by psycholinguistic experiments (see Murphy 1990).

References

Bauer, L. 1978. *The grammar of nominal compounding*. Odense: Odense University Press.
Bauer, L. 1979. "On the need for pragmatics in the study of nominal compounding". In *Journal of Pragmatics* 3: 45–50.
Bauer, L. 2001. "Compounds". In *Language Typology and Language Universals*, M. Haspelmath et al. (eds.), 695–707. Berlin: de Gruyter.
Brandt, L. and Brandt, P. A. 2002. "Making sense of a blend". In *Apparatur* 4 (2): 62–71.
Butt, M. et al. 1999. *A grammar writer's cookbook*. Stanford: CSLI.
Copestake, A. and Briscoe, T. 1995. "Semi-productive polysemy and sense extension". In *Journal of Semantics* 12 (1): 15–68.
Copestake, A. and Lascarides, A. 1997. "Integrating symbolic and statistical representations: the lexicon-pragmatics interface". In *Proceedings of ACL-EACL 1997*: 136–143.
Coulson, S. 2000. *Semantic leaps*. Cambridge: Cambridge University Press.
Coulson, S. and Fauconnier, G. 1999. "Fake guns and stone lions: conceptual blending and private adjectives". In *Cognition and function in language*, B. Fox et al. (eds.). Stanford: CSLI.
Croft, W. 1990. *Typology and universals*. Cambridge: Cambridge University Press.
Downing, P. 1977. "On the creation and use of English compound nouns". In *Language* 53 (4): 810–842.
Fanselow, G. 1981. *Zur Syntax und Semantik der Nominalkompositionen*. Tübingen: Niemeyer.
Hatcher, A. G. 1951. *Modern English word-formation and Neo-Latin*. Balitimore: John Hopkins.
Hatcher, A. G. 1960. "An introduction to the analysis of English noun compounds". In *Word* 16: 356–373.
Huang, S. 1998. "Chinese as a headless language in compounding morphology". In *New approaches to Chinese word formation*, J. L. Packard (ed.), 261–283. Berlin: de Gruyter.
Johnston, M. and Busa, F. 1999. "Qualia structure and the compositional interpretation of compounds". In *Breadth and depth of semantics lexicons*, E. Viegas (ed.), 176–187. Dordrecht: Kluwer Academic.

Kaplan, R. M. and Bresnan, J. 1995. "Lexical-functional grammar: a formal system for grammatical representation". In *Formal issues in lexical-functional grammar*, M. Dalrymple et al., 29–130. Stanford: CSLI.

Libben, G. 1998. "Semantic transparency in the processing of compounds: consequences for representation, processing, and impairment". In *Brain and Language* 61: 30–44.

Liberman, M. and Sproat, R. 1992. "The stress and structure of modified noun phrases in English". In *Lexical matters*, I. A. Sag and A. Szabolcsi (ed.), 131–182. Stanford: CSLI.

Lock, C. 1997. "Debts and displacements: on metaphor and metonymy". In *Acta Linguistica Hafniensia*. 29:. 321–38.

Murphy, G. L. 1990. "Noun phrase interpretation and conceptual combination". In *Journal of Memory and Language* 29: 259–288.

Nguyên, Đ.-H. 1997. *Vietnamese language*. Amsterdam: John Benjamins.

Pollard, C. and Sag, I. A. 1987. *Information-based syntax and semantics*. Stanford: CSLI.

Pollard, C. and Sag, I. A. 1994. *Head-driven phrase structure grammar*. Chicago: University of Chicago Press.

Pustejovsky, J. 1991. "The generative lexicon". In *Computational Linguistics* 17 (4): 409–441.

Rhyne, J. R. 1976. "A lexical process model of nominal compounding in English". In *American Journal of Computational Linguistics* 33: 33–44.

Ryder, M. E. 1994. *Ordered chaos: the interpretation of English noun-noun compounds*. Berkeley: University of California Press.

van Santen, A. 1979. "Een nieuw voorstel voor een transformationelle behandeling van composita en bepaalde adjectief-substantief kombinaties". In *Spectator* 9: 240–62.

Søgaard, A. 2002. "En introduktion til den kognitive lingvistik". In *Apparatur* 4 (2): 4-12.

Søgaard, A. 2003. "A compound algorithm". Presented at *Computational Linguistics in the Netherlands 2003*. Antwerpen: University of Antwerpen.

Spencer, A. 1991. *Morphological Theory*. Cambridge: Basil Blackwell.

Wierzbicka, A. 1985. *Lexicography and conceptual analysis*. Ann Arbor: Karoma.

Zwicky, A. M. 1993. "Heads, bases and functors". In *Heads in grammatical theory*, G. G. Corbett et al. (eds.), 292–315. Cambridge: Cambridge University Press.

Chapter 15

Inalienability and possessum individuation*

Frantisek Lichtenberk

University of Auckland

1. Introduction

To what extent are the syntactic structures of a language arbitrary and to what extent are they motivated by functional or cognitive factors? Clearly, these are empirical questions, and each case must be considered on its own merit. There is, however, increasing evidence that many aspects of the syntax of individual languages are not arbitrary. This is not to claim that all of syntax is motivated by functional and/or cognitive factors, nor is it to claim that functional and cognitive factors *determine* syntactic structures. One of the challenges for linguistics is to investigate the interplay between functional/cognitive factors and language structures. A given cognitive factor may turn out to motivate one or more syntactic patterns in a language; but one and the same cognitive factor may also motivate quite different syntactic patterns in different languages. It is the latter kind of case that will be discussed here. Specifically, we will be concerned with the notions of inalienable possession and possessum individuation. It will be argued that the latter notion provides an explanation for the properties of certain syntactic patterns in several genetically and/ or geographically diverse languages. We will also consider the link between possessum individuation and inalienable possession, and with the appearance of the latter category in the language family in question. After a brief discussion of the distinction between inalienable and alienable possession in Oceanic in section 2, we will investigate attributive possessive constructions in one Oceanic language, Toqabaqita, in section 3. It will be argued that in Toqabaqita the notion of possessum individuation underlies the uses of two different types of possessive construction. In section 4 it will be shown that the same factor is relevant to syntactic patterns in other languages, Oceanic or not, even though not all of the constructions in question are attributive possessive noun phrases. Emergence of the inalienable–alienable contrast in Oceanic will be the subject of section 5. Some concluding remarks will be made in the closing section.

2. Inalienable and alienable possession in Oceanic languages

A feature characteristic of Oceanic languages (a subgroup within Austronesian) is the existence of more than one type of attributive possessive construction. In keep-

ing with tradition, "possessive construction" is used here as a technical term for one
or more types of noun phrase that encode a variety of relations between two entities,
the "possessum" and the "possessor". The range of relations includes true possession, i.e., ownership, but also many others. Thus, for example, *my plane* may refer to
a plane I own or to a plane I will travel on. This is well known, and there is no need to
rehearse it in detail. I mention it here only because it will be of some relevance later.
In fact, we will deal here primarily with possessive constructions that do not express
true possession, such as, for example, *my head*, meaning the head which is part of
my body. Nevertheless, as will be seen later, there is a link between such possessive
constructions and those that do, or at least may, express true possession. Examples
(1) - (4) from Manam, an Oceanic language, illustrate two basic types of possessive
construction. In (1) and (2) the possessum noun carries an "adnominal" suffix that
indexes the possessor:

(1)   *ae-gu*[1]
      leg-1SG:AD
      'my leg (part of my body)'

(2)   *maloŋa-miŋ*
      voice-2PL:AD
      'your voices'

In (3) and (4) the same adnominal suffixes are attached to possessive classifiers rather than to the possessum nouns. Compare (3) and (2), and (4) and (1).

(3)   *ʔulu   ʔana-miŋ*
      breadfruit POSS.CLASS-2PL:AD
      'your breadfruit (to eat)'

(4)   *ogi ne-gu*
      axe POSS.CLASS-1SG:AD
      'my axe'

Notice that Manam has two different possessive classifiers, *ʔana* and *ne*. Similar kinds of distinction between possessive constructions where affixes indexing
the possessor occur on the possessum noun and one or more other constructions
where they occur on a possessive classifier are widespread in Oceanic. In terms of
the semantics of the two basic types of possessive construction — without and with
a possessive classifier — a distinction is usually made between inalienable and alienable possession. The general pattern is that constructions in which an affix indexing the possessor appears on the possessum noun encode inalienable possession, while constructions with possessive classifiers express alienable possession,
although there are also various idiosyncrasies in many languages. A language may
have more than one subtype of possessive construction for alienable possession.
Manam has two. One, with the possessive classifier *ʔana*, is used with items of food
and drink, as in (3) above, and also with certain other items that are metonym-

ically related to food and drink, for example 'garden' (where food is grown) or 'spoon' (used to eat food with). The other, with *ne* as the possessive classifier, is used for all other kinds of alienable possession.

The other type of possessive construction, where the affix indexing the possessor appears on the possessum noun is used — in Manam and other Oceanic language — to express inalienable possession: close, intimate, inherent kinds of relation between possessum and possessor. These include body-part relations (the possessum is part of the possessor's body), as in (1) above, and more generally parts of a whole, for example a branch of a tree; bodily liquids, such as blood; natural bodily "products", such as excreta, sweat, saliva, footprints, voice (as in (2) above); mental states, such as fear; traits and attributes, including names (as in 'My name is Bob'). Typically also included are kinship terms.

The possessive system of a language may be fluid to some degree; that is, one and the same noun may occur in the possessum position in more than one type of possessive construction to express different concepts or different kinds of relation between possessum and possessor. In examples (5), (6), and (7) from Manam the noun *ʔusi* occurs as possessum in three different possessive constructions, the first one without a possessive classifier and the other two with different classifiers:

(5) *ʔusi-gu*
     skin-1SG:AD
     'my skin (the skin of my body)'

(6) *ʔusi ʔana-gu*
     skin POSS.CLASS-1SG:AD
     'my skin (for me to eat, e.g., chicken skin)'

(7) *ʔusi   ne-gu*
     loincloth POSS.CLASS-1SG:AD
     'my loincloth' (worn wrapped tightly around one's body)

3. Inalienable possession and possessum individuation in Toqabaqita

Toqabaqita, spoken in the Solomon Islands, also has more than one type of possessive construction, but its possessive system is somewhat different from the usual Oceanic type with possessive classifiers, such as the one in Manam, illustrated above. Toqabaqita has two types of possessive construction. In one, the possessum noun carries a "personal" suffix that indexes the possessor, just as one finds throughout Oceanic, and with qualifications that I will discuss later it may be said to express inalienable possession:[2]

(8) *gwalusu-na*
     nose-3SG:PERS
     'his/her nose (part of his/her body)'

(9) *thata-ku*
     name-1SG:PERS
     'my name' (the name I bear)

The categories included in Toqabaqita inalienable possession are the usual ones mentioned earlier: body parts, parts of a whole, bodily liquids, bodily products, voice, name, etc. Included also are some, but not all, kinship terms.

The other type of possessive construction has no marking, either on the possessum or on the possessor, and there is no possessive classifier either. The expression of the possessum is followed by the expression of the possessor. This construction is used to express alienable possession, but not exclusively, as we will see later. Unlike the usual pattern in Oceanic, Toqabaqita makes no distinctions within the category of alienable possession, such as between items of food/drink and others. Pronominal possessors are encoded by means of independent personal pronouns rather than as affixes. Compare (10) and (11) below and (8) and (9) above, respectively.

(10) *fanga nia*
      food 3SG:IP
      'his/her food'

(11) *biqu nau*
      house 1SG:IP
      'my house'

In the discussion that follows I will refer to the construction in which the possessum noun carries a suffix indexing the possessor as "synthetic", and the other construction where the sole expression of the possessor is a separate phrase as "periphrastic".

Some kinship terms occur in the synthetic construction, while others occur in the periphrastic construction. In many such cases there appears to be no semantically-based pattern. For example, the word for 'mother' occurs in the synthetic construction, but the word for 'father' in the periphrastic construction. Rather, what appears to be the case is that those kinship terms that are old etyma continue, with some qualifications discussed further below, to occur in the synthetic construction, which was the case in Proto-Oceanic (see section 5), while those that are lexical innovations or replacements of original etyma occur in the periphrastic construction. There is then a trend in the language for the kinship terms to become formally dissociated from the other types of inalienable possession. Most of the discussion of inalienable possession in Toqabaqita below will focus on categories other than kinship terms.

As in other Oceanic languages, there is some fluidity in the Toqabaqita possessive system; that is, some nouns can be used in either type of possessive construction, with some accompanying semantic differences. For example, the noun *fote* is used in the synthetic construction when reference is being made to the possessor's shoulder blade, as in (12), but it is used in the periphrastic construction when reference is being made to the possessor's canoe paddle, as in (13).

(12) *fote-ku*
shoulder.blade-1SG:PERS
'my shoulder blade'

(13) *fote   nau*
paddle 1SG:IP
'my paddle'

The noun for 'head' is used in the synthetic construction when reference is being made to the possessor's own head as part of his or her own body, as in (14); but it is used in the periphrastic construction when reference is being made to a head that is not part of the possessor's own body, for example, a fish head he or she is going to eat or nibble on, as in (15).

(14) *gwau-ku*
head-1SG:PERS
'my head (part of my body)'

(15) *gwau nau*
head 1SG:IP
'my (e.g., fish) head'

Such fluidity is fairly straightforward, and this too is not something that will be discussed any further.

What we will focus on will be cases where one and the same noun may appear as possessum either in the synthetic construction or in the periphrastic construction and in both cases what is being expressed is inalienable possession. This is exemplified in examples (16) to (22). In (16) *maa* 'eye' occurs as possessum in a synthetic construction, but in (17) and (18) it occurs in periphrastic constructions.

(16) *maa-ku*
eye-1SG:PERS
'my eye(s)'

(17) *maa mauli   nau*
eye be.on.left.side 1SG:IP
'my left eye'

(18) *maa nau   naqi*
eye 1SG:IP this
'this eye of mine'

Clearly, there is no difference in inalienability: in 'my left eye' and in 'this eye of mine' the relation between the possessum and the possessor is as inalienable as in 'my eye' or 'my eyes'.

Similarly, in (19) the nouns for 'hand/arm' and 'foot/leg' appear in synthetic constructions, while in (20) the same nouns occur in periphrastic constructions. In both cases, reference is being made to the possessors' own hands/arms and feet/legs, and there is no difference in inalienability/alienability.

(19)   ...kera   anikaba-a   **qaba-na**   ma **qae-na**   laqu
        3PL:NONFUT handcuff-3:OBJ hand-3SG:PERS and foot-3SG:PERS also
        boqo.
        ASSERT
        '... they handcuffed his hands as well as his feet.'

(20)   ...keki   tekwa-si-a   **roo qaba nia** **ki ma roo qae nia ki.**
        3PL:FUT stretch-TRANS-3:OBJ two arm 3SG:IP PL two leg 3SG IP   PL
        '[He told them] they should stretch out both of his arms and both of his legs.'

And the noun for 'name' occurs in a synthetic construction in (21) but in a periphrastic construction in (22), even though, here too, there is no difference in inalienability/alienability:

(21)   **Thata-mu**   ni   tei?
        name-2SG:PERS FORE who?
        'What (lit.: who) is your name?'

(22)   **Rua-na**   thata qoe   ni   tei?
        two-3SG:PERS name 2SG:IP FORE who?
        'What's your second/other name?'

The question, then, is: why does one and the same noun sometimes appear as possessum in a synthetic construction and sometimes in a periphrastic construction when there is no difference in inalienability/alienability? There is one obvious syntactic difference: in inalienable possession, when the possessum noun is not in the scope of a modifier other than the possessor NP, it is the synthetic construction that is used; and when the possessum noun is in the scope of a modifier other than the possessor NP, it is the periphrastic construction that is used. The relevant modifying element may be a verb (17),[3] a demonstrative (18), a cardinal numeral (20) or an ordinal numeral (22). One could then give a formal explanation: the synthetic construction is grammatical only if the possessum noun is not in the scope of a modifier other than the possessor NP. Although such a rule would account for the data, it would miss the point. It would not tell us *why*, when the possessum noun is in the scope of a modifier other than the possessor NP, it is the construction that otherwise serves to encode alienable possession that is used. Before I offer an explanation, it is necessary to consider the nature of the distinction between inalienable and alienable possession in some detail. I will start by giving a few definitions and characterizations of these two categories:

Haiman (1983: 783): "there is a closer conceptual link between a possessor and an inalienably possessed object than between a possessor and an alienably possessed object".

Heine (1997a: 10, 1997b: 85): "Items that cannot normally be separated from their owners are inalienable, while all others are alienable.". And Heine again: "The inalienable category has also been called, for example, 'intimate', 'inherent', 'inseparable', or even 'abnormal', while the alienable categories have been labelled 'non-intimate', 'accidental', 'acquired', 'transferable', or 'normal'...." (1997a: 10).

Chappell and McGregor (1996a: 4): "Whereas inalienability denotes an indissoluble connection between two entities — a permanent and inherent association between the possessor and the possessed — the complementary notion of alienability refers to a variety of rather freely made associations between two referents, that is, relationships of a less permanent and inherent type ...."

Bally (1996 [1926]): 33) speaks of the notion of "personal domain" as it is relevant to inalienable possession: "The personal domain includes or can include objects and beings associated with a person in an habitual, intimate or organic way ..."; and "... each phenomenon, action, state or quality which affects any part whatsoever of the personal domain, automatically affects the whole person.".

Most definitions of inalienable possession characterize the nature of the relation between possessum and possessor in positive terms, as the existence or presence of a close, intrinsic, organic link between the two. On the other hand, Nichols (1992:117) characterizes inalienable possession quite differently: "The term *inalienable*, then, refers not to a semantic constant having to do with the nature of possession, but to whatever set of nouns happens to take inalienable possession marking in a given language." (original italics).

Putting Nichols' statement aside for now (I will return to it later), there is general agreement that in inalienable possession there are close physical and/or conceptual links between possessum and possessor. In alienable possession, on the other hand, the links between possessum and possessor are not close.

In most Oceanic languages, the degree of closeness of the conceptual link between possessum and possessor is iconically reflected in the structures of the possessive constructions. In synthetic constructions, which encode inalienable possession, the possessum noun itself carries the possessor-marking affix; see the Manam examples (1) and (2) and the Toqabaqita examples (8) and (9) further above. The possessum has very little "conceptual autonomy" (to adopt Langacker's (1991) term) vis-à-vis the possessor, and the close conceptual bond between possessum and possessor is reflected by a structural bond. On the other hand, in constructions used to express alienable possession, where the links between possessum and possessor are much looser, where the possessum has a much higher degree of conceptual autonomy vis-à-vis the possessor, the possessum noun does not carry any marking of the possessor. The possessor is encoded elsewhere, either on a possessive classifier, as in Manam (examples 3 and 4), or by a separate possessor NP in the case of Toqabaqita (examples 10 and 11). Conceptual separateness is reflected by structural separateness.

The structural bond between possessum and possessor in constructions expressing inalienable possession is not unique to Oceanic; it is, in fact, common in other languages that make a grammatical distinction between the two types of posses-sion. Nichols (1992:117) says that "[i]n terms of its grammatical form, inalienable possession always involves a tighter structural bond or closer connection between possessed and possessor, and the tightness of the bond can be described in terms of head and dependent marking." And: "... the inalienables take marking which is more nearly head-marking or less dependent-marking than the marking of aliena-bles." (ibid.).

The iconic reflection of the close conceptual bond between possessum and pos-sessor in inalienable possession through a tight structural bond has also been discussed by Haiman (1983), who says that this is part of a more general pattern whereby "[t]he linguistic separateness of an expression corresponds to the concep-tual independence of the object or event which it represents." (p. 783). Furthermore, following a suggestion by Greenberg, Haiman suggests that "[i]n no language will the linguistic distance between X and Y be greater in signaling inalienable posses-sion, in expressions like 'X's Y', than it is in signaling alienable possession." (1983: 793).[4] This prediction is upheld in Toqabaqita: inalienable possession is expressed either by a synthetic construction, where there is no separation of the expression of the possessum and the expression of the possessor, or by a periphrastic construc-tion also used to express alienable possession. However, this too does not explain why there is separation of the expression of the possessum and the expression of the possessor when the possessum is in the scope of a modifier other than the pos-sessor NP.

The factor that is relevant here is that of *possessum individuation*. Following Hop-per and Thompson (1980), by individuation I mean here the distinctness of an en-tity from its own background, specifically the distinctness of the possessum from the possessor. When there is no modification of the possessum noun other than by the possessor NP, the possessum is not individuated with respect to the possessor: it is viewed more as an aspect of the possessor. Rather than 'my eye' or 'my eyes', a more accurate translation of (23) would be 'the eye aspect/part of me'; and a more accu-rate translation of the possessive constructions in (24) would be something like 'the hand and the foot aspects/parts of him' rather than 'his hands and feet':

(23)   *maa-ku*   = (16)
       eye-1SG
       'my eye(s)'

(24)   ... *kera*   *anikaba-a*   *qaba-na*   *ma qae-na*   *laqu*
       3PL:NONFUT handcuff-3:OBJ hand-3SG:PERS and foot-3SG:PERS also
       boqo. = (19)
       ASSERT
       '... they handcuffed his hands as well as his feet.'

Significantly, the synthetic possessive construction is unmarked with respect to number. Out of context, *maa-ku* in (23) above may refer to the speaker's one or both eyes. In (25) below, both eyes are presumably involved. (Note that with inanimate subjects, the singular subject-tense markers are often used even if the subject is semantically plural.)

(25)   *Maa-ku*   *qe*   *biibiingala.*
         eye-1SG:PERS 3SG:NONFUT be.sleepy
         'I'm sleepy.' 'My eyes are sleepy.'

In (26), either one or both eyes may be intended:

(26)   *Maa-ku*   *e*   *fii.*
         eye-1SG:PERS 3SG:NONFUT hurt
         'My eye hurts.' Also 'My eyes hurt.'

The exact identity or number of the eyes involved is not relevant. What is more relevant is the affectedness of the person: 'I hurt with respect to the eye aspect/part of me'. Bally (1996 [1926]:33) similarly says: "The part of the body directly affected is only the medium for a condition which spreads to the whole system."

However, a possessum may be given more identity through specification: for example, my left eye rather than my right eye, both of my eyes rather than just one. Of course, the possessum always has some specification because it is related to its possessor, but this kind of specification does not give it identity vis-à-vis the possessor. It is through specification other than via the possessor that the possessum achieves individuation vis-à-vis the possessor. Although the possession is still inalienable, the possessum is given more identity of its own, and in that way it is conceptually more separate from, more conceptually autonomous with respect to, the possessor.

This means that the distinction between the synthetic and the periphrastic possessive constructions in Toqabaqita is ultimately based not a distinction between inalienable and alienable possession but on possessum individuation, even though the notion of inalienability is relevant because it is only in inalienable possession that there can be a difference in degrees of possessum individuation. In alienable possession the possessum is always individuated, and it is always the periphrastic construction that is used, regardless of whether the possessum is in the scope of a modifier other than the possessor NP or not:

(27)   *waqi   nau*
         basket 1SG:IP
         'my basket'

(28)   *waqi   baqita nau*
         basket be.big 1SG:IP
         'my big basket'

(29)   *waqi   nau   naqi*
         basket 1SG:IP this
         'this basket of mine'

The synthetic construction is used when the possessum is not individuated, which can happen only in inalienable possession. The periphrastic construction is used when the possessum is individuated: always in alienable possession, and when an inalienable possessum has been individuated vis-à-vis the possessor through specification.

As mentioned earlier, only some of the kinship terms in Toqabaqita can occur in the synthetic construction. With those kinship terms also, individuation affects the choice of a possessive construction, although the details are different from those found with terms other than kinship. Some of those kinship terms have related compound counterparts whose meanings are more specific than the meanings of the basic terms. The basic terms occur in the synthetic construction, while the corresponding compound terms occur in the periphrastic construction. Here is one example. The basic term *thaina* can be used to refer to one's mother, one's mother's sister and one's father's brother's wife. It occurs in the synthetic construction:

(30)   *thaina-ku*
       mother-1SG:PERS
       'my mother, my mother's sister, my father's brother's wife'

There is a related compound form *thaina-rua*, which only refers to one's mother's sister, and it occurs in the periphrastic construction:

(31)   *thaina-rua   nau*
       mother-two 1SG:IP
       'my mother's sister'

Arguably, referents of *thaina-rua* are more individuated than referents of *thaina* because they are specified more closely: 'mother's sister' as opposed to 'mother/mother's sister/father's brother's wife'.

4. Grammatical relevance of possessum individuation in other languages

Individuation has been shown to be relevant in various parts of the grammar in many languages, as shown by Hopper and Thompson (1980) and many others. Haiman (1985) also discusses the relevance of individuation to grammar, although in the area of possession he focuses on the conceptual distance between possessum and possessor as reflected in morphosyntactic distinctions between inalienable and alienable possession, rather than specifically on possessum individuation. He echoes his own earlier (1983) statement: "A separate *word* denotes a separate *entity*; a bound morpheme is less likely to do so." (Haiman 1985: 140, original italics). It turns out that Toqabaqita is not the only language where the notion of possessum individuation in inalienable possession has grammatical relevance. Very much the same situation seems to exist in Kwara'ae, a close relative of Toqabaqita, at least with respect to body-part nouns (Deck 1934). Given the close relatedness of the two languages, the use of the periphrastic construction rather than the synthetic one for inalienable possession when the possessum is individuated is a development that most likely happened in a proto-language from which the two languages are descended, rather then being the result of indepedent developments. It is, therefore, more instructive to look farther afield. In Toqabaqita (and Kwara'ae), possessum individuation is relevant in attributive possessive constructions. This is also the case in Kosraean, another Oceanic language. Although Toqabaqita and Kosraean are genetically related, the relationship is not very close. The relevant patterns are quite different in the two languages and are clearly the results of independent developments. According to Lee (1975), Kosraean inalienable nouns can occur in a suffixed form, a free form, an impersonal form and a construct form. It is the first three forms that will be relevant here. The suffixed form corresponds to the Toqabaqita synthetic possessive construction: the possessum noun carries a possessive suffix that indexes the possessor:

(32) *niyac-l*
       leg-3SG:POSS
       'his or her leg' (Lee 1975: 63)

In alienable possession, the possessive suffix is added to a possessive classifier:

(33) *ik   osrawac-l*
       fish POSS.CLASS-3SG:POSS
       'his (or her) raw fish' (Lee 1975: 104) (*Osrawac* is a possessive classifier used when the possessum is raw, uncooked food.)

In inalienable possession, then, the possessum noun carries a possessive suffix, but only when it is not modified by an adjective or a numeral: "[w]hen an inalienable noun is modified by an adjective or by a numeral, only the free form or the impersonal form can be used." (Lee 1975: 238); the suffixed form cannot be used. In the first example below there is no adjective or numeral, while in the subsequent two examples there is an adjective. In the set of examples that Lee gives to illustrate the difference between the suffixed forms on the one hand and the free and the impersonal forms on the other, there is a lexical possessor NP. In (34), with a suffixed form, the possessor is encoded twice, by the possessive suffix on the possessum noun and by a possessor noun phrase, the latter being grammatically optional.

(34) *paho-l   Kuhn*
       hand-3SG:POSS K.
       'Kuhn's hand' (Lee 1975: 239)

Examples (35) and (36) illustrate the free and the impersonal forms, respectively. In neither case does the possessum noun carry a possessive suffix. Instead of a possessive suffix, there is what Lee calls a "preposition" *kacl* 'of him', followed by the possessor NP. In the free form in (35) the element *lwac* means 'one member of a pair, one side, one part of a limb'.

(35) *lwac   po   lacsac   kacl   Kuhn*
     one.of.pair hand left.side of.him K.
     'Kuhn's left hand' (Lee 1975: 239) (*Po* is the free form of the noun 'hand'.)

(36) *paho lacyot   kacl   Kuhn*
     hand right.side of.him K.
     'Kuhn's right hand' (Lee 1975: 239) (*Paho* is the impersonal form of the
     noun 'hand'.)

It is not clear from Lee's discussion when it is the free form and when it is the impersonal form that is called for. Be that as it may, what is important is that the suffixed form, with its indexing of the possessor, cannot be used when the possessum
has been individuated through modification. Different data from Lee's grammar
of Kosraean are discussed, from a different perspective, by Hopper and Thompson
(1984), who suggest that possessum individuation is, or may be, a factor in the use of
the different types of possessive construction.

Outside of Oceanic, possessum individuation is relevant in French, although in
ways that are quite different from those in Toqabaqita and Kosraean. Bally (1996
[1926]), in his discussion of French, says that the definite article, in addition to its
other functions, serves to express indivisibility, inseparability of the possessum and
the possessor, the possessum being in the possessor's "personal domain":

(37) *serrer   la main à quelqu'un*
     squeeze the hand to someone
     'shake someone's hand' (Bally 1996: 56)

However, when the possessum noun is modified, a possessive pronoun is used instead of the article:

(38) *serrer   sa   main robuste*
     squeeze one's hand strong
     'shake his/her strong hand' (Bally 1996: 56)

As Bally (1996: 56) puts it: "... the concept of the integral part disappears once the
object is characterised in any way."; and: " ... in all these cases (with possessive modification), the object acquires a personality of its own, detached from the individual
of which it forms a part.". In fact, a possessive pronoun rather than the definite article may be used even if the possessum noun has no adjective:

(39) *J'ai   mal à ma jambe.*
     I:have pain at my leg
     'My leg is aching.' (Bally 1996: 56)

Bally (1996:56) says that (39) can mean "'the leg which always aches'". It is the note-
worthiness of the leg that individuates it and gives it more salience. The fact that a
possessive pronoun may be used when there is no modifier demonstrates that it is

possessum individuation rather than possessum modification that is the relevant factor.

In Toqabaqita, Kosraean and French, possessum individuation is relevant at the level of the noun phrase, but that is not the only possibility. In Mayali (Australian), it is relevant at clause level. Mayali has extensive incorporation of nouns into verbs (Evans 1996). Possessums that refer to body parts are typicallly incorporated, with the possessor external to the verb. Example (40) has no incorporation, while in (41) the possessum noun has been incorporated into the verb:

(40) *Bamurru*   *a-bom*   *gun-godj.*
      magpie.goose 1-shoot:PAST.PFV IV-head
      'I shot the magpie goose in the head.'

(41) *Bamurru*   *a-godj-bom.*
      magpie.goose 1-head-shoot:PAST.PFV
      'I shot the magpie goose in the head.' (Evans 1996: 65)

According to Evans (1996: 97), "[w]ith body part nominals in Mayali, incorporation is clearly the unmarked choice whenever this is grammatically sanctioned.[endnote omitted]" Cases where body part possessums are not incorporated are relatively rare, and non-incorporation is determined by discourse factors, specifically foregrounding:

> In all Mayali examples where body parts do not incorporate, there is clear evidence that, for one reason or another, they are being foregrounded. This may result from conjunction, contrast, and when emerging as a distinct discourse participant in their own right.   (Evans 1996: 98)

The next example illustrates non-incorporation due to the participant emerging as a distinct discourse participant: the noun for 'pus' is incorporated at first, but it is not incorporated in the last two sentences:

(42) a. *Gun-dulk barri-me,*   *barri-nud-gorrhge-ng.*
          IV-stick   3A:PAST-get:PAST.PFV 3A:PAST-pus-burst-PAST.PFV
          'They picked up a stick, and they burst his pus out.'
          ...
          ...
          ...
      f. *Gun-nud ba-rrolga-ng*   *an-ege.*
          IV-pus   3:PAST-arise-PAST.PFV III-that
          'All the pus rushed out.'
      g. *Gurlba gun-nud bi-rrelkge-ng*   *rowk, ragul.*
          blood IV-pus 3/3:PAST-spatter-PAST.PFV all   red.eyed.pigeon
          'Blood and pus spattered him all over, the red-eyed pigeon.' (Evans 1996: 100)

Evans (1996: 100) explains the difference between incorporation and non-incorporation of the noun 'pus' in the following way:

> In the first few lines [only line (a) is included in (42)], disposing of the pus is being
> viewed as an action carried out for the benefit of *wirriwirriyak* [black-faced cuckoo
> shrike], and it remains in the unmarked incorporated position. But by line (f) the
> pus emerges (literally) as an independent participant, spattering over *ragul's* face
> and hence accounting mythologically for his 'red eyes', and at this point it becomes
> an external argument.

In earlier discussion Evans shows that it is both possible for nouns referring to physically separate body parts to incorporate and for nouns referring to parts that are
not separate not to incorporate. He adds this concerning the passage in (42): "[i]t
seems unlikely, then, that it is simply the physical separation of the pus which is responsible for non-incorporation here." (Evans 1996: 100).

For a body part to be a discourse participant in its own right and to have high discourse salience is to be individuated. Note again the iconicity: conceptual separation results in grammatical separation, except that in Mayali the possessum noun is
separated from the verb, rather than from the expression of the possessor, as is the
case in Toqabaqita and Kosraean.

There is another area of grammar where possessum individuation is of relevance
in some languages, namely "external possession". In their survey of external possession in European languages König and Haspelmath (1997) point out that, in general, constructions with an external possessor are not possible when the possessum
noun is modified by a non-restrictive adjective.[5] They give the following pair of examples from Russian (originally in Levine 1984). In (43) where the possessum noun
'breast' is not modified by an adjective, an external possessor is possible; while (44),
where an adjective modifies the possessum noun, is "considerably *less* acceptable
(Levine 1984: 498, original italics):

(43)   *On položil golovu ej   na grud'.*
       he put   head   her:DAT on chest
       'He put his head on her breast.'

(44)   [??]*On položil golovu ej   na upruguju grud'.*
       he put   head   her:DAT on firm   breast
       'He put his head on her firm breast.' (Levine 1984: 498)

König and Haspelmath say they cannot provide a definitive explanation for this re-
striction, but they do suggest that it may have something to do with the referential
properties of the possessum: the possessum is specific, via its relation to the possessor, and there is no need for its establishment in discourse using specification. (A
different kind of explanation with respect to the same phenomenon in French is
put forth by Vergnaud and Zubizarreta 1992.) There is, however, another possibility.
I have argued above that possessum specification gives it individuation and hence

more salience. In very much the same vein, Levine (1984: 498) says this about modified possessums: "[t]he presence of the modifier characterizes the body part more explicitly and individuates it with respect to the possessor, and more generally, to the event." However, constructions with external possessors give relatively high salience to the possessor (see, for example, Payne and Barshi 1999a and other contributions in Payne and Barshi 1999b). Most likely, then, constructions with external possessor and modified inalienable possessums are ungrammatical or of low acceptability because there is a clash in salience: modification gives salience to the possessum and externalisation gives salience to the possessor. To the extent that it is non-restrictive modification of possessums that results in such a clash in salience (Levine does not specifically mention non-restrictive modification, although all three examples he gives do involve non-restrictive modification), this suggests that non-restrictive modification gives more salience to the possessum than restrictive modification does. This, in fact, is not surprising. Restrictive modification serves primarily to identify the referent (for example, her left breast (rather than her right breast)), while non-restrictive modification serves to highlight some properties of the referent (her firm breast).

We have seen examples from several genetically, typologically and/or geographically diverse languages where possessum individuation is of grammatical consequence. There is no direct link between possessum individuation and the grammatical structures involved. In Toqabaqita, Kosraean and French, possessum individuation is relevant at the level of the noun phrase; in Mayali and Russian it is relevant at the level of the clause. In Toqabaqita and Kosraean it has to do with the type of attributive possessive construction involved, but the details are quite different in the two languages; in French with the choice of a possessive pronoun rather than the definite article; in Mayali with non-incorporation of possessum nouns into verbs; and in Russian with restrictions on external possessors. It is the cognitive factor of possessum individuation that is the cross-linguistic commonality, not some structural correspondences among the languages involved.

5. Emergence of the inalienable–alienable grammatical contrast

The low degree of possessum individuation in inalienable possession (unless there is specification of the possessum) has additional, historical relevance, which has to do with the emergence of the inalienable–alienable grammatical distinction itself. Nichols (1992) and Heine (1997a) both argue that the rise of an inalienable category is an epiphenomenon of certain morphosyntactic developments affecting possessive constructions. The kind of scenario they propose is that at one stage in the history of a language, there was no formal distinction between alienable and inalienable possession, and more likely than not the possessive construction was synthetic, head-marking, with the possessor indexed on the possessum noun. At a later stage, a new pattern of marking develops which, for some reason, is used only with certain possessums or when the relation between possessum and possessor is of a certain kind. The new morphosyntactic pattern comes to mark alienable possession, and the old pattern, by default, comes to be associated with inalienable possession. Nichols and Heine differ from each other, however, in the kinds of factor they see as leading to the emergence of an inalienable–alienable distinction, and the respective historical scenarios they postulate account for the two main morphosyntactic types of inalienable possessive construction in existence. One cross-linguistically common type involves a synthetic, head-marked construction, where an affix on the possessum noun indexes the possessor, just as is the case in Toqabaqita; alienable possession is frequently dependent-marked or there is no marking (Nichols 1992). (However, in Toqabaqita the unmarked, periphrastic construction is used with individuated possessums, which may involve inalienable possession.) The other pattern is for inalienable possession to have no formal marking, while alienable possession does have some marking (Nichols 1992, Heine 1997a).

For Nichols, the development of an inalienable–alienable distinction is in essence a structural one: "The term *inalienable*, then, refers not to a semantic constant having to do with the nature of possession, but to whatever set of nouns happens to take inalienable possession marking in a given language." (1992:117, original italics). On this view, the grammatical distinction between inalienable and alienable possession is a consequence of purely structural developments. According to Nichols, the inalienable–alienable distinction is strongly associated with head-marked possession. In inalienable possession, the possessor is typically or obligatorily expressed, whereas this need not be the case in alienable possession. For whatever reasons, a new morphosyntactic pattern for possessive constructions may develop in a language that, however, does not apply across the board. It applies when a possessive construction encodes an instance of alienable possession, but does not apply when originally the same construction encodes an instance of inalienable possession, presumably because of the frequent or even obligatory expression of the possessor on the possessum. A common pattern is for independent personal pronouns to replace/renew possessive affixes, and this may result in the development of two types of possessive construction: one that continues the earlier head-marked pattern, and a new one where the possessive affixes have been replaced by independent personal pronouns. The new pattern is used in cases where the possessor need not be expressed, that is, in cases of alienable possession, and as a consequence, the old, head-marked pattern comes to be associated with inalienability. On the face of it, this scenario appears to fit Toqabaqita. In this language, inalienable possession with no individuation of the possessor uses head-marking, while alienable possession (and inalienable possession with individuated possessums) uses no marking: instead of suffixes indexing the possessor, independent personal pronouns are used. Importantly, a possessor cannot be encoded simultaneously by a suffix on the possessum noun and by an independent pronoun. While (45) with an independent pronoun encoding the possessor and (46) with head-marking are both grammatical, (47), with both a suffix on the possessum noun and a coreferential possessor pronoun, is not:

(45) *fanga nau*
      food 1SG:IP
      'my food'

(46) *gwau-ku*
      head-1SG:PERS
      'my head'

(47) **gwau-ku   nau*
      head-1SG:PERS 1SG:IP
      ('my head')

Possessor-indexing suffixes and possessor-indexing independent pronouns are in complementary distribution, and the Toqabaqita situation appears to fit Nichols' scenario. However, historical evidence tells a more complex story. It is true that early in the history of the Austronesian family there were only head-marked possessive constructions, like the one in (46). At a later stage a system of possessive classifiers developed for alienable possession, as will be discussed further below. The periphrastic construction (as in (45)) does not directly continue the synthetic construction (as in (46)), with the independent pronoun replacing the personal (possessive) suffix. Rather, it more directly continues a construction where the possessive suffix was attached to a possessive classifier rather than to the possessum noun. The historical development is shown in a schematic form in (48):

(48) Stage a: only [POSSESSUM-poss.suffix] construction exists;
      Stage b: system of possessive classifiers develops for alienable possession: [POSSESSUM POSS.CLASS-poss.suffix]; [POSSESSUM-poss.suffix] used for inalienable possession;
      Stage c (present-day Toqabaqita): [POSSESSUM POSS.CLASS-poss.suffix] has been replaced by [POSSESSUM POSSESSOR.pronoun] used for alienable possession and for inalienable possession when the possessum is individuated; [POSSESSUM-poss.suffix] is used for inalienable possession when the possessum is not individuated.

While it is true that in present-day Toqabaqita the independent personal pronouns are used to encode possessors whereas in Stage a the possessive suffixes were used in that function, there was an intermediate stage (Stage b) with a system of possessive classifiers. Toqabaqita has retained none of the possessive classifiers. It was the classifier constructions that the periphrastic possessive construction with independent personal pronouns replaced.

Nichols' scenario accounts for why in many languages inalienable possession is associated with head-marking, which is the historically older pattern, while alienable possession has a different pattern. It also accounts for why it is inalienable possession that retains the older pattern: because of the frequent or obligatory expression of the possessor. At the same time, Nichols says that the inalienable and the alienable categories are not "cross-linguistic semantic constants" (1992: 117), because the content of the inalienable category is not the same across languages. There are two basic types of relation between possessum and possessor that frequently figure in inalienable possession: one is kinship, and the other is body parts or more generally parts of a whole. However, not all languages subsume both of these types in their inalienable category: in some only body parts/parts of a whole are, and in some only kinship relations are. It is for this reason that Nichols says that the inalienable–alienable distinction is primarily structurally based: the inalienable category is that to which the new system of possessive marking did not extend. (Recall also that in Toqabaqita only some kinship terms occur in the synthetic constructions; those that are lexical innovations occur in the new periphrastic construction.)

On the other hand, Heine (1997a) sees the process of emergence of a formal inalienable–alienable distinction as grammaticalization: the morphology used to encode attributive possession is eroded, and simple juxtaposition is left to mark the possessive relation. Renewal by periphrastic means takes place, often using a locative, ablative or comitative marker. This marker may later fuse onto the expression of the possessor. Heine suggests that this kind of process is more likely to affect possessive constructions when alienable, rather than inalienable, possession is being expressed. This is because in the former case the fact that a possessive relation exists may not be obvious and so it may need to be made explicit. In inalienable possession the presence of a possessor is strongly implied, and so the extra marking may not be necessary. Heine's scenario accounts for the fact that inalienable possessive constructions, when not head-marked, are likely to have no morphological marking, while alienable constructions are likely to have marking. However, it does not account for the frequent correlation of inalienable possession and head-marking discussed by Nichols.

Both Nichols and Heine provide important insights into how an inalienable–alienable grammatical opposition may develop in a language, and they are of some relevance to the Oceanic case. Comparative evidence in Austronesian suggests the existence of a single, synthetic, head-marked possessive construction in early stages of the history of the family. There was no formal distinction in attributive possessive constructions between alienable and inalienable possession. Then, at a later stage, a grammatical distinction did develop, although that process took a different route from that hypothesized by Heine. Rather than locative, ablative, comitative or some other case marking being utilized, a system of possessive classifiers developed (Lichtenberk 1985). A system of possessive classifiers was clearly present at the Proto-Oceanic stage, but there is some evidence of possessive classifiers already at the Proto-Eastern-Malayo-Polynesian stage, but no evidence at earlier stages of Austronesian; see Figure 1 for an Austronesian family tree.

Proto-Oceanic had classifiers for different kinds of alienable possession. It had a classifier for items of food and objects associated with food (for example, objects used in food preparation or for food storage); the same classifier may have also been used for subordinate/passive possession, where the possessor is "the patient, target,

Austronesian

Formosan[a]   Malayo-Polynesian (MP)

Western MP[b]   Central MP   Eastern MP

South Halmahera–   Oceanic
West New Guinea

Manam,
Toqabaqita,
Kosraean,
Fijian,
etc.

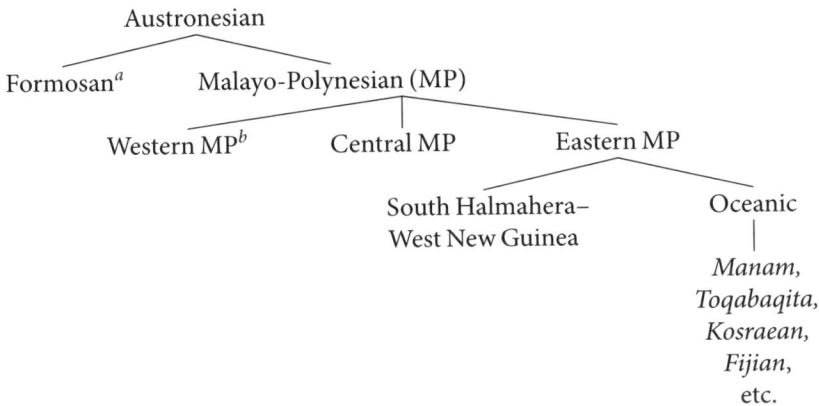

Figure 1. Subgrouping of Austronesian (Pawley 1999; after Blust, various publications)
([a] Possibly more than one subgroup   [b] Possibly not a subgroup)

or involuntary experiencer" (Pawley 1973:162), although there is no agreement on this among Oceanic linguists (cf., for example, Pawley 1973, Lynch 2001 and Lichtenberk 2002). It also had, at least, a classifier for items of drink and objects associated with drinks, and a general classifier used to express any other kind of alienable possession. There was no classifier for inalienable possession: inalienable possession was expressed by a synthetic, head-marked construction, which was the original pattern. The Manam examples (3) and (4) in section 2 exemplify an "alimentary" classifier (in Manam, the same classifier is used for food and drink) and a general classifier, respectively. The Proto-Oceanic food classifier derived from the word for 'food'. The drink classifier had some relation to the verb for 'drink'; whether there was a related noun for 'drink' is uncertain. The etymology of the general classifier is unknown. The basic structure of the Proto-Oceanic alienable possessive constructions was most likely that shown in (49) (Lichtenberk 1985):

(49)   POSS.CLASS-poss.suff. POSSESSUM (POSSESSOR)

The possessive suffix on the classifier indexed the possessor. In addition, the possessor could be encoded by means of a separate noun phrase.

Most likely, possessive constructions with classifiers were the result of morphosyntactic reanalysis, as illustrated in (50), from stage (a) to stage (b):

(50)   Stage a: [food-my] [taro]
       Stage b: [FOOD.POSS.CLASS-my taro]

At stage (a), the possessive construction was *food-my*, with which *taro* was in apposition. The noun phrase in apposition with a possessive construction specified more closely the nature of the possessum, such as the kind of food involved. Over time, the appositional structure came to be reanalyzed as a possessive noun phrase:

at stage (b) the original possessum had become a classifier, and the classifier and the erstwhile appositive noun phrase had come to form a possessive noun phrase in which the latter was the head.

The emergence of the inalienable possessive category in Austronesian was the consequence of the development of overtly marked alienable possession, just as postulated by Nichols and by Heine. Why did the classifier system not extend to inalienable possession? The answer lies in semantic/pragmatic differences between alienable and inalienable possession, regardless of whether there is a morphosyntactic distinction between the two or not. In alienable possession, the range of the kinds of relation between possessum and possessor, although not open-ended, may be quite large (see, for example, Seiler 1977, cited in Heine 1997a: 155; and Taylor 2000). A coconut, for example, may serve as food for the possessor, or as drink, or as something to be planted, or as something to be made into copra, and so on. Furthermore, in alienable possession there is often no one relation between possessum and possessor that is the dominant, natural, expected or default one. A possessive classifier serves to specify more closely the nature of the relation: a food classifier, a drink classifier, a general classifier (for any kind of relation between possessum and possessor other than food and drink). The following examples from Fijian illustrate:

(51)   *na   ke-qu*   *niu*
ART POSS.CLASS-1SG:POSS coconut
'my coconut (to eat; e.g., the flesh is grated and cooked with food)'

(52)   *na   me-qu*   *niu*
ART POSS.CLASS-1SG:POSS coconut
'my (esp. green) coconut (to drink)'

(53)   *na   no-qu*   *niu*
ART POSS.CLASS-1SG:POSS coconut
'my coconut (e.g., one I am going to sell)' (Loata Vuetibau, pers. comm.)

Development of possessive classifiers for alienable possession is well motivated. In inalienable possession, on the other hand, there is a dominant, default relation between possessum and possessor: it is an inherent, intimate relation, where the possessum is part of the possessor, the possessum is a natural product of the possessor, the possessum is a kin of the possessor's, etc. (see, for example, Barker 1995 and Partee 1997[6]). In the absence of any specification to the contrary, it is this default relation that is being encoded. If, however, the relation between possessum and possessor is not of the default kind, special marking, by means of a possessive classifier, is called for. This is illustrated by the next two examples from Manam. For 'my skin', if the skin is part of the possessor's body, no special marking is present:

(54)   *ʔusi-gu*   = (5)
skin-1SG:AD
'my skin (the skin of my body)'

On the other hand, if the relation between an otherwise inalienable possessum and its possessor is not of the default kind, a classifier is used:

(55) *ʔusi ʔana-gu*   = (6)
       skin POSS.CLASS-1SG:AD
       'my skin (for me to eat, e.g., chicken skin)' (*ʔana* is an alimentary, food/drink possessive classifier)

It is the existence of an inherent relation between certain possessums and possessors that obviates formal marking. That which is normal, expected need not be marked (see, for example, Haiman 1985 and Dixon 1994).

The emergence of the inalienable category in the history of Austronesian was a happy coincidence of iconic and economic motivation (Haiman 1983, 1985). When the possessive classifier system began to develop, it did not extend to cases where there is a close, inherent, default relation between possessum and possessor. The survival of the synthetic, head-marked possessive construction to mark inalienable possession was thus doubly motivated.

6. Concluding remarks

Both the use of the periphrastic and the synthetic possessive constructions in Toqabaqita and the emergence of the inalienable–alienable grammatical distinction in the history of Austronesian are motivated by cognitive factors: individuation or non-individuation of the possessum vis-à-vis the possessor in the case of the former, and the nature of the semantic/pragmatic relations between possessum and possessor in the latter, specifically the existence or non-existence of an inherent, default relation between the two. Possessum individuation is also relevant in other languages, where its grammatical manifestations are quite different.

While one must be careful in doing linguistic analysis, not to impose categories of one language onto another language, it is also true that "no language is an island" (Singh and Wee 2002: 522). Typically, very much the same cognitive factor is relevant in different languages, without this being due to genetic links or contact between them. Thus, different languages may have very similar grammatical structures, such as synthetic possessive constructions to encode relations between possessum and possessor when the former is not individuated from the latter, as opposed to other, non-synthetic constructions used when the possessum has a relatively high degree of conceptual autonomy from the possessor. Iconicity is the more general relevant factor here; and iconicity is implicated in a variety of other grammatical patterns in languages. And secondly, very much the same cognitive factor can be implicated in quite different grammatical constructions in different languages: possessum individuation is relevant, in different ways, to noun phrases in Toqabaqita, Kosraean and French, but, also in different ways, to certain clausal patterns in Mayali and Russian.

Notes

* In revising this paper I profited greatly from comments by participants at the Symposium on the version presented there.

1. The following conventions and abbreviations are used in glossing the examples: 1, first person; 2, second person; 3, third person; 3/3, third person minimal subject acting on third person minimal object; III and IV, noun class prefixes; A, augmented number; AD, adnominal; ART, article; ASSERT, assertive; DAT, dative; FORE, foregrounder; FUT, future; IP, independent personal pronoun; NONFUT, nonfuture; OBJ, object; PAST, past; PERS, personal; PFV, perfective; PL, plural; POSS, possessive; POSS.CLASS, possessive classifier; SG, singular; TRANS, transitive. The Manam and Toqabaqita data come from my field notes. The sources of the data from the other languages are as stated. I am grateful to Loata Vuetibau for the Fijian data. In some cases, morphemic glosses have been added and in some the original glosses have been adjusted for the sake of uniformity.

2. The personal suffixes of Toqabaqita and the adnominal suffixes of Manam correspond to, and sometimes are cognate with, what in the grammars of other Oceanic languages are called "possessive" suffixes.

3. Toqabaqita has only one adjective; in other cases, noun modification is done by verbs.

4. Later, Haiman (1983: 795) says that that generalization may need to be revised as follows: "In no language will the phonological expression of inalienable possession be bulkier than that of alienable possession."

5. I am grateful to Martin Haspelmath for drawing this study to my attention.

6. Barker's category of "lexical possession" includes inalienable possession, but it also includes cases that in Oceanic languages would not normally be encoded by possessive constructions used for inalienable possession, such as *John's book*, meaning the book that John wrote (Barker 1995: 86–87).

References

Bally, Charles. 1996. "The expression of concepts of the personal domain and indivisibility in Indo-European languages." In Chappell and McGregor (eds), 1996b, pp. 31–61. (Translated from the French by Christine Béal and Hilary Chappell. Originally published as L'expression des idées de sphère personnelle et de solidarité dans les langues indo-européennes, in Franz Fankhauser and Jakob Jud (eds), 1926, *Festschrift Louis Gauchat*, pp. 68–78. Aarau, Switzerland: H.R. Sauerländer.)

Barker, Chris. 1995. *Possessive descriptions*. Stanford: CSLI.

Chappell, Hilary and William McGregor. 1996a. "Prolegomena to a theory of inalienability." In Chappell and McGregor (eds), 1996b, 3–30.

Chappell, Hilary and William McGregor (eds). 1996b. *The grammar of inalienability: A typological perspective on body part terms and the part-whole relation*. Berlin and New York: Mouton de Gruyter.

Deck, Norman C. 1934. *Grammar of the language spoken by the Kwara'ae people of Mala, British Solomon Islands*. Reprint No. 5. Wellington: Polynesian Society.

Dixon, R. M. W. 1994. *Ergativity*. Cambridge: Cambridge University Press.

Evans, Nicholas. 1996. "The syntax and semantics of body part incorporation in Mayali". In Chappell and McGregor (eds), 1996b, 65–109.

Haiman, John. 1983. "Iconic and economic motivation". *Language* 59: 781–819.

Haiman, John. 1985. *Natural syntax: Iconicity and erosion*. Cambridge: Cambridge University Press.

Heine, Bernd. 1997a. *Possession: Cognitive sources, forces, and grammaticalization*. Cambridge: Cambridge University Press.

Heine, Bernd. 1997b. *Cognitive foundations of grammar*. New York and Oxford: Oxford University Press.

Hopper, Paul J. and Sandra A. Thompson. 1980. "Transitivity in grammar and discourse." *Language* 56: 251–299.

Hopper, Paul J. and Sandra A. Thompson. 1984. "The discourse basis for lexical categories in universal grammar." *Language* 60: 703–752.

König, Ekkehard and Martin Haspelmath. 1997. "Les constructions à possesseur externe dans les langues d'Europe." In *Actance and valence dans les langues d'Europe*, Jack Feuillet (ed.), 525–606. Berlin: Mouton de Gruyter.

Langacker, Ronald W. 1991. *Foundations of cognitive grammar*, vol. 2, *Descriptive application*. Stanford: Stanford University Press.

Lee, Kee-dong (with the assistance of Lyndon Cornelius and Elmer Asher). 1975. *Kusaiean reference grammar*. Honolulu: University Press of Hawaii.

Levine, James S. 1984. "On the dative of possession in contemporary Russian." *Slavic and East European Journal* 28: 493–501.

Lichtenberk, Frantisek. 1985. "Possessive constructions in Oceanic languages and in Proto-Oceanic." In *Austronesian linguistics at the 15th Pacific Science Congress*, Andrew Pawley and Lois Carrington (eds), 93–140. Canberra: Pacific Linguistics.

Lichtenberk, Frantisek. 2002. "The possessive-benefactive connection." *Oceanic Linguistics* 41: 439–474.

Lynch, John. 2001. "Passive and food possession in Oceanic languages." In *The boy from Bundaberg: Studies in Melanesian linguistics in honour of Tom Dutton*, Andrew Pawley, Malcolm Ross and Darrell Tryon (eds), 193–214. Canberra: Pacific Linguistics.

Nichols, Johanna. 1992. *Linguistic diversity in space and time*. Chicago and London: University of Chicago Press.

Partee, Barbara H. 1997. "Genitives – A case study." Appendix to Theo M.V. Janssen, 1997, Compositionality. In *Handbook of logic and language*, Johan van Benthem and Alice ter Meulen (eds), 464–470. Amsterdam: Elsevier; and Cambridge, Mass.: MIT Press

Pawley, Andrew. 1973. "Some problems in Proto-Oceanic grammar." *Oceanic Linguistics* 12: 103–188.

Pawley, Andrew. 1999. "Chasing rainbows: Implications of the rapid dispersal of Austronesian languages for subgrouping and reconstruction." In *Selected papers from the Eighth International Conference on Austronesian Linguistics*, Elizabeth Zeitoun and Paul Jen-Kuei Li (eds), 95–138. Taipei: Academia Sinica.

Payne, Doris L. and Immanuel Barshi. 1999a. "External possession: What, where, how, and why." In Doris L. Payne and Immanuel Barshi (eds), 1999b, 3–29.

Payne, Doris L. and Immanuel Barshi. 1999b. *External possession*. Amsterdam/Philadelphia: John Benjamins.

Seiler, Hansjakob. 1977. "Universals of language." In *Sprache and Sprachen: Gesammelte Aufsätze*, Hansjakob Seiler (ed), 207–229. Munich: Wilhelm Fink.

Singh, Rajendra and Lionel Wee. 2002. "On so-called triplication in Colloquial Singapore English and Thao: A response to Blust." *Oceanic Linguistics* 41: 514–522.

Taylor, John R. 2000. *Possessives in English: An exploration in cognitive grammar.* Oxford and New York: Oxford University Press.

Vergnaud, Jean-Roger and Maria L. Zubizarreta. 1992. "The definite determiner and the inalienable constructions in French and in English." *Linguistic Inquiry* 23: 595–652.

Chapter 16

Resultativeness in English

A sign-oriented approach

Marina Gorlach
The Metropolitan State College of Denver

This chapter is a brief analysis of the suggested lexico-grammatical category of re-sultativeness and the various language tools used for its representation in English, focusing on one of such tools — the post-NP position of a particle in transitive phrasal verbs. My assumption is that the semantic function of the discontinuous phrasal construction (V NP Prt) is to express an action viewed together with its re-sult (outcome, goal, consequence, endpoint, etc.), whereas the continuous phrasal construction (V Prt NP) can indicate actions viewed as either resultative or not. In the terms of markedness, the discontinuous phrasal construction is assumed to be marked for the semantic feature of result and the continuous one — unmarked. Testing this hypothesis, I will bring the data illustrating the non-random distribu-tion of the two forms in various literary texts and also present the findings of the comparative analysis of the forms occurring in the English-Russian translation of the phrasal constructions of two types. Finally, I will expand the study of the re-sultative/neutral-for-result oppositions to other language forms and show that such oppositions underlie many traditional categories of the English verb: lexical pairs, verb complements, categories of tense, aspect, voice, and mood. Resultativeness, if recognized, is then a unique lexico-grammatical category cutting across many dif-ferent layers of the language structure and having diversified ways of manifestation in English.

The present chapter discusses the category of resultativeness in English as one of the proposed universal categories cutting across multiple elements of the language structure. I will suggest a definition of this linguistic category and analyze the lex-ical and grammatical means of its representation.

English exploits a variety of lexical, morphological, syntactic, and prosodic tools to express the meaning of result. Phrasal constructions, or combinations of the transitive phrasal verb with the NP, play a significant role in conveying resulta-tive meaning due to the combined effect of their lexical complexity, morphological structure, syntactic mobility, and prosodic flexibility. I will illustrate my assumption with the phrasal constructions of two positional types:

(1) continuous construction   V Prt NP   *She broke up the glass.*
(2) discontinuous construction V NP Prt   *She broke the glass up.*

The hypothesis to be tested is that the continuous phrasal construction (C) may or may not convey the meaning of the result of the action, while the discontinuous one (D) always makes a specific claim for result associated with its 'resultative' word order.

The category of result, or resultativeness, rather frequently used in passing by many linguists and scholars, did not seem to require a definition since it has never been treated as a category in its own right. It has been regarded as a subcategory of either perfective aspect, which itself aroused no little controversy, or the passive voice (cf. Comrie 1976, Hirtle 1975, Jespersen 1924, Nedjalkov 1988, and others). It has also been attributed to the semantics of certain word classes, usually particles (cf. Bolinger 1971, Forsyth 1970, Quirk et al. 1982), or even morphemes (-en) (cf. Chafe 1970). I will attempt to show the inadequacy of merging resultativeness with 'aspectual', 'passive', or any other role, or confining it to them. I will present some of my findings showing the special position and legitimacy of resultativeness for a particular group of phrasal constructions and then expand it to various parts of the language structure.

Since this volume is devoted to the diversity of language theories and their different approach to language structure and since this study is performed in the framework of the sign-oriented theory, my approach to the syntactic and semantic problems will differ significantly from formal syntax or semantics. I think it would be appropriate to mention some of the central concepts of the sign-oriented theory applied in this study — the invariant meaning and the non-synonymy hypothesis.

The sign-oriented method revolves around the notion of a linguistic sign, defined by Saussure as an inseparable unity of sound signal and concept. Since the linguistic sign applies in a non-discriminative way to any language form, such as phoneme, morpheme, word, phrase, clause, sentence, text, word order, zero morphology, intonation, and stress, it has a potential to replace the autonomous levels of morphology and syntax and bridge the gap between these two domains, which are actually interdependent and inseparable, the distinction between them being to a great degree artificial and "illusory" (Saussure 1959 [1916]:136).

The conceptual part of the linguistic sign to which Saussure refers as invariant meaning and which is usually rather general and abstract, is not given in advance and should be postulated individually for each sign. It integrates all the possible contextual messages or dictionary meanings the sign may convey. Each signal corresponds to one meaning, and any change in signal brings about change in meaning. One signal — one meaning correlation underlies every sign system and is essential for communication of meaning, following the universal principles of economy of effort, efficiency, and intelligence (cf. Tobin 1991). This non-synonymy principle is best presented in Bolinger (1977:x): '[...] the natural condition of a language is to preserve one form for one meaning, and one meaning for one form.'

For the purposes of my study, I will view the phrasal verb as a single linguistic sign whose invariant meaning is semantically more complex than a simple sum of its constituents' meanings. If we compare the meaning of a phrasal verb to that of an underlying simple verb, we will notice that after adding a particle, phrasal verbs acquire not only a different lexical meaning, but also an additional common meaning — that of result used here as an umbrella term for all and any of the following: outcome, consequence, completion, goal, destination, endpoint, etc.

The fact that the meaning of a phrasal verb is more resultative than that of a simple verb has been recognized by many scholars studying phrasal verbs (Bolinger 1971, Jackendoff 1997, Kennedy 1920, Kruisinga 1931, Live 1965, Tenny 1994, Tobin 1993):

> The notion of resultant condition is essential to phrasal verbs. [...] the phrasal verb pictures the action as leading to a conclusion.   (Bolinger 1971:96)

In sign-oriented terms, it means that the invariant meaning of a phrasal verb can be regarded as its lexical meaning plus the meaning of result. But what is the role of the word order in expressing this meaning?

The alternating word order in phrasal constructions with nominal direct objects is part and parcel of the English language, and despite the prescriptivists' pressure, both variants are presently established as well-formed. But their coexistence in the language still makes many linguists wonder why the speaker should always make a choice between the two. Is this choice arbitrary or meaningful? Some grammarians regard the choice of one word order variant over the other as random and requiring no special attention (Murphy 1985). Others explain it by the requirements of rhythm, stress, style (Kroch and Small 1978), register (Kilby 1984), the length of the object (Biber 1995, van Dongen 1919, Quirk et al. 1982), or its news value (Erades 1961). Many authors discuss the relationship between the word order and idiomatic/non-idiomatic meaning of the phrasal verbs (Bolinger 1971, Palmer 1974, Tenny 1994), or between the word order and the focus structure of the utterance (Dehé 2002). Numerous articles assert that one construction is the result of the transformation performed on the other, and the further dispute is aimed at defining which structure should be regarded as underlying and which as derivative (Legum 1968, Stowell 1981, Fraser 1976).

My hypothesis doesn't contradict any of these views, but approaches the problem differently. I suggest that each word order type of the phrasal construction conveys its own meaning and plays its own role in discourse. As Bolinger (1971:ix) puts it: '[...] any word that a language permits to survive must make its semantic contribution; and the same holds for any construction which is physically distinct from any other construction.'

Given the signal of the two phrasal constructions — the order of the elements — is different, they are two different linguistic signs which are bound to have difference in meaning, although not necessarily a gross one. Now the task can be narrowed down to finding and defining such difference, however slight it might be.

Let us analyze the following system of oppositions:

to break the glass–*to break up the glass*–*to break the glass up*

I am going to assume that the resultative meaning is expressed stronger as we proceed to the right:

to break the glass (9) either process or result
to break up the glass (5) greater possibility for result
to break the glass *up* (5) compulsory claim for result

In support of this assumption I will analyze some language data culled from the authentic texts by British and American authors.

(1)   'It sure does explain things. This whole deal: the van, the furniture, it's just cover. Those two guys are coke runners. Two suitcases full of cocaine. Jesus.' He got out of the chair and against Mudge's protests shut the suitcase. Then they *checked its mate*. It was just as full. He lifted first one, then the other.   (Foster 1987:144)

In this example, checking the suitcase is reported as a step in the chain of actions the characters performed after having been captured by two drug runners and locked in their van, and the action expressed by the verb *check* is reported as making no claim for its result or outcome. As discussed in Tobin (1993), the invariant meanings of synonymous simple verbs often constitute result-based oppositions, as, for example, in *do* versus *make*:

"She didn't know what **to do to make** things happen.
My uncle **does** business in Europe and **makes** a lot of money."   (Tobin 1993:45)

In these examples *do* is the unmarked member of the opposition expressing the meaning of either process or result, whereas *make* is the marked one, making a specific claim for the result of the action. I assume that the analysis of the lexical pair 'check-examine' might show that the invariant meaning of 'check' is unmarked for result, though to the best of my knowledge, such analysis has not been performed yet. As many other simple verbs, this lexically unmarked for result verb can acquire resultative meaning if combined with a particle:

(2)   "Doctor, my men and I spent the night *checking out every Don Vinton in Manhattan and all the other boroughs*. We even covered New Jersey and Connecticut." He took a ruled sheet of paper out of his pocket and showed it to Judd.   (Sheldon 1970:107)

In this case, the emphasis is put not on the activity itself, but rather on its goal. The meaning of the phrasal verb *check out* integrates the process and its intended completion (result), implies a thorough and comprehensive search, exhausting all possibilities and having in view a very definite result. The C construction may be regarded as composed of result and process gradients, which makes it more resultative than the simple verb phrase, though not necessarily marked for result.

(3)   As both Vandervoort and Wainwright knew, there were devices used by criminals to decide whether a credit card in their possession could be

used again, or if it were 'hot'. A favourite was to pay a headwaiter twenty-five dollars *to check a card out*. (Hailey 1975:49)

The headwaiter in this example is bribed for a very clear purpose — to make sure whether a credit card is reported as stolen or its disappearance has not yet been noticed by the owner. The D construction is used to express the claim for the result of the action, or, in other words, its invariant meaning is marked for the semantic feature of result. Throughout these three examples the resultative meaning is expressed with increasing intensity, which falls in line with our hypothesis. It is also reinforced by the grammatical forms in which the phrasal verbs appear: in (2) it is gerund which is unmarked for result, in (3) the phrasal verb is used as infinitive, the marked for result verb complement (cf. Fradkin 1991 and others).

In order to focus on the semantic distinction between the phrasal constructions, I will compare them in minimal or near-minimal pairs differing only in the word order, keeping the other factors (style, register, degree of idiomaticity, length of the object, etc.) basically identical.

(4)   'The secretary told me you were rehearsing this morning, Miss Lambert,' the young man remarked. 'Does that mean *you're putting on a new play*?'   (Maugham 1985:16)

In this example, the C construction denotes the process of staging a new spectacle, focusing more on the process of the action and making no claim for its result. The meaning of the process in this case is also emphasized grammatically by the progressive form deemed as marked for process by many authors (cf. Battistella 1990, Fradkin 1991, Tobin 1993, and others).

(5)   Because he was practically penniless, he moved into the room in the Hotel Lincoln where Craig was living and in the five months that it took *to put the play on* they were together twenty-four hours a day.   (Shaw 1973:63)

The phrasal construction in (5) is composed of exactly the same lexical elements as (4) differing only in the word order. The meaning of result or accomplishment is essential in the context — the play was ready for presentation and its staging was finished within a limited period of time, five months. The use of the marked D construction seems to serve the purpose of expressing the resultative meaning in this context.

The relationship between C and D constructions as an opposition of unmarked/marked for result forms can be further illustrated by the following examples with contrastive word order:

(6)   Craig hesitated. Unconsciously, he patted his coat over his wallet. He knew he had five hundred dollars in American money and about two thousand francs in his wallet. Superstitiously, in memory of the time he had been poor, he always carried a lot of money with him. *Turning down requests for loans*, even from people who were strangers, was invariably painful,

almost impossible, for him. He regarded this trait, rightly, as a weakness in his character. He always remembered that in War and Peace, Tolstoy had used Pierre Bezouchov's new-found ability *to turn down supplicants for money* as a sign of maturity and ripening intelligence.   (Shaw 1973:85)

The use of the C construction, especially in the gerund form, denotes that the character dreads the process of refusing people even more than the consequences of such action. The unmarked construction in (6) conveys the meaning of both process and result.

(7)   It is common knowledge that at least on one occasion he was offered the top position at one of the most prestigious studios in the industry. It is said he *turned the offer down* in a brief telegram, "Have already deserted sinking ship. Craig."   (Shaw 1973:28)

Unlike in (6), the emphasis in (7) is placed on the result of the action, and the marked form is selected to convey the message of finality and irreversibility of the action when the character declined the offer deemed to be unique and flattering by many.

If our assumption is justified, it should allow us to predict the choice of one or another form in texts of different types. The following group of examples is taken from the book of recipes for preparing biscuits. Culinary books usually offer the techniques of cooking tasty things; although they always have in view the final product, they still focus more on the nature and sequence of the operations. Consequently, we should anticipate that the unmarked constructions occur more frequently in recipes. The analysis of the data supports this supposition:

(8)   ...*drop in the vanilla essence and egg yolk.*
...put the flour and sugar into a bowl and *rub in the butter* until the mixture resembles fine crumbs.
...*roll out the paste* on a floured board.
...put the icing sugar into a small pan and *stir in the lemon juice.*   (NJ Cuisine 1985:239–241)

Another prediction can be made about school textbooks: we can anticipate the higher frequency of the C constructions in the contexts where the students are instructed on how to use various methods and strategies of learning. The meaning of such texts is process-oriented, which presumes that they use more unmarked for result forms:

(9)   – Read the text below about a surprising new development in computers. Now read again and *fill in the blanks*, keeping the following in mind.
– If the relative pronoun is followed by a subject+verb, we can *leave out the relative pronoun*. If it is followed by a verb, we cannot *leave out the relative pronoun.*
– The only preparation you need is *to set aside the things you'll need during the exam*: pens, pencils, eraser, your dictionary, a bottle of water and

perhaps a sandwich or two.
- Think of what you want to say. In English or in your mother tongue, *jot down any thoughts you have on the topic.*
- Organize your thoughts! Group similar ideas together. *Cross out any irrelevant ideas*, then number the groups in a logical order. You now have an outline of your essay.
- Find the repeated structures on both sides of the bolded connectors and *fill in the missing words.*
- If the missing word is a part of a phrasal verb, and the verb is given, *look up the base form.*   (From:*Top Marks* 1997)

The D constructions are used in the textbooks very rarely and usually in the cases where the completion of the action is strongly stressed:

(10)   Important: **Read the whole passage through** before doing the exercise. (*Top Marks* 1997:74)

It is interesting to contrast two groups of examples from instruction manuals for electric appliances referring to similar actions and using similar verbs.

(11)   a.   **Turn on the radio** by rotating the volume control knob clockwise. To increase the sound volume, turn the knob clockwise. **Turn off the radio** by rotating the knob counter clockwise until a slight click is heard.   (Sanyo Radio Model 5050)
        b.   Turn clockwise **to switch the unit on** (a click is felt). Continue turning to increase the volume. Turn fully counter-clockwise **to switch the unit off.**   (Aiwa stereo car cassette receiver CS W6604)

In (11a), the unmarked for result phrasal construction is used to describe the manner of performing concrete actions. In (11b), the marked form making a specific claim for result indicates the desired effect of the action, its goal. Moreover, the grammatical form of the phrasal verb, the infinitive, contributes to the resultative meaning of the D construction in this case being marked for result (see references above). As the data show, the distinction in word order reflects different ways of perceiving actions from the point of view of their result rather consistently.

The meaning of the C construction used in (12) below may be regarded as either process or result:

(12)   'Well,' Murphy said, raising his glass, 'here's to my boy.' He *gulped down a third of his drink.* 'It's wonderful finally catching up with you. In person. You don't hand out much information in your letters, do you?'   (Shaw 1973:51)

Murphy's consuming only a third of his drink leaves no feeling of completion, but rather invites continuation. However, in (13) the meaning conveyed by the D construction is explicitly resultative: the glass is empty.

(13)   The routine of the mornings. After breakfast, he and Brenner sprawled in swimming trunks in the sun, the manuscript of Brenner's new play open on the table between them and Brenner saying, 'What about as the curtain comes up on the second act, the stage is dark, and she comes in, goes over to the bar, you only see her in silhouette, she pours herself a drink, sobs then *knocks the whole drink down* in one gulp . . .?'   (Shaw 1973:66)

The reinforcement in this case is rather lexical than grammatical because the adjective *whole* and the resultative phrase *in one gulp* contribute to the created effect of fulfillment. The choice of the marked word order type is therefore one of the ways to convey the message of the result of the action working simultaneously with other language tools.

In many languages, including Russian, the distinction between resultative and non-resultative forms of the verbs is expressed morphologically. In Russian the verb always appears in one of the two forms, imperfective or perfective. Although I do not identify the category of resultativeness with the perfective aspect, I find it legitimate to assume that there is a higher possibility for the result-oriented English forms to be translated into Russian by the perfective verbs, while the neutral or process-oriented forms are more likely to be translated by the imperfective verbs. The functions of the Russian perfective as presented in Forsyth (1970: 8) correspond to the semantic functions of the resultative forms: 'The perfective verb is consequently used whenever emphasis is placed upon such a new state of affairs produced by the action, i.e. the result or consequences of the action.'

If there exists some pattern in systematic representation of one type of the phrasal constructions by the Russian perfective and the other — by the Russian imperfective, the assumption that they have difference in meaning would receive additional support. I anticipate that the D constructions will be translated into Russian more frequently by the perfective forms and rarely by the imperfective forms. In order to check this hypothesis, I have compared the phrasal constructions found in 'Theatre' by Maugham and their translation into Russian (transl. by Ostrovsky 1982). Among 95 phrasal constructions occurring in the original English text, 79 (83.2%) were continuous and 16 (16.8%) discontinuous, which is consistent with the general tendency of the unmarked forms to occur more frequently. Their translation into Russian showed the distribution of the forms set out in Table 1.

Table 1. Translation of the Phrasal Constructions into Russian

Type of construction	Total	Translated by the perfective	Translated by the imperfective
Continuous	79 (100%)	54 (68%)	25 (32%)
Discontinuous	16 (100%)	15 (94%)	1 (6%)

As can be seen from the this table, the C constructions can be translated into Russian by both perfective and imperfective forms, whereas the D constructions are in most cases (94%) translated by the perfective forms, which supports the view that their meaning is more resultative and their distribution more restricted.

To illustrate this point, let us return to example (4) and compare the English form with its Russian translation:

(4)   'The secretary told me you were rehearsing this morning, Miss Lambert,' the young man remarked. 'Does that mean *you're putting on a new play?*'   (Maugham 1985:16)
      – Секретарша сказала мне, что вы были на репетиции сегодня утром, мисс Лэмберт, — заметил юноша. — Вы собираетесь *ставить новую пьесу?*   (Ostrovsky 1982:7)

(4)   *ставить   новую пьесу*
      put on-IMPERF new   play
      'put on a new play'

The C construction is translated into Russian by the imperfective form *ставить*, which makes no claim for the result of the action. The analysis of other English texts and their translation into Russian shows the same asymmetrical pattern: the D constructions are almost never translated by the imperfective Russian verb. I assume that the systematic translation of the D constructions by the marked for result Russian verb forms reflects the fact that they are preserved for result-oriented contexts.

The following examples are cited from a fantasy novel "The Time of the Transference" by A.D. Foster and its translation into Russian by S.Anisimov (2002):

(14) "If it's a party, why weren't we invited? You know how old shelldrawers likes *to show off your music.*"   (Foster 1986:442)
      – Если у них вечеринка, что ж нас не пригласили? Ты же знаешь, как костлявый комод любит *демонстрировать твою музыкальность.*   (Anisimov 2002:283)

(14) *демонстрировать твою музыкальность*
      show off-IMPERF   your   music skills
      'to show off your music'

The C construction used by Foster to indicate an action with no claim for its completeness or result is translated by the imperfective form of a verb performing the similar non-resultative function in Russian. In the same novel, the D constructions are consistently translated from English by the perfective forms:

(15) "You need an excuse to stand up to him? Okay — tell him that your sweet, demure little Talea badgered you unmercifully until you had no choice but to stumble over and pretty-please ask him *to shut his exalted self up.* For the rest of the night, at least …"   (Foster 1986:443)
      – Ах, тебе нужно оправдание, чтобы предстать перед ним?

Ладно, скажи ему, что твоя милая скромница Талея безжалостно пилила тебя, пока не осталось ничего другого, кроме как пойти и преподнести его разбушевавшейся милости нижайшую просьбу **заткнуться** — хотя бы до утра.   (Anisimov 2002:285)

(15) *его разбушевавшейся милости... заткнуться*
      his exalted   self ...   to shut up-PERF
      'to shut his exalted self up'

Talea, Jon-Tom's wife, cannot sleep through the racket made by somebody in the neighboring tree. Sending Jon-Tom to calm the tree's residents down, she has in view the outcome of this mission, not the action itself. The D construction in English and the perfective form in Russian are both tools to express the result-oriented meaning of her utterance.

We may also compare the translation of the minimal pairs into Russian. I will use the example from Hailey's novel «The Moneychangers»:

(16) Innes nodded his approval. 'Then let's keep it that way. We'll **pick Eastin up** for questioning as soon as we've finished here but he mustn't be warned. He's still at the bank?'   (Hailey 1975:105–106)
      – Тогда давайте поступим следующим образом. Как только закончим с формальностями, **допросим Истина**, но предупреждать его заранее нельзя. Он все еще в банке?   (Izosimova, Tarasov 1993:73)

(16) *допросим Истина*
      pick up-PERF Eastin
      'pick Eastin up'

(17) 'In that case do it my way. Don't **pick up Eastin** tonight. Give me until morning.' 'I'm not sure,' Innes mused. 'I'm not sure I can.'   (Hailey 1975:107)
      – В таком случае давайте поступим, как я предложил. Не **трогайте Истина** сегодня. Дайте мне время до утра.
      – Я не уверен... — Иннес колебался. — Не уверен, что имею на это право.   (Izosimova, Tarasov 1993:74)

(17) *трогайте Истина*
      pick up-IMPERF Eastin
      'pick up Eastin'

The D construction in (16) is translated into Russian by the perfective form *допросим*, whereas its counterpart in (17) — by the imperfective form *трогайте*. The two constructions occur in the same novel, one page apart. They belong to the same style and register, have the same one-word object, and the same degree of idiomaticity. The only difference between the two is the word order and this is probably the reason for translating them by the different aspect forms of the Russian verbs.

The similarity in structure, function, and meaning existing between the D type of phrasal constructions and the so-called resultative constructions, such as *hammer the metal flat,* has recently drawn a great deal of linguistic attention (cf. Carrier and Randall 1992, Jackendoff 1997, Levin and Rappaport 1995, Nedjalkov 1988, Simpson 1983, Tenny 1994):

> *He painted the barn red.* (Diver 1986)
> *She slept the night away.* (Jackendoff 1997)
> *Sylvester cried his eyes out.* (Levin and Rappaport 1995)

Tenny (1994) claims that "English verb-particle constructions and resultative secondary predicates are very similar syntactic constructions" (156). She applies the term 'verb-particle constructions' only to the D constructions, which may indicate that the meaning of result is frequently associated with the particular word order.

As can be seen from the prior studies, the resultative meaning can also be expressed in many other ways, which should be all brought into system and analyzed in order to gain a wider understanding of resultativeness and its place in the language structure. The first serious attempt to approach the concepts of process and result as a primary distinctive feature of language was made by Tobin, who defined it as "a fundamental semantic distinctive feature which cuts across almost all traditional categories: verb, noun, adjective, infinitive, gerund, participle, particle, auxiliary":

> ... language may reflect two fundamental ways of viewing actions, states, or events; either as focusing on the (ongoing) *process* involved in the action, state, or event, or, alternatively, from the point of view of the *result* (outcome, endpoint, consequence, completion, destination, or telic or teleological goal). (Tobin 1993:15)

The reason that the category of resultativeness has not been recognized as a part of the English structure lies probably in the sophisticated set of devices the language exploits for its manifestation. Any category can only be distinguished and studied adequately if it has its own means of expression in language. The category of resultativeness in English seems to be different from the traditional categories because it has multiple representations and uses various tools of expression. The previous analyses in this field provide several separate systems of result-based oppositions, each of them dealing with a particular phenomenon, lexical, morphological, or syntactic. In search for an orderly system, I attempted to unite them into one integral linguistic subsystem. As it appears, almost every linguistic category, either lexical or grammatical, reflects a relationship of forms that are marked or unmarked for result.

Resultativeness occupies a peculiar place in the language structure because it is not restricted to one affix or auxiliary, tense or aspect form. It cannot be accounted for by only the lexicon or grammar. Unlike other categories, it is expressed by the oppositions of unmarked/marked forms throughout all language levels and subsystems: morphemes, auxiliaries, lexical pairs, compounds, verb complements, tense, aspect, and voice forms, syntactic patterns, types of sentences, word order, stress, and intonation, as shown in Table 2. As can be seen from this scheme, the distinctive feature of result can be traced in numerous parts of the language structure, and the markedness opposition based on this feature can be viewed as a part of many systems of English forms.

Table 2. The result-based oppositions in the language

LEXICON

Lexical pairs:
do/make, begin/start, till/until
(cf. Tobin)

Simple verbs/phrasal verbs:
fight/fight off, eat/eat up
(cf. Bolinger 1971, Gorlach 2000, Jackendoff 1997, Kennedy 1920,
Kruisinga 1931, Live 1965, Tenny 1994, Tobin 1993)

GRAMMAR

Morphemes	Constructions
-ing/-ed (-en); -en/-ed (cf. Fradkin, Huffman, Tobin)	non-resultative/resultative (cf. Carrier and Randell, Jackendoff, Levin and Rappaport, Simpson, Tenny)
Auxiliaries: *be/have; be/get* (cf. Battistella, Benveniste, Dik, Tobin)	**phrasal constructions:** **continuous/discont**inuous **(cf. Bolinger, Gorlach, Tenny, Tobin)**
Verb complements: gerund/infinitive present participle/past participle (cf. Fradkin, Huffman, Tobin)	**Other possible candidates** (further investigation is required)
Tense: present/past present/future (cf. Battistella, Tobin)	Sentences: statements/questions statements/negations statements/exclamations non-emphatic/emphatic (cf. Battistella)
Aspect: progressive/perfect (cf. Battistella, Comrie, Fradkin, Khlebnikova, Tobin)	Questions: Yes/No questions/Wh-questions
Voice: active/passive (cf. Andersen, Beedham, Nedjalkov, Tobin, van Schooneveld) *be*-passive/*get*-passive (cf. Bolinger, Tobin, Vanrespaille)	Yes/No questions/alternative questions non-tag/tag-questions Mood: indicative/imperative indicative/subjunctive

The study of the result-based oppositions, especially in phrasal constructions, leads us to the following conclusions. First of all, I should suggest the definition of resultativeness: it is a lexico-grammatical category reflecting a fundamental way of perceiving actions and events integrally with their actual or potential result, which is sometimes characterized by a fixed marked word order. This linguistic category serves as reflection of the human perception of entities in general as process- or result-oriented. Resultativeness is an atypical independent category which exploits diversified language forms for its realization. In verbs the result-based oppositions occur on several levels. In simple verbs such oppositions are based on the degree of resultative meaning in their lexical meaning or on the grammatical form they appear in. The invariant meaning of the phrasal verbs always contains the element of result superimposed on their lexical meaning. The two positional variants of the phrasal constructions, continuous and discontinuous, reflect different degrees of result in their meaning. The C phrasal construction may denote either process or result, while the D construction is marked for result, i.e. makes a specific claim for result in all cases. The D constructions can be viewed as a particular type of resultative constructions, where the particle functions as a resultative phrase: **to break** the glass **up.**

References

Andersen, P.K. 1991. *A New Look at the Passive.* Frankfurt am Main, Bern, New York, Paris: Peter Lang.

Battistella, E.L. 1990. *Markedness: the evaluative superstructure of language.* Albany: State University of New York.

Beedham, C. 1982. *The Passive Aspect in English, German and Russian.* Tubingen: Gunter Narr Verlag.

Beedham, C. 1987. "The English passive as an aspect". *Word* 38:1.1–12.

Benveniste, E. 1971. *Problems in General Linguistics,* trans. M.E. Meek. Miami: University of Miami Press.

Biber, D. 1995. *Dimensions of Register Variation: A cross-linguistic comparison.* Cambridge University Press.

Bolinger, D. 1971. *The Phrasal Verb in English.* Cambridge MA: Harvard University Press.

Bolinger, D. 1977. *Meaning and Form.* London: Longman.

Carrier, J. and Randall, J. 1992. "The argument structure and syntactic structure of resultatives". *Linguistic Inquiry* 23:2.173–234.

Chafe, W. 1970. *Meaning and the Structure of Language.* Chicago and London: The University of Chicago Press.

Comrie, B. 1976. *Aspect.* Cambridge University Press.

Dehé, N. 2002. *Particle Verbs in English: Syntax, information structure and intonation.* Amsterdam and Philadelphia: John Benjamins.

Diver, W. 1986. The grammar of modern English. Columbia University, ms.

Erades, P.A. 1961. "Points of English syntax XL". *English Studies* 42:56–60.

Forsyth, J. 1970. *A Grammar of Aspect.* Cambridge University Press.

Fradkin, R. 1991. *Stalking the Wild Verb Phrase*. Lanham, New York, London: University Press of America.

Fraser, B. 1976. *The Verb-Particle Combination in English*. New York: Academic Press.

Gorlach, M. 1983. Nouns derived from phrasal verbs by conversion and ways of their translation into Russian (in Russian). Pyatigorsk: Pyatigorsk Pedagogical Institute of Foreign Languages, M.A.dissertation.

Gorlach, M. 2000. "Resultativeness: constructions with phrasal verbs in focus". In *Between Grammar and Lexicon*, E.Contini-Morava and Y.Tobin (eds), 255–286. Amsterdam and Philadelphia: John Benjamins.

Hirtle, W.H. 1975. *Time, Aspect and the Verb*. Québec: Les Presses de l'Université Laval.

Huffman, A. 1989. "Teaching the English tenses". *Columbia University Working Papers in Linguistics* 10: i-iv, 1–153, xvi-xxi.

Jackendoff, R. 1996. "Conceptual semantics and cognitive semantics". *Cognitive Linguistics* 7:93–129.

Jackendoff, R. 1997. "Twistin' the night away". *Language* 73:3.534–559.

Jespersen, O. 1924. *The Philosophy of Grammar*. George Allen and Unwin.

Kennedy, A. 1920. *The Modern English Verb-Adverb Combination*. Stanford University Press.

Khlebnikova, I. 1973. *Oppositions in Morphology: as exemplified in the English tense system*. The Hague: Mouton.

Kilby, D. 1984. *Descriptive Syntax and the English Verb*. Kent: Croom Helm Ltd.

Kroch, A. and Small, C. 1978. "Grammatical ideology and its effect on speech". *Linguistic variation: models and methods*, 45–55. New York: Academic Press.

Kruisinga, E. 1931. *A Handbook of Present-day English*, part II: English accidence and syntax, v.1, 5th ed., Groningen: P.Noordhoff.

Legum, S. 1968. "The verb-particle construction in English: basic or derived?" *Papers from the Fourth Regional Meeting of the Chicago Linguistics Society*, B.J. Darden, C.J.N. Bailey, and A. Davison (eds), 50–62. Chicago: Chicago University Press.

Levin, B. and Rappaport, M. 1995. *Unaccusativity: at the syntax-lexical semantic interface*. Cambridge MA: MIT Press.

Live, A.H. 1965. "The discontinuous verb in English". *Word* 21:428–451.

Murphy, R. 1985. *English Grammar in Use*. Cambridge University Press.

Nedjalkov, V. 1988. *Typology of Resultative Constructions*. Amsterdam and Philadelphia: John Benjamins.

Palmer, F.R. 1974. *The English Verb*. London: Longman.

Quirk, R., Greenbaum, S., Leech, G. and Svartvik, J. 1972. *A Grammar of Contemporary English*. London: Longman.

Saussure, F. de. 1959 [1916]. *Course in General Linguistics*, C.Bally and A.Sechenaye (eds), with the collaboration of A.Riedlinger, translation and introduction by W. Baskin. New York: The Philosophical Library.

Simpson, J. 1983. "Resultatives". *Papers in Lexical-functional Grammar*, L. Levin, M. Rappaport, and A. Zaenen (eds), 143–157. Bloomington: Indiana University Linguistics Club.

Stowell, T. 1981. *Origins of Phrase Structure*. Ph.D. dissertation, Cambridge MA: MIT Press.

Tenny, C. 1994. *Aspectual Roles and the Syntax-Semantics Interface*. Dordrecht, Boston, London: Kluwer Academic Publishers.

Tobin, Y. 1990. *Semiotics and Linguistics*. London: Longman.

Tobin, Y. 1993. *Aspect in the English verb: process and result in language*. London: Longman.

van Dongen, W.A. 1919. "*He put on his hat* and *He put his hat on*". *Neophilologus* 4:322–353.

Vanrespaille, M. 1989. "The English *get*-passive". *Papers from the Cognitive Linguistics Symposium*, Duisburg.

van Schooneveld, C. H. 1988. "Paradigmatic structure and syntactic relations". *The Prague School and Its Legacy*, Y. Tobin (ed), 109–121. Amsterdam and Philadelphia: John Benjamins.

Sources of data

Davidi, M.S., Revesz, R. and Spitz, Sh.R. 1997. *Top Marks*. Tel Aviv: Eric Cohen Books, Onda Publications Ltd.

Foster, A. 1986. *The Time of the Transference*. New York: Nelson Doubleday, Inc.

Foster, A. *The Time of the Transference*. Transl. by V.Anisimov (2002). Moscow: Expro Publ.

Hailey, A. 1975. *The Moneychangers*. London and Sydney: Pan Books.

Hailey, A. *The Moneychangers*. Transl. by Izosimova and Tarasov (1993). Moscow:Vsjo Dlja Vas.

Maugham, W. S. 1985. *Theatre*. Moscow: Vysšaja Škola.

Maugham, W. S. *Theatre*. Transl. by G.Ostrovsky (1982). Moscow: Raduga Publ.

Shaw, I. 1973. *Evening in Byzantium*. New English Library.

Sheldon, S. 1970. *The Naked Face*. New York: A Dell Book.

The New Jewish Cuisine, 1985.

CHAPTER 17

Encoding speaker perspective: Evidentials

Ferdinand de Haan
University of Arizona

1. Introduction

The main point of this paper is to argue that evidentiality is a deictic category, not a modal one, despite many current assumptions in the literature (see e.g. Palmer 1986, Willett 1988, Frawley 1992).[1] I will argue that the basic meaning is to mark the relation between the speaker and the action s/he is describing.[2] Evidentiality thus fulfills the same function for marking relationships between speakers and actions/ events that, say, demonstratives do for marking relationships between speakers and objects. Evidentiality is not a priori concerned with the modal aspects of the prop-osition although it must be stressed that (epistemic) modality may enter the picture at some point. Anyone listening to linguistic information containing evidentials is free to interpret that information however they wish but that does not make modal-ity part of the basic meaning of evidentiality. Rather the situation is similar to the Past tense in English, which can have modal interpretations but that does not mean that modality is part of the basic meaning of the Past tense in English.

Evidentiality is traditionally divided in two main categories: *direct evidentiality*, which shows that the speaker has directly witnessed the action, and *indirect* evi-dentiality, which shows that the speaker has no direct evidence for his/her state-ment, but has other sources for making the statement. Typical direct evidential cat-egories are *visual* and *auditory* evidence, stating that the speaker has respectively seen and heard the action. Indirect evidentials can be *inferentials*, which mean that the speaker has inferred the action from available evidence, and *quotatives* (also re-ferred to in the literature as reportative or hearsay evidentiality), which states that the speaker knows about the event from being told by another person. It is not un-usual to think of these two categories as representing different degrees of commit-ment to the truth of the action: indirect evidentials show that the speaker is not as committed to the truth of what s/he is saying than when a direct evidential is used. This view may be correct in some cases, but this is not the reason why evidentials are employed. It is argued here that they are used to denote the relative distance be-tween the speaker and the action. A speaker will use an indirect evidential to state that the action takes/took place outside the speaker's deictic sphere, whereas the use of a direct evidential shows that the action takes or took place within that deic-tic sphere.

The body of this paper consists of the following sections: section 2 discusses some reasons why a modal interpretation of evidentiality is not appropriate. Section 3 deals with the relation between first person and evidentiality. Section 4 discusses visual evidentiality while section 5 covers the relation between inference and deixis. Section 6 discusses the similarities and differences between auditory evidentials and quotatives. Section 7 compares evidential and demonstrative systems. Section 8 draws some conclusions.

2. Evidentiality and epistemic modality

The relationship between epistemic modality and evidentiality seems obvious, especially when looked at from the perspective of English. A typical view is Palmer (1986) who divides epistemic modality into judgments, speculation about the action described, and evidentials, assessment based on some type of evidence.[3] From that perspective it is indeed not hard to conclude that there is a link between the two categories. In English *must*, for instance, both interpretations appear to be present, since strong Epistemic *must* is indeed used to make an assessment that an action took place based on some type of evidence. A more limited approach is taken by Van der Auwera and Plungian (1998: 85–6) who only admit inferentiality as a modal category, but not the others.

As argued in De Haan (1999), there is no good reason to consider evidentiality a part of epistemic modality or even to consider them to be interchangeable terms. Evidentiality *asserts* the evidence, while epistemic modality *evaluates* the evidence. A good example which shows the difference is shown in (1). This example from Dutch is part of a newspaper account of murders committed in January of 1929 by a craftsman called IJje Wijkstra. The victims were four policemen who came to his house in the woods to arrest him on charges of abduction. This is a historical account and direct evidence does not come into play here. The evidential used is the verb *moeten* 'must' which can be used for both evidential uses and epistemic uses. In this example the epistemic reading is not present. The evidential occurs in the last sentence.

(1) *IJje Wijkstra was timmerman en klompenmaker, hij stroopte, was op zijn vrijheid gesteld en had een hekel aan autoriteit. Maar voor IJje hield de wereld niet op bij de harde strijd om het dagelijkse bestaan. Hij las boeken over spiritisme en occultisme, waagde zich aan Hegel en Nietzsche en **moet** zelf een boek hebben geschreven, 'Dualisme van het Heelal', al is het manuscript daarvan nooit gevonden.*

"IJje Wijkstra was a carpenter and maker of wooden shoes, he was a poacher, loved his freedom and hated authority. But for IJje the world did not end with the harsh struggle for daily survival. He read books about spiritualism and the occult, dared to tackle Hegel and Nietzsche and **alleg-**

edly wrote a book himself, called 'Dualism of the Universe', but the manuscript has never been found." (*Dagblad van het Noorden*, 11 Feb. 2003)

The use of *moet* in (1) is not epistemic. The author does not evaluate the evidence but rather asserts that there is evidence to support the statement that Wiekstra wrote a book. He does not state what that evidence is and indeed the evidence itself is in general never stated when *moeten* is used as an evidential. The author also does not evaluate the evidence but rather leaves the matter open whether there actually was a manuscript or not. In its epistemic reading, the author would evaluate evidence and, given the status of *moeten* as a strong modal verb, would believe that it is very likely that there is or had been a manuscript. This can be compared to English *must* which is wholly evaluative, as example (2) shows:

(2)   He must have written a book himself called 'Dualism of the Universe', but the manuscript has never been found.

Sentence (2) has to be interpreted in such a way that the speaker believes that there likely was such a manuscript. In no way can (2) be interpreted as a neutral statement about the existence of evidence. Hence English *must* is not an evidential.

The next point regarding the status of the verb *moeten* in (1) above concerns the status of the context. Note that the evidential only occurs in the very last clause of the text fragment. The other sentences are without any qualification whatsoever. Again, the difference between the sentences with or without the verb *moeten* is not one of relative confidence in the truth of the statement. The difference is rather the difference between *confirmed* and *unconfirmed* information. This terminology is due to Friedman (1986, 1999, *inter alia*), who has analyzed South Slavic evidentiality in this manner.

The use of *moeten* in the last sentence indicates that the statement contains an unconfirmed fact. The author wishes to indicate that there is evidence of Wiekstra having written a manuscript, but that he could not confirm it, and explicitly states why. The only thing that could confirm the fact, the manuscript itself, is not found. All the other statements in the fragment (1) are independently verifiable and verified. The author does not use the verb *moeten* in these sentences to mark them as confirmed. Despite the fact that the last statement is an unconfirmed one, the statement is not presented as uncertain, merely as unconfirmed. Recall that this is a factual article in the newspaper genre, in which speculation is generally not encouraged (unlike, say, an editorial). The author presents a fact as unconfirmed and, crucially, it is up to the reader (and/or hearer) to interpret the truth value of the unconfirmed fact. Since the reader/hearer has to do that anyway, regardless of whether an evidential is present or not, it is not part of the meaning of *moeten*. Hence, evidentials do not have an intrinsic epistemic component. Any epistemic value comes from the contextual interaction with the hearer (reader). Note that this is different from real epistemic modals, because there the epistemic value is determined by the speaker (and the hearer can still disagree with that value).[4]

Having shown that epistemic modality may not be the underlying meaning of evidentiality, the rest of this paper investigates the interaction of speaker viewpoint and evidentiality, and the link between deixis and evidentiality.

Anderson and Keenan (1985:259) start their article on deictic marking in a typological framework with the following definition: "Following standard usage, we consider as *deictic expressions* (or *deictics* for short) those linguistic elements whose interpretation in simple sentences makes essential reference to properties of the extralinguistic context of the utterance in which they occur." Although Anderson and Keenan, do not discuss evidentiality, this definition covers evidential usage very well.[5] Their usage makes crucial reference to the extralinguistic context. For instance, an auditory evidential can only be used in those situations in which the speaker has heard the action or event he/she is describing. This also implies that that action or event is capable of making sounds. Each individual evidential category has similar extralinguistic properties. As with deictic expressions like demonstratives, evidentials have as deictic center the speaker of the utterance. The speaker and its grammatical correlate first person singular, therefore has special properties in evidential systems. This is the topic of the next section.

3. First person and evidentiality

As the presumed deictic center of evidentiality, first person singular occupies a special position in evidential paradigms. There is an apparent incompatibility between indirect evidentiality and first person subjects. The reason is of course that it is very hard to have only indirect evidence for actions in which the speaker himself was the main participant.

In Tuyuca (E. Tucanoan; Barnes 1984:258, 261), there is no morpheme for First person, Inferential, Present tense because of the incompatibility of present tense and inferential evidence (there is a separate form for First person, past tense, however).

A similar situation is found in Komi (Finno-Ugric, Permian; Baker 1983, Leinonen 2000, Leinonen and Vilkuna 2000). There are two past tenses in Komi, usually referred to as the First and Second Past tense. The Second Past tense is used to denote indirect evidence. It is defective in that it has no separate First person morpheme, at least not in Standard Komi. A sample paradigm is shown in Table 1 (Baker 1983:69).

The different usages of the Past tenses are shown in example (3a) below. The use of the First Past in the final verb marks direct evidence while the use of the Second Past on the verb *vöć-ömyd* 'do-PST2.2SG' shows that the speaker was not present at the act of doing. Thus, the different uses mark different deictic distances between speaker and action. This can also be seen in (3b) where the action took place outside of the speaker's presence, hence the use of the Second Past. Note that in neither case there is a marked difference in epistemic modality: all actions are presented as true.

Table 1. Past tenses of Komi *munny* 'to go'

	First past	Second past
1SG	mun-i	—
2SG	mun-in	mun-ömyd
3SG	mun-is	mun-öma
1PL	mun-im	—
2PL	mun-innyd	mun-ömnyd
3PL	mun-isny	mun-ömaös'

(3) a. *Sidzkö myjkö   abu na sidzi vöć-ömyd   kydz me tšöktyl-i*
       so   something NEG yet so   do-PST2.2SG as   I   order-PST1.1SG
       'So, something you have not done as I told you to.' (Leinonen 2000: 427)

     b. [It is morning. A. wakes up, looks out of the window and sees that the
         courtyard (or the street) is wet]
         vojnas   zer-öma
         night.INESS.3SG rain-PST2.3SG
         'It has rained last night.'   (Leinonen and Vilkuna 2000: 499)

Although Standard Komi does not have separate forms for First person Second Past, such forms do occur in certain dialects (Leinonen and Vilkuna 2001: 502, Baker 1983: 79–80). These forms are identical to the corresponding 3rd person forms (i.e. *-öma* for 1SG, *-ömaös'* for 1PL). When such forms are used, the speaker disavows any responsibility for his actions ("I didn't know what I was doing, but . . ." according to Baker 1983: 80). The speaker performs a deictic shift from 1st person participant to 3rd person bystander[6] and effectively makes a separation between speaker and subject even though both are the same person.

   In the case of Komi, the choice of tense, and consequently the choice of evidentiality, is motivated by deictic forces, or as aptly put by Baker (1983: 79): "The [Second Past] tense reflects the narrator's deliberate spacing of himself from the action of the verb."

4. Visual evidentiality

The category of visual evidentiality refers to the deictic situation in which the speaker is in visual distance of the action described. Pure visual evidentials are relatively rare (as opposed to general direct evidentials), and, based on the WALS database, the presence of a visual evidential implies the presence of at least one other direct evidential (either an auditory evidential or a nonvisual direct evidential).

   It was argued in De Haan 2003 that visual evidentials typically come from deictic sources, such as tense morphemes or spatial deictic morphemes. In this section I will discuss two cases involving each scenario.

Table 2. The visual evidential paradigm in Tuyuca (Barnes 1984: 258)

	Past	Present
3SG. MASC.	-wi	-i
3SG. FEM.	-wo	-yo
3PL.	-wa	-ya
3SG. INAN, 1/2	-wɨ	-a

In Tuyuca (E. Tucanoan; Barnes 1984), visual evidentiality, and evidentiality in general, is expressed as a portmanteau morpheme together with person, number, gender, and tense. The paradigm is shown in Table 2.

Examples are shown in (4) below. In (a) the Past tense form is shown, and in (b) the Present is used, which involves a Progressive construction with an auxiliary verb. In both cases the speaker was/is in visual distance of the action.

(4) a. *díiga apé-wi.*
        soccer play-VIS.3SG.MASC.PAST
        'He played soccer (I saw him play).'   (Barnes 1984: 257)
     b. *díiga apé-gɨ   tií-i.*
        soccer play-3SG.MASC AUX-VIS.3SG.MASC.PRES
        'He is playing soccer.'   (Barnes 1984: 259)

Interestingly, the Visual evidential in Tuyuca is used not only to report on events witnessed personally, but also for cases in which strictly speaking a visual evidential cannot be used, namely (a) in a compound, resultative, construction to describe the end result of a state or event when the state or event itself was not seen but the end result was (example (5a)), and (b) for timeless events that are known to the speaker, such as "two plus two equals four" and an example is shown in (5b).

(5) a. *wesé sóe-ri-gɨ nĩí-wi.*
        field burn-RES-MASC.SG AUX-VIS.3SG.MASC.PAST
        'He burned his field. (I saw his field and it had been burned)'
     b. *ã́nã wãmɛ̃kɨti-yo.*
        Ana is.called-VIS.3SG.FEM.PRES
        'She is named Ana.'   (Barnes 1984: 259)

Strictly speaking, an Inferential should have been used (which is present in Tuyuca) in (5a) instead of a Visual evidential because the act of burning was not witnessed by the speaker, only the end result. This shows that visual presence of the speaker at any stage of the process can override the normal evidential used, in this case the Inferential. Note that the use of the Visual in no way implies that the action is more certain than it would have been if an Inferential had been used. In either case the speaker was not present at the act itself.

Sentence (5b) is the kind of sentence which would probably be expressed without an evidential were it not for the fact that evidentiality is an obligatory category in Tuyuca. The Visual is apparently the default category for cases like (5b) and it shows that there are some uses of the Visual which are non-evidential in nature. In this respect it is interesting to compare the Visual morphemes in Tuyuca with the usage of their cognate morphemes in the related languages Tucano and Carapana. Examples are shown in (6) below. The Carapana morphemes appear to be simple tense morphemes, without any evidential interpretations, while the corresponding morphemes in Tucano are general direct evidentials. The analysis is that the evidential interpretations in Tuyuca are the result of a shift from pure tense morphemes to hybrid tense/evidential morphemes (a shift attested in many languages around the world).

(6) a. Carapana (E. Tucanoan; Metzger 1981:34)
     pa-wõ
     work-3.SG.FEM.PAST
     'She worked.' (no evidential reading)
   b. Tucano (E. Tucanoan; West 1980:29)
     ní-wõ
     be-3.SG.FEM.PAST.DIRECT
     'She was.' (witnessed past)

It appears that the Eastern Tucanoan languages are in various stages of this shift. The use of the Visual evidential in cases like (5b) is likely a remnant of the old tense system.

The next language we will consider is Sanuma, a Yanomami language spoken in Brazil and Venezuela (Borgman 1990:165 and *passim*). Visual evidentiality is expressed by a mix of spatial and temporal deictic morphemes. There is an interesting distinction between past witnessed events and present witnessed ones. In the past, an action or event is located with respect to its temporal distance from the present (Table 3), while in the present, actions are located with respect to the position of the speaker (Table 4), i.e. spatially.

In (7) examples of the Past tense forms are shown, and (8) shows some examples with Present tense evidentials. The form *kule* 'near speaker' in (8a) appears to be the default form, inasmuch as it is the only evidential that can be used with all verbs.

Table 3. Past witnessed morphemes (Borgman 1990:169)

Morpheme	Gloss
ke/kehe/kuhe	immediate past (same part of day)
kupi/köpi/kipi	recent past (same 24-hour period, but not same part of day)
kupili/köpili/kipili	distant past (yesterday or before)

Table 4. Present witnessed morphemes (Borgman 1990:166)

Morpheme	Gloss
kule	Near speaker
kulai/kulaai	Fairly near, having been seen by the speaker, but at the moment hidden by some obstruction
kulati/kulahati	Farther away from the speaker but on the same level
kulali/kulahali	Upriver or across the river or even on land when there are one or more low spots or valleys between the speaker and the other person or object
kulatili	Far away inland from the river
kulakili	Far away downriver
kupoli/kupoholi	Up above in air, tree, etc.
kupokili	Down below in hole, earth, etc.
kimati/kuimati	Going away from speaker on same level
kimani/kimahani/ kuimani/kuimahani	Going away from speaker upriver or across river
kimakili	Going away from speaker downriver
kimi	Toward speaker

All other evidentials have restrictions of some kind placed on them (see also (9) below)

(7) a. *ipa sai   ha hama töpö hasu-ki   ke*
        my house by visitor 3PL pass.by-FOC IMM.PAST.WIT
        'The visitors passed by my house.' (p. 28)

    b. *ī   naha ī   a   ku-la-so   kupili.*
        REL like   REL 3SG say-EXT-FOC DIST.PAST.WIT
        'Like that that one finally said.' (p. 153)

(8) a. *hi   ti-nö   a   hīta   ku-le.*
        stick CLASS-INST 3SG stand.upright PRES.WIT-near
        'It is standing upright by means of a stick.' (p. 23)

    b. *hi   ai   kutiata pö kalol(o)-a ku-lai.*
        this other canoe 3PL float-DUR PRES.WIT-obstructed
        'There are other canoes floating here (beyond the trees).' (p. 166)

Example (9) below shows a typical deictic shift. The speaker is not near the action, and therefore the action is not witnessed at the precise moment of speech. However, the two are close enough in the mind of the speaker to warrant the use of *kule* 'near speaker'.

(9) *ī   na töpö ku kule.*
    REL like 3PL say PRES.WIT
    'That is what they are saying.' (p. 166) (the speaker had just come from a conversation in another house and reports what they are talking about)

The use of these evidentials with first person subjects can yield interesting results. Some forms in Table 4 above would seem incompatible with a first singular subject, namely those like *kuimati* 'going away from speaker on same level.' Nevertheless, such examples do occur. Sentence (10), from a personal narrative about an attempt to find fresh tapir tracks shows that the two are perfectly compatible. This deictic shift appears to be motivated by pragmatic and/or stylistic reasons (see also p. 168, ex. (672) for an explanation of a similar case). Note that the Present tense is used, even though a past event is described.

(10)   *hena tehe   ma   tu   kase hamö sa   samo   kuimani*
       early TEMP water CLASS edge along 1SG go.upriver PRES.LOC
       'The next morning I go away upstream along the bank of the river.' (p. 243)
       [Text 2, line 3 (personal narrative, reciting a past event)]

5. Inferentiality

The evidential category of inference is used for those instances in which the speaker has not witnessed the action personally, but has witnessed evidential traces of that action.[7] An example is shown in (11), from Tuyuca (Barnes 1984: 260) in which the action, the rotting of the plant, was not observed but rather deduced from the end result.

(11)   *bóahõã-yu.*
       rot-INFER.OTHER.PAST
       'It rotted.' (Said of a plant after pulling it up to examine it.)

Although the inferential is usually grouped with the quotative to form the category of indirect evidentiality (see e.g. Willett 1988 and Palmer 2001), it is in fact a hybrid direct/indirect evidential category, because the speaker is aware of the evidence for the action. Thus, in example (11) above, the Inferential can be used because the speaker has personally witnessed the evidence. If s/he had not, then the Inferential would not have been used.

This is why many languages make a distinction between witnessing an event and witnessing the result of an event in their choice of complement clauses (see Dik and Hengeveld (1991), Frajzyngier (1991, 1995), among others, for a discussion of perception verbs and their complements). A common example is (12), from English:

(12)   a.   John saw Mary cross(ing) the road.
       b.   John saw that Mary had crossed the road.

Sentence (12a), with its infinite embedded clause, is used to denote witnessing of an event, while (12b), with a finite embedded clause, is used when the result of an action is witnessed, but not the action itself. Hence, (12a) denotes simultaneity of perception and action, while (12b) denotes that perception is subsequent to the action (as also evidenced by the choice of verb tense in the embedded clause). This pattern occurs frequently across languages.

This hybrid nature of inferentiality is also found in languages with grammaticalized evidentials. In some languages inferential morphemes are grouped with quotatives, while in other they are grouped with (parts of) direct evidentials, which are typically the nonvisual sensory meanings. And of course they can group with neither of these two other categories. I will present here two languages which show these two cases.

In Patwin, the evidential *–boti* can be used for both Inferential and Quotative. Example (13a) shows the Inferential use and (13b) the Quotative use. This means that in Patwin the morpheme *–boti* functions as a general indirect evidential.

(13)   Patwin (S. Wintun; Whistler 1986: 70)
    a.   *ma-ne:n*   *we:ł tiwnana hara:-boti.*
        your-mother salt buy   go-INDIR
        'Your mother must have gone to buy salt.'
    b.   *yirma haybaɂa-boti pi.*
        leg.OBJ hurt-INDIR   he
        '(He told me) his leg hurts.'

Kashaya Pomo shows that an inferential evidential may be combined with direct evidence. The Inferential morpheme *–qa* can be used for inferring an action (as shown in (14a) below) but also for denoting sensory evidence from smell, taste and touch, as shown in (14b).

(14)   Kashaya Pomo (Pomoan; Oswalt 1986: 38)
    a.   *mu cohtoc-qa/mu cohztoc^{h}q^h*
        he leave-INFER
        'He has left.' (Said on discovering that the person is no longer present)
    b.   *cuhni: muɂt'a-q^h.*
        bread cook-INFER
        'Bread has been cooked.' (on coming into a house and detecting an odor)

Kashaya Pomo has separate evidentials for Auditory and Visual evidence and so these evidential notions are not grouped together with Inferentials. That does not mean that they can't, as witnessed by the following example from Hualapai, a Yuman language from Arizona (Watahomigie *et al.* 1982).

The evidential morpheme *–o* can refer to visual evidence as well as inferential evidence (this in itself is unusual), depending on its placement in the verb. If the evidential is placed verb-finally it denotes visual evidence (see example (15a) below). If, however, *-o* is placed immediately after the verb root, as in (15b), it has an inferential interpretation.

(15)   Hualapai (Yuman; Watahomigie *et al.* 1982: 392)
  a.   *Jóhnach   sma:kyunyo.*
       John(a)-ch sma:-k-yu-ny-o
       John-SUBJ 3:sleep-SS-AUX-PAST-VIS
       '(I witnessed that) John slept.'
  b.   *Jóhnach   wa:hm   a:mokyuny.*
       John(a)-ch wa:-h-m   a:m-o-k-yu-ny.
       John-SUBJ house-DEM-by 3.go.by-INFER-SS-AUX-PAST
       '(I have evidence that) John went by the house.'

When the morpheme *–o* has an Inferential interpretation it can be used to denote a wide variety of evidence, as the following quote illustrates: "When the speaker has not actually witnessed the event, but has deduced the occurrence from some other evidence (e.g. some trace of the event such as some left-over food on the table, the wrinkled sheet on the bed, etc.; hearing the noise that sounds like someone playing; smelling something being cooked; and so on), the speaker may use the evidential marker *-o* just before the same-subject marker *-k*." (Watahomigie *et al.* 1982: 393–394). The last two elements of the list of evidence in the quote refer to auditory and nonvisual, nonauditory sensory evidence, respectively. This means that in Hualapai direct evidentiality, excluding visual evidence, can be grouped with inferential evidence.

The grouping of any kind of direct evidence with inferentials is hard to reconcile with the theory that evidentiality is a modal category. It could conceivably be argued that types of evidence have different truth values in different languages (i.e. inferential evidence has a different, lower, truth value in Patwin than in, say, Kashaya Pomo), which would allow direct evidence to be classified with the Inferential in Kashaya, but not in Patwin. This would mean, however, that evidentiality as a category cannot be compared from language to language and thus that evidentiality is no uniform category which can be studied from a typological point of view.

In a deictic view, no such problem exists. When inferentials are grouped with (kinds of) direct evidence, the deictic presence of the speaker to the result of the action is highlighted. This places the speaker in the sphere of the action and the fact that the action itself may not have been witnessed becomes unimportant. When inferentials are kept separate the fact that there is a temporal separation between the action and the speaker is brought to the forefront. In the first case, the speaker's presence at the place of the action is deemed to be more important than the action itself. In the second case the action is more important than the fact that the speaker is now at the place where the action took place.

6. Auditory evidentiality vs. quotative

Although these two evidential categories are usually not thought of as having much in common, they do have in common the fact that the speaker receives auditory input in both cases. In the case of the quotative the input is verbal, namely a description of an event relayed by a third person. In the case of auditory evidentiality the input consists of sounds from the event itself. In this respect the relation between these categories is identical to the one between visual and inferential (see example (12) above), and it should come as no surprise that this distinction is marked in the complement clauses of verbs like 'to hear', as in (16) and (17) below. The difference between the (a) and the (b) sentences is that the (a) sentences show the hearing of the singing, while the (b) sentences mark the hearing of the report of the singing.

(16)   a.   I hear Sally sing.
       b.   I hear that Sally had sung.

(17)   a.   I heard Sally's singing.
       b.   I heard of Sally's singing.

There are differences and similarities between the role of the speaker in both cases and this can be reflected in the coding of the evidential. In the case of the (a) sentences the speaker serves as the experiential center of the act of hearing, but in the (b) sentences s/he is the recipient of the act of somebody else's report. In other words, the deictic relation between the speaker and the action is closer in the (a) sentences than in the (b) sentences. The relationship between the speaker and the perception is the same in both cases, as argued above, since in both cases the speaker receives auditory input.

Languages with grammaticalized evidentials for both evidential categories therefore have two options: (a) to encode these two categories with different morphemes or (b) with the same morpheme. If a language chooses option (a), which is by far the most common choice, based on the WALS data, the difference in deixis is highlighted. When option (b) is chosen, the similarity in perception is marked and the speaker fulfills the same deictic role, recipient of perception.

When the two types are marked differently, typically (but not necessarily) the quotative will be derived from a 'say'-verb, and the auditory evidential from a 'hear' verb. The path from a 'say'-verb to a quotative has been extensively documented in many languages. An example from Ocotepec Mixtec (Alexander 1988: 190) is shown in (18), in which the Quotative particle *chi* is derived from the verb *káchi* 'to say' (there is no auditory evidential in this language).

(18)   *uu vwélta n-sahá de   chi.*
       two time   COM-do he.RES QUOT
       'He did it two times, they say.'

Auditory evidentials appear to be routinely derived from the verb 'to hear'. Examples (19) are from Koasati (Muskogean; Kimball 1991: 206–7) where the Auditory evidential –*ha(wa)* comes from the verb *há:lon* 'to hear'.

(19)   a.   *nipó-k   aksóhka-ha*
            meat-SUBJ char-AUD
            'It sounds like the meat is charring.'

b. *ihá:ni-k   atawohlí:ci-ha*
earth-SUBJ reverberate-AUD
'One can hear the earth reverberating.'

What is of interest here is the fact that there are languages in which there is a formal correspondence between the auditory evidential and the quotative and with full grammaticalization. Two such languages are Nenets (Perrot 1996) and Sanuma (Borgman (1990), see also section 4 above). In Nenets, a Samoyedic language of Russia, the morpheme *–wonon* (and its allomorphs, such as *-won*) are used for both types of evidentiality. This morpheme is a suffix, placed after the verb root, but before the person suffix. Examples are:

(20) a. *pydoʔ to-won-doʔ*
they come-QUOT-3PL
'They are coming, it is said.'
b. *pyda laxanā-wonon-da*
he   speak-AUD-3SG
'He is speaking, it is perceived.'   (Perrot 1996: 162)

In Sanuma the particle *ha* (or *a*) denotes both auditory evidence and quotative evidence. It is a preverbal particle. Its origin is unknown, although it may come from the verb 'to hear', which is *hini*. Some examples are shown in (21). Examples (a) and (b) show the Auditory evidential reading, example (c) and (d) the Quotative:

(21) a. *wa namo hu a-so-lö   noai   ha,   au   nao   a   wani*
2SG hunt go leave-FOC-DIR INDEF.PERF upon your mother 3SG DEPR
ha   huama hisa   hāto-ma
AUD converse at.home secret-COM
'After you had gone out hunting, your mother conversed secretly at home.' (p. 92)
b. *. . .ti   a   thama-ti ku-a   kölö-a*
wood AUD do-CONT be-DUR LOC-DUR
'. . .he is down there making firewood.' (p. 99)
c. *kolo   hamö ai   töpö a   wele-o-ki*
bottom LOC   other 3PL QUOT go.downriver-PUNCT.ITER-FOC
'Others are going downriver.' (p. 178)
d. *ĩ   a   sai   ha töpö a   ku-ki*
REL 3SG house at 3PL QUOT be-FOC
'They stay at that house.' (p. 187)

In neither Nenets or Sanuma does there appear to be a formal difference between the two readings. Borgman (1990: 212) states that sometimes the Sanuma examples are ambiguous between the two readings. Indeed, out of context (and none is provided), it is not possible to determine whether the speaker in sentence (21a) above learned about the action directly or indirectly. Nevertheless, from the examples in the Sanuma grammar it appears to be the case that the auditory interpretation occurs almost always with verbs of speaking, such as *ku* 'say', *kateha* 'discuss', or at least denoting situations describing activities that make noise (as in (21b) above). In its quotative interpretation, the particle *ha* occurs with all types of verbs. The same is true for the Nenets examples, but due to the limited amount of data no fixed conclusions can be drawn from that.

In both languages it would seem that the quotative reading is much rarer than the auditory evidential reading. Perrot (1996: 163) makes an explicit statement to that effect regarding Nenets, and out of the 22 Sanuma examples with the particle *ha* in Borgman (1990) only four have a quotative interpretation. This particle only occurs twice in the accompanying texts, both cases with the auditory evidential reading. The text in which they occur is a mythical text, a genre in which normally we would expect quotatives to occur, but this is not the case. One of the examples is shown in (22):

(22) ĩ   a   hekula pö ama pö a   to-pa   kölö
      REL LOC spirit   PL song PL AUD join-EXT LOC
      'It is down there that the songs of the *hekula* spirit are clear.'
      (p. 238–239), [TEXT 1, line 29 (myth)]

The facts of Nenets and Sanuma are hard to reconcile with a modal account of evidentiality, given that auditory evidence and quotative are usually analyzed as having different levels of confidence (see e.g., Palmer 2001). In a deictic-based theory it is easy to account for these data if one recognizes that what is encoded here is the deictic relation between the speaker and the perception, which is the same in both cases.

Thus, quotatives typically mark distance between speaker and action. As is the case with inferentials, they mark that the speaker was not present at the space and time of the action. When inferentiality and hearsay evidentiality are encoded by one and the same morpheme to form a general indirect evidential, it is this aspect that is highlighted. But as we have seen in the discussion of Sanuma and Nenets, there are other deictic relations that can be encoded, such as the relation between perception and speaker.

7. Spatial deixis

In this section it will be shown that spatial deictic elements, commonly referred to as demonstratives, are organized remarkably like evidential systems. While a full discussion is beyond the scope of the present paper, the demonstrative systems discussed here do point further to a close link between deixis and evidentiality.

Spatial deictic forms can be either based on fixed reference points (e.g., the cardinal points like *north*, or geographical features, such as *upstream*, *inland*) or on points relative to the speaker and/or hearer. A full deictic system is usually made up of a combination of these two possibilities. It is the latter, the location of objects relative to the speaker, which interests us here due to its obvious connections to evidentiality.

In many languages, a visible/invisible distinction is made in their demonstrative system. This happens for instance in Native American languages of the Pacific Northwest, perhaps most notably in the Salishan languages, in certain Australian languages and the Oceanic languages of New Caledonia. In (23) the definite demonstrative system of Yidin[y] for humans and inanimates (Dixon 1977:181) is shown. Such systems can be mapped without problem onto the direct/indirect evidential distinction.

(23)   Human   Inanimate
'this'   yiɲdu-   yiŋgu-
'that'   ɲuɲdu-   ɲuŋgu-
'far, invisible' yuɲdu-   yuŋgu-

Such deictic elements can extend their meaning to temporal relations as well. In Ouvea Iaai (New Caledonia; Ozanne-Riviere 1997:96, citing Ozanne-Riviere 1976), some spatial deictic elements denote temporal deixis as well, as shown in (24) below. These data reinforce the link between the various deictic categories, including evidentiality.

(24)   Spatial   Temporal
-ang   near speaker   near in time
-e   near hearer   near in time
-lee   far from speaker and hearer   distant future
-jii[8] down; toward sea   past; introduces past relative clauses

In example (25) from Cèmuhî (New Caledonia; Ozanne-Rivierre 1997:97; Rivierre 1980:156–7), the parameter of (in)visibility plays a role in spatial and temporal deixis.

(25)   Spatial   Temporal
cè   near speaker   present tense
ne   distant, visible
naa   distant, invisible future tense

Although they appear to be rare, there are languages that, in addition to a distinction in (in)visibility, make an auditory distinction in their spatial deictic system as well. Already mentioned in section 5 is the case of the Mihilakawna dialect of Southern Pomo (Pomoan, Hokan; Oswalt 1986:37), where the demonstrative no- 'that' is used for objects that are invisible but audible. (Pomoan languages in general make distinctions between visible and invisible objects). Another such language is Nyêlâyu (New Caledonian; Ozanne-Rivierre 1997:97–8), which is related to Cèmuhî. Nyêlâyu has four deictic suffixes, as shown in (26).

(26) -*ija*   near speaker
     -*êlâ*   distant, visible
     -*ili*   distant, invisible, audible
     -*imi*   absent, known

The use of audible demonstratives corresponds closely to the use of auditory evidentials. In Nyêlâyu, the audible demonstrative can only be used if there is no visual contact between speaker and the object. Obviously, the object must be capable of making a sound, hence the acceptability of *wang-ili* 'boat-AUD', but the ungrammaticality of *doo-ili 'pot-AUD' (Ozanne-Rivierre 1997: 98). This is identical to the usage of auditory evidentials, which are used when there is no visual evidence available, but a visual evidential will be used when such evidence is present.

Given the similarity between spatial demonstrative systems and evidentials, it should come as no surprise that there are languages that use the same morpheme for an evidential and a demonstrative meaning. Such a language is Quileute (Wakashan; Andrade 1933: 204–205), which makes a distinction between visible and invisible objects and between known and unknown (to speaker) objects. It does so in the pronominal as well as the demonstrative system. There is a formal identity between Quotative and the 3SG(/PL).FEM pronoun, as analyzed by Andrade. An example is shown in (27):

(27) a. *hé-tkul-i-**ku**-l-ač*
        '**It is said** that he is sick'
     b. *hé-tkul-i-**ku**-ku*
        '**It is said** that she (invisible, unknown) is sick'.

The data in this section show that there is a conceptual link between demonstrative systems and evidential systems. This conceptual link is made explicit in languages like Quileute.

8. Conclusions

In the previous sections the relationship between various evidential categories and deixis was discussed. Based on this discussion I propose to add evidentiality to the category deixis as an example of *propositional deixis*. An evidential grounds an action or event with respect to the speaker, just as a demonstrative grounds an object with respect to the speaker. In other words, the relation between a proposition and an evidential is analogous to the relation between a noun (phrase) and a demonstrative.

Evidentiality has been considered to be a modal category, but based on the data discussed here such a view cannot be maintained. I do not wish to deny any relation between evidentiality and (epistemic) modality, but such a relation is secondary at best. It should not be thought that epistemic modality is part of the basic meaning of evidentiality but it can be added as a pragmatic feature.

Since I have argued for an analogy between demonstratives and evidentials, let us look at each category in modal view. It is fairly common to regard propositions with a quotative as less reliable than those with a direct evidential. To the best of my knowledge, a noun phrase containing an 'invisible, unknown' demonstrative have never been analyzed that way. Objects out of view have never been analyzed as being "less likely to be in existence" than objects in plain view. That does not necessarily mean that this is not a possible analysis in a given language, but modality is not considered to be part of the basic meaning of demonstratives. For that reason it is equally premature to talk of epistemic modality as being the basic meaning of evidentiality. Viewing the world in terms of relative truth may very well be a Western way of life. It would be wrong to assume a priori that other cultures share this outlook.

Abbreviations

AUD	auditive	LOC	locative
AUX	auxiliary	MASC	masculine
CLASS	classifier	NEG	negation
COM	completive	OBJ	object
CONT	continuative	OYHER	1 / 2, 3PL
DEM	demonstrative	PAST	past tense
DEPR	depreciatory	PERF	perfect
DIR	direction	PL	plural
DIRECT	direct evidential	PRES	present tense
DIST.PAST	distant past	PST1	first past
DUR	durative	PST2	second past
EXT	extent of action	PUNCT	punctiliar
FEM	feminine	QUOT	quotative
FOC	focus	REL	relativizer
IMM.PAST	immediate past	RES	resultative
INDEF	indefinite	SG	singular
INDIR	indirect evidential	SS	same subject
INESS	inessive	SUBJ	subject
INFER	inferential	TEMP	temporal
INST	instrumental	VIS	visual
ITER	iterative	WIT	witnessed

Notes

1. I am very grateful for the audience at the Boulder symposium for helpful remarks. I am especially grateful to Janet Barnes, for discussing Tuyuca data, to Marja Leinonen, for discussing the Komi data, to Marianne Mithun, for discussing Pomo data, as well as general helpful hints, and to Zygmunt Frajzyngier and David Rood for general comments. None of them is in any way responsible for the conclusions I have drawn here.

2. The material for this study is drawn from the World Atlas of Language Structures project (Haspelmath et al., forthcoming).

3. In the second edition, Palmer (2001), evidentiality and epistemic modality share equal billing under the heading of *propositional* modality, and some cases are discussed in which the link between evidentiality and epistemic modality is not obvious (pp. 29–31). Nevertheless, Palmer remains committed to the view that evidentiality is a modal category.

4. This analysis is a synchronic one. In no way is it implied here that evidentials cannot turn into epistemic modals (or, indeed, vice versa, as has happened in Dutch). The pragmatic forces can certainly become conventionalized. This, however, is a separate issue and has no bearing on the present discussion.

5. Frawley (1992:387 and *passim*) subsumes evidentiality under epistemic modality (similar to Palmer 1986) and gives a deictic account, based on the relative distance of the epistemic modal to the actual world. This *epistemic* deixis is not what is meant in the present paper. Rather, I propose a conventional definition of deixis for evidentiality, namely relative distance to the speaker.

6. This use is very similar to the use of English *one* in *One reads books* for *I read books*.

7. This section is based on De Haan 2001.

8. This is an example of a deictic morpheme based on geography, not on the speaker.

References

Alexander, R. M. 1988. "A Syntactic Study of Ocotepec Mixtec". In *Studies in the Syntax of Mixtecan languages, Vol. 1*, C. H. Bradley and B. E. Hollenbach (eds), 151–304. Dallas: Summer Institute of Linguistics.

Anderson, S. R. and Keenan, E. L. 1985. "Deixis". In *Language typology and Syntactic description Vol. III, Grammatical categories and the lexicon*, Timothy Shopen (ed.), 259–308. Cambridge: Cambridge University Press.

Andrade, M. J. 1933. "Quileute". In *Handbook of American Indian languages, Vol. 3*, Franz Boas (ed.), 149–292. Washington: Smithsonian Press.

Baker, R. W. 1983. "Komi Zyryan's second past tense". *Finno-Ugrische Forschungen* Band XIX, Heft 1–3, 69–81.

Barnes, J. 1984. "Evidentials in the Tuyuca Verb". *International Journal of American Linguistics* 50, 255–271.

Borgman, D. M. 1990. "Sanuma". In *Handbook of Amazonian Languages, Vol. 2*, D. C. Derbyshire and G. K. Pullum (eds), 15–248. Berlin: Mouton De Gruyter.

De Haan, F. 1999. "Evidentiality and Epistemic Modality: Setting Boundaries". *Southwest Journal of Linguistics* 18, 83–101.

De Haan, F. 2001. "The Place of Inference within the Evidential System". *International Journal of American Linguistics* 67, 193–219.

De Haan, F. 2003. "Visual evidentiality and its origins". Ms. University of Arizona.

Dik, S. and Hengeveld, K. 1991. "The hierarchical structure of the clause and the typology of perception verb complements". *Linguistics* 29, 231–259.

Dixon, R. M. W. 1977. *A grammar of Yidiny*. Cambridge: Cambridge University Press.

Frajzyngier, Z. 1991. "The de dicto domain in language". In *Approaches to Grammaticalization*,

Vol. I, E. Traugott and B. Heine (eds), 219–251. Amsterdam: Benjamins.

Frajzyngier, Z. 1995. "A Functional theory of Complementizers". In *Modality in Grammar and Discourse*, J. L. Bybee and S. Fleischman (eds), 473–502. Amsterdam:: Benjamins.

Frawley, W. 1992. *Linguistic semantics*. Hillsdale, NJ: Lawrence Erlbaum.

Friedman, V. A. 1986. "Evidentiality in the Balkans: Bulgarian, Macedonian, and Albanian". In *Evidentiality: the linguistic coding of epistemology*, W. Chafe and J. Nichols (eds), 168–187. Norwood: Ablex.

Friedman, V. A. 1999. "Proverbial Evidentiality: On the Gnomic Uses of the Category of Status in Languages of the Balkans and the Caucasus". *Mediterranean Language Review* 11, 135–155.

Haspelmath, M., Dryer, M., Comrie, B. and Gil, D. Forthcoming. *World Atlas of Language Structures*. Oxford: Oxford University Press.

Kimball, G. D. 1991. *Koasati Grammar*. Lincoln: University of Nebraska Press.

Leinonen, M. 2000. "Evidentiality in Komi Zyryan". In *Evidentials: Turkic, Iranian, and neighboring languages*, Lars Johanson; Bo Utas (eds), 419–440. Berlin: Mouton de Gruyter.

Leinonen, M. and Vilkuna, M. 2000. "Past tenses in Permic languages". In *Tense and Aspect in the Languages of Europe*, Ö. Dahl (ed), 495–514. Berlin: Mouton De Gruyter.

Metzger, R. G. 1981. *Gramática popular del Carapana*. Bogotá: Instituto Lingüístico de Verano.

Oswalt, R. L. 1986. "The evidential system of Kashaya". In *Evidentiality: the linguistic coding of epistemology*, W. Chafe and J. Nichols (eds), 29–45. Norwood: Ablex.

Ozanne-Rivierre, F. 1997. "Spatial references in New Caledonian languages". In *Referring to Space, Studies in Austronesian and Papuan Langauges*, G. Senft (ed), 83–100. Oxford: Oxford University Press.

Palmer, F. R. 1986. *Mood and Modality*. Cambridge: Cambridge University Press.

Palmer, F. R. 2001. *Mood and Modality, second edition*. Cambridge: Cambridge University Press.

Perrot, J. 1996. "Un Médiatif Ouralien: L' auditif en Samoyède Nenets". In *L' Énonciation Médiatisée*, Z. Guentchéva (ed), 157–68. Louvain-Paris: Peeters.

Van der Auwera, J. and Plungian, V. 1998. "Modality's semantic map". *Linguistic Typology* 2, 79–124.

Watahomigie, L. J., Bender, J. and Yamamoto, A. Y. 1982. *Hualapai Reference Grammar*. Los Angeles: American Indian Studies Center, UCLA.

West, B.. 1980. *Gramática Popular del Tucano*. Bogotá: Instituto Lingüístico de Verano.

Whistler, K. W. 1986. "Evidentials in Patwin". In *Evidentiality: the linguistic coding of epistemology*, W. Chafe and J. Nichols (eds), 60–74. Norwood: Ablex.

Willett, T. L. 1988. "A Cross-Linguistic Survey of the Grammaticization of Evidentiality". *Studies in Language* 12, 51–97.

CHAPTER 18

Distinguishing between referential and grammatical function in morphological typology

Edward J. Vajda
Western Washington University

This chapter argues that the contrast between derivation and inflection, which continues to inform most typological approaches to word formation, is useful for describing only a few of the most basic cross-linguistic differences in morphology. I begin by pointing out several gaps and inconsistencies in the traditional division of languages into analytic, synthetic, and polysynthetic types. Next I propose replacing (or at least augmenting) the morphology-specific categories of derivation and inflection with a system of functions based on a combination of two well-accepted linguistic contrasts that apply beyond morphology as well. The first involves the distinction between the three types of linguistic expression: referential (denotative, or real-world semantic) meaning, on the one hand, and two grammatical subsystems, on the other: discourse functions[1] and phrase structure rules. The second contrast is the structural difference between head and modifier, which has been applied semantically and in phrase structure, but here is also applied to the discourse layer of language. The resultant model, which I call 'Holistic Grammar', permits a more fine-grained approach to morphological typology, and also better integrates morphology with the syntactic and lexical components of language by avoiding primary dependence on notions unique to word formation. Next I demonstrate how Holistic Grammar is useful for comparing languages with rich affixal morphologies, the so-called polysynthetic languages, and propose a new way to compare verb agreement strategies across languages. Finally, I apply this scheme to the verb morphology of Ket, an endangered isolate spoken in Central Siberia that has hitherto defied typological characterization, comparing Ket subject/object agreement with that of better-known polypersonal languages.

1. Some gaps and inconsistencies in the traditional system

Linguists became keenly interested in typology long before they developed sophisticated theories of morphology. Ever since the days of Wilhelm von Humboldt, morphologists have categorized languages into isolating, analytic, synthetic and polysynthetic types. Subsequent advances in linguistic theory, including those offered by Edward Sapir (1921),[2] have contributed surprisingly little toward providing a more rigorous application of these traditional categorizations. In section 2, I will argue that this impasse developed because the functional dichotomy between derivation and inflection which informs this system is too imprecise to be of real value in understanding many key differences across languages in how lexemes or their grammatical forms are constructed. Even the few generalizations that can be elucidated by using these notions as morphological primitives — for instance the seeming continuum "isolating-analytical-synthetic-polysynthetic" — prove upon closer inspection to contain notable gaps and inconsistencies. To give the traditional typology its due, inflection is useful from both a descriptive and explanatory viewpoint in that languages with little or no word-internal morphosyntax (analytic languages) tend to use word order to express phrasal head/modifier relationships, while synthetic languages are free to use word order for pragmatic purposes. Also, languages weak in both derivation and inflection (isolating languages) tend to be correspondingly richer in productive patterns of conversion or root compounding. But the traditional typology is incomplete even by its own internal measure in lacking a designation for a language that is rich in inflection but poor in derivation. I propose the term 'conglomerating' for such languages, which rounds out the old derivation/inflection-based morphology as follows:

(1)   A basic morphological typology using derivation and inflection as functional primitives
Isolating: poor in both derivational and inflection affixes (Chinese)
Analytic: rich in derivation, poor in inflection (English)
Conglomerating: poor in derivational affixes but rich in inflection (Ket)
Synthetic: rich in both derivation and inflection (Latin, Russian)

As indicated in Table 1, one example of a conglomerating language is Ket, an isolate spoken by about 300 people near the Yenisei River in Central Siberia. I will return to Ket morphology in section 4.

What, then, is a polysynthetic language? On the face of it, this term would appear to be available to describe any particularly rich florescence of affixal morphology. However, there are two problems with how the word is actually used which limit its efficacy. First, a language is normally called "polysynthetic" only if it is richly synthetic in a way that differs fundamentally from the type of synthesis found in Indo-European languages. As is known, most Indo-European languages use suffixes to express grammatical categories, with a propensity for multiple exponence in a single suffix. Observe, for instance, the following Lithuanian words:

(2)   Lithuanian nouns
rank-a   *rank-omis*
hand-INSTR.SG   hand-INSTR.PL
'with the hand'   'with the hands'

Lithuanian verbs (Ambrazas 1997)
dirb-si-me   *dirb-davo-me*
work-FUT-1PL   work-PAST.FREQ-1PL
'we will work'   'we had been working'

Lithuanian nouns allow only one desinence, which normally expresses two distinct functions (case and number); verbs sometimes allow two desinences, but one of these likewise shows multiple exponence (person + number agreement). Now consider some examples from Hungarian (3) and Qazaq (4) — two richly synthetic languages that, perhaps unfairly, are *not* generally regarded as polysynthetic:

(3) Hungarian noun suffixation (Törkenczy 1997:62)
    kez-ek-vel
    hand-PLURAL-INSTRUMENTAL.CASE
    'with hands'
    kalap-jai-m-é-i-t
    hat-PLURAL-1SG.POSSESSOR-EXTERNAL. POSSESSUM-PLURAL-ACC
    'the ones that belong to my hats (used as a direct object)'

(4) Qazaq (Turkic) verb suffixation (Kozhakhmetova 1989)
    žas-ba-baq-siŋ-dar
    write-NEGATIVE-FUTURE-2SJ-PLURAL
    'you all will not write'

Hungarian and Qazaq are clearly richer in grammatical categories than even the most synthetic of Indo-European languages. Yet they tend to express many of the same morphosyntactic categories. In fact, Hungarian and Turkic affixal grammar differs from Indo-European mainly in the general absence of multiple exponence. Linguists usually avoid calling Turkic and Uralic languages 'polysynthetic', apparently because their type of synthesis — aside from the lack of multiple exponence and a concomitant penchant for agglutination — is little more than an elaboration of the same type of synthesis common to Indo-European.

Bantu and Athabaskan languages, by contrast, *are* considered polysynthetic, at least by virtue of their complicated verb morphologies. Functionally, verb forms in these families differ most obviously from Indo-European in that they cross-reference the object as well as the subject.[3] Even more striking, however, is the fact that they intersperse their grammatical morphemes among the verb's referential morphemes, rather than keeping them together in a single, segregated morphosyntactic zone:

(5) Navajo (Faltz 1998:324)
    ch'í-ná-náá-nish-d-zid
    out-revert-again-PAST.1SG.SJ-INTRANSITIVE-wake
    'I woke up again'

(6)   Swahili (Dimmendaal 2000:180)
     wa-li-ni-it-i-a-ni
     3PL.ANIM.SJ-PAST-1SG.ANIM.OBJ-call-APPLICATIVE-FINITE.VERB-what
     'What were they calling me for?'

The verb in these languages differs radically from the other parts of speech, which do tend to have discrete, word-like stems onto which grammatical affixes are concatenated. Rather than a word-like form, a verb stem in Swahili or Navajo involves a positional formula that often contains grammatical affixes interspersed between two or more disjunct referential morphemes. This formula, as well as the disjunct positioning of the referential morphemes, is probably residue left from a time when at least some of the verb's referential components were expressed as separate words sporting their own grammatical affixes. Ultimately, the verb stem itself inherited this phrase-like morpheme formula when the process of univerbation stranded referential morphemes among their own grammatical affixes. This sort of lexicalized position class is entirely lacking in concatenative languages such as Turkic or Hungarian, whose stems resemble Indo-European. Not surprisingly, languages that use such formulaic stems in at least one part of speech (most commonly the verb) are typically regarded as polysynthetic.

"Indo-Eurocentrism" is by far the lesser of the two problems affecting the typological label 'polysynthetic', however. More serious is the fact that richly synthetic languages that do get labeled 'polysynthetic' differ among themselves in ways that elude clear characterization in any typological scheme using derivation and inflection as descriptive primitives.

For example, Eskimoan and Wakashan languages are routinely (and, by any measure, justifiably) regarded as polysynthetic, yet both differ radically from Bantu and Athabaskan. These families are characterized by concatenations of suffixes expressing a rich array of referential functions. Neither contains anything resembling the position-class based stems of Athabaskan or Bantu. Instead, polysynthesis in Eskimoan and Wakashan involves long agglutinations of affixes expressing meanings that tends to coincide with free content words in other languages:

(7)   Central Siberian Yupik polysynthesis (de Reuse 1992:164)
     yughagh-vig-ghllag-nge-yug-tugh-t
     pray-place to do (preceding verb)-big (preceding noun)-acquire (preceding noun)-want.to (do preceding verb)-INDICATIVE-3PL.SJ
     'they want to acquire a big church'

(8)   Nootka polysynthesis (Sapir 1921:133–134)
     inikw-ihl'-minih-'is-ita-a
     fire-in.house-several-small-former-VERB
     'several small fires were burning in the house'

Some Eskimoan affixes can even be mildly recursive (de Reuse 1992), another morphological feature that is wholly alien to the Bantu/Athabaskan type of polysynthesis.

Observe that a key difference exists between the otherwise similar Yupik (Eskimoan) and Nootka (Wakashan) types of polysynthesis illustrated by examples (7) and (8) — a difference that cannot be captured by the traditional derivation/inflection dichotomy. Each of the Yupik base suffixes specifies a particular form class category (noun-creating or verb-creating) together with its specific referential content. For instance, the suffix -*vig*- not only conveys the semantic-head notion of 'place,' it also converts a verb base into a noun meaning 'place to do the event specified by the preceding stem.' This fusion of real-world referential content with form-class specification is typical of base affixes in all Eskimoan languages. In Nootka, by contrast, form class is specified by a separate suffix that is otherwise functionally vacant, while the semantically rich affixes preceding it are intrinsically neither verbal nor nominal. A hallmark of Wakashan polysynthesis, in contrast to Eskimoan, is the form-class neutral status of most referential affixes.

These and other key typological differences cannot receive an adequate assessment using the traditional morphological notion of derivation — a category that conflates form-class creation together with referential aspects of the stem. The following sections argue that derivation and inflection are in fact epiphenomena of two more basic, non-morphology specific features of language. These features do permit typological differences such as those evident among Eskimoan, Wakashan, and other richly synthetic languages to be described clearly and elegantly.

2. The problem with derivation and inflection, and a new system of typological primitives

Functionalist studies of morphology (for example, Bybee 1985) accurately point out that derivation and inflection represent a continuum rather than a discrete functional dichotomy. But this truth has never been squared with the sharp dichotomy that does exist between syntactic patterns (defined as rules capable of expressing meaning when combined with lexemes but lacking intrinsic referential meaning of their own) and content words (minimal free forms with their own referential meanings). It is common to regard derivational affixes as helping to form new lexemes and thus approximating content words in function, while inflections approximate function words or syntactic rules. If inflection is the syntactic portion of morphology, and derivation the referential portion (ignoring for the moment the issue of form-class marking discussed above), then why is the distinction between them so fuzzy? Why does it fail to reflect the sharp difference between phrase structure and referential meaning prevalent in the syntactic component of language? To elaborate upon a well-known Chomskyan metaphor, why do "colorless green ideas" behave one way in syntax, but quite another in the morphology as it is conceived of in terms of a contrast between "lexical derivation" and "syntactic inflection"?

A solution to this conundrum accrues from two observations. One problem, already discussed above, is that the notion of lexeme creation, or derivation, confounds two profoundly different linguistic functions. The first is the expression of referential meaning; the second is form-class (part-of-speech) marking, which clearly belongs to the grammatical rather than referential layer of language even though it is routinely subsumed under "lexical derivation." For example, the English words: *dark* (adjective) vs. *darkness*, and *darken* vs. *darkening* (noun) are synonymous referentially, but differ sharply in form class. Recall that in Nootka, referential expression and form-class marking are kept morphologically discrete, while in Yupik, as in English and many other languages, they are often fused in a single affix. Subsuming both functions together under "derivation" obscures this typological distinction.

The second observation that sheds light on the inadequacy of the traditional system is that it never takes into account the structural difference between head and modifier. This distinction can be applied to each of three long-recognized functional layers of linguistic expression to establish a new system of typological primitives. These three functions are: (1) referential (denotative meaning, or semantic content that exists independent of the speech act itself), (2) discourse (connotative, stylistic, pragmatic, or any grammatical feature that mechanically references the speech situation or its participants), and (3) phrasal (grammatical features unrelated to the speech situation itself). Note that the application of the head/modifier distinction to the discourse layer of language is innovative in this analysis.

A typology that replaces the fuzzy notions of derivation and inflection with the clear-cut dichotomies between referential, discourse, and phrasal function — subdivided into their possible head vs. modifier roles — yields the scheme shown in (9). It is important to note that the resultant categories represent abstract functions rather than morphemes or other concrete units of linguistic expression. A given lexeme, morphological operation, or syntactic pattern may express only one of these categories; or it may express two or more of them simultaneously (see (9)). This model of language is "holistic" in the sense that it employs a unified set of functional parameters to describe morphological operations and their relation both to lexemes as well as to syntactic rules. Yet morphology remains a distinct component in Holistic Grammar that cannot be reduced to the mere interaction of lexicon and syntax. The (partial) autonomy of morphology accrues from the process-oriented association between item and arrangement in morphological operations. Both syntactic rules and morphological operations represent processes; but the patterns of phrase structure have no meaning apart from the lexemes or morphological categories that provide their input[4]. A morphological operation, on the other hand, is intrinsically bound up with a specific meaning (either denotative, connotative or phrasal), even when it involves no unit of form apart from the process of change being applied to its base input. One example of a morpheme-less morphological operation would be the rule of subtraction that formally differentiates masculine and feminine adjectives in French by deleting the word-final consonant of the former. Another would be reduplication, which produces a meaningful change in the base via a rule that adds no independently existing morpheme form as part

(9) The Holistic Grammar Model

	Lexicon (l)	Morphology (m)	Head-modifying (m)	Syntax (s)
	(Item only)	(Item + arrangement) Head-creating (h)		(Arrangement only)
Referential function (r)	Lr lexical stems, content words, idiomatic phrases, modifying function words	Mrh basic referential meaning[a] (includes any idiomatic morpheme combination)	Mrm referent modification without idiomatic meaning (plural, aspect, valence, size, shape, intensity, etc.)	Sr subcategorization rules (referential constraints on phrase structure)
Discourse function (d)	Ld exclamations shifter words, discourse particles (deixis, style, pragmatics) sentential adverbs	Mdh discourse creation[b] subsumes any style-marking devices	Mdm discourse modification (all deictic categories: vocative case, tense, mood, person, evidential, viewpoint)	Sd functional sentence perspective, transformational rules
Phrasal function (p)	Lp non-discourse function words	Mph form-class marking (morphological modifications that explicate marking of syntactic phrase structure form classes)	Mpm non-form class changing (agreement; most noun cases)	Sp phrase structure rules (non-discourse syntax)

[a] In the scheme proposed, combinations involving two or more roots are either free syntactic phrases (created by the phrase structure rules, an Sp function) or new lexemes (idiomatic phrasal compounds, an Mrh function). Stylistic (connotative) differences in meaning are regarded as head properties in the discourse layer of the model. Just as every word capable of expressing phrase-related functions must belong to a particular form class and every content word must express a basic referent, every morpholexical process must belong to a particular stylistic subsystem of the language (be it the so-called "neutral style" or some more narrowly defined discourse sphere).

[b] Stylistic (connotative) differences in meaning are regarded as head properties in the discourse layer of the model.

of the process. Morphology might best be defined as the set of all processes in language that are limited to a particular meaning or set of meanings[5]. Syntactic rules, on the other hand, help express meaning yet lack any specific semantic content of their own. And phonological rules neither have meaning nor create meaning (apart from contributing to stylistic contrast), yet still form part of the functional system of language. Finally, the lexicon deals with meaningful units apart from the processes that create them.

As shown in (9), Holistic Grammar makes the claim that six distinct functions are fundamental to all morphological expression: 1) referent creation (abbreviated Mrh), 2) referent modification (Mrm), 3) discourse creation, or style marking (Mdh); 4) discourse (deictic) modification (Mdm); 5) form-class creation (Mph); and 6) phrasal modification (Mpm). All morphological processes (affixation, compounding, etc.) fulfill at least one of these functions by definition, and may express two or more of them simultaneously. Which among these six functions tend to get expressed through multiple exponence by a single morpheme or morphological operation is in itself an important typological parameter. Languages can thus be categorized both in terms of: 1) which functions tend to be expressed affixally (or by compounding, transfixation, subtraction, or another formal type of morphological operation), as well as in terms of 2) which functions share a fused morphological expression. Finally, some morphological patterns follow universal tendencies; others are more language-specific; and still others are linked to one another by various types of structural implicature.

How do the traditional categories of derivation and inflection actually pair up with the six morphological functions of the new model? Holistic Grammar redefines most derivational affixes as expressing either referent creation (Mrh) or form class creation (Mph) or both. It redefines most inflectional affixes as expressing either phrasal modifying (Mpm) or discourse modifying (Mdm) function or both. Referential modifying (Mrm) and style creating (Mdh) affixes are the least easily characterized in terms of derivation and inflection. Style creating features may attach to the lexeme, the phrase, the entire sentence, or be separate from lexical and phrasal systems altogether. Consequently, sometimes they seem inflectional, sometimes derivational. And sometimes they seem unlike either process (as, for example, in "un-friggin-believable").

The affixes that cause the most ambiguity for the old derivation/inflection split are those that express a referent modifying (Mrm) function. From the perspective of their intrinsic semantic content, these morphemes comprise a single, clear-cut functional category. But they differ with regard to the factor of their additional involvement in the grammar (defined here as the set of structural patterns that involve lexemes but extend beyond the individual lexeme). The morphemes used for deictic and phrasal modification are grammatical by definition, since their presence follows mechanically from the use of lexemes in specific discourse contexts or phrase structures. But referential categories such as number, gender, size, shape, animacy, intensity, and so forth, are real-world semantic features that need not, in and of themselves, play an extra-lexical role in the language system. Which referent modifying categories play an additional, grammatical role is an important typological parameter that depends on the language in question. Here, the notions of 'inflection' and 'derivation' are useful only up to a point. For example, the English plural suffix -*s*, like the category of noun plural in all languages, is referent modifying (Mrm), but it is also involved in subject–verb agreement; and its regularity and productivity make it especially "inflection-like." The Mandarin Chinese plural suffix -*men* plays no such role (in this way, it more resembles English referent modifying suffixes such as -*let* in 'cloudlet'). Plurality is expressed in formal fusion with grammatical categories such as case or agreement only in select families, such as Indo-European, whereas number and case are usually kept separate in families such as Turkic or Uralic. Diminutive and augmentative affixes in Indo-European languages do not interact with grammatical categories such as declension and gender. In Bantu, however, these categories are bound up with grammatical agreement. Other richly synthetic languages implicate none of their referent modifying categories in their grammatical system. Nootka provides an excellent example in having an unusually large array of referent modifying morphemes (plurality, size, shape, and various spatial details, such as being located on an island, near a river, etc.). All of these semantic categories remain aloof from the language's non-referential layers of function, yet appear very "inflection-esque" in terms of their productivity and regularity. Finally, Russian verb aspects play an obvious grammatical (discourse-related) role, yet their morphological expression is not generally predictable from a formal point of view. It is therefore practically meaningless to assign the term "derivational" or "inflectional" to affixes such as those that mark aspect in Russian, since their "derivation-like" formal irregularity stands at odds with the "inflection-like" regularity of their grammatical functions. The six categories of Holistic Morphology offer the typologist a more precise descriptive apparatus to differentiate between the inherent meaning of referent modifying morphemes, on the one hand, and their involvement (or lack of involvement) in expressing various non-referential functions, on the other.

To give a very preliminary example of how Holistic Grammar can be mustered to characterize a single language's overall morphological type, let us take a cursory look at affixation in English:

(10)   A holistic description of English morphology with emphasis on affixation

> **Mrh. Referent creation** is defined as the expression of basic denotative, real-world meaning, regardless of the mechanics of the speech situation, and separated from metagrammatical categories such as form class. In English, this basic, content-word function is frequently expressed by a bare root or idiomatic root compound. However, referent creating (Mrh) affixes are also fairly well represented and tend to be Stratum I affixes (in other words, they are integrated with their base in a single phonological word): *alcohol-ic*, *in-just-ice*, *re-ceive*, *com-pare*, *de-fy*, *in-ept*, etc.

(Prosodic features often serve to help distinguish morphological functions, but they need not be completely isomorphous with any particular function.) Like Eskimoan, English is rather rich in Mrh affixes that simultaneously mark form class (Mph function): *damn-ation, teach-er, green-ness, work-able*, etc. Referent creating affixes in English tend not to agglutinate unless they also alter the stem's form class: *act-iv(e)-ity*.

Mrm. Referent modification is defined as the explication of some aspect of denotative meaning intrinsically associated with the basic referent (inalienable or inherent notions such as size, shape, plurality, intensity, repetition), without the creation of any idiomatic or metaphorical meaning (affixes that create such meanings belong to the previous category, Mrh, since they express new referents). Referent modification in English is often achieved simply by adding lexical modifiers during phrase creation rather than by a morphological operation. Referent modifying (Mrm) prefixes in English usually belong to Stratum II (in other words, the do not form a single phonological word with their base): *re-write, de-louse, co-author, **non**-compliance*. Some Mrm affixes are mildly recursive: *re-re-write, **anti-anti**-war, **great-great**-grandmother*. This type of morphological recursion (where the same affixal form is repeated without intervening morphemes) appears to be unique to this functional category across languages, though most Mrm affixes are not recursive. English Mrm suffixes belong to Stratum I: *poet-ess, green-ish, cloud-let, gos-**ling***. English is somewhat poorer in the affixal expression of referent modifying categories, and affixes expressing them tend not to agglutinate (unlike Nootka) except in the cases of prefixal recursion mentioned above, though plural suffixes may follow another Mrm suffix: *tigr-ess-es, cloud-let-s*. (The traditional category of 'inflection' is useful when applied to English plural suffixes, cf. p. 405.)

Mdh. Style creation is a head-creating rather than a modifying aspect of the discourse layer of morphology, since it marks the basic sociolinguistic type of speech situation by specifying the identity, gender, or status of one or more participants in some way or another. Style creation subsumes all connotative meaning as well as other stylistic features of the morphology. English has few purely style-marking affixes, though certain morphological processes such as clippings and partial reduplications of the type *helter-skelter, wishy-washy* tend to express Mdh function by their very nature. Ideophonic affixes in other languages likewise belong here. So do hypochoristic affixes such as the somewhat old-fashioned *-kins* in *Bobbykins*, in contrast to true diminutive suffixes such as *-ette* in *kitchenette*, which fulfill a referent modifying (Mrm) function. The mildly productive suffix *-let* is functionally more diverse. In *cloud-let* this suffix is Mrm (a cloud specified as being referentially small) and Mdh (poetic style marking), whereas in *eyelet* it expresses Mrm together with Mrh functions (but lacks any special stylistic, or Mdh, function), since it helps create the basic referent: e.g. *eyelet* means "a small snap" rather than "a small eye". The propensity for various types of multiple exponence in the suffix *-let* may explain its weak productivity, since several specific factors must all be fulfilled simultaneously for any one of its lexical sub-patterns to apply. As might be expected, multiple exponence involving two or more Holistic functions seems in general to constrain a morpheme's productivity.

Mdm. Discourse modification (deixis) is defined as any function that mechanically (rather than referentially) signals the particular details inherent to the speech situation, minus the stylistic marking of the speech act or its participants (Mdh). Mdm functions include all of the traditional deictic categories, such as tense (*work-ed*), as well as person marking or viewpoint specification. The English verb agreement suffix *-s* (*he work-s*) fulfills two deictic functions (tense and person), as well as one phrasal modifying function (Mpm) — subject–verb agreement. Comparative and superlative suffixes also belong here: *old-er, old-est* because they express a modification of one part of the message in relation to another part. Recall that deictic affixes are normally regarded as inflections in the old typology.

Mph. Form class creation is defined as the form-class status (i.e. part of speech) of the word itself, minus the word's referential meaning. Unless they also express a new referent (Mrh function), form-class marking affixes in English tend to be Stratum II suffixes and are always added outside of affixes that express Mrh or Mrm functions: *quick-ly, think-ing* (deverbal noun). Such pure Mph affixes behave in a very "inflection-like" way, but could never be called inflections since form-class specification is supposed to be a "derivational" feature. Mph affixes can agglutinate in English, with each new affix canceling the previous one out: *anti-dis-es-tablish-ment-ari-an-ism*. Recall also that many affixes in English simultaneously fulfill both Mrh and Mph functions. English is moderately rich in Mph affixes, though conversion is also a common means of form class change. This functional component also subsumes participial and gerundive affixes, such as English *-ing*,[6] (as well as infinitival affixes in languages that contain them)

Mpm. Phrasal modification is defined as any function relevant to the phrasal syntax other than form-class specification itself. Mpm affixes include phrase-dependent features of morphology such as agreement, case, and subordination. This is by far the poorest affixal category in English, which is why English is considered an analytic language. Only a few Mpm suffixes have survived from the language's more synthetic Indo-European heritage and they never agglutinate. They also occur in morphological word-final position: *who-m*, he *see-s*. The possessive /s/

in *John's* or *students'* has even become a phrasal enclitic (e.g. *the student who dropped by your office's book is here*).

Other analytic or synthetic languages could be analyzed in similar fashion to reveal interesting features that cannot be described so clearly based on the old derivation/inflection dichotomy. Section 3 will illustrate how the six functional categories of Holistic Morphology can help define the differences between various types of polysynthetic languages. Section 4 will show how this new system provides a natural cross-linguistic typology for verb-internal subject-object agreement.

3. Polysynthesis revisited

Languages with rich morphologies differ even more strongly among themselves in how their affixes express the six morphological functions discussed above. Some of these differences have already been touched upon. Turkic and Uralic (cf. examples 3 and 4 above) tend to express phrasal and discourse modifications (Mpm and Mdm) separately from referent modifications such as plurality (Mrm) as well as from form-class marking (Mph). Wakashan languages (ex. 8) are extremely rich in affixes of referent modification (Mrm), and these affixes play no role in form-class marking (Mph). Eskimoan (ex. 7) is rich in affixes that simultaneously create a new referential head (Mrh) as well as specify the form class (Mph). Bantu languages (ex. 6) mix referent-modifying (Mrm) functions such as animate/inanimate with the phrase-modifying (Mpm) feature of noun-class agreement. The complex array of postpositions and semantically vivid spatial case suffixes in languages like Hungarian also fall within the function of referent modification (Mrm). In languages such as Navajo (ex. 5), where verbs display complex interdigitations of grammatical (Mpm or Mdm) and referential (Mrh or Mrm) morphemes, the positional selection of the grammatical morphemes itself fulfills a special form-class defining (Mpm) function, since the feature of position-class distinguishes verb stems from stems belonging to other parts of speech. The same will prove true of Ket verb stems (cf. section 4 below). In languages where all referential stems are concatenative, the juxtaposition of grammatical affixes in relation to referential morphemes fulfills a purely phrasal- or discourse-modifying function and has no role in distinguishing one form class from another. The use of position class as a morphological head-creating category (i.e. a form-class defining category) does not even enter into the old typology, which is based on morpheme form alone. For this reason, notions such as derivation and inflection are of little value in explaining one of the key traits of languages with non-concatenative morphological stems.

Holistic morphology, in particular, offers a better way to compare differing strategies of subject/object agreement in polysynthetic (as well as less richly synthetic) languages. As is known, languages with morphological noun/verb agreement can differ in several ways, in addition to the basic fact of whether agreement is expressed on the subject/object NPs, verb-internally, or both. The basic semantic and syntactic traits of verb agreement cross-linguistically have been surveyed in Dixon (1999). A language's overall agreement strategy can be accusative (sometimes called 'nominative'), where all subjects trigger the same marking. Or it can be ergative (sometimes called 'absolutive'), where any intransitive subject triggers the same marking as the direct object of a transitive verb. The final possibility is found in the so called active/agentive or active/inactive systems surveyed by Mithun (1991). These are of two types. Most active/agentive languages are split-S, whereby some intransitive verbs always cross-reference their subjects as active participants, and others always cross-reference their subjects as inactive participants (usually with the same marking as is triggered by an object patient); Lakhota (discussed in Mithun 1991) provides a clear example of such a language, where active vs. inactive subject agreement is lexically conditioned for each verb. A few active/inactive languages are fluid-S, where at least some intransitive verbs allow either active or inactive cross-referencing of the subject depending on the real-life situation being referenced; Tsova-Tush (Holisky 1987), a North Caucasian language related to Chechen, is an example of this rare type. Next, a language may use more than one of these agreement strategies based on the expression of some discourse-related function, such as using accusative marking for present and future tenses but ergative or split-S in past-tense verb forms; Georgian (Harris 1981) provides a classic example of such a language[7]. Third, subject and object markers might be concatenated onto a discrete morphological stem, as in most familiar languages of Europe and Asia, so that finite verb stems do not differ radically from stems of other parts of speech; or they may be interdigitated between the referential morphemes, so that the finite verb as a part of speech involves a morpheme position formula that radically distinguishes it from nouns and other parts of speech (this occurs in Athabaskan and Bantu, for example). Finally, it is possible that a language could vary its agreement strategy for purposes other than grammatical agreement (i.e. Mpm or Mdm function), per se. For example, different speech styles could require different agreement strategies; this would constitute a stylistic, or Mdh, split in agreement. Or, even more unexpected, a verb's individual agreement strategy could represent an idiosyncrasy not dictated by any overarching discourse or phrase-related considerations at all; in other words, the choice of agreement strategy could serve as a basic component of referential expression (an Mrh feature). The next section examines the only documented case of a language (Ket) that uses verb-internal actant agreement in this way. The chart in (11) illustrates how all of these differences in subject–verb agreement strategies can be described in terms of the Holistic Model.

Note that the model in (11) categorizes the possible functional roles played by verb agreement in the language overall. All languages with verb-internal agreement markers use them in verb-phrase creation; in other words, verb agreement is a phrase-modifying (Mpm) feature of every language that contains it. But languages with verb agreement differ in terms of what *additional* features their agreement system expresses. Language such as Indo-European, Turkic, and many others, use verb agreement for no other function than to link the subject with its verb as part of a finite verb phrase. In other languages, verb agreement is involved in expressing other types of linguistic function, as well. For example, Tiddim Chin (Tibeto-Burman)[8] additionally uses the choice of agreement as a stylistic marker (an Mdh function). Georgian (1981) requires different agreement strategies for different tense and mood forms, so that the choice of agreement strategy expresses a discourse modification (Mdm) function. And in languages that use an active/agentive agreement strategy, agreement plays a role both in phrasal modification and referent modification (Mrm). Finally, in languages with so-called templatic verb stems (Bantu, Athabaskan, for example), the morpheme positions involved in verb agreement help distinguish the verb from other form classes in the language, so that agreement additionally plays a role in form-class creation (Mph).

Perhaps the most striking detail in (11) is the assertion that there exists a language that uses agreement morpheme positions as a part of its system of basic referent creation (Mrh), in addition to several of the other purposes discussed so far. Only one such language has been documented. This language is Ket, an isolate spoken by a few

(11) A Holistic comparison of possible functions expressed by actant agreement

	Head-creating function	Head-modifying function
Referential function	Mrh Choice of actant marking strategy depends idiosyncratically upon the stem's basic referential meaning (documented for Ket).	Mrm Actant marking is split more or less predictably based on the semantic roles of event participants (in any language with active/agentive marking; examples include Lakhota, Tsova-Tush).
Discourse function	Mdh Actant marking is split based on speech style (reported in Tibeto-Burman; cf. Henderson 1965) (documented in Georgian and some other languages).	Mdm Actant marking strategy is split to reflect tense, mood, person, or functional sentence perspective. Different person markers (or person-marking strategies or positions) also belong to this function.
Phrasal function	Mph Actant position selection in any language with non-concatenative finite verb stems (where it helps distinguish finite verbs from words of other form classes) (Athabaskan, Bantu, Ket).	Mpm Actant position selection in any language with concatenative verb forms (no form-class split in stem type). Transitivity-based actant marking strategies (accusative, ergative) also belong here, as does any language with verb agreement.

hundred people in central Siberia. Section 4 examines Ket morphological typology in greater detail. It turns out that the scheme of Holistic Morphology is extremely useful for comparing Ket morphology with that of other polypersonal languages.

4. Ket finite verb morphology

Most of this section is devoted to explaining the basic features of Ket actant (i.e. subject/object) agreement, which are discussed exhaustively in Vajda (2003) and Vajda (in press). First of all, Ket morphology is noteworthy for its overall paucity of referential affixes. New referential stems are created mostly through conversion or root compounding rather than affixation. Conversion is also the favored means of changing form class, though a handful of purely form-class changing affixes do exist (for example, the suffix -s, which nominalizes most other parts of speech: *nánbèt* 'to bake bread' → *nánbèts* 'baker'; *úgdè* 'long' → *úgdès* 'length', etc.). Because Ket is rich in grammatical (Mdm, Mpm) affixes, it would not be appropriate to call it 'isolating.' In section 1 above, I offered the term 'conglomerating' as a typological designation for a language that is rich in grammatical affixes (i.e. phrasal and/or discourse modifying) affixes yet poor in referential (i.e. Mrh or Mrm) affixes.

The most unusual feature of Ket morphology, however, appears in the language's polypersonal finite verb forms. A finite verb conveys the deictic categories (Mdm) of tense (preterite vs. non-preterite) and modality (indicative vs. imperative), as well as the phrasal category (Mpm) person/number/class agreement with the subject and direct object (which I have called "actant agreement"). The Ket verb's complexity derives mostly from how the process of referent creation (Mrh) interacts with the grammatical feature of subject/object (=actant) agreement. In what appears to be a morphological quality unique to Ket and its extinct Yeniseic relatives, the positions that express subject/object agreement are selected as part of the verb's lexical entry rather than by a general grammatical rule, even though the morphs that occupy them are chosen by regular agreement rules during verb phrase formation. This technique divides the verbal lexicon into five productive conjugations, alongside about a dozen moribund patterns. Vajda (2003) argued that Ket has no typological alignment grammatically speaking, since every stem chooses its agreement strategy idiosyncratically. The lexical entry of each Ket finite verb consists of, in addition to one or more purely referential morpheme shapes, a positional formula that predetermines the positional configuration of its agreement markers. Every permissible configuration must conform to the position-class formula given in (12). But which particular configuration will be used in any given stem cannot be predicted in the grammar based on syntactic functions, semantic roles, or any other stem feature. In other words, the actant marker configuration is itself an important feature of what allows each individual verb stem to convey its individual referential meaning. It thus contributes to referent creation (Mrh function) in the same way that declensional classes and more conventional types of conjugation classes do in many other languages. All Ket finite verb-stem formulas follow a model consisting of the following ten position classes:

(12) Universal position-class formula used for all Ket finite verb forms
       (P = position class)

P8	P7	P6	P5	P4
valence	incorporate	**valence**	adposition	durative /a/or **valence**

P3	P2	P1	P0	P–1
valence	*past tense or imperative*	**valence**	base	**valence**

Darkened captions indicate possible subject-object (=actant) agreement positions, which are chosen referentially and idiosyncratically yet filled with grammatically determined morpheme shapes. Italics mark the tense/mood slot; the other slots (P7, P5, P0) are completely referential.

Vajda (2001; in press) argues that the position-class model, or template, shown in (12) represents an amalgam of five lexically competing allo-templates, each of which licenses a productive subject-object marker configuration called an "actant conjugation." These conjugations — labeled Active, Possessive, Absolutive, Coreferential Absolutive, and Coreferential Inactive — are shown in (13) below. Conjugation membership is lexically specified for each finite verb stem and can only be explained as deriving from (generally opaque) diachronic processes of stem creation, even though all five are grammatically equivalent in that each expresses subject/object agreement. In terms of its overall agreement system, modern Ket is neither accusative, nor ergative, nor active/stative (neither split-S nor fluid-S); nor is there any kind of grammatical or stylistic split in actant agreement. The use of actant agreement as a component of referent creation insures that Ket has no basic grammatical alignment typologically speaking.

The charts in (13) show how the various actant positions function in different conjugations. A hyphen marks slots never filled by any form belonging to the given conjugation; labels identify slots that may or may not be filled depending on the stem in question, though P0 is always filled. In Modern Ket, P7 is also filled in all productive stem patterns, making most finite verb stems discontinuous binomial constructs with their grammatical markers interdigitated between the purely referential morphemes. The relative positions of grammatical markers in the verb largely obey the scopal rules for morpheme ordering laid out in Rice (2000). However, the choice of actant conjugation, as well as the position of the grammatical affixes in relation to the purely referential portions of the verb (P7, P5, P0) cannot be predicted by any rules of universal syntax and therefore must be regarded as idiosyncratic features of individual stems). Table (13) illustrates these conjugations schematically as well as in terms of example verbs.[9]

(13) Five lexico-grammatical sub-formulas (each stem specifies one as part of its lexical entry)

Active conjugation (a basic active/inactive marking strategy)

P8	P7	P6	P5	P4
active animate agent (person/class)	incorporate	—	adposition	durative marker or **3animate patient**
P3	P2	P1	P0	P−1
3neuter patient (plural)	*past tense or imperative*	**1, 2 patient** base **animate**	**active**	

Examples

déqsàq 'I hear' [*di8-eq7-(s)-aq0* 1sj^8-L^7-L^0]

dʌ́bbàk 'she drags it (once)' [*də8-b3-bak0* 3F.sj^8-3N.O^3-drag^0]

dìgdàqsaq 'I go to the river for a few days and return' [*di8-igda7-k5-(s)-aq0* 1sj^8-*igda*^{7}-ADES^5-go^0]

dītʌ́ʌl 'I get cold' [*di8-təəl0* 1sj^8-freeze^0]

ī daésàʁut 'the sun rises' [*da8-es7-a4-qut0* 3F.sj^8-up^7-D^4-one.moves^0]

daqayaʁan 'she grows big' [*da8-qa7-a4-qan0* 3F.sj^8-big^7-D^4-INCEPT^0]

dítàɾamin 'we are lying prone' [*di8-t5-a4-damin0* 1sj^8-SU^5-D^4-PL.sj^0]

datóqǹìbèt 'she keeps stepping' [*da8-toq/ŋ7-bet0* 3F.sj^8-footstep/s^7-make^0]

Possessive conjugation (incorporated possessive proclitics cross-reference the subject)

P8	P7	P6	P5	P4
—	incorporate	—	—	durative marker
	+ subject agreement			
P3	P2	P1	P0	P−1
non-agreement	*past tense or imperative*	non-agreement	base	—

Examples

dkútòlejbata 'she **whistles**' [*d/kutolej7-b3-a1-ta0* her/whistling^7-IC^3-R^1-extend.INTR^0].

ablákèjbata 'I am clapping' [*ab/lakej7-b3-a1-ta0* my/clap^7-IC^3-R^1-extend^0]

Absolutive conjugation (ergative/absolutive marking strategy)

P8	P7	P6	P5	P4
transitive subject	incorporate	**intransitive subject or direct object** marker	adposition	durative
P3	P2	P1	P0	P-1 .
non-agreement	*past tense or imperative*	—	base	**transitive subject (any plural)**

Examples:

báyàvɾa 'I hear' [*ba6-k5-a4-b3-da0* 1s.sj^6-ADES^5-D^4-IC^3-sound.extends^0], *dabágdèŋúyàvet* 'she often drags it' [*da8-bakdeŋ7-u6-k5-a4-bet0* 3F.SJ[8]-drag[7]-3N.O[6]-ABL[5]-D[4]-ITER[0]]

àbátaʁan 'I sweat' *a7-ba6-k5-d/a4-qan0* heat[7]-1S.SJ[6]-ADES[5]-IIT/D[4]-INCEPT[0]]

úgbùn 'she slips' [*u6-k5-b3-un0* 3F.SJ[6]-ABL[5]-IC[3]-slip.MOM[0]]

éjbàyaptʌl 'I freeze to death' [*ej7-ba6-k5-a4-b3-təəl0* kill[7]-1S.SJ[6]-ADES[5]-D[4]-IC[3]-freeze[0]]

uyàtn 'she goes' [*u6-k5-a4-tn0* 3F.SJ[6]-ABL[5]-D[4]-go[0]]

Coreferential absolutive conjugation (ergative–absolutive with double subject marking)

P8	P7	P6	P5	P4
subject	incorporate	redundant subject marker	adposition	durative /a/ or 3 anim object

P3	P2	P1	P0	P−1
3 neuter object	past tense or imperative	1, 2 object	base	subject (animate class pl)

Examples

dakútòlejbuksa 'she whistles' [*da8-kutolej7-bu6-k5-(s)-a0* 3F.SJ[6]-whistling[7]-3RS[6]-ABL[5]-event.extends[0]]

dígdàvatsaq 'I go to the river for a few hours and come back'
[*di8-igda7-ba6-t5-(s)-aq0* 1SJ[8]-igda[7]-1S.RS[6]-SU[5]-go[0]]

dabútòlok 'she shuddered' [*da8-bu6-t5-o4-il2-ok0* 3F.SJ[8]-3RS[6]-head[5]-D[4]-PT[2]-move[0]]

súgbàyonden 'I returned' [*di8-suk7-ba6-k5-o4-in2-den0* 1SJ[8]-back[7]-1S.RS[6]-ABL[5]-D[4]-PT[2]-go[0]]

Coreferential inactive conjugation (a mixture of accusative and active marking traits, with double subject marking as well)

P8	P7	P6	P5	P4
active or transitive subject (person/class)	incorporate	direct object	adposition	durative marker

P3	P2	P1	P0	P−1
inactive inanimate-class subject	past tense or imperative	redundant subject marker (person/ number)	base	—

Examples

dígdàddaq 'I go to the river (and remain there)' [*di8-igda7-a4-di1-daq0* 1SJ[8]-igda[7]-D[4]-1S.RS[1]-go[0]]

sítòna 'he woke up' [*sit7-o4-in2-a0* wake[7]-3M.SJ[4]-PT[2]-state[0]]

dahúnàjarij 'she slips' [*da8-hun7-a4-(j)-a1-dij0* 3F.SJ[8]-slip[7]-D[4]-3S.RS[1]-ITER[0]]

da.ájàtij 'she grows' [*da8-a4-(j)-a1-tij0* 3F.SJ[8]-D[4]-3S.RS[1]-grow[0]]

díndìɾuk 'I moved aside' [*di8-in2-di1-duk0* 1SJ[8]-PT[2]-1S.RS[1]-move.away[0]]

It is the presence of multiple, idiosyncratically contrasting agreement patterns such as these that render Ket noun/verb agreement a referential feature of the verb stem. In other words, it is the multiplicity of roles played by each agreement position across the verb system as a whole that render them referential components of each particular verb form. The examples below, which are adapted from Vajda (in press), illustrate why the various Ket subject/object agreement strategies cannot be regarded as being governed by any overarching grammatical principle. They demonstrate that every referential class of Ket verbs — whether based on event individuation (aspect) or participant individuation (semantic or valence) — contain verbs belonging to more than one conjugation. Consequently, there are many synonyms or near synonyms across the various conjugations, as demonstrated when the examples in (13) are juxtaposed semantically (14–18) rather than grouped according to conjugation membership:

(14) Conjugational synonyms or near synonyms in Ket

Active: *déqsàq* 'I hear' [*di8-eq7-(s)-aq0* 1SJ^8-L^7-L^0]

Absolute: *báyävɾa* 'I hear' [*ba6-k5-a4-b3-da0* 1s.SJ^6-ADES^5-D^4-IC^3-sound.extends^0],

Active: *dʌ́bbàk* 'she drags it (once)' [*d´8-b3-bak0* 3F.SJ^8-3N.O^3-drag^0]

Absolute: *dabágdèɲuyavet* 'she drags it (often)' [*da8-bakdeɲ7-u6-k5-a4-bet0* 3F.SJ^8-drag^7-3N.O^6-ABL^5-D^4-ITER^0]

Possessive: *dkútòlejbata* 'she **whistles**' [*d/kutolej7-b3-a1-ta0* her/whistling^7-IC^3-R^1-extend.INTR^0].

Coreferential absolutive: *dakútolèjbuka* 'she whistles' [*da8-kutolej7-bu6-k5-(s)-a0* 3F.SJ^6-whistling^7-3RS^6-ABL^5-event.extends^0].

(15) Verbs meaning 'make a trip down to the riverbank' (*igda* = to the riverbank)

Coreferential absolutive	Active conjugation	Coreferential inactive conjugation
Single short round trip	Single longer round trip	Single trip without return
di8-igda7-ba6-t5-(s)-aq0	*di8-igda7-k5-(s)-aq0*	*di8-igda7-a4-di1-daq0*
1SJ^8-*igda*^{7}-1s.RS^6-SU^5-go^0	1SJ^8-*igda*^{7}-ADES^5-go^0	1SJ^8-*igda*^{7}-D^4-1s.RS^1-go^0
dígdàvatsaq 'quick trip'	*dígdàksaq* 'medium trip'	*dígdàddaq* 'long trip'

(16) Derivational patterns that build involuntary causatives

Active subject marking: *dītʌ́ʌl* 'I get cold' [*di8-təəl0* 1SJ^8-freeze^0]

Inactive subject marking: *sítòna* 'he woke up' [*sit7-o4-in2-a0* wake^7-3M.SJ^4-PT^2-state^0]

Absolutive subject: *àbátàʁan* 'I sweat' *a7-ba6-k5-d/a4-qan0* heat^7-1s.SJ^6-ADES^5-IIT/D^4-INCEPT^0]

Coref. Absolutive: *dabútòlok* 'she shuddered' [*da8-bu6-t5-o4-il2-ok0* 3F.SJ^8-3RS^6-head^5-D^4-PT^2-move^0]

Coref. Inactive: *dahúnàjarij* 'she slips' [*da8-hun7-a4-(j)-a1-dij0* 3F.SJ^8-slip^7-D^4-3s.RS^1-ITER^0]

Absolutive + P3 *b*: *úgbùn* 'she slips' [*u6-k5-b3-un0* 3F.SJ^6-ABL^5-IC^3-slip.MOM^0]

éjbàyaptʌl 'I freeze to death' [*ej7-ba6-k5-a4-b3-təəl0* kill^7-1s.SJ^6-ADES^5-D^4-IC^3-freeze^0]

(17) Subject marking in anti-causatives

Absolutive: *úyätn* 'she goes' [*u6-k5-a4-tn0* 3F.SJ[6]-ABL[5]-D[4]-go[0]]

Active: *ī daésàʁut* 'the sun rises' [*da8-es7-a4-qut0* 3F.SJ[8]-up[7]-D[4]-one.moves[0]]
    dáqàyaʁan 'she grows big' [*da8-qa7-a4-qan0* 3F.SJ[8]-big[7]-D[4]-INCEPT[0]]

Coreferential Inactive: *da.ájàtij* 'she grows' [*da8-a4-(j)-a1-tij0* 3F.SJ[8]-D[4]-3S.RS[1]-grow[0]]
    díndiɾuk 'I moved aside' [*di8-in2-di1-duk0* 1SJ[8]-PT[2]-1S.RS[1]-move.away[0]]

Coref.Absolutive: *súgbàyonden* 'I returned' [*di8-suk7-ba6-k5-o4-in2-den0* 1SJ[8]-back[7]-1S.RS[6]-ABL[5]-D[4]-PT[2]-go[0]]

(18) Derivational patterns that build iteratives or distributives

Special P0 morpheme: *dítaràmin* 'we are lying prone' [*di8-t5-a4-damin0* 1SJ[8]-SU[5]-D[4]-PL.SJ[0]]

Special P7 morpheme: *datóqỳíbèt* 'she keeps stepping' [*da8-toq/ŋ7-bet0* 3F.SJ[8]-foot-step/s[7]-make[0]]

Non-agreement P3-1: *ablákèjbata* 'I am clapping' [*ab/lakej7-b3-a1-ta0* my/clap[7]-IC[3]-R[1]-extend[0]]

A fuller analysis of Ket finite verb stem patterns (Vajda 2003) reveals that although the choice of actant agreement is often completely unpredictable, it sometimes is partly predictable based on notions of event or participant individuation. For example, Coreferential Absolutive stems sometimes convey certain types of quicker than usual events (cf. example 15 above). And Coreferential Inactive stems sometimes express "auto-instrumental" actions (where the subject's own body (hand, eye, foot, etc) fulfills the instrument role and specifically excludes the possibility that an alienably-possessed tool was used). However, these very same meanings are often expressed by stems belonging to other conjugations, so that the role of agreement strategy (i.e. actant conjugation) in conveying such specific Mrm (referent modifying) functions is too sporadic to be used as a global predictor of agreement marking. More evidence of the unpredictable, referent-marking function of Ket actant agreement could be provided, but the data presented should suffice to demonstrate that, although Ket has a rich system of verb-internal actant agreement, it has no typological alignment grammatically speaking due to the idiosyncratic role that agreement plays in basic referential expression.

In concluding this section it would be germane to ask how such an unusual and seemingly cumbersome morphological technique could ever have arisen in Yeniseic. Vajda (2003) suggest that the proto-Yeniseic linguistic forerunner of Ket originally contained a series of base-initial valence prefixes that contributed idiosyncratically to basic referential meaning (Mrh) in some stems; in other stems they helped express transitivity and semantic valence according to predictable patterns (Mrm). These prefixes appear to have been **d-* for valence decrease, and a voiceless fricative (possibly **¬-*) for valence increase of various sorts, and they operated much like the analogous "classifiers" found in Athabaskan languages today. The Athabaskan valence-decrease *d-* and valence-increase ¬- likewise play an idiosyncratic and unpredictable lexical role (Mrh function) in some stems, and a predictable referential modifying (Mrm) role in other stems. In time, the Yeniseic consonantal prefixes underwent phonological attrition due to the influence of the surrounding Turkic and Samoyedic languages, which did not tolerate anlaut consonant clusters. This led to their retention only before vowel-initial base (P0) morphemes and their elision elsewhere (though they left traces even here in the form of tonal and consonant ablaut in the following syllable). Because proto-Yeniseic morphology appears to have been, like Modern Ket, 'conglomerating' (i.e. poor in any type of referential affixation), no other referential affixes were available to replace the eroded valence prefixes. Instead, the grammatical agreement marker series themselves were co-opted for use in novel combinations to help signal differences in referential meaning. Note that Modern Ket actant conjugations — just like the valence-changing consonants reconstructible for proto-Yeniseic (and the valence-modifying "classifier" consonants of modern Athabaskan) — may contribute either to the basic referential meaning (Mrh) or help individuate the semantic roles of the event participants (Mrm). And so it turns out that a morphological feature of Yeniseic not even represented in the traditional isolating-analytic-synthetic-polysynthetic continuum (i.e. the language's age-old conglomerating morphological bent) seems to have been responsible for the rise of actant conjugations in Modern Ket.

5. Conclusion

The Holistic Model identifies the functional niche into which Ket actant agreement fits, so that the language's unique typological features can be meaningfully compared with the more familiar ones documented for other polypersonal languages. As it turns out, Ket is unusual only insofar as it uses the choice between several competing verb agreement strategies as a referential feature of each individual stem. By contrast, in other polypersonal languages with verb-internal subject/object markers, the agreement strategy represents a uniform grammatical feature of the verb system in general and plays no idiosyncratic role in the expression of referential categories of meaning. Because of historical changes that eroded certain valence prefixes, verb agreement in Ket has simply taken on a referential function in addition to its original phrase-building function. It also becomes clear that the Ket verb, among polysynthetic structures, bears more similarity to verbs in other "non-concatenative" languages such as Bantu and Athabaskan, where position class likewise fulfills a special function in form-class creation by radically distinguishing finite verbs from other word types. Thus, Ket verb agreement is involved, in one way or another, in expressing three distinct functions in addition to noun/verb agreement, per se: (1) referent creation, or Mrh, since the choice of agreement strategy is a component of the basic stem rather than dictated by an overall rule, (2) referent modification, or Mrm, in Active Conjugation and Coreferential Inactive Conjugation, where it marks the class of the subject and object; and (3) form-class creation, or Mph, for formally distinguishing verbs from other parts of speech. Simply calling Ket subject/object agreement markers 'inflections' completely misses the referential function expressed by the positional configuration of these morphemes within the verb complex.

Instead of merely replacing 'inflection' and 'derivation' with alternate labels, or dividing them into subcategories that fail to address the ambiguity between form and function inherent in these notions themselves, the Holistic Model demonstrates them to be epiphenomena of two clear-cut functional oppositions that operate beyond morphology: head vs. modifier structure, and referential vs. grammatical (i.e. discourse and phrasal) function. This short chapter has barely introduced the system's descriptive potential. If applied rigorously, Holistic Grammar offers the promise of achieving a more fine-grained and all-inclusive set of typological designations than has hitherto been available to morphologists.

Morpheme glosses used in the Ket examples in Section 4

ABL	ablative adposition (usually denotes motion away or an external change of state)
ADES	adessive adposition (usually denotes motion towards or an internal change of state)
AC	animacy classifier
AN	animate class
AL	applicative affix (adds an extra theme- or instrument-role argument to the stem)
AP	animate-class plural subject
AT	atelic (appears in some verbs lacking a built-in completion point)
D	durative marker (appears in many verbs denoting states or temporally complex events)
F	feminine class of referent
IC	involuntary causative (marker found in many stems denoting accidental action or natural process)
IIT	marker that appears in inchoatives with an incorporated theme-role argument
IMP	imperative affix
INCEPT	inceptive or inchoative
INTR	intransitive
ITER	iterative (multiple actions or events, or a single event progressing in increments)
L	any lexical element that defies clear semantic definition apart from the rest of the stem
M	masculine class of referent
MOM	punctual, momentaneous (specifically a single event rather than repeated events)
MT	classifier of mental states and attitudes
N	inanimate class of referent, either singular or plural
O	direct object agreement affix
PL	plural referent
PT	past tense (preterite) affix

R	resultative infix (derives stative intransitives from telic transitives)
RS	redundant subject agreement
S	singular animate-class referent
SEMEL	semelfactive (instantaneous or quicker-than-usual event)
SJ	subject agreement
SU	superessive adposition (marks verbs involving superficial contact with a surface)
TR	transitive

Notes

1. The discourse component of the proposed model includes all functions that mechanically align the message to the speech act or its participants. In other words, it subsumes speech style marking and functional sentence perspective, as well as deictic grammatical features such as person, tense, mood, evidentiality, and spatial viewpoint. The phrasal component subsumes grammatical features that are not speech-act dependent, such as agreement. The referential component includes all aspects of semantic content not tied mechanically to the speech act.

2. However, Sapir's typology was particularly innovative in treating multiple exponence as a key morphological feature, an idea I develop further in the scheme presented below.

3. Languages with polypersonal verbs (i.e. verbs that internally cross-reference one or more syntactic terms or semantic roles in addition to the subject or agent) are normally regarded as polysynthetic on this basis alone.

4. Word-order patterns are bound up with specific meanings only insofar as lexemes subcategorize for specific phrasal orderings, examples being the relative order of adjective vs. noun in Romance languages. Subcategorization rules (Sr in the scheme above) could be defined as lexeme-specific constraints on phrase structure patterns.

5. This scheme can accommodate both morpheme-based and word-based approaches to morphology, depending on what is viewed as the output and what as the input. A word-based approach takes two or more lexemes as the input and compares them to produce an output in the form of some characterization of morphological similarity/dissimilarity). A morpheme-based approach takes a base or stem as the input and subjects it to some operation (perhaps involving a discrete morpheme such as an affix, perhaps not) to produce an output (a complete word-form). Also, in a morpheme-based approach the six functions of Holistic Morphology can in theory serve as *either a trigger or a constraint* on the application of a morphological operation.

6. English gerunds and participles formed with the Mph suffix -*ing* do not concatenate with verb-modifying (Mpm, Mdm) affixes: thus, (*his*) *working* would be the gerundive formation from either *he works* and *he worked* (rather than *worksing or *workeding). Languages differ typologically in the degree to which they tolerate the retention of grammatical affixes during a change in form class (Mph). In Ket, for example, finite verbs converted into attributive adjectives or temporal adverbs do retain their agreement and tense/mood affixes (cf. Vajda, in press).

7. In languages such as Georgian, where case markers also help coordinate the subject and object with the verb, the tense- or mood-based grammatical split in agreement strategy

means that the case markers likewise fulfill both phrasal (Mpm) as well as discourse (Mdm) functions, since the type of agreement strategy used on the nouns helps signal tense or mood as well as noun/verb agreement on the phrasal level.

8. I thank Stefan George for his information.

9. A key to the abbreviations used in the glosses accompanying these examples can be found at the end of this article.

References

Ambrazas, Vytautas (ed) 1997. *Lithuanian grammar*. Vilnius: Baltos Lankos.

Bybee, Joan. 1985. *Morphology: a study of the relation between meaning and form*. Philadelphia and Amsterdam: John Benjamins.

de Reuse, Willem J. 1992. "The role of internal syntax in the historical morphology of Eskimo." In *Morphology now*, Mark Aronoff (ed), 163–178. Albany: State University of New York Press.

Dimmendaal, Gerrit J. 2000. "Morphology." In *African languages: an introduction*, Bernd Heine and Derek Nurse (eds), 161–193. Cambridge: Cambridge University Press.

Dixon, R. M. W. 1999. "Semantic roles and syntactic functions: the semantic basis for a typology." In *Chicago linguistics society* 35(2): 323–341.

Faltz, Leonard M. 1998. *The Navajo verb: a grammar for students and teachers*. Albuquerque: University of New Mexico Press.

Harris, Alice C. 1981. *Georgian syntax: a study in relational grammar*. New York: Cambridge University Press.

Henderson, Eugénie J. A. 1965. *Tiddim Chin. A descriptive analysis of two texts*. London: Oxford.

Holisky, Dee Ann. 1987. "The case of the intransitive subject in Tsova-Tush." In *Lingua* 71:103–132.

Kozhakhmetova, Khadisha. 1989. *Sorok urokov po kazakhskomu jazyku*. Alma-Ata: Zhalyn.

Mithun, Marianne. 1991. "Active/agentive case marking and its motivation." In *Language* 67: 510–546.

Rice, Keren. 2000. *Morpheme order and semantic scope: word formation in the Athapaskan verb*. Cambridge: Cambridge University Press.

Sapir, Edward. 1921. *Language: an introduction to the study of speech*. New York: Harcourt, Brace and Co.

Törkenczy, Miklós. 1997. *Hungarian verbs and essentials of grammar*. Chicago: Passport Books.

Vajda, Edward J. 2001. "Toward a typology of position class: comparing Navajo and Ket verb morphology." In *Proceedings from the Fourth Workshop on American Indigenous Languages* (Santa Barbara Papers in Linguistics, 11), ed. Jeanie Castillo, 99–114 . Santa Barbara, CA: University of California, Santa Barbara.

Vajda, Edward J. 2003. "Ket verb structure in typological perspective." In *Sprachtypologie und Universalienforschung* 56(1/2): 55–92. Berlin: Akademie Verlag.

Vajda, Edward J. (in press). "Ket morphology." In *Morphologies of Asia and Africa*, Alan Kaye (ed). Winona Lake, IN: Eisenbrauns.

Index

In the series *Studies in Language Companion Series* the following titles have been published thus far or are scheduled for publication:

A complete list of titles in this series can be found on the publishers website, **www.benjamins.com**